Paul Against the Idols

Paul Against the Idols

A Contextual Reading of the Areopagus Speech

Flavien Pardigon

FOREWORD BY
William Edgar

PICKWICK *Publications* • Eugene, Oregon

PAUL AGAINST THE IDOLS
A Contextual Reading of the Areopagus Speech

Copyright © 2019 Flavien Pardigon. All rights reserved. Except for brief quotations in critical publications or reviews, no part of this book may be reproduced in any manner without prior written permission from the publisher. Write: Permissions, Wipf and Stock Publishers, 199 W. 8th Ave., Suite 3, Eugene, OR 97401.

Pickwick Publications
An Imprint of Wipf and Stock Publishers
199 W. 8th Ave., Suite 3
Eugene, OR 97401

www.wipfandstock.com

PAPERBACK ISBN: 978-1-62564-795-5
HARDCOVER ISBN: 978-1-4982-8742-5
EBOOK ISBN: 978-1-7252-4948-6

Cataloguing-in-Publication data:

Names: Pardigon, Flavien, author. | Edgar, William, 1944–, foreword.

Title: Paul against the idols : a contextual reading of the Areopagus speech / Flavien Pardigon.

Description: Eugene, OR: Pickwick Publications, 2019 | Includes bibliographical references and index.

Identifiers: ISBN 978-1-62564-795-5 (paperback) | ISBN 978-1-4982-8742-5 (hardcover) | ISBN 978-1-7252-4948-6 (ebook)

Subjects: LCSH: Paul—the Apostle, Saint | Bible—Acts—Criticism and interpretation, etc. | Theology of religions (Christian theology) | Natural theology | Athens, Attica, Greece

Classification: BS2595 P172 2019 (print) | BS2595 (ebook)

Manufactured in the U.S.A. 01/31/19

To Paul and Alison Wells
teachers, mentors, friends, fellow-servants of Christ,
and much, much more

Q. 1. What is the chief and highest end of man?

A. Man's chief and highest end is to glorify God, and fully to enjoy him forever.

—Westminster Larger Catechism (1648)

Contents

Analytical Outline | ix
Foreword by William Edgar | xiii
Preface | xvii
Abbreviations | xx
Introduction | xxv

Part One: Contextualizing and Orienting Our Reading of the Areopagus Speech

Matters of Introduction | 3
Chapter 1: Luke's Theology | 6
Chapter 2: Luke's Use of the Old Testament | 40
Chapter 3: Luke's Narrative Setting for the Story of Paul in Athens | 81

Part Two: A Contextual Reading of the Areopagus Speech

Chapter 4: The Narrative Frame for Paul's Areopagus Speech (Acts 17:16–22a, 32–34) | 101
Chapter 5: Beginning an Oration (Acts 17:22–23) | 130
Chapter 6: The Creator-God Is Lord of Heaven and Earth (Acts 17:24–25) | 144
Chapter 7: Incriminating Evidence: The Divine Design for Mankind (Acts 17:26–27) | 161
Chapter 8: Convicted of *Lèse-Majesté* (Acts 17:28–29) | 185
Chapter 9: Eschatological Proclamation of Judgment (Acts 17:30–31) | 200
Exegetical Epilogue: Paul the Servant-Figure in Luke's New Exodus Judgment | 217

Conclusion | 221

Appendix: Some Further Reflections on the Subject of Theology of Religions | 223

Bibliography | 227
Index of Modern Authors | 255
Index of Scripture Citations | 263
Index of Ancient Sources | 277

Analytical Outline

Introduction | xxv
    Christianity, Religious Pluralism, and the Book of Acts   xxv
    Joining the Conversation   xxvii
    The Goal and the Journey   xxix

Part One: Contextualizing and Orienting Our Reading of the Areopagus Speech

Matters of Introduction | 3

Chapter 1: Luke's Theology | 6
    Luke's Theology in Past and Recent Scholarship   6
    Some Important Features of Luke's Theology   8
    The Acts of the Triune God   11
    The Divine βουλή   12
    The Consummation of Yahweh's Work of Salvation   15
    The Church as Restored Israel: Weaving Ecclesiology, Soteriology, and Christology Together   20
        The Challenge of the Jewish Rejection of Jesus   21
        The Challenge of the Increasingly Gentile Makeup of the Church   23
        The Lukan Portrayal of Salvation   28
        The Place of the Atonement in Luke's Soteriology   30
        Jesus the Messiah-Servant   32
    Conclusion   39

Chapter 2: Luke's Use of the Old Testament | 40
    Introductory Considerations   40
        The Importance of the Old Testament for Luke   40

How Luke Uses the Old Testament 46
Luke's Hermeneutic 52
    Beyond the "Promise and Fulfillment" vs. "Proof from Prophecy" Debate 52
    Lukan Hermeneutic and Typology 60
    Scripture Interpreting History and History Illuminating Scripture 63
    Conclusion: The Variegated and Pervasive Influence of the Old Testament on Luke-Acts 65
The Programmatic Role of the Book of Isaiah for Luke-Acts 66
    Isaiah and the Psalms in Luke-Acts 66
    The Significance of Isaiah for Luke-Acts 68
    Luke's Use of Isaiah 70
        The Awaited Restoration of Israel 70
        Isaiah's New Exodus and Lukan Theology 71
        Isaiah's New Exodus and Luke's Macro-Narrative 79

Chapter 3: Luke's Narrative Setting for the Story of Paul in Athens | 81
    On Textual Ambivalence and the Reading of Stories 81
    The Athens Episode in the Book of Acts 86
    Paul in Athens and Luke's New Exodus 88
        The Anti-Idol Polemic in Isaiah 89
        Salient Anti-Idol Polemic Passages in Luke-Acts 92

Part Two: A Contextual Reading of the Areopagus Speech

Chapter 4: The Narrative Frame for Paul's Areopagus Speech (Acts 17:16–22a, 33–34) | 101
    Acts 17:16–34 Is a Literary Unit 101
    A Cascade of Events 104
        The Precipitating "Crisis" 105
        The Pragmatic Articulation of the Early Narrative (μὲν οὖν . . . δέ) 106
    Paul's Ministry in Athens Prior to the Areopagus Speech 109
        Paul's Prolonged Proclamatory Activity 110
        Luke's Characterization of Paul's Audience 112
            The Composition of the Audience 112
            Three Defining Traits 114
                Idle Curiosity 114

Arrogance and Mockery   116
Ignorance and Confusion   117
The Forensic Atmosphere   118
Socratic Undertones   119
An Understated but Evocative Judicial Setting   120
Conclusion: What the Areopagitica Is and What It Is Not   126

Chapter 5: Beginning an Oration (Acts 17:22–23) | 130
Introductory Considerations: Dealing With "Irreducible Ambiguity"   130
Heeding Luke's Narrative Cues   133
Conclusion: Dramatic Irony and the Δεισιδαιμονεστέροι Ἀθηναῖοι   141

Chapter 6: The Creator-God Is Lord of Heaven and Earth (Acts 17:24–25) | 144
The Sentence Structure and the Isaiah 42:5 Allusion   144
Table 1: Isa 42:5 LXX and Acts 17:24–25 | 145
The Transcendent Creator-God   147
The Self-Sufficient Beneficent God   156
Conclusion: Yahweh Alone Is God   160

Chapter 7: Incriminating Evidence: The Divine Design for Mankind (Acts 17:26–27) | 161
Introduction   161
The Sentence Structure   162
A Post-Babel Perspective on the Creation of Mankind   166
Yahweh's Sovereign Providence over History   170
On (Not) Seeking and Finding the True God   175

Chapter 8: Convicted of *Lèse-Majesté* (Acts 17:28–29) | 185
Structural Considerations   185
Why Paul Is Not a Pantheist   187
Reading Aratus in Its Lukan Context   191
Drawing Incriminatory Deductions   193
On the Dynamics of Quoting Pagan Poetry   197

Chapter 9: Eschatological Proclamation of Judgment (Acts 17:30–31) | 200
Introduction: The Hortatory Climax of Paul's Speech   200
The Final Turning-Point in Redemptive History for the Nations   202
An Eschatological Transition   202
A Culpable "Unknowing" of Epochal Proportion   204

God Is Done Ignoring the Nations   208
The Resurrection of Jesus Inaugurates and Defines the "Last Days"   211

Exegetical Epilogue: Paul the Servant-Figure in Luke's New Exodus Judgment | 217

Conclusion | 221

Appendix: Some Further Reflections on the Subject of Theology of Religions | 223
The Areopagitica and Inclusivism   223
The Areopagitica and Theology of Religions   225

Index of Modern Authors | 255
Index of Scripture Citations | 263
Index of Ancient Sources | 277

Foreword

THERE ARE MANY CAUSES for the recent surge of interest in world religions. Ever since the explorations of Asian religions that came into vogue in the 1960s, many in the West have held a fascination for certain blends of Hinduism, Yoga, Buddhism, ayurvedic medicine, and the like. Most often embracing these views was selective, as was the case of the Beatles returning from India with their long hair and a song, "Within You, Without You," mingling the sitar and tabla with a rock feeling, but without giving up their bank accounts or middle-class lifestyles. Young people in those days were often searching for alternatives to what they perceived to be the conformist, moralistic culture of the West.[1] In the bargain, though, a number of serious students of Asian religions explored them more deeply, resulting in the establishment of serious academic fields of comparative religions or of specialized studies in various religions.

Another contributor to the greater interest in world religions is the more recent trend termed "post-secular society."[2] This expression, describing characteristics predominantly of the West, is not meant to deny the fact of secularization, but to argue that alongside the decline of Christian influence we can observe a resurgence of *religion*. Jürgen Habermas, himself a liberal secularist, argues that citizens must be open to considering the influence of religion, if only because Western culture is so rooted in a Judeo-Christian heritage. He detects three major reasons for the shift toward the post-secular: (1) Global conflicts where religious language is often used to baptize one side or both have had the effect of diminishing the secular zeal of many; (2) Politics which emphasize values increasingly promotes religious voices. (3) Immigration often brings people to "secular" countries who bring with them their strong religious way of life.[3]

The resurgence of Islam, the prominent role of religion in political discourse, as well as the resilience of broad religious belief and practice in places such as the

---

1. For a summary of such yearnings see, Paul Oliver, *Hinduism and the 1960s: The Rise of a Counter-Culture* (London: Bloomsbury Academic, 2014).

2. See, *Post Secular Society*, Peter Nynäs, Mika Lassander, Terhi Utriainen, eds. (Piscataway, NJ: Transaction Publishers, 2012).

3. Jürgen Habermas, "Secularism's Crisis of Faith: Notes on Post-Secular Society." *New Perspectives Quarterly* 25 (2008) 17–29.

United States, has created something of a crisis of faith among sociologists.[4] Peter L. Berger, a former leader in secularization theory, has changed his mind about the validity of forecasts about the abandonment of religion in the modern world. Modernity, he discovered, is not the predictor of religious decline once heralded by a majority of sociologists. World leaders have made unexpected acknowledgments of the importance of religion for understanding our planet. Former Prime Minister of Great Britain Tony Blair has converted to Roman Catholicism, and created the Faith Foundation, which aims at promoting religious literacy. "You cannot understand the modern world unless you understand the importance of religious faith," he affirmed. His main concern is to bring about better comprehension in order to avoid the threat of extremist religion.[5] When Pope Benedict XVI visited France, putatively the most secular country in Western Europe, then President Sarkozy rather shocked French secularists by calling for dialogue with religion, the refusal of which would be "a cultural and intellectual error."[6]

Partly because of these shifts, Christian theology has become more aware of the challenge of world religions than it ever was. Roman Catholic theology, especially since Vatican II, has taken a strong interest in the identity of those outside the church. Rather than the "we-they" tone of previous generations, the advocates of *aggiornamento* meeting from 1962 to 1965 have moved resolutely toward being inclusive as far as possible. The following statement from *Nostra Aetate* gives the idea:

> The Catholic Church rejects nothing that is true and holy in these religions. She regards with sincere reverence those ways of conduct and of life, those precepts and teachings which, though differing in many aspects from the ones she holds and sets forth, nonetheless often reflect a ray of that Truth which enlightens all men. Indeed, she proclaims, and ever must proclaim Christ "the way, the truth, and the life" (John 14:6), in whom men may find the fullness of religious life, in whom God has reconciled all things to Himself (2 Cor. 5:18–19).

While this statement does not deny access through the Roman Catholic Church, it leans over backwards to acknowledge insights from other religions. The expression "reflect a ray of that Truth which enlightens all men" is telling. While endorsing Christ as "the way, the truth and the life," it rather modestly sees in him only "the fullness of religious life," whatever that may mean. This kind of statement opened the door

---

4. Peter L. Berger, "The Desecularization of the World: A Global Overview, *The Desecularization of the World: Resurgent Religion and World Politics*, Peter L. Berger, ed. (Washington, DC: Ethics & Public Policy Center, Grand Rapids: Eerdmans, 1999), 1–18.

5. http://tonyblairfaithfoundation.org/foundation.

6. http://www.telegraph.co.uk/news/picturegalleries/worldnews/2825797/Pope-Benedict-XVI-visits-France-and-meets-Nicolas-Sarkozy-and-Carla-Bruni-Sarkozy.html?image=1.

for further bridges into various religions. Karl Rahner (1904–84) asked Catholics to recognize "Anonymous Christians."[7]

Among Protestants considerable energy has been expended on the subject of the "unevangelized" or the "unreached." Missionary theologians such as Hendrik Kraemer (1888–1965) and J. H. Bavinck (1895–1964) paved the way in the twentieth century toward a greater consciousness of religions such as Hinduism and Islam. Their goal as conservative Christians was to improve the effectiveness of evangelization of adherents to non-Christian worldviews. More recently two groups have emerged which have sought to argue for a kind of syncretism. The first is generally known as "inclusivists." They assert that there are other paths to salvation than consciously professing faith in Jesus Christ. The second is called the "insider movement." This group affirms that converts to the Christian faith need not abandon the social or cultural practices of their former religion. Thus, while following Christ at some level, it is permissible to pray in a Mosque, or even to call oneself a "Hindu Christian." While the present volume does not address the particular representatives of these approaches in any detail, the exegesis of the biblical texts will certainly speak to the issues involved.

A few, more orthodox theologians, have tackled some of the issues surrounding world religions. Among the most notable are Daniel Strange, who has extensively analyzed "inclusivism," and has sought to discover a truly biblical theology of religions.[8] Another conservative, David Garner, has done significant work on the "insider movement" which claims that one can be an authentic Christian while remaining inside one's social and cultural heritage, including religious practices which on the surface would seem quite foreign to the Christian faith. Garner is ultimately critical of this view.[9] But much more work needs to be done.

Accordingly, this volume by Flavien Pardigon is a most welcome addition to what we can hope is a growing body of literature by conservatives addressing the questions surrounding the theology of religions. Among its many virtues, *Paul Against the Idols* combines insights into the arguments of the various "inclusivists" with sound, detailed biblical exegesis. The focal point of this study is Paul's speech in the Areopagus, recorded in Acts 17:16–34. This remarkable discourse is significant because it is the fullest missionary address recorded in the Book of Acts, one which is addressed to a mixed audience including Epicurean and Stoic philosophers. The speech is a model of apologetic persuasion. Not strictly an evangelistic outreach, but

---

7. Karl Rahner, *Theological Investigations*, vol. 14, David Bourke, trans. (London: Darton, Longman & Todd, 1976), 283.

8. Daniel Strange, *The Possibility of Salvation Among the Unevangelised: An Analysis of Inclusivism in Recent Evangelical Theology* (Milton Keynes, UK: Paternoster, 2002); Daniel Strange, *"For Their Rock Is Not As Our Rock": An Evangelical Theology of Religions* (Nottingham, UK: Apollos, 2014).

9. David Garner, "High Stakes: Insider Movement Hermeneutics and the Gospel." *Themelios* 37.2 (2012) http://legacy.thegospelcoalition.org/themelios/article/high_stakes_insider_movement_hermeneutics_and_the_gospel.

rather an apologetic communication, it is also rich with implications for the sorts of questions raised by the current debates.

Dr Pardigon convincingly demonstrates that Paul's discourse, when understood in its fullest context, is both a radical critique of idolatry and a clarion call for faith in Christ as the only way for salvation. The critique of idolatry draws on the Old Testament, particularly the Book of Isaiah. Here is where we find the heart of Pardigon's argument about world religions. Over against inclusivists, he shows that when the Areopagus discourse is read in context, it cannot be understood as setting forth any real common ground between the gospel and other religions. When Paul quotes the local poets (Acts 17:28) he is not endorsing their basic views, but rather noting insights that emerge in spite of their fundamental framework. When he notes the Athenian Altar to the Unknown God, he is not suggesting they had taken the first steps toward the truth. Indeed, the discourse is a strong attack on human religions. At the same time, Paul does not end with a negative critique, but goes on to proclaim the "good news," as Dr Pardigon underscores. The author of Luke-Acts finds in the triumph of the gospel a "New Exodus," where the Lord gathers his people from Jerusalem to the end of the earth (Acts 1:8; 28:11–31). As such Paul's message heralds not only the impending judgment against all unbelief but also an appeal to repentance, which is at the heart of any sound gospel message.

This book displays extraordinary hermeneutical competence. The author demonstrates a thorough acquaintance with the history of interpretation and the most relevant commentators. Most of all, the book sets forth an orderly, logical and persuasive argument for the uniqueness of the Christian worldview, and the centrality of the gospel of salvation. While not a sociology nor a history of religions, it is a focused theological analysis which should serve the reader as a most appropriate place to begin before moving on to any wider considerations. This volume is a more than welcome addition to the literature on a subject that will only increase in importance.

William Edgar

Professor of Apologetics,
Westminster Theological Seminary

Preface

This book is a substantial revision of a PhD dissertation submitted to the faculty of Westminster Theological Seminary (Philadelphia) in December 2007. The degree was awarded by the Trustees and Professors of the seminary in May 2008.

I was originally led to study this passage in the Acts of the Apostles because of its (mis)use by so-called "inclusivists" in the field of Theology of Religions to defend the notion that the Christian God is somehow at work redemptively in non-biblical religions or ideologies. They allege that Paul's attitude towards his pagan audience in Athens is rather positive while his words affirm the truth of their (incomplete) knowledge of God and the legitimacy of their worship. So much so that he is keen to adopt their own poets to build his argument and message. Later I discovered that this line of interpretation was not only common among evangelicals, but was typical of distressing trends in missiological thinking and method (of which the so-called "Insider Movements" and the "CAMEL method" are avatars) whose influence and impact are increasingly felt worldwide.

The fundamental thesis and argument of the dissertation have not changed, though the manuscript has undergone some serious modifications. I daresay that the version you hold in your hands is a significant improvement on the original as a result. My principal concern all along the process of revision has been to increase the clarity of expression and the quality of argument, not to "popularize" the book content or idiom. That entailed "trimming" one full chapter and a few more bits in order to focus almost exclusively on the hermeneutical and exegetical core. It necessitated the translation of various footnotes to the main text. It called for hunting down obscure and muddled language, excessively long or complex sentences, undesirable semantic borrowings from my non-English native language, and infelicitous word choices or syntax. It also required catching up with the scholarship and updating (or filling some gaps in) the bibliography. Finally, I sought to use consistent theoretical frameworks and language to flesh out what were originally "mere" linguistic and narratological intuitions.

Before anything else I must express my deepest gratitude to the God and Father of our Lord Jesus Christ for sustaining my family and me by the grace of the Spirit through both the initial writing and the recent revision of this book. These were not always easy days, but he saw us through all challenges and difficulties. In all things he has shown himself faithful to his covenant promises and infinitely merciful.

There is no question in my mind that this book, like all books, is the fruit of a team effort. Literally hundreds of people have prayed and loved us through both the writing of the dissertation and the production of this book. Some have even read parts of the manuscript and suggested edits at various points in the double process. These friends' encouragement, care, and support over the years has been and remains invaluable. My family and I can never repay our debt in one lifetime, but be assured that you have hoarded treasures in heaven.

I was strongly encouraged to get my dissertation published by a number of missionaries and church leaders in the Majority World, who insisted on the relevance and importance its content has for their context and ministry. Dr Daniel Strange pointed me to a publisher who, he thought, could be interested in my work—and he was right. My thanks go to Wipf and Stock Publishers for accepting this book under their Pickwick Publications imprint. I want to express my great appreciation for their patience and for kindly granting multiple extensions as the completion of the work was delayed for one reason or another over the years.

I am extremely grateful to my field committee at Westminster Theological Seminary for allowing me to research and write a highly interdisciplinary dissertation that stretched the boundaries of our department nearly to the point of bursting. Westminster's historic tradition of weaving together exegesis, biblical theology, systematic theology and apologetics is both exemplary and unique. My book is a tribute to the faculty of this illustrious institution. My advisor, William Edgar, was unwavering in his support even when I was wading through uncharted waters. The external reader, G. K. Beale, offered extensive and extremely helpful feedback on the work and is therefore responsible for many of its subsequent improvements.

There are no words to express the immense privilege it was to be a part of the community at Tyndale House in Cambridge for the past four years. Of course the library holdings are remarkable (and effectively complemented by the various university libraries). I am convinced, however, that the most profitable contribution that Tyndale makes to its guests' scholarship is found in the innumerable conversations pursued over coffee or lunch. Thank you so much to Peter Williams, Simon Sykes, and all the staff for welcoming me into this extraordinary place and for your friendship. Thank you to the too-many-to-be-named readers who have listened, encouraged, challenged, stretched, corrected, taught, sharpened, and shaped me, and who have pushed me to always do better while warning me regularly against the temptation and idol of academic perfectionism. In this latter regard, a special mention goes to Dirk Jongkind and Katy Smith.

It goes without saying that any remaining weakness or error is my entire and exclusive responsibility.

Our local congregation (Cambridge Presbyterian Church) has been a home and a family to us for the past five years. Thank you for taking us in, loving us, and giving us the opportunity to serve Christ and his Bride among you.

To Inyange—my beloved wife—and Timothée, Nastasja, Agapée, Eden and Hosanna—my dear children: you have made great sacrifices for this book to come into being. Your partnership with me in the gospel is the *sine qua non* of everything I do. You make life infinitely more interesting and exciting. May the Lord Jesus Christ repay you a hundredfold in return for the husband and father you keep on giving away in his service. *Je vous aime de tout mon cœur.*

My sole purpose in publishing this book is to glorify God the Father, the Son, and the Holy Spirit, and to contribute to the edification of his global Church. *Soli Deo gloria!*

Abbreviations

AB	Anchor Bible
ABD	*Anchor Bible Dictionary*. Edited by David Noel Freedman. 6 vols. New York: Doubleday, 1992
AnBib	Analecta Biblica
ANRW	*Aufstieg und Niedergang der römischen Welt: Geschichte und Kultur Roms im Spiegel der neueren Forschung*. Edited by Hildegard Temporini and Wolfgang Haase. Berlin: de Gruyter, 1972–
ANTC	Abingdon New Testament Commentaries
ASNU	Acta Seminarii Neotestamentici Upsaliensis
BAFCS	The Book of Acts in Its First Century Setting. Bruce W. Winter, series editor. 5 vols. Grand Rapids: Eerdmans, 1993–96
BBET	Beiträge zur biblischen Exegese und Theologie
BECNT	Baker Exegetical Commentary on the New Testament
BDAG	Danker, Frederick W., Walter Bauer, William F. Arndt, and F. Wilbur Gingrich. *Greek-English Lexicon of the New Testament and Other Early Christian Literature*. 3rd ed. Chicago: University of Chicago Press, 1999
BDF	Blass, Friedrich, Albert Debrunner, and Robert W. Funk. *A Greek Grammar of the New Testament and Other Early Christian Literature*. Chicago: Chicago University Press, 1961
BegC	*The Beginnings of Christianity*. Part 1: *The Acts of the Apostles*. Edited by Foakes Jackson, F. J. and Kirsopp Lake. 5 vols. London: Macmillan, 1920–33
BETL	Bibliotheca Ephemeridum Theologicarum Lovaniensium
BHT	Beiträge zur historischen Theologie
BibInt	Biblical Interpretation Series
BNP	*Brill's New Pauly: Encyclopaedia of the Ancient World*. Edited by Hubert Cancik. 22 vols. Leiden: Brill, 2002–11

BSLib	Biblical Studies Library
BST	The Bible Speaks Today
BThS	Biblical and Theological Studies
BZAW	Beihefte zur Zeitschrift für die alttestamentiche Wissenschaft
BZNW	Beihefte zur Zeitschrift für die neutestamentliche Wissenschaft
CBET	Contributions to Biblical Exegesis and Theology
CNT	Commentaire du Nouveau Testament
CRINT	Compendia Rerum Iudaicarum ad Novum Testamentum
DJG	*Dictionary of Jesus and the Gospels*. Edited by Green, Joel B., Scot McKnight, and I. Howard Marshall. Downers Grove: InterVarsity Press, 1992
DSS²	García Martínez, Florentino. *The Dead Sea Scrolls Translated: The Qumran Texts in English*. 2nd ed. Translated by Wilfred G. E. Watson. Grand Rapids: Eerdmans, 1996
EKKNT	Evangelisch-katholischer Kommentar zum Neuen Testament
EPRO	Etudes préliminaires aux religions orientales dans l'empire romain
ESV	English Standard Version
ET	English translation
FAT	Forschungen zum Alten Testament
FRLANT	Forschungen zur Religion und Literatur des Alten und Neuen Testaments
HThKNT	Herders Theologischer Kommentar zum Neuen Testament
ICC	International Critical Commentary
JB	Jerusalem Bible
JSNTSup	Journal for the Study of the New Testament Supplement Series
KEK	Kritisch-exegetischer Kommentar über das Neue Testament (Meyer Kommentar)
KJV	King James Version of the Bible
LCL	Loeb Classical Library
LD	Lectio Divina
LNTS	The Library of New Testament Studies
LSJ	Liddell, Henry George, Robert Scott, Henry Stuart Jones, and Roderick McKenzie. *A Greek-English Lexicon*. 10th ed. Oxford: Clarendon, 1996
LXX	Septuagint
LDGNT	Runge, Steven E. *The Lexham Discourse Greek New Testament*. Bellingham, WA: Lexham Press, 2008–14
LNTS	The Library of New Testament Studies

MT	Massoretic Text
NA²⁷	Nestle-Aland, *Novum Testamentum Graece*. 27th ed. Stuttgart: Deutsche Bibelgesellschaft, 1995
NA²⁸	Nestle-Aland, *Novum Testamentum Graece*. 28th ed. Stuttgart: Deutsche Bibelgesellschaft, 2012
NASB	New American Standard Bible
NEG	Nouvelle Edition de Genève
NICNT	New International Commentary of the New Testament
NJB	New Jerusalem Bible
NovTSup	Novum Testamentum Supplements
NPNF¹	*Nicene and Post-Nicene Fathers*, Series 1. Edited by Philip Schaff. 1886–89. 14 vols. Reprint, Grand Rapids: Eerdmans, 1988–91
NSBT	New Studies in Biblical Theology
NTD	Das Neue Testament Deutsch
NTG	New Testament Guides
NTSI	The New Testament and the Scriptures of Israel
OBO	Orbis Biblicus et Orientalis
PNTC	Pillar New Testament Commentary
AcBib	Academia Biblica
SA	Studia Anselmiana
SBLMS	Society of Biblical Literature Monograph Series
SBLSP	Society of Biblical Literature Seminar Papers
SBLSymS	Society of Biblical Literature Symposium Series
SNTG	Studies in New Testament Greek
SNTSMS	Society for New Testament Studies Monograph Series
SNTW	Studies of the New Testament and Its World
SP	Sacra Pagina
SR	*Studies in Religion*
SSEJC	Studies in Early Judaism and Christianity
SubB	Subsidia Biblica
SVF	*Stoicorum Veterum Fragmenta*. Edited by Hans Friedrich August von Arnim. 4 vols. Leipzig: Teubne, 1903–24
TDNT	*Theological Dictionary of the New Testament*. Edited by Gerhard Kittel and Gerhard Friedrich. Translated by Geoffrey W. Bromiley. 10 vols. Grand Rapids: Eerdmans, 1964–76
TNTC	Tyndale New Testament Commentaries

ABBREVIATIONS

TOB	Traduction œcuménique de la Bible
UBS[4]	*The Greek New Testament.* 4th ed. United Bible Societies, 1983
WBC	Word Biblical Commentary
WC	Westminster Commentaries
WUNT	Wissenschaftliche Untersuchungen zum Neuen Testament
ZECNT	Zondervan Exegetical Commentary on the New Testament

Introduction

Christianity, Religious Pluralism, and the Book of Acts

Porphyry (AD 232–304), an influential Neoplatonist, put this challenge to the Christians of his time:

> If Christ declares Himself to be the way of salvation, the Grace and the Truth, and affirms that in Him alone, and only to souls believing in Him, is the way to return to God, what has become of men who lived in the many centuries before Christ came? . . . What, then, has become of such an innumerable multitude of souls, who were in no wise blameworthy, seeing that He in whom alone saving faith can be exercised had not yet favored men with His advent? . . . Why, then, did He who is called the Savior withhold Himself for so many centuries of the world?[1]

These words capture quite well the typical reaction of any follower of the traditional cults and/or philosophies in the Roman Empire. The unheard-of-before exclusivity and the suspicious novelty of Christianity were both a puzzle and a moral blemish in their eyes.[2] What kind of a god could ever require that all other gods and their multi-secular ancestral worship be forsaken? And how immoral it would be for any god to bypass most of mankind and limit his dealings to such a weak, provincial (barbarous!) and insignificant people as the Jews? The emergence of Christianity in

---

1. Porphyry's fifteen-volume work *Against the Christians* is mostly lost, except for numerous citations preserved in Christian authors seeking to answer his attacks. Kinzig, "Pagans and the Bible," 755n21, gives a useful list of existing critical collections of these fragments. Our quote is found in Augustine, *Epistulae* 102.8 (ET *NPNF*[1], 1.416).

2. "That a divine being would extend his wrath even beyond this dualism [being at war with all rivals] and send down suffering upon human beings simply for their failure to offer him regular cult seemed an even more blasphemous idea." MacMullen, *Christianizing*, 18. At the same time, it should be clear that "polytheism is rather the scheme of life that defines a *particular kind* of tolerance—the kind that places a missionizing Christianity outside its limits." Rowe, *World Upside Down*, 167 (emphasis original).

what may have been the most religiously pluralistic world to ever exist was a shock and a challenge for both sides.³

Though the question of how to make sense of this religious diversity and its history remained mostly academic or dormant in the Western world for most of the period known as *Christendom*, it sprouted some new shoots with the "age of discovery" of the fifteenth and sixteenth centuries. The worldwide colonial expansion and the missionary efforts that ensued were fertile ground for its further growth. The nineteenth and twentieth centuries saw its boughs and foliage develop and take up a significant place in scholarly circles and in the general population's awareness, as well as in Christian theological debates and ecclesiastical movements.⁴ Due to a variety of factors (democratization of international travel, omnipresent media, globalization, mass immigration, secularization, etc.) most people in the world today are confronted by the often-disorienting experience of the very real and concrete plurality and diversity of faiths and personal convictions.⁵ In many ways, it appears that we are nearly back to where we started: Christianity has to explain and justify its place and uniqueness in a world where its claim to exclusivity and morality is no longer either evident nor plausible in society's eyes.

In this context, the book of Acts is a crucial and unparalleled resource for all who are interested in the history of the emergence of Christianity in the ancient Mediterranean world⁶—and the incredible transition from a modest Palestinian Jewish origin to the dominant position in the Empire through persecution—, its ability to coexist and dialogue with other faiths or how it should construe and proclaim its peculiar message, the gospel, in any new context. Within this book, the episode that might have captured the attention and imagination of most of its students—whether historians, artists, biblical scholars, theologians, missiologists, or missionaries—is without question the story of Paul's sojourn in Athens and the oration he delivered before the elites of that glorious city. This discourse—a.k.a. the "Areopagitica" and the "Areopagus

---

3. See, for example, Gill, "Behind"; Winter, "Public and Private"; and Lane Fox, *Pagans and Christians*. Scott Hafemann puts it this way: "Indeed the pluralism of the modern world is no more dramatic than that faced by Israel or Paul . . . and our situation looks tame in comparison." Moreover, he adds: "To assert the One God of Israel and Jesus as his Messiah, *the* Son of God, was just as startling and exclusive then as it is now (cf. 1 Co 8:5–6; Php 2:9–11)." George et al., "Responses to Inclusivism," 56. Useful treatments of religion in the Roman Empire include MacMullen, *Paganism* and Klauck, *Religious Context*.

4. To the point of being deemed by many "one of the most pressing theological issues in recent years" (Zuck, "Possibility of Salvation Review," 497) and of leading to the appearance and rapid development of "Theology of Religions" as a distinct field of study (see Kärkkäinen, *Theology of Religions*, 22). A "theology of religions" is the study of the phenomenon of religious pluralism from a theological—in contradistinction to a philosophical, sociological, psychological, or comparative—methodological perspective. As is probably obvious, in this book we are concerned with a specifically *Christian* theology of religions.

5. See Taylor, *Secular Age* for arguably the most illuminating analysis of our times in this regard.

6. As is now commonly recognized by most scholars. See the argument in Hengel, *Zur urchristlichen Geschichtsschreibung* (ET *Earliest Christianity*).

speech"—has become the biblical *locus classicus* for the study of Christianity's encounter with a religiously diverse world in the form of ancient Graeco-Roman paganism, both cultic and philosophical.[7] It is the only biblical or extra-biblical record of a full (summarized but reporting the whole argument) apostolic missionary address to so-called "pure pagans," i.e., pagans with no connection whatsoever with the synagogue and the biblical faith.[8] It is strictly *sui generis*.

Joining the Conversation

The uniqueness of both book and pericope has led to intense scrutiny and extensive study by people with diverse interests, concerns, expectations, and methods. This has produced innumerable debates and competing interpretations. So much so that Luke-Acts has been labelled a "storm center in modern scholarship."[9] The scholarship is so diverse and expansive that almost forty years ago the great scholar Joseph Fitzmyer had to concede that no one could "cope with all the numerous interpretations that have been proposed for the various problems in the book [here Luke's Gospel] under discussion."[10] One direct result of this situation is an unending flow of publications, a problem recently captured by C. Kavin Rowe in a striking manner: "the fact is that the secondary literature on Acts is no longer full to the brim: it has now burst the dam and threatens to wash away the text of Acts in a torrent of scholarly glossolalia."[11] The same is, unsurprisingly, true of the Areopagitica.

We will not, therefore, attempt to provide a complete survey and history of past scholarship, but refer the reader to the standard specialized studies on the subject and the introductions of technical commentaries.[12] This history illustrates almost perfectly

---

7. "Paganism" here refers to the complex and pervasive religious, cultural, political, and social tapestry constitutive of life in antiquity, in contradistinction with Judaism and Christianity. Though greatly diverse in terms of beliefs and practices, it shared enough fundamental elements constitutive of a basic "world and life view" ("story" or "grammar") to be identifiable as a distinct entity. In this regard, we use the term (together with its cognate "pagan") in the same way it is commonly used by scholars of classical antiquity. For a useful discussion of the terminology and concepts, see Lane Fox, *Pagans and Christians*, 26–47.

8. Paul and Barnabas' words in Acts 14:15–17, though addressing "pure pagans," do not constitute a proclamation of the Christian gospel, but are meant to prevent the Lystrans from sacrificing to them (vv. 14, 18).

9. Part of the title of the famous 1966 essay by Van Unnik, "Luke-Acts."

10. Fitzmyer, *Luke*, 1.3.

11. Rowe, *World Upside Down*, 11. For an idea of the magnitude of the challenge, the reader is encouraged to glance at the bibliography provided by Keener, *Acts*, 4.3781–4082, which, though of titanic proportion (typeset on three columns in a very small font), still shows gaps in the English-speaking literature (not to mention German, French, Spanish, Italian, etc.).

12. For the history of scholarship on Acts up to the 1980s, see Gasque, *History of Interpretation*. For an impressive survey of most noteworthy publications from 1950 to 2005, see Bovon, *Luke the Theologian*[55]. For a recent survey of the extreme variety of scholarly opinions and methods up to the early 2000s, see Penner, "Madness in Method."

Thomas Kuhn's model for scientific progress through paradigm shifts.[13] For much of the past two centuries, the historical-critical model of scholarship was dominant, even hegemonic, taking a number of different shapes as it faced new challenges. It is not until the 1980s and 1990s that hermeneutical models of a different nature (linguistic and literary especially) began to have an impact on biblical studies in general and Luke-Acts in particular. They have become a lot more "mainstream" in the 2000s, but have not replaced altogether the historical-critical paradigm (yet?). It seems that we are currently in a transitional period of development where various new models and perspectives are suggested and tested, challenging former ways of conceiving and approaching the field and its object of study.

Certain "classic" publications can be seen as harbingers of changes to come, as they are like monuments crystallizing the fruits of the then dominant paradigm while also identifying shortcomings or problems and giving space to new perspectives and ideas. For example, the five-volume series *The Beginnings of Christianity* (1920–33) marks a transition from the models coming from F. C. Baur's historical reconstruction of earliest Christianity, the *Religionsgeschichtliche Schule*, *Tendenz*, and source criticism to the form criticism pioneered in Lukan studies by Cadbury and Dibelius that would dominate the following decades. This began a subtle shift from an exclusive concern for determining "what actually happened" (in modernist historical terms) to how Luke writes about it. In a similar manner, the commentaries on the book of Acts by Haenchen and Conzelmann and the collection of essays edited by Leander Keck (*Studies in Luke-Acts*, 1966), though still significantly dependent on Dibelius' and Vielhauer's framing of the issues, did open the methodological door to insights coming from Luke's compositional activity and legitimized—stimulated—a scholarly interest in his theology for its own sake.[14]

Finally, it seems that the last major turning point in the history of Acts scholarship occurred with the publication of the commentaries on Acts penned by Fitzmyer, Barrett, Jervell, and Witherington (all published in 1998).[15] These were the apex of long scholarly careers for the first three, in which they showed themselves both significantly indebted to and profoundly critical of the inherited paradigms and of the exe-

---

13. Cf. Kuhn, *Structure of Scientific*.

14. See the critiques of these four scholars offered by Robinson, *Weg des Herrn*; Flender, *Luke Theologian*; Franklin, *Christ the Lord*; Kümmel, "Accusations"; Marshall, *Luke*; and Wilckens, "Interpreting Acts." "In conclusion, it would be unjust to fail to recognize the positive value of the work of Dibelius. His emphasis on Luke as an author with literary ambition, as a historian who is not concerned simply to chronicle a series of events but who wishes to commend the Word of God to his readers, and as a theologian who sees the hand of God at work in history in his own day—these have all been valid and have led to a very fruitful period of study of the Lucan writings." Gasque, "Speeches," 250. Yet, as William Kurz rightly notes, these scholars' recognition of the literary dimension of Luke's work was made from within a *historical-critical* paradigm, not yet a truly literary or narrative one (*Reading Luke-Acts*, 3–5; so also Moyise, "Intertextuality and Historical," 24, 32).

15. Together with the five-volume series The Book of Acts in its First Century Setting (1991–96) and its companion Marshall and Peterson, *Witness*, from an evangelical perspective.

geses they spawned. Hence all of them affirmed the historical significance of (Luke-) Acts, the theological importance and originality of its author, the literary quality of his work, the Old Testament and Jewish rootedness of its thought, and its embeddedness in the Graeco-Roman world of the first century AD. The work of these four scholars can thus serve as a suitable window into earlier conversations *and* a stepping stone toward those started by a generation of scholars sharpened by deconstructionism and benefiting from the literary methodological watershed that accompanied it.[16] This is the mediating role they play in Part One of this book.

The Goal and the Journey

In spite of their great interest in the story of Paul in Athens, missiological and theological studies that see in the Areopagitica an exemplar[17] and a source for their reflections are generally "light" exegetically and uninformed of the (recent) specialized scholarship (whatever the particular theological shade of the author). In one way or another (more or less theoretically sophisticated), Paul's address is construed as a model of "contextualization" in cross-cultural gospel communication (even of a constructive inter-religious dialogue).[18] Rarely do such studies involve original and technical exegesis. Instead they tend to adopt "common places" (in their particular community) about the speech and its import and/or repeat the opinions of "biblical experts"—often the

---

16. That paradigm shift in biblical studies started in the late 1970s and early 1980s, beginning with OT studies (see Alter, *Art of Biblical Narrative*; Sternberg, *Poetics*; Talbert, "Shifting Sands"; Kurz, "Narrative Approaches"; and Hatina and Kozowski, "Introduction," 1–12). For a solid introduction to the insights and methodological explorations that have occupied researchers in the past two decades, see (in chronological order) Witherington, *History Literature Society*; Bartholomew et al., *Reading Luke* (the whole Scripture and Hermeneutics series is profitable for a perspective on current trends in broader biblical hermeneutics); Vanhoozer et al., *Theological Interpretation*; Hays et al., *Reading the Bible Intertextually*; Hatina, *The Gospel of Luke*; and Adams and Pahl, *Issues*. Surprisingly, the appropriation of modern linguistics in NT studies has been rather limited so far—in spite of Barr's bombshell *The Semantics of Biblical Language* (1961) and the publication of a journal like *Semeia*—, except for a few scholars (e.g., Fanning, Porter, Carson, Silva and Poythress). There is a renewal of interest in the topic however, and a volume like Runge and Fresch, *Greek Verb Revisited* offers hope that we might see significant advances in the (near) future.

17. Though a variety of nineteenth century scholars saw in the Areopagitica a *failure*, typically explained by the fact that Paul sought to adjust the kerygma to his philosophical audience (in contrast with 1 Cor 2:1–2), this theory is typically associated with the name of William Ramsay (and his apologetic book *St. Paul*; see Dibelius' reproof in "Areopagus," 73). This judgment, though proved to be erroneous many times (e.g., Hemer, "Speeches II," 258), keeps on reappearing occasionally: see, e.g., Pervo, *Profit*, 65, 72; Klauck, *Magic and Paganism*, 74; and the multiple references in Keener, *Acts*, 3.2677n3791.

18. Random examples include: Bossuyt and Radermakers, "Rencontre"; Charles, "Engaging"; Losie, "Paul's Speech"; Flemming, *Contextualization*; Span, "Areopagus"; Mbuvi goes further than many would when he writes: "Paul's assessment of the Athenian religion suggest a perspective that willfully engages the religious world and convictions of the other *with the aim of mutual edification.*" "Missionary Acts," 153 (emphasis added).

exponents of older scholarly paradigms—,[19] rarely engaging meaningfully the scholarly debate and the interpretations that would challenge their views. It seems to us that if this biblical story is to play the critical role it deserves in our theologizing about other religions and in determining how to communicate effectively and convincingly with their followers, we cannot be content with such expedients. Our purpose is to offer an original, current, and in-depth exegetical study of Luke's text that engages with the best and most influential biblical scholarship past and present. The results of our analysis should provide a solid foundation for the appropriation of the Areopagitica's import with a view to theological elaboration and missiological application. We will therefore limit ourselves to offering some *preliminary* theological and missiological reflections as they relate to the particulars of the text "as we go."

The vexing multiplicity of interpretations of Paul's Areopagus speech results from the diversity of (philosophical, historical and theological) presuppositions held by students of the text combined with the associated variety of hermeneutical theories and exegetical methods. Making sense of this problem and offering a solution acceptable to most is not within the purview of this book and will not be attempted. Yet, in order to help the reader follow the argument developed throughout the book, it is necessary to make a few hermeneutical points, trusting the interpretation of the text as a whole to demonstrate the validity of the approach adopted. A better interpretation should not only make sense of more data than its alternatives, it must also be able to account for the variety of scholarly opinion.

The biblical scholarship of the past two hundred years has generally tended toward a form of heuristic atomism and dimensional partiality (or myopia), both inherited from modern empirical sciences. This issue is compounded, of course, by the hyper-specialization of the field, the exponential growth of the literature, and the sophisticated nature of some exegetical techniques. This multiplicity of perspectives itself, however, should alert us to the complex nature of the object we are seeking to understand and thus warn us against the dangers of reductionistic and partial methods of study. Rather, it is of the utmost importance that we include *all* determinative dimensions (at least as many as possible) in our investigation. In our case, that means paying attention to the historical, theological, linguistic, literary, narrative, canonical, intertextual, and rhetorical aspects in a *holistic*, i.e., organic, unified, interconnected, and dynamic manner.[20]

19. E.g., self-professed evangelicals like Clark Pinnock and John E. Sanders depend heavily on Roman Catholic thinkers (like Schlette and Legrand) and the critical scholarship of Dibelius, Haenchen and Conzelmann. It seems that the fragmentation of the text produced by the latter's exegetical methods comports well with the former's method of arguing and theologizing (and conviction that the Bible includes truly diverse points of view). For a substantial study and sustained critique of Pinnock's theology (the "father" of "evangelical inclusivism"), see Strange, *Possibility of Salvation*.

20. An eclectic approach is not sufficient, for it still applies itself to the text's various elements in a disparate and disconnected (possibly haphazard and arbitrary) manner, *pace* Tannehill, *Acts*, 4 and Given, *Paul's True Rhetoric*, 43–44. On the contrary, "it is impossible for us to think in non-interdisciplinary ways." Rowe, *World Upside Down*, 8. Our methodology, therefore, seeks to be integrative in a

INTRODUCTION

The field of semantics has taught us that meaning, whether of a word, a sentence, or a pericope (even a book) is determined or produced by its context, or, better, its (intersecting) contexts. The setting of the Areopagitica is thus constituted by the linguistic specificity of Koine or Hellenistic Greek, the "cultural encyclopaedia" of the first-century Graeco-Roman world, the message and theology of the author, the literary devices Luke used in composing his work, the micro-narrative framework of Acts 17:16–34 and the macro-narrative of Luke-Acts, the rich intertexture of book, story and speech, and the scriptural history of God's work of salvation on behalf of his people culminating in the life-death-resurrection-ascension-heavenly session of Jesus and the expansion of the early church. We must hence affirm the methodological heuristic *priority* of the textual evidence, of course, and will therefore focus on the Lukan—rather than Pauline—meaning of the speech.[21]

Just like the episodes of a story develop what precedes and prepare what follows, so the chapters in this book build on one another and should all be read in sequence. Part One introduces the scholarly context in which our own research is happening and the interpretive conversation we are joining. It also serves to contextualize and orientate our reading of Acts 17:16–34. The four sections that compose it have a bit of a narrative texture and are more an intellectual journey than an encyclopaedic *exposé*. The first one is a rapid overview or statement of where we stand concerning traditional questions of introduction. Chapter 1 discusses some key features of Luke's theology which provide the broader context and some structuring elements of his text and message. We conclude that an essential aspect of Luke's theology is its dependence on the OT. Chapter 2 looks at Luke's variegated use of the OT and explores the programmatic role that the book of Isaiah and its "New Exodus" theme have for Luke-Acts as a whole. Finally chapter 3 quickly maps the macro-narrative context of Paul's ministry in Athens to situate the story in Luke-Acts. Part Two is made up of our exegesis of the entire pericope. It begins with an analysis of the narrative frame of the episode that Luke has provided for the speech (chapter 4). Chapters 5–9 contain the analysis of each segment of the speech in sequence. An "Exegetical Epilogue" offers some final considerations of a synthetic nature in conclusion of Part Two.

---

manner consistent with the redemptive-historical hermeneutical trajectory set by scholars such as G. Vos, H. Ridderbos, N. Stonehouse, R. Gaffin, M. Silva, and V. Poythress.

21. This is a methodological statement, not a judgment on the historicity of the story or the speech. The point is that the Areopagitica is Lukan in at least two crucial ways: first, we agree with the scholarly consensus that the speech in its current form is a *summary* reported by Luke, not Paul's *ipsissima verba* (verbal overlap is not thereby a priori excluded); even more significantly, it is now an integral and organic part of Luke's composition, serving his purposes and communicating his thought. That means that its primary interpretive context is Lukan (which is not necessarily true of its substance, but that is a second-order theological consideration); any other would be speculative or foreign. Our conviction is that Luke is (faithfully) reproducing Paul's argument and meaning with his own words and in his own way, rather than a purported compiling of bare facts.

PART ONE

Contextualizing and Orienting Our Reading of the Areopagus Speech

If there is anything pleasant in life, it is doing what we aren't meant to do. If there is anything pleasant in criticism, it is finding out what we aren't meant to find out. It is the method by when we treat as significant what the author did not mean to be significant, by which we single out as essential what the author regarded as incidental. Thus, if one brings out a book on turnips, the modern scholar tries to discover from it whether the author was on good terms with his wife; if a poet writes on buttercups, every word he says may be used as evidence against him at an inquest of his views on a future existence.

—Ronald Knox, *Essays in Satire*, 98

The principle of contextual interpretation is, at least in theory, one of the few universally accepted hermeneutical guidelines, even though the consistent application of the principle is a notoriously difficult enterprise. Occasionally, however, one is left with the uncomfortable feeling that biblical scholars take exception to the principle itself.

—Moisés Silva, *Biblical Words and Their Meaning*, 138

Matters of Introduction

THOUGH QUESTIONS OF INTRODUCTION are of importance for the interpretation of any biblical document,[1] a full discussion of those issues for Acts is beyond the purview of the present book. We consider that the Third Gospel and the Acts of the Apostles have a common author,[2] the Luke of the tradition[3] mentioned in Col 4:14, 2 Tim 4:11

---

1. "Attention to matters of introduction is important and necessary. For if the Bible is a historical document, then it is not an isolated phenomenon. No matter about the uniqueness of its origin and contents—precisely because these are historical, it is not isolated. That is, the biblical documents have contexts in which they are embedded. Each has a milieu in terms of which it is to be understood, a historical background apart from which it is intelligible only in a strictly limited fashion." Gaffin, "Place and Importance," 148. At the same time, one must recognize that the biblical text also has what could be called a "self-contained nature," by which we mean that its message is intelligible on its own. The best discussions of introductory matters are those that rely primarily on an inductive study of the Scriptures rather than on speculative historical (or theological) reconstructions and subjective correlations with extra-biblical materials. Cf. the helpful discussions of the issue in Fitzmyer, *Luke*, 1.6 and Rowe, *World Upside Down*, 10–12.

2. Historically, only very few scholars—e.g., A. W. Argyle, A. C. Clark and J. Wenham—have denied a common authorship. The large majority of scholars consider that the same author wrote the two volumes, including those questioning the literary unity of Luke-Acts. Fitzmyer, *Acts*, 49, offers a good overview of the debate and the evidence for a single author. For a recent denial, see Walters, *Assumed Authorial Unity*, thoroughly critiqued by Joel B. Green, "Luke and Acts," 109–12.

3. The main argument against this identification is a number of discrepancies perceived between the so-called "Paul of Acts" and "Paul of the (undisputed) Epistles." The second is a late dating of the book. Many contemporary scholars accept the Luke of the tradition as the author of Luke-Acts, however. They typically consider that the perceived discrepancies were exaggerated by earlier scholars (in particular because of their own theological agendas, e.g., Wilckens, "Interpreting Acts") and can be explained by the fact that Luke was a "sometime companion" of Paul who presents facets of Paul's life and character not disclosed in his letters, due to different audiences, situations and purposes. See the discussion of authorship in Fitzmyer, *Luke*, 1.35–53; Witherington, *Acts*, 51–57, 167–70; and Keener, *Acts*, 1.402–22. For an extensive survey of the ancient church tradition regarding the authorship of Acts, see Barrett, *Acts*, 1.30–48. Contrast the discussion of the picture of Paul in Acts in Vielhauer, "Paulinism" with Jervell, "Paul in Acts"; Jervell, "Unknown Paul"; Porter, *Paul in Acts*; and Keener, *Acts*, 1.221–57.

and Phlm 24.[4] He was a serious historian,[5] an original theologian,[6] a skilled writer and storyteller.[7] He is familiar with the canons of Graeco-Roman rhetoric and historiography (but is no slave to them), shows great knowledge of the Greek OT,[8] and is conversant with Jewish traditions of scriptural interpretations.[9] We consider that the book of Acts was composed "toward AD 70"[10] in an unknown location.[11] The Alexandrian text is almost universally considered to be the closest to Luke's original, yet certain Western variants can be illuminating and deserve consideration.[12] Though the Gospel of Luke and Acts are distinct writings, they were clearly conceived as one single work[13]

---

4. See Witherington, *Acts*, 57–60.

5. See Stonehouse, *Witness of Luke*, 32–45; Hengel, *Earliest Christianity*; Hemer, *Hellenistic History*; Fitzmyer, *Acts*, 124–27; and the defense of Luke's historical reliability running through Witherington, *Acts*.

6. Contra Conzelmann, *Theology of Luke*; cf. Marshall, *Luke*; Joel B. Green, *Theology of Luke*; Jervell, *Theology of Acts*; Marshall and Peterson, *Witness*; and Bock, *Theology*.

7. "Luke is a littérateur of considerable skill and technique. His literary methods serve his theology as his theology serves them. In short, Luke's theology of history has a grandeur all its own." Schubert, "Structure," 185. "L'auteur des Actes est un conteur" Marguerat, *Première histoire*, 10. See his chapter "Comment Luc écrit l'histoire," 11–43; cf. the excellent Aletti, *Quand Luc raconte* and Aletti, *L'art de raconter*; F. Scott Spencer, "Acts and Modern"; and Rowe, *Early Narrative*, 9–17.

8. The term "Septuagint" in its narrower technical sense refers to a particular Greek translation of the Pentateuch (third century BC) only, not to a complete Greek OT. In fact there were a good number of Greek translations available for the various books of the OT in Luke's time, some of which were found in collections. "Strictly speaking, there is really no such thing as *the* Septuagint." Jobes and Silva, *Invitation*, 30 (see survey of the various versions in chapter 1). We will use the term "Septuagint" (or its common abbreviation LXX) in this book in its broadest sense to refer to the Greek OT in general, as is commonly done in the literature. References are made to the critical text found in Rahlfs, *Septuaginta*.

9. This is particularly evident in Stephen's and James' speeches (Acts 7:2–53; 15:13–21); cf. Bauckham, "James and the Gentiles"; Bowker, "Speeches in Acts"; Kugel, *Bible as It Was*, 22; and Enns, *I&I*, 147–48.

10. The expression is from Marshall, *Gospel of Luke*, 48. A second-century date for Acts has been recently defended by Tyson, "Date of Acts" and Pervo, *Dating Acts*, but failed to convince. Cf. Fitzmyer, *Acts*, 51–55; Schnabel, *Acts*, 27–28 (who holds to a pre-70 date); and Keener, *Acts*, 1.383–401.

11. Most modern scholars agree that it is not possible to decide, and that it is irrelevant for the interpretation of the book. The simple fact that Acts does not provide enough evidence to determine its place of composition shows how unimportant that issue is. See Fitzmyer, *Acts*, 54–55; Jervell, *Die Apostelgeschichte*, 86; and the dismissive conclusion of Rowe, *World Upside Down*, 11.

12. "Der westliche Text ist dann der älteste Kommentar zur Apostelgeschichte." Jervell, *Die Apostelgeschichte*, 61. The classic defense of the opposite position is Boismard and Lamouille, *Texte occidental*.

13. See Barrett, "Third Gospel." Henry Cadbury is credited with being first to argue for the literary unity of the two volumes and coining the expression "Luke-Acts" in 1927 (*Making*). This position became the general scholarly consensus, though it has been challenged by some: see, e.g., Dawsey, "Literary Unity"; Parsons and Pervo, *Rethinking*; and Rowe, "Literary Unity"; cf. the debate in Verheyden, *Unity of Luke-Acts*; Gregory and Rowe, *Rethinking the Unity*; Adams and Pahl, *Issues*; Litwak, *Echoes of Scripture*, 35–47; Joel B. Green, "Luke and Acts"; and the review in Patrick E. Spencer, "Unity of Luke-Acts." It seems that the emerging consensus is that the two volumes can legitimately be read conjointly or severally in distinct canonical contextual frames: see Verheyden, "One Work" and Bock, *Theology*, 57–61.

of "theological history" in continuity with OT historiography.[14] Luke-Acts is aimed at a group of *Christians* who were familiar with the Christian kerygma as well as the OT and its interpretive traditions, though probably in various degrees.[15]

There is not one sole purpose that can account for the whole of Luke-Acts.[16] Luke is not a single-issue writer! One can yet detect an overarching or undergirding concern in Luke's two-volume work: Theophilus and his fellow readers appear to have been in need of reassurance concerning the legitimacy of the Christian church's message and promise of (Israel's) salvation.[17] Luke's response to this soteriological question is primarily christological and ecclesiological: Jesus of Nazareth is the prophesied/promised Messiah-Servant and his Spirit-inhabited ἐκκλησία is the eschatologically reconstituted—i.e., faithful and true—Israel. It is therefore the legitimate heir to Israel's eschatological salvation. This ecclesiological argument is itself based on christological, historical, pneumatological, and theological developments.

---

14. "But whatever the Greek, Hellenistic, and Roman components of Luke's historiography may have been, his own conscious intention was to write history in biblical style or, rather, to write the continuation of the biblical history." Dahl, "Abraham in Luke-Acts," 152–53. See also Witherington, "Editing," 346–47; Jervell, "Future of the Past"; and Litwak, *Echoes of Scripture*. "Genre" as a concept and its application to a work like (Luke-)Acts is greatly debated among scholars (and has always been) and its heuristic usefulness is often dubious. Some representative recent contributions to that discussion are Adams, *Genre of Acts* (somewhat traditional in outlook) and Bale, *Genre and Narrative Coherence* (questions profitably many common assumptions about genre).

15. See Jervell, *Theology of Acts*, 11–17; Jervell, "Mighty Minority"; Barrett, "What Minorities?"; Witherington, *Acts*, 63–65; and Moscato, "Audience of Luke-Acts," It is important to realize that Luke intended his book to be read to/by a wider audience than the "Theophilus circle," even though the latter must have been his first readership. See the significant methodological points made by Rowe, *World Upside Down*, 10–11 in this regard.

16. See Van Unnik, "Book of Acts"; Fitzmyer, *Acts*, 55–60; Jervell, *Die Apostelgeschichte*, 86–89; and Witherington, *Acts*, 68–74. Such a conclusion accounts for the number and variety of proposals that have been made by scholars. It also militates against the notion that Luke would have written his books for a narrow and well-defined group with a limited number of questions (it would be quite a time-consuming and expensive *ad hoc* response!). Luke's work addresses the needs of the church at large, though it was probably occasioned by the situation of a particular group of believers. See Bauckham, *Gospels for All*.

17. See, for example, Litwak, *Echoes of Scripture* and Wendel, *Scriptural Interpretation*. Thus, Yahweh is indeed fulfilling his promises of redemption to Israel: "This is the ground of the *aspheleia* that Luke promises to Theophilus. Readers of this Gospel are meant to come to the final page with a secure sense of the utter reliability of God's plan for Israel and the world." Hays, "Liberation of Israel," 116.

CHAPTER 1

Luke's Theology

Luke's Theology in Past and Recent Scholarship

CRITICAL SCHOLARS OF THE nineteenth century questioned Luke the historian. Those of the twentieth deprecated Luke the theologian. He has not only been accused of being a poor theologian, but also of betraying the church's original kerygma.[1] As Beverly Gaventa notes: "Conzelmann's work, taken together with the insights of Rudolf Bultmann, Ernst Käsemann, and Philip Vielhauer, led to the characterization of Luke's theology as theology of glory, in contrast to Paul's theology of the cross. Luke came to be regarded as a representative of early Catholicism who had replaced the kerygma of earliest Christianity with a historicized life of Jesus."[2] It was claimed especially that Luke had no atonement soteriology and that he had abandoned the earliest church's imminent eschatological expectation.

This conclusion has been carefully refuted by a number of scholars.[3] As early as 1966 Ulrich Wilckens offered a devastating critique when he wrote:

> This, then, is not the area in which to differentiate between Paul and Luke. The fact that at the present time it is being done anyway can be traced to the exegesis not of Luke's writings but of Paul's. It is Paul, interpreted existentially, who is so sharply set against Luke as the great but dangerous corrupter of the Pauline gospel. But the existentially interpreted Paul is not the historical Paul. And the essential points of theological criticism leveled against Luke are gained not so much from early Christian tradition itself as from the motifs of a certain modern school of theology which disregards or misinterprets essential aspects of early Christian thought. Recognition of these errors may well enliven the discussion of Luke's theology; for Luke, thus freed, is given

---

1. According to Fitzmyer, this negative attitude is responsible for the small number of synthetic theologies of Luke, and also for the fact that the few that exist end up focusing on defending Luke's historical value and attacking Conzelmann's theories (Fitzmyer, *Luke*, 1.143).

2. Gaventa, "Toward a Theology," 147.

3. For example, Ridderbos, *Coming*; Marshall, *Luke*; Morris, "Luke and Early Catholicism"; and Hengel, "Kerygma oder Geschichte."

the possibility of greatly stimulating our own thinking without compelling us to choose between himself and Paul.⁴

Thus, Aletti can write in full confidence: "Que Luc soit un théologien, et un grand, nul ne le nie aujourd'hui : l'ouvrage de François Bovon, qui porte précisément ce titre, l'a souligné comme il se doit, en reprenant les résultats les plus saillants de l'exégèse contemporaine. Il n'y a donc pas lieu de revenir sur ce point."⁵ And yet, Luke's christology, soteriology, and eschatology, the focus of the scholarly discussion, remain much debated to this day. Gaventa contends that "a major reason why neither Conzelmann's thesis nor any of those proposed by his critics has conquered the field concerns the method to be used for identifying Luke's theology, as Talbert argued."⁶ She identifies four main competing approaches. The first one is the redaction-critical school, which finds Luke's theology in the modifications and additions he makes to his sources. A fatal problem with this approach is that it ignores the possibility that the author may have selected the material in his sources because it represented his viewpoint in the first place—an issue compounded by the difficulty to identify Luke's sources in Acts.

The second—used by Cadbury, Dibelius, and Vielhauer—locates Luke's theology in the speeches. Two essential but questionable assumptions of this approach are that Luke has composed the speeches himself (being constrained by his sources for the narrative "frame") and that narrative cannot communicate theology. The third approach is based on the identification of a few texts that are deemed to provide the key to the whole book. However, "at present, we can only wonder how any single text may be regarded as the interpretive focal point for a narrative as complex and many-faceted as Acts."⁷ Finally, some scholars identify one particular theological theme or concern as "the" theology of Acts. Besides the obvious reductionistic flaw of such an approach, it is striking that few scholars ever concern themselves with the relative position and interdependence of such themes or concerns with one another. Gaventa concludes that the problem is simply that scholars fail to take into account the *narrative* nature of Acts, and want to see in it merely a casing or a prison for a theological argument or demonstration.

More recently, Fitzmyer, Witherington, and Jervell, being aware of this problem, demonstrated a greater sensitivity to the literary and integral nature of Luke-Acts. Yet all of them come somewhat short of the ideal.⁸ Fitzmyer still relies on form criticism

---

4. Wilckens, "Interpreting Acts," 76–77.
5. Aletti, *Quand Luc raconte*, 8–9, referring to Bovon, *Luc le théologien*.
6. Gaventa, "Toward a Theology," 147, citing Talbert, "Shifting Sands," 395.
7. Gaventa, "Toward a Theology," 149. Full discussion on pp. 148–49.
8. Kavin Rowe comes to the same conclusion when evaluating earlier studies (including those of Fitzmyer and Jervell; he does not mention Witherington at any point in his study, but does not mince his words concerning Bock) of Luke's use of κύριος in relation to his christology. See Rowe, *Early Narrative*, 8–9 (2–9 for full survey).

and has a tendency toward the "key texts" approach.⁹ Though Witherington puts much emphasis on the narrative nature of the New Testament elsewhere,¹⁰ he tends to fall in the "speeches" category because of his focus on rhetorical matters. Jervell is probably the one author who comes closest to an approach that takes into account the whole of Acts and its literary nature. His interpretation, however, is limited by the fact that he looks at Acts largely (though not entirely) independently from the Third Gospel, and by its "theological themes or concerns" perspective—ecclesiology being the driving force in the writing of the book, leading him to "excise" important texts and themes that do not fit his system.¹¹

It seems that of the three, Jervell comes closer to the truth: "His theology is to be found not within, but behind his narrative account, where we have his theological presuppositions."¹² This fact implies that we must pay attention to the entire book as we have it, and not merely to one part or aspect of it, in order to be able to discern Luke's theology. It also entails that much of it is never made explicit by the author. But is it really sufficient? Rowe, it seems to us, is perfectly correct when he states: "Jervell is not wrong in what he affirms—that Luke's presuppositions have to do with his theology—but in what he denies: that the narrative itself does not bring forth Lukan theology." Of course Luke's theology does play a determinative role in his understanding of the events recounted and in the purpose of his writing, but also in what he seeks to communicate and how he does it. So Rowe, highlighting two essential points, continues: "the Gospel [the same is true of Acts], in other words, is *a narrativizing of his theological presuppositions*; moreover, we have access to Luke's theological presuppositions only on the basis of an understanding of the meaning generated by the narrative."¹³

Some Important Features of Luke's Theology

It was customary at some time to claim that the explicit theology found in Luke-Acts showed a number of *primitive* features (therefore "pre-Pauline"), as if coming all the

---

9. The former is obvious in Fitzmyer, "Lucan Picture." For the latter see his discussion of Luke's eschatology in Fitzmyer, "Mary" where one single verse, Luke 16:16, is largely driving the argument.

10. For example, Witherington, *NT Story*.

11. Cf. Moscato, "Critique of Jervell."

12. Jervell, *Theology of Acts*, 10. This runs in the face of Barrett's own position (defending the historical-critical method), who denies literary criticism much use in Acts and any depth beyond the surface of the text—rejecting especially *any theological current behind the narrative*—and disallows the notion that Luke was trying to communicate any theology beyond the basic Christian gospel, thus destroying the unity of the narrative. Cf. Pao, "Review of Barrett," 349.

13. Rowe, *Early Narrative*, 13n46 (emphasis ours; see further pp. 189–96). Rowe refers the reader to Paul Ricœur, Hans Frei, Eric Auerbach and James Barr on the articulation of narrative and theological presuppositions. Surprisingly, he does not mention Aletti whose narrative approach, however, is quite akin to his.

way from the original Jerusalem community.¹⁴ Besides failing to take into account the narratival nature of Luke's theology, this is typically based on historical-critical methods that start by breaking the unity and integrity of the text and reads the resulting bits and pieces through the lens of a speculative reconstruction of what the theological evolution of the earliest church *must* have looked like, considering Luke to have written late in that process. The hermeneutical crux became whether this putative primitive character applied to Luke's own theology or to that of the characters depicted in his narrative and if it ought to be defined as "history" or "theology."¹⁵ However, as Rowe has shown, Luke's christology (at least!) is sophisticated and develops narratively throughout his Gospel (and, we would add, some more in Acts), so much so that his theological proximity to Paul or John can be affirmed.¹⁶ Hence, through the use of dramatic irony, Luke is able to merge a "post-Easter" so-called "high" christological perspective (affirming the shared identity of the man Jesus with Yahweh) with a "pre-Easter" historical situation through his clever use of the title κύριος.¹⁷

In the past decades scholars have been much more likely to discern a properly "Jewish" flavor to the theology found in the book of Acts. As could be expected, they explain it, once again, either as a result of history (the early church was made up of Jews) or theology (Luke himself is Jewish in mind-set). The extent of the application of the qualifier varies from author to author. For example, Fitzmyer and Witherington think Luke to be a Gentile who was acquainted with OT and Jewish thought (possibly a former God-fearer), while Jervell considers he might have been an ethnic Jew. Though Jervell's conviction that Luke offers us the most Jewish theology in the NT points us towards the truth, his enthusiasm needs to be moderated.¹⁸ Martin Hengel

---

14. "You find the most archaic and very old titles going back to the church in Jerusalem exactly in Acts and very often only here in the New Testament." Jervell, "Lucan Interpretation," 85.

15. Witherington's focus on the canons of ancient historiography comfort his opinion that there is not one christology but a variety of christologies found in Acts. "Rather, he [Luke] is trying to present the variety of Christologies which he found in his sources. He is not interested in ironing out the divergences and differences between his sources, . . . Luke acts as a historian in his handling of these matters, but not one without theological interests." Witherington, *Acts*, 153. Of course, one would want to know what kind of "variety" and "divergences" Witherington has in mind. Is a "christos-Christology" divergent (and therefore potentially incompatible and contradictory) from a "kurios-Christology" or are those merely different facets of a single christological construct so that if someone were to affirm both at the same time he would remain consistent? Besides, we *must* question the dichotomy between Luke's own christological convictions (Luke the theologian) and those of the early church he relays to his readers (Luke the historian) underlying his argument. It is an unjustified presupposition that flies in the face of the narrative-theological unity of Luke's authorial output, treating him like a mere compiler of putative sources.

16. In contract to the typical opinion in modern NT scholarship: Rowe, *Early Narrative*, 28. Here Rowe has especially the claim that Luke's christology is "low," i.e., presenting Jesus essentially (or exclusively) as a human being in view.

17. "Κύριος further expresses what it means to write a Gospel in that its use points to the essence of the Lukan christological task: to write a pre-resurrection life with post-resurrection theology and knowledge." Rowe, *Early Narrative*, 218.

18. Jervell, *Theology of Acts*, 13.

rightly points to the fact that other NT books—he mentions James and Revelation, to which one could certainly add Hebrews or 1 Peter—contain significantly Jewish ideas and that Acts contains a number of not-so-Jewish ideas too.[19] This feature, though, is consistent with the more-recently-recognized originality of Luke's thought. Hence most scholars today, in agreement with Wilckens, defend Luke as a theologian in his own right, whose theology is both distinct (it is Luke's theology, not Paul's or James') and in continuity with the kerygma of the early church.[20]

Another crucial element is the fact that Luke may (and does) assume a certain amount of knowledge on his readers' part, whether in terms of theological commonly-held beliefs in early church, OT and Second Temple Jewish traditions,[21] or what he has narrated earlier in his two volumes. This latter point is important in light of the debates that rage concerning what Luke does not say about theological themes that are considered to be central or essential to the primitive kerygma by modern scholars. It seems clear that the reason Luke does not spend a lot of time explicitly discussing Christ's atonement and its soteriological value in Acts is that he is writing to *Christians* whom he expects to be familiar with his Gospel.[22]

In fine, and in continuity with the preceding point, it is important to recognize that the theology expressed in Luke-Acts generally progresses consistently with the narrative itself (though see Rowe's point about Luke's use of κύριος above).[23] Thus, Fitzmyer shows also that certain themes found in a seed form at one point are developed at a later point in the narrative, sometimes a much later point, so that the one and the other are located in different volumes.[24] In the end, Luke's thought demonstrate a

---

19. Hengel, "Jude Paulus," 361n128.

20. In this regard Fitzmyer fully agrees with Wilckens and affirms that there is a greater theological agreement between Paul and Luke than is usually assumed, while identifying a number of true differences between the two. See Fitzmyer, *Luke*, 1.7–8, 28, 161.

21. The influence of so-called "Second Temple Judaism" on first-century Christianity—including Gentile Christianity—is now commonly recognized (though in a variety of degree), rejecting F. C. Baur's tendentious historical reconstruction. In the same way, the history of the "separation of the ways" between Christianity and Judaism as distinct religions is being re-evaluated. For provocative and stimulating suggestions that their unity lasted until after the end of the first century AD, see Boccaccini, *Middle Judaism* and Boyarin, *Border Lines*; cf. the (more conservative) recent collection of essays in Schwartz and Tomson, *Jews and Christians*.

22. For helpful articulations of the relationship of Luke's two volumes in this regard, see Thompson, *Acts of the Risen*, 29–48 and Larkin, "OT and Soteriology."

23. Parsons and Pervo, as well as Jervell, claim that Luke's theology is *different* and not just in progression between the two volumes. Fitzmyer, however, recognizes a deeper theological unity between the two volumes which develops alongside the narrative itself. Witherington argues that Luke's christology and soteriology follow the progress of fulfillment of the history of salvation, with the resurrection being a crucial turning-point. See Parsons and Pervo, *Rethinking*, 84–114; Fitzmyer, *Acts*, 49; Jervell, *Die Apostelgeschichte*, 108–9; Witherington, "Salvation and Health," 154; and Stenschke, *Luke's Portrait*, 44–50.

24. Fitzmyer, *Luke*, 1.7.

clear redemptive-historical structure and sensitivity. Something rather unsurprising for such a historian-theologian-*littérateur*.²⁵

The Acts of the Triune God

Most contemporary commentators agree that the title traditionally ascribed to Luke's second volume, "Acts of the Apostles," is somewhat of a misnomer.²⁶ In the first place, the term "acts" (πράξεις) was used to indicate "a specific Greek literary form, a narrative account of the heroic deeds of famous historical or mythological figures,"²⁷ which does not fit with the nature of the book. Secondly, the narrative certainly does not tell of the life and works of *all* the apostles. Except for more-or-less brief mentions of various characters (such as the Eleven/Twelve, John, the two James', Barnabas, Stephen, and Philip), it primarily focuses on Peter and Paul, the latter being called an ἀπόστολον only in Acts 14:4, 14 (together with Barnabas). "Moreover, the author tends to ascribe the achievements or exploits of Peter and Paul to the risen Lord or his Spirit or to God rather than to the apostles themselves."²⁸

Many scholars have noted that the main character in the Third Gospel is Jesus and that the Holy Spirit is prominent in Acts.²⁹ In fact, as Witherington notes, some have called Luke's second volume "the Acts of the Holy Spirit."³⁰ The person and work of the Spirit are particularly significant in Luke's writings in general, but they seem to take the lion's share in the second volume. Hence, e.g., the Spirit's power effects the conception of Jesus, he inspires the prophets, he empowers and leads Jesus, he teaches the disciples and emboldens them to witness, etc.³¹ At the same time, the Spirit remains dependent on the other two persons of the Trinity: he is fundamentally God's

---

25. This makes the task of offering a synthetic Lukan theology quite challenging, since an exclusively synchronic approach is insufficient. One must take into account the diachronic dimension of Luke's writing. That explains Bock's method in Part Two of his book: "This pattern of analysis uses two chapters for a topic for all our major categories, moving from literary order to a logical structure." Bock, *Theology*, 100. This redemptive-historical dimension makes all the more necessary a "holistic" approach that looks at Luke's work as a whole and denies the validity of atomistic approaches, thus confirming Gaventa's methodological assertion discussed earlier.

26. E.g., Fitzmyer, *Acts*, 47–48; Witherington, *Acts*, 2; Jervell, *Die Apostelgeschichte*, 56–58; and the title of Alan Thompson's monograph: *The Acts of the Risen Lord Jesus*.

27. Fitzmyer, *Acts*, 47.

28. Fitzmyer, *Acts*, 48. Fitzmyer cites Acts 1:8a; 3:12–16; 4:10, 30; 13:2; 15:4, 12; 21:19 as examples.

29. This distinction might be crystallized in the fact that "The Gospel focuses mostly on the vertical universalization of the salvation while Acts focuses on the horizontal spread of salvation across all geographical and ethnic boundaries. Jesus is the one savior for all peoples." Witherington, *NT Story*, 81.

30. Witherington, *Acts*, 72.

31. "The Holy Spirit is the key that makes proclamation, salvation, liberation, and strenuous discipleship possible." Witherington, *Acts*, 71. Cf. Jervell, *Theology of Acts*, 43–54 and Fitzmyer, *Luke*, 1.227–31.

Spirit and Christ's Spirit.³² It is Jesus who baptizes with the Spirit (Luke 3:16; 11:13; 24:49), it is the risen Christ who pours the Spirit of power and prophecy on the church (Luke 24:49; Acts 1:5, 8; 2:1–6), and the Spirit's activity allows the church to proclaim and live out the gospel of Jesus-Christ.³³

But whatever the relative positions of Christ, the Spirit or the apostles (or their Jewish and Roman enemies) in both volumes, the Father (typically referred to simply as "God" by Luke) is the one at work ultimately. "At the heart of his [Luke's] salvation message, however, is the new thing that God has done in Christ through Christ's life, death and resurrection which in Luke's view makes possible a sort of salvation not previously available at all and only occasionally hinted at in some of the later Jewish prophets."³⁴ Luke-Acts is wholly consecrated to the depiction of the triune God's activity in human history.³⁵ God—viz., Yahweh, the "God of Abraham, the God of Isaac and the God of Jacob, the God of our fathers" (Acts 3:13)—is hence at the very heart of Luke's theology, Father, Son and Holy Spirit working together according to their respective economic properties.³⁶

The Divine βουλή

"Luke's idea of history is, in the strictest sense of the word, theo-logically determined. God is the only *causa*, the motor and driving force in history, the only master of history."³⁷ God, in Luke-Acts, is absolutely sovereign over history and his activity is the interpretive key of the historical process.³⁸ Since God's activity at this point in history

---

32. So much so that Jervell writes: "The Spirit is an impersonal, active force, God's creative and prophetic presence in the history of the people." *Theology of Acts*, 44. This is an excessive judgment, for the Holy Spirit performs *personal* actions in Acts, e.g., in 16:7 and 2:26, texts cited by Jervell himself. In the same way, his repeated claim that Luke's christology has a "tone of subordination" is excessive, since, for example, Christ is depicted as holding a number of divine roles and prerogatives. It seems that Jervell fails to properly reckon with the *economic* relationship of the three members of the Trinity in their *opera ad extra* where the Father has a functional (not ontological) preeminence.

33. See Thompson, *Acts of the Risen*, 125–43.

34. Witherington, "Salvation and Health," 165.

35. "But Luke is interested in more than just mundane history and causation. He is interested in the divine guiding of and interfacing with human lives and events. He wants to show how God, God's Word, and God's Spirit are alive and active in the process of human history." Witherington, *NT Story*, 81. When Witherington writes that "the focus is actually on events, not on persons or personalities, even of God" (*Acts*, 72), he is not denying the revelatory nature of those events, but he is asserting Luke's focus on God's *activity*. This is consistent with his focus on ancient literary genres and his rejection of the identification of Acts as an ancient biography.

36. "Das Zentrum seines theologischen Denkens ist *Gott* als der Gott Israels." Jervell, *Die Apostelgeschichte*, 92.

37. Jervell, "Future of the Past," 106.

38. This fact probably explains why Luke's work is no mere history, but is truly theological-history, since he finds the meaning of all historical facts, events and causality in the direct and sovereign activity of the God of Israel: "But because Luke offers salvation history, the main cause in this process is God. And not God seen as divine providence or *deus otiosus*, but as the continuously acting God in

is redemptive, Luke offers almost exclusively a "salvation-history."[39] More than that, since God's salvific activity is limited to Israel (understood as God's chosen people rather than the ethnic-political entity descending from Abraham/Jacob), Luke focuses on, and basically limits himself to, Israel's history.[40]

The cue to God's absolute control over history is "βουλή, God's counsel, determination, decree, and will. The word points not only to the will of God, but even to the fact that God himself carries out his will and fixes the times for its execution (as he does in Acts 1:7; 13:37; 17:26; Luke 21:24; cf. 1:10)."[41] This word and the concept that it used to denote are extremely significant for Luke's theology.[42] It is used in Luke-Acts to express the fact that God has preordained or predetermined all events in history. It is like a script that God is following as his work of redemption unfolds before our eyes.[43]

This divine plan explains why Luke speaks frequently of God having predetermined certain events, such as Jesus' death (Luke 22:22), his appointment as Judge (Acts 10:42; 17:26, 31) or Paul's conversion (Acts 22:14; 26:16). It is also the reason behind the necessity ascribed by Luke to what Jesus does or says or to various Christians' activity. Luke uses frequently the impersonal verb δεῖ to express this idea.[44] It is very important to note that this historical necessity is associated with both God's sovereign plan and with the Scriptures.

---

all the processes of this history. . . . This exceeds by far the limits set for historians in antiquity." Jervell, "Future of the Past," 114–15, i.e., Graeco-Roman historians, not Jewish ones.

39. See Fitzmyer, *Luke*, 1.181.

40. Jervell, *Theology of Acts*, 19. Jervell here challenges what was a scholarly consensus evident in Conzelmann and echoed in Fitzmyer. Jervell is convinced that, for Luke, there is no history but Israel's history, on the ground that God is at work (i.e., redemptively) exclusively in it. On the other hand, Conzelmann and others complain that Luke destroyed the original kerygma by making Christ and the early church a part of "world history" (Fitzmyer does not go as far, but he believes nevertheless that Luke seeks to integrate the Jesus story into world history). It seems that both sides err by making absolute and exclusive claims. Jervell is right to point to the focus of Luke on Israel's history and to relativize the importance of Luke's connections between the history of Jesus and the early church and that of the larger world (viz., the Roman Empire). At the same time, one cannot just ignore this connection. This is especially true in the light of the fact that the salvation Luke has in view comes from Israel but is meant for the whole world, as is evident from his concern for the mission to the Gentiles, and its *telos* is Rome.

41. Jervell, "Future of the Past," 106.

42. The word itself clearly belongs to a peculiarly Lukan usage: it is used nine times in Luke-Acts (Luke 7:30; 23:51; Acts 2:23; 4:28; 5:38; 13:36; 20:27; 27:42), for a total of twelve occurrences in the whole New Testament. Luke uses also the Greek word θέλημα six times (Luke 12:47; 22:42; 23:25; Acts 13:22; 21:14; 22:14).

43. Moessner, "Script of Scriptures." For a substantial treatment of the subject, refer to Squires, *Plan in Luke-Acts*.

44. Fitzmyer, *Luke*, 1.180 offers a complete list of passages where Luke uses δεῖ Fitzmyer also notes that both Mark and Matthew use it only once each. See also Luke's use of the adjective ἀναγκαῖον in Acts 13:46. This confirms how insistent Luke is on God's absolute sovereignty and how important it is for his theology and narrative.

The execution of God's plan is often described in terms of fulfillment of prophecy and/or promise. As a matter of fact, this notion of fulfillment is already at the heart of the first verse of the Gospel: "a narrative of the things that *have been accomplished among us*" (διήγησιν περὶ τῶν πεπληροφορημένων ἐν ἡμῖν πραγμάτων). Luke uses this notion of fulfillment not only in relation to OT prophecy and promises, but also in relation to other OT passages that were not originally prophetic in nature, to larger textual units without more precision (like the whole of Scripture or of one of its parts) and to other events with no explicit or direct scriptural reference (especially to Christ's death).[45] Jervell makes several interesting points when he argues that Luke's use of the promise and fulfillment motif is not a simple one to one pattern (as it has often been construed), but is a more complex one. In particular, he notes the fact that frequently in Luke's writings the fulfillment of a promise (or a set thereof) brings along new promises or may be only partial and therefore points to a future consummation.[46] He also points to the complex dynamic of God's continued faithfulness to his people (and the promises he made to them) in the face of their faithlessness, sin and idolatry.[47] In other words, the dynamic process of promise-fulfillment is like the engine driving all of human history forward to its consummation at the parousia.

In this context, (biblical) history functions as both the source and proof of the present and of the gospel. The past, with its promises (already fulfilled or not), determines and explains the present. History, whether past or present, therefore determines and proves the future (for example, Jesus' resurrection is the proof of the final judgment in Acts 17:31), it is the guarantee (because itself the fulfillment of promises) of the eschatological consummation of all promises and prophecies of God.[48] The reason why history functions in that manner is God's eternal plan (ontology) which is

---

45. As noted by Fitzmyer, *Luke*, 1.180.

46. "The time of the church is the time of fulfillments of past promises, but even in the fulfilling of promises new promises are given. Thus, the outpouring of the Spirit is a fulfilled promise, but at the same time the fulfilling points to the consummation with the apocalyptic signs (Acts 1.4; 2.1ff., 17ff., 33). The time after the coming of the Messiah is even a time with fulfillment and promises, partly but not yet completely fulfilled (Lk. 9.31,41; 22.16; 24.26–49; Acts 1.4–11; 3.24, etc)." Jervell, "Future of the Past," 107.

47. "God's answer to the people is given through his constant [*sic*] renewed promises. . . . The decisive factor in the history of the people is not their faithfulness or faithlessness, not the sins or the piety of the people, but exclusively the faithfulness and grace of God. This is said very clearly (Acts 13:17–25)." Jervell, "God's Faithfulness," 33. Jervell offers a very interesting discussion in which he argues that because of who God is, the essential and ultimate sin is idolatry, which he identifies with breaking the Law, especially the first commandment (*Theology of Acts*, 18–20). This is perfectly consistent with Witherington's description of idolatry as man's attempt to fashion and control God (in the context of Stephen's speech of Acts 7) in *NT Story*, 133. In fact, even idolatry—and the associated ignorance—is within God's control and can only happen because he permits it or as a result of his judgment: Acts 7:42; 14:15–16; 17:30 (Jervell, "Future of the Past," 107).

48. Jervell, "Future of the Past," 107–9.

revealed by the Holy Spirit in the OT Scriptures (epistemology) offering thus the key to decipher redemptive history.[49]

The Consummation of Yahweh's Work of Salvation

All through the Luke-Acts narrative, we see promises being fulfilled partially or entirely, and new promises being made also; at the end of the day, however, there is only one event left pending: the parousia.[50] The term "parousia" is a convenient way to refer to a cluster of interrelated events: Christ's return (what the terms refers to *sensu stricto*), the consummation of all things, the final resurrection, the final judgment, etc.[51] If this is so, then it means that everything else has been fulfilled,[52] and therefore the church in Luke-Acts lives in the "last days."

Jesus Christ is not *Die Mitte der Zeit* (i.e., the "mid-point" of salvation-history; it is the German title of Conzelmann's *Theology of St. Luke*), but the *climax* of God's salvific activity (especially in the resurrection, which is emphatically God's act, often expressed by a divine passive), the final link in the history of salvation.[53] The eschatological age has been inaugurated by the coming of Israel's Messiah (it is therefore also the messianic age) and the universal spread of the Word about the salvation he brings to his people.[54] His coming was the final divine act. Through him God accomplished

---

49. "The place of Scripture in Luke's theology is clear. He wants to say that Scripture contains everything—πᾶς is a favorite word for Luke—about the message and life of the church. Scripture is the source for the past history of Israel, for the contemporary history of Israel, namely the church, and even for what is going to happen in the future. Further, it is the key to understanding history. Scripture belongs to the past and Luke is well aware of the fact that Scripture is a historical document. . . . The Scriptures not only are a mirror of history, but also create history. Therefore everything in this past has a future." And therefore: "The historian Luke does nothing but interpret the Scriptures. This is why his subject is only the history of salvation." Jervell, "Future of the Past," 109, 110.

50. See Jervell, *Die Apostelgeschichte*, 112.

51. The parousia is explicitly associated with the final judgment in Acts 10:41–43 and 17:30–31. In fact, Jervell notes that the Areopagus speech contains, as we have it, no gospel but only a reference to judgment, that Jesus is presented as the judge of the whole world, but not its savior, and that the "time of ignorance" has ended. This is one of his arguments against its being a missionary speech. See Jervell, *Theology of Acts*, 114.

52. At least proleptically. All promises that remain unfulfilled, or were only partially fulfilled, will reach their completion or consummation in the cluster of events surrounding the parousia, and can therefore by subsumed under that single category.

53. Contra Conzelmann: "Luke has no idea about the Jesus-event and the time of Jesus as 'Die Mitte der Zeit,' but Jesus means the inauguration of the last and final epoch of salvation history." Jervell, "Future of the Past," 105. Cf. Jervell, *Theology of Acts*, 31, 34, 94.

54. Witherington, *Acts*, 124. Witherington also points to the incomparable impact that the so-called "Christ-event" had on the theology of the (Jewish) early Christians. The coming of Christ transformed radically their understanding of eschatology and ecclesiology as well as soteriology and theology proper, in a way that has no precursor in Second Temple Judaism. In particular, he points to how Jesus' resurrection forced Paul to rethink entirely his eschatology. See Witherington, "Jesus as Alpha."

something unique, viz., a salvation of a kind not available before.[55] The coming of Christ and the establishment of the church (to be understood as the eschatologically restored Israel) are the unmistakable proofs that the last days are upon us, since they are the clear fulfillment of the OT prophecies.[56]

Scholars are quite divided on this particular point, though. Since Conzelmann's classic study, many have considered that Luke, when faced with the "delay" of the parousia, had abandoned all hope of an imminent return of Christ. Having relegated it to a distant "end-time," he concentrated his attention on the "today" and the anchoring of an institutional church (often referred to as *früh Katholizismus* or "early Catholicism") in history, thereby de-eschatologizing the kerygma.[57] Conzelmann recognized that one could still find *Naherwartung* passages in Luke's Gospel, but he saw them as a holdover from his sources (Jervell's category of "history"). In diametrical opposition to his views, Andrew Mattill—focusing on similar texts, including Luke 16:16 and Acts 17:31—argued that the parousia was still imminent in Luke-Acts.[58]

The truth is probably somewhere in the middle.[59] Most scholars today would agree that Luke does not present an exclusively imminent expectation of the parousia, but that he has not either reduced it to a footnote. Hence, Stephen Wilson believes that both strands are present in Luke-Acts because Luke faced both a renewal of apocalyptic fervor and an outright loss of faith in the church, due to the delay of Christ's return.[60] Eric Franklin (Gaventa generally agrees with his view) believes that Luke is trying to respond to the crisis in the church produced by the delay by reaffirming the promise of the return. The ascension narrative of Acts 1 binds Jesus' return to the promise of the Spirit and the universal mission, in such a way that the remainder of Acts demonstrates that the parousia is certain since the two other promises have been fulfilled.[61] Franklin's view is perfectly consistent with the so-called "promise-fulfillment pattern" in Acts. He seems, however, to be content with too little and to avoid dealing with the real issue by shifting the focus from timing to certainty.

It seems to us that the best understanding of the matter is the so-called "inaugurated eschatology" advocated by Earle Ellis and Herman Ridderbos among others.[62]

---

55. Witherington, "Salvation and Health," 155, 165.

56. Jervell, *Die Apostelgeschichte*, 106.

57. Conzelmann himself did not think that Luke represented *früh Katholizismus* (only traces of it could be found in Acts), but his view is often associated with this opinion in other scholars. See Conzelmann, "Luke's Place," 304 and Gaventa, "Toward a Theology," 147.

58. Mattill, *Luke and Last Things*. See the broader discussion of Luke's eschatology in Gaventa, "Eschatology" and Fitzmyer, *Luke*, 1.231–35.

59. Here we leave aside Helmut Flender's singular idea that Luke translated eschatology into the vertical categories of Platonism (*Luke Theologian*).

60. See Wilson, "Lukan Eschatology."

61. See Franklin, *Christ the Lord*.

62. See Ellis, "Eschatology in Luke" or Ellis, *Eschatology in Luke*; Ridderbos, *Coming*. Jervell lists the following alternative proposals also: delayed eschatology, individual eschatology, imminent

This view argues that the *eschaton* (especially under the category of the eschatological kingdom of God which was inaugurated by Jesus) is already experienced by the church, but that it is so only proleptically or partially.[63] The fullness is still to come, the consummation remains future. It seems that Jervell and Witherington come close to that view, though they do not use the expression "inaugurated eschatology" itself.[64] Jervell's assessment of the evidence (including the pattern highlighted by Franklin) leads him to conclude, rightly in our opinion: "Even if Luke here has no particular time-reference, the consummation is obviously not too far away."[65]

This point has far-reaching consequences for our understanding of Luke's eschatology in particular and of his theology as a whole. First of all, Conzelmann's trifold scheme of Lukan salvation-history ("Period of Israel," "Period of Jesus," "Period of the Church 'under stress'"), which is appropriated and adapted by Fitzmyer (without its original existentialist core), must be rejected in favor of one similar to Jervell's "the time of Israel before Christ, the time of the church and the time of consummation."[66] Secondly, one must also abandon the common use of the term "eschatology" to refer exclusively to a chronologically-defined "end-time," in other words, to a "futurology."[67] Rather, "the last days are a chain of occurrences, a historical process, ending with the parousia."[68] In other words, human history from beginning to end is to be seen and interpreted in terms of eschatology understood as a continuous and dynamic

---

eschatology, future eschatology, and present eschatology (*Theology of Acts*, 107n212).

63. Beale suggests that this *eschaton* should be understood in terms of *new creation*, an approach that is consistent with our understanding of Luke's eschatology as New Exodus. See Beale, "Eschatological Conception."

64. Witherington comes nearest it when he writes: "Basically, [Luke] seems to see the coming of Jesus and what ensues thereafter as the fulfillment of promises God made long ago to his people in the Hebrew Scriptures. In other words, he believes that *Jesus inaugurated the coming of God's eschatological dominion on earth*, a fact which must be proclaimed to all as 'Good News.'" Witherington, "Salvation and Health," 155n44 (emphasis added).

65. Jervell, *Theology of Acts*, 112, esp. n. 229; cf. Jervell, "Apostelgeschichte," 228. That being said, this "closeness" might sometimes need to be understood not so much in chronological terms as in relational or spatial ones, in a similar way to what Witherington writes about Paul's own eschatology in "Transcending Imminence." The discussion would certainly gain depth by taking into account Geerhardus Vos' "modified scheme" of Pauline eschatology, in which the world to come (realized in principle) overlaps with this world (or "age") in the period between Jesus' resurrection and his parousia. See Vos, *Pauline Eschatology*, 38.

66. Jervell, "Future of the Past," 111. This structure could be reformulated as "time of promises, time of fulfillments, time of consummation" or as "times before the end, beginning of the end, end of the end." This structure fits very well with the inaugurated eschatology described by both Ridderbos and Vos in Paul and the Gospels. For an early critique of Conzelmann's scheme, see Goulder, *Type and History*, 142–44.

67. This is particularly the case with Conzelmann, Fitzmyer, and Gaventa. In his discussion of Lukan eschatology, Fitzmyer clearly understands the term in this restricted and misleading way (reference in n. 58 above).

68. Jervell, *Theology of Acts*, 108.

process.⁶⁹ How could it be different if all of history is preordained by God's plan of salvation, history is the sphere of his sovereign activity, and Jesus is its climax?⁷⁰

It is therefore not surprising that Luke's kerygma is Jesus Christ himself, that is, Jesus Christ identified with the kingdom of God in both its present and future dimensions.⁷¹ The disciples certainly understood that Jesus' resurrection and the promise of the Spirit had everything to do with the establishment of the kingdom (hence their question in Acts 1:6). Jesus' answer (1:8) did not dispel that belief, but simply introduced a tension between the already and the not yet of this kingdom.⁷² Scholars struggle to pinpoint the exact transition to the "last days" (whether it is Jesus' resurrection, ascension or Pentecost),⁷³ most likely because in Luke's eyes all of those events—one should include Jesus' life and death on the cross to that list in light of the story of Simeon in Luke 2:25–32—constitute one single eschatological reality: God's final act to save his people.⁷⁴

In that context, Pentecost (and its corollaries) is presented by Luke emphatically as an eschatological event of the utmost importance. Two OT passages are particularly conspicuous in this context. The entire story is narrated in terms drawn from Isa 66:15–19, an eschatological text speaking of storm, fire, nations, and languages.⁷⁵ The second is the prophecy of Joel 2:28–32 quoted in Peter's speech (Acts 2:17–21). Three points must be noted: first, this prophecy concerns the pouring out of the Spirit on God's people

---

69. "From an eschatological point of view, Luke describes a development that comprises all of history." Jervell, "Future of the Past," 105.

70. Here, it is worth noting a correlated sub-theme that runs through the book of Acts. Witherington rightly points to the fact that the Roman emperor worship and its realized eschatology (the emperor was supposed to have established for good a reign of peace and prosperity) was a serious (Witherington thinks it was the main) competitor to Christianity at the time. This obviously means that eschatology and God's role in it would have been crucial to first-century Christians. Witherington, "Salvation and Health," 148. See, further, his comments on 1 Cor 15 in *Conflict and Community*.

71. Fitzmyer, *Luke*, 1.153.

72. Kingdom is a major eschatological term in the Gospels. Its choice in relation to the fulfillment of Joel's prophecy and the restoration of Israel/establishment of the church cannot be fortuitous on the part of Luke. Cf. Jervell, *Theology of Acts*, 109n220.

73. Fitzmyer's view that Luke's double reference to the ascension makes it the caesura between two salvation-historical periods misses completely Luke's point, in our opinion. It seems much more reasonable to conclude that the *narrative* sequence resurrection, promise of the "power from above," ascension (in Luke) and promise of the Spirit, ascension and Pentecost (in Acts) as a construction emphasizing the *unity* and *continuity* of those elements as one single redemptive-historical (eschatological) event. This point is reinforced by two other considerations: the strong parallelism that Luke builds between the role of the Spirit in Jesus' life and ministry and the role he plays in the disciples' or early church's life and ministry (including in baptism and at Pentecost); Peter's speech in Acts indicates that Jesus pours the Spirit he has received from the Father when he ascended as a direct result of his death and resurrection (Acts 2:33, 32). See, further Gaffin, *Perspectives*, 14–20. Fitzmyer's argument is made in "Ascension" and "Today."

74. "The kingdom of God is always present after Jesus, but the day of his coming lies in the future." Jervell, *Theology of Acts*, 109.

75. Noted by Jervell in Jervell, *Theology of Acts*, 107.

in the context of its *restoration*; second, Peter modifies slightly the original wording, making it thereby explicitly an *eschatological* prophecy; and third, of course, he claims that it is *now* being fulfilled in the eyes and ears of his audience.[76] At Pentecost, it is the people of God, the Israel of God, the messianic community, which is reconstituted, and this people is the church led by the Twelve. This church is the eschatologically Spirit-endowed people of God, i.e., this world has entered the last epoch in the (redemptive) history of Israel in accordance with God's OT promises.[77]

Pentecost is also key to the consummation of God's plan of salvation. Not only are his people (the exclusive recipient of salvation) restored, but they are now spreading God's Word and kingdom (and therefore salvation) under the guidance, empowering, and emboldening of the eschatological Spirit of God![78] This witness of the church to Jesus—the Christ—is itself presented in eschatological overtones. In fact, even the persecution suffered by the church in response to this Spirit-induced witness is an eschatological sign confirming that these are the last days.[79] More than that, the witness of the church in its worldwide dimension is both a signal that the last days have dawned and the proof or guarantee of the consummation of God's plan—i.e., the final judgment of all flesh at the parousia (in view of Jesus' answer to the disciples' question in Acts 1:7–8)[80]—as much as Jesus' resurrection, the very heart and substance of the church's witness.

How can eschatology be such a hermeneutical key to history both past and present? It can be so because the present (and the past, to some extent) are the fulfillment of the OT. The Scriptures are the true interpreter of history and of the early church's experience (as regards either the coming, suffering and resurrection of the Messiah, the outpouring of God's Spirit, or the mission to the Gentiles, for example) because they contain the revelation of God's βουλή, the blueprint of (redemptive) history. The age of the church is the age of fulfillment of God's Word (the Old Testament). This is why Luke focuses more on prophecy (or prophetically-read passages) than on stories—a feature prominent in other NT books.[81] At the end of the day, for Luke it is not the eschatological experience (even of the Messiah, of the Spirit of

---

76. As is well-known, Peter replaces the original "after these things" (LXX: μετὰ ταῦτα) with "in the last days" (ἐν ταῖς ἐσχάταις ἡμέραις). "Luke's alteration can only mean that the turning-point has already taken place, the expected new age has arrived." Jervell, *Theology of Acts*, 108.

77. See Jervell, *Theology of Acts*, 18–25, 43–54.

78. The Spirit is the distinguishing mark of God's people, as the Cornelius story (told three times) demonstrates. It is he who gives boldness to the church's preaching and produces "signs" and "wonders." This Spirit also leads the people of God to obedience to the law, to a "perfect" and exemplary (eschatological) community life. Similarly Thompson, *Acts of the Risen*, 125–41.

79. Jervell, *Theology of Acts*, 108; cf. Thompson, *Acts of the Risen*, 54–67.

80. Jervell, *Theology of Acts*, 111.

81. Witherington, *NT Story*, 136. Even so, the OT as a whole functions as a "frame" for Luke's writings.

prophecy or of the signs and wonders) but *Scripture* that reveals to the church that it is living in the last days.[82]

According to Gaventa, the core and main point of the eschatology of Acts is to be found in its first two chapters. Those chapters contain several important eschatological pronouncements (which she sees as programmatic). Chapter 3 contains a few more of those. "After this point in Acts very few explicitly eschatological statements occur."[83] The operative word here is "explicitly," it seems. Jervell explains that same fact by noting that Acts presupposes the eschatology of Luke's Gospel, adding no major development to it but only bits and pieces.[84] Yet he would strongly object to the idea that eschatology in Acts is limited to a few *explicit* statements in the speeches. On the contrary, he recognizes that eschatology is presupposed at all times.[85] If this is so, then Luke's biblical eschatology is critical for understanding his work, whether in part or *in toto*.[86] It is not only essential to Luke's interpretation of history (understood in terms of God's redemptive activity in and through Israel), it is also fundamental to his writing about that history.

The Church as Restored Israel: Weaving Ecclesiology, Soteriology, and Christology Together

Luke's eschatology implies that "Das *Hauptthema* ist die Restitution des Gottesvolkes durch den Messias Jesus."[87] In the words of David Moessner: "Luke presents the proclamation of the risen Christ, his resurrection or exaltation, and especially his rejection/crucifixion as the three critical components of the fulfillment of God's saving 'plan' for the world which has been announced in advance in Israel's Scriptures."[88]

Witherington similarly states that Luke sees the content of his two volumes as the fulfillment of the OT prophecy concerning God's final act of salvation. He rightly

---

82. Jervell, "Future of the Past," 109. This point is very important, for it entails that one cannot find in *history* the explanation of *theology/Scripture*, but the reverse. Thus the historical narrative penned by Luke is to be read in light of his *biblical theology*.

83. Gaventa, "Eschatology," 34.

84. Jervell, *Theology of Acts*, 107.

85. Jervell, *Theology of Acts*, 114–15. For example, he notes that it is part of all missionary speeches to the Jews (with their summaries of salvation history). We would add that it is also in the background of the Areopagitica (which Jervell does not recognize as a missionary speech) and its explicit reference to the final judgment. Gaventa seems to grant such an implicit role to eschatology in Acts when she writes, that "[Conzelmann's] viewpoint does not adequately recognize that there are three promises in [ch. 1] vv. 6–11 and that v. 11 is as concerned to affirm the reality of the parousia as it is to deny that the parousia is imminent. Moreover, the fact that the first two promises are fulfilled over and over again in Acts surely means that the third can also be trusted." "Eschatology," 37.

86. Hence Witherington argues that this is one of three points that must be kept in mind in order to appreciate the contents of the book of Acts (*NT Story*, 23).

87. Jervell, "Apostelgeschichte," 227.

88. Moessner, "Script of Scriptures," 221.

points out that Luke did not consider his work to be merely a continuation of OT history or Jewish historiography, but had to do with God's *eschatological* intervention (revelation)—implying a certain discontinuity with those earlier writings—therefore constituting a "new sort of Scripture" (one of fulfillment and climax).[89] At the same time, however, this characteristic entails a deep and essential continuity: God's eschatological act of salvation in Christ results from God's promises to Israel, issues from that people's history.[90]

This fact has several corollaries. By his heavy use of the Scriptures (which are God's revelation of his will, works, and words) Luke shows God to be the one Savior, and therefore the Messiah and salvation are God's gifts to his people.[91] The Christ himself receives from the Father the divine prerogative of salvation (just as he also receives the divine prerogative to judge the whole world) and is, thus, in a sense only derivatively the Savior. The history of salvation—that of God's redemptive activity—is exclusively Israel's history, and so Jesus of Nazareth, Israel's Messiah, is the final and climactic link in that history, taking it to its end-point.[92] In the end, one must conclude that for Luke "*extra Israel nulla salus est.*"[93]

The Challenge of the Jewish Rejection of Jesus

If salvation belongs to (and is therefore limited to) Israel, then the question of the relationship of the church to Israel and to Israel's salvation becomes paramount.[94] Therefore, even if we were to grant Jervell that ecclesiology is the primary concern of the author of Acts (rather than soteriology or christology), we would have to qualify his judgment by adding that the primacy of ecclesiology is only prima facie, for soteriology (which is inseparable from christology) is the underlying concern of the author.[95]

---

89. Witherington, *Acts*, 124. Cf. Witherington, "Salvation and Health," 155.

90. "Luke presupposes the history of Israel, and he does so *expressis verbis* as he is the only New Testament author who twice gives detailed representations of the history of Israel (Acts 7.2–53; 13.17–25). Further, his use of the Scriptures demonstrates that salvation comes from the past, namely from the history of Israel, from the promises and patterns in God's words and acts throughout that particular history." Jervell, "Future of the Past," 105–6.

91. Jervell, *Theology of Acts*, 94. Cf. Luke 1:47 (Mary's song in response to Elizabeth's prophetic utterance); Acts 5:31; 13:23. "In Jesus Christ, God's activity in the history of Israel is manifested. The key figure in this history, and so also in christology, is God himself." Jervell, *Theology of Acts*, 30.

92. For Luke, there is a sense in which only Israel's history is worthy of consideration because it is the exclusive arena of God's saving activity and purposes. The history of the nations is one of ignorance and idolatry in which God is redemptively absent, one that is borne of God's patience and judgment. Cf. Jervell, *Theology of Acts*, 18–25, 94–100.

93. "Israel is the one and only people of God destined for salvation." Jervell, "Future of the Past," 123.

94. As we have seen earlier, this very question is a the heart of Luke's authorial purposes.

95. Jervell himself hints at this qualification, since he recognizes that this soteriological dilemma is behind Luke's argument concerning the identity of the church with Israel understood as the (true or restored) people of God. See the summary paragraph of his thesis in *Theology of Acts*, i.

Luke's answer to this critical issue might be that, "in accordance with the idea that the history of Israel is the history of God's saving acts, *salvation through Messiah-Jesus at the end of times can be found only in Israel, that is in the church.*"[96]

The question hence becomes: How can the church be Israel when many Jews reject its gospel? The answer is to be found in the *eschatology* of the people in God's plan. The church is Israel in its final historical stage, at the point when God restores it eschatologically, according to his promises found in the OT—such as the programmatic Isa 61:1–2 used in Jesus' inaugural sermon (Luke 4:18–21) and Joel 2:28–32 used in Peter's Pentecost speech (Acts 2:15–21).[97] Israel (understood as the nation as a whole) has *not* rejected the Messiah Jesus nor the gospel: it is divided over it.[98]

In the first place, the book of Acts shows that the gospel of Messiah Jesus is warmly received by throngs of Jews (and God-fearers).[99] As a matter of fact, Luke records several "mass conversions" of Jews and God-fearers, but none of "pure" Gentiles.[100] From the very beginning of the church's existence and proclamation (Acts 2) thousands of Jews repent and believe in Christ. But at the same time, almost in a dialectical manner, the more the gospel is received by Jews, the more it is opposed by other Jews.[101]

All through the book, there is a powerful dynamic at work which rends the Jews into two groups: faithful/believing Israel, i.e., the church, and faithless/unbelieving Israel, which is no Israel at all.[102] This dynamic is already at work in Luke's Gospel,

---

96. Jervell, *Theology of Acts*, 96 (emphasis ours).

97. In Luke 4, Jesus announces that the prophecy of Isaiah 61—concerned with the eschatological Servant being anointed with the Spirit in order to restore God's people—is accomplished in him: this story follows his being anointed by the Spirit at his baptism and his successful journey-testing in the desert for forty days, an obvious allusion to Israel's Exodus. In Acts 2, Peter affirms that the Joel prophecy of the eschatological pouring of the Spirit over Israel is accomplished right then and there. Those two OT passages indicate that the eschatological/restored Israel would be "the people of the Spirit," to use Jervell's expression (cf. Jervell, *Theology of Acts*, 43–54). See further our discussion of Luke's use of Isaiah's New Exodus below (pp. 71–80).

98. Cf. Jervell, *Theology of Acts*, 34–43 and Jervell, "Divided People."

99. "Through the interpretation of the resurrection of Jesus and the mass conversions Luke sketches a picture of Israel for whom the promises are fulfilled, for the enthronement of the Messiah on David's throne has taken place (Acts 2:29–36) and a great part of the people has been converted." Jervell, *Theology of Acts*, 39.

100. "The basis of Luke's idea is the mass conversions among Jews and 'half-Jews,' the Godfearers (2:41, 47; 4:4; 5:14; 6:1, 7; 8:4, 12; 9:31, 35, 42; 11:21, 24, 26; 12:24; 13:43; 14:1, 21; 16:5; 17:4, 11f.; 18:8, 10; 19:20; 21:20). There is not a single report of a mass conversion of 'pure' gentiles, that is, of people outside the synagogues." Jervell, "God's Faithfulness," 34.

101. See Jervell's argument that the primary, if not exclusive, source of opposition to, and persecution of, the early church and the apostle Paul are unbelieving Jews, and that therefore Acts can in no way be meant to be an apology for Roman authorities in *Theology of Acts*, 100–106.

102. The multiple meanings of the term "Israel" can be confusing. Here Jervell means that unbelieving Jews (viz., members of national or genetic Israel) prove themselves not to be part of God's "true" people (viz., the spiritual or Spirit-endowed Israel). The latter group are the only legitimate heirs of God's promises and salvation, the former has cut itself off from them. Cf. Jervell, *Theology of*

where we see the Jews joining hands with Rome to get rid of the legitimate King of Israel, the Son of David. It develops with the growing opposition depicted along the narrative (especially during Paul's journeys in Asia Minor and Macedonia) as well as with Paul's several judgment pronouncements about turning to the Gentiles which bookmark his preaching ministry (Acts 13:40–41, 46–47; 18:6; 28:25–28). In fact, the opposition to and persecution of Jesus in the Gospel (together with his woe pronouncements against Israel) and of the early church (paradigmatically in the person of Stephen) and Paul in the Acts bring to its climax a long-standing OT theme: the persecution (and murder) of God's prophets (in the line of Moses). This gives therefore to the situation an eschatological and Scriptural explanation, demonstrating that the church is the final persecuted remnant of Israel which, alone, will escape the imminent impending judgment of the nation.[103]

As this dynamic develops, Luke demonstrates that the believing Jews, i.e., the church, are the restored Israel. The first, and maybe the most important, argument is that Jesus of Nazareth was indeed the promised Messiah. This is achieved primarily by demonstrating that Jesus' suffering, death, and resurrection were part of God's plan of salvation, and hence was prophesied by all of Scripture.[104] The corollary to the coming of the Messiah is that "now" is the messianic age, the "last days." The church is hence shown to bear the signs of the last days, in contradistinction with unbelieving Israel. The principal proof is, of course, the pouring of the Spirit and his work in and through the church.[105] Prophetic witness, boldness in proclamation, and accompanying signs and wonders are all demonstrating that the church has received God's eschatological blessing. Two other important fruits of this eschatological pouring of the Spirit—re-creation of Israel—are: the institution of the Twelve (the "patriarchs" of restored Israel; cf. Luke 22:28–30) and the Spirit-filled, law-abiding, life of the earliest church (Luke 24:49; Acts 2–6; cf. Jer 31:31–34).[106] Unlike the obdurate Jews—who are jealous, conniving, and even murderous—the church experiences the life, peace, and holiness of the kingdom of God in its community.

The Challenge of the Increasingly Gentile Makeup of the Church

This leads to another question: How can the church be Israel when it harbors increasing numbers of Gentiles? Luke's answer lies in his presentation of the mission to the

---

Acts, 35–43.

103. Moessner offers a very helpful discussion of this pattern in "Paul in Acts."

104. Jervell, *Theology of Acts*, 25–35. For studies of the identity-forming and legitimizing use of the OT Scriptures in contrast to other contemporary Jewish groups in Luke-Acts, see Sterling, *Historiography*; Newsom, *Self as Symbolic Space*; Litwak, *Echoes of Scripture*; and Wendel, *Scriptural Interpretation*.

105. See n. 78 above.

106. Jervell, *Theology of Acts*, 54–61, 75–82.

Gentiles: "While Luke is happy to speak of Jesus' appearance on earth as God's bringing to Israel a saviour (Acts 13:23) his view of the scope of Jesus' rulership is not limited to Israel."[107] The narrative of the book of Acts has a decidedly *centrifugal* direction, of which Jesus' programmatic charge in 1:8 is an iconic expression.[108]

The exact referent of the expression ἕως ἐσχάτου τῆς γῆς ("till the end of the earth") and their relation to the end of Acts is disputed among scholars. Jervell understands it as referring to the Diaspora, and therefore excludes a mission to the Gentiles: "Man sollte nicht vorshnell an Heiden denken. . . . Das 'bis ans Ende der Welt' ist dann in erster linie als die jüdische Diaspora zu verstehen. . . . Die Apg zeigt, dass 'das Ende der Erde' nicht einem Endpunkt kennzeichnet, sondern den Weg des Evangelium durch die ganze Welt. Rom ist als Ziel für die Judenmission verstanden, aber die Mission geht 28,30 über Rom hinaus."[109] A similar view is held by Daniel Schwartz who thinks that Palestine is the referent, and therefore is only the beginning of the church's mission.[110]

A common argument is that Rome would never have been considered "the end of the earth" in the first-century Empire, but rather its center. Moreover, some claim, Acts is ending in an open-ended manner which seems to indicate that the mission has not reached its goal at that point. The expression must therefore be a more "literal" reference and Rome is only a necessary step towards it.[111]

Nevertheless, many scholars recognize that the most natural reading of this phrase in light of the *storyline* of Acts is that Rome is in view somehow.[112] For one thing, from a Jewish (or Palestinian) point of view such as we find in the Third Gospel, Jerusalem would be the center of the world, and Rome, standing as the representative of the "nations" (the "world" outside the Holy Land), could then be referred to as "the end of the earth." As a matter of fact *Pss. Sol.* 8:15 speaks of Pompey as having come from "the end of the earth."[113]

Finally, we would argue that the Book of Acts closes on a note of both completion and openness which can be better explained in terms of Luke's inaugurated eschatology as an instance of the "already and not yet." This is especially convincing when

---

107. Witherington, "Salvation and Health," 158.

108. Bauckham, *Bible and Mission*, 27–54, offers an excellent discussion of the centrifugal nature of redemptive history in the Bible.

109. Jervell, *Die Apostelgeschichte*, 116.

110. Schwartz, "End of Gē"

111. See the classic Van Unnik, "Ausdruck"; Ellis, "End of the Earth"; and Witherington, *Acts*, 809, 110–11.

112. See *Acts*, 206. The point was already argued at length by O'Neill, *Theology of Acts*, 54–70.

113. Witherington mentions this piece of evidence, but he is not swayed by it. We wonder whether his evaluation of its import is due to his conviction that the key to Luke's mind-set is the Graeco-Roman world rather than the Jewish one, thus understanding him as following the typical Hellenistic historical practice of arranging the data by geographical area and therefore ethnic groups (κατὰ γένος). See Witherington, *Acts*, 110–11, 290–301, 783–93.

one recognizes the Isaianic background for Acts 1:8, as was argued by David Pao.[114] When Paul (and the gospel with him) reaches Rome, the end of the earth is reached *representatively* and *proleptically*, though the consummation—the kingdom covering the whole planet earth—is still to come.[115] This, it seems to us, is confirmed by Jesus' words to Paul in a dream reported in Acts 23:11 (cf. 13:47).

The "plot" of Acts follows the pattern established by Jesus in 1:8, and therefore chronicles a very significant movement or transition for the early church. This movement is first expressed in terms of the "from Jerusalem to Rome" journey of the gospel (though it is not exactly a straight line).[116] It is also materialized in the change of focus from Peter to Paul—the one a Palestinian Jew (Aramaic-speaking), the other a Diaspora Jew (Greek-speaking)—with an intermediate, "mixed" situation in Acts 6–8.[117] These features are interwoven with the recurring transition from a Jewish audience to a Gentile one (reminiscent of Rom 1:16: "to the Jew first and also to the Greek").[118]

Luke is not content, however, with merely describing what happened, he clearly sets out to justify it. The mission to the Gentiles is presented as being orchestrated by God himself, as being part of his plan. Maybe the first event to be noted is Pentecost, where pilgrims from all over the Empire were present and believed (though they were either Jews or proselytes). The second would be Philip's ministry in Samaria, to

---

114. Pao, *Acts and INE*, 91–96.

115. For the concept of "representative geography," see Bauckham, *Bible and Mission*, 55–81.

116. This aspect is basically recognized by all scholars, e.g., Witherington, *Acts*, 69 and Fitzmyer, *Acts*, 119. Cf. the hermeneutical and theological reflections on this geographic movement offered by Scobie, "Canonical Approach"; Marguerat, "Luc-Actes entre"; and Marguerat, *Première histoire*, 97–122. Witherington makes the illuminating observation that the direction in Acts is the opposite as the one in Luke's Gospel: rather than being centrifugal—away from Jerusalem, the center—there it is centripetal—towards Jerusalem. Salvation comes from Jerusalem, and therefore Jesus *must* (δεῖ) die and rise there. It is important to note that the Gospel begins and ends in the Jerusalem temple, and that many key events happen in the city and the temple precincts (so also Fitzmyer, "Jesus," 255 and Joel B. Green, *Theology of Luke*, 12). In fact, the temple scenes of the infancy narratives announce and interpret the key elements of the remainder of the story. Acts opens in Jerusalem, where the disciples are commanded to stay and wait for the gift of the Spirit, and from where they would spread God's salvation to the whole world. The Stephen narrative concludes this "Jerusalem period" and commences the story of the worldwide mission by introducing Saul/Paul and the persecution that will force the first Christians out of Jerusalem and Judaea (as noted by Doble, "Something Greater," 182).

117. Paul appears first as "a young man named Saul" in 7:58 and begins persecuting the church in 8:1. Peter disappears from the narrative after chapter 12, making a short appearance in chapter 15 for the Jerusalem council. Even Luke's usage for Paul's name marks the transition: he uses exclusively "Saul" (Σαῦλος, a Jewish/Hebrew name) until 13:9—where he explains that he "was also called Paul" (Παῦλος, a Grecized Latin name)—after which he uses exclusively "Paul."

118. This transition is very often presented as the result of the Jews' rejection of the gospel, consistently with the theme of the divided people discussed earlier. Yet, contra Jervell, this is not exclusively the case, for Paul's proclamation of the gospel to the Gentiles in Athens, Lystra or Ephesus, for example, does not follow any Jewish rejection (or even a prior proclamation to Jews in the latter two). It is important to note also that the "Macedonian call" of Acts 16 makes no reference whatsoever to the Jewish need for, or rejection of, the gospel. The evangelization of the Gentiles cannot therefore be limited to a second-rank duty in either Luke's or Paul's eyes.

the Ethiopian eunuch and the cities of the coast (those would have been considered "mixed" but still related to Israel), in which we see the Spirit moving Philip from one place to another (in a way reminiscent of Elijah's story in 1 Kings 18).[119] The third is a major turning point in the book: the conversion of Cornelius (a Roman attending the synagogue) and his household. This story is told three times in the book of Acts (chap. 10, 11 and 15), showing its great significance, and is introduced by Peter's vision in which God declares the distinction between (ritually) clean and unclean to be dispelled. Furthermore, Paul's conversion—itself told three times—emphasizes the commissioning and sending of Paul to the nations (9:15, where Gentiles precede Jews in the list; 22:21; 26:17-18). Another Lukan triplet is Paul's announcing that the message of salvation is going to the Gentiles after it's being rejected by his Jewish audience (13:46; 18:6; 28:28).

Luke is careful to show that God is leading the church to preach salvation to the Gentiles either by direct revelation or through his sovereign guidance of events, as in the case of the Pauline and Herodian persecutions of Acts 8 and 12.[120] In fact, all through the book we see God using the opposition to, and persecution of, the church by both Jewish and Roman authorities as a means to propagate his word "to the end of the earth."[121] More than that, Acts shows God's good pleasure in the mission by pouring his Spirit on Gentiles (which convinces the apostles and elders of the church in Jerusalem in Acts 11) together with the Spirit-produced signs and wonders that accompany it.[122]

The Jerusalem Council and its decision are central to Acts. The position of the story (right in the middle of the book) and the narrative differences between what precedes it and what follows (especially what disappears in the second part, like the Twelve, Peter, speeches laden with OT citations, etc.) show that this episode is of utmost significance in the history of the early church. Its position at the climax of the string made of the Cornelius episode followed by the ministry of Philip and the first trip of Paul and Barnabas, together with the arguments presented by Peter, Paul/Barnabas and James (with a cumulative effect) and the fruits of the "Jerusalem Declaration" (which comes from both the Holy Spirit and the leaders of the Jerusalem church, including the Twelve) illustrated in the subsequent narrative, can but only make a deep impression on the reader: the

---

119. Thompson suggests that Samaria represents the Northern Kingdom so that Luke has in mind the reunification of the Davidic kingdom promised in Ezekiel 37. In a similar way, he sees the eunuch as the sign that the outcasts are also included among God's people in fulfillment of Isaiah 56. See Thompson, *One Lord*, 96-98 and *Acts of the Risen*, 112-18.

120. This is the case for the three persons of the Trinity: God, the risen Christ and the Spirit.

121. Hence Paul's last and climactic "missionary journey" is his transfer from the prison in Caesarea to his house-arrest in Rome which, narratively begins with his arrest in the temple precinct in Jerusalem.

122. Jervell explains that theme in terms of the Gentiles' joining or incorporating the "Israel of the Spirit": "Diesem 'Israel des Geistes' (2,17ff) schließen sich die Heiden an, was als Erfüllung der göttlichen Verheißungen verstanden wird. . . . Weil die Heindenmission als Schrifterfüllung gesehen wird, wird sie als Gottes Werk und Initiative erkennbar." "Apostelgeschichte," 227.

mission to the Gentiles was an essential part of God's eschatological work of salvation in and through the church, the restored Israel.

The final proof that this mission was willed by God, and the one that might be the most weighty in Luke's evaluation, is that the mission to the Gentiles was revealed by God in the OT. It starts with the Joel 2 passage, which affirms that the Spirit of God will be poured on "all flesh" (πᾶσαν σάρκα in Acts 2:17; LXX Joel 2:28; cf. MT 3:1: כָּל־בָּשָׂר), understood by Luke to include the nations also.[123] Paul concludes his speech to the unbelieving Jews in Pisidian Antioch (13:47) with the words of Isaiah 49:6 ("I will make you as a light for the nations, that my salvation may reach to the end of the earth," ἕως ἐσχάτου τῆς γῆς, identical to 1:8), which originally were addressed to the Servant of the Lord in the context of the future restoration and purification of Israel, but that Paul appropriates for the church and its mission to the world. Most significant is James the Just's *pesher*-like speech in Acts 15:16–17, which weaves citations from several OT prophecies together with Amos 9:11, appealing thus to an entire body of OT teaching concerning the Gentiles in the last days.[124] This passage is especially striking since it teaches not only that the Gentiles would join with Israel in the messianic age, but that they would do so as *Gentiles*!

Faced with this evidence—and taking into account that the Messiah is, as the Isaianic Servant, true and eschatological Israel—we can only conclude with Witherington that "Luke is then trying to show that Jew and Gentile united in Christ is the true Israel."[125] God's eschatological salvation requires incorporation and participation in the people of God, and therefore even Gentiles can receive it—in accordance with God's plan—in the restored Israel, the Spirit-endowed church.[126]

---

123. Actually, it really starts in Luke 2:30–32, with Simeon's prophetic prayer echoing Isa 52:10; 42:6; 49:6; and 46:13.

It is important to note that though the referent of the expression "all flesh" in Joel is exclusively the nation of Israel (this is indubitable from the context, contra Kaiser, *Mission in OT*, 71–72), Luke clearly means the expression to include the Gentiles among the recipients of the eschatological gift of the Spirit (so Van de Sandt, "Fate of Gentiles"). Rather than concluding that Luke corrects Joel's message in doing so (Van de Sandt's interpretation), it seems better to deduce that Luke understands the eschatological/restored Israel to be made up of both Jews and Gentiles (cf. Stuart, *Hoseah-Jonah*, 260–62).

124. "The speech of James in Acts 15.13–21 plays a key role in Luke's account of the Council of Jerusalem (and therefore in his whole account of the origins of the Gentile mission). . . . After all, the matter under discussion is one of *halakhah* (15.5), which could only be decided from Scripture. It is therefore left to James to provide the clinching argument: that according to Scripture itself the Gentiles who, it predicts, will join the eschatological people of God will do so as Gentiles." Bauckham, "James and the Gentiles," 154.

125. Witherington, *Acts*, 73.

126. Jervell mentions Peter's sermon in Acts 10:34–43 as making this very point clear to his Gentile audience (*Theology of Acts*, 96–97).

The Lukan Portrayal of Salvation

Salvation in Luke-Acts is a divine gift: "Salvation in the Lukan sense of the term is something that comes from and properly belongs to God. . . . Salvation is something humans can only receive, not achieve."[127] Christ's authority to save and heal comes from his Father.[128] Jesus, the Messiah, is himself a gift from God to his redeemed people (just like the Holy Spirit, is given by the Father to Jesus who then pours it on the church): "And there is salvation in no one else, for there is no other name under heaven given among men by which we must be saved" (Acts 4:12). This Jesus is the *one* and only savior for *all* people, and therefore he must be proclaimed to all nations. This universalistic emphasis in Luke's soteriology is noted by all. It sets him apart from the other synoptic Evangelists and places him near Paul.[129]

Witherington notes that the book of Acts has a "horizontal" universal dimension in that the good news reaches the end of the world, beginning with Jerusalem, while the Third Gospel has a "vertical" universal dimension in that the same good news reaches up and down the social scale. "The spread of this good news even to the least, last, and lost is made clear in the paradigmatic speech in Luke 4:18–21 where Jesus quotes Isaiah 61."[130] Luke's two volumes demonstrate his interest for the poor, the oppressed, the possessed, the imprisoned, the diseased, the disenfranchised, women and children. Hence the depiction of the Spirit empowering the earliest church to minister to such as these: Acts 5–6, e.g., shows the community intent on taking care of those in needs, especially the widows. But Luke is no liberation theologian, for in his view the gospel is as much for the "least" as for the wealthy and the powerful, whether he be "righteous" or an oppressor himself.[131] This salvation is truly for *all*.

Not only is it for all people, but it affects every aspect of life. It has a social and physical dimension, even if the spiritual is preeminent. The social dimension is clear in Jesus' inaugural sermon (Luke 4), of course, but also in his restoration of social outcasts such as tax-collectors (Levi in Luke 5, Zacchaeus in Luke 19, the hero of a parable in Luke 15; cf. the comments on his ministry in 7:34 and 15:1), lepers or prostitutes as well as his care for the poor (such as the widow of Luke 7). The physical dimension is obvious in the numerous healings and exorcisms that Jesus (and his disciples) perform. Hence the response to John the Baptist's query about his messiahship:

---

127. Witherington, "Salvation and Health," 157.

128. Jervell, *Theology of Acts*, 95. Witherington points to the fact that "After the initial Jewish reference to God as saviour in Luke 1, the rest of Luke-Acts concentrates on Jesus as the one who fulfills that role, indeed exclusively so." Witherington, "Salvation and Health," 158. Moreover, he remarks that Luke is the only synoptic Evangelist to apply the noun σωτήρ to Jesus ("Salvation and Health," 157).

129. See the short but interesting discussion of this dimension in Fitzmyer, *Luke*, 1.187–92. This universalism, however, is not to be understood as "Jews plus . . ." but as a reconstituting of Israel itself, according to Fitzmyer who, here, agrees with Jervell.

130. Witherington, *Acts*, 69; see also Joel B. Green, *Theology of Luke*, 76–94.

131. Witherington comments: "They, too, were captives who needed to be set free, whether from money, power, or pious religiosity." Witherington, *Acts*, 71.

"the blind receive their sight, the lame walk, lepers are cleansed, and the deaf hear, the dead are raised up, the poor have good news preached to them" (Luke 7:22). As these two aspects recede to a secondary position in Acts, the spiritual dimension of salvation becomes much more prominent than it was in the Gospel.[132] In summary, "The whole gospel must be proclaimed to the whole person in the whole world, for there is one, all sufficient Savior for all, and therefore all must be for this one."[133]

Luke mostly speaks of salvation in present terms, though it has a future dimension also. Thus Witherington writes: "when σωτηρια/σωζω occurs and is used in a theologically loaded sense in Luke-Acts [in contrast with its more mundane usage], the large majority of the time he focuses on the present reality and benefits of salvation," whether those are social, physical, or spiritual.[134] This is fully consistent with Luke's conviction that salvation is God's act fulfilling his OT promises in Jesus, the Messiah. It is a fully present reality, awaiting its ultimate consummation.[135]

Luke's concept of salvation certainly includes a number of this-worldly benefits,[136] which are basically the same as the ones found in Jewish and Graeco-Roman literature under the name of "salvation." But they are almost incidental to the gospel itself and its proclamation, and they are certainly not the focus of Luke's soteriology: "It is especially the frequent, almost purely 'spiritual', use of this language [of salvation] to refer to conversion, forgiveness of sins, cleansing of the heart and its eternal personal benefits that makes Luke's work stand out from the non-Christian sources. Also, the christocentric focus and preoccupation of Luke's salvation language makes it stand apart."[137]

Witherington here points to an essential aspect of all NT thinking which is certainly true of Luke-Acts: soteriology and christology are inseparable.[138] Jervell expresses it this way: "The significance of the Jesus-event is, first and foremost, salvation."[139] But the converse is also true: "Salvation is linked exclusively with Jesus (Acts 2:21; 4:12; 13:23; 16:31; Luke 1:69; 2:11; 19:9)."[140] Interestingly, Luke does not

---

132. Cf. Witherington, *Acts*, 143. This is perfectly consistent with Luke's redemptive-historical sensitivity: the most important dimension of salvation takes its full place *after* the resurrection and the pouring of the "power from on high."

133. Witherington, *Acts*, 72.

134. Witherington, "Salvation and Health," 161. Luke depicts the future aspect of salvation as the entrance into God's dominion and participation in the messianic banquet following Christ's return.

135. See Fitzmyer, *Luke*, 1.222.

136. See Jervell, *Theology of Acts*, 100.

137. Witherington, "Salvation and Health," 156–57, 164.

138. "Part of what it means to recognize the synthetic thinking of the New Testament writers involves seeing that Christology in the New Testament is so bound up with soteriology that it is quite impossible and wrong methodologically to consider the person of Christ apart from his works. Often the christological and the soteriological statements come together and arise out of each other." Witherington, *Many Faces*, 232.

139. Jervell, *Theology of Acts*, 94.

140. Jervell, *Theology of Acts*, 97. Or, more precisely: "Das Heil is ausschliesslich mit dem Kommen

bind salvation to any discrete part of Jesus' life and work. Instead he ties the same soteriological benefits to all of them, viz., his life, death, resurrection, and ascension.[141] Moreover, he does not explain in what way those elements are the causes of salvation (or any part thereof). The conclusion to be drawn is evident: it is as a whole that Jesus' life and work accomplishes salvation for God's people.[142]

Luke is not very specific as to what exactly "salvation" is, according to Jervell. He mostly speaks of it in general terms, without specifying its content very precisely. Jervell's explanation of this trait seems correct: "Luke presupposes that his readers know what salvation means and that it contains various elements hard to put into one simple formula."[143] Scholars agree that in Luke-Acts "salvation" generally refers to the forgiveness of sins, a theme that becomes more prominent in the second volume (though it encapsulates all of Christ's life and work in Luke 24:46–47 already).[144] This is due to Luke's "keen sense of historical development and process," which allows him to give due weight to the soteriological and redemptive-historical (hence eschatological) turning point of Pentecost.[145] Finally, "sin" seems to be understood mainly in relational terms rather than in moralistic ones, and therefore the forgiveness of sins brings about the restoration of Israel's (and its members') relationship/communion with God. Sin's definition is thus itself God-centered. It has to do with people's actions against God, their "debt" in God's sight. In this context, forgiveness of sins provides the repentant believer with peace and (eternal) life.

The Place of the Atonement in Luke's Soteriology

The final aspect of Luke's soteriology that must be addressed is one that may have drawn him the most fire from certain critical scholars: the place of the atonement (if

---

und Werk des Messias verbunden" Jervell, *Die Apostelgeschichte*, 104.

141. See the relevant texts in Jervell, *Die Apostelgeschichte*, 104–5. At the same time, one must say that the resurrection of Jesus—seen as God's saving act for his Messiah—is preeminent in connection with salvation. Cf. Jervell, *Theology of Acts*, 97-98 and Thompson, *Acts of the Risen*, 71–83.

142. Jervell puts it this way: "That means that you cannot isolate any single phase; rather the whole sweep is redemptive." *Theology of Acts*, 97, elaborating on Glöckner, *Verkündigung*.

143. Jervell, *Theology of Acts*, 95. Rather than assuming, like a number of critical scholars, that Luke had no developed soteriology, it seems much wiser to assume that soteriology was a well-known Christian teaching in the church. Once again, Paul's (existentially-reinterpreted) focus on soteriology is used to judge Luke's lack thereof in an unfair and contextually-insensitive manner. Luke's concern is in a different place, and he can simply assume his readers' knowledge of the common faith of the church and of the content of his first volume.

144. See, e.g., Fitzmyer, *Luke*, 1.222-24; Jervell, *Theology of Acts*, 99–100; and Witherington, *Acts*, 143.

145. "Luke believes that with the sending of the eschatological Spirit the eschatological blessings of God's divine saving activity, including release from sins, begin to manifest themselves more fully and repeatedly." Witherington, *Acts*, 144.

any) in Lukan thought.¹⁴⁶ Jervell is willing to concede that Luke does not really speak of sacrifice or atonement in relation to Jesus' death, but that it is God's "plan" for effecting the salvation of his people. He is convinced that Luke knew of Jesus' death being understood as atonement and sacrifice (as is shown by Luke 22:19-20, 24:46-47, and Acts 20:28) and does not deny it, but that he "thrusts it into the background for some inscrutable reason."¹⁴⁷ Luke clearly presents Jesus' death as having saving significance, but it seems that his focus is more on showing that Messiah's suffering and death were part of God's plan, and that therefore Jesus is the true Messiah.¹⁴⁸

Not everybody is satisfied with this explanation, however, and Witherington sets out (with others) to defend Luke's soteriology and the place it gives to the cross against its critics. In particular, Witherington looks carefully at Acts 5:31 and what it reveals of Luke's soteriology. This text seems to teach that Jesus was not assuming fully the role of savior before his death-resurrection-ascension (in accordance with Luke's historical sense): "It is only after his death on the cross that he can offer repentance to Israel (especially for her role in what happened on Golgotha) and forgiveness of sins. It is also only then that Jesus can send the Holy Spirit who, in Luke's theology, is seen as Christ's agent bringing salvation to the world (Acts 2:33-38, 47; 10:15-18)."¹⁴⁹ Witherington fully agrees with Moessner at this point, who argues that Jesus' crucifixion/rejection, resurrection/ascension, and the proclamation thereof are the three critical components of God's βουλή (announced beforehand in the OT) for Luke.¹⁵⁰ This, together with Luke 24:45-49, shows clearly that "for Luke, Christ's death and resurrection are *at the very heart* of God's saving plan for humankind which is revealed in the Scriptures."¹⁵¹

---

146. So Fitzmyer, *Luke*, 1.219-20 reports that C. H. Dodd, J. M. Creed, E. Käsemann, G. Voss, H. Conzelmann, H. J. Cadbury and even C. H. Talbert consider that Luke ascribes no real meaning to the cross and does not regard Jesus' death as a sacrifice or an expiation for sin. Fitzmyer retorts that even if it were true that Luke had no clear atonement theory, he nevertheless indubitably considered Jesus' suffering and death as the means through which salvation was effected by God. Nowhere can one find Luke saying or implying that salvation was realized in spite of them.

147. Jervell, *Theology of Acts*, 98, cf. 31n44. Here Jervell seems to have a more positive opinion about this issue than in earlier writings such as "Paul in Acts," 305-6, where he claims that Luke only had a "rudimentary understanding" of the atonement.

148. Howard Marshall agrees with this view. He thinks that it explains why the resurrection is more prominent than the cross in Luke's writings, for it demonstrates God's approval of Jesus as Messiah. He adds that such a presentation of the story of Jesus and the early church is truer to the context of the early church which Luke is describing in Acts, where "there was probably little development of a theology of atonement." Marshall, "Christology," 131; cf. Joel B. Green, *Theology of Luke*, 64-68.

149. Witherington, "Salvation and Health," 158.

150. After studying a number of passages (Acts 1:15-26; 2:14-40; 3:12-26; 4:23-31; 5:27-42; 8:26-40; 9:1-18; 13:13-52; 15:1-21; 26:1-23), Moessner concludes convincingly: "We have seen, therefore, that Luke configures the death of Jesus as an atoning event through the interweaving of the stories of Israel's rejection of their Messiah and of God's overarching purpose for this rejection in God's plan (βουλή) for all humanity." Moessner, "Script of Scriptures," 249.

151. Witherington, "Salvation and Health," 159 (emphasis ours). Thompson argues that the focus on Jesus' resurrection in Acts presupposes and builds upon the Gospel's focus on his death, where it

It is therefore erroneous to claim that Luke has no, or at least no adequate, theology of the cross and the atonement. The fact that Luke does not spell out all the implications of Jesus' death is no argument, especially since Acts 20:28 makes clear that Luke knew and *approved* the idea of Jesus' shed blood being the means through which God creates and gathers the ἐκκλησία.[152] Moreover, William Larkin has shown that paying attention to Luke's use of Isaiah sheds much light on his soteriology. Hence, Luke construes the whole of Christ's passion (and not one discrete element only) as the fulfillment of Isaiah's prophecy. Moreover, he uses Isaiah 53:12 (Luke 22:37; 23:34) as a pointer to the larger Isaianic theme of the Servant (especially seen as the "suffering Servant"), which he uses to interpret Jesus' own suffering and death. Larkin's conclusion is that "Luke's soteriology does indeed have vicarious atonement as its foundation. Because its presentation concentrates on the objective historical basis, not the explicit theological interpretation that may be built on it, this aspect of Luke's soteriological thought is often missed."[153]

Jesus the Messiah-Servant

Thus Luke's soteriology—with all its connections to God's redemptive plan prophesied in the OT, to the eschatological and climactic nature of the salvation offered, and to the Holy Spirit who restores (re-creates) God's people (bringing together both Jew and Gentile, oppressed and oppressor)—truly centers around the person of Jesus of Nazareth.[154] This should not really be surprising. In the end, the question that proves to be central is how Jesus could be Israel's Messiah and the Lord of the whole world when his life was one of suffering that ended with the most despicable death possible?[155]

First of all, Jesus is a man (Acts 2:22; 17:31), a Palestinian Jew. Luke paints that portrait very carefully: Jesus was born in Bethlehem (Luke 2:6-7) of Mary, the bride of Joseph, a man of Davidic lineage (explaining the trip to Bethlehem for

---

is understood in line with the OT theology of the atonement, especially as expressed in Isaiah 53. See Thompson, *Acts of the Risen*, 83–88.

152. As noted by Witherington, "Salvation and Health," 159n59.

153. Larkin, "OT and Soteriology," 335.

154. "[Luke] knows that salvation is given only to the people of God and comes from no one but the Messiah, who stems from that same people. Everything in the church hangs on belief in the true Messiah." Jervell, *Theology of Acts*, 25. In other words, "Jesus ist der Messias des Gottesvolkes." Jervell, *Die Apostelgeschichte*, 93.

155. For a rather exhaustive study of the evidence concerning how the ancient world was repulsed by the crucifixion and its victims, see the classic Hengel, *Crucifixion*. In particular, one cannot overestimate the aversion that the crucifixion inspired to first-century Jews in the light of the well-known Deut 21:23 ("a hanged man is cursed by God") and of their own history. At the same time, see Boyarin's provocative argument that the notion of a suffering, (vicariously) dying and resurrected Messiah was congenial and even present in Jewish thought prior to the advent of Christ in *Jewish Gospels*, 129–56. If he is correct, then the issue would not be so much how the Messiah could go through such experiences, but whether Jesus was that Messiah. Christian christology would then have naturally grown out of its Jewish soil rather than been a radical innovation alien to it.

the census; Luke 1:27; 2:4; 3:31), circumcised the eighth day, presented to the Lord in the temple, raised in Nazareth (4:16), etc.[156] Moreover, Luke insists heavily on Jesus' "humanness," not just his humanity: he has human reactions and is unusually compassionate with others.[157]

But at the same time, there is much about Jesus that is not merely human. Fitzmyer discusses a number of peculiar traits that "transcend" Jesus' human condition. This list includes the virginal conception through the power of the Spirit (Luke 1:34–35), the exceptional guidance of the Spirit throughout his ministry (Luke 3:22; 4:1, 14, 18; 10:21), his unique relationship to the Father (Luke 1:32; 2:49; 3:22; 9:35; 10:21–22; 23:46; Luke's peculiar use of "Son of God," of which 3:38 seems to us to be fundamental), his resurrection from the dead (Luke 24:6a; Acts 2:24–32) and, of course, his ascension (Luke 24:51; Acts 1:9).[158] The title "Lord" (κύριος), especially in its definite form "the Lord," which Luke uses for both God and Jesus, clearly places Jesus on the same level as Yahweh, without completely identifying the two.[159] In fact, as Rowe has shown in *Early Narrative Christology*, these instances together with Luke's strategic interplay of vocative uses (in his character's mouths) with nominative ones (in narratorial comments) and the subtle narrative correction other terms of address (like ἐπιστάτα or διδάσκαλε) are very effective means to affirm the common divine identity of Jesus with the Father. Finally, Fitzmyer highlights three passages he considers *may* explicitly call Jesus "God": Luke 8:39; 9:43; and Acts 20:28.[160] Besides this evidence adduced by Fitzmyer, a very significant element that must be highlighted is Luke's ascription of a number of exclusively *divine* roles and prerogatives to Jesus. That includes forgiving sins (e.g., Luke 5:18–26; the Pharisees make explicit the link between doing so and deity), being the Savior (which Luke makes clear is a divine privilege in Luke 1:47), judging the whole world at the end of time (Acts 10:42; 17:31), and worship (from the disciples in Luke 24:52). In conclusion, we can say that though Luke stresses Jesus' humanness, he simultaneously reveals Jesus' divine roles and nature in a discreet but effective manner.

As has been noted several times before, the christology of Luke-Acts develops as the narrative progresses. This is particularly evident with Luke's use of titles and names in connection with Jesus. Examples include "Son of Man" which is frequent

---

156. Both Fitzmyer and Jervell make this point emphatically: Jervell, *Theology of Acts*, 29 and Fitzmyer, *Luke*, 1.192.

157. Noted by Fitzmyer, *Luke*, 1.193; see the fascinating portrait drawn by B. B. Warfield in "Emotional Life."

158. Fitzmyer, *Luke*, 1.193–94.

159. Fitzmyer notes that Jesus is never called "Father," a name/title that is exclusively used for Yahweh/God. He is very hesitant to conclude that Luke's use of "Lord" meant that Jesus was God, though he recognizes that it is not impossible. Cf. Fitzmyer, *Luke*, 1.202–4 and Rowe, *Early Narrative*, 7, 208–10, who points out the shortcomings of Fitzmyer's method and conclusion.

160. Though Fitzmyer remains cautious, he certainly is open to the idea that Luke actually refers to Jesus when using "God" in those verses. It is particularly the case for the last two. See Fitzmyer, *Luke*, 1.218–19, 740, 810 and *Acts*, 680.

in the Gospel, but appears only once in Acts in Stephen's vision (7:56)—depicting the Son of Man standing, whereas he is sitting in the Gospels.[161] Though Jesus is called "Savior" in Luke 2:11 (in the angels' proclamation to the shepherds; the only time in the whole Gospel), he fully takes on that role only in Acts, where the title is used of him twice in direct relation with his exaltation/ascension: once in Peter's response to the Sanhedrin, 5:31, and once in Paul's synagogue sermon in Pisidian Antioch, 13:23.[162] As C. F. D. Moule has argued, Luke uses christological terms and titles in a historically-sensitive manner, "with a clear historical perspective on the differences between the pre- and post-resurrection situation and the pre- and post-resurrection community of Jesus' followers."[163] Thus, as Rowe argues (going beyond Moule), Luke is able to combine theological affirmation and historical verisimilitude.[164] The resurrection-ascension is the turning point of redemptive history, even for Jesus, and it is therefore also the turning point of what Witherington and Rowe call Luke's "narrative Christology."[165]

"[Luke] has a highly independent and distinctive selection and use of titles. He employs some seemingly very old christological titles, mostly only to be found in Luke's works within the New Testament, and going back to the church in Jerusalem."[166] Depending on how scholars define what is a title, they produce different lists.[167] Nev-

---

161. Witherington notes that this is the only use of the expression outside of the Gospels and Revelation's quote of Daniel 7, in which it is not titular but analogical. Witherington, *Many Faces*, 154.

162. See Witherington, "Salvation and Health," 158. Witherington's excursus on christology studies that dimension of Luke's use of the titles "Christ" and "Lord" (*Acts*, 147–53).

163. Witherington, *Many Faces*, 154–55, referring to Moule, "Christology of Acts."

164. See his helpful critique of Moule's approach in Rowe, *Early Narrative*, 208–16.

165. Witherington, *Acts*, 152. As a matter of fact, Luke does not provide a systematic exposition of his christology. Instead, he tells the story of Jesus from his birth to his exaltation in heaven where he reigns as Lord over all (with the promise of his return as Judge on the last day).

166. Jervell, *Theology of Acts*, 26. Like others, Jervell considers the christology in Luke-Acts as a whole to be primitive, even pre-Pauline. This fact cannot, according to him, simply be explained as "historic," as if it had no bearing upon Luke's own theology as well as that of the Christians he was writing for. Rather, Luke's christology is Jewish-Christian in both character and origins, as it is deeply rooted in the Scriptures and in Jewish traditions. Witherington disagrees with Jervell on this point: in his eyes, Luke's christology is significantly influenced by the Hellenistic background of its author and audience (see Witherington, *Many Faces*, 153). He makes his case mainly on the basis of Luke's use of "Lord" and "Savior" in a polemical manner against the Roman Emperor worship. Fitzmyer—in accordance with his tendency towards a perspective akin to the *Religionsgeschichtliche Schule*—finds that some elements come from the OT and Jewish traditions, some from the Hellenistic world, some are a mix of both, and a number are impossible to decide.

It seems to us that the substance—and even form—of Luke's christology is essentially Jewish-Christian, though Luke does interact apologetically and polemically with the Hellenistic world (as well as the Jewish world), especially as regards official Emperor worship and its accompanying eschatology/soteriology.

167. For example, Jervell lists "the holy," "the righteous one," God's agent to Israel, God's servant, a man of God, "the prophet," leader, prince. Other titles (such as "Son of Man," "Son of God," and "Son of David") are considered under the categories of "kyrios" and "Christos" (*Theology of Acts*, 26–28). Fitzmyer discusses Messiah/Christos, Lord/the Lord, Savior, Son of God, Son of Man, servant,

ertheless, all generally agree that the two most significant titles used by Luke are, by far, κύριος—the most frequent—and χριστός—often deemed the most important. The two are combined once (χριστὸς κύριος in Luke 2:11) in the theologically very dense proclamation of the angel to the shepherds, to define and denote the σωτήρ who has just been given to mankind by God in the city of *David* (!). Yet, however much titles can offer a window into Luke's christology,[168] we must heed Jervell's words carefully: "In the Gospel of Luke christology is worked out *above all by a series of stories*, rarely by titles and never by exact definitions of the identity of Jesus. When writing Acts Luke obviously assumed that his readers knew those stories."[169] At the end of the day, it is clear that an essential feature of Luke's christology is to proclaim and explain—even offer an ἀπολογία for—Jesus the promised (eschatological) Davidic Messiah.[170]

Hence Eduard Schweizer has shown that Luke builds a strong scriptural argument to demonstrate that Jesus fulfills diverse messianic OT strands, and especially that he is the fulfillment of the promised Davidic king's and the nation of Israel's divine sonships.[171] In a similar fashion, Jervell claims that in Luke-Acts χριστός defines all titles.[172] In other words, all other titles must be understood under the category of Christ's messiahship as they refer to divers facets of—or perspectives on—that essential and all-defining character of Jesus' life and work. Jesus thus fulfills all the promises of God to Israel, he is God's Messiah who brings salvation to Israel in the last days. It is especially noteworthy that while Luke's application of various names and titles to Jesus is different before and after the resurrection, it is not so with the term Christ.[173]

---

prophet, king, Son of David, leader, holy one, righteous one, judge, teacher and God (Fitzmyer, *Luke*, 1.197–219). And Witherington focuses almost exclusively on "Lord" and "Christ," mentioning only other titles as they relate to these two (*Acts*, 147–53).

168. For example, it is generally considered that χριστός is often merely a name in the NT (especially when combined with Ἰησοῦς), having lost its messianic titular denotation. But this is clearly not true in the case of Luke, with whom the term retains its titular value most of the time. Cf. Grundmann, "Christ Statements."

169. Jervell, *Theology of Acts*, 26 (emphasis ours).

170. Cf. Witherington, *Many Faces*, 157 and Witherington, *Acts*, 152.

171. Schweizer concludes: "Thus, the question of the relation between the unique divine sonship of the coming Davidic king and that of the whole people of Israel, still open in postbibical Judaism (cf. Ps. Sol. 17), is answered in the New Testament by the person of Jesus Christ, fulfilling the old Davidic prophecies and incorporating the church in his status as the Son of God." "Concept," 191. Witherington refers approvingly to Schweizer's argument in *Acts*, 152.

172. Jervell, *Theology of Acts*, 27.

173. "In the christological titles employed by Luke there is no distinction between the earthly and the exalted Christ as if we had to do with two different epochs theologically." Jervell, *Theology of Acts*, 27. This characteristic is perfectly consistent with the fact that at Jesus' baptism the heavenly voice declares "You are my beloved Son; with you I am well pleased" (Luke 3:22), while in Acts 13:33 Paul states that Jesus' resurrection is the fulfillment of Ps 2:7 ("You are my Son, today I have begotten you"). These two passages are remarkably similar, especially in light of Jesus referring to his crucifixion (and resurrection?) as a baptism in Luke 12:50. One should add that both passages are clearly parallel with Gen 22:1 (when God calls Abraham to sacrifice Isaac, his only son whom he loves) and Isa 42:1, which speaks of the Servant of the Lord who is given the Spirit (the same Spirit received by Jesus at his

As Messiah, Jesus is king, that is, he is the Son of David who will reign on David's throne for ever.[174] As such he is also the Savior, though, of course, in an unexpected way: his inaugurated salvation is spiritual, not at all political or military.[175] Jesus is the Son of God, a title which is primarily messianic as its relation to the "Servant of the Lord" shows.[176] For Luke this title is equivalent (at least functionally) to "Son of Man,"[177] which comes directly from Dan 7:13 where it refers to the eschatological ruler of the earth, who receives dominion over "all peoples, nations, and languages," and whose kingdom is everlasting (in contrast with the various kingdoms and empires that preceded it). The resurrection, which is the demonstration that Jesus is the Messiah/Son of God (Acts 13:33), is also the *proof* that he has been appointed *Judge* of the whole world (Acts 10:42; 17:31).[178] In line with his Davidic lineage, Jesus is presented as the eschatological prophet, the final and messianic prophet-king.[179]

---

baptism) to bring justice to the *nations!* (Echoed in Isa 61:1–2, the text of Jesus' first recorded preaching in Luke 4.) Another interesting connection is Jesus' promise that the disciples themselves would be baptized with the Holy Spirit in Acts 1:5 (in contrast to John's baptism which was with water).

174. Jervell notes that Luke uses the title "Son of David" more than any other NT writer (Jervell, *Theology of Acts*, 28). Luke uses it in his Gospel but not in Acts, though the concept itself is repeatedly present. As Son of David, Jesus restores the kingdom to Israel (Luke 1:32–33; Acts 1:6–8), he is king of the Jews (cf. Luke 19:38, his triumphal entry into Jerusalem and the accusation brought forth against him by the Jews before Pilate, Luke 23:2–5—where "Christ" and "king" are corollaries if not synonyms—, and Luke 23:37–38).

175. Yet the use of this title could well be polemical at times, in opposition to the Emperor's worship in which the term σωτήρ was very important. See Witherington, "Salvation and Health," 157–58. Here we use "spiritual" to refer primarily to the *modus operandi* of the redemption/salvation at work between Jesus' two comings, it is not meant to limit its effects and efficacy to the "religious" sphere of human life only. Luke makes it clear that Jesus' salvation is concerned with all aspects of life (physical, social, economic, political, etc.).

176. Luke uses "Son of God" many times in his Gospel, but only once in Acts (9:20). He uses the title "servant"—παῖς, a reference to the "Servant" in Isaiah which echoes the figure of Moses, ὁ παῖς τοῦ θεοῦ/κυρίου (e.g., Josh 13: 8; 14:7; 2 Chr 6:34; 24:9)—not only for Jesus (Acts 4:30) but also for Israel (Luke 1:54) and for David (Luke 1:69; Acts 4:25).

177. It is obvious in Luke 22:69–70, where Jesus calls himself "Son of Man" and the Jews ask in response: "Are you the Son of God, then?" It is intriguing that, just like for "Son of God," Luke uses "Son of Man" many times in his Gospel but only once in Acts (7:56).

178. Here it is important to remember that in OT times, one of the most prominent roles of the king/ruler is to *judge* his people. This is evident in the case of Moses (Exod 18:14–26), the rulers of the book of Judges, and preeminently in the person of Solomon, the wisest judge that ever was and the king of the most expansive, peaceful and prosperous Israel (who built the first Jerusalem temple, a privilege denied his father David).

179. Luke is the only NT writer to call David a prophet (Acts 2:30), though the prophetic nature of his Psalms is often recognized or assumed in Second Temple Judaism and the NT. Cf. Kugel, *Bible as It Was*, 22. Jervell offers a very interesting study of Luke's understanding of David as "the prophet *par excellence* in the scriptures"—after Moses, of course (*Theology of Acts*, 65–69). Moreover Luke presents Jesus as Moses' promised "prophet like me" of Deut 18:15 (see Moessner, "Jesus and Wilderness" and Moessner, "Luke 9:1–50"), and builds a number of parallels between he and the prophets Elijah and Elisha of 1 Kings (see the various publications of Thomas Brodie on the subject, especially *Luke the Literary* and "Imitation and Emulation").

Two more elements need to be mentioned here. First, Jesus defines himself as a prophet in Luke's

Even the title "Lord" (κύριος) is messianic in character for Luke.[180] Its use for both God and Jesus (it is sometimes impossible to decide which is in view) certainly expresses the unity of the two (and some kind of equality) as well as the fact that Jesus exercises God's prerogative to rule over (re-established) Israel and the whole world.[181] Luke is emphatically clear that Jesus enters into his reign with his resurrection-ascension (which entails at the same time Christ's exaltation/glorification as a heavenly king and his bodily absence), which leads some scholars to speak of an "exaltation" christology.[182]

This picture of Jesus could certainly be considered a form of "theology of glory" if it were not for one more prominent element in Luke's christology: God's promised Messiah was not an always-victorious warlord, but a suffering servant who died a criminal slave's death on behalf of sinners.[183] In consequence, Fitzmyer makes the following claim: "The idea of a suffering Messiah is found nowhere in the Old Testament or in any Jewish literature prior to or contemporaneous with the New Testament. This has to be maintained, despite what Luke himself attributes to 'Moses,' 'all the proph-

---

Gospel, especially in relation with his suffering/persecution and death in Jerusalem (which he prophesies!). This theme of the persecuted prophet is then transferred to the disciples in the book of Acts (see Moessner, "Paul in Acts" and Moessner, "The Christ Must"). Second, Jesus is unique as a prophet in that he receives the Spirit of prophecy in such a way that he can in his turn dispense that same Spirit to his disciples so that the church becomes an eschatological prophetic community as is indicated in Peter's Pentecost sermon (see Witherington, *Many Faces*, 164).

Finally, it is noteworthy that Luke mentions the *Jewish guards* mocking Jesus as a *prophet* after his arrest, but not the *Roman soldiers* mocking him as *king* (in fact, Pilate seems to recognize Jesus' regal status as far as the Jews are concerned in the passion narrative). Matthew tells only the second event, while Mark includes both.

180. Jervell notes that χριστός and κύριος are often combined or used interchangeably (*Theology of Acts*, 29).

181. This is clear from the use Peter makes of Ps 110:1 in Acts 2:34–36. Jervell mentions only Israel in his discussion, but he seems to miss the fact that both in the OT and the Third Gospel, the restoration of God's kingdom involves the nations also, as the ones who will be subjected to the messianic rule (willingly or forcefully) or seek refuge under his wings (e.g., Isa 2:3–4; 14:1–4; 19:18–25). Maybe his failure to take into account this dimension of OT eschatology explains his failure to give its due place to the Gentile mission in Acts. Cf. Bauckham, *Bible and Mission*; Wright, *Mission of God*; and Kaiser, *Mission in OT*.

182. "But it can be said at once that the Acts' Christology is consistently 'exalted' in type. Although there are phrases which in a later context could be classed as adoptionist—Jesus is twice called ἀνήρ (2:22; 17:31; cf. Luke 24:19)—there is never any doubt that he is more than a mere prophet or rabbi of the past." Moule, "Christology of Acts," 166. Witherington adds: "This is also why the sending of the Spirit is so crucial in the Lukan scheme of things. If Jesus is absent, the church must have some source of divine power and direction, and the Spirit provides both." *Many Faces*, 155. See also Thompson's argument against the notion of an "absentee christology" (a phrase coined by Moule; "Christology of Acts," 165, 179–80) in *Acts of the Risen*, 48–54. Cf. Jervell, *Theology of Acts*, 33–34.

183. A notion that would have been shocking or offensive to both Jews and Gentiles, though for different reasons. The book of Acts shows that the Holy Spirit must enable people to accept this suffering Christ and Lord through faith, in a way that is perfectly consistent with Paul's summary of his evangelistic ministry: "we preach Christ crucified, a stumbling block to Jews and folly to Gentiles, but to those who are called, both Jews and Greeks, Christ the power of God and the wisdom of God." (1 Cor 1:23–24).

ets,' and 'all the Scriptures' in his Gospel (24:27, 46). Nor does any other New Testament writer ever speak of Jesus as a suffering Messiah. This is an exclusively Lucan theologoumenon."[184] Fitzmyer is right as far as the lexical combination "suffering" and "Messiah" is concerned, but he is mistaken as concerns the presence of the notion in either group of writings.

Fitzmyer flatly rejects the connection that many see between the Messiah who suffers and the Isaianic figure of the Suffering Servant.[185] The only argument he gives against it, however, is that an identification of the Servant with the Messiah is found in the Jewish literature only in the *later* tradition.[186] But his judgment is too harsh here, and quite a few scholars would strongly disagree with his assertion.[187] In the first place, we should not push aside so lightly Jesus' words concerning the OT's prophesying his suffering and death. Secondly, Fitzmyer seems to overlook the fragmentary nature of the extant Second Temple Jewish literature, and thus the gaps that must exist in our knowledge of earlier Jewish traditions. One must also grant the possibility that later documents might preserve earlier traditions otherwise unknown to us, a basic principle of textual criticism. Thirdly, even if he were correct, he does not consider the possibility that Luke and other early Christians could have made the connection themselves without a Jewish forerunner. This is a particularly questionable premise since it would imply that Luke invented the whole concept of a suffering Messiah *ex nihilo*. However, if he is not creative enough to connect the life of Jesus with the Suffering Servant of Isaiah's prophecy when the two have so much in common, how could he be creative enough to produce such a revolutionary concept as a suffering Messiah? On the contrary, Larkin's argument that Luke's use of Isaiah 53:12 in Luke 22:37 points to the fact that Luke did identify Jesus with Isaiah's Suffering Servant stands on much firmer ground.[188]

As Luke seeks to explain how the Messiah could suffer and die at the hands of his own people (ironically joining hands with the very enemy they hoped the Messiah would destroy!), he is not content with a merely human or horizontal explanation, though he mentions the Jews' "ignorance" (Ac 13:27).[189] Instead, he seeks to demonstrates that Jesus' "death and resurrection are solely God's work."[190] Jesus' suffering was a necessity (Luke 17:3; Acts 9:22; 17:25; 22:37; 24:7, 26, 44)[191] because it was willed by

---

184. Fitzmyer, "Jesus," 259; see also Fitzmyer, *Acts*, 200.

185. As do, e.g., Jeremias, "παῖς θεοῦ" and France, "Servant of Yahweh."

186. Fitzmyer, *Luke*, 1.200.

187. E.g., Hengel, "Effective History" and Boyarin, *Jewish Gospels*, 129–56.

188. "The method by which Luke worked out the fulfillment of Isa 53:12 in his passion narrative was to treat the verse as a text, the basis for a theme that would constantly recur throughout the narrative. The narrative of the historical events becomes an interpretive midrash on this OT text. The theme is that Jesus, though innocent, suffers as a condemned criminal according to the action of men and the plan of God." Larkin, "OT and Soteriology," 332–33. Cf. Rowe, *Early Narrative*, 180–81.

189. We discuss the interpretation of this passage in chapter 9 (pp. 205–7).

190. Jervell, *Theology of Acts*, 31.

191. Jervell, *Theology of Acts*, 96.

God and because it was at the heart of his plan of salvation. Luke proves his point by showing extensively that the Scriptures prophesied the Messiah's suffering, death, and resurrection (Luke 18:31–33; 24:26–27, 44–47; Acts 2:24–36; 3:18–21; 4:10–12; 13:33–37; 17:2–3; 26:22–23).[192] As Moessner has aptly demonstrated, Luke argues that Jesus' suffering/death, resurrection/ascension, and the proclamation thereof, are the substance of God's plan of salvation, i.e., they are God's chosen means of effecting salvation for his people.[193]

Conclusion

To conclude our quick overview of the most determinant aspects of Luke's theology as we find it in his two volumes, let us highlight three salient features.

The first—and maybe most striking—trait of Luke's construct is the intricate intertwining of all the different theological threads discussed above: each one depends on, supports, explains, and expands the others. In its respective way, each doctrine—God's sovereign redemptive activity according to his plan, inaugurated eschatology, the church as the restored Israel, the final divine act in redemptive history in and through the person and work of the promised suffering Messiah—is central to the system and can be used as a vantage point to study the others.

The second point is that Luke's theology cannot be extracted from Luke-Acts on the basis of a few discrete passages. Though his thought transpires in a number of explicit statements, it is only as one takes the whole of his narrative as *narrative* into account that a proper understanding can be attained. In fact, "loosing a statement from its narrative mooring as a means to determine specifically *Lukan* christology immediately involves a methodological confusion. In the act of disengaging any statement or passage from the narrative, the means of identifying what is Lukan are actually lost, for the Lukan context itself is rendered irrelevant as meaning-determining discourse."[194]

Finally, however much Luke's thought is in dialogue with the Graeco-Roman world (as in the case of the Emperor worship), its basis and content are found primarily—if not exclusively—in the OT as *the* hermeneutical key for Jesus' life and work, as well as its sequel in the early church.

---

192. Jervell, *Theology of Acts*, 30–31.

193. "We can now sum up 'the plan of God' for Luke's 'second' volume. The rejection/suffering/death of Messiah Jesus, his raising up to the 'throne' of God, and his preaching of this light to Israel and the nations constitute the three 'necessary' components of God's saving action, the three moments of the *script* of all the Scriptures. Jesus' resurrection and enthronement forms the hinge which unites the suffering-crucified one to the suffering-exalted one who preaches through his suffering apostles-witnesses to the ends of the earth." Moessner, "Script of Scriptures," 248–49 (emphasis original).

194. Rowe, *Early Narrative*, 190–91 (emphasis original). The same is, obviously, true of all theological topics.

CHAPTER 2

Luke's Use of the Old Testament

THE PREEMINENT INFLUENCE OF the OT on the writers of the NT is now commonly recognized among scholars, in good part thanks to the pioneering work of C. H. Dodd and Barnabas Lindars.[1] Otto Piper at one time even argued that the OT Exodus motif was determinant not only for the NT as a whole, but especially was behind the Gospel pattern itself.[2] This should not be a surprise since, as Klyne Snodgrass puts it, "the Hebrew and Aramaic Scriptures were, of course, the only Bible the early Christian thinkers and writers had. . . . [A]ll Christians would have been engaged in relating the two most important realities of their lives—the Scriptures and Jesus Christ."[3]

Introductory Considerations

The Importance of the Old Testament for Luke

Luke is no exception in this regard, and so the OT Scriptures are extremely significant to him as he seeks to make sense of what Yahweh has done in Jesus Christ, of how he fulfilled his promises of salvation to Israel.[4] Acts, just like the rest of the NT, shows that the early Christian communities were generally well acquainted with the OT.[5] Luke

---

1. The classic presentations of their views are found in Dodd, *According to* (later summarized and furthered in Dodd, "OT in the New") and Lindars, *NT Apologetic*.

2. Piper, "Unchanging Promises" and Piper, "Origin" both following in the steps of Piper, "God's Good News."

3. Snodgrass, "Use of OT," 29. He further qualifies this statement by adding that the Christians who did not know those two languages had access to the same Scriptures through the Septuagint. Witherington echoes the same conviction when he writes: "It is so often forgotten in the Church that there was no New Testament in the so-called New Testament era." *NT Story*, 5.

4. See Fitzmyer, "Use of OT," 534. The earliest Christians were very conscious of their living in the age of fulfillment of the OT. This is without question the reason why Luke reads the Scriptures primarily through a christological and eschatological lens, consistently with the early Christian practice. See Witherington, *Acts*, 124.

5. See, e.g., Witherington, *NT Story*, 14–17. The exact level of access to and familiarity with the OT found among early Christians is still engendering quite a bit of debate among scholars. Possibly the strongest recent defense of the view that they were very limited is Stanley, *Arguing with Scripture*, especially pp. 38–61. Stanley challenges nine commonly held assumptions concerning Paul's readers,

can be quite subtle and succinct in his references to the OT, and therefore appears to assume or expect much from his readers, just like other NT writers do.[6]

---

mainly on the basis of two premises: books (including, the various OT scrolls) were very expensive and therefore rare; the literacy rate in the Empire was very low across the board. These two "historical facts" together make it highly unlikely that many Christians would have been able to study or even read the OT, including in its Greek versions. In fact, he claims that the NT writers themselves must have had a very limited access to those books.

Stanley's two premises are not as solid as he takes them to be. Porter and Dyer argue against Witherington on these very same points ("Oral Texts?" 329–32; cf. Porter and Pitts, "Paul's Bible" and Porter, "Paul and His Bible"). They muster a variety of historical studies that provide solid evidence to question both notions that books were expensive (and rare) and that literacy rates were very low. Besides, Stanley's argument is problematic methodologically. First, he rejects or ignores the majority of the historical evidence available to us concerning earliest Christianity: viz., the NT writings (*primus inter pares*, the book of Acts) and the knowledge we have about first-century Jewish religious communities. Claiming that we do not have any direct historical evidence for the earliest Christian church, he then constructs a picture of the recipients of the Pauline epistles exclusively on the basis of what is known of the Graeco-Roman world of the period. But such a method is unacceptable from a historiographical point of view (see the argument of Hengel, "Historische Methoden" and Hengel, *Earliest Christianity*), and it leads Stanley to develop a picture of the early church that runs in the face of the evidence that the NT presents and represents.

First, the NT pictures the earliest church as being heavily Jewish—whether ethnically or ideologically—rather than Gentile (cf. Jervell, "Early Christianity"; Jervell, "Mighty Minority"; and Barrett, "What Minorities?"). Second, it depicts a church that is thoroughly Scripture-centered in all its facets, with leaders (whether the apostles or the elders) deeply acquainted with its texts, teachings, and interpretation (see, e.g., Jervell, *Theology of Acts*, 61–75). Third, we see teaching in its various forms was at the heart of the church's life, activity and identity, and is primarily and essentially *scriptural*.

Yet, one must take note of Stanley's arguments against excessively optimistic opinions of the early Christians' access to and acquaintance with the OT. First, scrolls of the LXX (especially a complete set of them) may not have been as common as Bibles are today. Second, it is quite reasonable to expect a diversity of both kinds and levels of literacy among Christians, limiting how many would have studied the Scriptures on their own. Third, it is quite likely that various levels of familiarity with, and comprehension of, the OT must have existed among Christians within each particular community (due to the diversity of background, ability, and longevity as a member of the church).

This being granted, however, there is no reason to doubt that, in time, Christians would have grown in their knowledge of the OT and in their ability to interpret and teach its contents (in the light of the apostolic teaching, of course). Learning does not have to be done in isolation: it can (and is often) accomplished *in community*. Moreover, one should not underestimate how sophisticated even strictly oral cultures can be, and how much information and skills they are capable to gather and pass on to their members (see the discussion offered by Bauckham, *Eyewitnesses*, 240–63). In any case, the early church would have had access to the writings of the OT, whether through the synagogues (the complete rupture with the church happened *after* the NT was composed), through notebooks or *testimonia*, personal memory of those who had memorized them when attending the synagogue, and even through the purchase/production of copies in many cases. After all, the church first settled in the main urban centers of the Empire and possessed some wealthy members such as, possibly, Theophilus, who *may* have been Luke's patron.

6. Witherington, *NT Story*, 110. Stanley rightly warns his readers against mistaking the "implied reader" with the actual original audience (Stanley, *Arguing with Scripture*, 38–39, esp. n. 2), but he wrongly makes this original audience the standard for interpreting the text. The study of the understanding of and reaction to the text that the original audience would have had (which he calls "rhetorical analysis") can be helpful in interpreting a text. However, such an endeavor is highly speculative, and it may restrict unduly the meaning of a text, especially the biblical text, to its "original" audience's ability. Besides the fact that little is known concerning the original audiences of the NT writings, it is

It seems quite clear that for Luke the OT Scriptures are, primarily or essentially, Israel's Scriptures.[7] Luke faces here the same legitimacy issue as he does concerning God, salvation and the Messiah. It is therefore not surprising that he addresses it in the same manner: since the church is restored Israel, the OT writings are her Scriptures.[8] And not only parts of the OT, but the whole of it. A particularly Lukan feature is his use of πᾶς ("all") in relation to the various parts of the OT. For Luke, *all* of Scripture is concerned with God's plan of salvation for Israel in the suffering Messiah (cf. Luke 24:44–47), and all of the OT is Scripture.[9] The OT prophets contain the gospel.[10] In fact, "The whole Gospel is read every sabbath in the synagogues as they read the Scriptures, Acts 15.21. In order to understand the Gospel you have to turn to the Scriptures, 17.3. If it is not there in the Scriptures, it is not a true Gospel."[11] This explains why Luke offers such a wide scope of citations in his two volumes, and also why he appropriates all the messianic titles and epithets he finds in the OT (including rare ones), in a way that is unique in the NT.[12] Luke's work of

---

also clear that the *intended* audience was generally wider than the original recipients (in the first century, one does not write a two-volume work like Luke-Acts for a small circle of readers). Moreover, the assumption that a writer would entirely restrain his intended meaning to the comprehension abilities of his readership—whether original, intended or implied—is rather questionable (see, e.g., Bauckham, *Gospels for All*).

Finally, from a theological perspective, one must also take into account the fact that the authorial intention is not limited to the human author, his ability, understanding, and aims, but ultimately includes the divine Author's revelatory purposes. Hence, a certain connotation or intertextual link may be significant for the interpretation of a particular passage, even though its original or intended audience may *not* have been able to identify and understand it, and its author may not have been conscious of (or intentional about) it and all its implications. See Poythress, "Divine Meaning"; Poythress, "Dispensing with Merely"; Hodge and Warfield, "Inspiration"; and Warfield, "Divine and Human."

7. So Jervell, *Theology of Acts*, 71–72.

8. Jervell, *Theology of Acts*, 61. And so the Scriptures themselves demonstrate the legitimacy of the church claiming them as her own!

9. Jervell rightly notes that though Conzelmann might be correct to say that "Scripture" for Luke is not a title for the entire canon, the Lukan use of "all" clearly implies the substance of what we now call "Scripture" in a canonical sense (Jervell, *Theology of Acts*, 61n104).

10. It is interesting that in the three speeches that include an indictment of the Jews for the death of Jesus (Peter's in Acts 3, Stephen's in Acts 7 and Paul's in Acts 13), this death "is coupled with a misunderstanding of the Prophets. Acts 3.17f. implies that Peter's audience had not understood the prophecies that Christ should suffer; Acts 13.27f. states the same thing more clearly; and in Acts 7.51f. Stephen accuses the Jews of resisting the Holy Spirit to the extent of murdering the prophets." Townsend, "Speeches," 159.

11. Jervell, "Lucan Interpretation," 84. This explains why the apostles constantly take their Jewish audiences to the Scriptures, as those are the basis on which the Jews may come to faith in Jesus Christ, as exemplified by the Bereans in Acts 17:11–12 (Jervell, *Theology of Acts*, 73).

12. See Witherington, "Finding Its Niche," 124 This is why Jervell considers Luke to be a "biblicist" (e.g., Jervell, "Lucan Interpretation," 88. Hence he writes: "It would be more proper to say that everything is Scripture, everything is important, everything is binding, and everything is God's or the Spirit's word. Luke is the fundamentalist—*sit venia verbo*—in the New Testament." Jervell, "Center of Scripture," 122.

history, literature, and theology is truly and essentially a biblical theology, i.e., a "scriptural theology."[13]

In consequence, Luke is not a "neutral" historian but is guided by the OT revelation of God's plan for history, which shows the true meaning of history to be redemptive in nature.[14] This means not only that Scripture provides (especially as it interprets the events recounted) the substance of Luke's narrative, but that it is what controls Luke's use of all other sources.[15] Scripture is determinative of Luke's writing: it governs both form and matter. Hence, Luke gives his reader a "preview" of the content of each volume through OT quotations and allusions (the various allusions in Luke 1–2; Isa 61:1–2 in Luke 4:11–12 and Joel 2:28–32 in Acts 2:17–21).[16] One can, with Fitzmyer, see in this "promise and fulfillment" pattern what guides Luke's ordered (καθεξῆς, Luke 1:3) account in Luke-Acts.[17] Beyond a mere appeal to OT prophecies, however, Luke's compositional method includes *syncrisis*, the drawing on particular stories and characters to shape his own.[18] Even Luke's language is deeply influenced by the OT—the LXX to be precise—in *both* parts of Acts, including the narrative material outside the speeches.[19]

There is yet one more significant role that the Word of God plays in the book of Acts: in a sense, it is the story's "main character," the only one in the spotlight of the narrative from beginning to end.[20] Most scholars agree that the book of Acts

---

13. Jervell, "Lucan Interpretation," 79, 81, 110.

14. "He is in no way a neutral observer, and he starts with the presupposition that the history he offers is the truth; and he aims at giving his readers security and assurance of the instruction of the church, that this history is the history of salvation. When he employs the Scriptures, not as historical documents, but as documents of the Word of God, there is neither independence nor impartiality." Jervell, "Future of the Past," 125. Jervell rightly notes that this fact sets him apart from ancient Graeco-Roman historians for whom independence and impartiality were essential and necessary qualities of a true historian.

15. Thus Jervell writes: "The Scriptures are a source in a special way, not only the main source with regard to material, but even Luke's means of control of any other employed source. Therefore his writing of history could be nothing but salvation history, which was given prominence in the Scriptures themselves." Jervell, "Future of the Past," 117.

16. See Joel B. Green, "Problem"; Witherington, *NT Story*, 81; Litwak, "Coat of Many"; and especially the analysis of Luke's technique as "framing in discourse" in Litwak, *Echoes of Scripture*.

17. Fitzmyer, *Luke*, 1.29.

18. "In some regards it is not surprising that Luke does not spend a lot of time retelling Old Testament stories. He believes he is writing about the age of the fulfilment of prophecies for a start, not a time of retelling old stories, and he also believes the emphasis must be on the Good News, the new thing that is happening. . . . Elizabeth is not Hannah, and neither John nor Jesus is really Elijah, but taking the Old Testament story as casting material or as background scenery or as subtext is a technique Luke uses." Witherington, *NT Story*, 136. See also Arnold, "Luke's Characterizing" and the early proposal of Goulder, *Type and History*.

19. Fitzmyer, *Acts*, 93. This is particularly significant since the large majority of explicit OT quotations are found exclusively in the first part of the book. This means that Luke's septuagintal phraseology cannot be explained merely in terms of "Semitic flavor" as a literary device suiting the Jewish context of the early chapters of the book.

20. As Fitzmyer notes, though the apparent "heroes" of the book are the apostles Peter and Paul, it

chronicles the progress of the Word from Jerusalem to Rome, beginning in Acts 1:8 (programmatic of what follows) and ending in 28:31, some considering Acts 13 to be a turning point.[21] Brian Rosner credits Conzelmann with being the first in modern times to recognize that theme as being central to the program of Acts. Conzelmann saw in this theme a clear expression of Luke's "theology of glory," obvious in the fact that God overturns every obstacle encountered by the Word in its triumphal spread to the end of the earth.[22] Fitzmyer represents the scholarly consensus when he affirms that the progress of the Word of God (or "of the Lord") is chronicled through the various summaries that are interspersed throughout the narrative of Acts: they "serve as signals to the readers, reminding them of the progress that the word of God is making despite the author's preoccupation with the narration of details."[23] It is quite significant that the last summary statement is found in 28:31, the ultimate verse of the book, the conclusion of the final "panel" or narrative section of the story.[24]

In fact, Luke's chronicling of the progress of the Word is not limited to the book of Acts, but begins in the Gospel already.[25] Fitzmyer argues that this theme is in view in "the things that have been accomplished among us" of Luke 1:1.[26] Following the geographical organization of Luke's two volumes, the Word goes first to Jerusalem (Luke) and springs thence to the end of the earth, i.e., ultimately to the whole world.[27] This structure makes perfect sense since Jerusalem "is not merely the place where Jesus suffered, died, and was raised to glory; it is also the place where salvation itself has been accomplished once and for all and from which preordained witnesses carry forth the kerygma about it."[28] Jerusalem is, simply, the place where salvation is springing from.[29] Hence the progress of the Word of God is truly the progress of the "Word

---

is clear that their role in the drama is to be the carriers of the Word of God, and that the latter is truly at the center—as we saw earlier, even that is true only insofar as the Word is the agent of *God*'s action (Fitzmyer, *Acts*, 120).

21. Cf. Fitzmyer, *Acts*, 119, 120 and Fitzmyer, "Use of OT," 536. That includes Barrett's commentary (*Acts*, 1.49).

22. Rosner, "Progress of the Word," 216. For Conzelmann's views, see his *Theology of Luke*.

23. Fitzmyer, *Acts*, 97. Fitzmyer offers a list of references for such summaries and discusses the three kinds he identifies in Acts on pp. 97–98.

24. As observed by Witherington, *Acts*, 810.

25. Fitzmyer, *Luke*, 1.192.

26. "Those events include not only what 'Jesus did and taught from the beginning' (Acts 1:1), but also the stage-by-stage spread of the Word of God from Jerusalem, the mother church, . . . and finally to Rome itself, "the end of the earth" (Acts 1:8; 23:11c; 28:14; cf. *Ps. Sol.* 8:15)." Fitzmyer, *Acts*, 56.

27. In fact, Luke's Gospel starts *and* ends in Jerusalem, a feature that sets it apart from the other Gospels, and Jesus goes twice to the Temple during his childhood, reinforcing this eschatological theme.

28. Fitzmyer, *Luke*, 1.165.

29. See Witherington, *Acts*, 70. There is a rich OT background to this theme, for both directions (toward and from Jerusalem), such as Isa 2:3–4; 61:11–12 and Mal 3:1: see Bauckham, *Bible and Mission*, 72–80. Pao argues convincingly that the movement under discussion is grounded in particular in the three stages of the Isaianic New Exodus, developing further Mark Strauss' insight (in *Davidic*

of salvation," the progress of salvation itself in and through the proclamation of Jesus, the Christ, God's salvation for Israel.³⁰

Many scholars are sensitive to Conzelmann's accusing Luke of having a *theologia gloriae*. All agree that Luke gives a powerful sense of the unstoppable nature of the advance of the Word.³¹ Yet most contemporary scholars rightly reject Conzelmann's accusation, and argue that there is no triumphalism at all in Acts. Opposition and persecution are pervasive and enduring throughout, and in fact they increase in intensity correlatively with the expansion of the Word itself.³² Yes, the Word is unstoppable, but it does encounter serious obstacles, including the persecution and sufferings of its heralds. In fact, the narrative includes a rather ironic dimension in that the very opposition to the Word ends up provoking or helping its progress (in a way that echoes the OT picture of God's laughter in Psalm 2, a very important intertext for the NT in general and for Acts in particular).³³ This impression is reinforced by the ending of Acts which highlights the fact that Paul could preach "with all boldness and without hindrance" (μετὰ πάσης παρρησίας ἀκωλύτως) in 28:31.³⁴ The first term has to do with Paul's Spirit-induced lack of fear (an eschatological feature), and the latter, the last word of Luke's two volumes (hence in a highly strategic and emphatic position), refers to the fact that nothing can stop the proclamation of the gospel of Jesus Christ.³⁵ The reason behind this situation is that the Word is God's agent of redemption,³⁶ its spread is God's own activity in the end time, and

---

Messiah) that "Jesus' journey should be understood against the Isaianic theme of the arrival of the salvation of God in Jerusalem." Pao, *Acts and INE*, 13; see also 249–50.

30. "It is, as we have seen, closely related to most of the other main strands of the theology of Acts, including the plan of God, salvation, witness, persecution, the Holy Spirit, Israel and the new people of God. It would be difficult to imagine a theme that is more comprehensive in scope." Rosner, "Progress of the Word," 233.

31. Witherington summarizes it with the expression "unstoppable word of God." (*Acts*, 816). For a rather complete study of the literary ways which Luke uses to convey this sense, see Rosner, "Progress of the Word." While comparing Luke's and Thucydides' method of using speeches in their respective writings, Aune makes this very interesting point: "In Thucydides speeches function as a commentary on events. In Luke-Acts, speeches are an essential feature of the action itself, which is the spread of the word of God." *NT Literary Environment*, 125.

32. See Rosner, "Progress of the Word," 233 and Gaventa, "Toward a Theology," 157.

33. Witherington notes that the trials of Paul are what advances the movement, spreading the word to Rome (Witherington, *Acts*, 73). There are many other examples of that dynamic throughout the book, including the Jews pursuing and persecuting Paul through Macedonia, leading him eventually to Athens, where he pronounces his most famous speech, though it seems he did not plan on going there at all!

34. Witherington is right to point out that Acts does not depict the proclamation of the gospel to the Emperor, since it does not include any reference to Paul's appearance before him. Witherington, *Acts*, 620. The narrative logic of the whole book implies it, though.

35. See Witherington, *Acts*, 814.

36. This is just another obvious connection with an important OT theme: "Just as there is in fact only one great sin for Isaiah, the contempt of the *tôrâ*, the Word of God (5:24; cf. 8:16, 20), so there is also only one message for the salvation of the world and that is the *tôrâ*, the Word of God (2:3), which

God is absolutely sovereign over all of world history,[37] inclusive of the nations.[38] It is striking how deeply rooted this theme is in the OT itself, especially in Isaiah's New Exodus.[39] There is no Graeco-Roman parallel to it.

How Luke Uses the Old Testament

It is necessary to address a few formal matters concerning Luke's use of the OT before we move on to Luke's hermeneutics. The first and maybe foremost question in this regard is: When or where is Luke actually using the OT? Though this question may seem to call for a simple answer, it is notoriously difficult to answer. Identifying OT references depends on the subjective ability of the reader to discern the hints and cues of the text, his pre-established understanding of Luke's hermeneutic and method of writing, as well as criteria for discerning what constitutes a quotation, an allusion, an echo and other subtle uses, together with determining which must be taken into account or should not.

For example, Fitzmyer and Jervell offer lists of distinct OT uses that cover mostly the same material but classify it differently.[40] The easiest to recognize OT usage is the quotation, of course, which typically involves an introductory formula of some kind and a "complete" passage. Even so, determining what constitutes a "quotation" in Acts

---

radiates throughout the nations." Vriezen, "Essentials," 135.

37. Witherington is one of the few commentators who makes this aspect explicit in his discussion of the subject (*Acts*, 816). It seems that the theme is introduced rather clearly by Luke himself in the words of Gamaliel: "So in the present case I tell you, keep away from these men and let them alone, for if this plan or this undertaking is of man, it will fail; but if it is of God, you will not be able to overthrow them. You might even be found opposing God!" (Acts 5:38–39). This passage is particularly *à propos* since: 1) it follows the disciples' prayer asking for God's enabling them to speak his Word μετὰ παρρησίας (4:29) after their first hearing before the council—a request immediately granted, using the exact same vocabulary (4:31); 2) it issues in their persecution (beaten and commanded to stop preaching, 5:40), their rejoicing and their continued proclamation in the temple and homes (in a way that can fittingly be described as "with all boldness and without hindrance," 5:42); 3) it prepares the way for the Stephen narrative (which will "cause" the first proclamation of the Word outside the walls of Jerusalem).

38. One cannot fail to see the Isaianic parallel or background to this. Pao discusses how the power of God and his Word (and therefore its progress) are essential to Isaiah's New Exodus theme: "In the Isaianic New Exodus, the supremacy of Yahweh is established through the contrast of the power of Yahweh with the futile efforts of the nations, their rulers, their deities, and their idols (and idol-makers). These four categories should not be viewed as four separate groups since they were understood as referring to the same entity." Hence "It is with this understanding that one can also appreciate the power of the anti-idol passages as one form of anti-imperialistic propaganda in that the divine power of the reigning political authority is called into question." This theme is built upon the depiction of God as the warrior who destroyed Egypt's army to save/liberate his people during the Exodus. Therefore, "In establishing the supremacy of the Lord of the early Christian movement, the author of Acts strips away the power of the nations and declares the early Christian community the sole possessor of divine truth." Pao, *Acts and INE*, 181–82.

39. Pao builds a strong case for the Isaianic background of this theme in *Acts and INE*, 147–80.

40. Fitzmyer, *Acts*, 90–91 and Jervell, *Theology of Acts*, 62–63. Cf. Moyise, *OT in the New*, 45–62.

is disputed by scholars, as is evident from comparing various editions of the Greek New Testament.[41] A second type of usage identified by Fitzmyer are phrases and allusions (defined as phrases that are not exact quotations) that Luke borrows from the OT and uses in his narrative without any formal introduction. Though Jervell recognizes the presence of such phrases, he does not list them as a distinct usage. On the other hand, he understands the historical résumés of Acts 7 and 13 as a distinct usage made up of recitals of *narrative and indirect* quotations, while Fitzmyer includes them among the quotations.[42] Finally, they both see in Luke's "global references" (Fitzmyer) or "summary references" (Jervell) a distinct usage that is peculiarly Lukan.[43]

Scripture quotations in Acts are found for the most part in speeches, rarely in the narrative, and never in Luke's summary statements.[44] This means that they are almost always found in the mouth of the characters of the narrative, but never on the lips on the narrator, which is quite significant since it means that Luke never uses the OT with his own voice to comment on the events being depicted. The OT text is thus an intrinsic part of the action, not an extrinsic comment on them. The large majority of quotations are found in chapters 1–15 (except for 23:5 and 28:26–27),[45] and happen in Jewish contexts: hence, no OT text is quoted in Peter's speech to Cornelius' household in chapter 10, while the Ethiopian eunuch is at least a God-fearer if not a proselyte. Yet Fitzmyer, together with virtually every contemporary commentator, recognizes that the OT is also very present in the second half of the book of Acts through phrases, allusions, and references, even in Paul's speeches to strictly pagan audiences.[46]

---

41. This is not only true of the differences between the two main critical texts (United Bible Society and Nestlé-Aland), but also of differences among the various editions of each of them. See the discussion in Fitzmyer, *Acts*, 90–91. It is interesting to note that Fitzmyer himself does not claim the same total number of quotations in Acts in two of his works. It may be due to the fact that in one case he is considering the number of *places* where Luke is quoting the OT, while in the other it is the number of individual OT *texts* quoted that he has in view. Compare the above reference (mentioning thirty-seven quotations) with "Use of OT," 534 (forty-five quotations).

42. Here the difference can be accounted for by the fact that Jervell considers them to be a peculiar type of quotation that needs to be distinguished, as it is used in a different way and for a different purpose. Moreover, he considers that usage to be exclusively Lukan: "We have no parallel to this in the New Testament. Hebrews 11 is a collection of examples, whereas in Acts 7 and 13 *a history as such is decisive*." Jervell, *Theology of Acts*, 62n107 (emphasis ours).

43. Those are references made to "all" the Scriptures, or "all" the prophets, as in Acts 3:18, 24; 10:43; 17:3, etc. Jervell mentions that there are only very few parallels to that in the rest of the NT, offering the following references: Matt 22:40; 26:56; John 1:45; 5:39, 46; 20:9; Rom 1:2–3; 3:21; 16:26; 1 Cor 15:3–4; Heb 1:1. Jervell, *Theology of Acts*, 62n108.

44. Fitzmyer, *Acts*, 91.

45. To be more precise, in Acts most quotations occur in chs. 1–4, 7, and 13, mostly in the speeches of Peter, Stephen and Paul (all addressed to Jews); on finds isolated quotations in the narrative in chs. 8, 15, 23, and 28. Fitzmyer, "Use of OT," 531.

46. "On the other hand, it is not surprising that there are no quotations from the OT in the speeches that Paul addresses to pagans in Lystra (Acts 14:15–17) or to the Athenians on the Areopagus (Acts 17:22–31). But there are allusions to the OT in both these speeches: one to Exod 20:11 in the speech at Lystra (Acts 14:15), and two in the speech to the Athenians, to Isa 42:5 in Acts 17:24, and to Ps 9:9,

Fitzmyer has studied extensively the introductory formulae in Acts and the contemporaneous Jewish literature.[47] The results of his research, which are generally accepted by other scholars, demonstrate that the formulae used by Luke are the same as those used by contemporary Jewish authors.[48] Intriguingly, *most* of Luke's quotation-formulae are *absent* from the LXX but *present* in Hebrew Qumran scrolls.[49] Finally, they show no relationship with the later rabbinical ways of quoting the Scriptures.[50] All this evidence taken together leads him to conclude: "The Lucan formulas are not in every instance an exact equivalent, but they resemble the Palestinian Jewish formulas enough to reveal how close the mode of citation actually is. In using such formulas, Luke thus shows his dependence on a genuine Palestinian Jewish custom of quoting Scripture in other writings. This is to be noted, because Luke is the evangelist who has been most influenced by his Hellenistic ambiance. Despite it, his interpretation of OT passages reveals his dependence on such Palestinian Jewish exegetical tradition."[51] This is perfectly consistent with the fact that the earliest church's use of Scripture depicted in Acts springs out of the matrix of first-century Palestinian Judaism.[52] This could also explain why, according to Jervell, Scripture is essentially an oral reality in Acts as it is intimately associated with the synagogue and the public reading that was typical in that context.[53] Finally, all agree with Fitzmyer that Luke's use of formulae clearly demonstrates his desire to show the continuity between the story of Jesus and the early church on the one hand, and the OT story of salvation on the other.[54]

The quotations in Acts are usually quite short (Joel 2:28–32 is the longest), and often partial.[55] This fact, combined with the use of "global" references, compels us to ask how familiar Luke was with the OT. Some scholars have suggested that Luke may

---

or 96:13, or 98:9 in Acts 17:31." Fitzmyer, "Use of OT," 532. Even Haenchen disagrees with Dibelius on this point (Haenchen, *Acts*, 528).

47. See in particular Fitzmyer, "Use of Explicit."

48. See Fitzmyer, *Acts*, 93 and Fitzmyer, "Use of OT," 526.

49. Being a translation of the OT Scriptures, and not a commentary, the LXX naturally contains very few introductory formulae. Unremarkably, all of them are found at the same points in the LXX and the MT (cf. the textual evidence in Fitzmyer, "Use of OT," 527–28).

50. See Fitzmyer, "Use of OT," 529. According to Fitzmyer, *Acts*, 93, they differ considerably from the formulae used in the Mishnah, a work he dates from ca. AD 200.

51. Fitzmyer, "Use of OT," 529; cf. Dupont, "Utilisation apologétique," 320–21.

52. Fitzmyer, "Use of OT," 524. This conclusion is supported and strengthened by his study of the content of the Qumran literature. See Fitzmyer, "Jewish Christianity."

53. Jervell, *Theology of Acts*, 63, 73. He is right to point to the fact that most of Luke's introductory formulae in Acts use the semantic field of an oral utterance, and only rarely "it is written." His judgment needs to be nuanced, however. First, as he himself notes (63n109), the Gospel uses almost exclusively the "it is written" type of formula. Moreover, Scripture is being quoted in various settings throughout the book of Acts (in fact, it rarely happens in a synagogue!), and in at least one instance the OT is read privately, viz., by the Ethiopian eunuch in Acts 8:30–35.

54. Though, as we have seen earlier, few agree on the exact nature of that continuity. See the generally balanced discussion of this issue in Arnold, "Luke's Characterizing."

55. Fitzmyer, "Use of OT," 530.

have used compendia of OT texts, called *testimonia* (a practice existing among the Jews of the time), but would not have had access to or used whole OT books.[56] Others, however, consider that Luke had a personal (i.e., first hand, not limited to tradition or *testimonia*) and substantial (i.e., texts in the context of the whole book they are coming from) knowledge of the scriptural material he used. For example, Jervell argues that these two features (global and focused quotations) demonstrate that Luke had studied personally and independently the Scriptures.[57] In particular, Jervell insists that Luke's interest in providing a summary of the message of Scripture as a whole does not mean that Luke extracts an ideology by disregarding the details and diversity of the individual writings. Though he recognizes a unified meaning to Scripture, he does not treat it *en bloc*. Jervell sees that in the fact that Luke never speaks of a singular "Scripture," but always of the plural "Scriptures," together with the fact that Luke makes a special effort to show where his quotations are coming from.[58]

That Luke was familiar with the Scriptures of the Old Testament is also supported by the fact that the text type he is using is overall quite consistent—when one takes into account Luke's editorial hand, the fact that he may sometimes quote from memory, that "quotations" may really be "allusions," etc.[59] Early in the twentieth century, William Clarke argued that the evidence was clear enough to identify which form of the septuagintal text Luke was using.[60] Though his specific identification has failed to convince, the scholarly consensus is that Luke is consistently using a text form close to the LXX.[61] One determinative observation is that Luke appears to always side with

---

56. For example Kilpatrick, "Quotations"; cf. the more recent Bauckham, "Kerygmatic Summaries." The original argument for the existence of *testimonia* in the early church was developed by Rendel Harris in various articles collected in Harris and Burch, *Testimonies* (but see the counter-arguments in Dodd, *According to*).

57. Jervell, *Theology of Acts*, 61–75, esp. 62–63. A number of studies set out to analyze Luke's hermeneutical methods and aims, too many to list. Examples include Van de Sandt, "Quotations"; Evans and Sanders, *Luke and Scripture*; and Wendel, *Scriptural Interpretation*, who shows that Luke was quite aware concerning method and significance of Scripture interpretation in relation to Judaism, to the point that it is a topic of concern for him in his two volumes.

58. Luke is certainly not the only NT writer who points out the origin of his quotations, but he does so in an extensive and meaningful manner. Hence, he is the only one to refer to the "*book of* Psalms" in the NT, for example (Luke 20:42; Acts 1:20). He even makes clear that a particular reference is from "the *second* Psalm" (Acts 13:33). Another peculiar feature of Luke is his focus on the *author* of the text mentioned (which goes beyond merely *naming* him), whether it is Joel, Isaiah, David, or Moses, a fact that Jervell interprets as Luke being "concerned about the human agency of the word of God." Jervell, *Theology of Acts*, 63.

59. Hence Pao criticizes a number of early studies of Luke's use of the OT because they underestimate Luke's theological contribution (and the modifications of the text this leads to), and sees in Martin Rese's work an improvement on this front (*Acts and INE*, 6–7; see Rese, "Funktion").

60. Clarke, "Use of LXX".

61. Fitzmyer represents rather well the general consensus on this particular point: see Fitzmyer, *Acts*, 91 and Witherington's agreement with him in *Acts*, 123. Fitzmyer builds on the fact that seventeen of the OT quotations in Luke-Acts are taken verbatim from the LXX while twenty-two more are close to it, though not exactly identical, with it. Yet, "in six instances the quotation is not close to

the Greek text of the OT when it differs from the MT, never the other way around. Finally, though some critical scholars have argued that Luke was only "proof-texting" and developing an ad hoc apologetic,[62] others have shown that his use of OT texts is at least knowledgeable and even quite sensitive to their original contexts.[63] Thus Carroll concludes: "Evidence surfaced that, on occasion at least, the quotations in Acts betray considerable reflection on the meanings of the larger passages from which the cited verses are drawn."[64] This being so, we must reckon (as Dodd did) with the fact that Luke may very well intend his OT references to point to their original literary and theological contexts, and even to function as "pointers" to a larger theme or tradition that runs through a number of OT books (and even later Jewish writings).[65]

According to Fitzmyer's tally, sixteen quotations are from the Pentateuch (ten in Luke and six in Acts), sixteen from the Prophets (seven in Luke and nine in Acts), and fourteen from the Psalms (seven in each).[66] Six years later, in *Acts*, his tally is slightly different but confirms the same trends.[67] This means he never quotes the historical books, except possibly 1 Sam 13:14 in Acts 13:22 (which is striking when one considers Luke's apparent desire to write biblical history), though he certainly makes many allusions or references to them (especially king David's story).[68] According to

---

the Greek text of the LXX at all, and it is impossible to tell whether Luke is conflating, quoting from memory, or using a Greek version different from the LXX." Fitzmyer, "Use of OT," 534.

62. "Older scholarship tended to see Luke's use of the Old Testament as 'apologetic' (proof from prophecy) but more recent work has found this description too narrow." Moyise, *OT in the New*, 61. Two classic defenses of the apologetic view are Sundburg, "On Testimonies" and Lindars, *NT Apologetic*, both of which were responding to Dodd, *According to*.

63. Dodd is an early example of such an interpretation. Though his theses had fallen in disfavor for a time, a number of recent scholars have argued convincingly for a similar position, defending Luke's use of OT texts as pointers toward their original narrative or theological context. See the discussion in Carroll, "Uses of Scriptures," 515–20 and the demonstration in Van de Sandt, "Minor Prophets."

64. Carroll, "Uses of Scriptures," 528. We would question a part of his argument, though. We disagree that the fact that Luke can "[ignore] contexts when he makes use of biblical texts" (Carroll, "Uses of Scriptures," 516) implies that he did not know or care about them. It seems that the evidence brought forth by Carroll demonstrates on the contrary that Luke was well acquainted with the texts' contexts and *purposefully* chose to ignore or adjust them for his own purposes. Doing so might shock modern critical scholars (and their canon of original intent), but it makes perfect sense for someone who is narrating the eschatological fulfillment of the OT taken as a whole, thus reading individual texts in a broader canonical context. It is neither a sign of ignorance nor of carelessness.

65. See Pao's argument for such an understanding of Luke's use of the OT (*Acts and INE*, 5–10), in which he uses the helpful concept of "evocations" of Scripture. "My use of the term 'evocation' in this study aims at highlighting the fact that the scriptural traditions recalled in the use of certain key words may be more profound than the content explicitly noted in the scriptural quotations and allusions." Pao, *Acts and INE*, 7.

66. Fitzmyer, "Use of OT," 532. That means that Luke quotes the OT explicitly in twenty-three instances in his Gospel and twenty-two in Acts (those are introduced with formulae), for a total of twenty-five OT passages in Luke and twenty-three in Acts.

67. Fitzmyer, *Acts*, 90.

68. This point shows the limits of looking primarily at the formal or explicit quotations and allusions while missing the more subtle, maybe even more fundamental, connections made by the NT

Fitzmyer, Acts contains *quotations* from Isaiah, Jeremiah, Joel, Amos, Habakkuk, and Malachi, but none from Ezekiel, Daniel (two "apocalyptic" books), or the Writings, except for the Psalms.[69] We see that Luke is consistent with the other NT writers since they *quote* also primarily from the books of Isaiah and the Psalms.[70]

From the above survey, it seems quite clear that past scholarship has tended to deal exclusively with explicit quotations—sometimes allusions—when discussing Luke's use of Scripture.[71] Thus, though Witherington and Jervell are keen to argue in a number of places against approaches confining themselves to formal quotations and the prophetic material, they themselves fail to discuss much else in their own commentaries. Now, one must concede that the identification of anything else than quotations (such as allusions, echoes, and more evocations) is notoriously difficult and runs the risk of sheer subjectivity.[72] Moreover, one must ask whether Luke "meant" all references to be picked up by his audience, or whether a number of stories, phrases, words and references were just "common stock," a familiar and therefore subconscious way of speaking (and thinking). We are thus led to ponder how much of Luke's knowledge of—and meditation upon—the OT does frame and drive his writing of

---

authors. Hence, Witherington is correct when he writes: "The tendency to focus too much on prophetic texts being fulfilled can cause one to overlook how often the New Testament writers grounded, illuminated, amplified, and explicated their proclamation of the gospel by the use of Old Testament stories. It is interesting that the material most frequently used is from the Pentateuch, particularly the foundational stories in Genesis, and to a lesser degree those from Exodus." Witherington, *NT Story*, 141; cf. Goulder, *Type and History*, 145–78.

69. Fitzmyer concludes his survey with the following words: "Thus Luke has quoted from those parts of the OT that he himself has mentioned in Luke 24:44, where he depicts the risen Christ appearing to the disciples" "Use of OT," 532.

70. For the NT writers, see Witherington, *NT Story*, 14; for Acts, see Dupont, "Utilisation apologétique."

71. Rather typical is Barrett who introduces the limits of his study with the following words: "It is arguable that references to OT characters, such as Abel or Lot's wife, are specific enough to be included among citations, but they will have to be set aside in the interests of what may legitimately be described as Scripture citing Scripture, that is, of passages where an Old Testament text is introduced by a citation formula and quoted literally (though not necessarily of course in complete agreement with any form of the OT text otherwise known to us)." Barrett, "Luke/Acts," 231. See the survey of scholarship provided by Litwak, *Echoes of Scripture*, 8–30.

72. Concerning the case of Acts 17:24, 31 in the various editions of the Greek NT, Fitzmyer writes: "Here modern editorial practice enters in, compounding the problem of how often Luke alludes to the OT. There is also the problem: Who sees the allusion? Luke himself, or the modern editor?" Fitzmyer, "Use of OT," 525n4. And he is only speaking about explicit uses at this point! In a similar way, Snodgrass expresses well the difficulty by asking a few probing questions: "What constitutes an allusion? Is one word in common between New Testament and Old Testament texts sufficient? Certainly not unless there is something in the New Testament context that suggests dependence on the Old Testament text. Does an allusion have to be a conscious allusion? Does it have to be an allusion that one could expect the readers to recognize? Frequently allusions are suggested that require a stretch of the imagination to accept." Snodgrass, "Use of OT," 46n54.

Luke-Acts (consciously or not), yet remains in the background, never emerging in a lexically-distinct manner.[73]

At the end of the day, David Pao is correct to conclude that the large majority of studies of Luke's use of the OT suffer from two major limitations: their focus on the christological use of OT citations (at the expense of other major themes) and the weight placed on explicit scriptural quotations (at the expense of other types of usage).[74] The direct consequence of such approaches is that the emphasis is placed solely on isolated quotations, thus failing to appreciate the wider patterns (or larger purposes) that exist behind them. This leads to a dichotomization of speech and narrative, to the fragmentation of the passage being studied. As Pao writes, "The relationship between the scriptural citations embedded in the Lukan speeches and the development of the narrative's wider plot has frequently gone unnoticed."[75] Though a number of more recent works have addressed the OT-based literary patterns structuring Luke's account, they have often limited their study to the Third Gospel,[76] or have not addressed the larger patterns that encompass the whole of the book of Acts.[77] In particular, they have failed to fully account for the programmatic role of the Isaianic citations, allusions and thematic emphases.

Luke's Hermeneutic

Beyond the "Promise and Fulfillment" vs. "Proof from Prophecy" Debate

In his discussion of the purpose of Luke-Acts, Fitzmyer defends the idea that showing the continuity between Judaism and Christianity is of primary importance for Luke (an insight generally adopted by contemporary Lukan scholars). According to him, this is especially visible in Luke's treatment of the OT data as prophetic or predictive of

---

73. Hence, Richard Hays developed a model for the identification of the more subtle references ("echoes") to the OT, seeking to limit the subjective dimension of such an endeavor, which he originally applied to Paul's epistles and recently to the Gospels (Hays, *Reading Backwards*). His "seven tests" (Hays, *Echoes*, 29–32) have been adopted by many scholars.

74. A typical example would be Bock, *Proclamation*, an otherwise useful book. It seems that such a narrow focus is typically due to historical-, source-, form-, and redaction-critical methodological commitments. Scholarship concerned with narrative and literary dimensions often seek to redress this deficit, e.g., Moessner, "Jesus and Wilderness"; Brodie, *Luke the Literary*; Swartley, *Israel's Scripture*; Joel B. Green, "Problem"; Arnold, "Luke's Characterizing"; Pao, *Acts and INE*; Litwak, *Echoes of Scripture*; and Mallen, *Reading and Transformation*.

75. Pao, *Acts and INE*, 8.

76. E.g., Drury, *Tradition and Design* and Ellis, *Canon and Interpretation*.

77. This is true of the valuable contributions of Thomas L. Brodie regarding Luke's use of the Elijah-Elisha cycle (references in the bibliography); Moessner, *Lord of the Banquet* looks at the Deuteronomic Exodus journey; and Mánek, "New Exodus" sees Jesus' life as a New Exodus event. See Pao's discussion in *Acts and INE*, 8–10. Since the publication of Pao's book, at least two more scholars have sought to correct this problem, *viz.* Litwak, *Echoes of Scripture* and Mallen, *Reading and Transformation*.

the events in Jesus' life and the history of the early church.⁷⁸ "This idea has been variously labeled as promise and fulfillment in Luke-Acts, or as the proof-from-prophecy motif."⁷⁹ As noted by Fitzmyer, this way of looking at Luke's use of the OT was first highlighted by Paul Schubert and Nils Dahl.⁸⁰

In his article "The Structure and Significance of Luke 24," Schubert makes two basic points: "(1) Luke 24 is held together by the proof-from-prophecy motif, and (2) this motif is Luke's central theological idea throughout his two-volume work."⁸¹ Dahl offered a more cautious and nuanced view, expanding the motif to all OT material (and not the prophetic only), seeing it as *one* chief device used by Luke in imitation of OT historiography,⁸² and recognizing a variety of functions to it.⁸³ The main reason for Luke's use of such a motif is his efforts to show the historical continuity between the Israel of old and the Jesus' story together with its sequel.⁸⁴ This view, obviously, presents Luke's use of the OT in a strictly apologetic light, and centers it around the person and life of Jesus. It is essentially—if not exclusively—concerned with a christological

---

78. Luke does so even when the particular Scripture in view formally lacks any prophetic character: "[Luke] makes passages that he quotes from the Pentateuch and the Psalter, texts that really have nothing to do with prophecy, into prophetic passages that not only announce God's message to humanity, as OT 'prophecy' was intended to do, but even into predictive passages." Fitzmyer, "Use of OT," 536–37. This way of using various types of OT passages as if prophetic in nature is called the "prophetic use of the scriptures" by Jack T. Sanders, "Prophetic Use" (cited by Fitzmyer).

79. Fitzmyer, *Acts*, 60.

80. Charles Talbert mentions other scholars representing that same view, all of whom are related to Yale (Schubert, Dahl, Minear and Luke T. Johnson were professors there, while Kurz received his doctorate there), except for one (Robert Karris, who claims that lineage nonetheless) in "Promise and Fulfillment," 91. See also Hays, "Liberation of Israel," 103.

81. As summarized in Talbert, "Promise and Fulfillment," 91–92. Both Talbert and Fitzmyer are critical of Schubert in that his study of Luke 24 seems to imply that only OT prophetic texts are concerned. On the one hand Fitzmyer claims that the whole of the OT is used for Luke's "proof-from-prophecy" argument in Luke-Acts, and not just the OT prophetic material (though he believes it is read as if it were prophetic), and therefore Schubert missed this larger dimension of Luke's argument. Talbert, on the other hand, thinks that Schubert actually includes the whole OT in the proof-from-prophecy motif, but that Luke 24 (vv. 5–9 and 44) also refers to Jesus' prophetic utterances prior to his passion, and that vv. 50–53 have no proof-from-prophecy element in them, thus preventing the motif from being *the* unifying element in the passage and therefore in Luke-Acts. See Fitzmyer, "Use of OT," 537 and Talbert, "Promise and Fulfillment," 92.

82. Many see in this motif a parallel with the way the Qumran community used the OT, and in particular with how it read its history (in its particular elements) in it. Talbert explicitly makes this connection, Talbert, "Promise and Fulfillment," 98, 99–100. For a discussion of Qumran's use of the OT related to this issue, see Bailey and Vander Broek, *Literary Forms*, 42–49.

83. As summarized in Talbert, "Promise and Fulfillment," 92. While Schubert seems to limit the use of the motif to emphasizing the continuity of the Jesus story and its sequel with the OT, Dahl adds to it the guarantee of the future fulfillment of yet-unfulfilled promises, to demonstrate the divine origin of the events and to develop an argument from antiquity. See Dahl, "Abraham in Luke-Acts" and "Purpose."

84. Following Dahl, Fitzmyer's writes: "The concern of Luke to stress the connection and the continuation between Judaism and Christianity is seen clearly in his use of the OT to interpret the Christ-event." *Acts*, 60.

reading of the OT Scriptures.[85] Luke's purpose in writing Luke-Acts is understood to be the defense of the legitimacy of Christianity in the eyes of *non-Christians* (usually the Romans, though it sometimes includes the Jews). The proof-from-prophecy motif is deemed to be his main (or only) weapon. This perspective leads one to construe Luke's use of Scripture in a mechanical and atomistic manner,[86] even as a kind of proof-texting allegedly similar to certain Second Temple Jewish apologetical methods.[87]

These problems with the proof-from-prophecy theory have been raised as early as 1965 by Martin Rese.[88] First, he sought to demonstrate the primary importance of Luke's theological contribution to his use of the OT, thus situating the discussion within the wider context of Luke's theological program and taking it beyond the mere mechanics of Scripture quotation.[89] By looking at the issue this way, Rese is able to discern a number of different kinds of uses, including scriptural proof (apologetic use), variations of the promise-fulfillment schema, typological, and hermeneutical (a way of using the OT to explain the present).[90] Identifying a larger variety of uses together with a broader theological context allowed Rese to argue convincingly against reducing Luke's appropriation of the OT to a simple proof-texting technique meant to foster a strictly apologetical purpose regarding outsiders.

Talbert builds upon Rese's insights and furthers his critique of the proof-from-prophecy/promise-fulfillment schemas. His argument is in two parts. The first follows Rese and argues that the proof-from-prophecy motif involves more than the OT (e.g., prophetic utterances by angels, human agents, and Jesus), and also that not all OT references follow that specific pattern.[91] In the second part, Talbert questions the determination of Luke's *purpose* on the sole basis of his use of the OT. First, he claims

85. See Dupont, "Utilisation apologétique" for a good example of the combination of a christological reading of the OT with an apologetical concern or purpose, though his personal view greatly exceeds the limitations of the proof-from-prophecy thesis.

86. Atomistic because the focus is on disconnected and discrete passages in both Acts and the OT. The larger patterns, themes, arguments or narrative structures are not taken into account, and so the logic, intertextuality and purposes of Luke's use of the OT remain hidden to the interpreter. Mechanical, because Luke's use of the OT is considered to be ad hoc (which implies that he does not know or take into account the larger context of the passage being used) and somewhat wooden with its "one-to-one" correspondence between promise and fulfillment and its attendant christological perspective. Luke's use therefore appears to lack theological depth, breadth, and finesse.

87. Other scholars have also made the connection between the use of the OT through *testimonia* and an apologetical (christological) purpose in Luke-Acts. See Bauckham, "Kerygmatic Summaries" and Snodgrass, "Use of OT."

88. Rese, *Alttestamentliche Motive*; his critique is furthered in Rese, "Funktion."

89. Pao identifies Bock, *Proclamation* as the most sustained critique of Rese's overemphasis on Luke's editorial hand in this context (*Acts and INE*, 7n25).

90. Talbert explains this last use as calling on OT passages to illuminate "present" events on the basis of their *resemblance*, without implying "fulfillment": "Behavior in the present is *like* this or that scriptural behavior in the past." "Promise and Fulfillment," 93. Talbert mentions Kilgallen, *Stephen Speech*, who argues for such a use as regards Luke's depiction of the Jews' opposition to Jesus in the light of their ancestors' opposition to the prophets of old.

91. Talbert, "Promise and Fulfillment," 93–95.

that some examples of the proof-from-prophecy motif do not serve to demonstrate the continuity between Israel and the church (for example, a number of promises/prophecies concerning Paul's life and death have no direct or immediate bearing on this issue). Second, he argues against the idea that one can discern Luke's purpose merely on the basis of the contents of his books, for it is necessary to take into account his *cultural* context in order to establish what role and impact the promise-fulfillment pattern would have had on Luke's original readers.[92] Finally, he rightly questions the notion that one can claim to explain Luke-Acts as a whole on the basis of only *one* of its themes, however essential it might be, but recognizes the complexity of properly organizing and relating all its various themes.[93]

Darrell Bock contributed to this debate by arguing for a "proclamation from prophecy" model.[94] Bock's exegetical work contends for moving away from an apologetical proof-from-prophecy schema to a kerygmatic (and therefore theological) one. The main shortcoming of his study was its concentration on Luke's *christological* use of the OT,[95] though his later essay "Scripture and Realisation" offers a fuller viewpoint. Bock argues that Luke's hermeneutic must be understood in the context of the overarching question of the relationship between the church and Israel (and its salvation), that is, in the context of his broader theological thought—which includes theology proper, soteriology, eschatology, and ecclesiology—in which christology is central but not the exclusive element or interest.[96] This approach is representative of the more recent scholarship on Luke's use of the OT, which has moved away from a mechanical to a hermeneutical outlook (though the two are interconnected), from a primarily apologetic explanation to a theological perspective (though apologetics remains a Lukan concern at one level or another),[97] and from a disconnected christological focus to an analysis of christology's role and function in Luke's theological system at large.[98]

---

92. According to Talbert such a study demonstrates that the proof-from-prophecy was used in the Mediterranean world to legitimate someone's religious or political ideas (hence encouraging conversion to the same) and of other types of utterances like not-yet-fulfilled prophecies, as well as to demonstrate the continuity with Israel's long history—thereby giving Christianity a claim to antiquity—and to provide evidence for God's providence in human affairs, especially as regards the rewarding and punishing of human behavior ("Promise and Fulfillment," 95–101).

93. Talbert, "Promise and Fulfillment," 101–2.

94. In Bock, *Proclamation*.

95. As noted by Pao, this leads Bock to end his study at Acts 13 on the (questionable) basis that there is no christological development beyond that point in Luke-Acts (*Acts and INE*, 7–8).

96. Bock offers three hermeneutical axioms and five scriptural themes that he sees as critical for understanding Luke's use of the OT. The axioms are: God has a design and this is a new era of realization; Christ is at the center of this plan; Scripture is the interpreter of the divine activity. The themes are: covenant and promise; christology; community mission and guidance; commission to the Gentiles; and challenge and warning to Israel.

97. See the interesting discussion of the apologetical value of Luke's use of the fulfillment motif in Peterson, "Motif."

98. In a nutshell: "Christology is not the goal of Luke's use of Scripture. It is a [*sic*] important port of call on the way to more comprehensive claims about God's plan and the promise's subsequent

It is important to note that though Bock uses the expression "promise-fulfillment" to describe Luke's perspective, he uses a more complete, complex and nuanced concept than Schubert or Dahl did (and therefore Rese or Talbert), viz., that of a *hermeneutical pattern* with variegated applications.[99]

Fitzmyer is quite typical when he defines Luke's use of Scripture as essentially prophetic in nature as well as global (the whole of the OT revelation is in view). Defined this way, the "promise-fulfillment motif" is found in all NT books: it is a typical and common approach in earliest Christianity.[100] Yet, there is more to Luke's (and the other NT writers') use of the OT. Luke's strong stress on the fulfillment of the OT in Jesus and the earliest church (which goes beyond fulfillment of specific prophecies or promises) is to be seen in relation to Luke's redemptive-historical understanding of the continuity between the two epochs.[101] Though Witherington is critical of Jervell's, Rosner's and Fitzmyer's emphasis on the continuity,[102] it seems that all would agree with his point that Luke's insistence on the eschatological and climactic nature of the history of Jesus and the early church implies discontinuity in a radical way also at some level.[103] In this regard, the very concept of "fulfillment" of one by the other effectively incorporates both dimensions in a balanced way.

It is because of this perspective that Jervell can write: "The centre of Scripture Luke locates in its *prophetic aspect*; this is true of the prophetic as phenomenon as well

---

realization. . . . The plan argues that Jesus is Lord of all, so the gospel can go to all." Bock, "Scripture and Realisation," 46.

99. In fact, both "promise-fulfillment" and "proof-from-prophecy" are used in the literature to refer to different concepts (cf. Fitzmyer, "Use of OT," 537). Thus sometimes the expression refers to a general outlook on the OT which takes different interpretative forms (it is then often combined with terms such as "pattern" or "motif"), or it is used with a similar meaning as Schubert's and Dahl's, but is then defined as merely one of the several ways in which Luke reads the OT. Litwak voices repeatedly his frustration concerning this diversity of conception and the frequent lack of clear definition that accompanies it (see especially *Echoes of Scripture*, 9–17).

100. Similarly, Witherington writes: "By this latter point I mean to stress that the earliest Christians saw themselves as living in the age of the fulfillment of the prophecies and various other Old Testament texts, and they believed these prophecies were fulfilled not only in the life and ministry of Jesus, but also in their own lives and times. They were living in the times when the Old Testament stories were all coming true." *NT Story*, 23. This seems more pronounced in Luke's writings, though. See Fitzmyer, *Acts*, 92; cf. Lindars, "Place of the OT."

101. Cf. Witherington, *NT Story*, 129 and Fitzmyer, "Use of OT," 525, 538.

102. See Arnold, "Luke's Characterizing," 300, for a summary of their views on that point. Cf. Witherington, "Finding Its Niche," 81–83. and Witherington, *Acts*, 35–39 (where the discussion revolves around the genre of Acts). Witherington is not satisfied with a definition that would make Luke-Acts into a mere prolonging of the OT narrative without recognizing the eschatological/qualitative leap that separates Luke-Acts from OT salvation-history. In his opinion, this discontinuity is inherent to the idea of "fulfillment."

103. They all insist heavily on that aspect of Luke's theology, as we saw earlier. Their insistence on the notion of continuity appears to be a reaction against the earlier German critical scholarship—typified by Dibelius—which studied Luke-Acts in (virtually) total abstraction from the OT in both content and form.

as of its content."[104] This explains Luke's interest in the prophetic *per se*, a characteristic made evident by the emphasis he places on Moses, the role of the Holy Spirit in prophecy and the production of the Scriptures, the prophetic ministry of Jesus (and that of others, like Simeon, Anna, Paul, or Agabus), and David as a writing prophet.[105] In fact, the members of faithful Israel are the sons of the prophets (Acts 3:25), a fact highlighted by both the presence and activity of the Spirit in the church (as well as in all of salvation-history) and the insistence on Israel's long history of rebellion against the Spirit.[106] Scripture is the word of prophets, that is, the word of the Spirit, the word of God himself. This is true not only of parts of Scripture (any kind of selection or *testimonia*), but of both the Scriptures as a whole and the whole of Scripture.[107] The "center of Scripture" (viz., the OT) is therefore "prophetic" in nature because *everything* in the Old Testament is awaiting its fulfillment in the New in one way or another.[108] This means that the whole of salvation history, the whole of Israel's history, as well as the whole of Jesus' life and his gospel are concerned and involved.[109]

All would agree that the person of the Messiah is the substance of the "center" of Scripture for Luke.[110] As many have argued, the suffering/death, resurrection/ascension and the proclamation of these facts to the whole world are the core of Luke's reading of the OT.[111] The identity of Israel's Messiah is at the heart of Luke's two-volumes—especially in relation to Jesus' life, death, and resurrection—and therefore calling Luke's hermeneutic "christological" cannot be entirely misleading. The problem is when christology becomes the exclusive and exhaustive explanation for Luke's use of the OT. Though christology is unquestionably preeminent, it is not so for its own sake but rather in service of a larger theological complex and of a more pressing issue, viz., the legitimacy of the Christian church's claim to Israel's heritage.[112] Here we

---

104. Jervell, *Theology of Acts*, 63 (emphasis ours). It is important to note that "center" here must be understood not as a "mid-point," but rather as the core or entirety of Scripture, as what ties all of its themes and parts together (Jervell, "Center of Scripture," 122).

105. Luke affirms that the whole Christian message is already present in Moses (noted by Jervell, *Theology of Acts*, 69–70). Additionally, Jervell observes that David is depicted as the father of the Messiah not only as king (a traditional connection in Jewish thinking), but also as prophet (a Lukan feature): Jervell, *Theology of Acts*, 65–66.

106. Jervell, *Theology of Acts*, 49, 65, and 72.

107. So Jervell, "Lucan Interpretation," 82–83.

108. See the interesting discussion of this point in Jervell, "Future of the Past," 105–8.

109. This is clearly visible in Luke 24 and in Paul's defense speeches (especially Acts 24:14 and 26:22), as well as in the pervasive use of πᾶς throughout the two volumes. See Jervell, *Theology of Acts*, 67–68; Jervell, "Lucan Interpretation," 83; and Jervell, "Future of the Past," 109.

110. Hence we can say that "the center of Scripture is also the center of the Christian message." Jervell, "Center of Scripture," 137.

111. Jacques Dupont, e.g., identified the same three features (though he distinguished between the proclamation of the gospel and reaching the end of the world). He considered that Luke's intention was to demonstrate the conformity of Jesus' life to the OT messianic tradition. See Dupont, "Utilisation apologétique," 322–24.

112. As the polemics of Acts 2 and 13 show, "the messiahship of Jesus and the salvation of Israel

are possibly touching on the heart of the issue: the prophetic, the christological, and the continuation of salvation-history in Luke's interpretation of the OT all have to do with God's redemptive plan (found in the OT) and with Jesus' place and role in its eschatological completion.[113] The whole theological system discussed in the preceding chapter, with its various themes and their mutual inter-relationships, is the proper context for and explanation of Luke's hermeneutic. The converse is true also.[114]

Of course, there is much debate over the specific structure of the promise-fulfillment schema in Luke-Acts. Conzelmann offered a three-stage pattern for Luke's salvation-history (basically: Israel before Jesus, Jesus, church), which Fitzmyer adopts and adapts. Some of Conzelmann's critics offered a two-stage alternative: promise and fulfillment.[115] Jervell rejects both Conzelmann's proposal and the promise-fulfillment explanation. As we have seen earlier, Jervell shows how promise and fulfillment are intertwined all through Luke's two volumes, developing a powerful historical (and narrative) momentum leading to the final "event," the parousia. Hence, he refuses a simple (simplistic?) identification of "promise" with the OT and "fulfillment" with the events narrated in Luke-Acts. According to Jervell, the dynamic of promise and fulfillment is at the heart of *all* of Scripture, including Luke-Acts—remember that he believes that Luke is self-consciously "writing Scripture," i.e., continuing the OT salvation history.[116]

Since the promise and fulfillment pattern is not limited to the Messiah but includes every aspect of the history and life of Israel (God's people), this means that the *whole* history of Israel is one of promise and fulfillment, and therefore that the time of the church (last redemptive-historical epoch before the consummation) is also one of *both* promise and fulfillment. In this sense, we can say that there is no "simple" prophecy in Luke-Acts. As Joel Green has convincingly argued, the dynamic at work in Luke's use of a promise-fulfillment scheme is one of both continuity and climax, one that is already present within the OT, continues between the Old and New Testaments,

---

are at stake when Scriptures are not understood." Jervell, *Theology of Acts*, 68.

113. Fitzmyer, *Acts*, 92; cf. Bock, "Scripture and Realisation," 41. It is important to keep in mind that Luke's books were written for the edification and encouragement of *Christians,* and not as an apology to "outsiders." At the same time, Peterson ("Motif") is correct to point out that these same Christians would have found in these two volumes much help for their efforts at commending and defending the faith.

114. Hence Luke's use of the title Χριστός for example, is a function of the promise-fulfillment scheme driving his interpretation of the OT. Cf. Jervell, *Theology of Acts*, 27–28.

115. Fitzmyer names Werner Kümmel, U. Luck, Charles Talbert, and François Bovon in that category ("Mary," 62). He rejects their proposal for two main reasons, the first being crucial. First, a binary scheme of that kind is insufficient in order to give a full account of Luke's view. Luke's promise-fulfillment pattern is much more complex than such a straightforward and neatly divided structure. Second (not that significant in our opinion) such a pattern is not distinct from Matthew or John. Though Fitzmyer is right to seek to preserve Luke's unique character, one should question the idea that Luke *could not* share such patterns with other NT writers, especially considering their common foundations in the OT and first-century Judaism.

116. See Jervell, *Theology of Acts*, 70–71.

and one that develops even within the NT itself. Thus we can see the same dynamic at work all the way through Luke's two volumes.[117] Because of such a movement at the heart of Luke's use of the OT in the composition of Luke-Acts, one must recognize that not only discrete promises are the object of fulfillment in the messianic age, but broader textual patterns as well.[118]

Witherington highlights a number of OT patterns used by Luke that were drawn from historical—not prophetic—materials, asserting that such material in the NT is too often missed or ignored by scholars.[119] Some are quite obvious or explicit (such as the Elijah/John and Elijah/Jesus connections), but a number are implicit and remain in the background.[120] Witherington's discussion, moreover, demonstrates the flexibility of such OT motifs and patterns. They are not used by Luke (or any NT writer, for that matter) in a mechanical and rigid manner, but they can be used in a creative way, in continuity with the history of their use within the OT and in Second Temple Jewish writings. The fact that Luke accessed the OT through its exegetical history was strongly emphasized by Rese, and finds expression in Swartley's concept of "tradition history."[121]

---

117. See Joel B. Green, "Internal Repetition." It is at work in each volume individually as well as between the two volumes. This is a much better way of accounting for how the narrative parallels in Luke-Acts form a complex motif characterized by both continuity and transformation.

118. Cf. Bock's discussion in "Scripture and Realisation," 43–49.

119. In particular, he shows how Luke used the Hannah-Samuel narrative to frame the story of Zechariah and Elizabeth in Luke 1, and how he represents both John the Baptist and Jesus as "Elijah" figures. In each case Luke's narrative is clearly drawing from and paralleling the OT story, while stretching and transcending its original contours (or giving it multiple fulfillments). Witherington, *NT Story*, 136.

120. Witherington notes the presence of repeated patterns throughout Luke-Acts, a phenomenon that Fitzmyer identifies as constituting a significant part of the parallels existing between (and structuring) Luke's two volumes. See Witherington, *Acts*, 102 and Fitzmyer, *Luke*, 1.164. Yet, they would undoubtedly join with Joel Green's approval of Praeder, who cautions "against what we might call parallelomania—i.e., the undisciplined ransacking of Luke-Acts for recurring patterns of narration—and urges readers (1) to be more forthcoming regarding their criteria for locating parallelisms and (2) not to confuse their findings with authorial intent." Joel B. Green, "Internal Repetition," 284; cf. Praeder, "Parallelisms in Luke-Acts." The term "parallelomania" was coined in 1962 by Samuel Sandmel (in "Parallelomania"), in the context of the comparison of the Gospels with the Qumran documents. It has since become a label for excessive and/or unwarranted quests for "parallels" between distinct bodies of literature.

121. See Rese, "Funktion." The idea that the NT writers read the OT from within a preexisting interpretive context is accepted by most today. Kugel, *Traditions* documents that context in a substantial and stimulating way. At the same time, one must also note that there is no *quotation* (only allusions or echoes) from Second Temple literature in any NT book, while only few minor elements possibly drawn from them have been identified in Luke-Acts (in Stephen's speech, for example). In *Israel's Scripture*, Swartley uses "tradition history" to refer to OT themes or patterns seen in the light of their interpretive history.

PART ONE: CONTEXTUALIZING AND ORIENTING OUR READING OF THE AREOPAGUS SPEECH

Lukan Hermeneutic and Typology

This type of reading of the OT has been described as "typology."[122] Hence, Denova considers that Luke is writing "typological history"[123] while Bock describes Luke's hermeneutic as "typological-prophetic."[124] Typology in the NT and Luke-Acts expresses the dynamic unity of Scripture (and of the OT writings with the NT events) in a manner that includes both progress and climax.[125] As such, typology is not only a hermeneutical tool or method, but also a form of historical understanding. Typology is fundamentally a historical interpretation, a historical hermeneutic.[126] This is consistent with Witherington's point that Luke's aim in writing Acts was not so much the validation, but rather the signification of the events, i.e., to bring out their meaning (and meaningfulness).[127] Such a reading and use of the OT is possible only in the context of a worldview that assents to God's plan for and sovereignty over (salvation-) history.[128] As Bock puts it, "The very premise behind reading history as involving promise and pattern is divine design and the constancy of God's character as he saves in similar ways at different times."[129] Jervell has a similar perspective. Thus he writes

---

122. See Goppelt, *Typos*. Lindars affirms that typology constitutes an important part of the New Testament's use of the Old, and that therefore it is more pervasive than appears on the surface, though a number of allusions are easily missed ("Place of the OT"). For a useful recent discussion of typology, see Seitz, *Figured Out*.

123. Denova, *Things Accomplished*, 230; a category used earlier by Goulder (e.g., *Type and History*, 34). See the discussion of her view of the use of the prophetic tradition for the structural patterns of Luke-Acts in Pao, *Acts and INE*, 15–17. On this point, Denova follows rather closely Jervell's position.

124. Bock, "Scripture and Realisation," 46–47. Though the use of typology in the NT is a well-known fact, some commentators avoid this language, probably because of its perceived abuse and misuse by others: "When employed to show the Christo-centric unity of the Bible, it may—and often does—impose an artificial unity upon Scripture and frequently results in an over-interpretation of the Old Testament." Anderson, "Exodus Typology," 178. Hence, for example, Snodgrass prefers to use the term "correspondence in history" ("Use of OT," 37n24). In spite of this semantic reluctance, frequently the same material and dynamics are in view when terms such as "allusions," "patterns" and "motifs" are being used.

125. Which might well be why authors such as Talbert and Denova prefer to use the concept of typology over that of promise-fulfillment, the latter tending to be of a "flat" and static nature.

126. See the helpful Anderson, "Exodus Typology," 177–79. David Baker says that modern scholars generally agree that typology is a kind of historical interpretation that is based on the Bible itself. See his discussion of definition in Baker, "Typology," 313–15.

127. Witherington, *Acts*, 69; he is building on Joel B. Green, "Internal Repetition."

128. Because it implies a teleological or, better, eschatological nature for time and history. Hence history is meaningful as such and it has a *telos* consistent with its nature and development. This biblical view of history runs totally contrary to the Graeco-Roman "vertical" or circular views found in both mythological and philosophical traditions. See the excellent discussion of this radical difference in Anderson, "Exodus Typology," 185–92.

129. Bock, "Scripture and Realisation," 47. An extremely important point needs to be made here: while scholars speak about promises and God's faithfulness in fulfilling them, they tend to do so in a somewhat abstract manner. In contrast, Bock highlights the fact that the promise and fulfillment pattern is to be seen in the context of the theme of the *covenant*. Hence he writes: "The theme of covenant

that, for Luke, "what has happened and what is going to happen in the church comes from history [Israel's history made of the patterns and promises of God's words and acts, all of which is recorded in Scripture]. If you want to know what is happening today and what is going to happen, you have to look to history. The future is there in the past as promises and as patterns in the Scriptures."[130]

Thus typology can and must be distinguished from allegory.[131] The former implies a *historical* continuity between the two elements connected, while the latter implies that the historical event is only a shell for an a-historical reality or truth. As such they are entirely different modes of historical interpretation, based on antithetical ontologies.[132] Foulkes defines typology as an interpretation of history that is theological, eschatological (we can therefore say historical or diachronic) and christological, a method that is deeply rooted in the OT itself.[133] In the light of our preceding discussion of Luke's theology and his use of the OT, this definition appears to be right on target.

Here one must be careful not to think that Luke's typological use of the OT is simple and straightforward, with a one-to-one correspondence between type and antitype.[134] Not only is there a historical or eschatological movement or progression

---

and realized promise is fundamental to Luke-Acts, since it was raised as early as Luke 1:54–55 (Abrahamic), and 1:68–70 (Davidic). This emphasis continues in Acts. All the covenants of expectation, or allusions to them, appear within the speeches in Acts." Bock, "Scripture and Realisation," 49.

130. Jervell, "Future of the Past," 107–8.

131. There is much debate on the precise meaning and contours of both "typology" and "allegory." We consider Jewett's argument in favor of seeing them as virtually identical to be mistaken, in agreement with Foulkes. It seems that Jewett's peculiar definitions blur the distinctions and miss the larger epistemological and metaphysical issues involved. We consider the interpretative method of the ancient Greeks, some of the church fathers and medieval scholastics to be properly "allegorical," in that it differentiates between the "true" or "spiritual" meaning of a story and its historical or literal sense. On the other hand, an exegetical method resting "on a genuine organic relationship between the original text and that in terms of which it is interpreted" (Jewett, "Concerning," 18) should be properly recognized as "typological." See Foulkes, "Acts of God."

In order to avoid abuses of what he calls "typological criticism," Goulder recommends three safeguards: "the need to supply catenas, and not single instances, of correspondences; the need for the coincidence of actual Greek words between type and antitype, and the rarer the better; and the need for a convincing motive for the evangelist to have composed his work in the way claimed." Goulder, *Type and History*, 10. Goulder understands Luke's method to be allegorical, really, since he considers the typological elements in the narrative to be symbolical and mythical, with only an occasional historical or factual kernel or basis (see his last chapter, "Symbol and History," 179–205).

132. "Allegory presupposes a view of existence which depreciates, if not abolishes, the meaningfulness of concrete, historical time. According to this view, man encounters reality by freeing himself from time and history and relating himself to that which is timeless and eternal." Anderson, "Exodus Typology," 178.

133. See Foulkes, "Acts of God," 342, 366. Hence typology is essentially redemptive-historical by nature. Cf. the helpful diagram ("Clowney's Rectangle") that Hugenberger offers as a slight elaboration of a private conversation with Edmund Clowney in "Introductory Notes," 340. Additionally, it is worth noting that "The word pair that perhaps best describes the structure of typology is type/antitype rather than scripture/interpretation." Bailey and Vander Broek, *Literary Forms*, 46.

134. As shows the example of the use of the Elijah-Elisha motif in the narrative of Acts

climaxing in Jesus Christ, but there are transformations of the original type. This happens mainly through the selecting of some features of a type (or even by using them like a photographic negative, as in the case of David's death in contrast with Jesus' resurrection), or by combining features from several different types (such as the prophets Moses, David, and Elijah in the case of the person of Jesus), or through the new light projected on the type by the history of the antitype itself.[135] It is rather striking that this phenomenon is not limited to the use of the OT by Luke-Acts but includes the use of Luke-Acts by itself![136] As Daube writes concerning the Exodus motif in the OT: "This often happens to patterns: they become independent of their original context and lose in meaningfulness.... Needless to say, new meanings may be gained where old ones are lost."[137] Jervell's failure to recognize the transformation of patterns and types in Luke's work is a major weakness.[138] This is particularly striking in his refusal to recognize the presence—not just its importance, but even its presence!—of the Gentile mission in the Book of Acts, and his need to demonstrate that the church in Acts is (almost) exclusively Jewish, forcing him to dismiss or explain away much textual evidence.

One must recognize that the modification/transformation (the "unfolding") of patterns, motifs and types is intrinsic to all typological or "promise and fulfillment" readings of the OT: "Typological interpretation refers to the way in which elements of the Hebrew scriptures are shown to correspond to elements in the Christian faith and thus further illumine God's salvific plan.... Interpretation of the Hebrew scriptures does take place, but in a way that is determined by its relationship to the N.T. concept."[139] In other words, "Scripture is an interpreter of those events [happening in Jesus' life and ministry], explaining them and their design. At the same time, the events themselves, as unusual and unique as they are, draw one to Scripture and seek explanation."[140] This means that Luke's use of the OT in its different forms—though controlled by a promise/pattern-fulfillment—is absolutely not *unidirectional*, a com-

---

1:9–11 (building upon an earlier transformative use in Luke 9:51–56). See Joel B. Green, "Internal Repetition," 292.

135. Koet provides an excellent example: "The Transfiguration story uses elements from different epiphanies to Moses. Luke does not use these stories as exact patterns for his description of God's epiphany to Jesus. He, rather, uses pigments taken from the stories about God's special relation with Moses to colour and to structure his version of the Transfiguration." "Why Does Jesus," 21.

136. Green gives a number of examples of how "narrative patterns" may echo (or reverberate) several times through Luke's narrative. Many were originally taken from the OT, but then the "antitype" becomes itself a "type" for an ulterior narrative. Green gives the example of the Cornelius story which at the same time parallels Jonah's and echoes the Zechariah/Mary and Saul/Ananias "complementary visions" with its Cornelius/Peter pairing. See Joel B. Green, "Internal Repetition," 293–95.

137. Daube, *Exodus Pattern*, 84–85.

138. This problem is highlighted by Pao when assessing Denova's study: see Pao, *Acts and INE*, 15–17.

139. Bailey and Vander Broek, *Literary Forms*, 45–46.

140. Bock, "Scripture and Realisation," 47.

mon critique leveled against such an understanding of Luke.[141] Inasmuch as Scripture interprets historical events, so also these events are revelatory and explain the Scriptures. The hermeneutical dynamic is bi-directional.

Scripture Interpreting History and History Illuminating Scripture

Thus, the Scriptures provide Luke with the necessary hermeneutical tools to interpret and explain the near past (Jesus' life and earliest church), the present (his and his readers' life), and the future. As Jervell argues, for Luke history as such has no meaning, only salvation history—that is history enlightened by Scripture—does.[142] The patterns of God's (redemptive) words and acts in the past (found in Scripture) are the spring from which the present salvation flows, together with the future expectation of the parousia.[143] Therefore, "prophecy" is necessary even for salvation history to have meaning, because God's acts of redemption are themselves in need of interpretation to be meaningful, in order to be truly revelatory.[144] This means that historical *facts* do not speak for themselves, but they must be interpreted by Scripture.[145] In this light, we may say with Dupont that the Scriptures are used by Luke not to *prove* (contra Jervell) historical events (in this case the death and resurrection of Jesus) but rather to *show* their messianic significance and their theological depth.[146]

Reciprocally, the historical events of the life of Jesus and of the primitive church themselves interpret the OT. The very fact of going back to the OT texts in search of meaning for historical events leads necessarily to a reappraisal of the meaning and reach of these same texts. Luke's reading was guided and informed by the very facts he was looking for in the prophecies, promises and patterns of the OT as a whole. Looking at the OT texts through the lens of their fulfillment in Jesus and the early

---

141. Bock refers in particular to Joel B. Green, "Problem" and Soards, *Speeches in Acts* for such a critique. His response to them is that he agrees that Luke's scheme is not unidirectional, but that this is consistent with a typological-prophetic fulfillment pattern. See Bock, "Scripture and Realisation," 47n11.

142. Jervell, *Theology of Acts*, 89. Obviously, the distinction made here between "history" and "salvation history" has nothing to do with the post-Kantian neo-orthodox dialectic of *Historie* vs. *Geschichte*.

143. See Jervell, "Future of the Past," 105–10.

144. See Jervell, "Acts and Early Christianity," 23. This point is very important, for it sets Luke-Acts directly in continuity with the OT historical books, especially the Pentateuch, where there is a constant interaction between God's acts (historical events) and God's words interpreting his acts. This principle is made explicit in the stories of both Abraham and Moses. In fact, one can see this revelatory pattern in the story of Adam and Eve in the garden of Eden already. See Gaffin, "Introduction," xv-xvii and Van Til, "Nature and Scripture."

145. Just as the days of Noah and those of Lot provide the pattern for understanding the days of the Son of Man in Luke 17:22–30 (Jervell, "Future of the Past," 109).

146. See Dupont, "Utilisation apologétique," 322–25.

church allowed Luke to see their fully developed or unfolded meaning and signification. "Thus the exact significance of the text was revealed in the event."[147] This is particularly evident in Luke's christology, for it brings together a number of strands that were probably understood in first-century Judaism to refer to *separate* eschatological figures.[148] In this regard Luke's interpretation of the OT is definitely christological, as is clear from Luke 24:44: Christ is literally the climax, the culmination, the endpoint of *all* of Scripture, and therefore his life and work reveal their full meaning in a final and ultimate fashion.[149] This is also why Luke may use non-prophetic material in a prophetic manner, as if the events recounted were "filling out" these OT texts.[150] Luke himself explicitly refers to such an enlightening of the Scriptures by the events surrounding the first coming of the Christ. This being said, one must emphasize that for Luke the OT Scriptures are *clear* and not obscure.[151] There is no "spiritual" (i.e., allegorical, esoteric or mythical) meaning hidden behind the text, only the literal. And yet, they must be "opened" to the audience.[152] Such "opening" is usually tied to Jesus' death and resurrection, but not exclusively, as Peter's Pentecost sermon makes clear.[153] Jesus is the one who opens them, either through his words or his works as they are proclaimed by his followers, because he *is* what they are all about. Jervell even points out that, in Luke-Acts, external events (which are guided by God and function within his redemptive work through Christ) often open the Scriptures to the people involved.[154] This "opening" does not provide any *new* content, but only brings out to full light what was always in the text.

Hence we see that there is a sort of "dialogue" happening between the events recounted by Luke in his two-volume work and the OT. As the early Christians—Luke included—were faced with the history of Jesus and the early church, they went back to their Scriptures seeking an explanation, an interpretation.[155] In this process we witness

---

147. Bock, "Scripture and Realisation," 48.

148. In the same way, Jesus' preaching, for example, clarifies the OT teaching about the Messiah-King and the kingdom of heaven. See Ridderbos, *Coming*, 27–36.

149. "The story of David and consequently of Israel is misunderstood when it is not interpreted as culminating in Jesus." Jervell, *Theology of Acts*, 67. Dupont thinks that this christological interpretation might well be the essence of Luke's use of the OT, in that the light shed by Jesus' death and resurrection—together with their proclamation by the early church—on the texts reveals their true meaning and significance ("Utilisation apologétique," 324–25).

150. Witherington, *Acts*, 124.

151. The Jews' misunderstanding is not due to a lack of clarity, but to their own ignorance and hardness of heart. Hence Jesus can challenge the Pharisees by asking them: "Have you not read . . . ?" in Luke 6:3.

152. It is explicitly the case for the Ethiopian eunuch (Acts 8:31, 35), the Jews (Acts 17:3), and for the disciples (Luke 24:32, 45), as noted by Jervell, *Theology of Acts*, 68.

153. Though Jervell claims it is *always* tied to these two events in "Center of Scripture," 137, he has a more nuanced position in *Theology of Acts*.

154. See Jervell, *Theology of Acts*, 69n116.

155. It is worth repeating Witherington's reminder that the OT was the only "Scripture" available

a mutual interpretation of the OT texts and the NT gospel/kerygma.[156] Therefore "[t]o characterize this relationship between text and event as one way by over-emphasizing either the text or the event is to fail to appreciate the complexity of the interaction between the two elements."[157]

Conclusion: The Variegated and Pervasive Influence of the Old Testament on Luke-Acts

In conclusion, we must agree with Witherington that "Luke's use of the OT . . . is a complex matter not easily deciphered or explained with simplistic formulae."[158] Though Luke reads the OT consistently with his theology and its redemptive-historical structure, his use of the OT is multi-faceted and even multi-layered. Building on a rich tradition of motifs and patterns found in the OT, he sheds a fresh interpretive light upon them all along his books. Through the use of both external repetition (by calling on the OT's own set of recurring themes and patterns) and internal repetition (by using the same themes and patterns repeatedly throughout his narrative), Luke creates a complex "intertextual web" which brings out the full meaning of both the historical events narrated and the OT Scriptures which prophesied them.[159] "The most striking thing about Luke's hermeneutical strategy is his insistent and skillful representation of *narrative continuity*, linking the story of Jesus seamlessly with the much longer narrative of God's promises to Israel and God's saving action to gather and redeem 'a people prepared for the Lord' (Luke 1:17)."[160]

Hence, for a proper understanding of Luke's work one has to be sensitive to the redemptive-historical and eschatological movement expressed through the many "reverberations" of OT patterns and stories that give his narrative its structure, shape, and movement. One cannot be content with a narrowly historical(-critical) account, but must pay attention to the theological, literary, narrative, and *intertextual* dynamics at work in Luke-Acts.[161] This is clearly indispensable since, as Barrett writes, the influ-

---

to the first Christians.

156. "Bible et message du Christ s'interprétaient l'un par l'autre." Dupont, "Utilisation apologétique," 289.

157. Bock, "Scripture and Realisation," 48.

158. Witherington, *Acts*, 124.

159. The expression "intertextual web" comes from Joel B. Green, "Internal Repetition," 293. Litwak wisely concludes: "In Luke's hermeneutics, the multi-purpose use of the Scriptures of Israel is complex, rich, and nuanced, and the last word on it has most certainly not been written." "Use of OT," 168.

160. Hays, "Liberation of Israel," 116. This achievement is crucial to the Lukan purpose of asserting the legitimacy of the church vis-à-vis Israel: "The question, so formulated, is a question about *intertextual narration as a culture-forming practice*. Communities form and maintain their identities through the stories they tell about their origins, history, and future destiny." Hays, "Liberation of Israel," 102 (emphasis original).

161. For kindred judgments, see Rowe, *World Upside Down*, 8 and Litwak, "Use of OT," 158. For

ence, whether literary or theological, of the OT upon the Lukan writings "is profound and pervasive. It is safe to say that there is *no major concept* in the two books that does not to some extent reflect the beliefs and theological vocabulary of the OT."[162] That includes the Areopagitica.[163]

The Programmatic Role of the Book of Isaiah for Luke-Acts

A quick look at the index of OT quotations and allusions of NA[27] (or NA[28]) shows that the books most referred to in the entire NT are, by far, the books of Psalms and Isaiah. Exodus would be third, closely followed by Genesis and Deuteronomy.[164] According to the editors of NA[27], there are more *quotations* of Isaiah than of any other (biblical or extra-biblical) writings in the NT, and possibly more *allusions* to the Psalms (though one needs to recognize the difficulty of identifying the latter). If the relative size of the two books is taken into account, then Isaiah is the book whose influence on the whole NT is at least the most apparent, if not the most significant.[165] Several studies have confirmed the place of Isaiah as a major (if not *the* major) source for both content (theology) and form (narrative structure) of various intertestamental and NT writings.[166]

Isaiah and the Psalms in Luke-Acts

So in the case of Luke-Acts, NA[27] lists seventeen quotations (five for Luke, twelve for Acts) and 113 allusions (seventy-one for Luke, forty-two for Acts) of the book of

---

a stimulating introduction to the field of biblical intertextual studies, see Moyise, "Intertextuality and Study." For a helpful recent collection of essays on the topic, see Hays, Alkier, and Huizenga, *Reading the Bible Intertextually*.

162. Barrett, "Luke/Acts," 231 (emphasis ours). And again, on p. 243: "Luke's use of the OT, which is co-extensive with most of the aims and interests that he has incorporated in his book."

163. "Acts 14:15–17; 17:22–31 are not exceptions; here too the influence of the OT is apparent." Barrett, "Luke/Acts," 244n5.

164. Piper's claim that Exodus would easily outrank both Psalms and Isaiah if the number of allusions to themes and motifs drawn from it were taken into account ("Unchanging Promises," 3) rightly points to the crucial impact that the Exodus narrative had on the first-century Christians' theology. However, though Piper recognizes the impact of the book of Exodus on other OT books (especially Isaiah, Hosea and Jeremiah), he does not discuss the possibility that many of the NT "Exodus themes" might have been mediated by other OT books, especially the prophetic ones. For other weaknesses in his study of the use of the Exodus in the NT, see Swartley, *Israel's Scripture*, 13 and Watts, *Isaiah's New Exodus*, 11–12. The same problem mars the otherwise valuable contributions of Mánek and Moessner to the study of the (New) Exodus in Luke-Acts.

165. Though the number of Isaianic quotations and allusions is not an unambiguous proof of the extent of the book's theological and compositional influence on the NT writers, it is certainly pointing in that direction. It may reveal Isaiah's importance in a way similar to the proverbial tip of the iceberg.

166. For example, Snodgrass, "Streams of Tradition"; Fekkes, *Isaiah and Revelation*; Watts, *Isaiah's New Exodus*; and Sawyer, *Fifth Gospel*.

Psalms, and sixteen quotations (nine for Luke, seven for Acts) and 107 allusions (seventy-four for Luke, thirty-three for Acts) of Isaiah. An intriguing issue in this context is the relationship between these two OT books. The similarity in thought and wording is striking—for example, between Isa 44:9–20, Ps 115:4–8 and 135:15–18, all examples of OT anti-idol polemic.[167] A number of oracles from Isaiah are so close to the text of particular Psalms that the question of dependence is inescapable; in most cases, however, it is impossible to determine which is the source of the other.[168]

In any case, it is clear that Luke (as well as other NT authors) was aware of this proximity. When discussing Luke's use of the title παῖς, David Seccombe notes that Luke seems to be drawing once from Isaiah (the Suffering Servant, as in Acts 3:13, 26) and another time from Psalm 2 (the Messianic Son/Davidic King, in Acts 4:27, 30). Commenting on this puzzling fact, he writes: "This, however, only serves to illustrate an important point: unlike us the NT writers were not interested in clearly differentiated OT title-themes. They believed in the essential unity of OT theology so that ultimately the messianic son of Ps. 2 and the suffering παῖς of Isaiah are identical."[169] Another example of such christological confluence is found in the words of the heavenly voice heard after Jesus' baptism, which seems to bring together Ps 2:7 and Isa 42:1.[170]

The author of Luke-Acts is neither naïve nor confused in this matter. On the contrary, he seems to bring together purposefully the diverse but complementary—or mutually-explanatory—strands found in these two books. A striking illustration of this dynamic is provided by Paul's speech in Acts 13. In this passage, Paul is developing a christological argument about Jesus in which he uses Psalm 16:10 to explain or interpret an Isaianic oracle (55:3) in order to demonstrate that the promises mentioned in both passages were intended for Jesus and not for David, as demonstrated by the resurrection of the former and the tomb of the latter.[171]

---

167. Michael Green highlights those passages in connection with the Areopagitica: "The whole approach is reminiscent of great passages in Isaiah and the Psalms where a stinging indictment of idolatry is delivered." Michael Green, *Evangelism*, 180.

168. Beale, "Isaiah 6:9–13," 258, notes that it is impossible to date the Psalms under consideration, and thus to determine which text was composed first. See esp. n. 3. Cf., however, Sommer, *Prophet Reads* (especially pp. 108–131) and Nurmela, *Mouth*, who study the intertextual interplay with other OT books (showing the Psalms to be prominent) in Isaiah 40–66.

169. Adding: "'Christ' is the dominant title for Luke; the Servant theme is subsumed under it." Seccombe, "Luke and Isaiah," 256.

170. Scholars are divided on the identification of the precise OT references used to compose this passage, but Koet argues that these two passages at least are almost certainly involved: Koet, "Isaiah in Luke-Acts," 60.

171. Koet also notes that "Van de Sandt . . . argues, that 55,3 is the only passage in Deutero-Isaiah alluding to a hope connected with the Davidic dynasty." Koet, "Isaiah in Luke-Acts," 68n44 (cf. Van de Sandt, "Quotations," 33n17). This fact is quite significant since Isaiah 55 concludes the section in the book that focuses on the figure of the "Servant," the New Exodus and on the anti-idol polemic. Luke is here merging two strands of OT tradition that are essential to his theology and the argument of his two-volume work.

There have been few studies of Luke's use of the Psalms. It might be because the book of Psalms appears to be a gathering of disparate materials (different authors, times, places, contexts, foci) and therefore it is difficult to discern a unified theological program or structure (unlike Isaiah).[172] Also, it seems that Luke's appeal to the Psalms serves largely and primarily his christology. This aspect of Luke's theological endeavors has been recently highlighted by Peter Doble, who notes the centrality of the Davidic element in Luke's interest in the Psalms.[173] Hence, it might be better to speak of the influence of individual Psalms or even clusters of Psalms on Luke, rather than looking for the impact of the book of Psalms as a whole. In any case, the massive impact of certain Psalms (e.g., 2; 16; and 110) on Luke's theology and narrative is undeniable, though it does not seem to have the same scale or programmatic nature as that of Isaiah.

The Significance of Isaiah for Luke-Acts

A number of studies in the last thirty years or so have sought to demonstrate that, of all the OT sources used by Luke, Isaiah—and especially its New Exodus theme—had the most substantial and significant impact on his writings.[174] Seccombe offered a solid demonstration of the "radical and searching nature of Luke's use of Isaiah"[175] on the basis of his examination of two themes found in Luke-Acts: the definition of Jesus' person and mission in his Nazareth sermon (Luke 4) and the "Servant" title.[176] His research showed that Luke did not merely "quarry" text-proofs from Isaiah, but that he had a deep appreciation for, and understanding of, his source. Luke's appropriation is not limited to discrete Isaianic texts, but, rather, he draws on wider themes.[177]

---

172. Though many scholars have given up on finding a logic to the ordering of the Psalter, there has been a renewal of interest in this issue recently. See Robertson, *Flow of the Psalms*.

173. Doble, "Psalms in Luke-Acts"; cf. Bonnard, "Psaume 72" and Dupont, "Interprétation des Psaumes."

174. For a survey of the scholarship on this point, see Pao, *Acts and INE*, 10–17.

175. Seccombe, "Luke and Isaiah," 259.

176. Seccombe mentions four other "obvious" proofs of Luke's peculiar interest in and familiarity with the book of Isaiah: long quotations in four passages, Luke's interest in the *book* of Isaiah, quotations *outside* the speeches (which he does exclusively with Isaiah), and his discussion of its interpretation in Acts 8. See "Luke and Isaiah," 252–53.

177. Though Luke is obviously not the only NT author to allude to or quote from Isaiah frequently (in fact Matthew *quotes* it more often than Luke), he might have appropriated its content the most extensively. Hence Seccombe gives the example of how Matthew quotes Isa 61:1–2 (58:6) and does no more with it, while Luke keeps returning to it in various contexts (Luke 4:18–19; 6:20–21; 7:22; Acts 10:38; NA[27] [not NA[28]] adds an allusion in Acts 4:27). When one takes into account the function of Isaiah 61 in the book of Isaiah (bringing together a number of key themes related to the New Exodus), it is impossible to explain Luke's usage as mere proof-texting (see Seccombe, "Luke and Isaiah," 253). According to James Sanders, the contrast between the two Evangelists seems to be that Matthew's use of the OT is often in dialogue with traditional interpretations of the text while Luke's is typically more direct or unmediated (James A. Sanders, "Isaiah in Luke," 16–17). For Matthew's subtle use of

The same sort of conclusion was reached by Dennis Johnson in his study of the Lukan use of the Servant Songs (Isaiah 42–53, 61) in relation to his ecclesiology and missiology. On the basis of his study of one quotation (Acts 13:47) and several allusions (Acts 1:6–8; 22:14–15, 18–21; and 26:16–18), Johnson is convinced that "indications in Acts suggest that the Isaianic servant songs *as wholes* lie in the background of Luke's presentation of the church, and particularly the church's apostolic leaders, as Spirit-empowered witnesses of Jesus the Lord."[178] Other studies arrive at similar conclusions regarding the extent of Isaiah's influence on Luke's thinking and writing, as well as the kind of knowledge of the scriptural data Luke demonstrates.[179]

David Pao was the first to show that Luke's dependence upon Isaiah can be seen not only in individual themes but in the overall structure, program, and message of Acts (Luke-Acts).[180] Pao argues that Isaiah's New Exodus theme is paradigmatic for Luke-Acts as a whole. He shows how texts that are key to the Isaianic program (especially 40:1–11, widely recognized by scholars as programmatic for the second part of the book of Isaiah, viz., chs. 40–55)[181] find their way through various types of evocations into programmatic passages of Luke's two volumes, such as Luke 4:16–30; 24:44–49; Acts 1:8; 13:46–47; and 28:25–28. Pao's extensive analysis of three themes common to Acts and Isaiah demonstrates the extensive dependence of the former on the latter and that Luke does not merely mimic Isaiah, but absorbs the material into his own subject matter and redemptive-historical situation. In the end, Isaiah's New Exodus pattern and theology provides Luke with the scriptural argument and material he needs for his own purposes, as he and Isaiah share a focus on God's restoration of Israel through his Servant.[182] Koet's study further confirms this line of thought.[183]

Scripture and his ability to communicate to a readership with various levels of comprehension, see France, "Formula-Quotations."

178. Johnson, "Jesus Against," 343 (emphasis original). The Isaianic passages concerned are part and parcel of the broader New Exodus theme of the book of Isaiah.

179. See, for example, James A. Sanders, "Isaiah in Luke" and James A. Sanders, "From Isaiah." Hence, "an examination of the evidence suggests that Luke did not merely utilize Isaiah as a source for prooftexts to support his own point of view. Rather, Luke had investigated Isaiah extensively and had a deep appreciation for Isaianic themes. *His mind was saturated with Isaianic texts and concepts*, which shaped his views." Moore, "To the End," 392 (emphasis ours).

180. Pao, *Acts and INE*.

181. See Snodgrass, "Streams of Tradition," 25.

182. But see the evaluation and critique of Pao's work offered by Beale, "Review of Pao." Beale concludes that Pao has made a generally convincing argument for seeing Isaiah as a major influence on Luke, though more inductive work is needed to decide whether it is *the* dominant influence or one among others. Pao's study is in continuity with the work of Watts on Mark and Fekkes on Revelation.

183. Hence Koet (in "Isaiah in Luke-Acts") writes that Isaiah functions somewhat like a "blueprint" for Luke-Acts. It is therefore key to understand Luke's work properly. Luke's knowledge of Isaiah was both extensive and personal, as demonstrated by Luke's narrative of Jesus' baptism and of the conversation of Philip with the Ethiopian eunuch. Such (extensive but not always explicit) use of Isaiah by Luke indicates that the OT book may have been generally well-known among Luke's audience. James Sanders also estimates that Isaiah was the "single most helpful book of the Old Testament" for the early church in its attempt at understanding the life and work of Jesus as well as its own identity and role as

Luke's Use of Isaiah

We saw earlier that one of Luke's primary concerns in writing Luke-Acts was the identity of the early church (especially in light of the Gentile mission) as a defense of its being the legitimate heir of all the promises to Israel. Pao has argued convincingly that one of Isaiah's most significant functions in Luke's works is precisely to establish the church's identity as the restored Israel.[184] In other words, Isaiah's New Exodus program, which serves as the spine of at least chapters 40–55 (though found throughout the book, it is most prominent there), is determinative for the author's purpose and program in Luke-Acts.

The Awaited Restoration of Israel

"The concern for the 'restoration' was shared by many of the interpreters of the scriptures of Israel throughout the intertestamental era."[185] The reason for this concern over the restoration of Israel (and the kingdom) was due to the fact that the Jews from this period generally considered that the promised restoration of Israel had not happened yet—at least not fully, if at all. The return of the exiles to Jerusalem in the sixth and fifth century BC failed to usher in the messianic age and to put an end to Israel's captivity and bondage. There is much debate about the Second Temple Jewish understanding and conception of this situation. It seems that a number of Jews thought that the nation of Israel was still in *exile* in spite of the return to Palestine, sometimes reinterpreting the concept of "exile" in spiritual terms. N. T. Wright has championed the view that all first-century Jews would have understood their condition to be a persistent "exile."[186] His position has been much critiqued and is in need of nuancing.[187] Other scholars have corroborated his fundamental insight that first-century Jews would have considered that Israel was still in need of restoration or re-gathering, and that some would have understood that to be a form of return from exile.[188] Michael Fuller offers an interesting analysis and taxonomy of Second Temple Jewish conceptions of the

---

witness ("Isaiah in Luke," 14–15).

184. See especially his second chapter, "Continuity and Discontinuity: The Significance of Isa 40:1–11 in the Lukan Writings," Pao, *Acts and INE*, 37–69.

185. Tiede, "Exaltation of Jesus," 279.

186. See especially Wright, *NT and People*, 215–338.

187. For example, Bryan, *Judgment and Restoration*, especially pp. 12–20. Bryan questions Wright's idea that *all* Jews would have understood the nation to be in exile in the first century BC. He argues for a broad diversity of opinions among Jews regarding the exact situation of Israel, and also for the fact that "exile" might not have been the most prevalent concept used to characterize it. See also Casey, "Where Wright" and Newman, *Jesus and the Restoration*.

188. For example, Evans, "Continuing Exile" lists additional texts in support of Wright's analysis. Cf. Pao's compact discussion in *Acts and INE*, 143–46.

situation of Israel, where he shows that "exile" was one strand among several, the one to which Luke-Acts belongs.[189]

In these circumstances, Isaiah's prophecies and promises of restoration (New Exodus) were the focus of much scrutiny on account of their perceived unfulfilled character.[190] Isaiah 40–55 was particularly significant for the development of Jewish theologies of the exile and the restoration.[191] This is apparent in a number of Qumran texts as well as in the later Targum Isaiah.[192]

Snodgrass' midrashic study of the various streams of traditions that sprung from Isa 40:1–5 (and how they were adapted in the NT) reveals how widespread and significant various themes of the Isaianic New Exodus were at the time.[193] In particular, it shows how a passage like Isa 40:3 ("A voice cries: 'In the wilderness prepare the way of the LORD; make straight in the desert a highway for our God.'") had become crucial for the first-century Jews' *self-understanding*.[194] Rikki Watts' conclusion to his study of the role of chs. 40–55 in the overall structure and message of the book of Isaiah may help understand why this was so: "In my view chapters 40–55 represent an explanation for the failure of the return from exile."[195] The returned remnant's continued idolatry and their commitment to an "idolatrous wisdom" (which causes their rejection of the "Servant" chosen by God) lead to further correction/punishment and the *delay of the New Exodus*,[196] that is, to a continuing exilic state (which can only cease with Israel's repentance and turning back to God).[197] If this is so, then Luke-Acts and its use of Isaiah must be understood in that same context.

Isaiah's New Exodus and Lukan Theology

Hence Luke's explanation of Jesus' exaltation—seen in the light of Isa 49:6—and the various Isaianic New Exodus themes of chs. 40–55 can only mean that the restoration of Israel has begun and is ongoing with Jesus' heavenly session and the Twelve's

---

189. Fuller, *Restoration*.

190. "The continuing unfulfilled promises in Isaiah occupied the mind of the ancient interpreters." Pao, *Acts and INE*, 30. This, Pao notes, is a major discrepancy between their and the early Christians' interpretation of the same passages, since the latter saw these as having been (and being) fulfilled in Jesus and the ongoing expansion of the church.

191. Pao, *Acts and INE*, 145–46.

192. See, for example, the Qumran pesharim on Isaiah in *DSS*^{2}, 185–91. According to Pao, the traditions behind the Targum Isaiah can be dated from the first century, which would make them contemporary with the NT.

193. Snodgrass, "Streams of Tradition." It should be kept in mind that these verses serve to introduce the following chapters and to summarize the (New Exodus) program developed there.

194. Snodgrass, "Streams of Tradition," 29.

195. Watts, "Consolation or Confrontation," 59.

196. See the references in Watts, *Isaiah's New Exodus*, 73n111.

197. Watts' conclusions on this issue seem to be confirmed and further developed by the findings of Beale, "Isaiah 6:9–13."

earthly session. Here we observe the apologetic dimension of Luke's programmatic use of Isaiah, affirming that its prophecy is eschatologically fulfilled "now." As Bock points out, the debate between early Christianity and its Jewish contemporaries was not whether the texts discussed were christological or soteriological in nature, but whether they were truly and finally fulfilled in Jesus and the church.[198] This conclusion is confirmed by the reaction of the Nazareth audience to Jesus' speech in Luke 4 (*à propos* Isa 61:1–2).[199]

In the light of the importance of Isa 40:3 for various Jewish groups' identity, Luke's use of the term ὁδός to identify the church would have been rather controversial.[200] This, together with the other aspects of Luke's use of Isaiah, confirms our earlier conclusion that ecclesiological concerns are primary in Luke-Acts (especially as regards which community is truly restored Israel and therefore the heir to God's salvation), to which other theological themes are subservient.[201] As Pao says: "One should be aware of the possibility that certain scriptural passages are quoted precisely because they are also quoted by other competing communities. The polemical function of the use of Scripture should, therefore, be noted."[202]

It is no surprise, then, that *all* the major themes of Lukan theology highlighted earlier in this chapter are at least present if not prominent in Isaiah, particularly in chapters 40–55. Luke's theology is theocentric in essence, and so is his reading of Isaiah.[203] Reading Isaiah in this manner does not constitute *eisegesis* because Isaiah itself is highly theocentric. Thus, Geerhardus Vos has shown that Isaiah's theophanic vision in the temple of the unique, most majestic and absolutely holy God of Israel (Isaiah 6) controls the prophet's career and message from beginning to end.[204] Hence,

---

198. See Bock, "Scripture and Realisation," 49n14. "The question was not 'Is a divine Messiah coming?' but only 'Is this carpenter from Nazareth the One we are expecting?' Not surprisingly, some Jews said yes and some said no. Today we call the first group Christians and the second group Jews, but it was not like that then, not at all." Boyarin, *Jewish Gospels*, 2.

199. This reaction makes perfect sense when the story is read in the light of its midrashic environment. See James A. Sanders, "From Isaiah."

200. See Pao's discussion of Luke's use of that term in the context of its role in Isaiah's New Exodus in *Acts and INE*, 59–68.

201. This is also the conclusion reached by Pao's extensive study of the role of the Isaianic material used in Luke-Acts (Pao, *Acts and INE*, 252).

202. Pao, *Acts and INE*, 252. This is especially true of Isaiah, as we have argued in this section. Seccombe is therefore probably right when he concludes: "What this study has shown is Luke's evident appreciation for this heritage as well as his thorough understanding of its source. . . . No doubt his depth of understanding is attributable in some degree to the controversy which surrounded the proclamation of Jesus as Christ in the hellenistic synagogues." "Luke and Isaiah," 259. Sterling, *Historiography* and Wendel, *Scriptural Interpretation* corroborate this insight.

203. See James A. Sanders, "Isaiah in Luke," esp. p. 25.

204. "We here discover the first outstanding feature of Isaiah's prophecy, what may be called its theophanic character. In every message he has to proclaim, in every interpretation of nature and history he is sent to make, we see rising up before us this same divine presence which rose up before the prophet in the temple. Self-manifestation of Jehovah is the fundamental aspect of every utterance or discourse." Vos, "Some Doctrinal Features," 274.

Isaiah's understanding of God is driven especially by the uniqueness and holiness of Yahweh, from which Isaiah draws a keen sense of the absolute chasm between what/who is God, and what is not-God.[205]

Sin, for Isaiah, is thus the ascription of divinity to any creature at the expense of the Creator and Lord of all things: it is a religious matter.[206] Because of who God is (the Lord, the Holy One), and because of the idolatry of the nations and Israel, Isaiah's ministry and message center on judgment, on the "Day of Yahweh."[207] These features are highlighted by Beale's study of Isa 6:9–13, which makes the case that these verses must be read as an anti-idol polemic, thus coloring all of the prophet's interaction with the people of Israel.[208] The same motifs of Yahweh's exclusive divinity and his absolute condemnation of idolatry are, naturally, at the very core of the anti-idol polemic found in Isaiah 40–55.[209]

This absolutely sovereign God has a plan for the history of the world.[210] This decree is like the master plan for the "work of Yahweh" in history,[211] a work through which Yahweh reveals himself to the whole world, a work that climaxes in both judgment and salvation.[212] As could be expected, this plan includes preeminently the eschatological New Exodus.[213] Hence most of Isaiah 40–55 is a revelation of that divine plan. Of course, the major development of the motif/program of the Exodus in Isaiah is its casting in a strictly *future-eschatological* mold. "Previous prophets, to be

---

205. "The theophany in the temple is clearly intended to place in the strongest possible contrast the absolute divinity of Jehovah and the relativity and dependence of created existence. Among all the prophets Isaiah was endowed with the keenest appreciation of the antithesis between God and not-God." Vos, "Some Doctrinal Features," 274.

206. "Even if there were not 2:2–4 and 6:3, the antithesis between Jehovah and the idols which pervades chapter 2 admits of no other construction than that divinity is the exclusive attribute of Jehovah. Because idols are the caricature of divinity, idolatry is the caricature of religion." Vos, "Some Doctrinal Features," 278. Vriezen comes to a similar conclusion: "In fact for Isaiah all sins are rooted in failure to recognize God, failure to believe, and the willful rejection of him. These failures Isaiah sees in all spheres of life, military and civil, profane and cultic; among the high and the low, priest and prophet. By these people God is not known as the living God who is the Holy, Glorious, and Mighty One. Therefore they wander into all sorts of ways but they do not choose the only way, the way of revelation. Proud and defiant, their lives come into conflict with God, and therefore they shall perish." Vriezen, "Essentials," 135.

207. Vriezen, "Essentials," 133.

208. Beale, "Isaiah 6:9–13."

209. See Pao, *Acts and INE*, 189–90.

210. See Vriezen, "Essentials," 142–44.

211. See Anderson's discussion of what we could call Isaiah's theology of history in "Exodus Typology," 179–80.

212. See Vos, "Some Doctrinal Features," 282.

213. Though many scholars recognize the significance of the Exodus for Isaiah, few seem to appreciate the fact that Isaiah is not merely using a variety of themes or motifs from Israel's founding story, but is recasting it as a whole, thus creating a new Exodus *program*. Recent studies such as Watts' and Pao's, however, have sought to remedy this lacuna. Cf. the following representative studies of the Exodus motif in Isaiah: Zakovitch, *You Shall Tell* and Daube, *Exodus Pattern*.

sure, had appealed to the memory of the Exodus. But it was Second Isaiah who, more than any of his prophetic predecessors, perceived the meaning of the Exodus in an eschatological dimension."[214]

A corollary to Isaiah's eschatologizing the Exodus is its universalization, a development accomplished through the casting of the Exodus into a future (promised) event and its reformulation in cosmogonic terms.[215] Hence, in Isaiah, the New Exodus is presented as a New Creation, emphasizing the radical "newness" of the eschatological work of God by which a new people is created.[216] This leads to a redefinition of the people of God in which an ambiguity arises concerning who exactly will make up this restored/recreated Israel. This very ambiguity allows various groups (in the first century AD and before) to call on Isaiah 40–55 in their competing with each another to establish their identity as the one "true Israel." Isaiah's adaptation of the ancient Exodus pattern to the eschatological future also involves a radical change concerning the agent who will accomplish Israel's deliverance: "In the past the arm/hand of Yahweh delivers his people through various mighty acts. In the New Exodus, the Word becomes the agent of the new creative acts."[217] One can also notice a progression—a redemptive-historical typological movement—in the person of the "Servant," who acts as "warrior-Yahweh" in the eschatological New Exodus, especially as concerns God's judgment of the idolatry of all nations, particularly Israel's.[218]

The impact of Isaiah's Servant Songs on the christology of Luke is widely recognized by scholars and therefore does not require much elaboration here. The use of Isaiah 61 in Luke 4 is a highly significant example of such dependence.[219] However, Luke's use of Isaiah 53 and the figure of the "Suffering Servant" is also of primary importance. Thus Dennis Johnson contends that the Isaianic song as a whole is in

---

214. Anderson, "Exodus Typology," 181. Anderson later (pp. 189–90) describes this eschatologization of the Exodus in terms of continuity and crescendo in relation to the Exodus—God's salvific act together with the anti-idol polemic it implies. As a matter of fact, Isaiah does not impose on the first Exodus an alien perspective, but he builds upon an intrinsic feature of the event. The Exodus was a de-creation/new creation that pointed proleptically to the final New Creation Isaiah has in view. This eschatological dimension of the first Exodus appears already in the Exodus narrative itself (see Dumbrell, *Covenant and Creation*, 100–104 and Dumbrell, *End of Beginning*, 167–71), in Ps 105 (where the plagues are seen as microcosmic de-creations; Lee, "Plagues Tradition"), and in early Judaism (e.g., Wis 19:6).

215. For more details, see Pao, *Acts and INE*, 55–59.

216. See Anderson's discussion of the contrast in Isaiah's New Exodus prophecy between the "old things" and the "new things" (Isa 43:18), and how even this is part of the anti-idol polemics: Anderson, "Exodus Typology," 185–88; cf. Bentzen, "Old and New."

217. Pao, *Acts and INE*, 59. It seems that the emphasis on the "Word" as the agent of salvation moves the focus away from the military deliverance imagery (Yahweh as warrior) to the (re-)creational imagery of the New Exodus. Since Yahweh created the universe by the power of his word, it seems rather natural that he would re-create it in the same manner.

218. See the fascinating chronicling of the development of the figure (and identity) of the Isaianic Servant in relationship with the "delay" of the New Exodus in Watts, "Consolation or Confrontation."

219. See Seccombe, "Luke and Isaiah," 253–55 and James A. Sanders, "From Isaiah."

Luke's mind when he considers Jesus' sufferings.[220] What is crucial in this regard is the connection existing between the Servant—identified with Jesus—and Isaiah's New Exodus. Mánek notes that Luke clearly links the two when he reports Jesus' words about his imminent "exodus."[221] Just as the Servant is key to Isaiah's anti-idol polemic, so is Jesus to Luke's. The elaboration from one to the other consists in that the Servant's function in Isaiah is to demonstrate that Yahweh alone is Lord/God, while in Luke-Acts Jesus is proved to be the Lord/God *also*.[222] Another significant feature is that just as there is fluidity in the exact identification of the Servant in Isaiah (from an individual, such as Cyrus or the "unknown" eschatological Servant, to a collective entity, such as Israel), so is there fluidity in Luke-Acts between Jesus and his disciples regarding his/their messianic role and function.[223] Related to that continuity and conjunction between Jesus and the church as "Servant" is their Spirit-generation into "sons" of God, another messianic title.[224]

Moessner highlights the connection between Jesus as Isaianic Servant and his unction by the Spirit when he applies the prophecy of Isaiah 61 to himself in Luke 4.[225] The link between the Spirit of Yahweh and the Servant fulfilling his mission as

---

220. See Johnson, "Jesus Against," 343–45, who cites Bock, *Proclamation*, 189 in support of his view.

221. Mánek, "New Exodus," 17. He also makes the observation that this "exodus" is God's *plan* for Jesus in order to effect the salvation (Exodus deliverance) of his people. There is debate among scholars about the exact reference in view: is Luke speaking solely of Jesus' death ("exodus" being a simple euphemism) or does he have the entire redemptive complex of death-resurrection-exaltation-Pentecost(-parousia) in mind? The latter is to be preferred on at least three counts: 1) Jesus is clearly and extensively characterized as a "second Moses" in Luke's Gospel (see Moessner, "Luke 9:1–50"); 2) Luke appropriates the rich imagery of the "way" from the Isaianic New Exodus which elaborates this Mosaic model; 3) Jesus' appearances for forty days between the resurrection and the ascension (Acts 1:3) seems to be a clear allusion to the forty-year wandering of Israel in the desert (see Goulder, *Type and History*, 147–48); 4) Luke is the only Evangelist using that term. Hence, Jesus' "exodus" is the preparation of the way for God to come and deliver his people by leading them out (ἔξοδος literally means "way out") of their slavery to foreign nations/gods. It is therefore more likely that Luke would understand Jesus' "exodus" as his complete redemptive work (see Moessner, "Jesus and Wilderness").

222. This is obviously the main point of Johnson, "Jesus Against," 350–51; cf. Pao, *Acts and INE*, 181–212.

223. For Isaiah, see Watts, "Consolation or Confrontation," 49–58. For the prophetic/messianic continuity between Jesus and his disciples, see Moessner, "The Christ Must." For the continuity between Jesus and Paul in particular, see Moessner, "Paul and Pattern"; Moessner, "Paul in Acts"; and Mather, "Paul in Acts." Moessner argues that Jesus and the disciples, especially Paul, are depicted as the "prophet like Moses." We would suggest that this pattern should be read not only in the light of the Deuteronomic figure of Moses and the Exodus (as Moessner does), but also in the light of the Isaianic Servant and the New Exodus, since there is good evidence that the latter is already an appropriation and adaptation of the former (the expression ὁ παῖς τοῦ θεοῦ/κυρίου used to refer to both in the LXX creates a strong link between the two figures). For the argument that the Servant is a "second Moses" figure, see Chavasse, "Suffering Servant" and Hugenberger, "Servant."

224. See Evans, "Jesus and the Spirit" for a stimulating discussion of the Spirit's role in engendering "sons of God"—including Adam, Jesus and the Gentile converts of Acts.

225. Moessner, "Ironic Fulfillment," 43.

witness is made explicit in several places in Isaiah.[226] That same link is prominent in Luke-Acts, as we have seen earlier.[227] The activity of the Spirit is a frequent theme in both Isaiah and Acts.[228] That activity is of an eschatological nature in Isaiah, a quality that is highly significant for Luke-Acts.[229] The Spirit is hence critical to Luke's appropriation of Isaiah's New Exodus, as he inaugurates and defines the messianic age and eschatological Exodus.[230]

Talking about Jesus' answer to his disciples (Acts 1:6, 8), Tiede argues: "The logic is directly from Second Isaiah: the promise of God's reign is not simply the restoration of the preserved of Israel, but the renewal of the vocation of Israel to be a light to the nations to the end of the earth. Have God's promises failed? No, the restoration which the exalted Jesus is now about to inaugurate through the Holy Spirit (the promise of the Father: Luke 24:49) is the renewal of Israel's prophetic calling in the world."[231] The prophetic/witnessing aspect of Israel's role in God's plan is significant in Isaiah's message of universal judgment. However, Israel's was disqualified from that mandate by her blindness, which is the result of her refusing to honor Yahweh as God (idolatry) and to accept his chosen agent of salvation—a herald tasked with carrying God's word/message of salvation to them.[232]

This rebellious and stubborn stance caused the failure of the return of the exiles and the postponement of the prophesied (Isaianic) New Exodus.[233] And yet, we see

226. See Walter Kaiser's discussion of Isa 42:1–4 and of how the endowment of the Spirit is related to the Servant's (here Israel) role as a witness in God's lawsuit against the idols: *Mission in OT*, 59.

227. For example, Dennis Johnson highlights several features of Acts 1:6–8 that are directly drawn from the Servant Songs: the expression ἕως ἐσχάτου τῆς γῆς, taken from Isa 49:6; the pouring of the Spirit (Isa 32:15; 44:1–8); God's people as witnesses; and God's salvation transcending the boundaries of Israel. See Johnson, "Jesus Against," 346–48.

228. Seccombe, "Luke and Isaiah," 253.

229. See the discussion of Isa 66:15ff. in Jervell, *Theology of Acts*, 107. Cf. Witherington, *NT Story*, 134, concerning the fulfillment of Isa 40:3 in Luke 1:17.

230. Pao, *Acts and INE*, 92–93.

231. Tiede, "Exaltation of Jesus," 286.

232. See Johnson, "Jesus Against," 347, 350, and Watts, "Consolation or Confrontation," 44–49. There are loud echoes of that theme in Luke-Acts, especially in the recurring motif of the rejection of the prophet/Servant sent to Israel. This crisis and its possible overcoming by God's grace is typologically represented in Saul/Paul's conversion: "Such suppositions regarding the subjective effects of Saul's blindness may well be correct. But *I* would suggest that in the first place Saul's physical blindness is a sign pointing to the blindness of Israel, the Lord's servant-witness." One finds hope in Isa 42:16–17, however, a text concerned with Israel's idolatry, so that "Like Israel, Saul could become a servant-witness who would bring light to the Gentiles, salvation to the end of the earth, who through his testimony would open blind eyes and turn the nations from darkness to light, *only* because his own blind eyes had been opened, his own darkness dispelled by Christ's light." Johnson, "Jesus Against," 351 (emphasis original).

233. See Watts, "Consolation or Confrontation," 49–58. The themes of "witness" and blindness are interwoven into the fabric of the Isaianic New Exodus via its anti-idol polemic. This polemic is set in the context of God's lawsuit against the nations/idols, and witnesses are called to the bar to support the case of each party. Israel is found incompetent as a witness because of her blindness and deafness, two features that most likely indicate the fact that she is herself idolatrous. This is supported by the

already in Isaiah itself the hope of a future (new) New Exodus in which the gods of the nations (and their worshipers) will be judged and God's people will be wrested from their sway once for all. This eschatological Exodus will be successful thanks to its agent, a Spirit-anointed Servant who will render light/sight to the elect people of God—thus leading them to repentance, i.e., the turning away from idols to Yahweh,—who will restore the kingdom and renew Israel's mission to bring the light of God's glory and salvation to the end of the earth—even to the outcasts of Israel and to the Gentiles.[234]

As we saw earlier, Isaiah's reworking of the Exodus pattern leads to a universalization of the New Exodus which opens the door of salvation to the Gentiles and other excluded groups—eunuchs, for example—in an unprecedented way at that point in biblical revelation history.[235] And yet, Isaiah's "universalism" remains limited: Isaiah displays concurrently a strongly "nationalistic" outlook on the future. This paradox has led to much debate, with scholars often concluding that this reveals an inconsistency on the part of the final author/editor of the book and considering that one aspect only could be original or normative. Van Winkle, however, proposes a more satisfying solution to that perceived contradiction:

> The tension between universalism and nationalism may be resolved by recognizing that for Deutero-Isaiah the salvation of the nations does not preclude their submission to Israel. The prophet does not envisage the co-equality of Jews and gentiles. He expects that Israel will be exalted, and that she will become Yahweh's agent who will rule the nations in such a way that justice is established and mercy is shown. This rule is both that for which the nations wait expectantly and that to which they must submit.[236]

As Pao has shown, it is a case where Luke expands the meaning of Isaiah's New Exodus much further than the prophet had apparently anticipated.[237] In a sense, Luke is doing to Isaiah's New Exodus program just what Isaiah has done to the pentateuchal Exodus pattern.[238]

Thus, just as the Word/*tôra* in Isaiah is the one and only message of salvation for Israel and the nations—that includes a condemnation of all forms of idolatry

---

running theme in Isaiah of the blindness/deafness (as well as lifelessness, immobility, and speechlessness) of the idols and the fact that all who worship idols become just like them. See, Beale, "Isaiah 6:9–13" and Beale, *We Become*, 36–70.

234. Watts, "Consolation or Confrontation," 56–59; cf. Pao, *Acts and INE*, 111–43.

235. "In Isaiah the Servant's mission is favourable to Israel and to the outcasts. In Acts Jesus as a Servant figure is favourable for one of the outcasts, mentioned in Isaiah: the eunuch, and Philip will baptize him as sign that he, too, belongs to God's people." Koet, "Isaiah in Luke-Acts," 65.

236. Van Winkle, "Relationship," 457.

237. Pao, *Acts and INE*, 217–45.

238. "The Exodus, then, is a 'type' of the new exodus which will fulfill in a more wonderful fashion, with a deeper soteriological meaning, and with world-wide implications, Yahweh's purpose revealed by word and deed in the beginning." Anderson, "Exodus Typology," 194.

as sin and rebellion against Yahweh and, therefore, of all idolaters,[239]—so also the Word/gospel in Luke-Acts is the one and only message/Way of salvation for all men everywhere—therefore opposing and condemning all other religions.[240] A Way was opened (prepared) by the Servant—who is "warrior-Yahweh"—through his ἔξοδος. As the Way expands, the Word travels along with it to reach God's elect (both Jews and Gentiles) and deliver them from the oppression of slavery to idols (judging and utterly condemning these to destruction, together with all who resemble them, i.e., their worshipers).[241] The Word/Way enables these people to turn away from their idols and return to God/Zion[242] This process effects the restoration/recreation of the eschatological Israel.[243]

The interpreter must reckon with the momentous influence that the book of Isaiah has on Luke's thinking and writing. Isaiah seems to be at the heart of every significant theme in Luke-Acts. At the same time, Luke is not merely repeating Isaiah's theology, but he is genuinely making it his own in light of his particular point in the history of redemption.[244] Hence, many of the differences or variations existing between the two biblical writers can easily be accounted for when we recognize that: 1) Isaiah is writing about distant future events while Luke writes almost exclusively about past history; 2) Isaiah announces the hope of God's saving act for his people while Luke writes of the time of the eschatological and climactic fulfillment of God's promises; 3) Isaiah's eschatological vision does not always distinguish clearly between the vari-

---

239. Vriezen, "Essentials," 135.

240. Johnson, "Jesus Against," 351.

241. Beale makes the case that Isa 6:13 is describing the judgment/destruction of the returned remnant in a way that continues the motif of the increasing resemblance of the idolater to his false god. Just as they become blind and deaf like them, they will also be felled and burned like them. See Beale, "Isaiah 6:9–13," 277–78.

242. "Of special interest is the reappearance of the phrase פנו דרך from 40:3 in 57:14 and 62:10 although the latter both speak of preparation of the way of the people while 40:3 speaks of preparation of the way of God. Similarly, the idea of a highway in the desert as a New Exodus theme in 40:3–4, which is developed from 11:16 and 35:8, reappears in 43:19 and 49:11." Snodgrass, "Streams of Tradition," 25. Snodgrass also notes that the Piel of פנה does not appear with דרך in the OT outside Isa 40:3, 57:14, 62:10 and Mal 3:1, a passage that also mentions the "way" being prepared for the coming of Yahweh to judge both his people and the nations. It is interesting to note here that this passage from Malachi is alluded to in Luke 1:17 and quoted in Luke 7:27, two programmatic passages for Luke-Acts.

243. See Pao, Acts and INE, 147–76.

244. Pao argues that there is one significant case in which Luke turns Isaiah's prophecy upside down. In Isaiah, the nations remain subjected to Israel, the latter being the center and raison d'être of the New Exodus. In Luke, however, the Gentiles are elevated to a status of equality with the Jews. Even more, Isaiah's New Exodus pattern begins with a stern condemnation of Israel but ends on the hope of their future conversion to Yahweh. Yet in Luke-Acts, according to Pao, the reverse is true: the first chapters of Luke's Gospel express great hopes but the last verses of Acts hint at Israel's potentially final rejection in favor of the nations, though the door is never definitely closed. "Here, one finds an example of a dramatic reversal of the "dramatic reversal" presented in the wider Isaianic context." Pao, Acts and INE, 108, see 217–45. Cf. Koet, "Isaiah in Luke-Acts," 78, who argues that Luke sought to highlight the (positive) availability of salvation to the Gentiles rather than the (negative) "writing off" of the Jews.

ous redemptive-historical stages included in his prophecy, while Luke writes with the precision of one who can look back at how God has accomplished his plan.[245]

Isaiah's New Exodus and Luke's Macro-Narrative

Though Luke is clearly drawing from a number of other OT books, stories, and themes (such as the Elijah/Elisha narrative and the book of Psalms), they seem to have a relatively limited impact on the overall narrative structure of Luke's two-volume work and the theological reflection it embodies. In a number of cases, as we have seen earlier for Ps 2:7, these OT texts are used to draw out the meaning of the Isaianic material in light of its historical fulfillment. Thus, Koet's detailed study of the *function* of the Isaianic material in Luke-Acts leads him to conclude that "Luke uses texts from Isaiah as a framework for his own work."[246]

This is where Pao's research is, possibly, the most helpful, in that it traces the key themes of Isaiah's New Exodus showing that they are not only present but determinative in Luke-Acts.[247] Hence, he offers a lengthy discussion of the significance of Isa 40:1–5 for Luke-Acts, beginning with Luke 3:4–6. This passage from Isaiah functions as a pointer to the entire New Exodus program, embedded as it is in 40:1–11.[248] At the same time Luke 3 defines the nature of the whole history narrated in Luke-Acts. Moreover, echoes of Isaiah 40:1–5 are found in a number of other pivotal texts such as Luke 1:17, 76 and Acts 13:23–26.[249] Pao also discusses the Exodus themes found in the Isaiah 40 passage as well as the function of the "way" terminology (which is found in 40:3) as an identity claim forged in the fires of the Exodus itself.

The next step in his study is to "show how specific Isaianic statements are used at critical points in the narrative of the Lukan writings to provide meaning for the development of the story in Acts."[250] This he does by offering an in-depth analysis of five

---

245. A telling example of this greater perspicuity would be the "two-stage" dimension of the eschatological coming of the Lord. This feature of the "last days" was not foreseen by any OT writer, except possibly Malachi, who seems to hint at it in Mal 3:1–5, seemingly elaborating on Isa 40:3 and the New Exodus theme (cf. Snodgrass, "Streams of Tradition," 25).

246. Koet, "Isaiah in Luke-Acts," 77.

247. Pao, *Acts and INE*, 38–69.

248. Which makes reference to all the major Isaianic New Exodus themes identified so far.

249. The limits of his study did not allow an in-depth and exhaustive study of the Isaianic (and other OT) evocations in the Third Gospel. Moreover, Pao is correct to point out the programmatic and determinative nature of chs. 3 and 4 for Luke-Acts as a whole. However, one could wish he had given more attention than he does to chs. 1–2, the so-called "infancy narratives." Though these chapters have often been treated like a foreign appendage (as Dibelius does), they are providing the setting for Luke-Acts, and thus an indispensable interpretive framework for its narrative. They play the role of "framing in discourse" which establish expectations and a narrative point of view for the reader. Cf. Joel B. Green, "Problem"; Litwak, *Echoes of Scripture*, 65–115; and Mallen, *Reading and Transformation*, 60–101.

250. Pao, *Acts and INE*, 70, which he does on pp. 70–101.

"programmatic" passages in both Luke and Acts. The first one, Luke 4:16–30, defines the person and mission of Jesus on the basis of Isa 61:1–2, one of the most significant New Exodus passages in Isaiah outside of chs. 40–55. The second, Luke 24:44–49, contains the "climax" of the appearances of the risen Jesus and is widely recognized as programmatic for the narrative of Acts. The allusion to Isa 49:6 in this pericope is particularly important because that same Isaianic text is evoked in both Acts 1:8 (with the phrase "to the end of the earth") and Acts 13:46–47 (in a formal quotation), and because it is a command to the Servant to bring God's salvation to the nations/the end of the world.

Pao focuses his attention on these two latter texts because both are determinative of the structure of the narrative of Acts: Acts 1:8 provides a general outline of the book; Acts 13:46–47 defines Paul's mission from that point (his ministry at Pisidian Antioch) on. At the same time, one cannot miss the fact that both passages have to do with the universal spreading of the word of God, especially to the nations. In fact, the latter is used explicitly to justify that direction of the apostle's ministry in the face of the Jewish rejection of the messenger.

Finally, Pao shows that the closing scene of the book of Acts (28:25–28), concludes the story of the New Exodus in Luke-Acts with an Isaianic oracle of condemnation (Isa 6:9–10), thus producing a striking contrast with the promissory and hopeful Isaianic references found in the early chapters of Luke's Gospel.[251] This oracle serves to highlight the rejection of the prophet like Moses—the Isaianic Servant—as a final justification for the mission to the Gentiles, that is, for the fact that the eschatological New Exodus actually reaches out to the nations while Israel refuses it—just as she also refused Cyrus, which led to the failure of the post-exilic Isaianic New Exodus.[252]

Hence it appears that Luke used the Isaianic New Exodus program as the canvas for his own New Exodus program. The entire narrative of Luke-Acts is at the same time bracketed by and articulated around summary and programmatic statements which determine its structure and meaning, while the work's major themes are playing off the essential components of Isaiah's New Exodus. "The Isaianic program becomes, therefore, the hermeneutical framework in which isolated events can be interpreted."[253] It constitutes therefore a primary interpretive lens in our study of Acts 17:16–34.

---

251. Pao, *Acts and INE*, 101–9.
252. So Watts, "Consolation or Confrontation."
253. Pao, *Acts and INE*, 110.

CHAPTER 3

Luke's Narrative Setting for the Story of Paul in Athens

On Textual Ambivalence and the Reading of Stories

THE LARGE MAJORITY OF modern scholarship on the Areopagitica falls essentially in two distinct and generally antithetical camps. On one side, we find those who, like Martin Dibelius, are convinced that the proper background of the speech is the Hellenistic thought world, especially its philosophical variety.[1] On the other, we find those who, like Bertil Gärtner, are convinced that the OT (typically understood to have been mediated through Hellenistic Judaism) is the hermeneutical key to the speech.[2] When one studies the speech and its surrounding narrative, one cannot avoid but being pulled in these two directions. The vocabulary and some of the concepts appear clearly of Hellenistic origin, while the substance of the speech is unmistakably Jewish-Christian. What are we to make of it?[3] Was Luke merely inconsistent (justifying Dibelius' comment that the speech is a *Fremdkörper* both in Luke-Acts and in the NT

---

1. Dibelius does separate the "Hellenistic" body of the speech (vv. 23–29) from its "Christian" conclusion (vv. 30–31), considering the latter to be merely "tacked" to the former. In his view, the body of the speech is strictly Hellenistic and philosophical in nature, with no trace whatsoever of biblical or Christian influence. Most of his followers, such as Haenchen and Conzelmann, are more moderate in their judgment and recognize that there is both biblical and Jewish influences on the content of the speech, generally considering it to be the kind of syncretism encountered in Hellenistic-Jewish works such as the Letter of Aristeas and the writings of Aristobulus or Philo. See Dibelius, "Areopagus" (Dibelius, "Paul in Athens" for a summary of his view); cf. Gasque, "Speeches," 249n98.

2. Gärtner's work has demonstrated that the entire content of the speech can be correlated with OT and Hellenistic-Jewish thought. He argued that Luke drew from the more uncompromising and polemic branch of Hellenistic Judaism responsible for various post-exilic LXX books and Second Temple Jewish writings, including the Qumran community scrolls. This is especially obvious in the speech's anti-idol polemic, for it is reminiscent of the "Jewish diaspora propaganda" appropriated by Wisdom of Solomon and Paul's letter to the Romans. See Gärtner, *Areopagus Speech*, 251–52; cf. Hanson, *Acts*, 182.

3. We agree with Joshua Jipp that a proper interpretation of the story "must account for the resonances of both Septuagintal and Hellenistic philosophical texts." "Paul's Areopagus Speech," 588. We are not swayed by his proposed solution, however.

as a whole)?⁴ Was he trying to synthesize both worlds into a form of Christianity that is evidenced in the second century AD, particularly among the Apologetic Fathers? Or is there more to this apparent ambivalence?

Mark Given makes an illuminating contribution to this issue.⁵ First, he argues that not only both aspects are present in the Areopagus speech, but they are intentional on Luke's part. Then, he suggests that the reason modern scholars tend to retain one over against the other is due to the fact that they read the text through the lens of either the original audience of the speech (whom he calls the "oratees") or the original readers of the book (the "narratees").⁶ Thus, when one chooses the former (as historical-critical scholars typically do), Greek philosophy and *paideia* become the all-determining hermeneutical key, while when one chooses the latter (as literary-critical scholars generally do) the OT becomes the sole focus of attention. Given's point is that both are intended by Luke—who uses a good number of *double-entendres* not only in the Areopagitica, but throughout the book—in a rather ironic and entertaining style of writing.⁷

It seems to us that Given has identified a significant key to understanding our passage and the history of its interpretation. On the one hand, that Luke is writing for a readership quite different from the original (depicted) audience of the speech should be self-evident. This is the case in at least two distinct ways. Historically, and crucially for the interpretation of the speech, the ones are *Christians* and the others are *pagans*, thus using a radically different cultural and religious framework.⁸ Narratively, they do not have access to the same interpretive context—the narrative framework (or

---

4. Dibelius, *Aufsätze*, 55, 65; cf. Dibelius, "Areopagus," 71. Earlier, Alfred Loisy, building on Norden, *Agnostos Theos*, suggested that a later redactor was responsible for the insertion of the story into Luke's original narrative: see *Actes*, 76, 659–83.

5. In Given, "Not Either/Or."

6. This distinction is similar to the one made by Hans-Josef Klauck between "narrated communication" and "communication via narration" (*Magic and Paganism*, 81). We should mention here the complementary distinction made by literary critics between the original and "implied" audiences. The former is the actual and historically-intended audience (which is basically unknown to us independently from the text), the latter is the audience that the modern scholar can reconstruct on the basis of the clues offered by the text. See, e.g., Kurz, "Narrative Approaches," 201 and Kurz, *Reading Luke-Acts*, 9–16. Gray suggests that the narrative framework of the Areopagitica indicates a plurality/diversity of implied audiences for the Areopagus speech ("Implied Audiences").

7. Marguerat credits Cadbury, "Commentary," 504, with the original recognition that this is a characteristic trait of Luke's method of writing, an insight he seeks to develop in his own study of the phenomenon ("Luc-Actes entre," 73–79). Marguerat notes that Luke uses both semantic and syntactic ambivalence frequently (Cadbury mentions that Plummer, *Luke* identifies 25 instances of the latter in the Gospel alone) and purposefully. This literary technique produces a narrative irony that elicits various responses from the reader: "there is a subtle irony which occasionally takes the form of brilliant parodies. . . . In the case of the hapless exorcists in Ephesus, laughter is the appropriate reaction, while we feel real compassion for the poor slave-girl in Philippi who proves to be a Gentile prophetess." Klauck, *Magic and Paganism*, 119.

8. This is highlighted by both Klauck, *Magic and Paganism*, 59 and Rowe, *World Upside Down*, 10, 179n16.

"plot") and theological background (or "grammar")—to make sense of the reported events and speech. Luke's intended readership shares in the narrator's omniscience (a literary "God's-eye view") concerning the meaning of the story and of Paul's message.[9] In other words, the narrator prepares and guides the readers so they experience the speech from his chosen point of view, thus ensuring they understand his intended meaning.[10] This guidance is provided first through the grand story being told in Luke's two volumes up to that point, and second through the narrative introduction to the speech which determines its specific mood and direction.[11] Both elements are inaccessible to the in-story audience, of course.[12] On the other hand, Luke is seeking to give his readers a sense of what "actually" happened and what was said on the occasion of Paul's sojourn in Athens, for their meaning is intrinsically bound with the events themselves.[13] Hence the "original" and characteristic Hellenistic and Athenian flavor of the speech and its narrative.[14] The ambivalence or incongruity encountered in this text cannot be explained meaningfully when the interpreter fails to appreciate the nature, dynamic, and purpose of Luke's writings. It is not a record of "brute facts" (an epistemological monstrosity anyway), but an *interpreted* history, a theological narrative and a work of edification intended for Christians.

Specifically, the interpreter must acknowledge the ambiguity built in Paul's speech, pay close attention to the dynamics it creates, and recognize the congruence of this feature with the circumstances in which the discourse is delivered. This kind

---

9. On narrative omniscience in Luke-Acts, see Moessner, "Ironic Fulfillment," 38–46.

10. On the notion of narrator's point of view, see Ricœur, "Narrative Function," 185–86, who builds on Scholes, et al., *Nature of Narrative*, 240–82; for the notion applied to Luke, see Arnold, "Luke's Characterizing," 302–06.

11. "To follow a story, then, is to understand the successive actions, thoughts, and feelings as having a *particular directedness*. By this I mean that we are pulled forward by the development and respond to this thrust with expectations concerning the outcome and the ending of the whole process." Ricœur, "Narrative Function," 182 (emphasis original). It is therefore essential to follow the natural sequence of narrative and character building, in order to understand any part thereof. See Darr, *Character Building* (cited in Stenschke, *Luke's Portrait*, 50). "Framing in discourse" is a narration technique providing the necessary keys to the reader/hearer for interpreting a narrative unit, and thus directing their expectations. Litwak relates this concept to Deborah Tannen's concept of "structure of expectation," Litwak, *Echoes of Scripture*, 1–3; cf. Tannen, "What Is."

12. The concurrence of the two points of view is what creates the irony of the story, for the reader ha access to both and "know better" than the in-story audience. "Irony is always the result of a disparity of understanding." Scholes et al., *Nature of Narrative*, 240. According to these authors and Ricœur ("Narrative Function," 185–86), irony is of the essence of narrative as such and is necessary to the emergence of the *histor*.

13. But he does so in a way that is meaningful to his audience, *not Paul's*. In a sense, Luke is translating—even exegeting—the story of Paul's ministry and discourse in Athens for his own audience. One could say that Luke does for his readers what Paul is depicted doing for his hearers in that very passage. Luke—as a historian—proves to be more aware of the historical and cultural distance that needs to be bridged than many modern historiographers.

14. Most scholars recognize that Luke captures skillfully the mood and distinctiveness of the city at the time. It is a literary achievement. See Pervo, *Profit*, 71–72.

of skillful ambivalence should be expected from an experienced apologist like Paul addressing a so-called "higher pagan" sophisticated audience.[15] It is the engine driving the narrative and the speech, moving the depicted audience from confusion to clarity—while the readers know the end-point of the speech from the beginning.[16] Given is correct: reading such a story is indeed pleasant and ironic. However, calling it "entertaining" fails to distinguish irony from humor and to give their due weight to the gravity of the subject matter and the seriousness of Luke's purposes.[17]

A number of recent studies have come to the conclusion that though the language of the speech is often Hellenistic or even philosophical in nature, its substance—that is, its point and message—are clearly biblical and Christian. This may reflect the increasing sensitivity of scholars to the literary nature of Luke's work and their turning away from excessively skeptical historical-critical methods (including form- and redaction-criticism). Hence, while Fudge could wonder "at the paucity of material treating its Jewish-Christian or Old Testament background and motivation,"[18] it is not so anymore. Of all the major commentaries published in the past thirty years, Barrett's might be the only one considering that Luke was substantially influenced by Hellenistic philosophy in the composition of the speech.[19]

---

15. A good illustration of this practice is the work of Cornelius Van Til, a twentieth-century apologist who often used the vocabulary of Hegelian absolute idealism and of various forms of Personalism to convey his confessional Reformed theology. Though some interpreters were confused by such an appropriation of the linguistic and conceptual world of philosophy, Van Til was rather effective in communicating the Christian world- and life-view in terms that were meaningful to his intended audience and in ways that struck at the core of their belief system. See, for example, Van Til, *Christian Theory* and Van Til, *Christianity and Idealism*.

16. Both verbal and dramatic irony are woven together in this passage, embodied in the "ambivalence" of both narrative and speech. The two kinds of irony are effective plot-forming devices that stir up the interest of the reader (see Ska, *Our Fathers*, 57–63). Given notes that ancient literature is not typically based on suspense to fuel the interest of the reader, but that the pleasure of reading was in discovering *how* the announced ending pens out (*Paul's True Rhetoric*, 46–47). In view of the evidence, historical, literary, and narrative, it is difficult to understand—and impossible to agree with—Marguerat's claim that Luke is letting his reader decide the meaning of a speech "à deux entrées" for himself until v. 31 ("Luc-Actes entre," 75–76).

17. Contra Given, "Not Either/Or," 364, and his longer argument in Given, *Paul's True Rhetoric*, 39–82. "Dernière précision : l'ironie au sens littéraire du terme n'est pas nécessairement comique. Elle n'est pas à confondre avec l'humour, même si son usage peut déclencher le sourire ou le rire. Elle se caractérise surtout par son caractère allusif ou suggestif qui laisse au lecteur la tâche de la reconnaître. En cela, elle est à distinguer du sarcasme ou de la moquerie qui sont d'ordinaire plus explicites, plus lourds et donc plus agressifs." Wénin, "Jeu de l'ironie," 159–60.

18. Fudge, "Apostolic Self-Consciousness," 193.

19. "[Luke's] criticism of popular polytheism and idolatry is at once philosophical and biblical" Barrett, *Acts*, 2.842. See also Marshall, *Acts TNTC*, 281–82, who follows a similar line of thought, claiming that Luke uses the philosophers against popular idolatry while showing they did not go far enough.
This dependence on Hellenistic philosophy is a point that Barrett makes a number of times in his writings, for it is an important argument in his claim that the so-called "Paul of Acts" is incompatible with the "Paul of the Epistles." Barrett develops this argument at length in his "Paul at Athens," in agreement with his earlier "Acts and Pauline Corpus." It is important to note, however, that, unlike

Building upon Gärtner's work, Hanson defended the idea that though the language of the speech is often Hellenistic in order to suit the audience concerned, its message is without question Christian.[20] This linguistic accommodation of the speech is supposed to facilitate cross-cultural communication, while eliciting and sustaining the attention of the in-story audience.[21] Michel Gourgues' fresh inquiry into the possible Hellenistic sources evoked by the Areopagitica reaches a very similar conclusion: "Les affirmations et les perceptions empruntées à la littérature et à la pensée philosophique, extraites le plus souvent de leur contexte et des réseaux conceptuels auxquelles elles se rattachent, fournissent comme un point de départ, une base minimale d'affinités, une sorte de terrain commun à partir duquel peut s'amorcer un dialogue."[22]

Hence, Gourgues affirms that even though the thought is without doubt biblical, it is expressed in a language borrowed from the Hellenistic world of thought. This should not be a surprise, for such adaptation is indispensable to make the biblical message intelligible to a pagan audience. At the same time, it does not necessarily imply a transformation of the biblical message itself, nor the equivalence or absorption of the concepts associated with the borrowed language.[23] Gaventa thinks this is the reason why the speech may appear to its modern readers to be "foreign" to Acts or the NT. "That impression fades on closer examination, however, when it becomes clear that much in the speech coheres well with the remainder of Luke-Acts."[24] When studied in its broader textual context, the speech reveals a great similarity of content with the rest of Acts, as well as a marked difference in form, better adapted to the audience of the speech.[25] There is therefore no ground for the notion that the Areopagitica

---

Dibelius, Barrett considers that the speech includes OT, Jewish and Christian material throughout, and not only in vv. 30–31. In this he demonstrates his self-professed general agreement with F. C. Baur's views, considering the Lukan church to be a *tertium quid*, i.e., a peaceful combination of Jews and Gentiles (though questioning Baur's chronology). See "What Minorities?" and *Acts*, 2.xli–xlii.

20. "In fact the language is often the language of contemporary philosophy, deliberately adopted to suit the philosophically minded audience which Paul is represented as addressing, but clothing ideas which are those of the early Gentile Church." Hanson, *Acts*, 182–83.

21. "While Paul utilizes the utmost in skill and erudition to ensure that the packaging of his message does not offend his audience, the content of the Christian apostolic kerygma inevitably is scandalous." Charles, "Engaging," 59. See 1 Cor 9:19–22.

22. To which he adds: "Cela dit, un examen attentif du discours manifeste que si les grandes affirmations se rejoignent pour l'essentiel et si les formules des poètes peuvent être utilisées pour traduire celles de l'Écriture, la distance reste parfois considérable entre l'univers de pensée auquel ces éléments sont empruntées et les données de la révélation." Gourgues, "Littérature profane," 269.

23. "Pour rejoindre une culture donnée, suggèrent ainsi les *Actes*, il importe que le mystère soit formulé dans un langage et dans des catégories qui lui soient accessibles." Gourgues, "Littérature profane," 267–68.

24. Gaventa, *Acts*, 247. Gaventa refers in particular to Schubert's work on the unity and progression of the content of the speeches throughout the book of Acts in Schubert, "Place." See also Schubert, "Final Cycle."

25. "These similarities suggest that the speech is a 'translation' of earlier Lukan themes into the local idiom, rather than an intrusion into the remainder of the book." Gaventa, *Acts*, 247. Translation, here, must include the idea that the target language and culture are being stretched and transformed

would be a piece of Hellenistic thinking with a Christian ending tacked on it or a synthesis of the two thought-worlds, however many the references to and parallels with pagan literature and philosophy can be identified.[26] The speech is thus not a special case—nor an anomaly—that would be incongruous with the general character and background of Luke-Acts that we explored it in the preceding chapters.

The Athens Episode in the Book of Acts

Paul Schubert accomplished quite a *tour de force* when he successfully challenged the scholarly opinion prevalent since Dibelius by showing not only that the Areopagitica was not a foreign body in Luke-Acts, but that it was part of a book-long development of speeches building one upon another.[27] Though a number of points he made have failed to convince, he has successfully demonstrated that the various speeches of Acts—including the Areopagitica—were interconnected and that all together they were presenting a consistent and complete message.[28] He also highlighted the fact that the speeches serve to structure and move the narrative of the entire book forward. Similarly, Marion Soards argues that "the speeches are a crucial factor in the coherence of the Acts account. The speeches in Acts are more than a literary device, or a historiographic convention, or a theological vehicle—though they are all of these; they achieve the unification of the otherwise diverse and incoherent elements comprised by Acts."[29]

Acts 17 is the last so-called "missionary speech" in the book of Acts. It is, therefore, the final and climactic proclamation of the gospel to an unbelieving audience, narratively speaking. The fact that Luke reproduces only two major missionary speeches of Paul, one to Jews and one to pagan Gentiles is telling—especially considering that, from 1:8 to 28:31, Acts chronicles the successful movement of the gospel of salvation from Jerusalem to Rome, from the Jews to the Gentiles. Maybe the concept of climax is not the best-suited in this case. It might be preferable to speak of a mountain range, each peak being the apex of a particular dimension of the story. In any case, the Areopagus

---

in the process: "Rather than positing conceptual equivalence between the former and the latter—the sine qua non for 'same-saying' or translation—the Areopagus discourse articulates a rival conceptual scheme. For Luke, pagan philosophy is not Christian discourse in a different language." Rowe, *World Upside Down*, 40.

26. Gourgues, "Littérature profane," 269. "After all, it is still a long way, across several abysses, from Luke to Clement of Alexandria, before Greek philosophers can rank alongside the Old Testament." Schubert, "Place," 257.

27. See Schubert, "Place," where he builds on his earlier insights in Schubert, "Structure."

28. Schubert says he set out to study those parallels because Dibelius and other interpreters of the speech neglected to do so ("Place," 253).

29. Soards, *Speeches in Acts*, 12. In the light of these studies, it is incomprehensible that Jervell would write: "from the point of composition and structure *no lines lead from the [Areopagus] speech to the other parts of Acts*." Jervell, "Acts and Early Christianity," 21 (emphasis ours). See, further, Jervell, *Die Apostelgeschichte*, 452–56.

speech comes at the end of the development—therefore in an apogean position—of the presentation and proclamation of the gospel to the nations in Acts.

At the same time, the Areopagus speech is closely connected to the latter speeches of the book, particularly the forensic ones. Among others, Schubert has made the case that the forensic speeches of chs. 21–28 are defenses of the gospel/kerygma in, through, or beyond Paul's personal defense.[30] This is part of a distinct but tightly-connected dynamic at work in the book of Acts: the transition from joyful reception of the gospel to violent or unjust persecution against its herald(s). For example, Acts 2 presents us with a crowd which, though at first mocking and incredulous, embraces in large numbers the gospel preached by Peter. The following chapters present the growing opposition and persecution faced by the disciples, ultimately leading to the dispersion of the church away from Jerusalem, James' murder, Peter's imprisonment, and Stephen's lynching. One of the well-known ironies of that story is, of course, that the emerging champion figure of this persecution, Saul of Tarsus, eventually becomes the preeminent carrier of the gospel to the pagans and to Rome (now himself in chains!), thereby fulfilling *proleptically* the "end of the earth" of Acts 1:8.

Paul's ministry embodies the same motif whether in individual events or as a whole. His first reported sermon in chapter 13 is received with great joy at first, but the following Sabbath sees the Jews reject and the Gentiles joyfully embrace the good news of salvation in Christ. From that point on, we see the same pattern repeated in nearly every city with a synagogue, to which a parallel motif is eventually added: Paul faces also a growing persecution on the part of the Gentiles, culminating in his arrest, jailing, and court appearances in chs. 21–28.[31] The stories reported in Acts 17 and 19 give a foretaste of what is to come by depicting early negative—even violent—responses of the pagan world to the proclamation of the gospel. Hence the Areopagitica is delivered in a judicial context, to a crowd quick to mock and dismiss its orator, and with relatively "meager" results.[32] Acts 19:23–41 shows how the broader pagan population reacted to the growth of the Word among their fellow-citizens and how they perceived it to threaten their religion—and their livelihood. In this perspective, the Areopagitica functions somewhat like a hinge between the time of the expanding proclamation of

---

30. Here we see the correlation of the theme of the progress of and opposition to the "Word of God" and that of the witness/Isaianic Servant/persecuted prophet in the person, life, and mission of Paul. See Schubert, "Final Cycle" and Neagoe, *Trial of the Gospel*, 175–217.

31. Luke is indicating the *telos* of this motif through prophetic announcements, indirect references, and narrative gaps in the characterizing parallels between Paul's and Jesus' life-stories. In this light, the end point of this plotline is unquestionably Paul's martyrdom in Rome (cf. Brosend, "Means of Absent Ends"). This meshes well with the rejected prophet/suffering Servant theme, which is intrinsic to the New Exodus pattern running through Luke-Acts.

32. Yet Jervell reminds us that nowhere does Acts depict a mass-conversion of Gentiles (e.g., "God's Faithfulness," 34; though see the response in Pisidian Antioch in 13:48–49). As others have pointed out, the Areopagitica receives the same *kinds* of responses as the other missionary speeches reported in the book of Acts .

the gospel and that of its defense through its principal herald: Paul. Once again, we observe a mountain ridge with several and successive peaks.

In this context, Paul's address to the Areopagus appears to possess a function and a weight that exceed what one would expect from a mere exemplary. Luke certainly intended the speech to provide some sort of model of apostolic proclamation to an educated pagan audience, a fact recognized by the large majority of scholars on all sides.[33] However it is of an even greater consequence in Luke's story, for Paul's speech possesses an eschatological and a universal significance. With Paul, the Word of God and the Way of salvation of the eschatological New Exodus have reached the cultural and religious heart of the inhabited world. The "light" of Acts 13:47 (Isa 49:6) has shone in one of the darkest place.[34]

Paul in Athens and Luke's New Exodus

We discussed key structural themes of the Lukan theological system in chapter 1. That theological construct provides the broader context for reading the Areopagitica. Now, we want to focus on a theological motif that is specially pertinent to the interpretation of Paul's address: the anti-idol polemic, a sub-theme of the New Exodus. This theme is developed by Luke in both the Gospel and Acts, though it is significantly more prominent in the latter. As we shall see below, the story of Paul at Athens is thus part of a string of passages in Acts progressively unfolding a theological motif, like a narrative "mountain ridge." This narrative and theological development adds to the evidence demonstrating that the Areopagitica is emphatically *not* foreign to Luke-Acts. David Pao offers the most extensive discussion of this theme in Acts to date, standing on the shoulders of earlier scholars who have studied this theme in the OT at large, in Isaiah in particular, in various NT books, and also in Acts.[35]

Polemical material against idolatry is spread through various parts of the OT, but it is remarkably concentrated in Isaiah 40–55, where it is an essential element of the New Exodus program.[36] This fact, however, does not mean that the anti-idol

---

33. Hence Dibelius, Haenchen, Conzelmann, Bruce, Marshall, and many other scholars agree that this passage is a climax in the book of Acts, and that it is meant to show the apostolic way to address the gospel to pagans (though cf. Schnabel, *Acts*, 744–48). William Ramsay's theory that 1 Corinthians (especially 2:2) indicates that Paul's speech in Athens was both atypically philosophical and a failure, which Paul himself would have subsequently repudiated altogether, fails to convince. See the conclusive arguments brought against it by Stonehouse, "Areopagus Address," 32–36 and Gempf, "Before Paul" (the latter based on recent archaeological and historical evidence).

34. Interestingly, Schubert, "Place," 261, also points the close similarity of Luke's theology of nature and history with that of so-called "Deutero-Isaiah" in relation to the Areopagitica.

35. The limits of this study do not permit a full discussion of the anti-idol polemics found in the OT, not even Isaiah. Besides the works discussed hereafter, we direct the interested reader to the following classic studies: Mánek, "New Exodus"; Anderson, "Exodus Typology"; Anderson, "Exodus and Covenant"; Daube, *Exodus Pattern*; Holter, *Second Isaiah*; and Fishbane, "Exodus Motif."

36. See Pao, *Acts and INE*, 182–83. Roth, "For Life," argues that the idol parodies contained in

themes and motifs found in Isaiah should be studied in isolation from the rest of the OT. On the contrary, since Isaiah draws from and contributes to a dynamic and wide-ranging OT tradition, its particular contribution should be understood in the context of that larger context.[37] In a similar manner, though anti-idol concerns are more or less evident throughout the NT,[38] it seems that it is a peculiar concern of Luke which finds a more focused expression in the book of Acts. And just as Isaiah is a primary background for Luke-Acts in general, so is it in this specific case: Acts is strongly indebted to the anti-idol polemic developed in the book of Isaiah.[39]

The Anti-Idol Polemic in Isaiah

Clifford's analysis of Isa 40:12–31 exposes the heart of the Isaianic anti-idol polemic:

> The series of rhetorical questions in Isaiah are designed to demonstrate that no deity was present as helper in the creation of the world (vv. 12–14), that the nations over whom the deities rule are insignificant before Yahweh (vv. 15–17), that idols are human handiwork and thus not fit representations of God, that the human rulers who serve the deities by ruling over the nations are powerless before Yahweh (vv. 21–24), that the deities even in their military might are under the control of the one God (vv. 25–26). . . . The purpose of these Joban questions seems to be to arouse Israel to an expectant confidence in the hidden rule of its God by successively dethroning all the powers it had come to believe held it in thraldom—the nations, their cults and kings, the patron gods of the nations' civic and religious institutions.[40]

Isaiah are interpolations from a later editor; many scholars reject his views on the basis of the literary unity demonstrated by the passages concerned. See Clifford, "Idol Passages."

37. For the extensive use of the Exodus tradition in the OT—especially its anti-idol polemic,—see the helpful Zakovitch, *You Shall Tell*. The book, however, is missing a number of important references where anti-idol polemics are at work in the OT. For example, Zakovitch fails to recognize the polemical anti-idolatrous and anti-mythical character of the story of creation in Genesis 1 and 2 (he considers the biblical story to be mythical). The book focuses especially on the so-called Deuteronomistic tradition. Besides offering some valuable insights into the books of Exodus and Genesis, Zakovitch argues that the books of Deuteronomy, Joshua, Judges, and 1–2 Kings revolve in good part around the issue of Israel's idolatry. Interestingly, the historical summary of Joshua 24 shows a clear affinity with Acts 7. Of great importance is the fact that the first two commandments of the Decalogue are explicitly and directly addressing idolatry—forbidding the worship of other gods than Yahweh (first) and the making of visual representations of Yahweh himself (second). See Zakovitch, *You Shall Tell*, 131.

38. For example, Paul's epistles to the Corinthians focus on the issues faced by *Christians* living in a pagan and idolatrous society (see Winter, "Theological and Ethical" and Winter, "Public and Private"). See also the programmatic 1 Thess 1:9–10 and the final and integrative exhortation of 1 John 5:21. The NT writing that concerns itself the most with the issue of idolatry may well be the book of Revelation, especially with its theme of Satanic "counterfeiting" (see Poythress, "Counterfeiting"). In a way, the anti-idol polemic theme runs through the entire canon of Scripture, literally from Genesis 1 (v. 1) to Revelation 22 (vv. 8–9).

39. As demonstrated in Pao, *Acts and INE*, 181–212.

40. Clifford, "Idol Passages," 459, 460.

An essential point made by the anti-idol polemic passages in Isaiah is that Yahweh alone is God, that he is God of the whole world. There is no other.[41] The corollary to this fact is that Yahweh also *rules* the whole world, that he presides over the history and destiny of all nations, even though they may not know him or recognize his sovereignty.[42] Finally, the prophet does insist on Yahweh's power and authority to *save his people* from their oppressors, that is, from the nations, their kings and their false gods.[43] This shows just how the New Exodus for Isaiah is truly a new Exodus.[44] In fine, the anti-idol polemic is an important element in the Isaianic New Exodus' focus on comforting God's people.[45]

The power and sovereignty of Yahweh is demonstrated primarily by contrasting him, his Word, and his Servant-witness with the impotent and lifeless idols (an apt representation of the deities they stand for), their silence and the blind nations (their witnesses).[46] This contrast is developed along several lines, the most important motif being the fact that Yahweh made all things (alone and without help), especially man who in turn made these idols with his hands. Isaiah contains several lengthy and ironic depictions (often called "parodies") of the process of manufacturing idols.[47] A direct corollary is the affirmation of Yahweh's control over history, which is demonstrated principally in two ways: through God's prophetic utterances and through his witnesses.[48] These polemics are generally set as trial scenes, a device

---

41. See Pao, *Acts and INE*, 189. This is consistent with Isaiah's vision in the temple and the defining impact it had on his entire life and message (see Vos, "Some Doctrinal Features").

42. Pao, *Acts and INE*, 181.

43. Pao, *Acts and INE*, 183, 191.

44. Pao, *Acts and INE*, 192. A casual reading of the Exodus story may fail to perceive the anti-idol polemic running through the story (in the "ten plagues," for example; but see Currid, *Ancient Egypt*, 108–20), and that the deliverance of Israel was not merely, essentially, or primarily political, but rather religious: it is a deliverance from idolatry. In the ancient Near Eastern world, political power and religion, kings and gods are all one (see the claims of Sennacherib and Yahweh's response in 2 Chr 32:1–22). Even so, that perspective is made explicit in passages such as Exod 12:12; 20:2–6; 32:1–10; Num 33:4; and Josh 24:23.

45. The tone is set in Isa 40:1: "Comfort, comfort my people, says your God."

46. "In the Isaianic New Exodus, the supremacy of Yahweh is established through the contrast of the power of Yahweh with the futile efforts of the nations, their rulers, their deities, and their idols (and idol-makers). These four categories should not be viewed as four separate groups since they were understood as referring to the same entity. Idols are, however, frequently singled out as the visual manifestation of the powers that oppose Yahweh. Similarly, in Acts, idols are identified as the symbol of those who oppose the Lord of the early Christian movement." Pao, *Acts and INE*, 181–82; cf. Clifford, "Idol Passages," 454.

47. "Significantly, four of the verbs used in 40:19–20 . . . to describe the creative acts of the idol-manufacturers are also used in Isaiah 40–55 to describe the creative acts of Yahweh. . . . The hierarchy established here among Yahweh, idol-fabricators, and idols should not be missed. Finally, the silencing of the idols seems to be intentional and the focus on the idol-fabricators should be understood as a rhetorical strategy that denies the existence of the power and status of idols." Pao, *Acts and INE*, 184n11.

48. "Most of the occurrences of *martus* in the Septuagint belong to its usage in the legal world and donate [sic] the witness before the seat of judgment." Mather, "Paul in Acts," 26.

used by Isaiah in particular when addressing the nations.⁴⁹ In this context, it is not surprising that "the trial speeches in Isaiah 40–55 are primarily concerned with the rival claims of power."⁵⁰

These Isaianic passages focus particularly on two key themes. The first is Yahweh's word, which foretold (foretells) what has happened (will happen), in contradistinction with the idols—and the deities they represent—which are silent, thus proving that all of history—including Israel's defeats and exile—is under God's control. The second is the Servant/Israel, who is an *eye*witness able and qualified to testify concerning God's sovereign and gracious activity in world history, while the idols/nations are blind, deaf, and mute.⁵¹ The first motif is painted especially with the contrast between (prophetic) word and silence and between sovereignty and impotence—particularly in terms of ability/inability to give one's people/nation military victory and deliverance. The second uses the antithesis between light and darkness or between sight and blindness (both metaphors for knowledge and ignorance), which definitively qualify and disqualify the respective witnesses called upon for the trial *qua* witness.⁵² It is quite obvious that the two lines of argument are interrelated, since the qualified witnesses are so by virtue of having *seen* Yahweh's powerful and saving hand at work and having heard his word,⁵³ while the nations are disqualified by the lack of the same.

The result is that as the nations and their gods are judged, God's people is vindicated and liberated, just like in the first Exodus (Exod 12:12–13). "Those who oppose the reign of Yahweh will thus be destroyed" because he is an all-powerful warrior battling impotent idols/deities/nations through the agency of the Servant on behalf of his people.⁵⁴ The book of Isaiah depicts in a number of places the destruction of idols, idolatrous trees, and their worshipers—both Israelite and Gentile.⁵⁵ It

---

49. Clifford, "Idol Passages," 453–54.

50. Pao, *Acts and INE*, 184n12, citing Melugin, *Formation of Isaiah*, 53.

51. For a fuller discussion of this theme of Israel as Servant and witness in the book of Isaiah, see Watts, "Consolation or Confrontation."

52. See Clifford, "Idol Passages," 463.

53. "The Lord's servant is a *martus* who can remember and speak in the courts of the Gentiles because the witness has seen and heard what the Lord has done and has known there are no other gods beside Yahweh. The Septuagint's usage is very close to the Lukan: those whom the Lord has chosen as witnesses share a peculiar knowledge of God that comes from the experience of salvation and a specific task of testifying before the Gentiles." Mather, "Paul in Acts," 27. In an interesting twist, though, the nations are called upon to judge "who is truly God, Yahweh or the deities of the Gentiles." Mather, "Paul in Acts," 26.

54. Pao, *Acts and INE*, 189 For the theme of Yahweh as a warrior in the Exodus tradition, see Dozeman, *God at War*. Yahweh's war/judgment against the nations and their gods is what opens the way of salvation (the ἔξοδος) for his people. A correlative theme in Isaiah—and in Acts—is the Word as the unstoppable agent of the New Exodus.

55. See Beale, "Isaiah 6:9–13," who highlights the fact that idol-worshippers resemble their idols in their final judgment and destruction (felled and burned like idolatrous trees), just as they did in their life (blind, deaf, and dumb)—itself a form of judgment, though one that is reversible through conversion. For a broader study of this biblical theme, see Beale, *We Become*.

is precisely this war/judgment that opens the "way" of salvation to God's people.[56] God's ability to save his people from the rule and oppression of the nations, their kings, their idols and their gods is the *absolute proof* to the *whole world* that Yahweh alone is God, that there is no other!

Pao points out that here is the very heart of the New Exodus program. Demonstrating that truth is the core of Isaiah's anti-idol polemic: "Yahweh is the sovereign one who is in control, and only the people that belong to him will survive. Again, the attack on the idols is an attack on the nations. The survival of the Israelite community is ensured by the power of Yahweh. It is only within this context that the Isaianic anti-idol polemic can be understood."[57] This point has a most important implication: the existence of the world, the course and end of history as well as every single aspect of human and national life all pivot around one fact: Yahweh alone is God. In other words, the meaning and significance of *all things* are determined by their covenant relation to—or rebellion against—the Creator who is Lord of heaven and earth. The whole of human existence and experience is thus by definition religious.

Salient Anti-Idol Polemic Passages in Luke-Acts

Rikki Watts has pointed out that, in Isaiah's oracles, Israel is disqualified from the role of witness in Yahweh's lawsuit because it is itself blind and deaf as a result of its idolatry (which was the cause of the Babylonian exile), a verdict that remains true of the remnant who have returned from exile.[58] Isaiah nonetheless proclaims a strong message of hope: God's eschatological promise to raise a new Servant who will redeem Israel from her exilic condition afar from God's presence and blessing—for though the nation is not in geographical and political exile anymore, it remains in spiritual alienation from God. This is where Isaiah's New Exodus and Luke's connect, for Jesus and the church are understood to be the eschatological fulfillment of this very promise of salvation.

Of course, idolatry is touched on in divers ways in Luke-Acts, many of which are implicit, implied or indirect. That it would be so should be expected, since most of the story in the book of Acts happens in the polytheistic world of the Roman Empire, where religion was integrated with every aspect of life.[59] Since our purpose here is to

---

56. "This final verse [Isa 46:13] also confirms the conclusion that the attack on idols is also an attack on the nations; and the affirmation of the power of Yahweh is at the same time a declaration of the promise of deliverance for the Israelite community." Pao, *Acts and INE*, 189.

57. Pao, *Acts and INE*, 185.

58. See "Consolation or Confrontation," 58–59.

59. "Investigating the problem of idolatry in the NT is a bit like examining an iceberg. All that is visible is the tip—the vocabulary of idolatry is not all that prominent in NT literature—yet underlying what is visible is a vast bulk, in our case an entire culture predicated upon what from a Judeo-Christian point of view could only be called idolatry. As a result the NT authors could assume much that did not need to be reported about their readers' religious and cultural environment." Achtemeier, "Gods

map the "mountain ridge" to which the Areopagitica belongs in order to acquire a context and an orientation for our reading, rather than do an exhaustive topical or plot analysis, we will limit our survey to passages concerned explicitly with idolatry—one in the Gospel and seven in Acts.[60]

We begin with Luke 4:1–13 not only because it comes first in the canon, but also because it sets the tone for every subsequent anti-idol passage.[61] This early pericope shows Jesus to be the antitypal/archetypal Servant resisting Satan's temptation to turn away from God and to trust, serve and/or worship another than him (whether his own person or Satan).[62] This narrative is tucked between the stories of Jesus' baptism—which concludes with the heavenly divine pronouncement "you are my beloved son" and is immediately followed by his genealogy which remarkably culminates with the words "son of Adam, son of God"—and of his first recorded sermon, in Nazareth. Both passages interpret Jesus' person and mission in terms of Isaiah's (suffering) Servant. Jesus' testing in the desert confirms that he is the promised Servant/Son of God—this pericope contains many echoes of the testing of both Adam in Eden and Israel (also God's son) in the wilderness after the first Exodus—who obeys perfectly the Father and therefore achieves the eschatological salvation of God's people.

Acts 7:2–53 records Stephen's defense against the charge of blasphemy, in which he recounts Israel's long history of turning away from God to idols, culminating with the implicit charge of having made the temple into an idol[63] and the explicit

---

Made with Hands," 43.

60. For a detailed study of the anti-idol polemic motif in these passages, see Johnson, "Jesus Against" and Pao, *Acts and INE*, 197–208.

61. Pao begins his study with the Areopagus speech because it is where the anti-idol polemic is the most explicit (especially because it clearly alludes to passages from Isaiah 40–55), then uses it to shed light on the other passages. This allows the climactic form of the polemic to illumine its less-developed expressions. Our own study, however, does the reverse for two reasons: our concern is to understand Acts 17 itself, not the broader theme; by approaching Acts 17 in this manner, we benefit from what Fitzmyer calls "the Lucan buildup" to the speech (*Acts*, 602–3).

Surprisingly, though Pao considers Acts 17 to be preeminent for his argument, he only dedicates *three* pages to its study, in which he passes by nearly completely the narrative framework and barely deals with v. 16 at all. Unsurprisingly, Beale accuses his analysis of this passage of being superficial. Beale points out in particular his failure to account for other influences evident in the text (such as various non-Isaian OT allusions, references to pagan thought, and the influence of Jewish and Christian traditions) and how they relate to, and interact with, the book of Isaiah and its anti-idol polemic. See Beale, "Review of Pao."

62. In contrast, Luke 24:52–53—the last sentence of the Gospel—shows the disciples *rightly* and *rightfully* worshipping the risen and just-ascended Jesus, as well as praising God in the temple. It is as if the cross-resurrection-ascension-session complex of events operates a redemptive-historical transition from Jesus being the Servant of Lord Yahweh to the church being the Servant of Lord Jesus. And yet, Jesus does not cease to be the eschatological Servant: he has merely moved to a different, consummated, phase in this role.

63. This accusation is already hinted at when the charge of blasphemy (Acts 7:11) is equated with "speaking against this holy place" (v. 13), but it becomes unmistakable when the temple is described as being "made by (human) hands" (χειροποίητος, v. 48) and then Stephen quotes Isa 66:1–2, *pace* Sweeney, "Stephen's Speech," 201–6. See further Beale, *Temple*, 216–32.

charges of opposing the Holy Spirit, of having murdered the Righteous One, and of not keeping the covenant-law. Thus, they are striving against God, a reminiscence of Gamaliel's words in 5:39.

Acts 8:4–24 tells the story of how the Samaritans came to faith in spite of the sway that Simon's magic had on them. Simon himself is characterized through the use of divine epithets, clearly though subtly indicating an idolatrous situation.[64] A strong contrast is built in this passage between Philip's message and wonder-making, which point exclusively to Christ, and Simon's magic, which points to himself. And yet, Simon is himself subdued in the end as he comes to faith and later accepts the rebuke of the apostles for his foolishness concerning the gift of the Spirit.

Acts 12:1–25 speaks of a king—Herod—who brutally oppresses the church for self-aggrandizement (it pleased his Jewish subjects, v. 3). Shortly after his plans fail miserably (in spite of an extensive guard, Peter escapes from jail thanks an angelic intervention), he dies at the hand of an angel from God in punishment for accepting to be praised as a god by his Caesarean subjects. By contrast, Peter immediately gives the glory to God alone for his miraculous escape. After Herod's death Luke tells of the church's enormous growth and expansion beyond Palestine.

Acts 13:6–12 tells of Elymas, a *Jewish* false-prophet who seeks to keep a Gentile (the proconsul Sergius Paulus) from turning to the true God by opposing the Word heralded by Paul and Barnabas. Paul calls him the "son of the devil" (together with similar epithets),[65] charges him with "making crooked the straight paths of the Lord,"[66] and asks the Lord to make him temporarily (physically) *blind*—when obviously Elymas is already *spiritually* blind. The proconsul, however, believes in response to this miracle and the "teaching of the Lord."[67] There is, once more, great irony in this situation, since Jesus called Paul "to open [the Gentiles'] eyes, so that they may turn from darkness to light and from the power of Satan to God, that they may receive forgiveness of sins and a place among those who are sanctified by faith in me" (26:18).

In Acts 14:5–19, Paul and Barnabas' refuse absolutely to be worshiped as divine beings, in stark contrast with Herod's and Simon's attitude earlier in the story.[68] This passage is the first to define explicitly the apostolic "good news proclamation"

---

64. Simon describes himself as "somebody great" (τινα ἑαυτὸν μέγαν, v. 9), while the entire population of Samaria considers him to be "the power of God that is called great" (ἡ δύναμις τοῦ θεοῦ ἡ καλουμένη μεγάλη, v. 10). This passage also makes mention of the fact that the people used to "pay attention" (προσεῖχον, used twice in vv. 10, 11) to him.

65. The scene is quite ironic, Elymas' Jewish name being Bar-Jesus, i.e., "son of Jesus."

66. Hence defining his action as an attempt to reverse Yahweh's promised work of salvation for his people (Isa 40:3).

67. This entire scene is preparatory for Paul's ministry in Pisidian Antioch (which follows immediately) by presenting Elymas as a type of unbelieving Israel and Sergius Paulus as a type of the gospel-receptive Gentile. Just like Elymas, Israel is not merely failing to be a light to the nations, it is striving to prevent them from being exposed to it.

68. In a similar manner, Peter refuses the worship of Cornelius by insisting that he is but a man like him, a clear parallel (Acts 10:25–26).

(εὐαγγελίζομαι, a term generally associated with the gospel in Luke-Acts) as *a call to turn away from idols* (τῶν ματαίων, "vain things") to the living God who made all things.[69]

Acts 19:11–20 recounts the story of how great numbers of both Jews and Gentiles in Ephesus and Asia came to fear God and extol Jesus' name, to repent of their occult practices and thus to destroy an astounding number of books of magic, the whole being summarized by Luke as "the word of the Lord continued to increase and prevail mightily."[70] Ironically, all of this happens because of the seven sons of Sceva, a Jewish high (or main) priest. Their disastrous attempt at exorcising in the name of Jesus demonstrates in a dramatic fashion that only Christians have access to the divine power and authority over the evil spirits, which is mediated through Jesus' divine lordship and authority—and that Jesus' name is not a magic formula.[71]

This story prepares the way for the last—and climactic—anti-idol polemic passage of the book: Acts 19:23–41. If Acts 7 is the apex of Luke's anti-idol polemic against the Jews and Acts 17 the climax of his anti-idol polemic against the Greeks, then Acts 19 paints the dramatic picture of the impact of Paul's ministry in its conflict with idolatry.[72] Perhaps the most significant element in this passage is that Paul's (successful) ministry is, once again, summarized as persuading people to *turn away from idolatry*.[73] It also exposes idolatry for being intrinsically motivated by personal interest.[74] Finally, it shows that people under the sway of idolatry will react with passionate violence to any *real* threat to their religion.[75]

---

69. An obvious parallel to 1 Thess 1:9–10. "Mark the vehemence with which all this is done by the Apostles: 'rent their clothes, ran in, cried out,' all from strong affection of the soul, revolted by the things that were done. For it was grief, indeed, a grief inconsolable, that they should needs be thought gods, and introduce idolatry, the very thing which they came to destroy!" Chrysostom, Homily XXXI, 195.

70. This way of phrasing the growth of the Word in this region clearly implies that the issue is overpowering or overcoming hostile forces in order to free people from their evil sway. Magic is an occult practice which in ancient times was generally associated with *chthonic deities*. It is therefore depicted as a particularly offensive form of pagan idolatry.

71. The fact that they were seven and the sons of a high (or main) priest makes them ideal representatives for the whole of Israel's priesthood. This story may suggest that even the Jewish priesthood has no access to God anymore, which would imply that national Israel as a whole is cut off from God.

72. Acts 7 does for Israel what both Acts 17 and 19 do for pagan Gentiles: it is an indictment of Israel's historic idolatry and her ongoing stiff-necked rebellion against God and his witnesses.

73. Note that here also idols are spoken of as "made with hands" and "not gods" (οὐκ εἰσὶν θεοὶ οἱ διὰ χειρῶν γινόμενοι, v. 26). The intriguing words of the town clerk in v. 37 may indicate that Paul avoided mentioning specific gods in his preaching, referring only to the physical objects of their worship and to the true God, just as we see him do in Athens. On the other hand, Demetrius seems to draw the right theological conclusion when he claims that the logical end result of Paul's ministry is "that the temple of the great goddess Artemis may be counted as nothing, and that she may even be deposed from her magnificence" (v. 27).

74. Whether the gain is about finances and respect (like here or with the pythoness girl in Philippi), or divine glory (Herod), or attention and amazement (Simon), or power over men or spirits (Elymas, sons of Sceva), idolatry is always about controlling the gods in order to obtain one's wishes.

75. The loss of personal gain and violent reaction are naturally correlative. This point was already

A few themes emerge from our swift overview. The most obvious—and the most central to Isaiah's anti-idol polemic—is that there is only *one* true God, Yahweh. All others are lifeless and powerless idols, inventions and creations of men. The second point—its correlative—is that this God will *not* share his glory and worship with anyone else, except with the risen Christ/Lord.[76] This one God is the sovereign Lord of the κόσμος who overpowers and masters (through his Word and Spirit) kings, nations, evil spirits, idols, deities, magicians, and so on. This divine lordship, power, and authority also belong to the risen and enthroned Christ—who is therefore himself Lord—and is shared with the church (especially its representatives) in a unique and exclusive manner through the Spirit.[77]

This sovereignty and authority—especially associated with the "name" of the Lord Jesus Christ—is what makes the Word ("word of the Lord," "word of God," "teaching of the Lord," etc.) grow, multiply, progress, and prevail irresistibly. In spite of the many enemies and opponents (some mighty) who seek to destroy or stop it, the word always prevails, being actually propelled forward by this opposition. And so it is for the heralds who carry this Word to the end of the earth.

---

made plain earlier in Acts 16:16–24. Paul's exorcism of a slave-girl with a spirit of divination in Philippi leads to his and Silas' trial-less beating and imprisonment, after her masters realize their financial loss.

76. This theme definitely follows the Old Testament teaching that God is a *jealous* God, as regards both his glory/worship and his exclusive relationship with his people, the locus of both his glory and worship among the nations. This final note is possibly where Jesus' deity appears most explicitly and strikingly in Luke's Gospel. Once again the resurrection appears to be *the* turning point as it exposes in full light the true and full identity of Jesus, the God-man.

77. Here we must differ with Pao's claim that "in Acts, the identification of the Lord is naturally made in reference to the risen Jesus." *Acts and INE*, 181n1. It is not sufficient to define this lordship merely as the fact that "everything is now under his control" either (Pao, *Acts and INE*, 210n83).

First of all, one needs to take into account the fact that in Acts the title κύριος can be used clearly of either God or Jesus, and that it is ambiguous in a number of passages (see Dunn, "ΚΥΡΙΟΣ"). Hence, though some of those uses entail or imply Jesus' ontological or eternal divinity, most—if not all—relevant passages for our purposes are concerned with Jesus' lordship as (human) *Messiah*. In this context Jesus' lordship is "derivative" in that it is conferred upon him by God in a proleptic manner at his baptism (effected by the heavenly declaration and the reception of the Spirit) and in a final manner after the resurrection and ascension (declared proleptically at the transfiguration, hinted at in Jesus' response to the disciples' question about the restoration of the kingdom, and infallibly demonstrated by the pouring of the Spirit at Pentecost). Hence, what is predicated of God as Lord is true of Jesus also, and reciprocally—except, of course, for the fact that one confers, and the other receives, the lordship and the prerogatives attached to it. If this is so, then we cannot define the heart of the anti-idol polemic in Acts as seeking to establish Jesus' lordship over all in a one-dimensional manner. This fact is especially important for the interpretation of Acts 17 as an anti-idol polemic.

Secondly, one cannot be content to define Jesus' lordship in Isaianic terms, however decisive they might be. Yes, Jesus is Lord as the Servant who acts on behalf of (the Lord) Yahweh and fulfills perfectly his mission, leading to his enthronement, but he is also Lord as the Davidic king under whose feet the Lord will put all his enemies (Acts 2:34–35, quoting Ps 110:1 [109:1 LXX], a very important and programmatic statement; see Doble, "Psalms in Luke-Acts"). As is well-known, Luke spends much effort demonstrating that Jesus is the eschatological Son of David through whom God "will rebuild the tent of David which has fallen" (Acts 15:16; see Dupont, "Cabane de David"). In Jesus God not only restores his people (releasing them from spiritual blindness and slavery) but he also restores the kingdom. See Franklin, *Christ the Lord*.

Jesus' representatives—they are so in several divers ways—, particularly Stephen and Paul in our set of texts, are "witnesses" in the Lord's universal trial of idolatry and idol-worshipers. As such their role is to convict their audience, both Jews and Gentiles, of the sinfulness and foolishness of idolatry (and of its abominable character in God's eyes), to summon them to turn from it in repentance to the only true God and Lord through faith in Jesus Christ. In doing so, they are truly giving sight to the blind and shining God's light in darkness, they are extending the eschatological "way" of salvation that has been opened for God's people by Jesus, who is the Servant/warrior/Davidic king/liberator. The battle for the final and universal establishment of Jesus' kingly rule produces increasingly violent conflicts, but it is sure to succeed in the end because God, the maker of heaven and earth, is waging war on behalf of his people.

With this macro-narrative framework in place, we now turn to Acts 17:16–34.

PART TWO

A Contextual Reading of the Areopagus Speech

L'entendement humain, comme il est rempli d'orgueil et témérité, prend l'audace d'imaginer Dieu tel que sa compréhension le porte ; parce qu'il est lourd et comme accablé d'ignorance brutale, il conçoit au lieu de Dieu toute vanité et je ne sais quels fantômes. Avec tous ces maux, il y a l'outrecuidance, qu'il ose tenter d'exprimer au-dehors les folies qu'il a conçues en soi touchant de Dieu. Ainsi l'esprit humain engendre les idoles, et la main les enfante.

—Jean Calvin, *L'Institution chrétienne*, 1.11.8

We need to remind ourselves, therefore, that while almost every word in Scripture is more or less polysemous *if considered in isolation*, that potential for ambiguity normally does not even occur to an individual in the course of reading substantive portions.

—Moisés Silva, *Biblical Words and Their Meaning*, 151

CHAPTER 4

The Narrative Frame for Paul's Areopagus Speech (Acts 17:16–22a, 33–34)

FROM THE "MACRO-NARRATIVE" OF (Luke-)Acts, we now focus on the "micro-narrative" of the Athens episode itself and set out on our exegetical journey. Luke's theology, his intertextual use of the OT, and the larger narrative of Luke-Acts provide a general and broad context for the story and, thus, for the speech. They are quite important for orienting our reading of the pericope. Luke's narrative frame, however, composes the immediate context for the speech, the one that is most directly determinative of its meaning.

Acts 17:16–34 Is a Literary Unit

Gärtner rightly emphasizes the fact that just as much as the Athens narrative is an integral part of Paul's second missionary journey, so the Areopagus speech and its narrative framework form an indivisible unit.[1] This is another case where the form-critical and similar methods clearly fail to account properly for the literary work of Luke and to understand ancient historiographical canons, especially those relating to the function of speeches.[2] The notion defended by Dibelius and others that the speeches have no actual connection with their narrative situation simply runs in the face of the textual and historical evidence.[3] As Pervo notes, focusing on Luke's putative

---

1. Gärtner, *Areopagus Speech*, 45. Stenschke, *Luke's Portrait*, 50, notes that this difference in method explains why Gärtner is more convincing than Dibelius, who sets the speech and narrative in tension with one another.

2. Gasque stresses these two points in his excellent critique of the approach adopted by Dibelius and his followers, including Haenchen and Conzelmann (see "Speeches").

3. Gasque, "Speeches," 240n47, makes the observation that Dibelius argues this point at length for the speeches in Acts in general in "Speeches and Historiography" (German original, 1949), using Acts 17 as an example (on p. 177), but he was arguing the exact opposite in "Areopagus" (German original, 1939). In the latter Dibelius finds that the close interrelationship between the narrative and the speech demonstrate that both were Luke's invention, with the exception of a few minor elements.

sources is unhelpful because it detracts from the indisputable unity of the episode.[4] This is why scholars today generally recognize the hermeneutical *necessity* of reading the speech in the context of the whole story, recognizing the well-crafted character of the episode and the fact that its narrative logic assists its interpretation.[5]

In this regard, Fitzmyer is correct to affirm that the introductory narrative "sets the tone" for the speech.[6] Yet, vv. 16–21 do more than setting the stage for the speech, they provide the necessary hermeneutical keys for the speech and the event as a whole: "A careful reading of vv. 16–21 thus creates a distinct *Vorverständnis* with which the reader then hears Paul's speech."[7] This interpretive relation is not unidirectional, however. There is a significant interplay and interdependence between the speech and the narrative: they illuminate and interpret one another.[8]

Dibelius and his followers not only claim that the speech is a foreign body in Luke-Acts, that it is disconnected from its narrative context, but also that the speech itself is composite and inconsistent.[9] Barrett, for example, asserts that Luke draws "illogical developments" out of vv. 22–29.[10] This kind of interpretation illustrates well Gärtner's point: what he calls the "philosophical interpretation" is wholly unable to discern the unity and integrity of the speech, and thus to uncover its inner logic. That type of interpretation is, first of all, self-contradictory since it claims that Luke completely invented the speech, so there was no constraints that would have kept him from giving his creation a strong coherence, especially since they recognize that he is an able writer everywhere else in Luke-Acts. Secondly, this method, though devised with the purpose of explaining the speech, actually destroys its meaning altogether.[11] We therefore concur absolutely with Gärtner's judgment that "if the choice lies between the dismemberment of a text and a homogenous conception of the same text, the latter is to be preferred."[12] Possibly the best evidence supporting the unity of the speech

---

4. Pervo, *Acts*, 426.
5. So Rowe, "Grammar," 36 and Neyrey, "Acts 17," 127.
6. Fitzmyer, *Acts*, 601.
7. Rowe, *World Upside Down*, 33.
8. So Witherington, *Acts*, 512; see also *BegC*, 4.208–9 and Stonehouse, "Areopagus Address," 6.
9. Dibelius famously claimed that the speech is a Hellenistic piece with a Christian ending "tacked on" it. Later critical scholars offer a more nuanced evaluation of the speech, but still contend that the thoughts presented in the speech are from disparate origins and form a more or less incoherent whole. See Conzelmann, *Acts*, 224–25 and Haenchen, *Acts*, 527–30. Barrett sees in this a characteristic shared with Stephen's speech: in both cases a Christian ending is added to an otherwise non-Christian body ("Paul at Athens," 151). By paying attention to the literary unity and flow of Stephen's speech, however, Witherington concludes that "the way it plots the trajectory of salvation history and the way it uses Old Testament stories are meant to lead the hearer to a Christian conclusion about Jesus and his followers. It is then a Christian reading of the history, though not overtly Christian in its content up to verse 52." *NT History*, 130. The same would be true of the Areopagitica.
10. Barrett, "Paul at Athens," 153.
11. See, for example, Gärtner, *Areopagus Speech*, 166–67, 168–69.
12. Gärtner, *Areopagus Speech*, 168–69.

comes from the rhetorical or literary analyses of the inner organization of the speech or of the episode as a whole (speech plus narrative framework). Recognizing the well-crafted nature of the pericope, many have shown that the speech has a natural flow, moving logically from one idea to another in spite of its compactness.[13] Des Places, in particular, has demonstrated that the final part of the speech—vv. 30-31, supposedly the only "Christian" element in the speech—is bound to the rest by a number of intertextual parallels.[14] Others have offered very detailed structural analyses—Pierre Auffret, Robert O'Toole, and Mikeal Parsons even suggesting chiastic arrangements for either the speech or the entire pericope.[15]

Because of the compact nature of the speech as it is reported by Luke, contemporary interpreters generally favor simple and straightforward outlines. In spite of an overall agreement concerning the general layout of the material, the proposals vary in detail.[16] We would suggest the following—we believe non-controversial—general outline for the pericope: 16-21,[17] narrative introduction; 22-23,[18] Paul's introduction

---

13. "The brevity of the Areopagus speech is matched only by the fine balance of its literary structure and the compactness of its content. . . . The train of thought moves smoothly and evenly." Schubert, "Place," 248. Parsons offers a fascinating list of literary and rhetorical features present in the speech, demonstrating the care taken by Luke in its composition (*Acts*, 249). See also: des Places, "Actes 17,27"; Dupont, "Discours à l'Aréopage"; Hemer, "Speeches II"; Porter, *Paul in Acts*, 118-24; and Witherington, *NT Rhetoric*, 70.

14. Des Places, "Actes 17,30-31."

15. Auffret, "Essai Sur" and Parsons, *Acts*, 245-48 for the speech; O'Toole, "Paul at Athens" for the entire pericope.

16. Two issues are involved in this disagreement. The first one is whether the speech is complete or not. If it is, then the interpreter should be able to find a balanced outline (which is our premise in this book). If not, assuming Paul is represented as being actually interrupted, then the speech is incomplete and the interpreter can offer a balanced outline only for the first part (vv. 23-29).

The second issue is how much the interpreter expects the speech to follow the rules of ancient rhetoric. When the interpreter focuses on the linguistic and thematic cues, like we do, he generally arrives to an outline similar to the one we are proposing. When, on the other hand, he seeks to correlate the speech with the canons of rhetoric, the interpreter must first determine the genre of the speech (and there is little agreement on this point), and then which parts of the speech match the various prescribed elements (recognizing that some may be missing or may be half a verse long). Rhetorical analysis of the Areopagitica has yet failed to elicit any substantial consensus among its proponents.

17. Keener, *Acts*, 3.2570-74, considers that v. 15 should be included in the pericope, forming the narrative transition together with v. 16. He is the only commentator we could find arguing for this view. Narratively speaking, his proposal has real merit, since both verses do serve to transition two distinct but causally-related stories. However, they function like a hinge, v. 15 concluding (and therefore belonging to) the earlier episode, and v. 16 introducing (and therefore belonging to) the subsequent narrative unit. We therefore consider that v. 16 alone marks the beginning of the Athens narrative. Rius-Camps and Read-Heimerdinger, *Message of Acts*, 338-40, also consider vv. 14-15 to be a transition from Beroea to Athens, which they entitle "Journey to Athens."

18. Gaventa, *Acts*, 246, prefers to include v. 23b (which announces the subject of the speech) in the second segment of the speech, but it seems more natural for it to be a part of Paul's introduction rather than of the development of his argument. Zweck and Witherington prefer to keep v. 23b (which they see as a *propositio*) distinct, and thus offer a four-part outline of the speech (Zweck, "Exordium," 96; Witherington, *Acts*, 518). Barrett, *Acts*, 2.825, is critical of formal analyses based on rhetorical categories. Though we agree with him that rhetorical analysis is not really suitable for such

(the great religiosity of the Athenians and the altar inscription); 24–29, critique of pagan worship; 30–31, call to repentance; 32–34, narrative conclusion. This outline might be improved to better plot the flow of the speech and its climaxing in vv. 30–31 by distinguishing the three constitutive elements of its central section: 16–21, narrative introduction; 22–23, introduction of the speech; 24–25, world Creator vs. pagan temple worship; 26–27, man's Creator vs. man's idolatrous quest; 28–29, Giver of life vs. lifeless representations; 30–31, call to repentance; 32–34, narrative conclusion.[19]

A Cascade of Events

Jervell captures the powerful irony of the Areopagus pericope when he notes that though Athens appears not to have been part of Paul's travel plans, Luke presents it as the climax of his missionary and preaching career.[20] It is clear from vv. 13–15 that Paul had no design to visit Athens nor any intention to minister there: he was forced to flee from Berea, was taken to Athens by the disciples and was awaiting his fellow-workers Silas and Timothy so that they could go on to their next station, Corinth (18:1).[21] Once again opposition and persecution further and drive the progress of the Word, not the apostles' plans.

Paul's "mission strategy" appears to have focused on large cities, especially capitals of Roman provinces, which were like hubs from which the gospel could reach entire regions. At the time of Paul's travels, Corinth was the capital of the Roman province of Achaea, rather than Athens—which was a *civitas libera et foederata*. Moreover, Athens had long lost its political and economic hegemony, as well as much of its population.[22] Estimates vary, but Haenchen holds to Keil's number of 5,000 inhabitants, while Longenecker claims that it could not be more than 10,000.[23] Horace speaks of *vacuae Athenae*.[24] Moreover, there is no known historical evidence of a church established by Paul in Athens. Yet, most commentators—if not all—recognize that the speech is

---

a short or summarized speech, we must appreciate the fact that all studies in that tradition discern a similar structure, irrespective of the various rhetorical labels used to identify each section. For the least, this implies that we are dealing with a complete argument, i.e., the outline of an actual speech or a typical pattern.

19. A few commentators note that the central part of the speech, vv. 24–29, is articulated around three negations, all of them in relation to proper worship. Pesch adds that the three are found in Isa 45:18, a key anti-idol text. Cf. Pesch, *Apostelgeschichte*, 2.137 and Tannehill, *Acts*, 215.

20. Jervell, *Die Apostelgeschichte*.

21. This is generally recognized by all scholars, but the following articulate the consensus particularly well: Bruce, *Acts NICNT*, 348; Johnson, *Acts*, 312; and Longenecker, *The Acts of the Apostles*, 979. Gray, "Implied Audiences," 207 adduces Acts 15:36 as further evidence that Athens was not part of Paul's "plan."

22. On Athens in that period, see Geagan, "Roman Athens" and Goette, et al., "Athens."

23. Haenchen, *Acts*, 517 and Longenecker, *The Acts of the Apostles*, 980.

24. *Epistulae* 2.2.81, cited in Haenchen, *Acts*, 517n2. In the same vein, Rackham, *Acts*, 306, calls it "a body without a soul."

set as the climax of Paul's missionary activity.²⁵ So why choose Athens? Most likely because Athens remained the cultural and religious "capital" of the ancient world, at least symbolically.²⁶ In terms of representative geography, when Paul's gospel engages Athenian culture and religion, it has engaged the best and therefore the entirety of Gentile (pagan) culture and religion.

The Precipitating "Crisis"

This *providential* change of plan (Luke has no room for "accidents" in his theology) launches a domino cascade that climaxes with Paul's speech. The second determinative step in the process is Paul's reaction at what he encounters in the city as he "goes through" it.²⁷ Paul observes (θεωροῦντος)²⁸ that the city is κατείδωλον, "overgrown with idols."²⁹ It is crucial to note that this is Luke's only—hence exhaustive—*description* of the city.³⁰ Narratively, Athens is thus characterized exclusively and entirely in terms of idolatry, using an intensive compound of the word εἴδωλον—itself a derogatory term.³¹ Paul's reaction to this setting is very intense, as the verb παρωξύνετο indicates.³²

---

25. Fitzmyer calls it "the most important episode in Pauline Mission II, the evangelization of what had been the most renowned city in ancient Greece." (*Acts*, 600).

26. Dupont, "Discours à l'Aréopage," 384.

27. Διερχόμενος γὰρ καὶ ἀναθεωρῶν in v. 23 may indicate that Paul made this observation when he arrived in the city (coming from the Piraeus, for example) or while wandering in the city like tourists did already in the first century (hence the popularity of "travel guides," such as Pausanias, *Description of Greece*). The use of the present tense for these two verbs as well as for ἐκδεχομένου in v. 16 (describing Paul's "waiting" for his collaborators) indicates a progressive action extending over a certain length of time. In light of the context, this fact favors the second possibility, though Paul is no "gawking tourist," judging by his reaction to the "effluvia of idolatry" (as Pervo, *Acts*, 424, puts it).

28. Another present participle, indicating an ongoing action or situation. The verb θεωρέω in itself denotes an active and attentive or lengthy activity, not a casual or accidental one.

29. Barrett, *Acts*, 2.824, echoing Wycherley's "a forest of idols." Wycherley, "Paul at Athens," 619–20 is the classic discussion of the meaning of this word, which appears to be a Lukan neologism. Wycherley notes that compound words with κατά are primarily used in reference to luxuriant vegetation and always to express a large amount of something. In his opinion, Luke must have deliberately used this word "with a touch of humorous exaggeration," which seems to underestimate the historic reality (so also Gill, "Achaia," 443–44).

30. Also noted by Stenschke, *Luke's Portrait*, 203. The archaeological evidence available to us shows that Paul's impression and Luke's description are very accurate. It resembles Pausanias' description of the city in the second century AD (*Descr.* 1). It is easy to understand why a first-century Jew like Paul would have been overwhelmed by the plethora of idolatrous objects (and buildings) of all kinds clogging the city, especially its innumerable herms. See the description in Hemer, "Paut at Athens: A Topographical Note."

31. See Klauck, *Magic and Paganism*, 75–76.

32. As Gill, "Achaia," 443, notes, Paul had encountered paganism and idolatry before. The vehemence of his reaction bespeaks the intensity of what he encountered in Athens: "Luc raconte qu'il a été plus enflammé à Athènes, car il y voyait régner une idolâtrie supérieure à celle qui existait coutumièrement en d'autres lieux." Calvin, *Actes*, 458.

Two things are important to note concerning this verb. First, Luke is using the imperfect indicative, indicating that this was not a temporary emotional reaction (punctiliar) but an ongoing state (durative). He is thereby characterizing Paul's frame of mind during his entire stay in Athens and setting the tone for ("framing") his subsequent activity as a whole (since he does not "re-characterize" him).[33] Second, Luke's choice of παρωξύνω cannot be innocent or accidental. The verb occurs only once in Luke-Acts and once elsewhere in the NT (1 Cor 13:5), while its cognate noun παροξυσμός appears only in Acts 15:39 (where it refers to Paul's and Barnabas' sharp disagreement over Mark that leads to their separation) and Heb 10:24. However, both occur quite frequently in the LXX. Its most characteristic (almost technical) usage is to denote Yahweh's wrath (often compounded by the use of the adjective μέγας and/or various cognates of θυμός and ὀργή) against idolatry and covenant-breaking.[34] Its meaning in Acts 17:16 is nicely captured by John Calvin: "[Luc] ne parle point là d'un simple courroux et il ne dit point qu'il a été offensé simplement par un tel spectacle ; il exprime une *ferveur admirable d'une sainte indignation* qui aiguisait le zèle de Paul pour qu'il se prépare à œuvrer avec un plus grand courage."[35] By framing the episode this way, Luke reveals his narratorial point of view, thereby supplying the reader with the necessary hermeneutical key to see through the prima facie ambivalence of the episode and the speech.[36]

The Pragmatic Articulation of the Early Narrative (μὲν οὖν . . . δέ)

This narrative technique is reinforced, at a linguistic level, by the use of μὲν οὖν in v. 17, an expression generally used to introduce a new scene or a new division.[37] With it Luke moves the story from Paul's reaction to Paul's response to the Athenian idolatry, viz., what he did in Athens. A crucial question for the interpretation of the whole episode is whether the transition entails a *causal* relationship between v. 16 and what follows. Gaventa, among others, argues that μὲν οὖν is merely transitional for two

---

33. Also noted by Stott, *Message of Acts*, 278.

34. Here is a sample taken from the three OT books used the most in Luke-Acts: Deut 9:7–8; 18–19; 31:20; 32:16, 19, 41; Ps 9:25, 34; 77:41; 105:29; Isa 5:24; 65:3. This intertextual background is noted by most commentators; for example, Witherington, *Acts*, 512; Bock, *Acts*, 560–61; and Peterson, *Acts*, 489n53 Cf. the identical use of παροργίζω (e.g., Judg 2:12, 14).

35. Calvin, *Actes*, 459 (emphasis ours). It is noteworthy that in spite of the possible ambivalence of this verb (see BDAG), we did not find any biblical scholar arguing that its positive meaning should be read in this text (though see Pervo, *Acts*, 426). Commentators may differ on the exact shade of meaning or connotation to adopt, but the LXX usage in a similar context does not leave any doubt that (holy) anger is intended.

36. So also Rowe, *World Upside Down*, 28 and Roloff, *Apostelgeschichte*, 257, who says that Paul's *heiligen Zorn* frames the Areopagus speech: "Mit der Schilderung dieser Reaktion wird bereits die Rede vorbereitet (vgl. V.29)."

37. See, e.g., Haenchen, *Acts*, 517 and Witherington, *Acts*, 513. Moule, *Idiom Book*, 162–64, lists four possible uses for the expression in general, of which two are possible here: resumptive and adversative; cf. Turner, *Syntax*, 337–38.

reasons: this is the most common way to use μὲν οὖν; she cannot understand why Paul would preach in the synagogue concerning Athenian idolatry.[38]

We see four reasons why her position is not convincing. First, Gaventa recognizes that the "repetition of this common practice momentarily distracts from the focus on idolatry." Rather than grappling with the narrative logic, however, she repeats the dubious idea that Luke includes this half verse out of literary "habit."[39] But it makes no sense for Luke to use a (useless) literary pattern that disrupts his story-line. A convincing explanation must be able to account for the text as we have it and its inner logic.[40] Besides, the picture is historically plausible, since there is archaeological evidence that some Jews or God-fearers in Athens might have succumbed to the surrounding syncretism and idolatry.[41]

Second, the verb διελέγετο describes what Paul did in *both* the synagogue *and* the agora.[42] It is one single activity being pursued in two places/contexts (at different times). So if Paul's ministry in the synagogue is not to be associated with the idolatry mentioned in v. 16—nor Paul's reaction to it—, neither is his interaction with people in the agora and the subsequent events. It is quite difficult to conceive what role v. 16 would then play in the narrative chain of events. The unity of action requires us to recognize that Paul's activity in the synagogue is related to the idolatry of Athens. Verse 17a cannot be used as an argument against attributing a consequential force to μὲν οὖν.

Third, besides the unity of action in v. 17, there is an obvious thematic continuity between the idolatry of v. 16 and the central concern of the entire pericope. Hence, the subsequent narrative and speech center around paganism and idolatry, even making reference to its extreme form in Athens (e.g., in vv. 18 and 22). Thus, the whole episode demonstrates a great level of unity, whether of theme, place, time or action. There is great continuity between v. 16 and the rest of the passage. This verse is part of the total narrative chain of events, which entails some form of causal relationship.

Fourthly, a consequential meaning is supported by a (function-based) linguistic understanding of the expression μὲν οὖν. Thus, Steven Runge argues that, in Greek,

---

38. Dunn captures the puzzlement of many: "Quite why Paul should debate with his fellow Jews and the usual God-fearers, presumably on the subject of idolatry, is not clear." (*Acts*, 232). He recognizes that this is the natural meaning of the text, however, and suggests two possible explanations: Luke's assumption that this is what Paul did, based on his habit; Paul accused the Jews of not protesting enough against idolatry. Gaventa, *Acts*, 248, asserts that it is "misleading" to entail that Paul's activity in the synagogue could be in reaction to Athenian idolatry. Keener, *Acts*, 3.2576, also refuses to link the synagogue with idolatry, except for the possibility that Paul found it to be a "more welcoming venue." Both therefore contradict the syntactially obvious. Muñoz-Larrondo, *Postcolonial Reading*, 201, goes even further and erroneously claims that no synagogue is mentioned in Athens (just as in Lystra!).

39. A view associated with Conzelmann, though she does not cite him. See Conzelmann, "Areopagus," 219.

40. See the discussion in Gray, "Implied Audiences," 208–10.

41. See Van der Horst, "Unknown God," 35–38; cf. Marcus, "Idolatry in NT," 111 and Hengel, *Judaism and Hellenism*, 261–67 on the issue in Judaism more broadly.

42. Also noted by Peterson, *Acts*, 489n53 and Schnabel, *Acts*, 724.

when particles are combined, each keeps its particular meaning and function.[43] In this case, μέν is a forward-pointing device marked with continuity and correlation (but unmarked for development), which creates anticipation.[44] Οὖν is backward-pointing and is marked with close continuity and development, which indicates "that what follows the particle is either inferentially drawn or concluded from what precedes."[45] Together, they express the fact that what follows (vv. 17ff.) is the direct result of what precedes (v. 16), while alerting the reader that something significant—in fact, the central focus of the development—is still to come.[46] Here, the pointed target is probably the new development unit beginning in v. 18, as indicated by the development marker δέ—here associated to adverbial καί. In this case, we would have the following pattern: v. 16, the precipitating initial event; v. 17, the initial response, a causal intermediate link that increases suspense and anticipation by delaying the dramatic resolution of the conflict;[47] v. 18ff., the ultimate complex of events pointed to by μέν, which is the focus of the author at this stage—since it describes what caused Paul to give his speech, the climax and resolution of the narrative unit.[48]

Hence, it is clearly preferable to understand μὲν οὖν in v. 17 to indicate that the subsequent Pauline activity is the result of his strong reaction to the surrounding idolatry: Paul's *response* to the Athenian idolatry is to proclaim Jesus and the resurrection, both in the synagogue and the agora.[49] This means that v. 16 provides the orientation necessary to understand not only the events reported in general, but especially the meaning and import of their apex: the speech before the Areopagus. As concerns the interpretation of the Areopagitica, it is not so much Paul's *emotional response* that is significant, but the *point of view* on idolatry that it reveals on his—and therefore the narrator's—part. In the light of the argument of the speech, we would say that Luke depicts Paul's dominant motivation to be Yahweh's glory, love for neighbor being a probable second (Luke 10:27 // Matt 22:38–40).

From this point on Luke's story picks up speed. Paul's speaking in the synagogue (presumably on the Sabbath) is introduced first, and then Luke quickly moves

---

43. Runge, *Discourse Grammar*, 19, 75.

44. Runge, *Discourse Grammar*, 54–55, 74–83.

45. Runge, *Discourse Grammar*, 43–48, here 43; cf. Levinsohn, *Textual Connections in Acts*, 137–41.

46. Contra those who claim it merely introduces a new scene or story, without indicating any causal or consequential force, like Moule, *Idiom Book*, 163; Pervo, *Acts*, 426n19; Schnabel, *Acts*, 723; or Gaventa, *Acts*, 248. For a fuller discussion of μὲν οὖν in narrative material in Acts, see Levinsohn, *Textual Connections in Acts*, 141–50.

47. This narrative device is noted by Gray, "Implied Audiences," 208.

48. Cf. Levinsohn, *Textual Connections in Acts*, 143–47. So also Rius-Camps and Read-Heimerdinger, *Message of Acts*, 3.341n76.

49. Especially in the light of the fact that it seems pretty clear that Paul originally had *no intention* of ministering in Athens. Something had to make him change his mind, and his strong emotional reaction is the obvious culprit. See Johnson, *Acts*, 312; Wilkinson, "Acts 17," 4; and Bruce, *Acts NICNT*, 349.

the reader to Paul's encounter with the Athenians.⁵⁰ Appositely, Paul debates with whomever he meets in the agora, the heart of life in Athens.⁵¹ The curiosity of some philosophers is pricked by this proclaimer of strange/new ideas. Their persistent confusion at Paul's message causes them to lead him to the Areopagus for an explanation—or defense—of his philosophical and religious ideas. At the apex of this chain of events, Paul orates the most famous speech in Luke-Acts. Once he is done, Luke concludes the episode with a very short summary of the results of Paul's ministry in Athens (the story has come full circle: v. 32 loudly echoes v. 18), and the story moves on to Corinth.⁵²

The speech reveals many connections with its narrative framework. Here it will suffice to note the following: idolatry (v. 16); audience's misunderstanding (vv. 18–20) together with the theme of ignorance/unknowing; Jesus and the resurrection ("foreign deities," v. 18); Paul's "indignation" and the pronouncement of judgment.⁵³ Fitzmyer is absolutely correct when he concludes that not only the speech and the narrative are well integrated, but the speech "constitutes an essential element of the narrative."⁵⁴ There is therefore no justification for ever alleging that the Paul of v. 16 is different from the Paul of v. 22!⁵⁵ The narrative shows how Paul, rather in spite of himself, is led by the Lord to be his witness before the highest authority of Athens, thus fulfilling his Christ-appointed mission (Acts 9:15).⁵⁶

Paul's Ministry in Athens Prior to the Areopagus Speech

It seems that much disagreement over the nature and meaning of Paul's Areopagitica could be resolved if scholars paid more attention to the preparatory narrative, especially the details of Paul's activity it contains. Too many students of this

---

50. "There is no comment on the attitude of the Athenian synagogue, which is dismissed in half a verse (17.17a): there were synagogues everywhere, but there was only one Athens, and Luke proceeds to deal with it as a special case." Barrett, "Paul's Speech," 71.

51. "In the agora at the foot of the Acropolis, where the citizens of Athens met to exchange the latest news, there was no lack of men ready to enter into debate with him about the nature of the divine being." Bruce, *Paul*, 238.

52. This narrative structure is without doubt meant to place all the emphasis on the speech, with a quick-paced action going crescendo up to the speech and a transition to the following story which is meant not to distract the reader from what has just happened.

53. Cf. Dunn, *Acts*, 230.

54. Fitzmyer, *Acts*, 601.

55. Contra Samuel, "Paul on the Areopagus," 21. Though other inclusivists might not be so bold as Samuel, they all consider Paul's words in v. 23 to indicate at least a change of mood or attitude on his part. Keener, *Acts*, 3.2574, sees a change of *tone* that demonstrates Paul's self-control.

56. Here, we are especially thinking of the call to be a witness before *kings*. In Athens—and a few other cities—the highest authority is not an individual, but a council: "According to Acts, therefore, just as Paul is brought before the στρατηγοί at Philippi, the πολιτάρχαι at Thessalonica, the ἀνθύπατος at Corinth, so at Athens he faces the Areopagus. The local name for the supreme authority is in each case different and accurate." *BegC*, 4.213.

speech—especially those interested in its missiological or theological import—still ignore the interpretive cues provided by the author, hence reading it practically as a self-sufficient or self-contained unit.[57] Yet, reading carefully Luke's depiction of Paul's activity in Athens prior to the Areopagitica greatly helps in discerning the nature and purpose of the speech, two key orienting factors for its interpretation. There are three specific features that must be highlighted.

Paul's Prolonged Proclamatory Activity

We read that Paul was "reasoning" in the synagogue and in the agora. The verb διαλέγομαι is used ten times in Luke-Acts out of thirteen for the whole NT. They are all located in chapters 17–24 of Acts, where they always describe *Paul's activity*. The verb is used four times to depict his speaking at a synagogue (17:2; 18:4, 19; 19:8), one time at Tyrannus' school (19:9), twice at a church meeting (20:7, 9), once in the temple (24:12), once before Felix (24:25), and once in both synagogue and agora (17:17). It is always referring to Paul's *public* proclamation of Jesus Christ and, with the exception of the church meeting, this proclamation is *evangelistic* in nature. Finally, it generally implies a situation where the audience interacts with the speaker, where there is address and reply, questions and answers, arguments offered back and forth.[58] It is therefore not surprising to read in v. 18 that the philosophers were "debating" with Paul.[59]

Though Acts 17:17 does not make explicit the precise meaning of διαλέγομαι, Luke's attentive (i.e., "competent") reader can easily determine it from the context, as he should. First, the activity it refers to is clearly depicted in 17:2–3.[60] Second, the phrase ὅτι τὸν Ἰησοῦν καὶ τὴν ἀνάστασιν εὐηγγελίζετο in v. 18[61] offers a condensed summary of what it is in view in v. 17.[62] The verb εὐαγγελίζω in Acts always means "to

57. For a recent example, see Higgins, "Key to Insider Movements."

58. Haenchen highlights this feature and also notes that, according to Plutarch, this method of teaching was used by the Peripatetic philosophers (*Acts*, 517n6).

59. Barrett notes that συμβάλλω is another Lukan term, used three times in Luke and four times in Acts, but nowhere else in the NT. Here he translates it "arguing," adopting a slightly more conflictual tone. The other uses of the verb in Luke-Acts are not uniform, but the rest of verse 18 appears to support Barrett's translation. See Barrett, *Acts*, 2.829–30; cf. BDAG and Culy and Parsons, *Acts Handbook*, 334; contra Rothschild, *Paul in Athens*, 29n21.

60. "And Paul went in, as was his custom, and on three Sabbath days he *reasoned* with them from the Scriptures, explaining and proving that it was necessary for the Christ to suffer and to rise from the dead, and saying, 'This Jesus, whom I proclaim to you, is the Christ.'"

61. The phrase is omitted by D gig, probably in order to avoid the association of Jesus and his resurrection with the pagan concept of deity (δαίμων/δαιμόνιον). So Metzger, *Textual Commentary*[2], 404 (who mentions Knowling in support of this explanation) and Holladay, *Acts*, 338.

62. Barrett observes that v. 18 "bears remarkable resemblance to the word of faith quoted by Paul in Rom. 10.9" (*Acts*, 2.824); similarly, Stenschke, *Luke's Portrait*, 205, and Klauck, *Magic and Paganism*, 78, highlight the clear christological nature of Paul's message; contra Jervell, *Die Apostelgeschichte*, 443, 377, and the puzzling: "Paul has already been preaching in Athens (Acts 17:17), *but Luke has not provided the content*; the Areopagus speech thus offers not only to the Areopagus (in the

proclaim the good news," while the content of the one "good news" is parsed diversely.⁶³ Hence, though the verb διαλέγομαι, especially in connection with the ἀγορά, would most likely bring the figure of Socrates to mind to an ancient Greek there is no doubt that Paul's preaching of the Christian kerygma is meant.⁶⁴ Hence, it is rather clear narratively that "Paulus tritt nicht als Philosoph auf, sondern als christlicher Verkündiger, was auch für die Erklärung der Rede entscheidend ist."⁶⁵

Another crucial aspect of Paul's activity that must be noted is one often neglected or missed by students of the Areopagitica. The rapid pace of the narrative is deceitful as one can easily get the impression that the events of vv. 16–20 happened in no time at all. But in reality, the story indicates that there was a certain length of time between Paul's arrival in Athens and his appearance before the Areopagus.⁶⁶ All the indicative verbs of verses 16–18 are in the imperfect tense, thus denoting an ongoing or repeated action/activity.⁶⁷ This means first that Paul was in town for a some time before he did anything, but also that his activity—whether proclaiming his message or debating with the philosophers—took place over a relatively lengthy period of time. That indication of duration is reinforced by the expression κατὰ πᾶσαν ἡμέραν ("every single day") and, as Schnabel notes, by the present participle used to describe the audience (παρατυγχάνοντας) in v. 17.⁶⁸ This means that at the point when Paul is taken to the Areopagus, his audience has had the opportunity to hear him present the gospel, to make objections, and to ask questions at length or on several occasions before.⁶⁹ This

---

narrative world) but also to Luke's own audience a summary of Paul's message for Athens." Keener, *Acts*, 3.2614 (emphasis added).

63. The *verb* is not used in Mark and only once in Matthew, but ten times in Luke's Gospel and fifteen in Acts. It also occurs six times in the book of Isaiah (all in the second half: 40:9 [2x]; 52:7 [2x]; 60:6; 61:1[!]). The content of the proclamation can be "Jesus and the resurrection" (17:18), "the Christ Jesus" (Acts 5:42), "the word" (8:4), "the kingdom of God and the name (of) Jesus Christ" (8:12), "Jesus" (8:35), "peace through Jesus Christ" (10:36), "the Lord Jesus" (11:20), "the promise to the fathers fulfilled for us in the resurrection of Jesus" (13:32), "that you should turn from these vain things to a living God, who made the heaven and the earth and the sea and all that is in them" (14:15), "the Word of the Lord" (15:35) or intransitively (8:25, 40; 14:7, 21; 16:10). Luke's use in 14:15 is particularly striking in view of the parallels existing between the two stories. It seems to imply that calling pagans "to turn from idols to the true God" is the same gospel as proclaiming "Jesus and the resurrection" (which, in 17:31, is intimately connected with the final judgment). Cf. Luke 1:19; 2:10; 3:28; 4:18 [citation from Isa 61:1], 43; 7:22; 8:1; 9:6; 16:16; 20:1.

64. Both Conzelmann, *Acts*, 139 and Barrett, *Acts*, 2.828 make this point.

65. Jervell, *Die Apostelgeschichte*, 444; contra Keener, *Acts*, 3.2565; cf. Rothschild, *Paul in Athens*, ix.

66. Haenchen is among the few who note this fact, though only in a footnote (*Acts*, 517n7). Kilgallen, on the contrary, strongly highlights the evidence indicating a "lengthy activity" (to use Haenchen's expression) of Paul in Athens prior to giving the Areopagus address. See Kilgallen, "Acts 17:22b–31."

67. Also noted by Rothschild, *Paul in Athens*, 28n19, who cites Smyth, *Greek Grammar*, 423–24, § 1890.

68. Schnabel, *Acts*, 724.

69. One textual variant (found in D(1) 614 *pc* syh**) makes the indication of an interval of time explicit by adding the words μετα δε ημερας τινας ("after a few days") at the beginning of v. 19. However, none of the indications of duration that we have identified is precise enough even to guess the

seems to entail, therefore, that the purpose of Paul's speech is *not* to present the gospel for the first time to his audience.

Luke's Characterization of Paul's Audience

Luke's characterization of the Athenian audience—especially who constitutes it and their frame of mind—is another crucial element for the interpretation of the story and speech.

The Composition of the Audience

Paul's ministry in Athens is far from being limited to a small or peculiar part of the population. According to Luke, Paul first proclaims his message to the Jews, to the God-fearers, and to "whomever" he happens to meet in the market place. This description implies that Paul did seek to address the *entire* population of Athens, without distinction of class or education. The philosophers[70] come into the picture in v. 18 only after Paul has been at work for some time already, and it is not entirely clear that they become the exclusive focus of either Paul's activity or Luke's narrative from that point on.[71] Whichever way one understands this transition, it is plain from vv. 32

---

length of either of the phases of Paul's activity. If we take as a cue the mention that Paul was waiting for Silas and Timothy to join him (whether in Athens or in Corinth, 17:15), then Paul's stay in Athens may have lasted up to a few weeks.

70. The reason why Luke singles out Stoics and Epicureans is debated. Two main lines of explanation can be identified. Some, considering that Luke invented the speech entirely, argue that these two schools were the ones with which Luke was familiar or simply that they were the most prominent and typical at the time (e.g., Barrett, "Paul's Speech," 72–75). Others who think that Luke reports a true event argue that, simply, these were the actual groups Paul interacted with (e.g., Winter, "Public and Private," 127). The correspondences identified between the content of the speech and the philosophy of these two groups can be adduced for either position. It seems to us that a both/and is the best explanation. Since Stoics and Epicureans were historically the most prominent and numerous schools at the time, they would quite certainly have engaged a "proclaimer of new/foreign things" debating with people in the agora like Paul did. Additionally, their position and reputation would make them ideal types or models for Luke's purposes when composing his narrative and choosing which episodes to include or not. Especially since their philosophies basically represent the two poles of philosophical thinking about the gods at the time (noted by Gärtner, *Areopagus Speech*, 48).

71. One could understand v. 18 as narrowing the focus to the philosophers alone, but the language of vv. 19–20 is not clear enough to require that interpretation. Also noted by Schnabel, *Acts*, 725. However, scholars focusing on historical and rhetorical questions tend to argue that the audience is essentially or exclusively made up of philosophers or members of the philosophically educated elite from then on (see, e.g., Neyrey, "Acts 17"; Haenchen, *Acts*, 517; Roloff, *Apostelgeschichte*, 255; Stenschke, *Luke's Portrait*, 205; Pervo, *Acts*, 428; and Keener, *Acts*, 3.2581). In contrast, those focusing on literary and narrative features tend to defend the continued participation of the general population in various ways (e.g., *BegC*, 4.211; Rothschild, *Paul in Athens*, 29n24; Gray, "Implied Audiences," 206, 212–13; and Wright, *Acts*, 2.90). It seems that if the philosophers are in the spotlight here, it is for two reasons: they took the "leadership" or control of the conversation when they joined it; they symbolically represent the "ideal Athenians."

and 34 that there were more than philosophers and Areopagites involved in the whole matter, since "other men" and a woman are mentioned.[72] Moreover, Luke's characterizing comment in v. 21 and Paul's address in v. 22 both refer to the "Athenians" indiscriminately.[73] Finally, the universal nature of Paul's call to repentance (τοῖς ἀνθρώποις πάντας πανταχοῦ, v. 30; τὴν οἰκουμένην and πᾶσιν, v. 31) confirms an all-inclusive point of view rather than one limited to a narrow segment of Athenian society.

It is significant that Luke would record the audience's response twice in a parallel manner: vv. 18–20 to Paul's initial proclamation in the agora and vv. 32, 34 to his speech before the Areopagus. This point is adduced by Haenchen—here building on Loisy—to argue that this is one of Luke's several uses of a stereotypical motif found in a clearer form in chapter 23 (with Pharisees and Sadducees).[74] Haenchen thinks that the Epicureans are the ones mocking, while the Stoics are interested and want to hear more (thus inviting Paul to expound his views more conveniently in a different location). This view has been developed further by Neyrey and is adopted by some recent commentators.[75]

There are several problems with this view, however. First, v. 21 is clear in its scope: *all people* residing in Athens were "curious," whether Athenians or sojourners. It is not limited to one party, group or category. Second, intellectual curiosity is not underlined in vv. 18–20, but rather incomprehension. In the end, what we observe in v. 18 are two activities expressing the very same kind of attitude/character of the crowd and the philosophers as a whole: jest/mockery and misconstruction/confusion.[76] Similarly—and in continuity with the portrait of vv. 18–21—it seems that the response reported in v. 32b should be understood as a dismissal, rather than a genuine desire for further information.[77] It appears that v. 34 records the only *positive* response to Paul's activity in the whole episode. The correlation of specific (and identifiable)

---

72. See Winter, "Introducing Gods," 85–87 for the archaeological evidence demonstrating that such could be the case even for an actual case before the council, and Spencer, *Journeying*, 183–84 concerning the historical plausibility of a woman being present.

73. Even though the expression may have been a customary address when speaking before the Areopagus court, a fact that may not have been known to Luke's readers. In any case, the court was representing—and acting on behalf of—the whole population of Athens by law.

74. Haenchen, *Acts*, 517–18, 526; cf. Loisy, *Actes*, 662; the view is mentioned with no further comment in *BegC*, 4.219.

75. Neyrey, "Acts 17," 127–29 builds on the chiastic structure proposed by O'Toole, "Paul at Athens," 186, where vv. 18 and 32 bracket the speech with parallel contrasting reactions. See also Klauck, *Magic and Paganism*, 78–79 and Keener, *Acts*, 3.2580–81. Barrett, *Acts*, 2.830, thinks that the philosophers as a whole are depicted as mocking, while the general public is confused (though cf. Barrett, "Paul's Speech," 71).

76. So also Kurz, *Acts*, 268–69.

77. Narratively speaking, the fact that no further interaction of any kind is recounted seems to confirm that line of interpretation.

groups with particular and contrasted reactions is not springing from the text, it is speculation forced onto it.[78]

Three Defining Traits

The characterization of this diverse audience representing the Athenian population is constructed through three key and interrelated features: curiosity, mockery/arrogance, and ignorance/confusion.

IDLE CURIOSITY

Verse 21 is particularly remarkable as it is one of the rare narratorial comments Luke makes in his two volumes. This fact, combined with its position at the apex of the narrative development and immediately prior to the focus of the episode (the speech), gives a high profile to the "curious"—nosy, entertainment-driven, busybody-like—character of the residents of Athens.[79] Already vv. 17 and 18 implied that the Athenians (Jews, God-fearers, passersby and philosophers) were intrigued concerning Paul and his message. But Luke's comment in v. 21 elucidates their behavior in vv. 17–20 and prepares the reader for both the speech and the response it will receive in v. 32.

Hence, the omniscient narrator offers a sharp and negative description of the Athenian *idle* curiosity.[80] "Luke's unusually direct authorial comment on this aspect of the Athenian character avoids the basic Greek terms for curiosity (e.g., πολυπραγμοσύνη, περιεργία). The Athenians nevertheless exhibit the behaviors typical of the busybody in ancient Greece and Rome."[81] This verse presents Paul's audience as one that is *not* seeking knowledge or truth—including the philosophers, who are

---

78. For example, Haenchen depends on an abstract and mechanical "literary motif," Neyrey on his identification of "ancient stereotypes," and Keener on the purported apologetic advantage of siding with the more prominent party. See n. 71 above for references. Acts 23 states the successful result of Paul's defense strategy, something that has no equivalent in Acts 17. The description found in vv. 18 and 32—just as in 21 and 34—is of a general nature, describing the general and characteristic attitude of Paul's audience. In this regard, Acts 2:7–13 is a much closer parallel than Acts 23 (also noted by Pervo, *Acts*, 427, 441). Cf. the discussion in Bock, *Acts*, 570–72.

79. The imperfect tense of the verb again marks the fact that this is a constant or typical (recurrent) trait, not a temporary or accidental one. Rothschild defines it as an "imperfect of customary action" (*Paul in Athens*, 30n32, citing Smyth, *Greek Grammar*, 424, § 1893).

80. Keener, *Acts*, 3.2612 notes the stylish Attic style of the verse and its hyperbole as evidence of irony on the author's part (cf. Culy and Parsons, *Acts Handbook*, 336). Similarly Marshall comments that Luke's "tone is distinctly sarcastic" (*Acts TNTC*, 285), while Rackham says that Luke "expresses the contempt of a serious Christian for the frivolous populace of Athens" (*Acts*, 306). Luke is not unique in this, however, since many ancient writers have scoffed at this notorious trait of the Athenians—including playwrights like Timocles, Diphilus, and Heniochus. See examples in Conzelmann, *Acts*, 140; Bruce, *Acts Greek*, 378; and Gray, "Athenian Curiosity."

81. Gray, "Athenian Curiosity," 110.

therefore no "noble seekers of truth"—but one that is intrigued by "novelty."[82] As Barrett puts it, "Paul had to deal with the Greek love of novelty, an unstable society, *more interested in entertainment than religion.*"[83] "Curiosity" was also treated by ancient moralists like Apuleius and Plutarch. Gray points the fact that the latter associates that trait with "superstition," for which he uses the term δεισιδαιμονία—used in the comparative degree in v. 22.[84] This picture furthers the negative ethos and portrayal of Paul's situation, increasing the narrative tension leading to the speech.[85]

So is v. 32b indicating a real intellectual interest on the part of a segment of the audience, some of whom believed after further interaction with Paul, according to v. 34? First, it is important to note that v. 34 is not a development of v. 32. The use of the phrase τινὲς δὲ ἄνδρες after the focus had moved to Paul in v. 33 prevents the immediate identification of the converts with any one of the two recorded reactions specifically. Moreover it is clear that v. 34 is the summary statement concluding the entire episode and not the speech scene only, though both are likely in view. Such summary statements in Acts always refer to what happened immediately before and there is no *narrative* indication of a further ministry of Paul after the speech that would have led to further fruits.[86]

Rather, the "curiosity" of the Athenians turns to mockery and dismissal once their initial confusion is dispelled. Note the contrast created by the use of the imperfect ἐχλεύαζον ("were mocking")—indicating an ongoing action with some duration—and the aorist εἶπαν ("said")—denoting a complete action with no further aspectual specification. The final phrase ἀκουσόμεθά σου περὶ τούτου καὶ πάλιν is nicely imprecise, indefinite and expresses no genuine commitment. In the end, the audience was never motivated by a true desire for knowledge, and now that the newness/foreignness is cleared, Paul is no longer entertaining.[87] Luke's mention of some who "attached themselves" to Paul and believed is rather surprising: "That some . . . should join and believe can then be read as a rather dramatic success."[88] Thus, we can

---

82. So also Jervell, *Die Apostelgeschichte*, 445 and Roloff, *Apostelgeschichte*, 258–59; contra Keener, *Acts*, 3.2613 and Morlan, *Conversion in Luke and Paul*, 105.

83. Barrett, "Paul's Speech," 72 (emphasis ours); cf. Witherington, *Acts*, 535. We would add that this attitude contrasts strikingly with the noble character displayed by the Bereans in Acts 17:11–12 (also noted by Stenschke, *Luke's Portrait*, 209–10, who is critical of Winter on this point).

84. Gray, "Athenian Curiosity," 111.

85. So also Rowe, *World Upside Down*, 32,contra Haenchen, Conzelmann, and Nock. Cf. Witherington, *Acts*, 517.

86. Note the use of the aorists κολληθέντες . . . ἐπίστευσαν. See Bossuyt and Radermakers, "Rencontre," 23; cf. Jervell, "Church of Jews," 19.

87. Gray, "Implied Audiences," 211, also notes the consistency of the portrait of the Athenians throughout, and concludes: "Luke constructs the scene so that the Athenians emerge as willfully ignorant."

88. Rowe, *World Upside Down*, 192n93. Hence, John Sanders' judgment that "His preaching was a success in that *those who were believers* became Christians" (*No Other Name*, 247 [emphasis ours]) simply runs in the face of the evidence.

see either two antithetical responses—the unbelief of v. 32 and the faith of v. 34—or three distinct ones—mockery, dismissal, and faith. But not mockery and interest that eventually leads to faith.

Arrogance and Mockery

Another less than praiseworthy trait of Paul's audience highlighted by Luke is the self-confident intellectual arrogance revealed by their sneering.[89] It is difficult to agree with Luke Johnson that v. 19 reveals an "elaborate politeness."[90] The evidence is rather that "the impolite are made to express themselves in (for the NT) unusually stylish Greek."[91] Hence, the first reported reaction of v. 18 is extremely demeaning. The use of the near demonstrative ὁ . . . οὗτος ("this one") in presence of the referent is markedly disparaging.[92] This is compounded by the use of σπερμολόγος ("seed-picker" or "babbler"), a characteristic derogatory Athenian slang-term "used of an inferior speaker of writer who picks up and uses as his own ideas that he has found in others."[93] This negative characterization is reinforced by the use of a double potential optative, therefore expressing something like: "What would this babbler say, if he could say anything that made sense!"[94] As Runge points out concerning another passage, "sarcasm is realized by the apparent mismatch between the form of address and the discourse context."[95] It is thus clear that the excessive stylishness of the invitation to speak in vv. 19–20 is ironic in this audience's mouth.[96] Finally, calling Paul a "herald" of "strange deities" radically misconstrues Paul's gospel and sounds somewhat dismissive.[97]

---

89. There is quite a bit of irony here, since these haughty people are simultaneously described by Luke as idle novelty-seekers who cannot make heads and tails of Paul's message. This ironic thread runs through the episode, especially via the theme of ignorance.

90. Johnson, *Acts*, 314; also Rackham, *Acts*, 311.

91. Barrett, *Acts*, 2.830.

92. See Barrett, *Acts*, 2.830 and Croy, "Hellenistic Philosophies," 23. For an explanation of the pragmatic effect, see Runge, *Discourse Grammar*, 372–73.

93. Barrett, *Acts*, 2.830; cf. Witherington, *Acts*, 514.

94. Bock, *Acts*, 562. "Ἄν with the optative here, may refer to the suppressed condition—if his words have any meaning." Hackett, "Discourse of Paul," 341. See also Culy and Parsons, *Acts Handbook*, 334, 96, and references. Stenschke, *Luke's Portrait*, 206, rightly highlights the fact that this is a *rhetorical* question, not a request for an explanation.

95. Runge, *Discourse Grammar*, 355.

96. This view is supported also by the fact that these unusually polite and Atticized requests come *after* the crowd *seized* Paul and while it is taking him to the council/court of the Areopagus. However one interprets ἐπιλαβόμενοι, the scene does give the impression that Paul was rather forcefully led to the court (cf. Luke 21:12, "they will lay their hands [ἐπιβαλοῦσιν] on you and persecute you . . . and you will be brought before kings and governors for my name's sake.").

97. At least such a summary of Paul's teaching shows a profound carelessness and lack of attention. So also Gaventa, *Acts*, 248.

Ignorance and Confusion

This leads us to the third key element in the characterization of Paul's audience: its utter misunderstanding of his message and identity.[98] Luke's skillfully-painted picture highlights this feature by playing against one another a sense of total confusion and the crowd's arrogance and grandiloquence.[99] This impression is produced first by the rapid cumulation of questions or phrases expressing misunderstanding and confusion containing cognates related to newness and strangeness (five in three verses), concepts that would be very similar in the Athenians' eyes.[100] This is reinforced by the numerous references to ignorance and the various cognates of "unknown" used by Paul in relation to his audience in the speech.

What may be the most striking about the audience's utterances in vv. 18–20 is that they do not contain one single bit of truthful information concerning the meaning of Paul's proclamation. The most substantive assertion they contain is that Paul "appears to be the herald of foreign deities (ξένων δαιμονίων)" in v. 18, itself a complete misrepresentation of Paul's identity and mission from the narrator's and reader's point of view.[101] All other statements are rather vacuous and indeterminate: τί ἂν θέλοι and δοκεῖ... εἶναι in v. 18; τίς ἡ καινὴ αὕτη ἡ ὑπὸ σοῦ λαλουμένη διδαχή in v. 19; ξενίζοντα ... τινα and τίνα θέλει ταῦτα εἶναι in v. 20. If all the reader had access to were the Athenians' words, he would be unable to reconstruct the contents of what Paul had been discussing with his audience, and would probably be quite disconcerted by the reference to "foreign deities" (not even "gods") in v. 18. The Athenians' utter failure to understand and render Paul's message is underscored by the ending of the verse, when the *narrator* intrudes in the story to elucidate the situation for his reader's sake, as if he could not rely on his (pagan) characters to do so.[102] The audience's confusion is quite remarkable when one considers that these words come in response to Paul's

---

98. Gaventa captures very well the situation in v. 18: "Whether disparaging Paul as a charlatan or a curiosity, both these initial responses conflict profoundly with Luke's presentation of Paul and the gospel." Gaventa, *Acts*, 249.

99. One cannot miss the irony and humor of Luke's portrayal of the Athenians' requests for an explanation revealing their utter ignorance (as we shall see hereafter) expressed through such an unusually stylish and Atticized wording! As Krodel puts it: "The sophisticated philosophers did not even understand him." Krodel, *Acts*, 64.

100. "More clear to many ancient readers than to modern ones would be the similarity in meaning between the charge of foreign (ξένων) deities, the strange (ξενίζοντα) words, the new (καινή) teaching, the love of novelty (καινότερον), and the worship of the unknown (ἀγνώστῳ) God. The adjectives would be felt to be nearly synonymous." *BegC*, 4.212; see also Norden, *Agnostos Theos*, 53n3.

101. This parallels the situation in Lystra where Paul's (and Barnabas') identity and mission are totally misunderstood by the population of the city. Though the audience's evaluation is much more flattering in Lystra than in Athens, it is no less wrong, for in both cases it is the exact opposite of what the apostles came to do and say (cf. Acts 14:15).

102. See Winter, "Introducing Gods" for one of the most detailed defenses of the historical verisimilitude of the "two deities" interpretation of "Jesus and the resurrection"; cf. Barrett, *Acts*, 2.831 for the standard argument against it.

proclamation and defense of the gospel over a period of time.¹⁰³ This situation exposes the profoundly and incorrigibly *religious*, *pagan* and *polytheistic* point of view of the audience—including the *philosophers*.¹⁰⁴ Narratively, the actions and words reported in vv. 18–20 thus seem to be caused by the philosophers'/Athenians' apparent desperation at ever making sense of Paul's witness to the risen Jesus.

The verbal echoes created by the various cognates of "foreign" and "new" tie vv. 18–20 and 21 closely together.¹⁰⁵ In vv. 18–20 they are used in a derogatory—even somewhat threatening—way by the audience in reference to Paul's teaching. However, in v. 21 the narrator employs them in his overall (omniscient) characterization of that very audience. Thus, though v. 21 is truly the climax of the narrative preparing the reader for the speech ("framing"), it completes the picture by effecting an ironic narrative reversal.¹⁰⁶ The hypocrisy and superficial interest of the Athenians are highlighted, as they are shown to be the true dilettantes in the story: those who charged Paul with novelty are the ones whose life is wholly spent on discussing (τι καινότερον ("something newer").¹⁰⁷ Their accusations against the hero of the story are sure to elicit a negative reaction on the part of the readers, while it prepares them for the apposite—witty, erudite, and well-crafted—response from Paul, and the fact that it will not receive the hearing it deserves.¹⁰⁸

The Forensic Atmosphere

One of the much-debated issues concerning the Areopagitica is whether it is a defense speech in a trial, a lecture at a more-or-less informal hearing, or simply the continuation of a friendly conversation in a more comfortable location. The determination of this point raises the dual question of the setting of the speech (the court or the hill)

---

103. "So Paul faced a communication problem in which the preacher says one thing and the audience hears another." Krodel, *Acts*, 64.

104. See Stenschke, *Luke's Portrait*, 208; Gray, "Implied Audiences," 211; and Rowe, *World Upside Down*, 28.

105. It is quite noteworthy that ξένος is used only here in Luke-Acts (v. 18, 21), ξενίζω is used only in v. 18 in this sense (the other six instances refer to hospitality: Acts 10:6, 18, 23, 32; 21:16; 28:7), and καινός is used only in vv. 19 and 21 in Acts (its five uses in the Gospel are referring to the new covenant: Luke 5:36 (3x), 38; 22:20).

106. See, for example: Klauck, *Magic and Paganism*, 80; Rowe, *World Upside Down*, 28–29, 32–33; and Keener, *Acts*, 3.2595–96, 2613.

107. The exact force of the comparative καινότερον has been quite debated in the past. Some, like Haenchen (*Acts*, 520), have considered it should be read with a superlative force ("newest"), as a way to underline the excesses of the Athenians' love for novelty. However, most scholars consider that Norden's argument (*Agnostos Theos*, 333–35) remains convincing: see Schneider, *Apg.*, 2.237; Rowe, *World Upside Down*, 196n125; and Keener, *Acts*, 3.2612. The point of the expression is that the Athenians seek whatever is newer than what they have heard before. Rowe points out the irony of the expression, as it denotes a comparison of the Athenians' preferred activity to Paul's preaching, which is solidly anchored in a long-standing tradition (*World Upside Down*, 33).

108. See Rowe, *World Upside Down*, 29, 33, 192n93, and Pervo, *Acts*, 425.

and of the nature (or genre) of the speech, both of which are significant for its interpretation. On this point, Lake and Cadbury present an intriguing argument in their commentary: they claim that Athens is the only place depicted in Acts where Paul does not encounter any persecution, yet they highlight many features of the passage that imply the contrary.[109]

Socratic Undertones

It is generally agreed that the episode contains a number of more or less subtle allusions to Socratic traditions.[110] Possibly the most obvious for Luke's original readers is the depiction of Paul's ministry in Athens with the terms διαλέγομαι and ἀγορά. Another is the mention of ξένων δαιμονίων, a reminiscence of the best-known charge leveled against Socrates since it led to his execution.[111] Such allusions *cannot* be accidental, and so must be intentional on Luke's part.[112] Since the charge is associated with Socrates' death sentence, it suggests that Paul is facing a perilous situation also. As a matter of fact, Josephus—who writes at about the same time as Luke—reports that propagating "foreign divinities" (ξένους δαιμονίους) was prohibited by law in Athens, and that it carried a *death penalty*.[113]

Most scholars note that the mention of ξένους δαιμονίους suggests a dangerous or threatening situation.[114] Yet a number also insist that Paul does not seem to be in *actual* danger at any point in the narrative. So Gaventa claims that "neither the questions asked in vv. 19–20 nor the responses in vv. 32–33 indicate that Paul is in any danger."[115] This poses two problems. First, in this view v. 18 must be merely transitional and not be a part of setting up the speech, which is contrary to the textual evidence and implies that much (a half) of the narrative material is not contributing significantly to the story (since vv. 16 and 17 are also transitional in Gaventa's opinion). Second, the speech is not considered to have any real impact on the narrated events, and so the ending of the story appears redundant as it merely lengthens a strictly static scene. That understanding violates the most essential nature of narratives, which must have a distinct beginning, middle, and end—typically, a crisis, an event/action, a resolution.[116] Gaventa, and others who argue in the same manner, appear to fail to

---

109. *BegC*, 4.208–11. The conviction that "it is unnecessary to exaggerate Paul's persecutions" (p. 211) seems to be directing the interpretation here.

110. For a maximalist perspective on (alleged) Socratic echoes, see Sandnes, "Paul and Socrates."

111. The same charge was also leveled against Anaxagoras and Protagoras according to Haenchen, *Acts*, 518n2.

112. Cf. *BegC*, 4.212. Rothschild, *Paul in Athens*, 59, claims these features are stereotypical.

113. Josephus, *Ag. Ap.* 2.266–68.

114. Fitzmyer adds that v. 20 expresses a "serious concern" on the part of the Athenians (*Acts*, 605).

115. Gaventa, *Acts*, 249; similarly Keener, *Acts*, 3.2602.

116. Cf. Ricœur, "Narrative Function," 181–83.

take into account the narrative change effected by the speech—in this case, at once a clarification and a reversal. Haenchen and Barrett do recognize this literary dynamic but consider it to be inconsistent with the actual events being depicted. Thus they affirm that the narrative is building tension and is meant to give a sense of a looming danger or threat, and that it indicates Paul's eventual escape in v. 33.[117] Yet, they claim, nowhere is Luke indicating that an actual legal proceeding is under way.[118]

An Understated but Evocative Judicial Setting

But is that really the case? First, the allusion to the charges against Socrates clearly points to a judicial situation, one that is neither friendly nor leisurely, but perilous, overcast with the threat of death.[119] This orientation is strengthened by the depiction of Paul addressing *formally*[120]—and therefore in one official capacity or another—the court of the Areopagus.[121] The expressions used in vv. 22 and 33 (ἐν μέσῳ τοῦ Ἀρείου πάγου and ἐκ μέσου αὐτῶν; cf. Acts 4:7) leave little doubt that a court, not a

---

117. Haenchen summarizes the dynamic this way: "So Luke conjures up the shadow of Socrates—without calling his name, we should take note!—and the reader feels Paul is here entering upon a dangerous adventure, and begins to breathe freely again when Paul finally 'goes out of their midst.'" Haenchen, *Acts*, 528; cf. Barrett, *Acts*, 2.833. Elsewhere Barrett remarks that Paul not only escapes from danger, but manages to win converts (v. 34)! ("Paul's Speech," 70).

118. Both Barrett and Haenchen are convinced that the story and the speech are pure inventions of Luke. They defend the view that in the end, Luke intends the Athenians' "curiosity" to be the motivation for the speech. They both defend the view that Luke's story is a composite of different motifs or materials, and Haenchen does not hesitate to conclude that the speech is inconsistent with its narrative framework (cf. *Acts*, 527–28). Similarly, Pervo, *Profit*, 45, recognizes that Luke is painting a trial scene with its full apparatus, but claims that Luke is inconsistent and the scene turns into a lecture. On the contrary, Rothschild, *Paul in Athens*, 29n26, argues that the climax of the speech makes sense *only* in a trial setting.

119. So Rowe, "Grammar," 39 and *World Upside Down*, 31; see the possible supplementary evidence adduced from Demetrius' accusations in Acts 19 in Rowe, *World Upside Down*, 195n121.

120. The speech shows formality in both language and organization. Moreover, v. 22 depicts Paul assuming the standing position of an orator (σταθείς) in an official situation—like a court setting—and addresses his audience with the customary greeting for the court (Ἄνδρες Ἀθηναῖοι), just as he does in other similar judicial settings.

121. Most scholars today agree that the court is in view (most recently Keener, *Acts*, 3.2600; cf. Lightfoot, *Acts*, 230 for the older, opposite view). The main argument raised against this interpretation is the perceived lack of clear legal proceedings. Some consider that "what happened" is that the philosophers were looking for a peaceful place to continue their conversation with Paul, away from the noise and agitation of the agora. However, as noted by Rowe, *World Upside Down*, 30, the agora *was* the normal and convenient place to hold such discussions. Moreover, if they had needed a more quiet place, they could have used the ποικίλην στοάν, the habitual meeting place of the Stoics on the edge of the agora—so much so that Gill, "Achaia," 444, expects it is where Paul's disputations happened. Finally, Paul's witness to the risen Jesus before the highest authority in Athens flows naturally from his Christ-given mission (Acts 9:15). As noted earlier, Luke records Paul's giving an account for his gospel proclamation before the ruling authorities in all major cities in fulfillment of his Christ-given mission. Cf. *BegC*, 4.213.

location (the hill), is primarily in view.¹²² This evidence is reinforced by the use of ἐπί in v. 19 to mean "before"—just like in Acts 16:19 and 17:6—¹²³ and the reference in v. 34 to Διονύσιος ὁ Ἀρεοπαγίτης, a member of that court.¹²⁴ Significantly, the verb ἐπιλαμβάνομαι is *always* used in similar contexts to depict the arrest or the forcible handling of someone, therefore indicating an adversarial situation.¹²⁵ As Haenchen writes: ἐπιλαμβάνομαι "sounds unpleasantly like an arrest."¹²⁶ Moreover, Bruce Winter has shown that vv. 18–20 contain a number of terms that are common in legal contexts, arguing on that basis that v. 19b should be translated as "we possess the legal right [δυνάμεθα] to judge [γνῶναι] what this new teaching is that is being spoken by you."¹²⁷ Finally, Keener's unsupported assertion that "capital sentences belonged to Rome by this period" fails to consider the fact that Athens was a free city at that time and therefore that its institutions wielded their full powers.¹²⁸ Thus, the Areopagus court must have possessed the authority to pronounce a death sentence. This historical context meshes well with the menacing atmosphere of the narrative and the court's reputation regarding "foreign gods."¹²⁹

---

122. See Bruce, *Acts Greek*, 379 and *BegC*, 4.219. Barrett points the fact that the expression ἐκ μέσου αὐτῶν is often used in Luke-Acts to depict someone "escaping" from a dangerous situation (Barrett, "Paul's Speech," 71). Barnes has argued that the court would have met on the hill again at that period, at least occasionally ("Apostle on Trial," 410). Rowe (*World Upside Down*, 30 and "Grammar," 37) thinks that, in consequence, Luke had no reason to be more specific and could have intentionally left the ambiguity stand, contra Nock, *Essays*, 2.831.

123. See *BegC*, 4.212 and Pesch, *Apostelgeschichte*, 2.135.

124. Adduced by Barrett, *Acts*, 2.885.

125. This verb occurs twelve times in Luke-Acts (out of eighteen in the NT): all the uses with a singular agent are positive (Luke 9:47; 14:4; Acts 9:27; 21:33; 23:19) and all the uses with a plural agent (especially crowds) are negative (Luke 23:26; 16:19; 18:17; 21:30; and, we argue, Acts 17:19), i.e., denoting at least constraint if not the use of force or violence. The same is actually true of the other NT occurrences, except for 1 Tim 6:19, where, though the agent is plural, it depicts a positive action (it seems to carry a forceful connotation nonetheless). Cf. Witherington, *Acts*, 515–16; Pesch, *Apostelgeschichte*, 2.134; and Rowe, *World Upside Down*, 29.

126. Haenchen, *Acts*, 527.

127. Winter, "Introducing Gods," 82. Wright, *Acts*, 2.84, considers vv. 19b-20 to be a "veiled and sarcastic threat." Though Winter makes a plausible case for the legal nature of the lexical content of the phrase, considering it to be an initial statement of the court itself is dubious, since v. 19 puts those words in the mouths of those leading Paul to the court. Moreover, it requires an emendation of the critical text to make 19b an affirmation, even though it is generally accepted to be a question—a determination supported by the Vulgate and the addition of πυνθανόμενοι in D(1) (614 *pc* syh**; see comments in Rius-Camps and Read-Heimerdinger, *Message of Acts*, 3.344–45). His overall interpretation seems guilty of reading into the text the results of Garland's study (*New Gods*) rather than drawing them out of it. Cf. Jipp, "Paul's Areopagus Speech," 574; Rowe, *World Upside Down*, 31, 194n112; Rowe, "Grammar," 38; and Schnabel, *Acts*, 728; contra Culy and Parsons, *Acts Handbook*, 335.

128. Keener, *Acts*, 3.2601. On Athens as *civitas libera*, see Gill, "Achaia," 441 and references in n. 99.

129. See Gill, "Achaia," 447. On the history of the court, see Martin, "Areopagus"; Rhodes, "Areopagus"; Geagan, "Ordo Areopagitarum Atheniensium"; and Geagan, *Athenian Constitution*. On the *topos* of the persecution, even death, of those introducing new gods to Athens, see Jipp, "Paul's Areopagus Speech," 572n22.

PART TWO: A CONTEXTUAL READING OF THE AREOPAGUS SPEECH

The context unmistakably indicates that something ponderous is at stake, and the unstated nature of the inquiry does not dispel the reader's concerns, on the contrary.[130] However, this undefined character of the process leads many to conclude that though the court is in view, there does not seem to be a clear motive nor legal proceeding.[131] Moreover, it appears the Areopagus council was the highest court of Athens at the time, and thus had jurisdiction over all matters of importance (including public teaching and religious questions).[132] This combination of factors probably helps explain the variety of opinions encountered among scholars and why no significant consensus has yet emerged on this point.[133] It seems to us that the way out of this impasse is to pay close attention to the narrative structure and development of the pericope as a whole (plot analysis) in light of its theological and intertextual context.

Hence, as we argued earlier, the events narrated in v. 18 eventually lead to the dragging of Paul to the Areopagus in vv. 19–20.[134] Verse 21 is not developing the *action* itself, nor does it disclose the motivation of the Athenians. Rather, it completes their portrait by exposing their true character. Looking at the structure of the pericope, we see the concerns of v. 18 being addressed in vv. 23 (the "foreignness" of Paul's teaching) and 31 (Jesus and the resurrection), the potentially threatening situation of vv. 19–20 is resolved in v. 33 (Paul leaves the scene without further ado),[135] and the Athenians' portrait of vv. 18–21 reaches its final stage in vv. 32 and 34 (confirming their arrogance and carelessness, though some come to faith unexpectedly and providentially). The thematic correlation of vv. 18 and 31 confirms that the focal point of the whole matter is Jesus and his resurrection. We see in v. 32 that the profuse confusion of vv. 18–20 has

---

130. As noted by Pervo, *Acts*, 425. Cf. Schnabel, *Acts*, 728–29, who questions the interpretation of Bock and Gaventa on this point.

131. Fitzmyer, *Acts*, 605, is quite typical of that position. Pervo, *Acts*, 428, comments that the author is "cagey" in his depiction of the event as a sort of trial.

132. Cf. *BegC*, 4.212; Barnes, "Apostle on Trial"; and Barrett, *Acts*, 2.832.

133. Haenchen, *Acts*, 517; Barrett, *Acts*, 2.830; Gaventa, *Acts*, 249; and Klauck, *Magic and Paganism*, 80 consider the motivation for the speech to be pure curiosity and desire for more information, on the basis of v. 21. Bruce, *Acts NICNT*, 362 (but see below); Gärtner, *Areopagus Speech*, 64–65; Dunn, *Acts*, 234; Longenecker, *The Acts of the Apostles*, 981; and Keener, *Acts*, 3.2603 think that Paul was "tested" or assessed for an official authorization to teach publicly in Athens. Bossuyt and Radermakers, "Rencontre," 23, argue that Paul is suspected of disturbing public order by introducing religious innovations. See also *BegC*, 4.213. Bruce, *Acts Greek*, 378 (!) considers that Paul is simply charged with introducing "strange divinities" without further elaboration. Winter, "Introducing Gods" argues that Paul was invited to determine whether he should undergo the legal process for the addition of a new deity to the Athenian pantheon. He is followed by Schnabel, *Acts*, 745 and Jipp, "Paul's Areopagus Speech," 572, though the latter is critical of Winter's depiction of the scene as a mild questioning. Finally, Barnes, "Apostle on Trial" argues that Paul was actually tried for *impiety*.

134. See our earlier discussion of the narrative development built around the use of μὲν οὖν . . . δέ.

135. Whatever the uncertainty over the nature of the proceeding, one thing is clear: "Paul left the court without condemnation." *BegC*, 4.212.

been dissipated by Paul's address, and now the audience is reacting to his message on account of understanding rather than misunderstanding.[136]

In the light of this evidence, it is indubitable that v. 18 furnishes the answer to the question of motive: Paul's audience was utterly confused by his message, which led them to suspect that he *might* have been heralding ξένους δαιμονίους, a serious transgression of Athenian law and customs.[137] Verse 21 discloses Luke's (and thus God's) point of view on Paul's audience and, probably, unveils the underlying cause of their persistent confusion.[138] This reading of the story provides a satisfactory rationale for why Paul would have appeared before the Areopagus council (or a committee thereof), a body that must have had little time for trivial matters. The language of the speech, which betrays or presupposes a formal/official context, comports well with this picture, confirming its heuristic strength.[139] At the end of the day, this line of interpretation alone provides a setting in which the content of the Areopagitica (with its various emphases) is fully at home.

---

136. The "low response" to the speech and ministry of Paul has been marshalled by some commentators together with 1 Cor 16:15 to argue against the "exemplary" nature of the speech. The classic exposition of this view is Ramsay, "Firstfruits." Though it can still be found in popular exposés, it is generally rejected by recent scholarship. For example, Barrett shows how such an understanding of Luke's presentation of Paul's mission in Athens (speech included) runs in the face of the author's overall purposes and arguments, especially the "unstoppable word" theme ("Paul's Speech," 70–71). In fact, many note that the *kinds* of responses depicted in our passage are identical with those encountered elsewhere in Luke-Acts: they are typical (see Krodel, *Acts*, 65). Moreover, Luke's depiction of the reactions produced by Paul's proclamation of the risen Jesus (which implies the *crucified* Jesus, obviously) are perfectly consistent with Paul's own description and explanation in 1 Cor 1:18–25 (as noted by Dunn, *Acts*, 225). Rather, it seems that Luke insists on the fact that even in a place like Athens Paul had converts, some of whom—represented by a member of the Areopagus and possibly a woman of high rank (cf. Acts 17:12)—were of social significance (see *BegC*, 4.219). This is especially remarkable in the light of the contrast thus created with v. 21 (cf. Winter, "Introducing Gods," 87). Finally, the mention of the house of Stephanas as the "firstfruits [ἀπαρχή] of Achaea" should not be construed to mean that the results in Athens were negligible or nonexistent (see Bruce, *Acts Greek*, 387). This interpretation reveals a misunderstanding of the concept of "firstfruits" which is not primarily *chronological*, but essentially *eschatological* and *representational* in both OT and Pauline theology. Paul's considering Corinthian Christians as the "firstfruits" of his ministry in Achaea is consistent with his missionary method concentrating on the capitals of Roman provinces and their representative function. See the study of this concept in Dennison, *Two-Age*, 41–43.

137. If this is the case, then the absence of explicit charges and judicial process may be simply explained by the fact that the Areopagus was examining Paul to decide whether charges should be pressed against him, but was successfully convinced against it by his argument. It should also be noted that the book of Acts contains a number of situations where Paul is cleared from all charges or suspicions immediately after a single apologetic speech. This is a recurring, maybe even typical, pattern.

138. It is to be expected that they did not pay close attention to Paul's words, since they deemed him to be a mere σπερμολόγος and an occasion for entertainment. This posture is sufficient to explain both the vagueness and the error of their reproduction of Paul's message as reported in v. 18. In any case, this verse plays the same characterizing role for the Athenians as v. 16 plays for Paul.

139. See Kennedy, *NT Interpretation*, 129–32 and Soards, *Speeches in Acts*, 96. Witherington, *Acts*, 517–21, agrees with Kennedy that Paul's anger establishes a judicial situation for the speech. According to him, Paul's aim is deliberative (he seeks to change his audience's beliefs and behavior regarding the Christian faith), but his means is forensic.

Lake and Cadbury point out that the narrative presents some "blurred" areas as to the exact nature of the proceedings and of the decision of the court, but that this feature is shared with other similar accounts in the book of Acts.[140] In particular, they point to Stephen's trial.[141] Even if one were to grant that Luke is not depicting an actual trial, there is no question that the whole story is painted in legal and judicial colors.[142] Either way, this literary feature has to be accounted for in the interpretation of the passage—the speech in particular. It should not be lightly dismissed as a historical improbability or a literary curiosity, for it has an unmistakable theological import: "Christianity is depicted in this episode in direct confrontation with pagan idolatry, Greek philosophy, and Athenian intellectual curiosity."[143]

The book of Acts is filled with courtroom-like scenes—some present actual trials, others "quasi-trials"—and uses a good amount of legal language.[144] One salient feature that the Areopagus story shares with these other passages is that the heart of the matter, the crux of the debate, is always the content of the message being proclaimed, not the word-bearer *per se*. In the case of Paul's "custody trials," the apostle himself expressly declares it to be the case.[145] Ultimately, it is not even the "gospel" as message that is in view, but the risen Jesus whose messiahship and universal lordship it heralds. This raises the question of the role played by the apostle in those scenes, and the answer can be found in Paul's retellings of his calling by the ascended Jesus: he is

---

140. "The matter scarcely ends like a trial with a clear-cut decision, but the account of trials in Acts is often blurred in this way." *BegC*, 4.212. For example, the episode at Philippi in Acts 16:16–40 (see Neagoe, *Trial of the Gospel*, 188–89).

141. *BegC*, 4.219. As we said earlier, the parallels between the two stories are numerous. Here it will suffice to highlight the following: 1) no trial is explicitly mentioned; 2) the "charges" are found on the lips of members of the crowd/mob (in Acts 7, those are witnesses serving therefore an actual judiciary function, which is probably true in Acts 17 *de facto* if not *de jure*); 3) the court is expecting an explication or defense regarding the testimony of the crowd; 4) the "charges" are of a religious nature; 5) the "charges" are liable to death in the applicable law; 6) Stephen and Paul appear before the highest local authority, one that has jurisdiction over religious, civil and criminal matters (with one significant difference: the Sanhedrin's authority is limited by the Roman rule, especially in regard to the death penalty); 7) the court does not deliberate or render a verdict; 8) yet the matter is definitely settled. Of course, the latter parallel is also the most striking contrast between the two trials: Paul leaves free, Stephen is *lynched* by a mob that appears to include members of the court itself! The fact that the "witnesses" are the ones starting the stoning (in apparent obedience to the Mosaic law) is only a parody of justice since: 1) they are *false*-witnesses; 2) the court did not pronounce any verdict; and 3) the Sanhedrin does not have the authority to sentence someone to death, even less to execute that person (this is the reason why the same Sanhedrin had to ask Pilate to "dispose" of Jesus for them).

142. "Regardless of the position which one reaches on the judicial matters, it remains clear that the author has once again cast his story in a trial form: charges are brought (17.18–19); Paul is 'taken hold of' (ἐπιλαβόμενοί αὐτοῦ) and 'led' (ἤγαγον) to the place of interrogation (17.19), where a formal response is offered (17.22–31)." Neagoe, *Trial of the Gospel*, 192. Cf. Conzelmann, *Acts*, 139, who denies any judicial proceeding is depicted, but nevertheless concludes that Luke "seeks . . . to create a mood."

143. Fitzmyer, *Acts*, 601.

144. On this general subject, see Trites, "Importance" and Neagoe, *Trial of the Gospel*.

145. Here we focus on Paul because of his immediate relevance to our study, but the same would be true in the case of Peter or Stephen, for example.

a witness (26:16; cf. 9: 15; 13:47; 20:24; 22:15; 23:11; and 1:8), the legal representative of the enthroned Son of David.[146]

This ties in with the theological and scriptural background discussed in the earlier chapters. The judicial atmosphere and setting created by Luke points the reader to the divine perspective over the events. In an ironic reversal of the situation, the heavenly tribunal breaks into the earthly "courtroom," the "trial" of Paul's message becomes God's eschatological and universal lawsuit against his rebellious creatures, and Paul is the Lord's "accusation witness" in the court case. As in the Isaianic New Exodus, this lawsuit centers on the people's idolatry (whether Jews or Gentiles are in view) and on defending the Lord's universal authority to rule and judge, as well as affirming his power to save his people. In other words, the worldwide encounter of the gospel with unbelief and idolatry is in itself an anti-idol polemic in Luke's eyes.

This biblical-theological perspective sheds more light on various features of the Areopagus narrative and its character. Paul's anger in v. 16 does not only give the tone for all his subsequent activity in Athens, including the speech, but it also mirrors and discloses narratively the divine judgment on the city. Paul's address is not merely a defense of his message (and possibly a way of escaping personal harm), but also Paul's eschatological testimony against all idol-worshippers and witness to the lordship of Christ. In short, it is the unstoppable agent of the New Exodus—the Word of the Lord—in action.

The Athenians' confusion and ignorance, as well as their arrogance and idle curiosity, characterize them specifically in their function as "witnesses" of their idols, highlighting the ways in which they "image" and resemble them. They are thus disqualified from the role of legitimate witnesses in God's court, and as a matter of fact we do not ever hear them speak in this capacity. All these elements of Luke's anti-idol polemic are undergirded by the various ironic reversals structuring the story, of which the most obvious and pregnant is that Jesus, the putative δαιμόνιον the Athenians would judge (vv. 18–20), is the divinely-appointed (Davidic) King who will judge the οἰκουμένη (v. 31). And that includes these would-be—counterfeit, truly—judges. If the mention of the resurrection in v. 18 is meant to refer to a consort goddess, then v. 31 contains a second ironic reversal: this other putative deity under investigation turns out to be the condemnatory juridical *proof* (πίστις) of Jesus' appointment as

---

146. See Trites, "Importance," 280–81.

judge of the world.¹⁴⁷ In that light, the response of the audience in v. 32 takes on a tragic and ominous significance.¹⁴⁸

Conclusion: What the Areopagitica Is and What It Is Not

In the light of the evidence discussed above, it seems we should (re)consider the nature—or genre—of the speech itself afresh and give a new hearing to Jervell's claim that the Areopagitica is *not* a missionary speech.¹⁴⁹ Traditionally, the discussion of the genre of this speech has been based exclusively on internal evidence, at the exclusion of the narrative framework.¹⁵⁰ Though such evidence is certainly significant it is only partial because the narrative defines what the circumstances, mood, and purpose(s) of the speech were.¹⁵¹ A paradigm shift towards a truly narrative/literary perspective must be operated, for the historical-critical paradigm has proved wanting.

So if one adopts the usual meaning given by scholars to the expression "missionary speech," Jervell can claim both the narrative evidence and the internal evidence

---

147. This theme of reversal is deeply embedded in the whole narrative of Acts (as well as in Luke's Gospel), and is developed especially through the interweaving of a number of Davidic Psalms, such as Ps 2, 110 and 118. A lot would deserve to be said here, but we must content ourselves with two programmatic passages that shed much light on our subject. The first is Acts 2:34–35, in which Peter quotes Ps 110:1 ("The Lord said to my Lord, Sit at my right hand, until I make your enemies your footstool") and uses it to argue that Jesus is both "Lord and Christ." It seems that this passage describes what is being actually fulfilled in the history of the early church (especially in the light of the conversation between Jesus and the disciples in Acts 1:6–8).

The second is Acts 4:25–26, quoting Ps 2:1–2: "Why did the Gentiles [nations] rage, and the peoples plot in vain? The kings of the earth set themselves, and the rulers were gathered together, against the Lord and against his Anointed." These verses are the scriptural foundation and heart of the disciples' prayer following the *first* persecution ever. They seem to also provide the interpretation of the subsequent story of Acts as they point to the rest of the Psalm: the nations revolt against God and his "anointed," i.e., his *Christ*, and in response God laughs in his anger and proclaims to the world that he has already placed his king in Zion, king who will rule and judge all the nations. It should be noted that the middle verse of the Psalm (v. 7), a promise made to the Messiah-King, is said by Paul to have been fulfilled in the resurrection of Jesus in Acts 13:32–33 (v. 34 tying it to Isa 55:3, a Servant Song).

See the excellent Doble, "Psalms in Luke-Acts."

148. As noted by Pao, *Acts and INE*, 196n40.

149. Jervell is one of the few to argue in this direction. He does so insistently in *Die Apostelgeschichte*, 55, 72, 379, 445, 452, 453, and *Theology of Acts*, 85, 88, 114.

150. This is, in good part, due to the influence of Dibelius' work and the general conviction of form-critical scholarship that the speech is a unit that stands on its own. It is also related to the notion that Luke composed the speech (and the narrative) in a manner similar to ancient historiographers, and therefore that its content has little to do with its narrative framework.

151. In this we fully agree with Kilgallen's method for determining the nature of the speech: "In this essay I propose that one begin the search for the nature of the Pauline discourse in Acts, not from a study of the speech itself, but from the vv. 16–21 with which Luke introduces the speech. Attention to some of the details of these circumstances should help clarify what kind of speech we have before us in Athens. In particular can we thereby begin to understand what kind of discourse this speech is *not*." Kilgallen, "Acts 17:22b–31," 419 (emphasis original).

in support of his denial.¹⁵² This being said, there is no reason to deny any *evangelistic* intention to the speech or a *missionary* context to the story as a whole. Though the speech does not expound the gospel (the good news of salvation) *per se*, it is meant to commend this very gospel and impress on the audience the ultimacy and urgency of its claims.¹⁵³ As a matter of fact, the narrative is pretty clear that Paul's missionary preaching is the very background and *raison d'être* of the speech, as well as its focal and end point. Verses 32 and 34 are typical of Luke's summary statement of an audience's response to the apostolic proclamation of the risen Jesus.

There is therefore no need to bemoan the purported absence of the "kerygma" in the speech or to speculate that the speech must be incomplete because Paul was interrupted.¹⁵⁴ First, the gospel has been proclaimed and discussed at length with the audience, as the narrative makes clear.¹⁵⁵ Second, v. 18 makes clear that what the Athenians had heard for some time—and were utterly confused about—was "Jesus and the resurrection," a succinct and apt summary of the Lukan gospel when not received with polytheistic ears.¹⁵⁶ Third, the teleology of the speech, so to speak, shows that all along this gospel was the focus of the speech (same key points in vv. 31 and 18). Fourth, the reactions in v. 32 imply that the speech has successfully clarified the *gospel*, because the audience finally demonstrates an understanding of what the reference to Jesus' resurrection actually meant.¹⁵⁷ Fifth, the call to repentance of v. 31 is the natural

---

152. The material written on this point is extremely abundant. Though there is much disagreement among scholars, all generally agree that the "missionary speeches" all share a number of patterns and themes (but not on how many or which they are or how essential to the definition they might be), and they generally purport to communicate what Jervell calls the "Jesus-kerygma." This is a very difficult question to answer for methodological reasons: speeches are used to define the criteria that in turn define the speeches. What is clear, however, is that one finds two quite distinct groups of speeches in Acts with a significant number of internal similarities in each case (whether in form, argument, or content). The first type could be called "missionary" in that it depicts a proclamation of the gospel, and the other "forensic" because it depicts people speaking in a judicial setting. The Areopagitica does not seem to fit well in either. See Porter's evaluation in *Paul in Acts*, 165. Besides the works already cited, the following are significant contributions: Dibelius, "Areopagus"; Dibelius, "Speeches and Historiography"; Dodd, *Apostolic Preaching*; Schweizer, "Concerning the Speeches"; Bauckham, "Kerygmatic Summaries"; see the survey in Padilla, *Speeches of Outsiders*, 16–41.

153. Yet, one must recognize that these features are also found in the forensic speeches, as Paul's defense before king Agrippa makes clear (see especially Acts 26:19–23, 27–29).

154. "The Athenian Discourse is an *opus infinitum*." Legrand, "Unknown God," 159n7. Cf., for example, Dibelius, "Areopagus"; Barrett, *Acts*, 2.825; Fitzmyer, *Acts*, 603; and Bock, *Acts*, 558.

155. Cf. the evidence above. As to the exact content of those communications, we find our cue in vv. 17 and 18. Verse 17 seems to indicate that the type and substance of Paul's proclamation were identical in the synagogue and the agora, however different the form it might have taken. Verse 18, of course, shows that the essence of the message announced was the meaning of Jesus' resurrection. Luke's reader is in no need of a fuller description of Paul's kerygma at this point in the book: he has indeed heard it before. Acts 13 is the most complete or developed record of the substance of Paul's preaching (and its form in synagogues), while Acts 17:2–3 just refreshed their memory. See Shields, "Areopagus Sermon," 25.

156. Cf. Neagoe, *Trial of the Gospel*, 192.

157. And that it was successfully defended since conversions are reported.

and proper conclusion of the speech, in that it summons the audience to change their beliefs and behavior in the light of what has been argued.

It is also clear that the Areopagitica is no *praeparatio evangelica*, as some scholars have claimed, but rather some sort of *defense* of the gospel.[158] The speech is not properly speaking a forensic speech—there are no specified charges against which Paul would be speaking[159]—and yet it is clearly apologetic in nature.[160] The Athenians' judgment on the "herald" in v. 18 evinces the fact that they estimate the gospel itself to be meaningless and insignificant. Paul's address redresses this injustice as it provides a successful ἀπολογία for its meaningfulness (in contrast to the foolishness of Athenian religion) and its eschatological—and therefore ultimate—significance.[161] In other words, in response to his audience's nonchalance, confusion, and threatening arrogance regarding his message, Paul provides a hermeneutical framework that enables the Athenians to make sense of the gospel and then confronts them with its claims, warnings and condemnation, hence pointing them toward the only escape route: repentance.[162]

Finally, the Areopagitica must be understood in the broader context of Luke's New Exodus, as argued earlier. This means that the forensic element in the speech is not only apologetical but also polemical: the speech is not only a *defense* of the risen Lord Jesus (whom the gospel proclaims), but it is also an attack against his enemies. Hence, the speech must be understood as an anti-idol polemic that not only brings God's anger (cf. v. 16) and judgment (v. 31) to bear upon the enemies of his Christ/king/Servant—including the idols, the deities they represent, and their worshippers—, but also proclaims and establishes his universal and eschatological

---

158. This is often claimed on the basis of 1 Thess 1:9–10, but this passage is used by Paul to encapsulate the heart of his message, not to describe its form. F. F. Bruce was a consistent proponent of this view over the years: Bruce, *Defence of the Gospel*, 46; *Acts NICNT*, 362; "Paul of Acts," 303; "Paul and Athenians," 11; "Paul's Use of OT," 74, 76; *Acts Greek*, 379; and *Paul*, 245; cf. Fitzmyer, *Acts*, 602 and Schnabel, *Acts*, 745.

159. Even if one takes v. 23 as an *apologia* against the accusation of introducing "foreign gods," this element remains secondary and almost negligible for the speech as a whole, since the rest of the speech and its conclusion are entirely focused on something else (idolatry and true worship). So also Kilgallen, "Acts 17:22b–31," 418; cf. Jervell, *Die Apostelgeschichte*, 453. See our earlier discussion of the forensic aspects of both narrative and speech.

160. The context for and content of this ἀπολογία strongly resemble what is in view in 1 Peter 3:14–16, another *locus classicus* for Christian apologetics.

161. Dunn comes to a similar conclusion when he writes: "From this we may deduce that Paul focused his teaching on the central features of the Christian message (cf. again 4.2; 23.6), and that without a context (knowledge of Jewish history and religion) it proved meaningless to them." Dunn, *Acts*, 234. See also Kilgallen, "Acts 17:22b–31," 424. Roloff's antithesis "defense" vs. "proclamation" (*Apostelgeschichte*, 258) is unsustainable.

162. We can therefore conclude that "it is evident from the speech that Paul gave (intended to give) no more explanation here about Jesus risen from the dead than he had given earlier . . . except to place the risen Jesus within Paul's explanation of 'the unknown god.'" Kilgallen, "Acts 17:22b–31," 422. Cf. Jervell, *Die Apostelgeschichte*, 444.

rule.¹⁶³ There is therefore no reason to see in the speech a "theological kerygma" that would somehow replace or negate—or simply be divergent from—the "christological kerygma."¹⁶⁴ The two are inseparable: the former establishes and implies the latter, while the latter always presupposes and requires the former. This, evidently, means that we should expect the heart and concern of the speech not to be abstract and philosophical, but existential and religious.¹⁶⁵

---

163. As in Ps 2 and 110:1. It is significant that trial scenes are a genre used by Isaiah in his New Exodus material to depict God's way of dealing with the nations (understood as the enemies of God's chosen people and therefore of God himself), often represented by their idols and rulers. See Pao, *Acts and INE*, 184.

164. Contra Legrand, "Unknown God," 159.

165. See Jervell, *Die Apostelgeschichte*, 444n214.

CHAPTER 5

Beginning an Oration (Acts 17:22–23)

Now that the broad and narrow contexts of the Areopagitica have been set, we turn to the speech itself.

Introductory Considerations: Dealing With "Irreducible Ambiguity"

The interpretive debate over the introduction of the speech seems to center around the precise meaning of δεισιδαιμονεστέρους—the comparative form of the adjective δεισιδαίμων, a NT *hapax legomenon* found neither in the LXX nor in the papyri.[1] The problem is that the word and its cognates are used by ancient Greek writers in three basic and distinct ways, often rendered in English as *religious, pious* and *superstitious* (in part under the influence of the ancient Latin terminology).[2] Though the "unfavorable" usage is predominant in the extant literature since Theophrastus (fourth century BC), both are attested until the fourth century AD in a variety of contexts—philosophical, literary and epigraphic.[3] Most scholars base their solution on the identification of this part of the speech as a rhetorical *captatio benevolentiae* or a complimentary *exordium*. In this perspective, the use of the word should be understood positively, whether wholly or in part.[4] More recently, the "irreducibly ambiguous" character of the term,

---

1. Spicq, *Notes*, 3.113.

2. See the standard lexicons, like BDAG, *TDNT*, and Spicq, *Notes*.

3. Cf. des Places, "Actes 17:22," 190–91 and des Places, "Deisidaimôn." The standard study of the word group remains Koets, *Deisidaimonia* (1929). See Martin, *Inventing Superstition* and Van Nuffelen, *Rethinking the Gods* for excellent recent treatments of the concept, its history, its language and the ideological, theological, philosophical, sociological and political contexts of its usages.

4. See, for example: Conzelmann, *Acts*, 140; Haenchen, *Acts*, 520; Zweck, "Exordium," 101; L. T. Johnson, *Acts*, 314; Dunn, *Acts*, 235; Fitzmyer, *Acts*, 606; Witherington, *Acts*, 518; Gaventa, *Acts*, 250; or Schnabel, *Acts*, 729. Some argue for a nuanced view, recognizing that though Paul would certainly not want to insult his audience from the start, he could not simply praise their religiosity in the light of vv. 16 and 23. Thus Conzelmann and Haenchen recognize that the reader knows this and therefore would not read 22b as praising pagan religiosity. See also Bruce, *Acts Greek*, 380; Jervell, *Die*

the *exordium*, and most of the speech has been deemed to be both intentional and meaningful, particularly when studied in a literary and narrative perspective.[5] Hence, the in-story audience would hear the introductory words positively while Luke's readers would know that he understands them negatively.

Barrett is correct to warn against the typical a priori assumption that this phrase is a *captatio benevolentiae* (and therefore a complimentary comment), making the methodological point that this determination should be made on the basis of the meaning of δεισιδαιμονεστέρους, not vice versa.[6] Rowe raises a further objection to this assumption: the evidence from Lucian and Apuleius indicates that it was *forbidden* to use complimentary *exordia* when addressing the Areopagus court.[7] So the determination of the actual semantic import of δεισιδαιμονεστέρους in this verse must draw from a broader set of considerations.

To begin with, it is important to make two lexicographic clarifications. First, the textual evidence we possess shows that the word group of δεισιδαίμων could carry more than two meanings and could have a variety of referents, in all relevant periods.[8] Though *most* (not all) can be grouped *grosso modo* in two broad categories ("positive/favorable" and "negative/unfavorable"), one ought to avoid oversimplification, abstraction or generality. Strictly speaking, the word is not *ambivalent* but *plurivalent*.[9] Second, when used unfavorably or pejoratively, the word does not mean "superstition" in the typical modern sense.[10] Besides a few exceptions (typically, skeptics and

---

Apostelgeschichte, 445n228; and Bock, *Acts*, 564. No contemporary scholar is willing to give the term (and therefore the *exordium* of the speech) a purely negative meaning, unlike Hanson, *Acts*, 178.

5. "The scholarly consensus now emphasizes Luke's artful use of ambiguous religious language that can be read in either way, for either rhetorical or ironical purposes." Gray, "Athenian Curiosity," 109–10. The various studies by Marguerat, Butticaz, Rowe, Jipp, Gray and Given are prime examples of this interpretive line.

6. Barrett, *Acts*, 2.836, in contrast to most commentators who seem to consider that identification to be self-evident. In our opinion, Barrett is correct to question the usefulness of formal rhetorical categories for such a short summary of a speech in the first place (*Acts*, 2.825). The absolute lack of consensus among rhetorical analyses, together with the various caveats each proposal requires, further support his skepticism.

7. Rowe, *World Upside Down*, 33; see Lucian, *Anach*. 19 (*De Gymn*. 19) and Apuleius, *Met*. 10.7. Many commentators mention the passage in Lucian, yet do not consider it as decisive. Keener dismisses this idea altogether, for "it would violate one of the most basic traditions of rhetoric" (Keener, *Acts*, 3.2627). Bruce is a notable exception (*Acts Greek*, 380) as well as Witherington (*Acts*, 520).

8. For a convenient summary of the various nuances encountered in our literature, see Koets, *Deisidaimonia*, 104–6.

9. "Many modern scholars in defining δεισιδαιμονία lose sight of its manifold meanings and give definitions which only fit the usage of certain writers." Koets, *Deisidaimonia*, 99.

10. Nearly all scholars dealing with "superstition" in the Graeco-Roman warn of that fact, though most keep on using the term because of a lack of a better equivalent. Two features are especially highlighted as being anachronistic for the ancient world: the concept of "supernatural" as distinct from "natural," and "rational" vs "irrational" explanations (the former being associated with science in particular). See especially Koets, *Deisidaimonia*, 99 and Martin, *Inventing Superstition*, 10–16; cf. the intriguing Smith, "*De Superstitione*," 2–3. For a history of the rise of the modern Western concept of

"atheists"[11]), the term was not used to condemn religion as such, but forms of religion that were considered inappropriate or offensive by some individual or group.[12] Therefore, its negative usage was primarily in contrast to "true" religion or piety.[13]

Frequently scholars consider Paul's (depicted) audience as an argument for a favorable sense. However, this determination is problematic, on any definition of the audience in view. As we saw in the preceding chapter, the narrative intimates that the audience is a variegated sample of the Athenian population (Areopagites, philosophers, and "crowd"). That implies a substantial diversity of perceptions of the world and of Athenian religiousness. Even if one were to limit the audience to the philosophers and members of the educated upper-class, the diversity of views and practice among them would prevent a uniform determination.[14] In any case, it is doubtful that philosophers—especially Epicureans—would have heard δεισιδαιμονεστέρους in a complimentary way, even if it were intended to be so.[15] The one other NT use of a cognate, δεισιδαιμονία in 25:19, though in a scene with many narrative similarities, is of little help. Placed in the mouth of a Roman official addressing Agrippa and Berenice in reference to internecine Jewish religious debates, the term is just as ambivalent.[16]

---

superstition, which taints modern scholarship, see Cameron, *Enchanted Europe*.

11. "'Atheism,' when used by ancient authors, refers more accurately to 'despising' or 'ignoring' the gods rather than to the more modern notion that beings superior to humans simply do not exist at all. Though ancient authors sometimes speak of 'atheists,' even apparently meaning people who deny the existence of the gods, it is strikingly difficult to find an actual atheist in the ancient world. All sorts of people were called 'atheists' (including Christians and Epicureans) who did not actually deny the existence of *any* god." Martin, *Inventing Superstition*, 25on6. Thus, "antiquity cannot be appraised from an eighteenth-century, or, later, from a Marxist, point of view. If we try to do so we see an atheist made in our own image, not in that of the Ancients." Meijer, "Philosophers," 227. For a provocative defense of the existence of "genuine" atheism in the ancient world, see Whitmarsh, *Battling the Gods*.

12. One could argue that in a number of cases the words δεισιδαίμων and δεισιδαιμονία do not carry a definite semantic content or referent, but express a value judgment or reveal an attitude on the part of the speaker or narrator. See the discussion in Gray, *Godly Fear*, 2–3.

13. This is particularly obvious in the works of Plutarch, who seeks in good part "to recall those suffering from the malady of superstition to a sober and sane piety, as well as to rescue the atheist from the perils of the opposite extreme." Moellering, *Plutarch on Superstition*, xiii. See especially his *Superst. and Is. Os*. The same is true of Theophrastus, who wrote an essay on piety (εὐσέβεια), known to us only through fragments preserved in Porphyry (fr. 584A–588).

14. See Martin, *Inventing Superstition*, 79–92.

15. See the challenge raised against Given's thesis in Martin, *Inventing Superstition*, 246n10. Keener thinks that the audience in general would have heard the term positively—though considering it an inapt word choice, but recognizes that Epicureans might have been an exception (*Acts*, 3.2628).

16. Hence Barrett, *Acts*, 2.835, considers it to be clearly positive (as Festus would not want to insult his regal audience); Witherington, *Acts*, 520 and 730, that it is clearly negative (the Latin term *superstitio* is always disparaging and often used to describe Judaism); Koets, *Deisidaimonia*, 25, that it would mean "religion" (neutral) for both speaker and hearer; Moellering, "Deisidaimonia," 471, that the strangeness of the controversy is intimated by the use of ἰδία rather than δεισιδαιμονία itself; Bruce, *Acts Greek*, 380, that it might have had a different meaning for each; and Martin, *Inventing Superstition*, 5–6, is unsure! An example of its disparaging use for Judaism is found in *Diogn*. 1:1; 4:1.

Lexicographical, historical, social, and cultural studies are crucial to define the cultural encyclopaedia of a text and the *semantic range* of the term under consideration, but they cannot determine the semantic import of a particular occurrence.[17] This is what context, in its various forms and levels, does.[18] At the end of the day, the precise import of the word is determined by the point of view of the "speaker," i.e., the (technically, "implied") narrator—Luke—and the character who is his mouthpiece, so to speak—Paul.[19] In the case of δεισιδαίμων and δεισιδαιμονία, it is the author's religious—i.e., *theological*—perspective on the referent that defines the specific signification they carry.[20] We must therefore pay close attention to Luke's point of view and the cues he furnishes to his reader.

Heeding Luke's Narrative Cues

The forensic (and adversarial) situation developed by the narrative framework (see chapter 4) is essential for understanding the speech. Paul is depicted as *formally* addressing the highest court of Athens, possibly under the threat of being charged with a serious crime having to do with religion. He assumes the position of a "rhetor" (σταθείς, v. 22) giving a public speech. His oration evidences various rhetorical features and a high style.[21] The expression "men of Athens" (ἄνδρες Ἀθηναῖοι) is a well-attested—probably customary or conventional—formula (typically headed by the interjection ὦ) found in the speeches of Thucydides and Demosthenes, for example.[22] It is quite similar in form to other introductory words in speeches addressed to crowds or courts in the book of Acts.[23]

---

17. We strongly concur with Rowe, "Acts and Cultural Explication," 247, on this point.

18. Linguistically-speaking, the context has a *determinative* function, i.e., "the context does not merely help us understand meaning—it virtually *makes* meaning." Silva, *Biblical Words*, 139 (emphasis original).

19. Narratively, one must pay attention to how the (depicted or implied) audience might have heard (read) the utterance, for it is a part of the (inter)texture of the story, and therefore is a constitutive element of the narration.

20. A point highlighted in *BegC*, 4.214 and Moellering, "Deisidaimonia," 469. Koets, *Deisidaimonia*, 20–21, notes a case in which two authors use this term for the same referent but intending opposite meanings.

21. Parsons, *Acts*, 249, goes so far as to claim that the speech is "lyrical" and euphonic, noting that Paul uses assonance (repetition of internal vowel sounds in neighboring words), alliteration (repetition of initial sound), reduplication (repetition of one or more words for amplification), antistrophe (repetition of last word in successive phrases), litotes (affirming by negating the opposite), and paronomasia (similar sounding words with dissimilar meanings). He adds the use of γε, including εἰ ἄρα γε (v. 27), and of two optatives to this list on p. 432.

22. Jacquier, *Actes*, 528; Witherington, *NT Rhetoric*, 70, cites Aelius Aristides, *Orationes* 1 as further evidence. A second-century AD example is found in Lucian, *Demon.* 11.

23. Cf. ἄνδρες Γαλιλαῖοι, 1:11; ἄνδρες Ἰσραηλῖται, 2:22; 3:12; 5:35; 13:16; 21:28; ἄνδρες Ἐφέσιοι, 19:35 (in the mouth of the town clerk); and ἄνδρες ἀδελφοί, 1:16; 2:29, 37; 7:2, 26; 13:15, 26, 38; 15:7, 13; 22:1; 23:1, 6; 28:17.

In this context, it appears extremely unlikely—really, impossible—that his very first sentence would be insulting or overtly critical of his audience's religious character.[24] The former would be completely unbecoming for a herald of the risen Christ whose characterization is patterned on Jesus' life and role as the Isaianic Servant.[25] Either would be a self-defeating strategy for someone seeking to bring his audience to repentance and faith.[26] Both would be sheer folly when addressing judges who hold one's fate in their hands! Finally, Paul's auditors are not jeering, mocking or interrupting the way ancients were prone to do when listening to public speeches they disliked or disapproved of.[27] At least, not yet: they will do exactly that in v. 32 and bring the scene to an end. Δεισιδαιμονεστέρους, therefore, cannot be *univocally* negative.

However, other considerations must be attended to. Of primary importance is the picture of Athenian religion that is painted before the reader's eyes. The most obvious trait is the intensity—even excess—of the Athenian religiousness.[28] Luke highlights this character in several ways. First, he emphasizes that the Athenians are δεισιδαιμονεστέρους in "all respects." The intensive κατὰ πάντα—a rare expression in the NT[29]—is placed in a marked position in the clause, raising its pragmatic profile and creating a topical frame.[30] This framing clarifies the extent of application of the following descriptor: the whole Athenian way of life is characterized as being intensely concerned with religious matters.[31] Second, the use of ὡς with a comparative adjective (such as δεισιδαιμονεστέρους) is intensive. Whether one understands the

---

24. Though see the caustic words with which the Cynic Demonax is reported to have begun his address to his judges in Athens, and yet was able to earn their good will in the end. Lucian, *Demon.* 11.

25. For the parallels drawn between Jesus, Paul and the Servant, see the various articles by Moessner on the topic ("Paul and Pattern," "The Christ Must," and "Paul in Acts") as well as Mather, "Paul in Acts" and Cerfaux, *Saint Paul*. It is worth noting the respectful attitude that Paul demonstrates toward the authorities in other forensic situations, even when treated unfairly (e.g., in Philippi, in Caesarea, or in Jerusalem: 23:1–5).

26. "Acts is clear that Paul is vexed by the idolatry (v. 16), but he finds it important to graciously show the way to the one God." Bock, *Acts*, 558. Cf. 1 Pet 3:16: "but do it with meekness and respect" (ἀλλὰ μετὰ πραΰτητος καὶ φόβου).

27. On ridicule in rhetorical contexts, see Keener, *Acts*, 3.2675.

28. A commonplace for ancient writers, both praisingly or mockingly. See Pausanias' claim that the Athenians' devotion to divine matters is superior to that of all other people (*Descr.* 1.17.1; 1.24.3). Cf. Sophocles, *Oed. Col.* 260; Josephus, *Ag. Ap.* 2.130; Strabo, *Geogr.* 9.1.16; Livy, *Hist.* 45.27. See further Jacquier, *Actes*, 529.

29. Elsewhere only in Acts 3:29; Col 3:20, 22; Heb 2:17; 4:15.

30. See the discussion of topical frames in Runge, *Discourse Grammar*, 210–16.

31. Well captured by Alexander, *Acts*, 2.151: "*In all things*, or in all respects, entirely, altogether." This is consistent with the nature and role of religion in the ancient world, as recent studies have demonstrated: "Ancient religion, that is to say, is a pattern of practices and beliefs inextricably interwoven with the fabric of ancient culture. Religion is not, however, just part of this fabric, ultimately passive and controlled by other more basic influences such as politics and economics, for example. Rather, religion is also constitutive of culture; it helps to construct the cultural fabric itself. Religion is, therefore, in the last resort 'indistinguishable from culture.'" Rowe, *World Upside Down*, 50–51, citing Young, *Biblical Exegesis*, 50. So also MacMullen, *Paganism*, 36, 40.

construction to have an elative ("very" or "extremely") or superlative ("most") force, its effect is to intensify the import of the adjective: the Athenians are δεισιδαίμονας in an exceptional, extreme, manner, above all men.[32] Third, the position of the phrase ὡς δεισιδαιμονεστέρους in the sentence is emphatic, being *focal* information placed before the verb.[33] Four, as indicated by the use of γάρ, v. 23a presents the grounds for Paul's assertion—therefore supporting and strengthening this characterization.[34] Paul singles out one object of worship among the many he encountered, raising its profile through the use of an ascensive καί. This creates what in discourse analysis is called a thematic addition, confirming the preceding proposition (v. 22b) by highlighting an extreme or unlikely example of what was in view—here probably with a touch of irony, maybe even sarcasm.[35] This discursive device makes the altar "to an unknown god" both prominent and representative.[36] The altar is a striking token of the Athenians' extreme polytheism, a tangible—one is tempted to write "monumental"—expression of their fear of neglecting *any* god.[37] Fifth, the reference to Paul's initial tour of the city brings v. 16 back to the mind of the reader, especially its characterization of the city of Athens as being "overgrown with idols" (κατείδωλον).[38] All this is what being δεισιδαιμονεστέροι means and looks like concretely for our author.[39]

32. See the excellent discussion in Barrett, *Acts*, 2.836.

33. In terms of "natural information flow," *topical* information is established or already-known elements that compose the mental picture necessary to understand what is being said. *Focal* information is non-established or new information communicated on that basis. The latter is usually the *raison d'être* of the discourse. See Runge, *Discourse Grammar*, 187–91 for that distinction, and 271–72 for the related concept of *emphasis*.

34. In terms of discourse analysis, γάρ introduces "background" material that explains what precedes. It does not advance the argument but is important to it, as it confirms the preceding proposition as a part of the audience's mental representation of the discourse. See the discussion in Runge, *Discourse Grammar*, 51–54. Paul's argument is resumed in v. 23b, as indicated by οὖν.

35. See Runge, *Discourse Grammar*, 339–48 for a discourse explanation of thematic additions.

36. The indeterminate translation ("an") seeks to render more literally the anarthrous inscription. So also Alexander, *Acts*, 2.152. The standard discussion of the relevant historical and archaeological evidence is Van der Horst, "Unknown God" and Van der Horst, "Altar of the 'Unknown God.'"

37. Especially in light of the Epimenidean story concerning similar altars told by Diogenes Laertius (*Vit. Philos.* 1.110). Both Pausanias (*Descr.* 1.1.4; cf. 5.14.8) and Philostratus (*Vit. Apoll.* 6.3) mention these altars (with inscriptions in the plural, but see Barrett, *Acts*, 2.838) as proofs of the exceptional or exemplary piety (even wisdom) of the Athenians. Hence, this altar inscription demonstrates the thoroughgoing idolatry of Athens, as noted by Conzelmann, *Acts*, 141. John Calvin comments that "[cela] était le signe qu'ils ne poursuivaient rien de certain" and then adds: "Or, quiconque sert Dieu sans aucune certitude adore seulement ses propres inventions au lieu de Dieu." *Actes*, 464. This is reminiscent of the frame of mind revealed by their confusion concerning "Jesus and Resurrection" in v. 18.

38. The link is both narrative and verbal, as Luke uses the verb θεωρέω in vv. 16 and 22b, and ἀναθεωρέω in 23a.

39. "La précision 'plus religieux que quiconque' [δεισιδαιμονεστέρους] fait allusion non seulement à l'autel érigé 'au dieu inconnu' (*Act.* XVII, 25), mais à toutes les représentations de divinités qui foisonnaient dans cette ville (*Act.* XVII, 16), où, plus qu'ailleurs, s'appliquait le mot de Plaute [sic] (*Satir.* 17): 'un dieu s'y rencontre plus facilement qu'un homme.'" Spicq, *Notes*, 3.116.

Furthermore, by recalling v. 16 Luke also reminds his readers of Paul's reaction to (and perspective on) such extreme idolatry (παρωξύνετο). In this manner, the narrative of v. 16 not only constitutes a frame of reference for the overall story, but for the speech itself. It must be noted that the word σέβασμα is consistently and exclusively employed to describe *idolatrous* objects of worship in the LXX and in Jewish writings, though it would have no negative connotation for Paul's depicted hearers.[40] The usage for βωμός is of the exact same nature and import. For Luke's reader, both are thus consistent with the denotation and connotation of the intensive compound of εἴδωλον used in v. 16—the latter being a derogatory term never used by pagans to speak of their own cultic images.[41]

It is at this very moment that Paul is shown doing something grammatically surprising, rhetorically striking and theologically far-reaching. Between v. 23a and 23b, he shifts from the original masculine gender of the inscription ("a god") to the neuter (ὅ, "that which"; τοῦτο, "this"). This shift is remarkable in such a well-crafted oration because it is grammatically awkward: a neuter relative pronoun and a demonstrative pronoun refer to a masculine antecedent![42] Neither the in-story audience nor Luke's readers could have missed it. Rhetorically Paul demotes what the Athenians took to be a god to an impersonal *object* of idolatrous worship: the move to a neuter relative pronoun highlights the undefined and indeterminate nature of the object of Athenian worship, depriving it of individuality and personality.[43] The referent becomes therefore the "divine" in an indeterminate, generic or abstract sense. This enables Paul to prevent any confusion between the Athenians' ultimately impersonal concept of the godhead and the absolutely *personal* God of his kerygma—who is introduced as ὁ θεὸς ὁ ποιήσας κτλ. immediately afterward, in v. 24.[44]

---

40. In the LXX: Wis 14:20; 15:17; Bel 1:27. Stonehouse, "Areopagus Address," 15–16 already makes this point. See also Barrett, *Acts*, 2.837 and Marshall, *Acts TNTC*, 286. Haenchen thinks that this is a carefully chosen word meant not to communicate any approval in Paul's mouth (*Acts*, 521).

41. Βωμός is a common Greek word for an altar on which offering are burnt. Used only here in the NT, it refers to a *pagan* altar, which is consistent with the LXX usage (see also *1 Clem.* 25:4). Out of 46 occurrences, only three refer to Yahweh's altar: Num 3:10; Sir 50:12, 14. All others refer to pagan or idolatrous altars. The NT, just like the LXX, always uses θυσιαστήριον to refer to Yahweh's altar, whether terrestrial or celestial (Matt 5:23, 24; 23:18, 19, 20, 35; Luke 1:11; 11:51; Rom 11:3; 1 Cor 9:13; 10:18; Heb 7:13; 13:10; Jas 2:21; Rev 6:9; 8:3, 5; 9:13; 11:1; 14:18; 16:7). On εἴδωλον, see the comments in Klauck, *Magic and Paganism*, 75–76.

42. This fact is highlighted by the textual variants that correct it back to the masculine gender (e.g., ℵ Ac E Ψ 33). These scribal corrections are also due to the fact that the use of the neuter seems to indicate that Paul was proclaiming an *impersonal* deity rather than the personal God of Christianity. See Barrett, *Acts*, 2.838.

43. Parsons, *Acts*, 246, puts it well: "The Athenians had been worshiping an object, nor a personal God, a 'what,' not a 'whom.'" See also Bruce, *Acts NICNT*, 356.

44. Also noted, e.g., by Klauck, *Magic and Paganism*, 83. What Marguerat, *Actes*, 2.157, calls "the anaphoric position" of the clause is a left dislocation, a discursive device used to introduce a new topic or character in a speech or narrative. See Runge, *Discourse Grammar*, 287–93. One of the effects of using that device here is to further highlight the already-present contrast between the two conceptions.

This initial shift and distinction is continued and reinforced by the consistent use of the neuter when Paul refers to the Athenian religion—except, of course, when quoting some pagan poet in 28b—and of the masculine for Paul's own argument (24, 25, 26b, 27, 28a, 29a, 30, 31b). In this respect, it is noteworthy that Paul chose an altar dedicated to an unnamed god when hundreds of named objects of worship would have been available. Such a move achieves several purposes: it crystallizes the extreme polytheism of his audience; it is a graven self-confession of ignorance concerning the divine realm and its nature as a whole;[45] it preempts the risk of being accused of blasphemy;[46] it precludes the confusion of Yahweh with any member of the Greek pantheon; and thus it consistently preserves the separation between the two religious thought worlds. Paul is in no wise equating the one true God, Yahweh, with an idolatrous and polytheistic "unknown god." "Rather, he is drawing their attention to the true God who was ultimately responsible for the phenomena which they attributed to an unknown god."[47] He is making use of the Athenians' creational *sensus divinitatis* (cf. v. 27) to connect with his audience, while simultaneously establishing a fundamental antinomy at the outset.[48]

The inscription on the altar is the starting point for what is arguably the most visible theme of the speech. As various scholars have noted, ἀγνώστῳ and ἀγνοοῦντες in v. 23 form an *inclusio* with ἀγνοία in v. 30, indicating that the Athenians' ignorance is central to the speech as a whole.[49] That it would be so was to be expected, since ignorance is a dominant feature of the characterization of Paul's audience and the narrative cause of Paul's speech. This being so, it is crucial to note that this denial of knowledge and understanding is not conceptualized in a merely intellectual or abstract philosophical (metaphysical) way—as has often been claimed—but in an emphatically *religious* one, with a particular focus on the concrete reality of the worship of God in thought and deed.[50] Hence, to state the obvious, Paul's point of contact is an *altar* inscription.

---

45. "Damit ist angezeigt, daß es sich nicht nur um Unkenntnis der Person oder des Namens des Enen Gottes handelte, sondern um eine (freilich ahnungsvolle) Unkenntnis bezüglich des 'Göttlichen' (vgl. V29 τὸ θεῖον) im allgemeinen. Der Anspruch des Redners geht dahin, die Hörer über den Unbekannten Gott aufzuklären, ihnen den Schöpfergott der Bibel bekanntzumachen." Schneider, *Apg.*, 2.238.

46. It seems that this was a standard practice of Paul's, in light of the Ephesian town clerk's words of defense in Acts 19:37.

47. Marshall, *Acts TNTC*, 286.

48. Contra Schnabel, *Acts*, 730, who claims that "Paul asserts that this god whom the Athenians worship (εὐσεβεῖτε) as 'unknown' (ἀγνοοῦντες) is the God he proclaims in the agora, . . . a divine being that is already present in the city and worshiped by the Athenians, a deity whose name, spheres of influence, power, and forms of appearance are unknown to them." On the contrary, we agree with Butticaz's conclusion: "Ce refus de toute continuité religieuse entre paganisme et foi chrétienne est on ne peut mieux manifesté dans la formulation *neutre* du v. 23." *Identité de l'Eglise*, 380 (emphasis original).

49. E.g., Gourgues, "Littérature profane," 245 and Soards, *Speeches in Acts*, 97. See the various elements forming the *inclusio* highlighted by Dupont, "Discours à l'Aréopage," 392.

50. Contra Dibelius, "Areopagus," 57–58. Unsurprisingly, then, "the speech possesses few of

Secondly, this altar is dedicated to *a* god that is unknown, not to *the* unknown god of either Gnosticism or some philosophical monotheism, even less to Yahweh![51] Finally, the inscription means, and is explicitly understood to mean, that this god is not-known by the Athenians, but not that it is *unknowable* in the absolute.[52]

Further evidence is available in the relative clause ὃ οὖν ἀγνοοῦντες εὐσεβεῖτε in 23b, for it draws out the signification of the inscription in Paul's eyes. While appropriating rhetorically the wording of the inscription, it plays several discursive roles. First, οὖν marks the resumption of the line of thought started in 22b which was interrupted by the invocation of supporting material in 23a (introduced with γάρ). Second, it indicates a new development in the discourse, one that draws an inference from the intervening supporting material.[53] Thus, the clause expands Paul's assertion in 22b in light of 23a.[54] Whether one understands ἀγνοοῦντες to relate adjectivally to ὃ ("what you do not know") or adverbially to εὐσεβεῖτε[55] (indicating *manner*, "ignorantly"), in

---

Hellenistic philosophy's requisite technical terms. Major Stoic themes, such as determinism, are absent. At times the author even seems to take measures to *avoid* the technical terms of philosophy." Rothschild, *Paul in Athens*, 5 (emphasis original).

In any case, the often-assumed post-Enlightenment dichotomy between (rationalistic, naturalistic and secular) philosophy and religion is anachronistic when read into the antique Graeco-Roman world—in any period of its history. Even the more skeptical and antithetical forms of philosophy, while being critical of ancient cults and inherited notions of the divine, engaged religious topics (including theology, the meaning and origins of rituals and festivals, and the role of religion in social and political realities) and often shared some of its basic concerns, values and presuppositions. Only "at one extreme stood the radical scepticism about the fundamental assumptions underlying religious belief. This criticism, however, remained abstract and theoretical, and either ignored or acquiesced in cultic practice." Attridge, "Philosophical Critique," 45. Critical scholarship has tended to project its own post-Enlightenment Western values and prejudices (especially against religion as such) on classical writers, thus reconstructing the ancient philosophers in their own image. This is particularly evident in many discussions of "superstition." See Gray, *Godly Fear*, 34–36; Martin, "Hellenistic Superstition"; Martin, *Inventing Superstition*, 10–18; and Van Nuffelen, *Rethinking the Gods*, 5–14, 231–41.

51. See Hackett, "Discourse of Paul," 348 and Conzelmann, *Acts*, 141. The scholarly consensus today is that Gnosticism is too late a phenomenon to be a direct background to the NT, thus Norden's argument is moot (*Agnostos Theos*, 56–83). On the recent debates concerning pagan monotheism, including the cult of Θεὸς Ὕψιστος, see especially Athanassiadi and Frede, "Pagan Monotheism" and Mitchell and Van Nuffelen, *One God*. Finally, it should be noted that "to many Greeks the god of the Jewish religion was definitely an unknown god *par excellence* because he could not be called by name and he had no image, not even in the inmost recess of his single, unapproachable sanctuary in Jerusalem." Van der Horst, "Unknown God," 35.

52. So Barrett, *Acts*, 2.839. That is narratively confirmed by the remainder of the speech, of course. Van der Horst, "Unknown God," explains that such dedications were used for gods whose name and function were not known at all.

53. See the discussion of the resumptive and/or inferential nature of οὖν in Levinsohn, *Discourse Features*, 126–29 and Runge, *Discourse Grammar*, 43–48.

54. As a left dislocation, it enables the speaker to introduce in a marked way a new topic that is grammatically the direct object of the main verb (καταγγέλλω) in a very compact way. That topic is thus identified as the focus of Paul's proclamation.

55. This verb occurs only twice in the NT (cf. 1 Tim 5:4). In general Greek usage it refers to an appropriate attitude or act of reverence and devotion in relation to either gods or people, including the Roman emperor. See Barrett, *Acts*, 2.838. It is never used in relation to Yahweh in either LXX or

view of what has been said so far, the point is clear.⁵⁶ And it cannot be that the Athenians really or actually worship the true God without knowing or realizing it!⁵⁷ On the contrary, through this representative example the speaker subsumes the whole of their devotion (and therefore way of life) under the category of ignorance.⁵⁸

The end of v. 23 confirms and reinforces both the fact that the focus is religious, rather than philosophical, and the fundamental antithesis between the Athenians and Paul. Hence, the speech is characterized as a *proclamation*—understood, of the Word of the risen Christ, in view of the strong rhetorical verbal linkage with v. 18 (καταγγέλλω and καταγγελεύς) and parallel with 17:3 and 13—, not a lecture.⁵⁹ Thus, though *some* of the in-story audience may have heard ἀγνοοῦντες in its typical philosophical sense—and therefore expect Paul to seek to augment their knowledge (and tickle their proverbial curiosity)—, the context indicates clearly (i.e., to the reader) that this is neither Paul's meaning nor intention. The speech is not a typical piece of philosophical or rhetorical oration. The theme of ignorance that is developed throughout the speech is intrinsically connected with the nature of Yahweh and his worship.⁶⁰ It is impossible to disentangle and isolate the two. Fundamentally, "ignorance" in this passage denotes the idolatrous (and therefore erroneous, offensive and condemnable) nature of paganism—whether popular or educated, even philosophical. It is important to note the *relational* dimension of this "un-knowing," marked by the shift to the neuter. The biblical concept of religion and worship proclaimed by Paul centers on a covenantal fellowship between a personal God and his people. That aspect is evident in vv. 27, 28, for example.

The emphatic use of ἐγώ—both grammatically redundant and in a pragmatically-marked position—in 23b simultaneously sets the speaker apart from and in

---

NT, though the noun εὐσέβεια is. In our text, it simply refers to the Athenian pagan religiousness. See Jobes, "Distinguishing" for an overview of the NT vocabulary for worship.

56. The latter seems to be preferable syntactically: see Culy and Parsons, *Acts Handbook*, 337. However, both *BegC*, 4.215 and Barrett, *Acts*, 2.838-39 make the case for the latter on rhetorical grounds, in spite of this consideration.

57. Contra Zweck, "Exordium," 96; Holladay, *Acts*, 341; L. T. Johnson, *Acts*, 315; Kurz, *Acts*, 271; Pinnock, "Toward an Evangelical," 365; and Sanders, *No Other Name*, 246.

58. Witherington puts it this way: "Paul is suggesting here that the Athenians have an inkling that such a God exists, as is shown by their actions, but they do not either really know or properly acknowledge this God." Witherington, *Acts*, 523. This emphasis on ignorance is quite ironic, of course, in view of Athens' intellectual and religious symbolism. See Stonehouse, "Areopagus Address," 19. It is probable that we have another example of dramatic irony here, since the term can denote a mere lack of knowledge, as noted by Rowe, "Grammar," 40n38.

59. See further Dupont, "Discours à l'Aréopage," 391-92. After making the same point, Stählin adds: "Paulus steht nicht als Philosoph unter den Philosophen, sondern als Prophet." *Apostelgeschichte*, 232; see also Litwak, "Israel's Prophets," 200. It is likely that v. 23 is part of Paul's in-story strategy to deny the charge of proclaiming "strange gods." So Rowe, *World Upside Down*, 34, and Keener, *Acts*, 3.2605, for example.

60. This is why O'Toole, "Paul at Athens," 185, argues that worship *is* the focus of the passage; cf. Stonehouse, "Areopagus Address," 10.

opposition to his audience.⁶¹ An antithesis is therefore established between the Athenians, who idolatrously revere the divine without knowledge, and Paul who proclaims it with knowledge and authority.⁶² Moreover, an antinomy is also implied between pagan idolatry (ignorance) and the Christian faith and message (revealing the true God). These are strengthened by the use of the verb καταγγέλλω, which indicates that the word of God is being "heralded," and consequently the message and its bearer carry God's commissioned authority.⁶³ The point is not that Paul intends to build on what the Athenians already knew, but to call them to a radical change—a μετάνοια.⁶⁴ This is a proper starting-point for a speech that negates typical pagan practices and culminates in a universal summon to repent. The reader witnesses a complete and surprising reversal of the original situation (depicted in vv. 18–22a), as the "babbler" is now the "herald" on whose message his "would-be judges" depend.⁶⁵

Luke thus continues to weave the reversal and irony of Ps 2 with the New Exodus of Isaiah into his narrative. The clearest OT parallel to our text seems to be Isa 45:14–15 LXX, where the nations, now in subjection to Israel, confess: Οὐκ ἔστιν θεὸς πλὴν σοῦ· σὺ γὰρ εἶ θεός, καὶ οὐκ ᾔδειμεν, ὁ θεὸς τοῦ Ἰσραηλ σωτήρ (the LXX differs significantly from the MT here). That this text is echoed here is supported by the obvious similarity of thought between the two passages in their respective contexts and the extensive echoing of Isaiah 45:14–25 in Paul's speech as a whole.⁶⁶ We could find only one other OT passage where, similarly, nations/Gentiles confess with their own mouths that they do not know Yahweh: Exod 5:2. To be precise, it is part of Pharaoh's denial of Moses and Aaron's first request by arguing: οὐκ οἶδα τὸν κύριον (LXX and MT are identical).

---

61. The "*your* poets" in v. 28 produces a similar rhetorical effect.

62. "The sentence taken as a whole makes two statements, one about the Athenians and one about Paul. The subjects are different, the verbs are different, but the objects are the same, as the relative construction shows (ὅ . . . τοῦτο)." Barrett, *Acts*, 2.838.

63. Interestingly, the verb καταγγέλλω is exclusively Lukan and Pauline in the NT: it is used twice in the LXX (2 Macc 8:36; 9:17); eleven times in Acts (never in the Gospel): 3:24; 4:2; 13:5, 38; 15:36; 16:17, 21; 17:3, 13, 23; 26:23; and seven times in Paul's epistles (Rom 1:8; 1 Cor 2:1; 9:14; 11:26; Phil 1:17, 18; Col 1:28). Luke's usage refers exclusively to the *proclamation* of the gospel of the risen Jesus. It refers nine times to the apostles' message (and, except for 4:2, always in reference to Paul and/or Barnabas), once to the OT prophets' (3:24) and once to the risen Christ's (26:23, associating it closely with Paul's own ministry). All of those are "authorized" messengers of God. Paul's apostolic authority is thus strongly affirmed here. See Stonehouse, "Areopagus Address," 23–25.

64. Contra a common (mis)interpretation of these verses, recently defended by Kurz, *Acts*, 271. See Rowe's excellent critique of that perspective in "Grammar," especially pp. 40–41. On p. 45, he concludes: "Rather [than a mere correction or adjustment], as the end of Paul's speech makes so clear, to shift from the 'unknown God' to knowledge of him is to move into and inhabit the way of life constituted by repentance and the recognition of the identity of the man who was raised from the dead."

65. As Wolfe cleverly puts it: "Thus a role-reversal occurs by which the defendant becomes the 'gnostic' to 'a-gnostics.'" Wolfe, "Rhetorical Elements," 277.

66. Though Dubarle's claim that the whole speech is directly framed on Isa 45:14–25 (Dubarle, "Discours à l'Aréopage") is excessive, his work does demonstrate extensive parallels between the two texts. Surprisingly, Pao does not discuss vv. 22–23 at all and therefore does not address this piece of evidence.

In view of the fact that this passage is the beginning of the original Exodus cycle with its archetypical anti-idol polemic, it is quite likely that Exod 5:2 is echoed in Isa 45:15, and thus mediately and faintly also in the Areopagitica. All this contributes to reinforce Luke's developing characterization of Paul as the Servant-witness against God's idol-worshiping enemies in the eschatological judgment.[67]

Conclusion: Dramatic Irony and the Δεισιδαιμονεστέροι Ἀθηναῖοι

The evidence shows without doubt that the introduction of the Areopagitica is plurivocal. The challenge for the interpreter is to distinguish properly between the various voices and to account for the dynamics created by their plurality and interaction. As Rowe says: "Through a deft use of dramatic irony, Luke unifies historical verisimilitude—and rhetorical skill—with theological judgment and, precisely in so doing, alerts the readers of Paul's speech to its multi-level discourse."[68] The speech and its introduction fit extremely well in the world of first-century Athens as we know it, as well as in the plot Luke has developed to this point. It is perfectly "in character."

In-story, the use of δεισιδαιμονεστέρους is very effective. It is a phenomenologically-accurate description of the Athenians, truly a common place. Semantically, the word is plurivalent and would have been heard in a variety of ways by different members of the audience. The pragmatic elements noted earlier would have favored the perception of a negative or critical note due to the intensification produced, but not made it explicit yet. It is improbable that any educated member of the audience would have perceived the word to be univocally or flatly positive.[69] It is more likely that the audience would have been intrigued or puzzled by it, perceiving the uncertain meaning of Paul's words. Their curiosity would have been pricked as they wondered what exactly this σπερμολόγος intended to communicate with this word, thus being moved to listen further—the only way to find out what he meant and who he meant it for. Rhetorically, such a approach would be quite effective, as it captivates the audience's attention, avoids immediate direct confrontation, creates a point of contact and subtly, but unmistakably, invalidates the charges intimated in vv. 18–20.

This kind of story-telling is quite engaging and stimulating for the reader, who is curious to find out how Paul is going to "get himself out" of this sticky situation. The term δεισιδαιμονεστέρους, just like σεβάσματα and βωμόν, is perfectly adapted to the

---

67. A portrait that fits very well with the figure of the prophet as Yahweh's messenger found in the OT, especially in Isaiah. The prophetic messenger typically carries a message of woe and speaks with the exact same authority as Yahweh (or the divine "council") who sent him. See the helpful Ross, "Prophet."

68. Rowe, "Grammar," 40.

69. Thus, we question the picture of the entire audience uniformly considering Paul's introductory words to be a wholesale praise of their religiousness. Contra, e.g., Klauck, *Magic and Paganism*, 81–82 and Given, *Paul's True Rhetoric*, 70.

situation, an apposite depiction of Athenian religiousness, without any definite prima facie value judgment implied.[70] It probably expresses something like "extremely religious" or "uncommonly devout" in reference to their type of religion.[71] This religion is depicted as idolatrous, polytheistic to the extreme and "ignorant" of the identity and nature of the divine. This picture is developed both narratively and intertextually, and v. 23 ensures that the reader will connect the dots. Several of the typical *topoi* associated with the figure of the δεισιδαίμων in a derogatory sense are present, explicitly or implicitly.[72] The allusion to Isaiah 45 alerts the reader to the nature and meaning of the event. Even the mood of the text echoes the ironic—occasionally sarcastic—tone of OT scenes depicting Yahweh's confrontation with and judgment of the nations, especially anti-idol parodies. Theologically, there is no doubt about the condemnatory perspective of the narrator and his "reliable orator," consistent with Stephen's in Acts 7.[73] The Athenian religiosity is not one in need of adjustment, complement or supplement (whether small or large), but one that must be replaced altogether by the gospel of Jesus Christ that the apostle Paul proclaims.[74] The speech is not highlighting the audience's knowledge but its ignorance, neither is it building on their natural theology but rather is affirming the absolute necessity of special revelation.[75] The Athenians—all of them—are characterized as the apex of idolatrous mankind, and therefore its symbolic representatives.[76]

All in all, Luke captures very crisply the complex religious reality of fallen mankind. The altar with its engraved confession of ignorance points to and presupposes an awareness of the divine, however confused and wrongheaded it might be.[77] As Dennis

70. Stonehouse, "Areopagus Address," 16–17, arrives at a similar conclusion. See Spicq, *Notes*, 3.116, for ambiguous uses in Plutarch and Diodorus Siculus, and Martin, *Inventing Superstition*, 83, for uses in Diodorus that are neither positive nor negative but merely descriptive.

71. A "superior devotion in the heathen sense." Alexander, *Acts*, 2.151–52. Barrett, *Acts*, 2.835, and Bruce, *Acts Greek*, 380, come to a similar conclusion.

72. For example: ignorance (e.g., Plutarch, *Superst.* 1 [164E], 11 [170E]; Diodorus Siculus, 32.12.1-2); confusion of gods with their representation as in idol worship (e.g., Plutarch *Is. Os.* 71 [379C–D]; Lucian, *Jupp. trag.* 7–13); extreme scruple and fear (e.g., Theophrastus, *Char.* 16; Plutarch, *Superst.* 3–4 [165D–167A]); excess in religious practices (e.g., Theophrastus, *Char.* 16); possibly, curiosity (see Gray, "Athenian Curiosity"). Besides the specialized studies mentioned earlier, see Attridge, "Philosophical Critique."

73. As rightly pointed out by Given, *Paul's True Rhetoric*, 74.

74. For it is very clear that their polytheistic idolatry is emphatically *not* the worship of Yahweh, the one God and Lord who raised Jesus from the dead, "because the object of their worship in such cases was not the true God, but a mere nonentity or vague abstraction." Alexander, *Acts*, 2.153.

75. "Indeed, as the thesis statement shows, proclamation of special revelation is needed for them to be able to make sense of the behavior they already exhibit." Witherington, *NT Rhetoric*, 71. See also Hansen, "Preaching and Defence," 316–17 and Rowe, "Grammar," 40–41.

76. It is therefore turning the text on its head to conclude that either Paul or Luke is commending the Athenians for their "pious behavior" (Samuel, "Paul on the Areopagus," 21) or considers the altar to be a preparation for the gospel (Higgins, "Key to Insider Movements," 161).

77. It is strikingly reminiscent of the very first paragraph of Augustine's *Confessions* (1.1.1) and its famous words: "you have made us for yourself, and our hearts are restless until they rest in you."

Johnson says, there is a sense in which the Athenians *know of* God at the same time as they *do not know* him.[78] They are entirely ignorant of either his identity or his nature, but they have a sense of the existence and presence of a transcendent or divine reality.[79] Paul exploits this ambiguity as well as the Athenian self-testimony of ignorance as a point of contact with his audience and a starting point for his discourse.[80] The budding anti-idol polemic of v. 23b is a fitting announcement of Paul's topic, for every section of the speech focuses on the interplay between the audience's ignorance and the failure to serve and worship the God of Jesus Christ in an acceptable way.[81]

(Translation by Carolyn J.-B. Hammond.)

78. Dennis E. Johnson, *Message of Acts*, 196. This paradox is the heart of Rom 1:18–23.

79. This is why Paul is so careful to distinguish the deity associated with the altar from the God who raised Jesus from the dead. It is a complete denial of the evidence to say that "in certain respects they did acknowledge the true God" as does Sanders, *No Other Name*, 246.

80. So also Alexander, *Acts*, 2.152; Bruce, *Acts NICNT*, 356; Owen, "Scope," 135n1; and Bock, *Acts*, 564.

81. At the same time, the allusion to Isa 45:15 LXX offers hope, since in this passage the nations voice their *former* ignorance of the fact that Yahweh was the one and only God and Savior. Thus, as mankind's idols are exposed and judged the way of deliverance and salvation is extended to those who *were* under their sway.

CHAPTER 6

The Creator-God Is Lord of Heaven and Earth (Acts 17:24–25)

The "unknown god" is now made known by Paul, and he is the one God who made all things and gives (natural) life to all creatures.[1]

The Sentence Structure and the Isaiah 42:5 Allusion

The use of a left dislocation in v. 24 is remarkable, as this type of construction entails either the introduction of or a shift to a new topic.[2] One would have expected Paul to continue with the topical frame in v. 23b and thus to use either a relative or a demonstrative pronoun here. This choice seems to serve three pragmatic purposes: first, it reinforces the distinction established previously between the referent of the altar inscription and the God of Paul's proclamation;[3] second, it allows Paul to re-characterize God and avoid confusion; third, it topicalizes what is specifically relevant or in view about this God for what follows. Verses 24–25 tell Paul's audience who the God he heralds is, and how far his rule extends. These two verses are framed by an *inclusio* formed with an allusion to the words of Isa 42:5.[4]

---

1. See Owen, "Scope," 135–36.
2. Runge, *Discourse Grammar*, 290.
3. Contra Smith, *God in Translation*, 308.
4. The similarity of language has long been recognized, though not all scholars see an allusion split between 24a and 25b. Cf. the discussion in Haenchen, *Acts*, 522; Pao, *Acts and INE*, 194–95; Beale, "Other Religions," 84–85; and Marshall, "Acts," 594. The number of echoes from the same section of Isaiah throughout the speech and the whole of Luke-Acts strongly supports this view in our opinion. Moreover, "Acts 17:24–25 alludes to Isaiah 42:5, which introduces a promise of Israel's restoration (Is 42:6) by God opening their eyes and delivering them from captivity (Is 42:7), as well as introducing a contrast between the uniquely true God and idols (Is 42:8)." Beale, *We Become*, 282. A variety of OT echoes and parallels have been suggested for these two verses, for example: Gen 1:1; 2:1, 7; Exod 20:11; 1 Kgs 8:17, 27; Ps 50:8–13; 145: 6 LXX; Isa 43:24 LXX; 45:12, 18; 66:1–2; Acts 7:48; cf. 1QH 1, 13–15. See Barrett, *Acts*, 2.839–40; Litwak, "Israel's Prophets," 204–06; and Butticaz, *Identité de l'Eglise*, 357–58 for more parallels, biblical and extra-biblical.

THE CREATOR-GOD IS LORD OF HEAVEN AND EARTH (ACTS 17:24–25)

Isaiah 42:5	Acts 17:24–25
κύριος <u>ὁ θεὸς ὁ ποιήσας τὸν οὐρανὸν</u> καὶ πήξας αὐτόν ὁ στερεώσας <u>τὴν γῆν καὶ τὰ ἐν αὐτῇ</u>	v. 24: <u>ὁ θεὸς ὁ ποιήσας τὸν κόσμον καὶ πάντα τὰ ἐν αὐτῷ</u>, οὗτος <u>οὐρανοῦ καὶ γῆς</u> ὑπάρχων κύριος οὐκ ἐν χειροποιήτοις ναοῖς κατοικεῖ
καὶ <u>διδοὺς πνοὴν τῷ λαῷ</u> τῷ ἐπ' αὐτῆς <u>καὶ πνεῦμα τοῖς πατοῦσιν</u> αὐτήν	v. 25: οὐδὲ ὑπὸ χειρῶν ἀνθρωπίνων θεραπεύεται προσδεόμενός τινος, αὐτὸς <u>διδοὺς πᾶσι ζωὴν καὶ πνοὴν</u> καὶ τὰ πάντα

The statement made in 24a is part of a chiastic structure made of two consequent affirmations about God and the respective implications each has for distinct aspects of pagan worship (in the center). It could be charted as follows:

  A God: Creator and Lord (24a)

    B Temples: God does not dwell in them (24b)

    B' Sacrifices and ceremonies: God does not need them (25a)

  A' God: Benefactor and Life-Giver (25b)

This ABB'A' structure supports a double thematic progression, from God the Creator to his being the universal Lord (A) to his corollary life-giving activity (A'), and from temple-building (B) to pagan sacrifices and ceremonies (B'). The fact that God is the maker of the universe implies that he is Lord of all things as well as the one giving to all creatures their existence or life. Because God is the universal Lord, pagan temples are wrong; because God gives all things to his creatures, pagan sacrifices are wrong. This simple chiastic structure indicates that the As (and thus Isa 42:5) are the reason for the denials of the focal point (the Bs), emphasizing the tension between the divine (creational and providential) reality and the folly of pagan cultic conceptions and practice.[5]

The first clause of v. 24 discloses the unique identity of the God proclaimed by Paul. Grammatically, it is a long predicate clause qualifying "God" (ὁ θεός).[6] As such, the phrase "who made the world and everything in it" is there to specify who (i.e., which and what kind of "god") Paul is talking about. The aorist participle (*perfective*) ποιήσας denotes a complete and finished act of creation (here, past from the speaker's vantage point), in contrast with the subsequent present participles (*imperfective*) denoting God's ongoing activity.[7] Ποιέω is the standard verb used in the LXX for God's creative acts, translating both בָּרָא and עָשָׂה in Genesis 1–2.[8]

---

    5. Cf. the structural analyses in Gourgues, "Littérature profane," 246 and Tannehill, *Acts*, 219–20.

    6. Also noted by Barrett, *Acts*, 2.839.

    7. Ellis et al., "Greek Verbal System" presents a convincing argument for the use of a linguistic aspect-prominent model to understand the Greek verbal system (see also Ellis, "Aspect-Prominence"). We adopt their aspectual taxonomy of "perfective," "imperfective," and "combinative" in this book. The aspectual import of the verbal forms is decisive for the semantic point we are making here.

    8. The verb κτίζω is used infrequently for the same, e.g., Gen 14:19, 22; Hos 13:4; Dan 4:37; Matt

The expression used in our text is all-inclusive, for it refers to both the κόσμος—the universe, essentially understood as a "space" here—and the creatures that fill it.[9] This conceptual combination is a common way of describing God's work of creation in its universal dimension in the OT.[10]

Fitzmyer claims that Luke is introducing a Hellenistic concept by using κόσμος, a word that denotes the "ordered world" in Greek writers, but this inference in unwarranted.[11] First, it is clear that Luke is motivated by a desire for brevity (a quality inherent to left dislocations), for stylistic variation (the very next clause contains the phrase "heaven and earth"), and possibly for a Hellenistic "sound" which would be an appropriate transition for his audience.[12] Secondly, it seems rash to draw from the occurrence of this one word the conclusion that Paul is depicted as using its *technical* philosophical meaning and appealing to its theoretical import. Especially in view of the biblical frame of reference within which it appears.

Κόσμος does not occur in the sense of "world" in the LXX, but its Hellenistic semantic range is consistent with its being used as a short-hand for the more extensive (and frequent) Hebrew phrases which express the idea of the whole universe, such as "heaven and earth" or "heaven, earth and the sea."[13] The term appears in several intertestamental Jewish writings with that meaning, however, indicating that there existed a "generic" usage among Greek speakers also.[14] More significantly, κόσμος is a rather common word in the NT, particularly in the Johannine and Pauline literature, always in the sense of "world" (though often with negative ethical-eschatological connotations). It is therefore not surprising that the other three Lukan occurrences (Luke 9:25; 11:50; 12:30) denote the wholeness or entirety of the created universe.[15] Finally, it must be noted that the typically biblical expression "Lord of heaven and earth" that follows immediately makes clear what was meant by κόσμος, at least for the reader.[16]

19:4; Mark 13:19; Rom 1:25; Col 1:16; Rev 4:11; 10:6.

9. Here Luke condenses significantly the text of Isa 42:5 LXX, using ὁ ποιήσας τὸν κόσμον καὶ πάντα τὰ ἐν αὐτῷ for ὁ ποιήσας τὸν οὐρανὸν καὶ πήξας αὐτόν ὁ στερεώσας τὴν γῆν καὶ τὰ ἐν αὐτῇ.

10. This is true of the original account of the creation of the universe in Genesis 1 as a whole. See also, e.g., Gen 1:26; 6:7; Exod 20:11; Ps 145:6 LXX; Job 34:13; Dan 4:37; Acts 4:24; 14:15; Rev 10:6.

11. Fitzmyer, *Acts*, 608. Pervo, *Acts*, 434, sees it as the "only concession" to philosophical language in the speech.

12. Suggested by Haenchen, *Acts*, 522. Cf. Marguerat, *Actes*, 2.158.

13. Marshall thinks this absence is explained by the lack of a one-word Hebrew equivalent (Marshall, "Acts," 594). The septuagintal usage of κόσμος draws exclusively on its "ornament" or "adorning" semantic range, both literally and figuratively. In the latter case, it is sometimes used to refer to the beings "populating" a creational space—especially the heavens—as in Gen 2:1; Isa 13:10; 24:21. In a few cases, the heavenly beings in view are associated with idolatry: Deut 4:19; 17:3; Ezek 7:20.

14. See Barrett, *Acts*, 2.840.

15. Though the notion of "order" is not in view or in focus, it is not incompatible in and of itself with a biblical understanding of creation, as the original creation account of Genesis 1–2 makes clear.

16. See Jervell, *Die Apostelgeschichte*, 446.

We may therefore conclude that Luke/Paul has aptly adapted the wording of Isa 42:5 LXX for his own purposes, yet without altering the thought world it conveys. Not all in the depicted audience would have heard the term κόσμος in a philosophical sense. The philosophers might, though they may not have expected a clear or consistent philosophical theory from Paul, whom they deemed a σπερμολόγος. Besides, Epicureans and Stoics held to very different cosmologies,[17] neither of which looked like the creational theology developed by Paul in his discourse. Finally, Luke has provided the reader with multiple intertextual, narrative and discursive frames of reference, all of which confirm a biblical creational meaning. So rather than reading Isa 42:5 through the lens of Hellenistic philosophy on account of the use of κόσμος, we ought to understand κόσμος through the lens of Isa 42:5 and the thought world it crystallizes.

In this regard, it is rather striking that the author did not choose a "creational" OT text here (such as Gen 2:1), but one that introduces the principal New Exodus section of the book of Isaiah. In fact, Isa 42:1–9 is the first of the so-called "Servant Songs," one that depicts the calling of the Servant in relation to *all nations* in Yahweh's eschatological salvation-judgment, in the broader context of a polemic against false gods and idols. In this perspective, three further observations deserve to be made. First, Isa 42:1–9 (especially 5–9) shares many themes with the Areopagus speech, as will appear through our study. Second, v. 6 is part of Simeon's prayer in Luke 2, serving to identify Jesus with the Isaianic Servant and to highlight the fact that he is bringing salvation and light to the *Gentiles*. Third, this same v. 6 is a very close parallel to Isa 49:6, the text used by Paul to justify his turning to the Gentiles in Acts 13:47 and the source of the expression "to the end of the earth" in Acts 1:8! It seems that Luke is weaving together the original universalism of creation with the eschatological universalism of God's salvation, i.e., the final Exodus and the New Creation.[18]

The Transcendent Creator-God

The use of the resumptive pronoun οὗτος in 24b and of the personal pronoun αὐτός in 25b make of their common antecedent, the Creator-God of 24a, the subject of all the subsequent verbs in vv. 24b–25.[19] As topical frames, they clarify for the hearer or

---

17. For a rapid but useful overview of the teachings of the two schools relevant to the Areopagitica, see Keener, *Acts*, 3.2584–95.

18. Luke is here merely echoing his source: "The new Exodus of the future, especially as predicted in the prophecies we call Deutero-Isaiah (Isa. 40–55), will be an event of universal significance precisely because the God who brought Israel out of Egypt is also the Creator and Ruler of all things." Bauckham, *God Crucified*, 10.

19. We use the capitalized "Creator" to express the absolute and strictly unique nature of this divine identity as it is conceived in our text and its OT background. Whether in the OT, Second Temple Judaism or early Christianity, that is the distinguishing identity that makes Yahweh, and Yahweh alone, God: "The uniqueness of the divine identity was characterized especially by two features: that the one God is sole Creator of all things and that the one God is sole Ruler of all things. To this

reader what is the vantage point from which what is said must be understood. In fact, God *qua* Creator is the frame of reference for the entire speech, and therefore the point of reference from which everything that is said must be understood.[20]

Grammatically, the participles in vv. 24–25 have a causal relation to the main verbs, which is made explicit in the NASB through the double use of "since." At the same time, they exegete the affirmation that God is maker of the world and all that is in it, drawing out critical corollaries most relevant to the situation at hand. Since God is the Creator of *all there is*, he is therefore also Lord of heaven and earth (an all-encompassing reference) and giver of life, breath and all things to all creatures (another all-encompassing reference).[21] It should be noted that this same line of thought is essential to OT anti-idol polemics, including Isaiah's.

The inference drawn by the speaker is that God is Lord with complete authority over whatsoever he created, i.e., over everything there is. His rule is absolute and universal. One finds in 24b the affirmation of a universal and permanent state of affairs: both κατοικεῖ—clearly gnomic here[22]—and ὑπάρχων—a present participle (*imperfective*) indicating the reason or ground for what is being denied[23]—express general or universal truths about God. Yahweh's lordship is constant, without change or end. The expression "Lord of heaven and earth" reiterates and therefore reinforces his claim to absolute and universal sovereignty,[24] "and that characteristic evokes how he should be acknowledged and worshiped."[25]

Here we must pause and ask whether F. F. Bruce is right when he claims that Paul's starting with God the Creator means that "no concessions are allowed to Hellenistic paganism."[26] Contrary to his assertion, many scholars have affirmed that a number of ancient Greek philosophers believed in a notion of creation, or even that

---

unique identity corresponds monolatry, the exclusive worship of the one and only God who is so characterized." Bauckham, *God Crucified*, 25.

20. The author does not let the hearer/reader lose sight of this fact, as αὐτός in 25a, ἐποίησέν in 26a, ὁρίσας in 26b, τὸν θεόν in 27a, αὐτόν in 27b, ὑπάρχοντα in 27c, ἐν αὐτῷ in 28a, τοῦ in 28b, τοῦ θεοῦ in 29a, τὸ θεῖον in 29b, ὑπεριδὼν ὁ θεός in 30a, παραγγέλλει in 30b, ἔστησεν and μέλλει in 31a, ὥρισεν in 31b, παρασχών and ἀναστήσας in 31c make clear.

21. Alexander says that it is so "by necessary consequence" (Alexander, *Acts*, 2.154).

22. See the discussion of the gnomic or generic use of the present in Wallace, *Greek Grammar*, 523–25 (who cites Acts 7:48 as a clear example on p. 524) and Fanning, *Verbal Aspect*, 208–17 (who cites both Acts 7:48 and 17:24–25 as examples on p. 208).

23. So also Barrett, *Acts*, 2.840. Note that ὑπάρχω (also in v. 29) is elegant and gives the speech an elevated style and a Greek flair. See Bruce, *Acts Greek*, 384 and Haenchen, *Acts*, 522.

24. It is important to understand that "the point here is not the *conservatio* but the *gubernatio*" of the world. Haenchen, *Acts*, 522. The same contrast is used by Schubert, "Place," 251.

25. Fitzmyer, *Acts*, 608, who cites the following parallels: Tob 7:17; 1QapGen 22:16, 21 (Aramaic paraphrase of Gen 14:19); Matt 11:25; Luke 10:21; to which we would add Acts 4:24, a significant anti-idol polemic parallel, where the rare δεσπότης (ten times in the NT; Luke is the only Evangelist to use it, once in each volume) occurs in the context of the affirmation of God's lordship over human political powers. Cf. Jervell, *Theology of Acts*, 19.

26. Bruce, "Paul and Athenians," 9.

the "Supreme God" was the father or maker of the world.²⁷ There is indeed literary evidence of a concept of creator-god, sometimes referred to as ὁ δημιουργός.²⁸ Hence, Barrett mentions Plato's *Timaeus* as an example of a text that, just like Genesis 1, attributes the creation of the world to divine causation.²⁹ Similarly, Marshall claims that Paul's words "could also have been accepted by the Greek philosopher Plato," while Dibelius asserts that vv. 24–25 (together with 26–27) "are intended to convey a Hellenistic doctrine of God."³⁰ Pervo draws the conclusion that "The God of Israel is, the narrator asserts, identical to the deity whom Greeks worship as creator and source of life and existence."³¹

After listing a large number of similar parallels from Greek writers, however, Fitzmyer and Gourgues both ask whether such resemblance is merely formal or truly substantial.³² And both conclude that the fundamental difference between the teaching of vv. 24–25—in fact, 24–29—and that of the Greek philosophers is the *nature* of the divine reality that is in view. We would add, as a necessary corollary, the nature of its relationship to the κόσμος. Though the various post-Hellenistic schools of philosophy held to distinct doctrines—and debated them publicly, frequently, and often vehemently³³—they shared various presuppositions and approaches, including a certain class etiquette.³⁴ Philosophers of that period often drew from various schools, so much so that certain ideas, principles and arguments became "common stock" for discussions of religious topics.³⁵

The Hippocratic literature evidences a turning point, when members of the intellectual elites started thinking about the gods and their involvement in the world along

---

27. See Bock, *Acts*, 565.

28. For example, *Timaeus* 28A, 29A. The term δημιουργός appears once in the LXX (2 Macc 4:1) and once in the NT (Heb 11:10), while the related verb δημιουργέω occurs three times in the LXX (2 Macc 10:2; 4 Macc 7:8; Wis 15:13) and none in the NT. In the LXX, two refer to conceiving something (evil deeds and a law), two to making idolatrous objects (altars and idols). In Hebrews, the reference is to God himself as the "builder" of the eschatological (heavenly) city: ἐξεδέχετο γὰρ τὴν τοὺς θεμελίους ἔχουσαν πόλιν ἧς τεχνίτης καὶ δημιουργὸς ὁ θεός. See further references to a "creator" in Parsons, *Acts*, 246.

29. Barrett, *Acts*, 2.840.

30. Marshall, *Acts TNTC*, 286; Dibelius, "Areopagus," 46. Cf. Downing, "Pagan Theism" and Downing, "Common Ground."

31. Pervo, *Acts*, 438.

32. Cf. Gourgues, "Littérature profane," 250–55 and Fitzmyer, *Acts*, 608.

33. Lucian, *Jupp. trag.* 34–52 provides an entertaining satirical glimpse of what these may have looked like.

34. As argued by Van Nuffelen, *Rethinking the Gods*; on "etiquette," see Martin, *Inventing Superstition*; the expression "post-Hellenistic" is used to characterize the period running from the first century BC to the second century AD. Concerning the various Greek philosophical systems of thought, we refer the reader to standard introductions, e.g., Jaeger, *Theology*; Clark, *Thales to Dewey*, 3–180; Bréhier, *Histoire*, 1.37–365; and Copleston, *Greece and Rome*.

35. On the surface, Paul's words in vv. 24–25 sound like the broadly-shared arguments against "popular" pagan cultic practice and conceptions, as noted by Rowe, *World Upside Down*, 35.

new lines.³⁶ Socrates, Plato, and Aristotle crystallized this new sensibility in systems that influenced greatly subsequent thinkers.³⁷ It produced what Dale Martin calls the "Grand Optimal Illusion":

> The important revolution in ancient thinking that Plato here represents (I do not believe he invented it) is not the assumption of hierarchy—that was everywhere in the ancient world—but the assumption that the different hierarchical scales *match one another*: that superior beings are superior with regard to morality as well as intellect, power, and beauty. Ontological hierarchy is matched by axiological hierarchy.³⁸

The Post-Hellenistic period saw a return to classical traditions, especially to Plato and Aristotle. This included a re-appropriation of "traditional religion" through a demythologizing philosophical interpretation of its myths, poets (especially Homer and Hesiod) and rituals, of which Plutarch's works are a prime example.³⁹ As Van Nuffelen has shown, these two categories—"cosmic hierarchy" and "ancient wisdom"—are the foundations for the philosophical thinking about religion during the historical period constitutive of the "cultural encyclopaedia" of the Areopagitica.

First, it should be remembered that, as we noted earlier, there is no distinct concept of "supernatural" in the ancient Greek world. "Nature" (φύσις)—or the "universe" (κόσμος)—is everything there is.⁴⁰ The gods—θεοί, δαίμονες, or δαιμόνια—are as much part of this whole as the rest, or they do not exist at all.⁴¹ Even the most apparently dualistic cosmologies assumed an ontological monism, a continuum from the lowest to the highest forms of being or existence.⁴² There is no true tran-

---

36. Note that they did not deny "divine intervention" as such, but reconfigured its modes, nature and extent. See Martin, *Inventing Superstition*, 36–50.

37. "In fact, the centrality of Plato and Aristotle for ancient philosophy and science meant that their notions of nature and divine activity within it exerted tremendous influence on other intellectuals for the duration of the ancient world." Martin, *Inventing Superstition*, 51, cf. 76–78. Martin presents Theophrastus as an excellent representative of this "new sensibility," pp. 21–35.

38. Martin, *Inventing Superstition*, 60 (emphasis original). It is important to note with Martin that this was not built on new evidence or arguments, but on socially-shared *assumptions*.

39. Especially *De Supestitione* and *De Iside et Osiride*. See discussion in Attridge, "Philosophical Critique," 75–77; cf. the fuller analysis in Van Nuffelen, *Rethinking the Gods*, 48–71.

40. So much so that for some of them, like Galen, it is itself divine. See Martin, *Inventing Superstition*, 117–19 and Klauck, *Magic and Paganism*, 84.

41. See Martin, *Inventing Superstition*, 14–15; Klauck, *Religious Context*, 354; and Meijer, "Philosophers," 224–27. This is true whether the gods are construed as the pantheistic Logos of Stoicism, the Platonic hierarchy of Ideas (whether Plato considered them to be gods or not), astral gods, Olympian gods (cf. *Timaeus* 40D, 41A), daimons and heroes (cf. MacMullen, *Paganism*, 79–80), or the materialistic, distant and uninvolved gods of Epicureanism (cf. Attridge, "Philosophical Critique," 51–53 and Klauck, *Religious Context*, 393).

42. "'Divinity' in the Greek world was basically a state of 'more or less,' referring to a relative position on a hierarchical scale from inferior to superior." Martin, *Inventing Superstition*, 183. Cf. Martin, *Corinthian Body*, 116 and Van Nuffelen, *Rethinking the Gods*, 160. This is true both ontologically and ethically: see the discussion of *isonomia* in Martin, *Inventing Superstition*, 229–37.

scendence, and therefore no true immanence either. Ultimate reality is, at the end of day, impersonal and abstract.[43] The "creator" is strictly an artisan: he gives shape, not existence, to the world; he works with pre-existing and eternal "stuff" (ὕλη); he is limited by the nature of that material and by what is "possible," whether defined in an abstract manner, as the Ideas (e.g., in *Phaedr.* 249C), or as the Logos.[44] Such a view of creation enables visible representations of divine realities.[45] It is therefore not surprising that the philosophers of the period commonly participated fully in the "popular" or "traditional" pagan rituals of their time. Some even became priests, like Plutarch who served the Delphi sanctuary.

In this light, the particular emphases of Paul's speech prove to be strictly polemical not only in relation to so-called popular paganism, but also in relation to these "higher"—pagan—philosophies.[46] Bruce was correct after all. Our interpretation must take full account of the fact that Paul begins his argument with the uncompromising affirmation that the one eternal, transcendent and personal God—of whom the local alternatives are *counterfeits* (religiously considered) and *functional equivalents* (sociologically and culturally considered)—is the Creator of everything that was ever made.[47] There is no space left for a demiurge, an eternal primeval substance, or a shape-giving impersonal principle in Paul's words.[48] His God gave the *prima materia* its existence as much as its shape. He is the one who *continually* sustains his creatures by providing them with life, movement and all they need to exist (vv. 25, 28). More-

43. See Owen, "Scope," 140.

44. Contra Keener, *Acts*, 3.2637. See Martin, *Inventing Superstition*, 111–13 on Galen's polemic with the Jewish and Christian view of the Creator's freedom to create things as he wished. It should also be noted that for Plato, the Demiurge was never considered in religious terms (to be worshiped), and that, contrary to what is sometimes said, the *Timaeus* does *not* teach a "beginning" to the world that could be related to the Christian notion of *creatio ex nihilo*. See Owen, "Scope," 138; Dennison, *Two-Age*, 1–10; and Clark, *Thales to Dewey*, 91–95, 146–69. The reference to *Phaedrus* comes from Meijer, "Philosophers," 244.

45. As noted by Rowe, *World Upside Down*, 34.

46. Contrary to interpretations that perceive a rapprochement with the audience or a convergence of views and/or arguments concerning "popular" paganism, e.g., Malherbe, *Paul and the Popular Philosophers*, 151; Balch, "Areopagus Speech"; or Schnabel, *Paul*, 1399–1400. Paul is not siding with *earlier* forms of these philosophical schools against his contemporaries either. They were just as compromised with "popular" forms of pagan idolatry anyway. See Winter, "Public and Private," 138–40; Gärtner, *Areopagus Speech*, 226–28; and Hansen, "Preaching and Defence," 309–10. Finally, "it is clear that, whether Paul had the philosophers in mind or not, they too, according to his principles, fell into idolatry of a subtler kind in so far as they were led to venerate the κόσμος as divine." Owen, "Scope," 142. Idols of the mind (ἐνθυμήσεως ἀνθρώπου) are no less idols than physical ones (χαράγματι τέχνης), as v. 29 indicates!

47. So also Fitzmyer, *Acts*, 608 and Shields, "Areopagus Sermon," 33; contra Legrand, "Unknown God," 164, who sees the "unknown god" as the actual starting-point of Paul's argument.

48. See Bruce, *Acts Greek*, 381 and Gourgues, "Littérature profane," 269. Keener's reduction of the exclusion of a demiurge to an argument "from silence" based on a summary statement (Keener, *Acts*, 3.2638–39) is missing the point, probably because he understands Paul's words from the depicted audience's point of view.

over, this God is not infused in or confused with this world, but he *transcends* it and rules over it as a Lord who has personality, wisdom, will and purpose (vv. 26–27).[49] The Creator/creature distinction is absolute. Yet the transcendent God is *immanently* present with his creatures, bestowing on them his good gifts and directing all their affairs (vv. 26–27; cf. 14:17).[50] Those various points strike directly at the foundations of all Greek philosophical systems, and do not offer any rapprochement as far as the *content* is concerned.[51] At the same time, there is enough *formal* resemblance that Paul's speech is intelligible to his audience in the end.

We must also point out that Paul is not depicted as arguing from the "first principles" that were the foundations of all Greek philosophical systems, but rather from the God of biblical revelation.[52] Neither is Paul arguing that Christianity is a better philosophy, either by claiming that the OT scriptures are the ultimate source of philosophical truth (as Josephus and certain second century Apologists do), or by demythologizing the OT or the Greek poets in the typical philosophical fashion of the time.[53] It seems, therefore, that the *crux* of the matter is the pagans' failure to recognize the transcendent-immanent Creator and Lord of all that is.[54] Alternatively, Dunn suggests that Luke is here developing the first principles of a natural theol-

---

49. See also Witherington, *Acts*, 535.

50. We therefore strongly disagree with Gärtner when he writes: "The way in which the Areopagus speech pictures God seems to bear traces of both the immanent and the transcendent conception of Him. The speech is not univocal on this point, but appears to be composed of disparate elements showing both Jewish-Christian and Stoic characteristics." Gärtner, *Areopagus Speech*, 170–71. Such a judgment seems based on the erroneous idea that the Jewish-Christian understanding of God centers exclusively or primarily on *transcendence*. Gärtner appears to be influenced by an existentialist (possibly Neo-orthodox) strand of theology, a peculiar perspective that is *not* representative of the common and traditional Christian understanding of God—even less of the biblical presentation of Yahweh/God—as being *both* transcendent and immanent. The immanence appearing in the Areopagitica does not owe anything to Stoicism but everything to the OT portrait of the transcendent God who is present among his people and at work in the world. Transcendence and immanence define and explain each other. See Bavinck, *RD 2* and Frame, *Doctrine of God*, especially pp. 21–115. Cf. the interesting comments on this issue in Tannehill, *Acts*, 215.

51. "At the same time, the narrative furthers the reshaping of the readers' religious imagination by placing its theological foundation in the transcendence of the Creator God over the world of images. That such a move is conceptually similar to the statement in Acts 14:15 is not mere coincidence. Much to the contrary, the similarity points to a fundamentally important part of Luke's narrative project vis-à-vis gentile converts: to break the connection between God and the world that underwrites pagan religion." Rowe, *World Upside Down*, 36.

52. A point Bruce makes emphatically in, for example, *Acts NICNT*, 355; *Defence of the Gospel*, 38; "Paul and Athenians," 9; and *Acts Greek*, 382. Greg Bahnsen develops Bruce's point further in *Always Ready*, 264–65. "Deliberately the nature of this God is defined not by Greek (ontological) categories but by a biblical quotation [viz., Isa 42:5]." Conzelmann, "Areopagus," 221.

53. On the differences with Josephus and the Apologists, see Wendel, *Scriptural Interpretation*, 147–48; contra Jipp, "Paul's Areopagus Speech."

54. See Owen, "Scope," 137. This is consistent with the fact that, in Luke-Acts, *sin* is essentially idolatry, the failure or refusal to acknowledge Yahweh as the one and only God, as in the first two commandments of the Decalogue. Cf. Jervell, *Theology of Acts*, 20.

ogy, meant to function as the foundation for critiquing his audience's own natural theology.[55] In the following discussion, we will use Bruce Shield's definitions of key expressions for clarity's sake:

> "Creation theology" and "theology of creation" are used synonymously to refer to the understanding of the creation of the universe by God and the universe as the creation of God. When the term "natural theology" appears, it refers to an understanding of God arrived at through philosophical speculation on the phenomena of the physical universe (nature). By "natural revelation" is meant God making something of himself known through nature.[56]

Based on these definitions, it is rather clear that the Areopagitica does *not* develop or sketch a "natural theology," but rather a "theology of creation"—and history.[57] It is evident from Paul's starting-point (and development) that what he presents to his audience is not a demonstration of God's existence and attributes from the order and rationality of the κόσμος or from πρόνοια ("providence") like the Stoics and some Hellenistic Jews did (e.g., Wisdom of Solomon), but rather an interpretation of nature and history on the basis of the nature and character of the God who is their Creator and Lord.[58] To use systematic-theological categories, Paul is using *special revelation* to bring out the meaning and import of *natural revelation*.[59]

Moreover Paul/Luke is not expounding a full theology of creation in these verses, so the elements included must serve a different purpose.[60] That God is Creator is known only by *special* revelation and faith, not by a reasoned argument based on natural revelation.[61] Paul, as an apostle or missionary, is the divinely-authorized carrier of that type of revelation.[62] Hence, Paul articulates his argument around Yahweh's prerogatives as Creator, Lord, and Judge of the whole world, in continuity with the pattern found in Scripture as a whole.[63] Our author is not using the premises or argu-

---

55. Dunn, *Acts*, 225.

56. Shields, "Areopagus Sermon," 23n2.

57. When considering vv. 30–31, we will see that this theology of creation and history is of a redemptive-historical nature.

58. Thus playing a very similar role to Gen 1:1 (ἐν ἀρχῇ ἐποίησεν ὁ θεὸς τὸν οὐρανὸν καὶ τὴν γῆν) for the creation accounts (the first polemic against pagan idolatry in the biblical canon) and everything that follows.

59. Cf. Shields, "Areopagus Sermon," 40. For substantial studies of those theological concepts and their relationship to Christian theologizing, see Bavinck, *RD 1*; Berkouwer, *General Revelation*; Demarest, *General Revelation*; and Frame, *DKG*. For an illuminating explanation of the interrelationship of the two kinds of devine revelation, see Van Til, "Nature and Scripture."

60. See Shields, "Areopagus Sermon," 35, 25.

61. In agreement with Heb 11:3, "by faith we understand that the universe was created by the word of God." See Owen, "Scope," 139; Barrett, *Acts*, 2.840; and Hanson, *Acts*, 178–79. See the denial of a merely "general revelatory" nature of the speech in Beale, *We Become*, 281.

62. See our earlier discussion of Paul's authority and the nature of his communication as indicated by the verb καταγγέλλω in v. 23.

63. Cf. Bruce, *Defence of the Gospel*, 38 and Bruce, *Paul*, 239. Our use of "Lord" both includes and exceeds Bruce's use of "sustainer," in keeping with Paul's usage here.

ments of the philosophical tradition.⁶⁴ The God of biblical revelation is his *principium* for human knowledge of the world and its history, as well as the Christian proclamation and defense of the gospel.⁶⁵

God's relationship to the world has immediate consequences for the way he ought to be worshiped. Because he is Creator, he is also Lord. Since he is Lord of the universe, how could he dwell in temples made by (human) hands?⁶⁶ Verse 24b (οὐκ ἐν χειροποιήτοις ναοῖς κατοικεῖ) is nearly identical to Acts 7:48a (ἀλλ' οὐχ ὁ ὕψιστος ἐν χειροποιήτοις κατοικεῖ), an intratextual link that connects the text of Isa 66:1–2 (cited as confirming evidence in 7:49–50, with minor variations) with Paul's polemic.⁶⁷ The main difference between the two Lukan texts is the use of "Lord of heaven and earth" (οὐρανοῦ καὶ γῆς ὑπάρχων κύριος) in 24a and "the Most High" (ὁ ὕψιστος) in 7:48a.⁶⁸ This parallel confirms the transcendent nature of the lordship in view, as well as the OT anchorage of Paul/Luke's thought. The remainder of both verses is virtually identical, with v. 24b using "temples" or "shrines" (ναοῖς)⁶⁹ while 7:48 leaves the referent of χειροποιήτοις indeterminate.⁷⁰

64. As argued by Bahnsen, *Always Ready*, 246. See also Rothschild, *Paul in Athens*, 5.

65. See Van Til, *Introduction to ST2*, 29–31 for a definition of the concept (the book for its application to systematic theology); Bavinck, *RD 1*, Part 3 and Van Til, *Survey of Epistemology* for fuller discussions.

66. Though the Stoics were critical of temples and shrines (examples in des Places, "Actes 17, 24"; Conzelmann, *Acts*, 141–42; and Gourgues, "Littérature profane," 251–53), their ground for doing so was different from Paul's. In their eyes, temples and shrines could not enclose the divine because it is in all things, and none of them could be "worthy" of the divine either, due to their ontological hierarchy. For Paul, the reason is that God is the *transcendent Lord* of heaven and earth, whose abode cannot therefore be delineated, defined, decided or controlled by any creature, including mankind. See Rowe, *World Upside Down*, 36.

67. Acts 7:49–50: "ὁ οὐρανός μοι θρόνος, ἡ δὲ γῆ ὑποπόδιον τῶν ποδῶν μου· ποῖον οἶκον οἰκοδομήσετέ μοι, λέγει κύριος, ἢ τίς τόπος τῆς καταπαύσεώς μου; οὐχὶ ἡ χείρ μου ἐποίησεν ταῦτα πάντα;" See discussion in Gärtner, *Areopagus Speech*, 208 and Gärtner, "Paulus." Alexander, *Acts*, 2.154 reminds his readers that Paul may have personally heard Stephen's speech. 7:41 roots the whole religious-covenantal history of Israel in the episode of the golden calf—the nation's archetypal sin of idolatry—using the expression ἐν τοῖς ἔργοις τῶν χειρῶν αὐτῶν (see Beale, *We Become*, 192).

68. See the LXX usage for this term, particularly in: Gen 14:18, 19, 20, 22; Deut 32:8; Psalms (22 times in reference to Yahweh), especially Ps 45:5; 46:3; 77:17, 35, 56; 82:19; 86:5; 96:9; Daniel (14 times); and Isa 14:14 and 57:15.

69. On the exact referent in our text, see the discussion in Rowe, *World Upside Down*, 34. Luke uses ναός to refer to a temple only six times: four in the Gospel, for the Jerusalem temple (1:9, 21, 22; 23:45, the rending of the inner curtain at the moment of Christ's death), and two in Acts, both for pagan temples (17:24; 19:24: the silver temples crafted by Demetrius). Otherwise, he mostly uses the word ἱερόν: fourteen times in the Gospel and twenty-four times in Acts. Of those, only one is not a reference to the Jerusalem temple: 19:27 (Demetrius speaks of the temple of Artemis). Surprisingly, Luke uses the word οἶκος a very common word in the LXX—only three times in that context, all of which are in Acts 7: two in the Isa 66:1–2 quotation, and the third (v. 47) preparing the way for that quotation, echoing its wording. The other references to Yahweh's temple in Stephen's speech—which is focused on Israel's idolatrous relation to it—are indirect (understood, implied or periphrastic), besides the use of σκηνή in v. 44 for the Mosaic tabernacle and in v. 43 in reference to Moloch (quoting Amos 5:25–27).

70. "[L]a Septante a érigé l'adjectif χειροποίητος *(fait de main d'homme)* en terme technique

The issue here is whether God "dwells" (κατοικεῖ) in *man-made* temples of any kind at all.⁷¹ The heart of the polemic is not whether God can be present in or be attached to a sanctuary *per se*,⁷² but whether it can be the exclusive *locus* of his presence, concern, and authority, and whether *man* can legitimately determine this *locus*.⁷³ Here it is important to note the contrast with v. 26, where God's sovereignty expresses itself in his authority to determine where peoples and nations are dwelling.⁷⁴ In light of v. 26, we can say that the *crux* of the matter is who, of God or man, has sovereignty over the other, this prerogative being considered in terms of making and defining dwelling places. Paul answers emphatically that God alone has this power and authority, for both himself and his creatures.⁷⁵

This theme is an important anti-idol theme in Isaiah. Not only is an idol fashioned by man and is carried to its place by him, but man decides its abode and *fastens*

---

de l'idolâtrie." Marguerat, *Actes*, 2.158 (emphasis original). Every single occurrence of the word in the LXX refers to an idolatrous object. Of its four other NT occurrences, see especially Mark 14:58 (together with its antonym ἀχειροποίητος) concerning the usage of this term in ancient literature, see Van der Horst, "New Altar," 66–67); Heb 9:11, 24; Eph 2:11 applies the term to circumcision. See also the occurrences of its antonym in 2 Cor 5:1 and Col 2:11. Cf. the discussion of the concept in Beale, *We Become*, 190–96. Even if the depicted audience would have sensed a negative connotation in the use of this term, they would not have measured its full force, contrary to Luke's reader.

71. The phrasing is such that only the "man-made temples" element is negated. It implies that God does "dwell" somewhere, but somewhere of a totally different kind, viz., the heavenly temple-palace-house (cf., e.g., Luke 3:21–22; 11:13; Acts 1:11; 7:55–56; 9:3; Heb 9:11, 24; Rev 4–5; 21:2).

72. This is a given in the OT. However, God's name and presence could be associated with no other place than the one chosen by *God* himself. For God's presence, see Exod 33:7–11; 40:38; Lev 16:2; 1 Kgs 8:10–11; Isa 6:1–8; for God's exclusive prerogative in choosing the place, see Deut 12:11; 14:23; 16:2, 6, 11; 23:16; 2 Chr 7:12; Neh 1:9; Ps 132:13–14. See further Beale, *Temple*, 222–28, 230–32. Moreover, "While God condescended to dwell in a handmade structure for a brief time in the Old Testament period and commanded Israel to worship him at that temple, his ultimate design was that his presence would break out of that human structure and spread throughout the earth through Christ, his Spirit and his people. Thus to continue to worship at the old architectural temple and not to worship Christ is to make an idol out of the temple." Beale, *We Become*, 191.

73. Cf. Witherington, *NT Story*, 132. Paganism's association of gods with particular places or peoples, and also with a limited sphere of concern and sovereignty (whether geographical or existential), finds its most concrete expression in the use of temples and shrines. The OT is full of illustrations of this principle, such as 1 Samuel 5–6. Cf. Gourgues, "Littérature profane," 250.

74. V. 26 uses both the present infinitive (κατοικεῖν) of the same verb and the cognate noun κατοικία. 26a proclaims God's absolute sovereignty to determine the mandate for mankind to cover the face of the earth (cf. Gen 1:28; 9:1; 11:8, 9), while 26b affirms his authority to fix the boundaries of all nations (cf. Genesis 10). Besides, the use of τέ together with ἐποίησεν indicates that v. 26 continues the theme of vv. 24–25, narrowing it down to a particular instance of the creational life-giving activity of God. Hence, it is clear that v. 26 continues and develops the polemic started in v. 24b.

75. "Because of the universality of his reign, God cannot be domesticated—not even by temples (v. 24)." Carson, "Athens Revisited," 392. Cf. Carson, *Gagging*, 500 and Soards, *Speeches in Acts*, 97. The NT makes explicit something that is mostly implicit in the OT: God dwells in a palace/temple/sanctuary that *he* has made for himself (in contrast with *man*-made temples), one that transcends and is outside the visible world. This idea is already present in the Isaianic image of the heavens being God's throne as well as in Solomon's prayer of 1 Kings 8 (see especially vv. 23, 27, 29–30, 33–34; cf. 12–13, 16, 20). It is asserted explicitly in Heb 8:1–5 and 9:11, 24, two passages building directly upon Exod 25:40.

it to make sure it will not move (Isa 46:7). Being able to decide another's dwelling place and the limits of his movement is therefore a function of one's authority and control over that other. Israel's idolatrous confusion on this point is the background for Yahweh's pronouncement in Isa 66:1–2 and 57:15.[76] Both texts emphasize at the same time God's transcendence—and inability to be constrained to a man-made temple—and his close presence with those whom he loves—the humble and repenting ones. This point is at the core of Stephen's speech: God is free to be with his elect *wherever* they might be. This polemic reveals an essential feature of idolatry: its purpose is to control the gods so as to secure or exact their benefaction.[77] Through it, man is seeking to become the master and make the god his servant.[78] This point is even clearer in the light of v. 25.

The Self-Sufficient Beneficent God

"After the polemic against the temple comes the attack on sacrifices."[79] There is a thematic progression here, from "hand-made temples" to "human service."[80] This progression is reinforced by the movement from God as Creator of the whole world, to God the giver of life, breath, and everything to his creature, i.e., man. The phrase πᾶσι ζωὴν καὶ πνοὴν καὶ τὰ πάντα could be understood in a generic way of all "breathing" creatures (since πᾶσι could be either masculine or neuter), therefore including animals (in the OT world a plant is not a "living being," i.e., a ψυχὴν ζῶσαν or נֶפֶשׁ חַיָּה). However, the context militates in favor of understanding the referent to be human beings (if not exclusively, at least primarily): first, the focus has shifted to *human* activity; second, the contrast is between *man's* activity toward God and God's activity toward "all"; third, the triad is part of the Isa 42:5 allusion, where these gifts concern "the people" and "the walking"; finally, this triad is very similar to the one found in 28a.[81] In fact,

---

76. Ancient Israel's idolatrous thinking concluded that because God's temple was in Jerusalem, the city and its population was safe, whatever they did. God was *bound* to the city and the people, and had no other choice but to protect and bless them.

77. Cf. the intriguing appropriation of this principle in existentialist terms in Bultmann, "Prédication."

78. However, this leads ironically to man being enslaved to his idols, as he develops an increasing dependence on them. See the analysis of this dynamic in Keyes, "Idol Factory."

79. Haenchen, *Acts*, 522. The verb θεραπεύω usually means "to heal" in the New Testament, but in the Greek literature and the LXX the term frequently denotes man's "service" to the gods or to Yahweh (e.g., Isa 54:17). See *LSJ*.

80. Though it is clearly implied that the "hands" that made the temples were human, it is only implicit in v. 24b, in contrast to v. 25a. This is consistent with the overall movement of the speech that will now dedicate several verses to the relationship of God with man and reciprocally (vv. 25–31).

81. "The threefold gift in 17:25 probably anticipates the threefold expression of dependence in the quotation in 17:28, which begins with the same opening element ('live')." Keener, *Acts*, 3.2644.

the two triads seem to form an *inclusio* framing a development concerned with God's providential care for his human creatures.[82]

The triad modifies the text of Isa 42:5 LXX in three ways: 1) Luke uses ζωὴν καὶ πνοήν instead of πνοήν and πνεῦμα;[83] 2) he substitutes "to all" (πᾶσι) for τῷ λαῷ (further defined in Isaiah as τοῖς πατοῦσιν αὐτήν, i.e., τὴν γῆν);[84] 3) τὰ πάντα, "and everything," is added, increasing the sense of totality.[85] The use of πᾶσι ... τὰ πάντα (cf. πάντας πανταχοῦ in v. 30), its assonance, and the paronomasia of ζωὴν καὶ πνοήν all contribute to making the expression emphatic.[86] By using three near-synonymous expressions, it produces a powerful statement of man's absolute and permanent dependence on God for the most basic element of his existence: his very life.[87] Stoics could also speak of the divine as the source of life, but they meant something radically different. Their pantheistic ontology considered the divine itself to be what animates all things. Paul, on the contrary, is speaking of something that is distinct from God and can therefore be communicated to his creature.[88] Thus, this verse affirms an absolute contrast between the divine and the human. And this contrast serves to highlight a radical antithesis: the God who gives life to man—something closely related to being his Creator, as in v. 26a—has nothing in common with the lifeless and impotent idols-deities that man manufactures to put and serve in "hand-made" temples.[89]

---

82. Barrett, *Acts*, 2.841, also thinks that both refer to human beings. Contra Gärtner, *Areopagus Speech*, 198, who considers that one triad speaks of creation at large (25b) while the other speaks only of mankind (28a).

83. The change is often understood as an effort to avoid confusion in the Christian reader who might have understood πνεῦμα to mean the Holy Spirit (for example, Haenchen, *Acts*, 522n7). Even if correct, this view does not account for the *choice* of words itself. It seems preferable to explain Luke's wording—and his motive—by the assimilation of the language of Gen 2:7 LXX, where Adam's coming to life is depicted as the result of God's breathing in him the πνοὴν ζωῆς. Cf. 2 Macc 7:23.

84. In the LXX and Luke-Acts λαός (singular) is consistently used to refer to the people of Israel. So much so that Van de Sandt reckons that out of the 79 uses of the word in the singular in Luke-Acts, only two do not refer to the whole or a part of Israel: Acts 15:14 and 18:10 ("Fate of Gentiles," 66n38). Isa 42:5, however, is a "universalist" passage where vocabulary typically referring to Israel (like λαός and γῆ) is used for the whole world and all of mankind. Hence, v. 6—used by Paul in Acts 13:47—defines the mission of the Servant in favor of the nations. Luke is therefore not changing the meaning of the passage, but makes it explicit and unambiguous.

85. Barrett notes that τὰ πάντα "is deliberately imprecise" (*Acts*, 2.841). It seems to be a general reference to everything people need for life—such as food and water—since the references to "life" and "breath" are very concrete and natural. It is not ontological in nature. The background of the triad is undoubtedly the OT, not Greek philosophy.

86. See *BegC*, 4.215.

87. See Barrett, *Acts*, 2.841. The present (imperfective) participle διδούς functions in 25b like ὑπάρχων does in 24b. It has a gnomic force, denoting a universal truth. It is describing the state of affairs since the creation of the first human being until the Parousia and the re-creation of all things. Man's dependence on God is *intrinsic* to his being a creature.

88. Contra Sanders, *No Other Name*, 245.

89. Barrett, *Acts*, 2.840–41. This point finds a further development in vv. 28–29 where *life* clearly sets God apart from idols.

Verse 25a reinforces this point. *Since* God is the giver of life and all that man needs for his existence, *then* he cannot be in need of man's sacrifices (or religious service in general).[90] God gives and man receives—not the reverse. Scholars often depict v. 25 as dealing with God's activity as the sustainer of his creation, a biblical notion. However, the connection between vv. 24 and 25 (and 26) indicates that God's characterization as universal *Lord* is here furthered. One of the characteristic virtues of lords, kings and emperors of the ancient world was to be the *benefactors* of their people and hence to bestow their generosity upon them. The idea of a mere sustainer tends towards an abstract ontology, while Luke is here continuing his depiction of Yahweh as the King of kings who reigns over mankind (cf. "every nation" in v. 26). This point is another example of anti-idol polemic, one that challenges both the pagan gods (cf. 1 Cor 8:5–6) and the rulers of the nations—including the Roman emperor.[91] Verse 25 shifts the context from the theological category of "creation" or preservation (v. 24a) to that of "common grace" or providence.[92] Anyway, the logic of the argument is at the same time simple and irresistible: God made all things, he is therefore Lord of all things (which means he alone legitimately owns them); God graciously dispenses what belongs to him to his creatures (who depend entirely on him for even the most elementary aspect of their existence); therefore it makes no sense to imagine that man could offer God anything he would genuinely need or lack.[93]

An obvious parallel to this thought is found in Psalm 50, especially vv. 7–15.[94] This psalm argues that Yahweh does not need man's sacrifice (e.g., he does not need

---

90. The present participle προσδεόμενος carries also a gnomic force. It asserts a general truth: God *never* benefits from—even less depends upon—man's service and offerings. Note that it is in the passive voice, God being its subject not its object. This reinforces the reader's sense of Yahweh's centrality and sovereignty.

91. Cf. Witherington, "Salvation and Health," 148; Krodel, *Acts*, 5; Baugh, "1 Tim 4:10"; and Joel B. Green, "Salvation."

92. Cf. Bock, *Acts*, 566. Theologically speaking, nothing is purely "creational" after the fall of Adam, but is always a combination of creation, common curse and common grace, moving towards the eschatological poles of eternal judgment or consummate redemption. See Van Til, *Common Grace* and Bavinck, "Common Grace." Verse 25 echoes Acts 14:17, itself a reminiscence of Luke 6:35 (cf. Matt 5:45).

93. Some scholars claim that the Areopagitica is joining hands with the Stoics—one could add probably the Epicureans—at this point, by teaching God's self-sufficiency or *aseity*. See, e.g., Dibelius, "Areopagus," 43–46. and Haenchen, *Acts*, 522n5, a point of view echoed by Samuel, "Paul on the Areopagus," 23. Such judgment, however, is once again arbitrarily translating Paul's biblical thought into philosophical and ontological categories foreign to the text. The Areopagitica is indeed affirming God's "self-sufficiency" and "aseity" here (cf. Carson, "Athens Revisited," 392 and Carson, *Gagging*, 500), but from a biblical, rather than philosophical, conception of God's nature. It does so in a way that would be understandable and would even sound "congenial" (so Gaventa, *Acts*, 250–51) to a philosophically-educated audience.

94. Dibelius ("Areopagus," 45) is incorrect when he asserts that the notion of God's self-sufficiency is found only twice in the LXX, in texts obviously dependent on Hellenistic ideas (viz., 2 Macc 14:35 and 3 Macc 2:9–10). *Pace* Haenchen, Psalm 50 (49 LXX) is very relevant to our passage, as vv. 12 ("If I were hungry, I would not tell you, for the world and its fullness are mine") and 13 ("Do I eat the flesh of bulls or drink the blood of goats?") make clear. It is also striking that v. 14 refers to Yahweh

food for his sustenance) and reiterates what he requires from his people (among others: justice, righteousness and true worship coming from faith and humility). Psalm 50 belongs to a group of OT passages depicting God judging Israel's (false) worship (for example, Isa 1:11–17; 29:13; and Mic 6:6–8).[95] As is typical in these texts, Yahweh first reminds his people that he does not need their sacrifices and that, therefore, he is not indebted to them in any way. He thereby dispels their idolatrous notions that they can coax him to bless them on account of their religious performances. God then reminds them that what he wants is not formal or external worship ("with their lips"), but one that is driven by a contrite heart—i.e., characterized by humility before Yahweh, repentance for one's sins and faith in God's mercy and salvific provision—and produces a life of mercy, righteousness, and justice. This family of texts composes the background of the Areopagitica's concept of God's self-sufficiency, Ps 50:12–13 possibly being its closest parallel.

The setting for both Acts 17:25 and Psalm 50 is not philosophical speculation, but *worship* that is consistent—or not—with God's self-revelation. This criterion is applied in our text to the Athenian—i.e., pagan—religion, thereby demonstrating its utter inadequacy in relationship to the true God. Through the radical contrast between God and man regarding who is dependent on who, it is the absolute antithesis between Yahweh and pagan idols/deities that is being highlighted. The God who made all things and gives life to all men has nothing in common with the gods men enclose in temples and who depend on their gifts and sacrifices.[96]

In contrast, the OT sacrificial system is designed entirely for the benefit of the people of Israel. Yahweh himself does not gain anything from it. The various sacrifices are all concerned with Israel's relationship with their God, whether they provide a means for their sins to be forgiven, for the cleansing of their impurity, the payment of their vows, the expression of their thanksgiving or a picture of their communion with him. Even Israel's tithes are ultimately for the people's benefit. It is when Israel thinks according to pagan wisdom about sacrifices that God rebukes her and corrects her mistaken opinion as in the passages cited above.[97]

---

as ὁ ὕψιστος, just like Acts 7:48. What disqualifies this psalm, according to Haenchen, is that it "does not speak about the θεῖον which is ἀπροσδεές." Haenchen, *Acts*, 522n5. The problem is that Acts 17:25 does not speak in that manner either! We hear of ὁ θεὸς ὁ ποιήσας ... ὑπάρχων κύριος, who is not served by human hands as if he "lacked" anything. Not only is the subject the *person* of God and not the divine nature, but the verb προσδέομαι is used in a common and non-philosophical (in fact, biblical) way, in continuity with the LXX usage (cf. Prov 12:9; Sir 4:3; 11:12; 13:3; 18:32; 42:21; it is a *hapax* in the NT).

95. See Bruce, *Acts NICNT*, 357n43.

96. A prominent argument in Isaiah's anti-idol polemics, especially the parodies. See Clifford, "Idol Passages"; Holter, *Second Isaiah*; and Pao, *Acts and INE*, 195.

97. See Waltke and Yu, *OT Theology*, 445–78 for a theological study of the tabernacle and the sacrifices in the Mosaic law; and Watts, "Consolation or Confrontation" for a discussion of Israel's use of "pagan wisdom."

Conclusion: Yahweh Alone Is God

Because he is Creator and Lord of all, God cannot be coaxed, manipulated, or coerced by man's religious devices, contrary to the way pagan worshipers relate to their gods and idols. Verses 24–25 constitute a powerful anti-idol polemic that indirectly but effectively "negates the whole pagan belief in gods"[98] as well as the metaphysical speculations of the philosophers. They further Paul's (and Luke's) vindication of Yahweh's sole claim to divinity, as well as of his absolute sovereignty and authority over (and independence from) all creatures (including the depicted audience) in all respects, especially religion. Those two verses continue and develop the themes of the Athenians' ignorance and of the offensive nature of their religious beliefs and practices in Yahweh's eyes, therefore implying the divine condemnation of the Athenians in particular and of paganism in general.[99]

---

98. Haenchen, *Acts*, 522–23.

99. "To hear clearly παροξύνομαι and κατείδωλος in Acts 17:16 is to understand 17:24–25 at the narrative theological level not so much as philosophical critique as a skillfully articulated charge of idolatry." Rowe, *World Upside Down*, 36.

CHAPTER 7

Incriminating Evidence: The Divine Design for Mankind (Acts 17:26–27)

Introduction

After some general comments on the first clause of verse 26, Witherington ominously states: "The text then becomes complex and highly debated."[1] Both the construction and the import of vv. 26–27 have been the cause of much scholarly debate, resulting in little consensus.[2] The wording would fit in either the biblical or the Hellenistic thought-world, yet carry radically different meanings.[3] In-story, that feature creates linguistic points of contact that make genuine communication between the two religious worlds possible.[4] It is in continuity with the pattern of narrative "ambivalence" we encountered in the speech so far.

Verses 26–27 are essential to Dibelius' argument in favor of a philosophical interpretation of the speech. In his eyes, one encounters in these verses a ("second") theme of an unmistakably Stoic (and therefore "Hellenistic" in contradistinction with "Jewish") origin and import.[5] Following his or similar tracks, some interpreters claim that these verses demonstrate that people can truly—i.e., savingly—seek and find God through providence and/or general revelation.[6] However, we concur

---

1. Witherington, *Acts*, 526.

2. Cf. Haenchen, *Acts*, 523. These verses are at the heart of the controversy crystallized in the works of Dibelius and Gärtner.

3. Barrett, "Paul at Athens," 148–49.

4. See the comments on vv. 24–29 in Stonehouse, "Areopagus Address," 26; Barrett, "Paul at Athens," 149, comes to a similar conclusion.

5. See Dibelius, "Areopagus," 32. Dibelius deems the speech to be a Lukan interpolation into an existing itinerary (a Pauline source): Dibelius, "Areopagus," 71–76 and Dibelius, "Paul in Athens." He opposes Norden's and Loisy's view that it is the work of a later editor of the book of Acts: Norden, *Agnostos Theos*, 3–83 and Loisy, *Actes*, 660–84; cf. Gärtner, *Areopagus Speech*, 38–41. For various views on the speech as an interpolation or a "foreign body," see Jervell, *Die Apostelgeschichte*, 444n214.

6. For example: Legrand, "Unknown God," 164–65; Samuel, "Paul on the Areopagus," 25–26; Pinnock, "Finality," 158; Pinnock, "Toward an Evangelical," 365; Sanders, *No Other Name*, 236, 260;

with Gärtner that this line of interpretation is possible *only* when one destroys the unity—and therefore the argument—of the speech.[7] For a proper understanding of these verses, one must not only pay attention to their intrinsic grammatical or syntactical structure and extensive OT background, but also to their contribution to the speech and narrative at large.

The Sentence Structure

First, it must be noted that vv. 26–27 form a single and complete sentence, distinct from what precedes and follows.[8] Τέ at the beginning of v. 26 marks a related but separate development in the discourse.[9] Verses 24–25 define the identity of the God (topical information) who is the subject of the main verb (focal information)—i.e., the one whose activity is the focus—of 26–27. Γάρ at the beginning of v. 28 indicates both that the verse is intimately connected with 27b (and what precedes more generally) and that it is a distinct discourse element presenting confirming or supporting evidence for the preceding claim (structurally, it is "offline" or "background" information).[10] Moreover, in vv. 28–29 Paul is not merely repeating himself but presents a supplementary (and complementary) argument to the one made in vv. 26–27.[11] Barrett himself must recognize that the various parts of these verses—in spite of the interpretative difficulties—hold well together.[12] Including v. 28 in this discourse unit would destroy its unity and make both its meaning and relationship to v. 29 incomprehensible.[13] The syntactical and thematic unity of vv. 26–27 seems to be confirmed by the *inclusio* formed with ἐποίησέν . . . ἑνὸς and ἑνὸς . . . ὑπάρχοντα.[14] Their integrity is

---

see also Kee, *Every Nation*, 215; Kurz, *Acts*, 273; and Pervo, *Acts*, 437–38; cf. the survey of the issue in Barrett, *Acts*, 2.845–46.

7. Gärtner, *Areopagus Speech*, 168–69. Barrett goes so far as arguing that the content of the speech is *illogical* as a result of its seeking to integrate elements common with Hellenistic thinking ("Paul at Athens," 153).

8. This is also highlighted by des Places, "Actes 17,27," 2 and Barrett, *Acts*, 2.841–42; contra Dupont, "Discours à l'Aréopage," 392–96. It is marked in UBS[4] by the capitalization of ἐν at the beginning of v. 28 (not in NA[27] or NA[28]).

9. It introduces an additional statement about the preceding "event" (the creation of the world and of living beings) that concentrates on a particular aspect of that event (creation of mankind). See the discussion of τέ solitarium in Levinsohn, *Textual Connections in Acts*, 121–36, 127–29 for this particular usage.

10. Another discursive connection that is often missed is the fact that Paul shifts to the first person plural in 27b ("each one of *us*"), thus preparing for the person and number of *both* 28 and 29. The shift is noted by Gaventa, *Acts*, 251.

11. Vv. 26–27 are concerned with God's original design for man, while vv. 28–29 focus on the folly of idolatry in the light of man's being the image of the living and acting God.

12. Barrett, *Acts*, 2.842.

13. Cf. the discussion in Gärtner, *Areopagus Speech*, 168–69.

14. The two verbs have God for subject and bracket the sentence, being respectively the very first and the very last words of the sentence. This *inclusio* seems to indicate that God is the acting

also marked by their bracketing with two near-synonymous triads, in 25b and 28a.¹⁵ Finally, the sentence is held together by repeated alliterations.¹⁶ These considerations taken together do not indicate independence from—or worse, incongruity with—the rest of the speech. On the contrary, they indicate that this sentence makes a unique and well-articulated contribution to the speech and its argument.

The second issue to be discussed is the inner relationships of the various parts of the sentence. The connection of the present infinitive verbs κατοικεῖν and ζητεῖν to their subordinate clauses is rather clear and undisputed.¹⁷ By contrast, the exact relation of those same infinitives to one another and to the main verb (ἐποίησεν), crucial to the understanding of the text, is disputed. A few scholars have suggested that ἐποίησεν functions as a helping verb for κατοικεῖν, while ζητεῖν is a final or purposive infinitive. The resulting meaning would be something like "he made them dwell (in order) to seek."¹⁸ This position has, however, been rejected by the large majority of scholars, including Dibelius.¹⁹

It is rather obvious that ἐποίησεν must be understood in relation to the ὁ θεὸς ὁ ποιήσας of v. 24a. The most conspicuous connection is probably the repetition of the verb ποιέω. But there is a stronger and deeper link: the subject of ἐποίησεν is the "God-ὁ ποιήσας-the-world-and-all-that-is-in-it" topicalized in vv. 24–25. Verses 26–27 thus prolong and develop the line of thought initiated in the preceding sentence. The person and activity of the universal Creator and Lord of 24–25 are now further considered in terms of his original design for mankind.²⁰ Moreover, it is virtually

---

subject, and that the matter at hand is his relationship as Maker and Lord to his human creature. This understanding is reinforced by the threefold reference to "men" at the beginning (ἀνθρώπων), middle (αὐτῷ) and end (ἡμῶν)—in the genitive plural, hence connecting them also through flexion and assonance—all in relationship to a verb whose agent is the Creator/Lord God (ἐποίησεν, ὁρίσας, ὑπάρχοντα).

15. The two express the same essential point emphasizing man's utter dependence on his Maker and Lord for what characterizes him as a living being. One does so through three nominal expressions, the other through three verbs. Even without such a tight thematic convergence the formulaic framing would set vv. 26–27 apart. Cf. the discussion in des Places, "Actes 17,27," 2.

16. Cf. Bruce, *Acts Greek*, 383. There are other features such as the repetition of words, cognates or referents.

17. The subordinate participial clause introduced by ὁρίσας (an aorist participle indicating both the antecedent and definitive nature of the clause) describes the conditions for the κατοικεῖν preordained by the one who "made" mankind. Ζητεῖν on the other hand commands a fourth class conditional clause qualified by a subordinate participial clause. Cf. Dupont, "Discours à l'Aréopage," 395–96.

18. See BDAG 840 (use 2, h); Pohlenz, "Paulus," 84–85; and Eltester, "Gott und Natur," 211n13.

19. In fact, Dupont declines to even discuss it, considering that "Il ne paraît pas utile de revenir sur *une discussion qui semble dépassée*" "Discours à l'Aréopage," 395n28 (emphasis ours). In spite of his judgment, this interpretation is adopted by Johnson, *Acts*, 315. Cf. the discussion in Barrett, *Acts*, 2.841–42.

20. The reference to God *qua* Creator in 26a implies the whole of vv. 24–25, including its assertion of God's lordship. Verses 26–27 continue and expand the same thought, drawing out relevant implications of that initial presentation of Yahweh. The perspective on God's relationship to his creatures does not suddenly turn into an abstract ontological conception. Man can only relate to God as

impossible to account syntactically for ἐξ ἑνός if ἐποίησεν is a helping verb.²¹ Besides, the first clause (at least) of v. 26 alludes to the creation story of Adam in Genesis. This strongly favors an absolute understanding of ἐποίησεν to mean "he made" in the sense of "he created,"²² in accordance with the septuagintal use of the verb ποιέω in the creation story.²³ All the evidence shows that ἐποίησεν cannot function as a helping verb in this sentence. Rather, as the principal verb, it establishes the topical information necessary for the subsequent elaborations.²⁴ This means that the two infinitive verbs relate directly and severally to ἐποίησεν.²⁵

Most scholars understand κατοικεῖν and ζητεῖν to be parallel, either final/purpose or epexegetical, infinitives expressing the divine purpose for human existence.²⁶ Though a difficult construction, it is perfectly possible. And it makes much more sense than the other option.²⁷ Whether the infinitives are final or epexegetical, their import is clear: they denote the twofold divine design for his human creatures.²⁸ It seems to us, though, that categorizing these verbs as final or purpose infinitives is preferable. First, they cannot be infinitives of result—a use sometimes indistinguishable from that of purpose—indicating the *outcome* of God's work of creation.²⁹ Paul's surroundings and audience represent the exact opposite of what was intended. The optatives of v. 27 and the remainder of the speech confirm that the purpose is not realized. Besides, if the author had wanted to express an actual or probable *result*, he would have used a different construction.³⁰ Second, it seems that the epexegetical category is too vague

---

simultaneously—and coterminously—his Maker *and* Lord. With this caveat in mind, see Witherington, *Acts*, 526. In consequence, we disagree with the claim in Soards, *Speeches in Acts*, 97 that the movement is from God's character (24–25) to God's interaction with humanity (26–27). First, the latter aspect is already central in 24–25, and this interpretation assumes a dichotomy between God's character and his activity that is contrary to the very point made by these verses. There is a transition, indeed, but it is one of focus: vv. 24–25 consider mankind as a creature in general, thus receiving all things from God; vv. 26–27 consider humanity in terms of its original—i.e., creational—design and purpose. Both are understood in the context of Yahweh's kingship and his covenant rule over Adam and his offspring. Strictly speaking the focus is on God, not man.

21. See Conzelmann, *Acts*, 142.

22. Cf. Wilson, *Gentiles*, 200–201.

23. Ἐποίησεν is used for the creation of mankind in Gen 1:26, 27 (3x). In 1:26 ποιέω serves to express God's design for the creation of man depicted in v. 27. It is likely that Luke's readers would make the connection between the ἐποίησεν of Acts 17:26 and the creation story in Genesis. See Marshall, "Acts," 595.

24. See the discussions in *BegC*, 4.216; Haenchen, *Acts*, 523; and Barrett, *Acts*, 2.841.

25. Contra Jipp, "Paul's Areopagus Speech," 582. Moreover, the single purpose resulting from the "helping verb" construction obscures the allusion to the Genesis story, which stresses man's mandate to "fill the earth" (1:28), the very point made by the κατοικεῖν clause. Cf. Witherington, *Acts*, 526.

26. See Fitzmyer, *Acts*, 609. For these two uses of the infinitive mood, see BDF § 390 and 394.

27. As noted in Conzelmann, *Acts*, 142 and Jervell, *Die Apostelgeschichte*, 447.

28. So Jervell does not even seek to decide whether it is one or the other (*Die Apostelgeschichte*, 447–48).

29. This is especially the case when the agent whose purpose is in view is the Almighty, whose eternal plan is infallible—a prominent theme in Luke's theology and narrative.

30. By using the genitive article τοῦ (cf. BDF § 400), or by using ἵνα with the subjunctive (cf. BDF

to be really helpful, as it covers much of the same ground as purpose and result.[31] This probably explains why several scholars seem to use the term in this context while understanding the two verbs as denoting the double "intention" or "design" of God for his creature, with no particular result being implied or expected.[32] Finally, the notion of a pre-existing "plan" or design is indicated by ὁρίσας (referring to an antecedent "bounded" action) together with the perfect participle προστεταγμένους.

In any case, it is clear that the two divine purposes are not causally related one to the other. Each infinitive is independently connected to the main verb, and therefore to the mainline of the discourse, which they develop.[33] They are thematically interrelated in the fact and the intention of the divine sovereign creation of mankind. This mutual independence is further indicated by two noteworthy structural features: first, the two infinitival clauses are asyndetic;[34] second, the first clause is clearly delineated by an *inclusio* formed by the first infinitive verb κατοικεῖν and the noun κατοικία, setting it apart from the clause starting with ζητεῖν.[35]

In consequence, the ὁρίσας participial clause of 26c is exclusively related to κατοικεῖν (26b) and has no relation whatsoever with ζητεῖν (27a): the "dwelling" and the "seeking" are described as strictly *parallel* purposes intrinsic to the divine design for human life.[36] Verse 27 ("seeking") does not indicate the cause or reason for the "dwelling" of v. 26.[37] Reciprocally, v. 26 does *not* describe "arrangements" designed to nudge man into "seeking" God, even less ways that would lead man to find him.[38] Thus, "in reality there is here no proof for the existence of God at all."[39] We must also

---

§ 369 and the discussion in § 388), for example.

31. "To a greater or lesser degree most adverbial infinitives are epexegetical, i.e., they modify a verb." Brooks and Winbery, *Syntax*, 142.

32. See, for example, *BegC*, 4.216; Dibelius, "Areopagus," 35 and Barrett, *Acts*, 2.841–42. It seems this choice is meant to avoid the confusion between purpose and result. However, most scholars who identify the infinitives as final clearly distinguish between the two and deny the latter. For example, Conzelmann, *Acts*, 142; Marguerat, *Actes*, 2.159; Culy and Parsons, *Acts Handbook*, 338–39; Pesch, *Apostelgeschichte*, 2.138; Roloff, *Apostelgeschichte*, 261; Schneider, *Apg.*, 2.240; and Witherington, *Acts*, 526.

33. Hence, Witherington notes that the allusions to Genesis 1–2 argue in favor of a parallel construction of the infinitives, since the narrative of the origins emphasizes man's mandate to populate the earth for its own sake. Witherington, *Acts*, 526.

34. Also noted by Jervell, *Die Apostelgeschichte*, 447.

35. See Dupont, "Discours à l'Aréopage," 395.

36. See Haenchen, *Acts*, 523n1 and Dupont, "Discours à l'Aréopage," 395n29.

37. So also Haenchen, *Acts*, 523–24 and Witherington, *Acts*, 528.

38. Contra Bruce, *Defence of the Gospel*, 42 and Gourgues, "Littérature profane," 255. Gourgues affirms that v. 26 is meant to describe ways provided by God to *know* God, even though he confesses that it is difficult to decide the exact meaning of the phrase, and therefore the precise nature of those ways. He concludes without any clear textual evidence that it must have to do with a vague "ordre ou d'une ordonnance inhérents au monde créé et à partir desquels il est possible de connaître Dieu."

39. Haenchen, *Acts*, 523n1; contra Dibelius, "Areopagus," 27–37. Haenchen sees in vv. 26–27 the double task appointed to mankind by God.

object to the idea that these verses would be developing—or even establish the possibility of—any (author-sanctioned) natural theology demonstrating the existence and nature of God on the basis of providential patterns identifiable by man.[40] Just like vv. 24-25, vv. 26-27 begin both syntactically and thematically with the God who made all things, gives life to all, and rules over all nations' destiny. It is from that exclusive vantage point that they exegete mankind's two creational mandates.[41] In other words, they simply continue Paul's theological *exposé* regarding the nature of God, man and history, one that gives Yahweh all preeminence and centers around man's service to and worship of the one God and Lord of all.

A Post-Babel Perspective on the Creation of Mankind

In that case, "the method of making (ἐξ ἑνός) must be seen in relation to the dwelling and seeking."[42] The most obvious point being made here is that mankind was created as a unity. The expression ἐξ ἑνός asserts a unity of origin while πᾶν ἔθνος ἀνθρώπων indicates that humanity as a whole is in view, a perspective reinforced by the subsequent παντὸς προσώπου τῆς γῆς. The contrast created by the juxtaposition of ἑνός and πᾶν is at the same time emphatic and striking, especially since πᾶν stands out in an alliterative phrase where virtually every other word begins with ε. Yet at the same time the ἐξ ἑνός is ambiguous, since ἑνός could be either neuter or masculine in gender. The former would mean either an abstract principle of "oneness" (as in Stoicism or Platonism) or a primordial ἔθνος ("from one nation he made every nation"), the latter a person.

Though the combination of πᾶν with ἔθνος is extremely frequent in the LXX (especially in the plural), the phrasing of v. 26 with ἀνθρώπων does not occur anywhere else in either the LXX or the NT and appears emphatic—though it might simply reflect classical usage.[43] Either way, the adjunction of ἀνθρώπων leaves no doubt as to what kind of "nation" is in view. It also dispels the ambiguity of ἐξ ἑνός, thus allowing this expression to be absolute in its denotation of the original oneness.[44] The reference to the creation account together with the use of ἀνθρώπων (a strong verbal link to ἀνθρωπίνων in 25a) make it clear that a human being is in view.[45] The general consen-

---

40. The conclusion that these verses are indebted to the Stoic argument from "providence" (i.e., from the order of nature and history produced by the Logos), is groundless, contra Gourgues, "Littérature profane," 256–57. The fact that the Areopagitica addresses the same aspect of reality in such a radically antithetical perspective demonstrates an apologetical and polemical intention.

41. To use systematic theological categories, Paul/Luke here interprets natural revelation through special revelation. We arrive as the same conclusion as we did for vv. 24–25. Cf. Stonehouse, "Areopagus Address," 26.

42. Barrett, *Acts*, 2.842.

43. As noted in *TDNT* 2.369. Cf. Montanari, *Brill DAG*, 594.

44. Contra Kurz, *Acts*, 273, who sees a reference to an original *couple* (viz., Adam and Eve).

45. The Western text (D E 𝔐 gig sy) seeks to make this identification explicit by the addition of

sus is that Adam is the "one."⁴⁶ There is further confirming evidence for this identification. For example, Jesus' genealogy in Luke's Gospel goes back to Adam (by contrast, Matthew's focuses on his Abrahamic and Davidic descent).⁴⁷ Moreover, the "dwelling" and the "seeking" of vv. 26-27 correspond neatly to Adam's kingly and priestly functions in Eden—"garden" depicted both as a kingdom and a sanctuary.⁴⁸ Finally, it is consistent with the framing of the whole of human history—from its inception to its consummation—with two individuals: to Adam the nameless "one" (creation) corresponds Jesus the nameless "man" (ἀνήρ, v. 31; final judgment).⁴⁹

The expression πᾶν ἔθνος ἀνθρώπων can itself be understood in two ways: "every nation of men" or "the whole nation/race of men."⁵⁰ The entirety and essential unity of humankind is denoted either way, but with different connotations: the former implies multiple nations, while the latter implies an undifferentiated unity.⁵¹ The majority of scholars opt for one form or another of the first interpretation, the standard meaning of πᾶς with a singular and anarthrous substantive in (classical) Greek. However, one consideration may favor the second possibility: Luke uses that same combination with the clear meaning of "whole" or "entire" to describe what is to be populated: ἐπὶ παντὸς προσώπου τῆς γῆς.⁵² Verse 26 would thus affirm that the "whole humanity" was to colonize the "whole earth," two concepts that are profoundly antithetical to Hellenistic thinking.⁵³ Either way the point is that by

---

αἵματος.

46. See Gaventa, *Acts*, 251 and Keener, *Acts*, 3.2645-47. The latter discusses the possibility of a reference to Noah.

47. See Witherington, *Acts*, 526.

48. See Kline, *Kingdom Prologue*, 6-85; Beale, *Temple*, 29-167; and Waltke and Yu, *OT Theology*, 209-83.

49. A parallel highlighted by Gärtner, *Areopagus Speech*, 230; Dupont, "Salut des Gentils," 154; Calloud, "Aréopage," 243; and Pervo, *Acts*, 440. Wilson rejects Gärtner's emphasis on this point. He deems it "unwarranted" and argues that if Luke had meant it, he would have made the reference to Adam unambiguous (Wilson, *Gentiles*, 213). However, the ambiguity is consistent with the character of the speech as a whole, and the name Adam would be meaningless to the depicted audience. The reference, however, is clear to Luke's readers in context. Once again, Luke simply shows himself to be a sophisticated and subtle storyteller.

50. See Turner, *Syntax*, 199-200.

51. In either case, the focus is the wholeness of the *one* humanity, whether looked at in a differentiated or undifferentiated manner. The point is not a "principial" movement from unity to multiplicity as in Posidonius (mentioned by Conzelmann, *Acts*, 142). Even if "every nation of men" is the proper interpretation, it would still mean that man is "l'unité d'une multiplicité" (Bossuyt and Radermakers, "Rencontre," 31).

52. This is Barrett's and Haenchen's position. Haenchen, *Acts*, 523n3, mentions that one scholar, B. Weiss, has suggested to translate this expression "on every face of the earth," but without gaining support from anyone else. Cf. Barrett, *Acts*, 2.842.

53. First, the ancient Greeks did not believe in the genetic unity of mankind, though the Stoics did teach that all men and all things were one in the Logos in a pantheistic manner (see Keener, *Acts*, 3.2645, 2648). Contra Haenchen, *Acts*, 523n2, there is no clear parallel in Greek mythology and thought to Adam as the father of all humans (see Barrett, *Acts*, 2.842 and Witherington, *Acts*, 526).

virtue of being Adam's offspring, every single human being is meant to "dwell" and to "seek." In consequence, all will have to give an account of their response to their God-given double mandate and are called to repentance in view of their failure (cf. τοῖς ἀνθρώποις πάντας πανταχοῦ in vv. 30–31).

Even though the focus is clearly on the original, or creational, design of/for mankind, the use of ἔθνος reveals a point of view that takes into account humanity's failure to fulfill its double mandate. This word is used in the Bible (whether Old or New Testament) to depict the human race in terms of its social, tribal, linguistic, geopolitical, and religious differentiation—implying its fragmentation.[54] It points therefore necessarily to a post-Fall, post-Flood, and post-Babel situation. Interestingly, the only time ἔθνος is used in the same context as Adam in the LXX is Deut 32:8. This passage speaks of the dispersion of the "sons of Adam" after Babel and has many interconnections with Paul's address, especially with v. 26.[55] As a matter of fact, the word ἔθνος does appear in the Genesis narrative for the first time in chapter 10, in the so-called "table of nations," a chapter that introduces the Babel story and anticipates the division of mankind that ensues.[56] It is intriguing that though Genesis 10 introduces the word (and concept) of "nation," it is altogether absent from the subsequent Babel narrative as a whole. Its next occurrence is in Yahweh's promise to Abram (Gen 12:2), while the remainder of chapter 11 contains the genealogy of Shem and Terah. Hence, Adam and Eve as well as their descendants down to Noah's sons are conceived in Genesis without racial or national distinctions. The division line among them, beginning with

---

They believed in a diversity of races, theirs being superior (of course) because "autochthonous," i.e., "sprung from the soil of their native Attica." Bruce, *Acts NICNT*, 357–58; cf. Bruce, *Acts Greek*, 382. Second, contra Dibelius, "Areopagus," 27–37, the text speaks of dwelling on the entire surface of the earth, while the Greeks believed that only two of the five zones of the world—the temperate ones— "were fit for and assigned to human habitation." Barrett, *Acts*, 2.843; cf. Haenchen, *Acts*, 523.

54. The identity of a "nation" in the ancient Near East was defined by its god(s), even more than by its ethnic composition (see Block, *Gods*). Moreover, ἔθνος, especially plural, is typically used by biblical writers to denote all peoples or tribes that are not bound covenantally to Yahweh, while Israel is the λαός, the chosen people (Luke-Acts follows that practice). Genesis 10 is in consequence foundational for both the OT and Jewish definitions of Israel's identity among the nations in its past, present and even eschatological dimensions (cf. Scott, "Geographical Horizon," 499–522). The choice of a loaded term like ἔθνος cannot be accidental. Luke could have used other words to depict mankind, had he wished to avoid its allusive power and connotations, e.g., γένος (used twice in vv. 28–29), πατριά, γενεά, or φυλή, all of which imply common descent.

55. Ὅτε διεμέριζεν ὁ ὕψιστος ἔθνη ὡς διέσπειρεν υἱοὺς Αδαμ κτλ. See Witherington, *Acts*, 527n236, who notes that v. 5 includes the notion of mankind's fallenness, including Israel's. See v. 9 also (ἐγενήθη μερὶς κυρίου λαὸς αὐτοῦ Ιακωβ σχοίνισμα κληρονομίας αὐτοῦ Ισραηλ) which revolves around the strict distinction between the "nations" and "Israel." Beale, *Temple*, 231n55, notes that the Palestinian Targum of this passage explicitly makes the connection with Babel. Cf. Marshall, "Acts," 595.

56. The exact meaning and grounds for the grouping of various peoples, regions or towns listed in the "table" are much debated among scholars, in ways quite similar to the debate surrounding the list found in Acts 2:9–12. One thing seems clear, however: the demarcation lines are not drawn along strict genealogical lines, but rather along territorial or geopolitical ones—two aspects inseparable from religious considerations in the Ancient Near East and in the OT *after* Babel. See Hays, *Every People*, 47–48.

Cain and Abel or Seth, is strictly covenantal and religious. "Israel" as a distinct people group emerges only with chapter 12, when Abraham is called *out* of his family, his nation, and their (his?) idolatry.[57] Babel is a major turning point in biblical anthropology, marking the beginning of mankind's division in distinct linguistic, geographic, national, ethnic, and religious groups. Genesis 10 is thus proleptic, anticipating the earth-shattering consequences of the following Babel episode.

It should be noted that the sin of mankind at Babel was its idolatrous claims to divine power and authority.[58] Genesis 11:4 reports its absolute refusal to "fill the earth" and its stubborn gathering into one πόλις.[59] The comment discloses the hubris of their resolve to reach Yahweh's dwelling place—therefore his presence, a privilege lost when Adam and Eve were cast out of Eden—by their own means and power, and for their own glory.[60] Babel thus represents the narrative climax of the story of humanity's absolute failure to fulfill its most essential creational purpose: the unity of the race is broken into pieces (implying competition and enmity), the "filling" of the earth becomes "scattering," and the "seeking" of the one God and Lord becomes turning away to all sorts of gods and idols.

It is quite remarkable that Genesis 1–11 does *not* contain any trace of polytheism or paganism, in spite of its chronicling of mankind's unrelenting and intensifying rebellion against its Creator and Lord. All depicted religious activity prior to Babel is immediately related to the one God, whether in a covenant-keeping and obedient way—demonstrating a true "seeking" and "knowing" of Yahweh as God and Lord—, or in a covenant-breaking and mutinous manner. In the case of Cain and Abel, for example, both are addressing their worship to the same God. And yet, only one sacrifice finds favor in Yahweh's eyes. The fact that Abel's is accepted and agreeable seems to be due to both the attitude of his heart and the form of the sacrifice, the latter expressing

---

57. Therefore, not even with Shem's or Terah's "generations" (the last uses of תּוֹלְדֹת/תּוֹלְדֹת in Genesis before the "generations" of Isaac in chapter 25).

58. Here, we see that the original design of unity and divine imaging are warped into a rebellious unification of the race to usurp God's glory, authority and creational purposes. The text makes abundantly clear that the crux of the passage is man's striving against God's rule in its refusal to fulfill Yahweh's creational purposes according to his ways. Mankind's success in this rebellion appears to be entirely dependent upon its unity, both ethnically and geographically. The original mandate to populate the whole earth becomes thus a threat in men's eyes (Gen 11:4) and thereafter a punishment from God (11:8, 9, repeated for emphasis), using each time a formula that is almost identical with that of Acts 17:26: ἐπὶ προσώπου (v. 4; προσώπον in 8, 9, with no change in meaning) πάσης τῆς γῆς.

59. The original mandate to fill the earth (1:28) is republished immediately after the Flood in 9:1 and 7 (emphatic repetition) following Noah's re-establishing of the worship of Yahweh with acceptable sacrifices (8:20–21). Noah is like a "second Adam" through whom the order and design of creation are restored (including the original mandates to "dwell" and "seek") and a covenant is made with all of creation (8:21–22; 9:8–17), in a post-lapsarian context.

60. The religious "seeking" of man is here at least as intense as that of the Athenians: the human race concentrates all its population, strength, means and efforts for one exclusive religious purpose: reaching God's abode. It is also just as misdirected, rebellious, idolatrous (pagan in its mode of thinking), sinful, and offensive to Yahweh.

concretely and tangibly the former. It is therefore not surprising that Deut 32:8–9 (and its reference to Babel) correlates the multiplicity of nations with the multiplicity of gods.⁶¹ This means that God's plan to unite all nations under one God and one Lord in Jesus Christ is at the same time the fulfilling of the creational purposes and the undoing of Babel's curse, since the "new Jerusalem" is at the same time God's kingdom, God's temple, God's people, and the "new heaven and new earth" (Revelation 21).⁶²

As a result of these various OT intertextual echoes, the frame of reference provided by the first clause of v. 26 combines the primordial design for all of mankind and man's failure to fulfill this mandate because of a sinful and perverted pursuit of it.⁶³ Eden is seen through the lens of Babel. This point of view means that the two (dependent) adverbial clauses of vv. 26–27 must be read in the light of the OT background of the main clause and, therefore, that they both depict simultaneously God's original design and man's failure to accomplish the purpose for his existence.⁶⁴

In fact, κατοικεῖν already points in that same direction. Its use with ἐπὶ παντὸς προσώπου τῆς γῆς is an unmistakable thematic reference to the original mandate of Gen 1:28 (echoed in 9:1, 7), implying that it has a stronger or broader meaning than merely "to reside."⁶⁵ And yet, the term itself does not occur in Genesis before the story focuses on the dispersion of the nations.⁶⁶ In any case, its use in v. 26 in conjunction with ὁροθεσίας and αὐτῶν suggests a situation where mankind is divided and the world is partitioned among various nations, thus confirming a post-Babel perspective.⁶⁷

Yahweh's Sovereign Providence over History

We must now turn our attention to what is possibly the most debated interpretive issue for this verse: the precise reference of καιρούς and ὁροθεσίας. Schubert claims

---

61. Also noted by Witherington, *Acts*, 527.

62. Acts 1:8 shares that same perspective: the spread of the church "to the end of the earth" leads to the turning of all peoples to the one God and one Lord. The gospel of Jesus Christ is therefore by nature a polemic against all forms of polytheism and idolatry. The speaking of tongues at Pentecost (2:1–11)—itself a proleptic sign of the eschatological new creation—is a sort of "anti-Babel."

63. James Scott aptly describes v. 26 as "foreshortening the story line of Genesis 1–10," and notes a similar compression in 1 Chr 1:1—2:2 in "Geographical Horizon," 541–43. Cf. Gärtner, *Areopagus Speech*, 151; Calloud, "Aréopage," 231, esp. n. 16; and Peterson, *Acts*, 493.

64. Thus Barrett, *Acts*, 2.842 notes the "biblical" (i.e., septuagintal) flavor of the language found in this passage.

65. Cf. Bossuyt and Radermakers, "Rencontre," 32, who think the verse depicts God's provision of both the time and space for man's habitation.

66. In Gen 9:27 (blessing of Japheth); 11:2 (the settling of mankind in the plain of Shinar); 11:31 (Terah's settling in Canaan); and 12:6 (the Canaanites were inhabiting the land). Even its cognate κατοικία does not appear before Exod 35:3 (and κατοικεσία in Ps 106:36 is a hapax).

67. Witherington makes reference to this evidence also. He translates the original singular κατοικίας by a plural, viz., "habitations." Witherington, *Acts*, 527.

that the evidence for their philosophical—i.e., natural—interpretation is supported by an "overwhelming evidence." We believe the opposite is true.[68]

First, it should be noted that the word ὁροθεσία appears only here in the whole Bible. Its cognate ὅριον, however, is used many times (mostly plural), though only once by Luke in Acts 13:50 (when Paul and Barnabas are driven out of the "district" of Pisidian Antioch).[69] Ὅριον occurs in a few passages that are immediately relevant to our text, viz., Gen 10:19; Exod 23:31; Deut 32:8; Isa 10:13; and Ezek 48:1–14. Witherington notes that ὁροθεσία is also rare in extra-biblical documents, "but what little evidence we do have suggests it normally means the boundaries that divide nations."[70] To be precise, the ancient evidence indicates that ὁροθεσία does not denote a boundary or limit as such, but rather the setting of territorial limits, of borders.[71] Conzelmann adds that D's variant for our text, κατὰ ὁροθεσίαν ("according to the boundary"), argues for the historical—i.e., national—interpretation.[72] Finally, the reference to "the whole face of the earth" also argues against Dibelius' natural interpretation based on the Hellenistic theory of "habitable zones."[73] It is interesting to note that though Bruce argues in favor of Dibelius' philosophical interpretation in his 1954 commentary, he explains it as referring to national boundaries on the basis of Daniel and Deuteronomy in 1990.[74]

The argument for a "natural" interpretation of καιρούς as "seasons" is based mostly on Ps 74 (73 LXX):17 and, more weightily, Acts 14:17.[75] The passage would

---

68. Contra Schubert, "Place," 255. See the helpful discussion on the inference of "dependence" from verbal or thematic parallels in Nash, *Christianity and the Hellenistic World*, 15–18.

69. Cf. Scott, "Geographical Horizon," 543. Ὅριον refers to the boundaries of a region or nation, and is often used in the plural for the region itself. See BDAG 723.

70. Witherington, *Acts*, 527, citing Eusebius, *Demonstr. Evan.* 4.9; cf. Wilson, *Gentiles*, 204–5 in support for this judgment.

71. See the discussion in Cadbury, *Acts in History*, 36 and Spicq, *Notes*, 2.631, who concludes: "l'ὁροθεσία est la *limitatio*, la détermination des frontières."

72. Conzelmann, *Acts*, 143. The only variant known for this element of the verse appears in D* and Irlat.

73. See discussions in Haenchen, *Acts*, 523 and Conzelmann, *Acts*, 143. Conzelmann also argues against Eltester's interpretation of ὁροθεσία as the boundary between land and sea (in mythical terms of order vs. chaos). Though it may claim Job 38:8–11 and Ps 104:5–9 for support (according to Marshall, "Acts," 595), it is totally absent from Luke's writings and from the OT background we have identified for the passage. Cf. Eltester, "Gott und Natur," 209–12.

74. Cf. Bruce, *Acts NICNT*, 358 and Bruce, *Acts Greek*, 383.

75. See Haenchen, *Acts*, 523 and Marshall, "Acts," 595. "We can understand also, in the light of this kind of repetition of similar material, how it is that Paul's words to the inhabitants of Lystra (Acts 14.15–17) have already provided a unique prelude to his Areopagus speech. That God has revealed himself by sending the rains and the seasons, by giving man food and gladness, is introduced in the chief sentence of this little 'sermon' as proof of God's existence. The Areopagus speech proceeds along similar lines and introduces these things in the same way as the speech in Lystra, by means of an affirmation of God's nature which is reminiscent of the Old Testament." Dibelius, "Speeches and Historiography," 170.

thus insist on God's *provisions* for human needs and well-being.[76] Though tempting in view of the parallel with the speech in Lystra, there are several insurmountable problems with this interpretation. First, as we have seen, it is clear that *national* borders are in view, not *natural* delineations, and therefore neither text called upon in support of this view is immediately relevant.[77] Second, though καιρούς can mean "seasons" in biblical Greek, it is always made clear by either a qualifying adjective (καρποφόρους in 14:17, a NT hapax) or a clear context, neither of which is present in v. 26.[78] Third, the attributive perfect participle προστεταγμένους indicates that the times in view have been determined or fixed in advance.[79] This conception is confirmed and reinforced by the aorist participle ὁρίσας in the subordinate clause. This means that the "times" in view are part of God's antecedent design and plan for man κατοικεῖν the "whole face of the earth," making the natural or meteorological interpretations quite unlikely. It is therefore clear that the emphasis of this clause is on God's *authority* over the nations which expresses itself in a sovereign *plan* (cf. 2:23) ordering both the distribution and the timing of the nations' inhabitation of the world.[80]

The reoccurrence of the same verb ὁρίζω in v. 31 (for the appointment of the universal judge; ἵστημι is used for the "setting" of the day of the trial) not only reinforces this temporal and historical interpretation, but points further to a redemptive-historical meaning. A connection with Daniel's "apocalyptic vision of world history" is therefore likely.[81] Especially in light of Luke 21:24, a Lukan "apocalyptic" passage, where the word "nations" is used three times, including in the expression καιροὶ ἐθνῶν.[82] Schubert's rejection of the historical interpretation on the ground that an "apocalyptic" interpretation of history is foreign to Luke's thought fails to understand the nature of both Daniel's vision and Luke's eschatology.[83]

76. See Soards, *Speeches in Acts*, 90; Bruce, "Paul and Athenians," 10; and Bruce, *Paul*, 241.

77. God's sovereign setting of natural boundaries and climactic conditions is a profoundly biblical concept, of course. In this way the Creator and Lord of creation reveals his great care for his creature and insures favorable conditions for the "filling" of the whole earth. However, the Areopagitica does not draw any inference from this that would look like an argument from nature, so a historical interpretation is preferable, as noted by Schnabel, *Acts*, 735. Cf. Witherington, *Acts*, 527, who also notes the difference of contexts between the two Lukan passages.

78. See Wilson, *Gentiles*, 203; cf. Barrett, *Acts*, 1.682.

79. Commenting on the variant προτεταγμένους (D* pc bo), which indicates more explicitly the anteriority of the appointment, Barrett, *Acts*, 2.842, notes that, in fact, the difference in meaning is minimal, since "if the times were appointed at all they were appointed in advance" by definition. In any case, such a variant is a witness to the fact that it was understood as referring to a divine appointment preceding the "times" themselves.

80. Cf. Alexander, *Acts*, 2.156 and Soards, *Speeches in Acts*, 97.

81. Conzelmann, *Acts*, 142. Dan 2:36–45 is the most-commonly identified intertext. The book of Daniel includes other examples of eschatological and epochal interpretation of world history, especially in chs. 7–9.

82. NA[28] lists several LXX parallels for it, including Dan 12:7. This connection is also made by *BegC*, 4.216.

83. Schubert, "Place," 255. This might be an over-correction of Conzelmann's (mis-)representation

INCRIMINATING EVIDENCE: THE DIVINE DESIGN FOR MANKIND (ACTS 17:26–27)

Lake and Cadbury conclude from their study that Luke employs the anarthrous plural καιροί in Luke-Acts as if it were a technical term, i.e., a redemptive-historical epoch.[84] The evidence strongly supports their view: of the five such uses in Luke-Acts (including Luke 21:24, the only occurrence in the Gospel), only Acts 14:17 would not fit that description, but this usage variation is marked by the adjunction of καρποφόρους. Both Acts 1:7 and 3:20 are part of a discourse or a discussion having to do with eschatological matters.[85] Interestingly, those two texts use καιροί and χρόνοι interchangeably to refer to epochs or periods of redemptive history, in a way similar to 17:26, 30.[86] Though Barrett slightly favors the natural interpretation in his commentary, he recognizes that the call to repentance of v. 30 is set in the framework of *Heilsgeschichte* in a way that is "adumbrated by one way of understanding v. 26."[87]

There is one last matter to discuss about the interpretation of this verse. Even though the redemptive-historical and national denotation is unquestionable, the "natural" interpretation may yet have something to contribute. And that could explain the indecisiveness experienced by various scholars.[88] In continuity with the OT background identified for the beginning of v. 26, it seems that here also Luke "compresses" Eden and Babel together, the creational (better than "natural") design and the post-Babel situation. If this were so, then just as ὁροθεσίας refers to God's sovereign allotment of the boundaries of the nations and would suggest his determination of the "boundaries" of the created world, so also καιρούς would denote Yahweh's predetermination of the epochs of world history (in a redemptive-historical perspective) and evoke his fixing of the various time divisions at creation (such as day and night, seasons, etc.). 1QM 10:12ff. is an example of such a use of creational categories in conjunction with historical ones.[89] Isaiah 45:15–25 is another one.

---

of Luke's eschatology as a rigid triple "periodization" of history. While rejecting the latter's interpretation, one must still recognize the "epochal" nature of Luke's (Scripture's, more broadly) understanding of redemptive history which it sought to explain. See our discussion of Luke's eschatology in chapter 1.

84. *BegC*, 4.216. Cf. Keener, *Acts*, 3.2649.

85. For a study of 3:20 in context, see Bayer, "Christ-Centered Eschatology." Note that this passage contains a call to repentance (v. 19) and speaks of ἄγνοια in relation to the audience's sinful opposition to God (v. 17), just like the Areopagitica.

86. We will later argue for a redemptive-historical and eschatological interpretation of v. 30 on the basis of τοὺς ... χρόνους τῆς ἀγνοίας and τὰ νῦν. Porter, *Paul in Acts*, 122, also sees v. 30 as evidence that καιροί in v. 26 should be understood in a redemptive-historical sense. Cf. Tipton, "Resurrection Proof," 46–47. In this context, Schubert is right to point to the fact that for Luke-Acts, there are only *two* "great historical epochs," though we would question the sharpness of his division and consider the resurrection—as the climactic and representative aspect of Jesus' work of salvation—to be the actual redemptive-historical and eschatological turning point of history. Cf. Schubert, "Place," 255.

87. Barrett, "Paul at Athens," 151; cf. Barrett, *Acts*, 2.844.

88. For example: Conzelmann, *Acts*, 143–44, who concludes that we might be asking too much from Luke on this issue; Barrett, *Acts*, 2.842–44; and Bock, *Acts*, 566.

89. Cited by some scholars, e.g., Marshall, *Acts TNTC*, 288; Conzelmann, *Acts*, 144; Barrett, *Acts*, 2.843 (together with other Qumran parallels); and Marshall, "Acts," 595. ET *DSS*[2], 102–3.

This Isaianic oracle evidences several striking verbal and thematic parallels with the Areopagitica. In particular, v. 18 depicts the Lord Maker (ὁ ποιήσας) of heaven and earth—who "divided" (using the verb διορίζω) "her" (τὴν γῆν is the antecedent of αὐτήν) so that it would be inhabited (κατοικεῖσθαι) and "made not to be empty" (οὐκ εἰς κενὸν ἐποίησεν)—concluding with the claim: ἐγώ εἰμι καὶ οὐκ ἔστιν ἔτι (echoed by the "I am the Lord and there is no other" of v. 22; cf. Isa 42:6, 8). This verse emphasizes the difference between the nations—who do not know God for he hides himself, who worship idols that cannot save and who will be put to shame—and Israel—God speaks clearly and openly to them for he is their God and Savior—in the past and the present. But it also calls the nations to turn to God and be saved (there is no other God and Savior than he, vv. 21, 22) in the midst of a trial of the nations that will force them to "bow their knee" in allegiance to him and in recognition that righteousness and glory are in him alone.[90]

Thus the polemic in v. 26 seems to function at two interrelated levels. Schubert is right to see a parallel between this verse and the long historical summaries of Acts 7:2–53 and 13:16–25.[91] In these texts Luke depicts Stephen and Paul recounting "lengthy treatments of God's dealings with Israel in its history" in a way similar to what 17:26 (27) and 30–31 do for the Gentile nations.[92] Wolfe argues that Stephen's speech in Acts 7 is a polemic establishing the proper view and interpretation of Israel's (redemptive) history, while Paul's in Acts 17 corrects the Athenians' erroneous understanding of history with the necessary redemptive-historical hermeneutical grid.[93] In other words, in the context of the whole speech, v. 26 develops a theology of history that serves as a polemic against the pagan understanding of the origins and history of the entire human race—whether popular or philosophical.

This verse continues therefore the anti-idol polemic of vv. 24–25 by proclaiming Yahweh's rule over all of mankind, not only in its creational and natural state but also in its fallen, fragmented and dispersed state, which is the only one Paul's audience— and every single human being since Babel—has ever known. As Porter says, it affirms God's sovereignty over the process of both the procreation and the dispersement of mankind.[94] Yahweh is the *one* God who is Creator and Lord of the *nations*. That means that he, and he alone, has the royal authority, prerogative and charge to *judge* them all, as well as the ability to save his chosen people from among them. This argument is

---

90. Isa 49:20; Jer 6:8; and Ezek 38:12 are the only examples we could identify of the use of ποιέω and κατοικέω in the same sentence in a similar context in either LXX or NT. See also Jer 26:19 and Ps 115:15–16 (113:23–24 LXX) for similar ideas but a different wording.

91. Schubert, "Place," 255–56.

92. Soards, *Speeches in Acts*, 98.

93. Wolfe, "Rhetorical Elements," 280. Once again, we see special revelation interpreting general revelation and the affirmation that man *never* reaches any knowledge of the true God on the latter's basis alone.

94. Porter, *Paul in Acts*, 122.

essential to OT anti-idol polemics, especially Isaiah's.⁹⁵ What is particularly striking is that the absolute affirmation of Yahweh's sovereignty and authority not only promise destruction for idols and idolatrous nations but are the very grounds for the call to idolaters to turn away from their false gods—who are nothing and cannot do anything for them—to the one and only Savior-God.⁹⁶

On (Not) Seeking and Finding the True God

Most—if not all—scholars would agree with Calvin's construal of Paul's argument when he writes: "Après que S. Paul ait traité de la nature de Dieu, c'est bien à propos qu'il entremêle cette [sic] avertissement, à savoir que les hommes doivent être diligents et attentifs à connaître Dieu, car ils ont été créés pour cela et sont nés à cette fin."⁹⁷ Yet, there is much debate over the background and precise meaning of ζητεῖν as well as over the possibility—or lack thereof—of man "finding" God on the basis of natural revelation alone.

Dibelius argues that "seeking" in this verse is of an "intellectual" (i.e., strictly epistemic) nature, that the speech is concerned with the "true knowledge of God," and that the import of this verse is therefore Hellenistic (i.e., philosophical), since the OT and Jewish concept of "seeking" is primarily volitional (i.e., existential).⁹⁸ Haenchen, however, questions the notion that Luke could have meant this phrase in purely intellectual terms, and defends the view that the proper background for it is the type of Hellenistic Judaism exemplified by Philo—a more syncretistic kind, according to him—that uses natural theology and grants the fact that Gentiles do seek God.⁹⁹ Barrett's challenge goes further, arguing that one should not make such a sharp distinction between the Hellenistic "intellectual" and the Jewish "existential" notions of seeking.¹⁰⁰

---

95. See Pao, *Acts and INE*, 196–97 and Calvin, *Actes*, 470–71. Gärtner, *Areopagus Speech*, 177, discusses the differences existing between this view of providence and the ones held by the Epicureans and Stoics philosophers.

96. Hence many commentators' mention of Isa 55:6 in this connection: ζητήσατε τὸν θεὸν καὶ ἐν τῷ εὑρίσκειν αὐτὸν ἐπικαλέσασθε ἡνίκα δ' ἂν ἐγγίζῃ ὑμῖν (note the use of "seek," "find" and "is near"), a passage that resembles v. 27 in our passage. See also Isa 42:6–9 and 45:18, 20–25.

97. Calvin, *Actes*, 470.

98. Dibelius, "Areopagus," 32–35; cf. Conzelmann, *Acts*, 144. Just as Dibelius' name is associated with the strictly "intellectual" interpretation, so is Gärtner's with the "existential." See the discussion in Owen, "Scope," 135n5. Dibelius' type of interpretation is followed by many inclusivists, for it confirms their idea that Paul is making use of pagan/Greek concepts, thus demonstrating that truth of a saving kind can be found in pagan culture and religion. See, for example, Samuel, "Paul on the Areopagus," 25 and Sanders, *No Other Name*, 245.

99. See Haenchen, *Acts*, 524n1. Haenchen thinks that the "nearness" of God—and therefore the seeking and finding also—is of a relational nature, just like a child with his caring parent.

100. Barrett, *Acts*, 2.844, 846. He thinks that Hellenistic Judaism made the intellectual dimension of the OT notion of seeking more explicit under the influence of Hellenistic philosophy.

Hemer, however, raises three issues that call for a much more radical critique of Dibelius' view.¹⁰¹ First, the latter's position is built on highly questionable assumptions coming from the *Religionsgeschichtliche Schule* concerning the "Hellenized" nature of early Christianity. Second, it is based on an artificial and fallacious polarization of OT/Jewish and Hellenistic concepts, associated with an unwarranted theologizing of words—including ζητέω, πίστις and μετανοέω—in a manner akin to what one finds in *TDNT*.¹⁰² At a methodological level this approach to semantics combined with the erroneous conviction that the intellectual association these words have in the speech precludes their having an OT origin explains why Dibelius interpreted the content of the speech, especially vv. 26–28, in strictly philosophical and Hellenistic terms. Yet, "None of these usages seem in any way unnatural for a speaker in a cross-cultural situation, rather the reverse, that this speech incorporates a running critique of the hearers' categories, and seeks to wean them away towards the initially unthinkable."¹⁰³ Finally, the comparison with Romans 1 is artificial and fails to account for the contextual differences existing between the two texts.

Contemporary scholars generally consider the use of ζητέω (and therefore εὑρίσκω) in v. 27 to be clearly—even thoroughly—biblical, recognizing the breadth and wealth of the OT background attached to it.¹⁰⁴ Isaiah 55:6 is hence often cited as a close parallel, together with Isa 51:1 and many other texts.¹⁰⁵ As a matter of fact, a computer search for ζητέω and its cognates in the LXX yields an overabundant harvest of texts concerned with "seeking God."¹⁰⁶ This illustrates the fact that this theme "is axiomatic for the biblical tradition."¹⁰⁷ As a result, it is so broad, rich, and complex that the kind of study it deserves would require substantially more space than we can afford here.

Before we highlight some salient features of the OT theme of seeking God, we must first address Haenchen's weighty objection to understanding ζητέω in this manner. His argument is based on the consideration that the "seeking of Yahweh" frequently required of Israel consists in obedience to the Torah, and that "this Torah

---

101. See Hemer, "Speeches II," 248–55.

102. This misleading approach to semantics used *TDNT* has been definitively dismissed by Barr, *Semantics*. See also Silva, "Review of TDNT."

103. Hemer, "Speeches II," 249–50.

104. Here we should be careful to distinguish between the meaning of the word and its thematic import. The verb ζητέω itself means "to seek" in Acts 17:27 (for its semantic range, see BDAG 428), but because it had become closely tied to the particular scriptural teaching of "seeking God" (or "God's face"), its use here infallibly evokes this scriptural tradition for the competent reader.

105. See the sample of texts adduced by Marshall, "Acts," 595; Butticaz, *Identité de l'Eglise*, 359; and Litwak, "Israel's Prophets," 207–08.

106. To do full justice to the theme one would have to include corollary themes such as "turning" to God and "following" his ways or commandments as well.

107. Johnson, *Acts*, 315.

was not revealed to the heathen; Paul's listeners still live in ignorance of God."[108] Haenchen is correct: the call or command to seek God in the OT belongs to Israel in the Mosaic economy; obedience to the Torah plays an important role in it; Paul's audience did not have access to the commandment; therefore they could not know they must seek Yahweh.

But Haenchen's argument fails on the following grounds. First, Paul is speaking of God's *creational* design, a mandate that antedates both the Fall and Babel—and therefore sin, mankind's division, and Israel's election—as well as the covenant of grace in either its Edenic (Gen 3:15), Abrahamic (Genesis 12, 15, 17), or Mosaic forms.[109] Second, it is not so much the Torah as the covenant of which the Torah is a part that is at the heart of the OT theme of seeking God. Therefore, the obedience to the Torah, however important it might be, is not the sum, nor the center, nor the primary dimension of what it means to seek God. Third, though the perspective of the Areopagitica on the original design is, indeed, post-Babel, and seeking God (with the assurance that he may be found) is a privilege springing from the first Exodus, it is applicable to Paul's audience because they are under the New Exodus economy. Finally, though the Athenians are ἀγνοοῦντες of God, Paul is calling them to repent unconditionally and to obey God's new covenant commands—in accordance with his role as "prophet like Moses" and Isaianic Servant—on the basis of his antecedent proclamation of the gospel—the New Exodus Word of God, a sort of "new Torah."[110]

The heart of seeking Yahweh in the OT is the covenant that God graciously gave to Israel. This covenant was established between the great King Yahweh and his vassal Israel on account of his making and freeing them.[111] In this compact, the suzerain makes promises to his subject, gives commands, and warns of the consequences for failing to obey. All those features are found throughout the OT passages calling Israel to seek Yahweh.

---

108. Haenchen, *Acts*, 524n1. He is arguing specifically against Gärtner, *Areopagus Speech*, 158, and concludes that the speaker does not specify how man is to seek God.

109. While in Eden, Adam and Eve did not have to "seek God" since they dwelt in the very palace/temple of Yahweh. The garden itself was the place where the Creator came to have fellowship with his creature, and there was no sin to keep them apart yet. The expression itself seems to appear for the first time in Exod 33:7 (where people "sought the Lord," probably in the sense of receiving guidance or justice from him in light of 18:15), therefore not only after the fall and Babel, but after the Exodus and the establishment of the Mosaic covenant, both of which are seen as a "new creation" of a "new humanity" that would belong to, serve and worship Yahweh in a unique fashion.

110. Note that the concepts of "knowing" or "not-knowing" are not primarily or exclusively intellectual, in terms of what is known *about* God (the French *savoir*), but personal and relational, in terms of knowing *God* (the French *connaître*). Of course, the latter implies, includes, and even requires the former—in order to know someone we must know something about that person—, but it is substantially larger. The theme of ἄγνοια in Acts 17 is not limited to a lack of information concerning God but is primarily concerned with the lack of a *proper relationship* between the creature and his or her Maker and King.

111. For Near Eastern parallels to the Mosaic covenant as it is found in both Exodus and Deuteronomy, see Kline, *Treaty* and Kline, *Biblical Authority*, 113–53.

Hence, the call is based on Yahweh's fundamental covenantal promises that he will be their God—concomitant with their being his people—and that he will dwell among them.[112] The corollary to this promise is that he will make himself found and that he will respond favorably. Hence the one seeking can do so with confidence, trusting God to do just what he said he would.[113] The typical context for the call to seek God, however, is Israel's sin, rebellion, and idolatry, together with their corresponding covenantal retribution: the loss of God's presence and favor, climaxing in the exile.[114] This withdrawal of God's presence is at the same time punishment and mercy, for it is meant to lead Israel to turn away from its sins and idols and back to Yahweh in humility and repentance.[115] Those who thus seek him find forgiveness, healing, salvation, as well as justice and a refuge when distressed, oppressed, or in danger.[116] Their true seeking produces joy and praise expressing themselves in covenant obedience and acceptable worship, both of which are so exclusively because of humble submission to God's Torah.[117] Those features fit very well with the content and argument of the Areopagitica, especially in light of vv. 30–31.[118]

Legrand is one of very few scholars who consider that v. 27 affirms the *actuality* (or factuality) of the seeking and, consequently, of the finding on the part of the Gentiles.[119] The majority of scholars recognize a certain ambivalence in the text and conclude that Luke/Paul affirms both the *possibility*, whether actual or theoretical, of man's seeking (and finding) God and its great uncertainty, many stating that it

---

112. For example: Exod 6:7; 29:45; Lev 26:12; Deut 12:11; 1 Kgs 6:13 (cf. 8:27); Ps 132:13–14; Rev 21:3.

113. See, for example: 1 Chr 28:9; 2 Chr 7:14; Ps 9:10; 27:4, 7–8; Prov 8:17; Isa 45:19.

114. For example: Deut 4:29 (15–40); 28:15–68; 29:21–27; 2 Chr 17:3–4; Ps 27:9; Hos 5:6; Amos 5:5–6.

115. Pride is the opposite of "seeking Yahweh" and leads both to idolatry and wicked practices (e.g., Ps 10:4; Hos 5:5; 7:10). That to "turn" in this context is virtually synonymous with "seeking" is obvious from Deut 4:29–30. For "seeking" as humbling oneself and repenting, see Hos 5:15; Isa 55:6–7; and the *locus classicus*, 2 Chr 7:13–14.

116. See respectively: Isa 55:6–7 (8–9); 2 Chr 7:14; Isa 45:20, 22 (an anti-idol passage); Exod 33:7, 9 (cf. 18:15; Mal 3:1); Ps 141:8. Note Prov 29:26: "Many seek (the LXX does not use ζητεῖν here, but θεραπεύω, used in Acts 17:25) the face of a ruler, but it is from the LORD that a man gets justice."

117. For obedience, see 2 Chr 15:12–15; 17:3–4 (in contrast with those who "seek Baal"); Prov 28:5; Isa 51:1; contrast 2 Chr 12:14. For worship out of joy, thankfulness and love, see: 1 Chr 16:10–11; 2 Chr 11:16; Ps 22:26 (21:27 LXX); 40:6 (39:17 LXX).

118. So also Witherington, *Acts*, 528. O'Toole notes that the expression "to seek God" appears only here in all of Luke-Acts. He therefore suggests that we should understand it in the light of the similar Lukan phrase "to seek Jesus." On that basis he concludes: "When Luke writes 'to seek God' in v 27, he directs us to what God has done in the resurrection of Jesus as v 31 indicates." O'Toole, "Paul at Athens," 195.

119. In spite of his acknowledgment of the fact that the construction of the speech lays great stress on the negative clauses. See Legrand, "Unknown God," 164–65, and Kurz, *Acts*, 272–73—who quotes Vatican I in support of the same view. Cf. the even more enthusiastic assessment in Pinnock, "Finality," 158; Pinnock, "Toward an Evangelical," 364–65; and Sanders, *No Other Name*, 236, 246, 260.

never *actually* happened.[120] For example, Barrett notes that confidence in the possibility of man's seeking is indicated by the fact that "God wills it" as well as the use of the verb εὑρίσκω, while the uncertainty is expressed by the form of the clause (εἰ ἄρα γε with optative), though modified or corrected by the final clause introduced by καί γε.[121] Soards adds to the positive evidence the following parallels in Acts: 10:34–35; 14:17; and 15:16b–17.[122]

It seems that the difficulty scholars have in interpreting this verse and in finding the right balance between "possibility" and "uncertainty" is due to their failure to fully take into account the structure of the sentence and its *complete* OT background. Hence, they flatten the redemptive-historical framework of the passage and are forced to try to make sense of the "seeking" in an absolute and univocal way, missing the various levels of nuance built into Luke's report of Paul's argument.[123] However, the point of view here is identical with that of 26a, namely, God's original (i.e., creational) design seen through the lens of the post-fall/post-Babel situation, here extended to the post-Abrahamic covenantal separation of Israel from the rest of the nations.

It is therefore God's original design for man that he should pursue fellowship with his Creator and Lord and hence serve and worship the one God in acceptable ways (according to the covenant of creation), God being immediately accessible to

---

120. As we have argued earlier in this chapter, the sentence structure for vv. 26–27 serves to express God's creational or original design, but not an actual state of affairs or a divine *telos* that will eventually obtain. This fact by itself precludes Legrand's interpretation but leaves the door open as to the level of probability of any man actually fulfilling his religious mandate.

121. See Barrett, *Acts*, 2.844–45; similarly, Tannehill, *Acts*, 219n22.

122. Soards, *Speeches in Acts*, 97, 98.

123. The same is true for most scholars' interpretation of the Cornelius narrative and its three tellings. The point of this story is not that pagans may "find" the true God in purely "natural" ways but that the wall of separation between Israel and the nations was taken down, and that God's New Exodus salvation is not limited to one ethnic group anymore. See Stenschke, *Luke's Portrait*, 148–64. The climax of this narrative complex (of which the Lystra story is an integral part) is the Jerusalem council and James' speech in Acts 15:16–20, a biblical argument bringing together several prophetic strands (Jer 12:15; Amos 9:11–12, an eschatological promise that the *nations* will "seek the Lord" in its LXX form; Isa 45:21, a New Exodus oracle) establishing that the eschatological New Exodus has begun, as is evident from the conversion of Cornelius' household. See Pao, *Acts and INE*, 236–42. For James' speech, see Bauckham, "James and the Gentiles."

It must also be said that though Cornelius serves as a "type" for the Gentiles in Luke's narrative, the passage makes clear that he is a believer in Yahweh and that his "good works" are according to Torah. Moreover, the story is very clear that he *needs* to hear the gospel of Jesus Christ from the mouth of a human herald, Peter. This extremely important episode is therefore far from teaching that the "unevangelized" have access to God's grace independently from his ordained Way, in fact it is emphasizing the fact that even Israel's "old covenant" is not valid anymore. Finally, the affirmation in Acts 14:17 that God has not left himself "without a witness" does not say anything about man's actual response to it. "Gärtner (*Speech*), Dibelius (*Studies*) and Pohlenz ("Paulus") have treated this subject, writing in terms of 'natural theology.' In this regard, the term 'natural revelation' is to be preferred, in order to make the necessary distinction between the Creator's initiation and human attempts at religiosity." Charles, "Engaging," 56n51. As a matter of fact, Acts 14:17 sounds rather like grounds for condemning the Lystrans' failure to seek and serve the true God (abundantly evidenced by their superstition and idolatry), thus functioning in a way similar to vv. 26–27 in the Areopagitica (see below).

his image/child/servant.[124] But the verse in its larger context greatly emphasizes a negative assessment of mankind's performance as we shall now argue. Hence Stonehouse writes:

> Paul is not describing contemporaneous pagan religion but rather is disclosing the divine purpose regarding man's religious response which was grounded in the creation of man and the divine rule over him. To man was appointed the privilege of religious fellowship with his Creator, and this was to be attained by way of a conscious seeking after God in response to the divine revelation. That goal had always remained, but in "the times of ignorance" it evidently remained distant and had not been reached.[125]

The first and most obvious indication of the negative evaluation of man's performance is the narrative framework of the speech, as we saw in our earlier study. It insists heavily on the fact that the Athenians do *not* know God, that they are religious *dilletantes* whose religion, in either its popular or "higher" form, is idolatrous and offensive to Yahweh.[126] The assumption or implication of the speech is therefore that mankind in general—Paul's audience especially—never *sought* (in the OT meaning of the term) and never *found* the true God.[127] Even though all human religious quest is due to man's created design,[128] it only ends in blindness, ἀγνοία, and utter idolatry when it is not according to God's covenantal revelation and ways.[129]

Second, the syntax of the clause itself suggests a high level of uncertainty or unlikelihood, even impossibility. It is grammatically possible that the optatives would reflect the highly classical report of the subjunctive mood in indirect discourse, but this is very unlikely on at least two grounds: style and syntax.[130] As far as

---

124. This original situation is echoed in the infinitive ζητεῖν, the use of εὑρίσκω for the intended result of the seeking, and the mention of God's nearness to "each one of us."

125. Stonehouse, "Areopagus Address," 27.

126. Keener, *Acts*, 3.2651, makes a similar point. Peterson, *Acts*, 498 cites Isa 45:20; Ps 14:2–3; Jer 10:1–16; and Wis 13:1–10, to show what every first-century Jew knew: Gentiles are ignorant and pray to gods who cannot save. Cf. Schnabel, *Acts*, 736.

127. So also Carson, "Athens Revisited," 393; Hanson, *Acts*, 180; Stenschke, *Luke's Portrait*, 216; and Rowe, *World Upside Down*, 37, 199n155.

128. What Fitzmyer calls man's "instinctive searching" (*Acts*, 610) and Calvin the *sensus divinitatis*, is exemplified in a climactic manner by the δεισιδαιμονεστέρους Athenians (v. 22). Cf. Krodel, *Acts*, 65. This certainly would justify defining the human being as *homo religiosus*, pace Berger, *Sacred Canopy*, 177.

129. See Thompson, "Uniqueness of Christ," 107–8 and Keyes, "Idol Factory." For a peek into the modern-day "groping" of man after the traces of the divine in his nature, life and environment, see Berger, *Rumor of Angels*.

130. For the use of the optative in indirect discourse, see Turner, *Syntax*, 129–31; BDF § 386; and Smyth, *Greek Grammar*, § 1862–1683, 2619. L. T. Johnson understands the clause to be an indirect question, but he does not argue his case (Johnson, *Acts*, 316). All other interpreters we have consulted conclude that the optative construction is meant to express a highly improbable fact. In any case, even if Johnson were right on this point, then the two optatives would merely continue to express the original design of 27a in an epexegetical manner and therefore would still not indicate either actuality

the former is concerned, it would represent a clearly Atticizing form that would be very surprising in the NT (and would be unique), even in this speech with its higher Greek style.[131] As far as the latter is concerned, it would be hard to see how this piece of indirect discourse fits in the syntactical structure of the sentence and verse. The use of εἰ ἄρα γε with the optative forms a fourth-class conditional, the construction that "grammaticalizes the most condition-laden form of conditional supposition in Greek."[132] The only way to express a less certain fact would be a straightforward negation, which was not an option for Luke in this sentence, since he meant to depict God's original design.[133]

Third, though more debated, the use of the verb ψηλαφάω seems to reinforce the pessimism of the clause. It is used only four times in the NT, but its three other uses are irrelevant to the interpretation of v. 27 for they are all concerned with the tangibility or physical reality of something.[134] In contrast, the evidence from both LXX and Greek literature—where the usage is consistently negative—is more helpful.[135] There it is used to describe the groping of a *blind(ed)* person (Isaac in Gen 27:12, 21, 22; Samson in Judg 16:26; Cyclops in his desperate efforts to catch Odysseus and his men in *Od.* 9.415–16), an "amateur guess" in Plato or the fumbling of someone in the darkness of night.[136] In the OT it is often used in the context of God's judgment: of idolatrous and sinful Israel, Deut 28:29 and Isa 59:10 (v. 7 is cited in Rom 3:15); of evil men in general, Job 5:14; 12:25 (cf. Gen 19:11 where ζητέω carries the same meaning); of Egypt with the ninth plague (γενηθήτω σκότος ἐπὶ γῆν Αἰγύπτου ψηλαφητὸν σκότος, Exod 10:21; using the cognate adjective); of idols in the anti-idol parodies of Ps 115:7 (113:15 LXX) and 135:17 (134:17 LXX).[137] "The image is not an encouraging one, even when coupled with

---

or probability.

131. As is well known, the optative mood is rare in the NT, especially in a classic usage. This clause contains two "real" optatives, a fact that certainly would have caught the attention of Luke's original readers and impressed on them his insistence on the unlikelihood of the seeking and finding.

132. Meaning that "the chance of a human finding God is, in other words, minimal." Porter, *Paul in Acts*, 122. So also Keener, *Acts*, 3.2652; Marguerat, *Actes*, 2.160, says it denotes a "possibilité hypothétique"; Jipp, "Paul's Areopagus Speech," 582, calls it a "conditional contrary-to-fact clause." See the longer discussion of the Greek conditional in Porter, *Idioms*, 254–67, 263–65 for the fourth-class type. Cf. Wallace, *Greek Grammar*, 484, 699–701 and Culy and Parsons, *Acts Handbook*, 339.

133. As Witherington notes, this construction in and of itself "sets this sentence off from Stoic thought since Stoics believed that God's existence could readily be inferred and known from examining nature." *Acts*, 528, in agreement with Wilson, *Gentiles*, 206.

134. Contra Bock, *Acts*, 566–67. Luke 24:39, Jesus' resurrection body; Heb 12:18, either positively for the mountain (Western text) or negatively in contrast with the phenomena observed by Israel at Sinai (Alexandrian text); 1 John 1:1, part of several expressions for the experience of the "word of life" by the apostles that legitimize their witness. Cf. Owen, "Scope," 135.

135. So Witherington, *Acts*, 528–29; cf. Barrett, *Acts*, 2.845; see references in Bock, *Acts*, 566–67.

136. See Witherington, *Acts*, 528 and Bahnsen, *Always Ready*, 258.

137. The reference here is to the fact that the idols do have hands, but are unable to "touch." The meaning could then be similar to the other NT uses, tough in a judicial context that is absent from them. Since those verses have a similar judicial context (anti-idol polemic) to Acts 17:27 and the fact

what follows it."[138] Just like the grammatical construction it belongs to, this verb depicts God's original design for man in a highly uncertain way, hence expressing the pre-Fall mandate from a post-lapsarian vantage point (see the discussion of ζητέω above).

Fourth, the force of the final clause in the sentence can be understood in at least three ways, depending on the meaning of καί γε. This combination can be either connective, adversative, or concessive.[139] It is impossible to decide on the basis of general grammar or NT usage.[140] The meaning must be ascertained by considering the relationship of 27c with 27a, 27b, and 28a. The clause continues and expands the thought initiated in 27a. The nearness of Yahweh is a powerful and necessary correlative to the original mandate for man to seek his Maker and Lord, one that was lost with the Fall. It was hence a prominent and preeminent part of God's covenant promises to Israel, indispensable to a renewed fellowship between Yahweh and his redeemed people.[141]

It must also be understood in relation to vv. 28–29, as indicated by γάρ.[142] Those verses are opposing the content of 27c–28 to the foolish idolatry of v. 29. In this light, it is pretty clear that the speaker does not mean to say that man has indeed sought and found God. On the contrary, the content of 27c appears to be asserted, at least in part, in *contrast* to that of 27b. Hence, 27c is in continuity with God's original design expressed in 27a-b, but is also in contrast to man's failure to seek and find God suggested by the OT background of this seeking, by the extreme uncertainty built in 27b, and by the anti-idolatry argument of 28–29.[143] The quotation from Aratus

---

that the idols have already been declared to be blind (among many other infirmities!), it seems better to translate the verb as "groping" here also. Once again, the idol-worshipper and his idol/deity look alike.

138. Witherington, Acts, 528–29. Similar judgment in Keener, Acts, 3.2652.

139. See the discussion of those different uses in Porter, Idioms, 191, 211–12. Most of the major commentators understand it to have a concessive force, an interpretation supported by the variants καίτοι ($\mathfrak{P}$74 A E 945. 1891 pc; Cl) and καίτοι γε (a 323. 1739 pc). However, Culy and Parsons, Acts Handbook, 340, argue that it cannot be concessive because ὑπάρχοντα cannot be adverbial but must be attributive to τὸν θεόν.

140. The only other NT occurrence of this exact combination is in Acts 2:18, where γε is added by Luke (for emphasis?) to Joel 2:29 LXX.

141. In fact, the Torah, in its moral and ceremonial aspects, is primarily there to make sure that such proximity of the Holy One with Israel would not lead to the destruction of God's people on account of their sin and moral corruption. Its purpose is to enable Israel to have fellowship with its God as well as to serve and worship him safely.

142. We postpone the discussion of the meaning of God's nearness in v. 27c to our study of vv. 28–29 below.

143. Though our interpretation differs from Gourgues', we can use his formula: "Dieu est à la fois lointain, en tant qu'il est difficile d'accès . . . et tout proche de chaque être humain" "Littérature profane," 246, cf. 256. It is the irony and tragedy of human existence, being so close to God and yet unable even to seek after him. Cf. Witherington, Acts, 529; Hansen, "Preaching and Defence," 316; and Porter, Paul in Acts, 148. On p. 168, Porter calls it "a picture of perpetual frustration. The image is of humans struggling to make contact with the divine, but not being successful, despite the proximity of the creator-God." The affirmation of the proximity heightens the severity of the failure (also noted by Stenschke, Luke's Portrait, 216). Witherington notes that though Dio Chrysostom at first appears

illustrates the dual aspect of v. 27 very well: the Greek poet did have a true insight concerning the divine (used and reinterpreted by Paul), and yet he totally fails to seek and find the one God and Lord.[144]

Fifth, one must take into consideration the structure of the whole speech and pericope. As far as the speech is concerned, it seems to form a simple topical chiasm: ABCB'A'.[145] A and A' (22–23, 30–31) speak of not knowing God; B and B' (24–25, 28–29) of its corollary, idolatry; C (26–27) functions as a foil that highlights the failure and the sinfulness of As and Bs.[146] It provides the proper standard or commandment by which mankind's "ignorance" and "idolatry" must and will be judged. It magnifies therefore the severity of man's sin and the folly of his idolatry, and thus reinforces his responsibility and culpability.[147] In this manner, the speech develops at the same time a theology and an anthropology, which together produce an hamartology by clarifying what sin is, thereby making idolatry utterly reprehensible for it is rebellion against Yahweh—both as God and Lord.[148]

In the light of the end-point of the argument, v. 27 must be understood as pointing already to the fact that the nations' "redemptive history" is described by Paul as "the times of ignorance."[149] And this ignorance is not due to God's absence or failure ("he

---

similar, in the end his teaching is absolutely different due to clearly opposite types of theism: Paul affirms and maintains a strict distinction between the Creator and the creature, which "requires a relationship of adherence to create fellowship." Finally, Betz and Smith, "De Iside et Osiride," 82, point to the contrast with the notion of proximity in *Is. Os.* 28 (362A).

144. Leading some scholars to describe vv. 27 and 28 as a "double failure" on man's part. See Owen, "Scope," 135 and Bahnsen, *Always Ready*, 259–60.

145. Which could be charted as follows:

    A Athenians' unknowing of God (vv. 22–23: "unknown God," "worship in ignorance," etc.)

       B Idolatry: pagan temple and ceremonies (vv. 24–25; contrasted with God's nature)

          C Man's double creational mandate (vv. 26–27: dwell and seek)

       B' Idolatry: crafting of lifeless idols (vv. 28–29; contrasted with life-giving God)

    A' All nations' unknowing of God (vv. 30–31: "times of ignorance")

146. Des Places and O'Toole offer a much more detailed chiastic organization of the speech and pericope, each with v. 27 at its center. They understand it to indicate that the heart of the speech and of the Athens narrative is the true worship of God. See des Places, "Actes 17,27" and O'Toole, "Paul at Athens," especially 194–95; cf. Jervell, *Die Apostelgeschichte*, 449. O'Toole adds that the branches of the chiasm show that for Luke true worship is *necessarily* connected to Jesus and his resurrection (one of the two main arguments of his article).

147. Cf. Larkin, *Acts*, 258.

148. Cf. Carson, "Athens Revisited," 394.

149. We could say that the nations' history is rather *un*redemptive (cf. Jervell, *Theology of Acts*, 19), contra those who would see it as a "pre-history" equal or similar to Israel's—e.g., Butticaz, *Identité de l'Eglise*, 376–79, 81; Higgins, "Key to Insider Movements," 161, 162; Pervo, *Acts*, 437; and Wilson, *Gentiles*, 217. It is important to insist on the *redemptive-historical* nature of this characterization. As Tipton, "Resurrection Proof," 46–47, notes, it is not people who are here deemed "ignorant," but entire historical eras! Cf. Strange, *For Their Rock*, 285–88, who uses the concept of "subversive fulfillment" (borrowed from Hendrik Kraemer) to understand the Areopagitica on this point.

did not leave himself without witness," Acts 14:17), but to mankind's.¹⁵⁰ As Rom 3:11 says (adapting Ps 13:2 LXX [MT 14:2]): "no one understands; no one seeks for God."¹⁵¹ Stonehouse concludes: "The concessive character of this statement indeed confirms the conclusion that the goal of finding God had not been attained, but it also reflects positively on an actual relationship of God to all men in the present situation."¹⁵²

And so Paul's speech is neither hopeless nor presenting a message of unqualified doom. Yahweh has accomplished the salvation of his people, a people that brings together Israel and the nations.¹⁵³ The New Exodus has come, and God is extending the Way of salvation through the progress of his Word. The darkness to which the nations have been condemned until now (τὰ νῦν of v. 30) is dispelled by the light of the gospel. As Paul utters words of condemnation for all idolaters, he is at that very moment fulfilling the words of Isa 42:6–7 concerning the Servant: "I am the LORD; I have called you in righteousness; I will take you by the hand and keep you; I will give you as a covenant for the people, *a light for the nations, to open the eyes that are blind, to bring out the prisoners from the dungeon, from the prison those who sit in darkness.*"¹⁵⁴

---

150. Soards, *Speeches in Acts*, 98, makes the same connection with Acts 14:17, and sees another parallel to this idea in 7:44—the "tent of witness" the fathers had in the wilderness. See also Calvin, *Actes*, 471–72 and Chrysostom, Homily XXXVIII, 235–36. One cannot but see a close parallel with Rom 1:19–23 and Ps 19.

151. See Wilkinson, "Acts 17," 7.

152. Stonehouse, "Areopagus Address," 27; cf. Rowe, "Grammar," 44n48.

153. Here we are reminded of Jesus's answer to the question full of pathos asked by the disciples concerning whether *anyone* could be saved found in the three Synoptic Gospels: "With man this is impossible, but with God all things are possible" (Matt 19:26 // Mark 10:27; Luke 18:27).

154. Note that v. 8 of Isaiah 42 is a piece of anti-idol polemic parallel to Acts 17:24b–25a, 29, while 24a and 25b are built upon an allusion to Isa 42:5. In the light of what has been addressed in the current chapter, there is no doubt that Paul is following a biblical and prophetic argument in vv. 26–27. Cf. Dunn, *Acts*, 235–36.

CHAPTER 8

Convicted of *Lèse-Majesté* (Acts 17:28–29)

IF THE SPEECH WAS "bilingual" so far, "verse 28 comes out fully on the Greek side, with a quotation, possibly two quotations."[1] These verses have often been seen in the past as injecting a good dose of Stoic pantheism into the speech.[2] They are therefore frequently used to defend inclusivistic theories and practices.[3] We will argue, as do virtually all contemporary NT scholars, that such is not the case: though the language is thoroughly Hellenistic, the import and the argument are strictly biblical.

Structural Considerations

Gärtner provides a helpful discussion of the relationship of v. 28 with 27 and 29.[4] He argues convincingly against the idea that this verse is providing the ground for both the nearness and the seeking. That is, against the view that v. 28 would be the climax of an argument establishing a natural theology on the basis of man's kinship with God—understood Hellenistically in relation to the Stoic Logos—, a point that would be made on the authority of a pagan poet. In this view, v. 29 begins an independent argument developing a mild polemic against idols.[5]

But, as Gärtner points out, the connection indicated by οὖν at the beginning of v. 29 renders this structure—and therefore its natural-theological interpretation—impossible.[6]

---

1. Barrett, "Paul at Athens," 150; cf. Gärtner, *Areopagus Speech*, 166.

2. Gärtner, *Areopagus Speech*, 177n2, gives a good list of earlier scholars of that opinion. Of prime importance are Norden, *Agnostos Theos*, 18–24; Dibelius, *Aufsätze*, 45–60; and Pohlenz, "Paulus," 90–95. "This verse combines οὐ μακράν, 'not far,' with a pantheistic triad and a pantheistic (Stoic) quotation." Conzelmann, *Acts*, 144.

3. For example, Samuel, "Paul on the Areopagus," 27 and Sanders, *No Other Name*, 245.

4. Gärtner, *Areopagus Speech*, 166–67.

5. "It is mild polemic; Deutero-Isaiah (40.19f.; 46.6 and especially 44.9–20) spoke more bitterly and mockingly. Even the Jewish hellenism of the Wisdom of Solomon (13.10–14.2; 15.7–17) criticizes more sharply . . ." Dibelius, "Areopagus," 55.

6. Gärtner, *Areopagus Speech*, 166.

This conjunction shows that v. 28 is part of the grounds upon which the anti-idol polemic is argued. The connection between the two verses is further strengthened by the repetition of the term γένος from the quotation in 28c in a marked position at the beginning of v. 29. This connection is reinforced by the use of two semantically related verbs (in fact, they are here synonymous), εἰμί and ὑπάρχω, being repeated: the occurrence of ἐσμέν in v. 28a and c (each time the final term of a formula), εἶναι at the end of 29, as well as ὑπάρχω in the final position in 27c (cf. 24b).[7]

Gärtner understands v. 28a to be a transition or a bridge between the argument of vv. 26–27 and that of vv. 28b–31, thus concluding the first and initiating the second by resuming the argument line of 24–25[8] (cf. the chiastic diagramming of the speech above), all at the same time. We can be more specific by looking carefully to the discourse development markers. Γάρ indicates that 28a introduces supporting or confirming information for the preceding line of thought. In view of our earlier structural analyses, that means vv. 24–27. This is confirmed by the use of ἐν αὐτῷ in 28a, which (re-)topicalizes the God of 24a (24–27, therefore). Ὡς καί in 28b indicates that what follows immediately further elaborates/confirms the support information introduced in 28a. Οὖν in 29a resumes the discourse mainline for which v. 28 provides background ("offline") information. It continues therefore the development started in v. 24 in view of the content of v. 28. This relation is further marked by the repeated γένος, in an emphatic position in 29a. Thus, v. 29 brings the argument of vv. 24–28 to a conclusion. Μὲν οὖν in v. 30 brings the whole speech to a conclusion in light of what is said in v. 29, thus tying the assertion of 22b with the call to repentance of vv. 30–31.[9] It should be noted that there are *no discontinuity markers* in the speech before v. 32 (with δέ marking a new narrative development). Thus, as Gärtner perceived, the rhetorical development of which 28 is a part "moves forward" toward v. 29 to finally reach its apex in vv. 30–31.[10] The speech increases its pace at this point, thanks to the accumulation of conjunctions and particles articulating the various elements of vv. 28–31: γάρ in 28a, ὡς καί in 28b, οὖν in 29a, μὲν οὖν in 30a, τὰ νῦν in 30b, and καθότι at the start of 31.[11]

---

7. Furthermore, αὐτῷ in 28a has for its antecedent τὸν θεόν of 27a, which itself refers back to ἐποίησεν in 26a, which is a resumption of ὁ ποιήσας in 24a. It is also connected to τοῦ in 28b and to the several explicit and implicit references to God in the subsequent verses.

8. The resumption is effected especially by the use of parallel tricolons affirming poetically God's role as the giver of life to mankind in both 25b and 28a. The latter is therefore an integral part of the anti-idolatry argument being developed all along the speech. See Gärtner, *Areopagus Speech*, 198, 222, respectively.

9. Hence des Places writes: "Alors que l'οὖν 'parénétique' de 29 introduisait la conclusion de la partie apologétique, le μὲν οὖν de 30 fait la transition entre les deux parties." "Actes 17,30–31," 526.

10. Cf. Gärtner, *Areopagus Speech*, 166–67.

11. In fact, this change of pace seems to start with v. 27 and its use of εἰ ἄρα γε and καί γε. By contrast, vv. 24–26 contain long and somewhat complex sentences with no strongly-marked transition.

Why Paul Is Not a Pantheist

Since Gärtner's groundbreaking study, scholars have generally understood v. 28a to clarify or add precision to the expression οὐ μακράν of v. 27c, bringing together the ideas that God is near to man, that he gives him life, and that mankind is his "offspring."[12] The question becomes then whether it does so in Stoic and pantheistic terms or not.[13] The expression ἐν αὐτῷ at the beginning of 28a was taken by Dibelius to imply at least a form of panentheism.[14] But the idea that man would be "in God" is the exact opposite of the Stoic teaching of "god in us."[15] It is therefore impossible to claim that v. 28a is affirming a form of Stoic pantheism on that basis. In the context of v. 28a (both in relation to what immediately precedes and follows), it seems better to understand the expression as indicating something like "in the power of."[16] Because of the influence of the LXX on NT Greek, especially Luke's, the ἐν should most likely be understood in an instrumental sense ("by"), indicating the source of life on which man is absolutely dependent.[17] In this case, the use of ἐν αὐτῷ rather than διὰ αὐτοῦ could add a connotation congruent with the idea of relational proximity between God and man affirmed by both 27c and 28b.[18]

Remains the issue of determining whether the triadic formula is of Stoic origin, and is thus meant to express a pantheistic view of man's nature. This has led to a debate between scholars who defend the idea that 28a is an actual quotation (from Epimenides) and others who consider the triad to be an original Lukan composition bringing together common Hellenistic ideas.[19] The introductory formula of 28b (note the plural: "τινες τῶν καθ' ὑμᾶς ποιητῶν εἰρήκασιν"), though placed after the triad, could possibly refer backwards and forwards and therefore present the triad as a quotation also.[20] But there are good reasons to limit its application exclusively to the quotation from Aratus in 28b. The most obvious is the formula's position which would be surprising if the speaker meant both 28a and 28b to be actual quotations. The plural

---

12. See, for example, Gärtner, *Areopagus Speech*, 179; Conzelmann, *Acts*, 145; Haenchen, *Acts*, 524; des Places, "Actes 17,27," 2; and Barrett, *Acts*, 2.846–47.

13. Stoics were pantheists and, therefore, when they taught that mankind was "the offspring of Zeus/god" (like Aratus in the text reproduced in 28b), they meant that man possessed a spark of the Logos. See Barrett, *Acts*, 2.848–49.

14. See Dibelius, "Areopagus," 47.

15. See Hanson, *Acts*, 180–81 and Witherington, *Acts*, 529. See also Bruce's argument against Schweitzer's idea that Luke is here teaching a "God mysticism" in Bruce, *Acts Greek*, 384.

16. See the discussion in *BegC*, 4.217.

17. See Witherington, *Acts*, 529.

18. See the discussion in Barrett, *Acts*, 2.846–47.

19. See, for the former: Stonehouse, "Areopagus Address," 27–31; Bruce, *Acts Greek*, 384–85; Bahnsen, *Always Ready*, 259; Dunn, *Acts*, 236; Porter, *Paul in Acts*, 120; and Longenecker, *The Acts of the Apostles*, 984; and the extensive defense of this view in *BegC*, 5.247–51. For the latter: Conzelmann, "Areopagus," 223–24 (Stoic) and Hommel, "Platonisches" (Platonic).

20. See *BegC*, 4.217–18.

and vague formulation is a conventional stylistic device, a cultured literary convention well suited to the style of the speech.²¹ Evidence shows that similar formulas were used when the identity of the author was certain or uncertain (at least to the speaker), or when the material quoted is found in several authors (and the Aratus citation has an extant very close parallel in Cleanthes).²²

In any case, the formula does not require *two* quotations, so the issue becomes whether one can identify the source of the quotation. In spite of Bruce's efforts to defend the idea that the triad comes from Epimenides' quatrain cited in Titus 1:12, the identification is not convincing.²³ First, the exact original form of Epimenides' verse is not known.²⁴ Its identification is therefore made principally on the basis of a passage of Isho'dad of Merv, a reading that has been strongly questioned by Pohlenz.²⁵ Besides, Luke's triad is neither in meter nor in the proper dialect.²⁶ In consequence, Marguerat concludes: "La thèse d'une citation en 28a d'un hymne à Zeus d'Epiménide de Crète ... a été abandonnée."²⁷

Both a Stoic and a Platonic source have been suggested, but the problem is that no exact parallel can be adduced in support of either.²⁸ To this absence of literary evidence, one must add the fact that the closest known parallels are found in the Pauline epistles. The conclusion that seems to impose itself is therefore that the triadic formula was composed by Paul or by Luke.²⁹ This is further supported by the fact that the closest parallel to the triad of 28a one can find in the literature is located in 25b—which no one claims is drawn from a preexisting source. Besides, it is well-known that the tricolon was "an old and frequent pattern in the Greek language, with nothing particularly philosophical about it, even though the tricolon was also used in

---

21. See Dibelius, "Areopagus," 50–51, especially n. 76; Cadbury, *Acts in History*, 49; Fitzmyer, *Acts*, 610–11; Renehan, "Classical Greek Quotations"; and Klauck, *Magic and Paganism*, 88.

22. See *BegC*, 4.218; Renehan, "Classical Greek Quotations," 42; Barrett, *Acts*, 2.848; and Thom, *Cleanthes' Hymn*, 65. For a full discussion of the various possibilities, see Rothschild, *Paul in Athens*, 68–71.

23. Bruce, *Acts NICNT*, 359 (esp. n. 49) and Bruce, *Acts Greek*, 384–85; cf. Fitzmyer, *Acts*, 610 and Haenchen, *Acts*, 524n3.

24. L. T. Johnson, *Acts*, 316.

25. Pohlenz, "Paulus," 101–4 (cited in Barrett, *Acts*, 2.847); cf. Gärtner, *Areopagus Speech*, 195n2.

26. Marshall, *Acts TNTC*, 289. Renehan, "Classical Greek Quotations," 38, shows that the phrase is not poetry. It is always possible that Luke/Paul might have quoted it from memory or simply given its general sense.

27. Marguerat, *Actes*, 2.161n41. In spite of this claim, the presence of an Epimenidean source has been defended recently by Keener, *Acts*, 3.2658–59 and Rothschild, *Paul in Athens*, 67–73.

28. Stoic source: Norden, *Agnostos Theos*, 19–24 ; Conzelmann, "Areopagus," 223–24; and Conzelmann, *Acts*, 145; cf. Gärtner, *Areopagus Speech*, 202 and Barrett, *Acts*, 2.846–47. Platonic source: Hommel, "Platonisches"; cf. Fitzmyer, *Acts*, 610 and Barrett, *Acts*, 2.847–48. Note that Epimenides cannot be considered a Stoic since he lived *before* the time of Zeno.

29. Barrett, *Acts*, 2.847, cites Rom 11:36, while Bahnsen, *Always Ready*, 260, points to Col 1:15–17. See Gärtner, *Areopagus Speech*, 195–98.

Greek philosophical writing."[30] Yet Barrett is right to point out that the absence of such formula in the extant literature is not sufficient to conclude that no Stoic ever said or wrote anything like it.[31] The historical question of the possible *source(s)* used by Luke or Paul remains open.

Thus, Luke/Paul may have cited a line from a poet now lost, brought together some Hellenistic "common places," or have invented the formula altogether. Whichever might be the case, they are now his words, incorporated in a broader discourse and story. Even if the author used material drawn from Hellenistic poetry or philosophy, its frame of reference in-speech is fundamentally theistic and biblical.[32] Thus it is indubitable that the triad's in-context meaning is *not* pantheistic, however much the form and wording might sound Hellenistic to Paul's depicted audience.[33] It should be noted, however, that the three verbs (ζῶμεν, κινούμεθα, ἐσμέν) belong to the septuagintal language of anti-idol polemic.[34] Hence they are used of typical elements of biblical and Jewish condemnation of idolatry: idols are lifeless/breathless, they cannot move (or do anything for either themselves or anyone else), and they are "vanities" (μάταια, Acts 14:15;[35] cf., for example, Lev 17:7; Isa 2:20; 44:9; Jer 8:19) or non-beings.

For a proper understanding, v. 28a must be read in relation to vv. 25b, 27c, 28b, as well as 24–27b and 30–31. As we saw earlier, the topical frame ἐν αὐτῷ in 28a makes the depiction of the person, identity and activity of Yahweh the interpretive framework to understand the new information introduced. In vv. 24–26, God is declared to be the Creator—and therefore the Lord—of the whole world, of mankind, and of the nations. As Lord/King, God is humanity's benefactor, dispensing life and all its necessities, as well as the one ruling over world history. Verses 26–27 affirm God's prerogative to assign mankind its double purpose, while 30–31 assert his prerogative to judge the inhabited world, having set a day and appointed a judge. The "seeking" of v. 27 and the call to repentance of v. 30—together with the affirmation of God's absolute authority over the nations and of his being the one God—establish Yahweh as the one who, alone, can save and deliver man from his estrangement from his Maker and from idolatry.

---

30. Fitzmyer, *Acts*, 610.

31. Barrett, *Acts*, 2.847.

32. Cf. Barrett, *Acts*, 2.846–48 and Bruce, *Acts Greek*, 385. Even Conzelmann concludes that "the intention of the statement as Luke uses it is not ontological—as if to say something about the essence of humanity as superior to nature. Rather it is intended as a criticism, aimed at the restoration of the proper kind of worship of God." Conzelmann, *Acts*, 145. He considers that is due to Luke's inability to interpret the formula. Barrett, however, argues that the shift in meaning would have occurred in the Hellenistic Judaism from which Luke would have received the formula.

33. So also Fitzmyer, *Acts*, 610; Stonehouse, "Areopagus Address," 27–30; and Bahnsen, *Always Ready*, 259.

34. As shown by Gärtner, *Areopagus Speech*, 219–23.

35. See the discussion in Rowe, "Acts and Cultural Explication," 254 and Rowe, *World Upside Down*, 21–22.

Verses 28a and 25b are very similar in at least three ways: they have a triadic form, they consist of a cumulation of expressions related to life, and they provide grounds for an explicit anti-idol polemic.[36] Structurally, 28a resumes the anti-idol polemic of vv. 24–25, adding to their attack on the temple and the sacrifices an attack on idol-making *per se*.[37] The supporting description of mankind's original design (vv. 26–27) is thus woven into the anti-idol argument also. Doing so both increases the weightiness of the argument against idol-making and makes explicit the grounds for man's indictment in God's tribunal. When the two triads are read together as they were meant to, it is obvious that their point is not to express an abstract philosophical ontology, but to proclaim Yahweh, the Creator and Lord, who alone gives man his life/existence and provides for its sustenance.[38] Verse 28a "sums up human existence."[39] The clear implication of both triads is man's absolute dependence on God's benevolent care.[40]

This notion of God's sovereign and providential care for his creature is at the heart of the connection between the nearness of 27c and the tricolon of 28a, as indicated by the use of γάρ.[41] Man's absolute dependence and God's royal provision for his subjects elucidate the manner in which God is always near his creature, and they imply that God's presence is inescapable (in either a positive or a negative sense; cf. Jer 23:23–24 and Ps 139:7–12).[42] It is as Maker and Lord that God is present in man's life and destiny, "so near as to constitute the environment in which we live, but in a personal sense."[43] Haenchen is correct: v. 28b confirms that God's nearness in 27c is to be understood not in a spatial (or ontological) but in a relational sense, the relationship being established and defined by God's creation of man.[44]

---

36. Cf. Gärtner, *Areopagus Speech*, 198 and Haenchen, *Acts*, 525.

37. Or one could say that v. 25 anticipates v. 28 (so Keener, *Acts*, 3.2644).

38. Thus, translating ἐσμέν "we have our being" "exaggerates its ontological implications. A far preferable translation is 'For by him we live and move and are' . . . which simply epitomizes all that has been said previously regarding God as the creator and sustainer of human life." Gaventa, *Acts*, 251, quoting L. T. Johnson, *Acts*, 312 (see also 316). This is confirmed by the use of ἐσμέν in 28b and of εἶναι in 29c. See also Klauck, *Magic and Paganism*, 87–88.

39. Fitzmyer, *Acts*, 610.

40. Cf. Witherington, *Acts*, 529 and Parsons, *Acts*, 247. The thought is similar to Acts 14:17, though with distinct imageries adapted to their respective audiences.

41. See Gärtner, *Areopagus Speech*, 179.

42. Cf. Stonehouse, "Areopagus Address," 26 and L. T. Johnson, *Acts*, 315.

43. Barrett, *Acts*, 2.847, based on the fact that ἐν αὐτῷ in 28a must be understood in relation to 27c.

44. Haenchen, *Acts*, 525.

Reading Aratus in Its Lukan Context

The verse from Aratus (ca. 315/310–240 BC) in v. 28b is tightly tethered to the triad of 28a (and therefore to 27c) by the use of ὡς καί ("as also" or "as even").[45] This conjunction is reinforced by their identical ending (ἐσμέν).[46] The speaker thereby indicates that the intended import of both sentences is analogous. Therefore, being "God's offspring" is another way of saying that "in him we live, etc.," that God created man, and that he is not far from us. The denotation is unquestionably God's original and ongoing providential gift of life to each human being (as Maker and Lord), while a personal—viz., familial and parental—dimension is added to the depiction of God's relation to man. Neither Luke's readers nor Paul's depicted audience could have missed the connection with ἐποίησεν ἐξ ἑνός in 26a. In light of the background of 26a discussed earlier, it is indubitable that the figure of Adam is behind the speaker's understanding and use of Aratus' poem.[47]

In this regard, the conclusion of Jesus' genealogy—"the son of Adam, the son of God" (Luke 3:38)—is illuminating as it encapsulates Luke's understanding of Adam's creational relationship to God. Haenchen does recognize a connection between the two passages, but he contends that in the Lukan genealogy "nothing more is intended than that he [God] created Adam."[48] He is correct to insist that Luke has Adam's *creation* in mind, rather than any other form of generation, whether procreation, emanation or Logos inhabitation. However, one cannot simply brush aside Luke's use of paternal language. It denotes more than bare creation, though certainly nothing less.

As we saw in chapter 1, Jesus' own status as messianic Son of God is intricately related to Adam's original created sonship, which it fulfills in an eschatological and redemptive manner.[49] Moreover, Adam's creation in the image (κατ' εἰκόνα) and after the likeness (καθ' ὁμοίωσιν) of God (Gen 1:26; cf. 27; 5:1, 3) is essentially or fundamentally his being covenantally constituted God's *son*.[50] This means that mankind has

---

45. It is generally agreed that the text is from Aratus, *Phaen.* 5, though it also resembles Cleanthes' *Hymn to Zeus* 4. This section of Aratus' poem is quoted by Aristobulus in a fragment known to us through Eusebius, *Praep. ev.* 13.12.6, in the context of his discussion of God's omnipresence in creation. Technical studies of these two poems (which address their appearance in the Areopagitica) are found in Kidd, *Aratus:* Phaenomena and Thom, *Cleanthes' Hymn*. Otherwise see the discussions in Fitzmyer, *Acts*, 611; *BegC*, 5.246–47; Cadbury, *Acts in History*, 51; and Edwards, "Quoting Aratus."

46. Which means that the word order of the tricolon was most probably chosen for literary reasons—ζῶμεν ties it to 25b and ἐσμέν to 28b—not to present an ontological scale, contra Hommel, "Platonisches," 198–99 (see Conzelmann, *Acts*, 144–45).

47. This is the general consensus among NT scholars, including those who consider that v. 28 represents a genuinely Hellenistic element in the speech. Contra Wilkinson, "Acts 17," 10.

48. Haenchen, *Acts*, 525.

49. On this topic, see the excellent Evans, "Jesus and the Spirit." The parallel existing between Luke's *covenantal* and *redemptive-historical* anthropology (and christology) and Paul's (in Romans 5 and 1 Corinthians 15) is unmistakable. See Murray, *Imputation* and Garner, "First and Last Son."

50. For a historical overview of the theological understanding of the nature of the *imago Dei*, see Berkouwer, *Man*, 67–118. For the understanding of the *imago* in terms of covenantal sonship, see

a unique and special relationship with the one God and Lord who made all things. This relationship was designed to be one of fellowship and love, and therefore of service and worship (cf. vv. 26–27). It also means that man was appointed the *representative* of God on earth, his vice-regent, the very icon or emblem of God's universal kingship.[51] Finally, and this might be the most obvious denotation of the Genesis description of Adam: mankind was to image or reflect Yahweh's nature and character.[52] "It is here that the terminology of this speech shows closest Hellenistic affinities, but to another audience Paul might have expressed the same thoughts in more biblical terminology by saying that man is God's creature, made in His image."[53]

And this biblical doctrine is precisely the end-point, the argumentative aim or apex of vv. 24–29. It is the linchpin of the condemnation of idolatry in v. 29, as indicated by the use of οὖν and the repetition in an emphatic position of γένος.[54] Rhetorically and argumentatively, 28b is a perfect hinge between, on the one hand, the proclamation of the Creator God and the divine-image-bearing nature of mankind and, on the other hand, the polemic against lifeless, man-made, idols of v. 29.[55] Discursively, οὖν in 29a marks the resumption of the development started in v. 26 (v. 28 contains "background information" supporting or confirming the precedent claim), itself a continuation of the argument started in v. 24 (indicated by τέ). In fact, vv. 24–25 and v. 29 compose a "frame of human ignorance" for vv. 26–28, highlighting the tension between original design ("potentiality") and reality.[56] Thus, 29a is a deft recapitulation of the whole line of argument that brings out clearly the grounds for the censure of 29b.[57] In this perspective, Hanson is correct in describing 28b as a witness

---

Herman Bavinck, *RD 2*, 530–80; Kline, *Kingdom Prologue*, 28–30, 40–42; and Waltke and Yu, *OT Theology*, 215–23. Marguerat's claim that "ici, l'effort d'inculturation atteint son point extrême et se cristallise dans une conceptualité inédite dans le NT : la descendance divine." (Marguerat, *Actes*, 2.160) is simply baffling.

51. Cf., e.g., Ps 2:1–12; 8:6–7; 110:1–7; Isa 42:1–9; Luke 20:41–43; Acts 2:32–36.

52. "Just as children reflect the image of their parents, so God's children should reflect him, which they do by reflecting the glorious attributes of his 'divine nature' (cf. Gen. 1:27) and not by not [sic] reflecting the unspiritual nature of handmade idols." Beale, *Temple*, 230. See also Beale, *We Become*, 197.

53. Bruce, *Defence of the Gospel*, 42. See also Barrett, *Acts*, 2.849; Bossuyt and Radermakers, "Rencontre," 34–35; and Parsons, *Acts*, 248.

54. Cf. Gärtner, *Areopagus Speech*, 166–67.

55. Also noted by Hanson, *Acts*, 181. Hence, "A force de fixer leur attention sur le détail de certaines considérations, plusieurs auteurs sont arrivés à perdre de vue le but qu'elles poursuivent; si l'on insiste sur la bonté de Dieu à l'égard des hommes ou sur la parenté des hommes avec Dieu, ce n'est pas qu'on veuille s'arrêter à ces idées pour elles-mêmes, mais pour mieux mettre en valeur l'erreur commise par ceux qui confondent la divinité avec des statues matérielles." Dupont, "Salut des Gentils," 153n1.

56. To use the language of Tannehill, *Acts*, 219–20.

57. The quotation in 28b and the introduction in 29a are so much alike in content, form and even wording, that, considering the fact that 28b was already repeating the content of 28a which itself was expanding on 27c, it seems the reader should feel somewhat overwhelmed by such (ponderous) insistence.

similar to that mentioned in 14:17.[58] Both belong to the kind that leaves idolatrous humanity without excuse in Yahweh's eschatological lawsuit (cf. Rom 1:18–32).

Drawing Incriminatory Deductions

The sentence structure of v. 29 possesses several noteworthy features. The main verbal clause (οὐκ ὀφείλομεν νομίζειν) is in an unmarked position, immediately following the summary statement of the principle/evidence it is drawing from. Follows the substantival infinitive clause, which starts with a long and redundant topical frame (χρυσῷ ἢ ἀργύρῳ ἢ λίθῳ, χαράγματι τέχνης καὶ ἐνθυμήσεως ἀνθρώπου) preceding the subject (τὸ θεῖον, in an emphatic position), the verb (εἶναι) and the predicate (ὅμοιον). The verse is thus bracketed by γένος . . . τοῦ θεοῦ and τὸ θεῖον εἶναι ὅμοιον.[59] This forms a simple chiasm in which God's likeness frames man's idolatrous attempts at representing the divine nature, thereby emphasizing the contrast and opposition between the two.[60]

One pragmatic effect of the sentence structure is to delay until the very end the elucidation of what it is exactly "we ought not to think."[61] This postponement increases the hearer's and reader's sense of expectancy, curiosity and suspense. It also brings out with greater sharpness the point of the comparison being negated. Thus, χαράγματι τέχνης καὶ ἐνθυμήσεως ἀνθρώπου foregrounds an aspect already communicated by χρυσῷ ἢ ἀργύρῳ ἢ λίθῳ. Besides delaying the elucidation of the author's meaning, this overspecification reminds the hearer/reader of a particular quality that was on the back burner of his or her mental representation but is now especially important in the context.[62] This thematic highlighting also ties up the meaning of v. 29 to the negations of vv. 24 (χειροποιήτοις) and 25 (χειρῶν ἀνθρωπίνων). In the end, the formulation communicates a thoroughly and emphatically negative judgment on the arrogance and folly—even absurdity—of idol-making.[63]

---

58. See Hanson, *Acts*, 180.

59. See also Alexander, *Acts*, 2.158. There is thus a double shift in focus through vv. 24–31: God is first in the spotlight (seen in relation to his creation, especially man), then man moves to the fore in 26a (seen in relation to his Creator, Lord, and Father), and now God is back in focus (in relation to sinful man who is about to be judged).

60. Τὸ θεῖον is a reference "to the property of being divine, divinity contrasted with an implicit τὸ ἀνθρώπειον, that which is human, and τὸ ὑλικόν, that which is material." Barrett, *Acts*, 2.850. Though the referent of τοῦ θεοῦ and τὸ θεῖον is, ultimately, the same being, the shift in perspective implied by the change of language augments the conceptual distance between the God proclaimed by Paul and the Hellenistic pagan notion of the divine, both popular and philosophical. It creates "un écran entre le dieu inconnu adoré par les Athéniens et le Dieu que Paul annonce. . . . Terme intermédiaire, il assure un passage tout en maintenant la différence." Dupont, "Discours à l'Aréopage," 419. See also Rowe, *World Upside Down*, 37 and Stenschke, *Luke's Portrait*, 217n522.

61. Marguerat, *Actes*, 2.161, puts it nicely: "ὀφείλω est le verbe du devoir moral."

62. On the various uses of overspecification, see Runge, *Discourse Grammar*, 317–26.

63. Cf. Jervell, *Die Apostelgeschichte*, 449, who comments that v. 29 makes every Athenian object

As a result, two key aspects of manufacturing idols are specially highlighted by the polemic: the material nature of the representation ("gold or silver or stone") and human creative activity ("the art and imagination of man"). The contrast between the divine nature and its material representations is not here specifically concerned with the spirituality of God vs. the materiality of idols, but with the fact that idols are *lifeless*, inert, impotent. This is clear from the principle behind the denial in 29a: the kinship of (somatic) mankind with God. Verses 24–28 make three foundational points in this regard: man is a living being; man is made and kept alive by God's sovereign and benevolent providence; man was created in the image and likeness of God. These propositions have two immediate and unmistakable implications: God is not only himself "alive"—a divine attribute revealed by man's very nature—but he is the Creator and giver of life itself. This fact entails that he is active and acting. Idols of "gold or silver or stone" are therefore the exact and absolute antithesis of who and what Paul's God is. Both the language and conception are taken directly from OT polemics.[64]

The second element highlighted is that such images are *man's* creations (ἀνθρώπου is strictly redundant and therefore emphatic in this context), or better, creatures—the one necessarily implies the other.[65] Hence, it is not only their material and lifeless nature that is reprehensible, but the fact that they were both imagined (designed) and crafted (created) by man.[66] As such man is the creator and lord (and

---

of worship, *including the altar "to an unknown god,"* reprehensible (*verwerflich*).

64. For the language of incomparability see, for example: Exod 15:11; 18:11; Ps LXX 34:10; 70:19; 88:7, 9; Isa 44:6, 8; 45:5, 6, 21; 46:9; Deut 32:39; Hos 13:4; Joel 2:27; cf. Ps 113: 16 LXX and Rev 13:4. For materials used and craftsmanship: Exod 20:3, 23; Deut 4:28–29; 32:31; Ps 113:12 LXX; Isa 40:18–20; 44:9–20; 46:1–7. For Yahweh being the only living and acting God: Deut 4:33; 5:26; Josh 3:10; 1 Sam 17:36; 2 Kgs 19:4, 16; Ps LXX 41:3; 83:3; 113:13–15; Isa 37:4, 17; 41:28; 46:1–7; Dan LXX 4:22; 5:23; 6:21, 27; 12:7; Hos 2:1 LXX; Esth 6:13; 8:12a-x LXX; cf. Acts 14:15; Matt 16:16; Rom 9:26; 2 Cor 6:16; Heb 9:14; 1 Pet 1:23; Rev 7:2; 15:7. Note that the expression "living god" is *never* used in the plural ("living gods") in either LXX or NT.

65. The use of the rare noun χάραγμα ("image") is remarkable. The noun does not occur in the LXX. In the NT, it is used only in our text and in the book of Revelation, where it occurs seven times to refer to the "mark" or "stamp" of the beast that is engraved or etched on the forehead of those who worship its image (Rev 13:16, 17; 14:9, 11; 16:2; 19:20; 20:4). The verb χαράσσω is used three times in the LXX, however. In Sir 50:27, it refers to writing in a "book." In 3 Macc 2:29, it refers to Jews who were marked or branded with the mark of the pagan god Dionysos by Ptolemy IV. In 2 Kgs 17:11 (cf. 6–23; not mentioned by Wilckens in his *TDNT* article), it refers to Israel's making of idols to provoke Yahweh to anger (using παροργίζω a verb built on the same pattern as παροξύνω in v. 16). In our passage it denotes all religious objects crafted by man. Cf. BDAG 876 and *TDNT* 9.416–17. It seems to have a similar import as the term γλυπτά, which is common in the LXX and always used of idolatrous objects. See, for example: Exod 34:13; Lev 26:1; Deut 7:5, 25; 2 Chr 28:2; Isa 10:10; 42:8, 17; 46:1: 48:5.

66. As Calvin puts it: "Quand S. Paul dit que Dieu n'est point semblable à de l'or ou à de la pierre ou du bois, et quand il ajoute, ensuite, *ou de la pierre sculptée par l'art et l'imagination des hommes*, il exclut la matière et la forme et, en même temps, il condamne toutes les inventions humaines qui défigurent la vraie nature de Dieu." Calvin, *Actes*, 475 (emphasis original). One does not have to choose between either a reference to life or to the image, contrary to what some scholars seem to think (see, e.g., Roloff, *Apostelgeschichte*, 264; Parsons, *Acts*, 248; and Rowe, *World Upside Down*, 38). Both are in

caretaker) of his own gods, an obvious reversal of the true relationship between the divine and the human. It is a *lèse-majesté* of cosmic proportion! Paul's polemic is therefore meant to show how absurd, offensive and grievous idol-making is *per se*, reaffirming the absolute sovereignty of God vis-à-vis man (and his idols, of course). Jervell summarizes it well: "Gott ist Schöpfer und Herrscher und kann deshalb nicht einem Ding, über das wir selbst herrschen, ähnlich sein."[67]

The polemic nature of v. 29 is so evident that it is acknowledged by all. What is debated is the nature and depth of the critique, and how relevant it would be to the philosophers in Paul's audience. Hence, Haenchen writes: "To the philosophers who were being addressed this polemic would of course have offered nothing new: it hit only Greek popular religion and not the enlightened philosophical Hellenism."[68] Such opinion, however, fails to take into account at least two key elements that our study has highlighted earlier. First, Paul's argument, especially as it relates to the person and nature of Yahweh, attacks the very foundations of Hellenistic thinking about the divine, whether popular or philosophical. Paul is not building on—supplementing, complementing, adjusting, correcting—the philosophers' critique of popular religion.[69] The Areopagitica is not addressed to one or another segment of the depicted audience with diverse or disparate individual elements.[70] No, Paul is challenging the whole pagan world and life view, replacing it altogether with a new narrative.[71]

Second, the notion of a Greek philosophy entirely free from the trappings of paganism and idolatry is, to put it simply, a myth.[72] True in general, it is even more so in the first century AD. In this regard, it is quite significant that Paul would quote a *poet*—typically an authority associated with traditional (popular) religiosity in contradistinction to the philosophers.[73] Greek philosophers, however, re-interpreted and appropriated the poets as "ancient wisdom" at least as early as Plato, the practice

---

view and are inseparably intertwined. Marguerat's neo-orthodox notion that it is God as "Tout-Autre" that is being affirmed (Marguerat, *Actes*, 2.161–62) seems to completely miss the point that the denial of comparability with idols is based on man's imaging of God and, therefore, on notions of kinship and resemblance.

67. Jervell, *Die Apostelgeschichte*, 450.

68. Haenchen, *Acts*, 525. See also Dunn, *Acts*, 236 and Pervo, *Acts*, 440.

69. Contra Balch, "Areopagus Speech," 79, who argues that "Luke-Acts guards the legitimate philosophical tradition against the Athenians who delight in novelties." Cf. Schnabel, *Acts*, 738; Talbert, *Reading Acts*, 156; Tannehill, *Acts*, 218; and Hansen, "Preaching and Defence," 310.

70. As in Witherington, *Acts*, 534–35; cf. similar judgments in Marshall, *Acts TNTC*, 281; Bruce, *Acts Greek*, 385; and Charles, "Engaging," 57.

71. See the excellent discussion in Rowe, "Acts and Cultural Explication," 263–65.

72. Contra Balch, "Areopagus Speech," it was not only the Epicureans and Stoics of Paul's time who were compromised with pagan idolatry, but they were so from the very beginning, as demonstrated by Winter, "Theological and Ethical." Religion in the ancient world was part of the warp and woof of all of life, it was public, inescapable. See MacMullen, *Paganism*, 36, 40 and Rowe, "Acts and Cultural Explication," 245n5.

73. For poets and philosophers as authorities in the ancient world, see MacMullen, *Paganism*, 9–10; Rothschild, *Paul in Athens*, 68–71; and Keener, *Acts*, 3.2653–57.

being almost universal in the first century AD.[74] They applied the same hermeneutical framework to the physical (artistic) representations of the gods also.[75] A good illustration is Dio Chrysostom (ca. AD 40–after 112), whose *Olympic Discourse*—basically an ode to Zeus declaimed in Olympia around the turn of the century—is frequently cited as a parallel for vv. 27–28.[76] He writes "let us name as the fourth [source of man's conception of the divine being, after the innate, the poets and the lawgivers] that derived from the plastic art and the work of skilled craftsmen who make statues and likenesses of the gods" and later calls them "interpreters and teachers" who speak with one voice with the poets, the lawgivers and the philosophers.[77] Plutarch uses the same demythologizing, philosophically-controlled, hermeneutic.[78]

Verse 29 condemns this "higher" conception with its symbolic interpretation of idolatrous representations just as much as the so-called "popular idolatry."[79] This verse not only critiques the confusing of lifeless material idols for the divine (like most Greek philosophers do, including Plutarch: e.g., *Is. Os.* 71 [379C–D]), but castigates the very process of idol-making in its *two* dimensions: craftsmanship and *imagination*. Though not a violation of any rule or standard, the word order of the expression τέχνης καὶ ἐνθυμήσεως is definitely unusual, surprising and remarkable, though—maybe especially since—the terms themselves are common in this kind of context.[80] Logically, and typically, imagination (conception) should precede art (realization). The Areopagitica's formulation highlights the imaginary and inventive (creative!) dimension of the process, an essential feature of idolatry that is common to both popular paganism and Hellenistic philosophy, and one that v. 29 condemns both solemnly and uncompromisingly.[81] As Peterson puts it: "Paul's argument is a challenge to all forms

---

74. Plutarch is typical in his way to handle the matter. The poets' imagination and exaggerations can lead to both atheism and δεισιδαιμονία (see his negative judgments in *Is. Os.* 20 [358E–F], 66 [377D–F] and *Superst.* 8 [169B–C]), but they also can be a source of truth when interpreted properly, i.e., philosophically (see his positive evaluation in *Is. Os.* 1 [351D–E], 45 [369B], 57 [374C] and *Superst.* 3 [165E, 166B]). See further the excellent Van Nuffelen, *Rethinking the Gods*, 48–71.

75. See the study of Varro's (116–27 BC) thought on this point in Van Nuffelen, *Rethinking the Gods*, 29–37.

76. Cohoon dates it to AD 97, Van Nuffelen to AD 101 or 105. Dio's thought is a combination of Socratic-Platonic, Stoic and Cynic ideas. See Weißenberger, "D. Cocceianus of Prusa."

77. *Dei cogn.* 44, 47, 48, translated by J. W. Cohoon. It is worth reading the whole section (44–48) as well as 60–61. Larkin, *Acts*, 259, cites Strabo 1.2.7–9 as a parallel. Cf. Barrett, "Paul at Athens," 150 and Kennedy, *NT Interpretation*, 130.

78. See, e.g., *Is. Os.* 9 (354C), 10 (354F–355A), 36 (365B–C), 71 (379C–E).

79. Also noted by Bruce, *Acts NICNT*, 361.

80. The first two genitives denote the means of the verbal idea implicit in χαράγματι, while ἀνθρώπου denotes its agent. See Culy and Parsons, *Acts Handbook*, 341. Concerning the order of τέχνης καὶ ἐνθυμήσεως, Barrett, *Acts*, 2.849–50, says that at the most one can speak of "inappropriateness," while Rothschild, *Paul in Athens*, 34n60, considers it to be "unexpected." She also notes that, interestingly, τέχνης καὶ ἐνθυμήσεως were both areas of Athena's peculiar patronage!

81. Cf. Alexander, *Acts*, 2.158 and Dennis E. Johnson, *Message of Acts*, 198. In this regard, the speech echoes the first two commandments of the Decalogue as well as the "great and first commandment" of

of religion which seek to make a god to suit the needs of the worshippers. Moreover, idolatry can take many forms, both intellectually (with false ideas about God) and practically (with the worship of created things rather than the Creator)."[82] Idols of the mind (heart) are no less idols than those made of gold, silver and stone!

On the Dynamics of Quoting Pagan Poetry

How should one understand the fact that Paul is citing approvingly pagan poetry then? There is absolutely no doubt that the line from Aratus (and the possible source material behind 28a) was meant by its original author to express a *pagan* belief in the Stoic Zeus. But it is just as clear, as we have shown heretofore, that Paul's point is thoroughly biblical and therefore antithetical to the original "authorial meaning."[83] The way Paul/Luke weaves this material into the speech shows that, first, he is very aware of its original meaning and frame of reference and, second, that he purposefully "transplants" it into a new framework, thereby giving it a radically different meaning.[84] This is what context and discursive frames do. So "words or phrases are not in and of themselves Stoic, Epicurean, Platonist, or anything else. Rather, they are 'Stoic' because of the interpretive framework in which they occur, viz. 'Stoicism.'"[85] Change the framework, as Luke/Paul does here, and you change the meaning.

To the question of whether the Athenians (the depicted audience) would have been able to perceive the semantic shift, the analysis of the text we have offered so far forces us to conclude that "by this time the men that heard him knew that Paul did not mean the same thing that their poets had meant when they too said that men live and move and have their being in God and that they are the offspring of God."[86] It was quite standard in the Graeco-Roman world to change the meaning of citations, so Paul is not depicted doing anything unexpected or strange in his audience's eyes.[87] In any case, whatever was the original meaning of the poetry quoted in v. 28, that material is now an integral part of—and contributes to—Luke's uncompromising and radically-biblical anti-idol polemic.[88] That is the very nature of intertextuality.

Luke 10:27 (// Matt 20:37; Mark 12:30), "you shall love the Lord your God with all your heart [καρδία] and with all your soul [ψυχή] and with all your strength [ἰσχύς] and with all your mind [διάνοια]."

82. Peterson, *Acts*, 501.

83. Contra Dibelius, "Areopagus," 46–47, 56.

84. In full agreement with Jervell, *Die Apostelgeschichte*, 449; Fitzmyer, *Acts*, 611; and Barrett, *Acts*, 2.847–48; but contra Conzelmann, "Areopagus," 224 and Conzelmann, *Acts*, 145. See also *BegC*, 4.218.

85. Rowe, *World Upside Down*, 40; cf. Rowe, "Grammar," 45.

86. Van Til, *Paul at Athens*, 11.

87. See Keener, *Acts*, 3.2664.

88. Cf. Witherington, *Acts*, 529–30 as well as Wilson, *Gentiles*, 208. "He does not put the gospel into the language of a pagan philosophical system but instead rejects pagan wisdom as leading to idolatry." Rowe, *World Upside Down*, 201n179.

Even so, we must still address what role or function this quote may have in the Areopagitica. It is a well-known fact that the speeches in Acts contain many scriptural quotations, except the speeches in Lystra and Athens.[89] This consideration has led a number of commentators to conclude that the Stoic material being quoted in v. 28 is meant by Luke (or Paul) to fulfill the exact same role for the Areopagitica that the OT Scriptures do for the speeches aimed at Jewish audiences.[90] Rhetorically speaking the two uses are indeed parallel, in that they both present the depicted audience with an evidence that carries authority in its eyes.[91] But this is about as far as the correspondence goes.

First, Luke's use of the Scriptures in his speeches is not monolithic but varied (as we argued in chapter 2), so one needs to be specific concerning *which* use in particular is in view. Second, the status and authority that the OT had for the majority of first-century Jews was quite different in nature from the kind that poets had for Hellenistic philosophers and educated elites.[92] Third, there is no question that Aratus and other pagan authors did not hold a comparable position as Scripture in Paul or Luke's mind. In fact, the use and position of καθ' ὑμᾶς ("your") makes clear and explicit the distance (chasm) between Paul and his audience on this point.[93] He does not claim Aratus as his own. On the contrary, this formulation perpetuates the antithesis initiated in vv. 22–23.[94] Both the depicted audience and the implied reader are aware of the rhetorical situation and understand that Paul does not ascribe to the saying(s) the same sense as their pagan author(s) did.

Moreover, the quoted material is not foundational to the argument, as if it established its weight, substance, or authority. The speaker does not base his argument or meaning upon it. The reverse is true, since the very meaning of the quotation and the triad is defined by what precedes. Its function is rather that of an illustration

---

89. It is, of course, commonly recognized that this absence is congruent with the respective settings of the speeches. Quoting the OT Scriptures to Lystrans or to Athenians would have made little sense, and would certainly not have strengthened Paul's argument in their eyes.

90. The classic statement of this view is found in Schweizer, "Concerning the Speeches," 214; cf. Pervo, *Acts*, 439. Such explanation is generally associated with the conviction that Luke invented the speeches altogether, and is therefore adapting their content to their supposed circumstances (like Polybius and Herodotus), though some more conservative scholars hold to it also. See, for example, Dunn, *Acts*, 236 and Longenecker, *The Acts of the Apostles*, 984.

91. See Witherington, *Acts*, 530, who connects such rhetorical strategy with one's sensitivity to the audience's "plausibility structures."

92. Luke was well aware of this fact, as is evidenced by the introductory formula he uses in v. 28. The καθ' ὑμᾶς is not an emphatic form, but a common Hellenistic expression substituted for the classic possessive ὑμετέρων. *That* is what communicates pragmatically that the audience might confer an authority of some sort to the cited text. Cf. the discussion in Haenchen, *Acts*, 525; *BegC*, 4.217; and Barrett, *Acts*, 2.848.

93. Being placed in an attributive position, the adjectival expression makes definite *which kind of* poets is denoted. It is highlighted at the expense of the substantive. Cf. Robertson, *Grammar*, 776.

94. The distance is not merely cultural in nature, contra Marguerat, *Actes*, 2.161. Cf. Klauck, *Magic and Paganism*, 88.

which a skillful orator uses to help bring his point across to his audience, appropriating one their cultural artifacts. He invades their thought world and imports his meaning into it. The speaker is making use of the Athenians' *sensus divinitatis* in exactly the same way as he did when referring to the altar "to an unknown god" in v. 23.[95] Paul/Luke recognizes a true insight is hidden behind the erroneous interpretation found in the pagan doctrine proclaimed by Aratus, one that can be redeemed or reclaimed and made to shine again by embedding it in a biblical framework that will give it its proper meaning.

Paul's use of Hellenistic language and cultural-religious icons is often described in terms of "translation." However, the dynamics of the semantic shifts operated by Luke's framing of the material is significantly more radical than merely "translating" the gospel in philosophical or Hellenistic terms. It denies the conceptual equivalence that "translation" requires or implies, and takes the adversary's meaning and worldview seriously.[96] It is no mere "plundering the Egyptians" but rather a "conquering the land." It is appropriation and reconfiguration, the process J. H. Bavinck termed *possessio*.[97] By doing so the apologist turns the Athenians' own weapons against them. He uses their own confession of "unknowing" (v. 23) and of being God's "offspring" (v. 28) as incriminating evidence demonstrating their failure and guilt.[98] This is very similar to the self-condemning silence of the idols and their "witnesses" in Isaiah's anti-idol trial scenes.[99] At this point, it is only perfectly natural for Paul to turn to the proclamation of God's coming universal judgment.

---

95. So also Stonehouse, "Areopagus Address," 29–30; concerning the *sensus divinitatis*, see especially Calvin, *Instit.*, 1.1–4 and Herman Bavinck, *RD 1*, 278–79, 319–20.

96. See the excellent discussion in Rowe, *World Upside Down*, 39–41, 49–51 and Rowe, "Grammar," 44–50. The principles of "translatability" and "cultural equivalence" are behind many of the theories and practices developed in missiological circles in the last half century, especially under the influence of cultural anthropology. They are a significant influence on—even a cause of—theories like inclusivism and methodologies like Insider Movements and CAMEL. They are at the heart of the reading of the Areopagitica presented in Higgins, "Key to Insider Movements" and Jennings, "Deity of Christ for Missions."

97. For the concept of *possessio*, see J. H. Bavinck, *Introduction to Missions*, 178–90 and Strange, *For Their Rock*, 322–29.

98. Cf. Wilkinson, "Acts 17," 10; Dennis E. Johnson, *Message of Acts*, 196; and Bahnsen, *Always Ready*, 259–63.

99. Even Barrett notes that this verse is "reminiscent" of Isaiah, even though the language sounds different and some of the key words in v. 29 are totally absent from the LXX. See Barrett, *Acts*, 2.850; cf. Dennis E. Johnson, "Jesus Against," 347–48, who lists the following parallels: Isa 41:1–4, 21–24; 42:18–19; 43:8–12; 44:8, 9, 17–20; 45:20–22.

CHAPTER 9

Eschatological Proclamation of Judgment (Acts 17:30–31)

Introduction: The Hortatory Climax of Paul's Speech

IN VIEW OF OUR study of the speech so far, we can confidently conclude that there is strictly no ground for Dibelius' judgment that vv. 30–31 represent the only Christian element of the speech, something "tacked on" a Hellenistic oration.[1] On the contrary, it is clear that the reported speech as a whole has a solid unity and is uncompromisingly Christian—or biblical—in both content and form.[2] The speech shows a solid lexical, thematic, ideological, and narrative unity and integrity, both internally and contextually, undergirded by various framing devices and by verbal repetition.[3] It has a natural and smooth flow, leading up to the hortatory climax of vv. 30–31.[4] The

---

1. Dibelius, "Areopagus," 56. Conzelmann considers this sentence to be the only *explicitly* Christian part of the speech, though he thinks that it properly belongs to the speech and that the "anthropological" element of the speech is framed in such a way that it also expresses a Christian message (Conzelmann, *Acts*, 146). A similar opinion was recently voiced by Keener, *Acts*, 3.2668. Other than the reference to the person of Jesus (without naming him, though!), what exactly makes these two verses more "Christian" than the rest of the speech, especially when read in its immediate narrative context?

2. Also noted by Dupont, "Discours à l'Aréopage," 407; Witherington, *Acts*, 531; and Barrett, *Acts*, 2.850.

3. For example: Jesus and the resurrection (vv. 18, 31); γνῶναι (v. 19) and ἄγνοια (v. 30); ἀγνώστῳ and ἀγνοοῦντες (v. 23) and ἄγνοια (v. 30); one man in relation to the whole world (vv. 26, 31); Paul's holy anger (παρωξύνετο, v. 16) that matches God's attitude towards idolatry evidenced in his eschatological judgment (v. 31; as we saw earlier, παροξύνω is used many times of Yahweh's response to sin, rebellion and idolatry in the LXX); the reactions of the crowd (vv. 18–19, 32); the speech covers past, present and (eschatological) future as it considers mankind's history from creation to final judgment (vv. 24, 31); the use of inflection, with θεός in all four cases (dative in v. 23, nominative in 24 and 30, accusative in 27, and genitive in 29). Besides our earlier discussion of various structuring features of the speech, see Gourgues, "Littérature profane," 245–47 and Jipp, "Paul's Areopagus Speech," 587.

4. So also Witherington, *NT Rhetoric*, 71 and Parsons, *Acts*, 248; contra Keener, *Acts*, 3.2674–75 and Marguerat, *Actes*, 2.162, who consider the speech to be rhetorically incomplete (though the author has said all he meant to). Witherington remarks that forensic speeches were building toward the decision of the judges, and "Neyrey has pointed out that in the forensic speeches in the latter half of Acts it is *always the resurrection* that brings us to the 'point of judgment.'" Witherington, *Acts*, 530

speech's message/argument is complete at that point, whether one perceives a narrative interruption at v. 32 or not.[5]

Contrary to what is sometimes claimed, μὲν οὖν in v. 30 is not merely indicating a new train of thought or a new development,[6] but rather an inference, a conclusion drawn from what precedes, viz., the whole speech. Even if a "not illative nor even consequential" but "merely . . . transitional" use of οὖν and μὲν οὖν was attested, it would only occur in *narratives* and not in speeches.[7] Yet, recent studies of the NT usage have shown that it is better to explain all uses as either resumptive or inferential.[8] In context, it seems quite clear that the expression in v. 30 must be understood in an inferential or illative manner. First, that would be consistent with all other non-narrative uses of μὲν οὖν in the LXX and the NT.[9] Second, as we saw earlier v. 29 is already resumptive of the line of argument started in v. 24 (using οὖν). So if v. 30 were to be also resumptive, one would have to ask the question, "resumptive of *what*?"[10] Finally, vv. 30–31 are clearly intended to serve as a conclusion to the whole speech, as demonstrated by their hortatory nature and their many verbal and thematic links to the rest of the speech, from v. 22b onwards.[11] The καταγγελεύς (v. 18) has come to the end of his anti-idol polemic; he thus logically calls his audience

---

(citing Neyrey, "Acts 17," 121n16 [emphasis added]).

5. Most recent scholars who discern a narrative interruption here consider that Luke (or Paul) has said all he wanted to say. The narrative device thus serves to highlight the most important element of his message: Jesus' resurrection. In consequence, Smith's comparative study of the rhetorical use of interruption in Luke-Acts and in ancient Greek narrative concludes: "if scholars agree that the speech is finished, and if there is no claim of interruption in the narrative framework, then we can conclude that 17:32 is not an interruption." *Rhetoric of Interruption*, 232 (231–32 for the full argument). Rather, it is a record of the audience's reaction (rejection) of the message of the resurrection, which serves a similar rhetorical purpose.

6. As, for example: Haenchen, *Acts*, 525; Peterson, *Acts*, 501; JB, KJV, ESV, TOB and NEG.

7. Robertson, *Grammar*, 1191, claims that Luke preserves such a purportedly Homeric and Attic idiom with his use of μὲν οὖν, but see Wallace, *Greek Grammar*, 674 and Denniston and Dover, *Greek Particles*, 470–81.

8. See οὖν in BDAG. See also the discussion in Levinsohn, *Discourse Features*, 126–29, 170–72 and Runge, *Discourse Grammar*, 43–49 from the perspective of linguistics. The resumptive use often possesses an inferential quality.

9. Per our accounting, μὲν οὖν is used in non-narrative texts seven times in the LXX (Gen 43:3; Exod 4:23 [twice]; 9:2; 4 Mac 1:7, 10, 22; Wis 13:16) and fourteen in the NT, six of which are in Acts (Acts 1:18; 17:30; 19:38; 25:11; 26:4, 9; Rom 11:13; 1 Cor 6:4, 7; 9:25; Phil 2:23; Heb 7:11; 8:4; 9:1). Except for 4 Mac 1:10 which could be resumptive (yet with a clear inferential nuance), all other occurrences are inferential.

10. As listed in Turner, *Syntax*, 337.

11. So also Bock, *Acts*, 569. Jervell, *Die Apostelgeschichte*, 450, is correct to note a change of tone at this point, but his characterization—from argument to proclamation—is erroneous. Besides the fact that such a dichotomy between proclamation and apologetic is artificial, he fails to account for the terminology used: Paul moves from proclamation (v. 23, καταγγέλλω) to command (v. 30, παραγγέλλει). Luke's language furthers and completes his characterization of Paul as the one who is endowed with divine authority by virtue of his prophetic role as New Exodus Servant sent to the nations.

to submit to the risen Lord Jesus Christ who will soon judge the whole human race—a divine regalian prerogative.[12]

The irony of the situation is to be noted. The Areopagus was to judge both Paul and "Jesus and the resurrection," but in the end Jesus is their judge on account of his resurrection and Paul is his herald announcing the judgment that is to come upon them. Though a natural conclusion for the reader, it is a surprising twist for the depicted audience. Paul does not even plead for the dismissal of the charges (or suspicions) brought against him![13]

The Final Turning-Point in Redemptive History for the Nations

Des Places is absolutely correct to highlight the forward-pointing nature of μέν in the expression μὲν οὖν in v. 30.[14] However, it seems highly unlikely that it would be anticipating the δέ in v. 32, since the former is part of the speech and the latter belongs to the narrative (unlike μὲν οὖν . . . δέ in vv. 17–18). Rather than preparing for the reaction of the audience, it is more natural to construe μέν as pointing to the second part of v. 30 introduced by τὰ νῦν—normally the related clause is immediately adjacent, unless the μέν clause is further developed—while δέ in v. 32 introduces a new narrative development unit.[15] Especially since the μὲν οὖν participial clause (ὑπεριδὼν ὁ θεός) functions as a circumstantial frame for what immediately follows.[16] Besides, this pragmatic understanding is concordant with the thematic content and contrastive relation of the two parts of the verse.[17]

An Eschatological Transition

Hence, one is confronted by the radical contrast—even antithesis—between two cosmic historical eras (τοὺς χρόνους τῆς ἀγνοίας and τὰ νῦν) heralded by Paul in vv. 30–31.[18] The chasm between the two is nothing less than eschatological, and thus of a

---

12. Just as Isa 45:20–24 does for Yahweh. See Pao, *Acts and INE*, 196–97.

13. Often noted by scholars, e.g., Schnabel, *Acts*, 739. Various elements of the speech implicitly deny the charges of introducing foreign gods, however.

14. See des Places, "Actes 17,30–31," 526. On the fact that μέν is always prospective, even when it is not followed by δέ, see Levinsohn, *Discourse Features*, 170–72 and Runge, *Discourse Grammar*, 75–83, especially 75–76 and note 7.

15. Our analysis therefore agrees with *LDGNT* here (accessed on Logos Bible Software, 6:38pm, April 27th, 2018).

16. See the discussion of this use of the participle in Wallace, *Greek Grammar*, 640–43 and Runge, *Discourse Grammar*, 250–55.

17. Barrett, *Acts*, 2.850, speaks of "adversative force."

18. "Elle délimite deux périodes dans la fresque historique qui va de la création au moment présent et invite à distinguer deux sous-séquences dont les contenus respectifs posent le problème du passage

redemptive-historical—rather than epistemic—nature.[19] The prospective μέν creates expectancy in the reader's mind, and makes the subsequent material introduced by τὰ νῦν the focus of attention. The placing of τὰ νῦν between the participial phrase ὑπεριδὼν ὁ θεός and the main verb παραγγέλλει (of which ὁ θεός is the subject) puts it in a prominent position, further raising its pragmatic profile.[20] Since τὰ νῦν functions as a temporal frame for what follows, the change of time reference in the discourse it expresses is strongly highlighted, thus sharpening the contrast between the two epochs.[21] This construction stresses the urgency of the divine command to repent, implying that something of paramount importance has happened.[22] Something so significant that, in consequence, God's activity in relation to mankind as a whole has changed dramatically.[23] God's βουλή has reached its climactic turning point.[24] The "now" is therefore indicative of the dimension of cosmic eschatology that was *realized* in the person and life of Jesus.[25]

Des Places observes that this kind of usage of "now" (νῦν or τὰ νῦν) is often associated with the eschatological judgment of the world in the NT.[26] This is certainly the case here. The phrase ἔστησεν ἡμέραν (v. 31) is suggestive of the scriptural theme of the ἡμέρα κυρίου, and contributes therefore to the eschatological mood of the passage.[27] Moreover, that the eschatological judgment is in view is made evident by the claim that God *is about to judge* (μέλλει κρίνειν) the whole inhabited world (τὴν οἰκουμένην) in v. 31. Μέλλει here denotes an imminent future, a *Naherwartung*.[28] As Tipton puts it: "the appointed day of judgment . . . looms imminent on the horizon of

---

direct du paganisme au christianisme." Calloud, "Aréopage," 221 ; cf. p. 239.

19. Contra Marshall, *Acts TNTC*, 290 (due to Paul's proclamation) and Kurz, *Acts*, 275 (due to full revelation in Christ).

20. Cf. Alexander, *Acts*, 2.159; Fitzmyer, *Acts*, 611–12; and Rowe, *World Upside Down*, 39.

21. So also Culy and Parsons, *Acts Handbook*, 341. On temporal frames, see Runge, *Discourse Grammar*, 216–20.

22. See Gaventa, *Acts*, 253.

23. "It is impossible not to hear the note of warning here: God's leniency is in fact over, and one must stop putting it to the test." Klauck, *Magic and Paganism*, 91–92.

24. The transition is emphatically not due to man but to God alone, as Soards, *Speeches in Acts*, 99, notes.

25. And not an "existential" moment of decision. See Tipton, "Resurrection Proof," 45–46, 47.

26. In des Places, "Actes 17,30–31," 528, agreeing with Dupont, "Repentir et conversion," 437n28.

27. Cf. des Places, "Actes 17,30–31," 530–31; Dubarle, "Discours à l'Aréopage," 186; and Bruce, *Acts Greek*, 386. The allusion is made especially plausible by the association of the theme with the prophecy of Joel quoted in Peter's Pentecost sermon, a passage that sets the tone for the entire book of Acts (see Evans, "Pentecost Sermon," 220 and Bayer, "Preaching of Peter"), as well as the various intertextual links between the two books (cf. Van de Sandt, "Fate of Gentiles"). It is also central to Malachi 3:1–2, a text quoted and alluded to in Luke's Gospel in relation to both Jesus' and John the Baptist's ministries (Luke 1:17; 7:27). Cf. the discussion in Pao, *Acts and INE*, 40–44.

28. Not an intended action, contra BDAG 628, §1.c.γ. Cf. 2 Tim 4:1 and Jas 2:12. See discussion in BDF §356; Jervell, *Die Apostelgeschichte*, 450n259; Barrett, *Acts*, 2.852; Fitzmyer, *Luke*, 1.233–34; and Rothschild, *Paul in Athens*, 35n65.

redemptive history."[29] This makes perfect sense in view of Luke's (inaugurated) eschatology, since for him the Parousia alone constitutes the "not yet."[30]

A Culpable "Unknowing" of Epochal Proportion

This eschatological "now" is contrasted with "the times of ignorance" (τοὺς χρόνους τῆς ἀγνοίας), which God "overlooked" (ὑπεριδών). To refer to "the proud history of Athens as 'times of ignorance'" in and of itself is quite "a bold move"![31] But Paul does not limit his judgment to his Athenian audience (in all its diversity), as if they singularly or uniquely among men were "not-knowing." While v. 23 anchors the argument in the reality of then-contemporary Athens (and is linguistically tied tightly with v. 30)—the symbolic apex of pagan religion in the ancient world and the narrative of Acts—, the purview has been universalized through the argument of the speech, to the effect that all of paganism—geographically and historically—is subsumed under the category of ἄγνοια.[32] The time reference is purposefully indefinite, emphasizing the contrast or antithesis with the situation in the redemptive-historical (eschatological) present.[33] The comprehensive quality of this statement is reinforced by the subsequent expressions τοῖς ἀνθρώποις πάντας πανταχοῦ (note the paronomasia) in v. 30, τὴν οἰκουμένην and πᾶσιν in v. 31.[34] All, whether Jews or Gentiles, must repent in light of God's past and future actions, each in accordance with its peculiar history and relation to Yahweh. It is in this perspective that the history of the *nations* is defined as τοὺς χρόνους τῆς ἀγνοίας. It is suggested by some commentators that Luke conceives of it as redemptively parallel (or equivalent) to Israel's or as a "pre-history" of Christianity, thus implying some form of qualitative continuity and a preparatory nature.[35] But this line of interpretation is faulty in two clear ways. First, it underestimates the radical

---

29. Tipton, "Resurrection Proof," 47–48.

30. In fact, the parousia is not only the last "stage" of eschatology that remains to be fulfilled, it is also presented by Luke as just about to happen. See Jervell, *Theology of Acts*, 114; Owen, "Stephen's Vision"; and Bock, *Theology*, 394–95.

31. Schnabel, *Acts*, 739.

32. Contra Kennedy, *NT Interpretation*, 130. Cf. Tipton, "Resurrection Proof," 46 and Lints, *Identity and Idolatry*, 119. For the use of χρόνος and καιρός in Luke-Acts, see Bayer, "Christ-Centered Eschatology," 45–48.

33. Conzelmann, *Acts*, 146, comments that we find world history being divided between *two* epochs (ignorance and proclamation unto conversion), apparently contradicting his thesis that Luke's *Heilsgeschichte* is made of *three* discrete periods (see especially his *Theology of Luke*).

34. The repetition of the adjective πᾶς and its cognate is emphatic and ties these verses in with the six other occurrences of πᾶς throughout the speech. Cf. Gaventa, *Acts*, 252.

35. It seems that the expression "pre-history" was first used by Vielhauer ("Paulinism," 37). It is repeated by Wilson (*Gentiles*, 217–18), Pervo (*Acts*, 437) and Butticaz. The notion of two parallel salvation histories—understood: of similar nature or value—is found, for example, in Butticaz, *Identité de l'Eglise*, 376–79, 81; Pervo, *Acts*, 440; and Marguerat, *Actes*, 2.162. However, see Flemming, "Contextualizing in Athens," 210.

nature of the eschatological turning point expressed in v. 30. Second, it equates too rapidly the meaning and referent of the noun ἄγνοια here with its only other Lukan use, in Peter's speech in the Portico (στοά) of Solomon (Acts 3:11–26).

Though Paul's and Peter's speeches share a number of formal features and include a call to repentance, they develop two distinct arguments in which ἄγνοια has a different referent. Hence, in Peter's speech, the term describes the manner (κατὰ ἄγνοιαν) in which one specific, chronologically-circumscribed, course of action was pursued, in stark contrast with its use in the Areopagitica.[36] That particular transgression of God's law was the rejection and murder of Jesus, the very instrument promised and sent by God for their salvation.[37] Those addressed are referred to as ὁ λαός (vv. 11, 12), ἄνδρες Ἰσραηλῖται (v. 12) and ἀδελφοί (v. 17), even though they are the Jerusalem-dwellers who, with their rulers (v. 17; see Acts 13:27, where Paul uses ἀγνοεῖν in a similar context; cf. Luke 23:13–25, 34a) committed this crime.[38] The God in view is not ἄγνωστος but Yahweh, "the God of Abraham, of Isaac, of Jacob, the God of our fathers" (v. 13), who has spoken by the prophets (vv. 18, 21, 22–23, 24, 25). Their act is not due to their lack of either information about or acquaintance with God, but to covenant rebellion. Peter's call to repent is conjoined with an exhortation to "return" (ἐπιστρέψατε) for the removal of their *sins* (τὰς ἁμαρτίας, note the plural). Amazingly, the auditors are told that their act was part of God's plan of salvation for his people (v.18). Finally, and logically, the repentance required in 3:19 concerns what they have done—presented as the climactic and eschatological iteration of Israel's characteristic rejection of God's servants in Peter's Pentecost sermon (2:23, 36), Stephen's speech (7:51–53) and in Jesus' polemical "parable of the tenants" (Luke 20:9–18)—not the ἄγνοια itself. Peter functions here as a "preacher of eschatological repentance to Israel" in continuity with the OT prophetic tradition.[39] In view of this evidence, it seems that we should consider carefully Dupont's suggestion that Luke uses two different concepts, drawn from distinct OT and Jewish traditions.[40]

On the one hand, in 3:17 κατὰ ἄγνοιαν seems to refer to what makes certain transgressions *atonable, and thus forgivable*, according to the Mosaic law (Lev 5:17–19; Num 15:22–31; cf. Ps 24:7)—in contradistinction with conscious or intentional

---

36. Especially as it forms an *inclusio* with ἀγνώστῳ θεῷ and ὅ ἀγνοοῦντες εὐσεβεῖτε (v. 23), which strikingly characterize the ongoing or permanent nature of pagan worship in Athens.

37. "Yet sin is also historical for Luke in a much more comprehensive sense: it characterizes the age into which Jesus comes—'this wicked generation' (Luke 11:29)—and is manifested in relation to him especially and in particular." Rowe, *One True Life*, 131.

38. And not the Romans, who are nearly relegated to the role of "instruments" in the deed. See Strahan, *Limits of a Text*, 70.

39. See the fuller discussion in Bayer, "Preaching of Peter," 262–65, who cites Jer 3:12–16; 7:3–25; 14:6–7; Ezek 18:30; Zech 1:3; 7:8–10; and Mal 3:7 in particular.

40. See Dupont, "Repentir et conversion," 436–40; Dupont, "La conversion," 461–65; Dupont, *Gnosis*, 1–6; and des Places, "Actes 17,30–31," 527–28.

ones for which there was no redemption possible.[41] Note that this category of sins do require expiation and reparation (hence the related body of legislation), and therefore carries both culpability and guilt. This same Mosaic provision appears to be behind Jesus' and Stephen's intercession on behalf of their tormentors in Luke 23:34 and Acts 7:60 (see also Acts 3:17 and 13:27; cf. 1 Tim 1:13).[42]

On the other hand, the statement in v. 30a refers directly to the post-Babel situation of the nations, depicted in vv. 24–29 and illustrated in vv. 16–23, 32 by its epitome, Athens.[43] Luke makes that clear through the use of οὖν (discussed above) and of the striking *inclusio* formed with v. 23, in which both the Athenians' object and mode of worship are defined by cognates of ἄγνοια: ἀγνώστῳ θεῷ and ὃ οὖν ἀγνοοῦντες εὐσεβεῖτε. The term ἄγνοια seems therefore to function here as a shorthand for mankind's rebellious and unbridled—i.e., restrained by God (Acts 14:16: ὃς ἐν ταῖς παρῳχημέναις γενεαῖς εἴασεν πάντα τὰ ἔθνη πορεύεσθαι ταῖς ὁδοῖς αὐτῶν)— idolatry.[44] This usage is typical of a distinct and consistent OT and Jewish characterization of the Gentiles, in which ignorance is closely associated to both idolatry and sinful living.[45] The same perspective appears in Eph 4:18 and 1 Pet 1:14—the only two other occurrences of ἄγνοια in the NT (cf. 2 Pet 2:12–13; Jude 10–11; Ign. *Eph.* 19.3)—as well as in other Lukan references to the redemptive-historical situation of the nations (e.g., Luke 2:31–32; 12:30; Acts 4:25–27, quoting Ps 2:1–2 LXX; 10:9–16; 15:29 [21:25]; 26:18; the events in Philippi and Ephesus). Dupont rightly concludes: "Le terme 'ignorance' ne tend aucunement ici à minimiser la faute des païens, comme

---

41. Our point is made on thematic grounds; see Strahan, *Limits of a Text*, 78–80 for an intertextual argument.

42. It should be noted "that the idea of the Jews acting in ignorance with reference to Jesus' death is peculiar to Luke." Epp, "Ignorance Motif," 56. Evans, "Prophecy and Polemic," 183–84, provides a helpful discussion of this OT background for Luke's soteriology in general. *Pace* Metzger, *Textual Commentary*[2], 154, we consider the logion of Jesus in Luke 23:34a to be original. See the defense of its originality offered by Nolland, *Luke*, 3.1141–42; Bovon, *Luc*, 4.368–69; and Dirk Jongkind: http://evangelicaltextualcriticism.blogspot.co.uk/2018/03/father-forgive-them-variant-in-luke.html (accessed April 27, 2018).

43. As Roloff comments: "Auch das Beste, Geistvollste and Reflektierteste an heidnischer Religiosität is letzlich 'Unwissenheit.'" Roloff, *Apostelgeschichte*, 265.

44. Cf. Klauck, *Magic and Paganism*, 91 and Gaventa, *Acts*, 252. Conversely, idolatry is therefore strictly defined as ἄγνοια, a complete lack of knowledge—i.e., understanding—of and acquaintance with the one true God and Lord. "This is one more nail in the coffin of the thesis that the writer of this speech regards pagan religion as possessing elements that can be incorporated like building blocks into the Christian edifice. No mention is made of true knowledge, but only of 'ignorance.'" Wilkinson, "Acts 17," 11.

45. Using various cognates of γινώσκω/γνῶσις and οἶδα in the LXX: e.g., Deut 13:7; Hos 5:15–6:6; Ps 78:6; Isa 45:20 (v. 22 calls them to "turn," ἐπιστράφητε); Jer 10:25; Sir 23:3; 28:7; Wis 14:22–31 (especially v. 27! ἡ γὰρ τῶν ἀνωνύμων εἰδώλων θρησκεία παντὸς ἀρχὴ κακοῦ καὶ αἰτία καὶ πέρας ἐστίν); *Jos. Asen.* 13.9. Gärtner notes that ἄγνοια is used in the LXX "as the translation of five Hebrew words, all of which mean sin or guilt. Sometimes we find ἁμαρτία parallel to ἄγνοια." Gärtner, *Areopagus Speech*, 234–35 (full discussion on pp. 232–37 and 93–95). So also Dubarle, "Discours à l'Aréopage," 186.

dans l'emploi qu'en faisait saint Pierre dans son discours aux Juifs (*Act.* III, 17) ; il exprime, au contraire, le désordre radical du paganisme."[46]

It is clear that in either case ἄγνοια cannot refer to a mere lack of information or propositional knowledge. The Jews have the OT Scriptures (Luke 23:27; 24:44, 46), the Gentiles God's general revelation (Acts 17:24–28; in 14:16–17 Paul says that the living God, the Creator, οὐκ ἀμάρτυρον αὐτὸν ἀφῆκεν in relation to πάντα τὰ ἔθνη).[47] The term must therefore denote at least faulty understanding and construal of the available information—something in itself culpable before God—and is associated with courses of action and ways of life and worship eliciting divine judgment.[48] It is no surprise, then, why ἄγνοια requires repentance for both Jews and Gentiles—μετάνοια/ἐπιστροφή (cf. Acts 20:21; 26:20, 23).[49] It is clear from his Gospel and Peter's Pentecost speech that to overcome ἄγνοια for Luke requires the intervention of God—Father, Son, and/or Holy Spirit—"to open the eyes" of the hearer/reader of the Word (for example: Luke 24:31, 44–49; Acts 1:8; 2:16–41; 8:30–38: 9:3–19).[50]

In the end, Barrett's witty paraphrase of Paul's point seems to hit the nail on the head: "This ignorance, which perverts the εὐσέβεια that accompanies it into δεισιδαιμονία, has been going on for a long time; the story of Athens is a record of χρόνοι τῆς ἀγνοίας. *From nature the Greeks have evolved not natural theology but natural idolatry.*"[51]

---

46. Dupont, *Gnosis*, 4; contra Keener, *Acts*, 3.2635–36, 2668. In Gärtner's words: "Ἄγνοια is thus one of the current terms for denoting the state of Gentiles, and this state is obviously stamped by ἁμαρτία." *Areopagus Speech*, 235. Interestingly, Epp, *Theological Tendency*, 48–50, argues that the variant ἀγνοίας ταύτης found in D and the Vulgate seeks to make clear that the ignorance in view in 17:30 is distinct from that in 3:17 (Witherington, *Acts*, 531n255, agrees but Pervo, *Acts*, 440n139, considers it a mere stylistic improvement). In any case, even if the two Lukan uses were of the same attenuating nature, ἄγνοια would still not entail innocence or guiltlessness. It would only mean that the sin concerned *can* be forgiven by following God's prescribed method: repentance (and faith).

47. The disciples themselves persistently fail to understand the Word, especially as concerns the nature of God's plan and Jesus' messiahship, in spite of Jesus' teaching and signs, including the resurrection. For example: Luke 9:32–35, 43–45, 54–55; 18:34; 22:24–27, 49–51; 24:25–27, 31, 44–49; Acts 1:6–8.

48. As vv. 24–29 make clear by narratively developing and disambiguating Paul's meaning and point of view in v. 23. Joel B. Green, *Conversion in Luke-Acts*, 91–96, and Strahan, *Limits of a Text*, 65–78, make a good case against reading ἄγνοια as a mere lack of information in Luke-Acts. However, their construal remains too narrowly intellectual in our opinion, and both fail to deal with the particular import of the term in Acts 17:30.

49. Joel B. Green, *Conversion in Luke-Acts*, 50, presents the textual evidence showing that the μετάνοια/μετανοέω and ἐπιστροφή/ἐπιστρέφω word groups are used essentially interchangeably in Luke-Acts for both Jews and Gentiles. More broadly, Green argues (pp. 49–53) against the fast distinction between conversion and repentance in Luke-Acts claimed by some (notably Nave, *Role and Function*).

50. Rowe, *One True Life*, 5, comes to a similar conclusion on this point.

51. Barrett, *Acts*, 2.850–51 (emphasis ours). As is commonly recognized, just as much as fear (δειλία) is at the heart of the negative definition of δεισιδαιμονία (Stobaeus, *Ecl.* 2.92 [*SVF* 3.98.42]; Andronicus, *[Pass.]* 3 [*SVF* 3.99.13]; Theophrastus, *Char.* 16.1, even—or especially—if that first line is an interpolation; see further references in Gray, *Godly Fear*, 49–50), ignorance is the root of that very

PART TWO: A CONTEXTUAL READING OF THE AREOPAGUS SPEECH

God Is Done Ignoring the Nations

This understanding of the import of ἄγνοια fits perfectly Paul's heralding of both God's past—but foregone—forbearance/abandon and present summon to repentance. The epochal transition marked sharply by the μὲν οὖν . . . τὰ νῦν construction is from God "ignoring" (ὑπεριδών)[52] the nations to his commanding every single human being to repent because of their impending trial and condemnation. God's inaction concerning the nations and their idolatry is over. The NT hapax ὑπεροράω, when used of Yahweh in the LXX always refers to his not (or no longer) caring for his people *in judgment* for their sin.[53] This participial circumstantial frame provides the backdrop against which the action of the main clause (παραγγέλλει . . . μετανοεῖν) must be seen.

In view of the contrastive nature of μὲν οὖν . . . τὰ νῦν, the aorist participle ὑπεριδών is better understood as being concessive in nature ("Although God overlooked").[54] It expresses what was true in the past, not what is true now: God is not overlooking the past in order to call to repentance.[55] Ἄγνοια is not an attenuating circumstance that would cause or ground the divine forbearance, *but rather the very sin* that has been patiently and graciously borne and is about to be judged (v. 31), therefore urgently requiring repentance.[56] God's judgment does fall on these times, and Luke's readers

---

fear (Plutarch, *Superst.* 1 [164E], 2 [165B–C]). Each time a cognate of ἄγνοια is used in vv. 23 and 30 it refers to a religious practice that an educated Athenian would have considered a topos of the figure of the δεισιδαίμων.

52. Spicq writes: "Selon l'étymologie, ce verbe signifie 'regarder par dessus, voir d'en haut' et en mauvaise part 'regarder de haut, mépriser, dédaigner'. Dans les Septante et les papyrus, seul ce second sens est attesté." Spicq, *Notes*, 2.899; see *LSJ* and Montanari, *Brill DAG* for the full semantic domain of the term. Of forty-two verses in which the verb occurs in the LXX, only four entail a positive evaluation of the course of action in view: Eleazar and the seven brothers and mother "despised" death and torture for the sake of God's law (2 Mac 7:11, 23; 4 Mac 1:9; 9:6). One wonders if Given is not confusing mere polysemy with double-entendre here (Given, *Paul's True Rhetoric*, 73), especially as it is difficult to see what meaningful effect the latter would produce.

53. Lev 26:37, 40, 43, 44 is a most striking example, as the same verb is used three times to refer to Israel's sin and once of God's judgment in response. In the MT Deut 3:26; Ps 77:59; and Zech 1:12 speak of God being angry (עבר), while Ps 9:22 and Isa 58:7 speak of God hiding (עלם). See also Josh 1:5; Esth 4:17g (Sinaiticus); Jdt 8:20; Ps 77:62; Job 6:14; Wis 19:22; *Pss. Sol.* 8:30; Nah 3:11. In all cases, the consequences in view of God's "overlooking," whether actual or potential, are disastrous and destructive for Israel or Judah. All uses with a human being as subject relate to sin in action—better, inaction—, attitude, or as a consequence of failing to keep God's statutes.

54. "The logical relation of the circumstantial participle to the rest of the sentence is not expressed by the participle itself (apart from the future participle), but is to be deduced from the context." BDF §417; so also Turner, *Syntax*, 153. On concessive participles, see Wallace, *Greek Grammar*, 634–35. Culy and Parsons, *Acts Handbook*, 341, arrive at the same conclusion, as do most commentators.

55. Contra Marguerat, *Actes*, 2.149, 162, NJB ("But now, overlooking the times of ignorance, God is telling . . ."), NEG, or TOB.

56. Contra Kurz, *Acts*, 275 and Holladay, *Acts*, 341, 346 (who translates v. 30a "so then, God turned a blind eye to that age of innocence"). See Shields' argument against Käsemann on this point in "Areopagus Sermon," 38. Pinnock's claim that to overlook meant "not to charge with guilt" is completely counterfactual (Pinnock, *Wideness*, 101). See further Carson's response in *Gagging*, 310.

know very well that God does not "wink at" (KJV) idolatry! So, on the one hand, God has not (yet) judged and punished in an eschatological manner their idolatry the way it deserved (an important aspect of common grace).[57] On the other hand, the circumstantial frame signals a "terrible divine abandonment": the general exclusion of the Gentiles from God's redemptive plan and activity since Babel.[58] "God had hitherto permitted the heathen to pursue their own way, without manifesting his sense of their conduct, either by sending to them special messengers to testify against it, as he did to the Jews, or by inflicting upon them at once the punishment deserved."[59] In the sub-eschatological dispensations of the covenant of grace God did reserve his redemptive and paternal correction for only one family of men: Abraham's.[60]

Thus, the bad news of v. 30b proves to be in the end also good news: the Gentiles *can* at last repent of their idolatry and thus escape the final and eschatological judgment that is awaiting them.[61] The nations have now (τὰ νῦν) crossed over from "the times of ignorance" (τοὺς χρόνους τῆς ἀγνοίας) to the "time of repentance" (καιρὸν μετανοίας).[62] This means leaving behind a history of postponed but inevitable doom to join Israel in the final and climactic moment of redemptive history.[63] Note the abrupt shift from the nations alone (v. 30a) to an emphatic reference to all

---

57. There is not the least sign of complacency on God's part, only postponement of his exacting justice, as is often recognized. See Hansen, "Preaching and Defence," 317; Haenchen, *Acts*, 525–26; McGiffert, *History of Christianity*, 260n (quoted by Bruce, *Acts Greek*, 385); L. T. Johnson, *Acts*, 317; Dennis E. Johnson, *Message of Acts*, 199; Jervell, *Die Apostelgeschichte*, 450; Barrett, *Acts*, 2.851; Witherington, *Acts*, 531–32; Tipton, "Resurrection Proof," 47; Stenschke, *Luke's Portrait*, 218; and Fitzmyer, *Acts*, 611, who notes that there is here no difference with the Paul of the Epistles, contra Dibelius, "Areopagus," 55–56, and all those who would argue that this verse is in tension with Rom 1:20 (like Parsons, *Acts*, 257, does).

58. The expression is from Dennis E. Johnson, *Message of Acts*, 193, speaking of the parallel point made in Acts 14:16 and Rom 3:25. Bock, *Acts*, 569, says about the same text that God "largely ignored them," playing nicely on the theme at hand. The thought is found in Isa 45:15, 17, 19. See our earlier discussion of the OT theme of seeking God. Van Til speaks of mankind being under God's "common grace" and "common wrath" simultaneously (Van Til, *Common Grace*, 74).

59. Hackett, "Discourse of Paul," 354–55. "God does not intervene to change the situation." Gärtner, *Areopagus Speech*, 230. See further Calvin, *Actes*, 476–77. Here Paul is answering a major question that would have puzzled his audience, just like it did Porphyry: why did Paul's God not make his displeasure felt before.

60. Cf. Deut 8:5; Ps 81:1–2; Acts 14:16; Rom 1:28. This discipline was fundamentally legal and forensic, i.e., covenantal in nature. See Dennis E. Johnson, *Message of Acts*, 193.

61. Highlighted already by Chrysostom, Homily XXXVIII, 237. Hence the reaction of Paul's Gentile audience in Pisidian Antioch (13:48)—ἔχαιρον καὶ ἐδόξαζον τὸν λόγον τοῦ κυρίου—after he described his commissioning from the Lord in the words of Isa 49:6! Cf. the story of the conversion of Cornelius' household reported three times in Acts 10, 11 and 15 (note 11:18).

62. To use the clever formulation from *2 Clem.* 8.2 (cf. 9.7; 16.1) to address Christians: μετανοήσωμεν ἐξ ὅλης τῆς καρδίας ἵνα σωθῶμεν ὑπὸ τοῦ κυρίου ἕως ἔχομεν καιρὸν μετανοίας.

63. In many ways, this redemptive-historical turning point is at the heart of all of Luke-Acts. See Dennis E. Johnson, *Message of Acts*, 199 and Barrett, *Acts*, 2.851; cf. L. T. Johnson, *Acts*, 317 and Dunn, *Acts*, 277. This fulfills the promise made to Abraham in Genesis 12:3 (see Bauckham, *Bible and Mission*, 28–36).

human beings (30b)—encompassing both Jews and Gentiles.[64] Yahweh is calling his eschatological and universal New Exodus people out of their exile among the nations, which are all defined by idolatry (including Israel, per Stephen's speech).[65] In these the last days (Acts 2:17), God exercises his royal authority over the whole world anew and therefore *commands* (παραγγέλλει) every single human creature to (re)turn to him in repentance and submission. No one is exempt. The emphatic present and universal nature of the statement is quite striking, especially since the Word has not yet reached ἕως ἐσχάτου τῆς γῆς (1:8) nor Paul Rome: "C'est la loi (le devoir-faire) qui est déterminée comme universelle, non l'annonce."[66] This worldwide royal decree is being disseminated by the heralds who expand the Way. "Now" is the age of the Christian proclamation of Jesus and the resurrection (both the occasion/cause and terminus of the address), the messianic age when the light shines into the darkness enveloping the nations.

The command from God is to repent, not to complement or supplement one's preexisting knowledge (a rather obvious point), nor merely to "change one's mind" (the most common philosophical usage for μετανοέω).[67] The argument of the speech, Lukan usage (cf. 2:38), the universal judgment in view (v. 31) and the eschatological nature of the summon all make clear that nothing less than a full-blown (biblical) religious repentance is required. Mankind must acknowledge and confess the sinfulness and guilt of its way, and henceforth make a radical break with it. That means to forsake wholeheartedly the entirety of their pagan beliefs and practices—that is their whole worldview and way of life—and to replace those with the Christian gospel

---

64. V. 30b could be rendered: "but now God orders to human beings that all people everywhere repent." The combination of τοῖς ἀνθρώποις and πάντας πανταχοῦ is doubly redundant while using the device of paronomasia (a "rhetorical refinement" [Barrett, *Acts*, 2.851] and "redoublement hymnique" [des Places, "Actes 17,30–31," 528]) to express the same idea as τὴν οἰκουμένην and πᾶσιν in v. 31, as well as εἰς πάντα τὰ ἔθνη in Luke 24:47 or ἕως ἐσχάτου τῆς γῆς in Acts 1:8 (the latter two noted by Dupont, "Salut des Gentils," 154). It is interesting that the nearly identical expression πάντας πανταχῇ is used to describe Paul's activity in 21:28 by the Jews from Asia.

65. Many identify Isa 45:15–24 as the background (Pesch, *Apostelgeschichte*, 2.140, adds 46:8 LXX). Isa 42:1–9 LXX is another obvious intertext: v. 6 is a promise to "my Servant" that he is to be given as "a covenant to the peoples, a light to the nations" (cf. Isa 49:6 which is cited in Acts 13:47 and forms the backdrop for 1:8) to open the eyes of the blind etc. (cf. Acts 17:27); vv. 1, 3 that he is to carry out judgment of the nations; and v. 9 ends the oracle with the words: "the former things have come to pass, and new things I now declare; before they spring forth I tell you of them." Strikingly, v. 4 declares: "the nations will hope on his name" (differing significantly from the MT's "the coastlands wait for his law"!). The second part of the book of Isaiah depicts Yahweh addressing the nations (Dupont, "Salut des Gentils," 154), focusing on his overcoming the idols and their worshippers (Beale, *We Become*, 282).

66. Calloud, "Aréopage," 240–41.

67. Contra Morlan, *Conversion in Luke and Paul*, 106 (supplementary knowledge); Rothschild, *Paul in Athens*, 35 and Thom, "Cleanthes' Hymn," 498—in the line of Vielhauer and Pohlenz—for the philosophical interpretation. See discussions in Dupont, "Discours à l'Aréopage," 411–16; Barrett, *Acts*, 2.852; Fitzmyer, *Acts*, 611–12; Witherington, *Acts*, 531, 534–35; Given, "Not Either/Or," 369; and Parsons, *Acts*, 248.

and church (both as community and *locus* of worship).⁶⁸ Salvation itself is at stake, forgiveness must be secured!⁶⁹ There is no "nuanced judgment" that would see both positive and negative aspects to paganism, praising their religiosity but making "a few negative comments" pointing to some "dark sides."⁷⁰ No, it is man *qua* idolater who is under God's wrath and judgment, and therefore it is idolatry (paganism) as such and as a whole that is man's sin. Worshiping anything or anyone else than Yahweh the Maker-Lord-Judge who raised Jesus the Christ is turning away from him and mutiny: "Worshipping false gods or worshipping the true God falsely arose from the same mechanism—creatures inverting their rightful place relative to their Creator."⁷¹ Such divine requirement of exclusivity was unthinkable for Paul's audience, something completely intolerable that would be the cause of much persecution for the Christian church under the Roman imperial rule.⁷²

The Resurrection of Jesus Inaugurates and Defines the "Last Days"

This epochal shift in redemptive-history happened according to God's plan and is the result of his decisive and eschatological work through Jesus.⁷³ The *raison d'être* or cause for this change is revealed in v. 31, as indicated by the strong causal conjunction καθότι.⁷⁴ The whole verse is elegantly crafted. Hence, the parallel expressions ἔστησεν ἡμέραν and ᾧ ὥρισεν bracket the main verbal idea μέλλει κρίνειν (forming a chiasm?) which commands three adverbial or circumstantial affirmations introduced by ἐν—indicating when, in what manner and through whom. The dependent clause starts

---

68. Discontinuity with and condemnation of sin are at the very heart of the biblical concept of μετάνοια. See Rowe, *One True Life*, 5, 133 and Rowe, *World Upside Down*, 41. It simply makes no sense to claim that vv. 30–31 depict Paul as "enlightening, not accusing" or that they present no discontinuity between the beliefs of paganism and Christianity like Samuel, "Paul on the Areopagus," 30–31, and Dibelius, "Areopagus," 55. Acceptance of the christological claims of v. 31 (and the gospel preached in the agora) is an integral part of what is commanded here (cf. Jipp, "Paul's Areopagus Speech," 586 and Rowe, "Grammar," 45).

69. Rightly highlighted by Dupont, "Repentir et conversion," 437, 440, 452, who sees a special connection between the concept of salvation in Luke-Acts and the Joel 3:5 (2:32 LXX) quote in Peter's Pentecost sermon.

70. As claimed by Legrand, "Unknown God," 164–66; Pinnock, "Toward an Evangelical," 364–65; Sanders, *No Other Name*, 246n70; and Samuel, "Paul on the Areopagus," 30. On the contrary, v. 30 makes very clear that the Areopagitica's "jugement sur le culte païen est purement négatif" (Dupont, "Discours à l'Aréopage," 420) for "tout égarement du sentiment religieux dans les voies de l'idolâtrie ou de la superstition fait injure à Dieu" (Dupont, "La conversion," 463).

71. Lints, *Identity and Idolatry*, 117.

72. "Pagans could tolerate anything except such intolerance." Marcus, "Paul at the Areopagus," 145. See the excellent discussion in MacMullen, *Christianizing*, 17–19.

73. The βουλή τοῦ θεοῦ is evoked by the use of the aorist verbs ἔστησεν and ὥρισεν, the latter echoing the ὁρίσας προστεταγμένους καιρούς of v. 26. See also Jervell, *Die Apostelgeschichte*, 450.

74. Barrett, *Acts*, 2.852, remarks that καθότι is used exclusively by Luke in the NT (viz., in Luke 1:7; 19:9; Acts 2:24, 45; 4:35; 17:31). It is relatively common in the LXX, however (sixty-seven times per our accounting).

with an emphatic πίστιν, part of a threefold π alliteration (a Greek favorite)[75] followed by a twofold α alliteration that brings the hearers and readers back to the starting point: Jesus and his resurrection (v. 18). Though καθότι is sometimes understood to indicate that the coming judgment is the motivation for man's repentance, this is true only in a derivative or consequential manner.[76] The mention of the preparatory proceedings for God's universal lawsuit is syntactically and causally related to God's *commanding* men to repent.[77] In other words, καθότι is used to indicate the reason for God's new activity in relation to idolatrous mankind: "It was not God's intention that men should continue permanently in this ignorance of his true being and worship in ignorant idolatry. *Now* . . . he is taking steps to end this situation."[78] This double turn of event (imminent lawsuit and divine injunction), however, is a rhetorically effective and pressing inducement to repent!

Pervo's statement that "the grounds for judgment are not stated" is rather puzzling in view of the evidence put forth by the speech and the entire episode.[79] It seems rather obvious that the trial initiated by Yahweh is against mankind's idolatry or, to be more precise, against mankind on account of its idolatry, as discussed above. On the one hand, vv. 22–29 make the case that Paul's God alone possesses the power, legitimacy, and authority to judge the whole world—by virtue of being its sole God-Creator-Lord-Benefactor.[80] On the other hand, they also supply ample evidence and the necessary witness to demonstrate man's inexcusable crime against that very same king and judge—idolatry is among other things a *lèse majesté*, a seditious covenant-breaking—therefore establishing his guilt and making his conviction inevitable. The cosmic-eschatological perspective of the situation is reinforced by several features: 1) Paul's argument starts with God the creator and ends with God the universal judge, thus being bracketed by the two poles of world history; 2) each pole has all mankind in view through the lens of one nameless though definite man, thus weaving together absolute universality and absolute particularity together; 3) past (even before creation itself), present and (eschatological) future are covered; 4) God's person, plan and activity pervade the whole (rhetorically marked by the

---

75. Dupont, "Discours à l'Aréopage," 405, thinks this explains the choice of the word πίστις in its otherwise common but unique in the NT sense of "proof."

76. For example, Dupont, "Repentir et conversion," 451 ("il faut se repentir parce que [καθότι] le jugement peut commencer d'un moment à l'autre") and Dunn, *Acts*, 237. This interpretation is often used to point the "un-Pauline" character of the passage, since Paul—we are told—would always speak of God's grace as the incentive for one's repentance. See Vielhauer, "Paulinism," 36, 45; cf. Wolfe, "Rhetorical Elements," 281.

77. So also Barrett, *Acts*, 2.852.

78. Barrett, *Acts*, 2.851 (emphasis original).

79. To which he adds the vague: "Presumably they would involve acknowledgment of the one true God and righteous behavior." Pervo, *Acts*, 440.

80. As far as the depicted audience is concerned. The evidence presented to the reader begins with v. 16 and ends at 34—in fact, is found throughout Luke-Acts and its OT intertexts.

use of inflection).⁸¹ The purpose of the upcoming judgment is to quench mankind's rebellion once for all (as in Isa 45:23–24).⁸²

Verse 31 now tells us that everything for the trial is in place and ready: the date has been set, the evidence and witness are gathered, and a competent and legitimate judge has been appointed to render the verdict.⁸³ The date of the court session is set to "a day," but no specific date is offered in line with Jesus' words to his disciples in 1:7.⁸⁴ This suggests both the eschatological nature of the "day" and its redemptive-historical imminence. In the ancient world, the setting of a date and appointment of a judge indicated that the trial was ready to start.⁸⁵ It is therefore urgent to be reconciled with the accuser for soon it might be too late, as in Jesus' parable (Luke 12:58 // Mat 5:25). Paul's speech leaves nothing to the present other than the call to repent: "On peut donc dire que le v. 31 donne toute sa valeur à la précision temporelle du v. 30 . . . Tout ce qui appartient déjà au passé (quatre aoristes) laisse entendre que le moment présent n'est plus très éloigné du redoutable jugement."⁸⁶ What is required is an *immediate* surrender, for no one can tell whether there will be a tomorrow.⁸⁷ "Today" is the day to repent, as in Isa 55:6 ("Seek the LORD while he may be found; call upon him while he is near"; cf. Acts 17:26–27).⁸⁸

---

81. For 1) see Bruce, *Acts NICNT*, 361; Pervo, *Acts*, 440; Rowe, "Grammar," 44; 2) see Calloud, "Aréopage," 242–43; Dupont, "Salut des Gentils," 154; Dupont, "Repentir et conversion," 454; Rowe, *World Upside Down*, 39; 3) see Klauck, *Magic and Paganism*, 91–92 and Rothschild, *Paul in Athens*, 35n65; 4) see Bale, *Genre and Narrative Coherence*, 202 and Parsons, "Progymnasmata," 58 (who points out that the inflection of θεός is also used by Paul in his speech before Agrippa in Acts 26). This structure forces us to read the beginning of the speech in view of its end, thus further clarifying what is meant by both the depicted speaker and the narrator.

82. Cf. Dennis E. Johnson, "Jesus Against," 352.

83. The notion of postmortem or final judgment was known to the Greeks, of course. Popular paganism spoke of an individual judgment after death, though not a final universal one (see Keener, *Acts*, 3.2671). Stoics believed in a final universal conflagration that involved the judgment of all according to the Logos, a major bone of contention with the Epicureans who denied anything of that kind (see Plutarch, *Superst.*, 3 [165F], 4 [166F–167A], himself a Middle Platonist; cf. Winter, "Public and Private," 136–38 and Balch, "Areopagus Speech," 79). To all of them, the idea that such judgment could be rendered by a man (not a god or something beyond the gods) and be grounded in the resurrection would sound quite strange, even preposterous (especially in the context of the Areopagus, a court whose purported founding myth explicitly denied the possibility of the resurrection: Aeschylus, *Eum.* 647–648). Cf. Calvin, *Actes*, 478; Kee, *Good News*, 64–65; Kee, *Every Nation*, 216; Porter, *Paul in Acts*, 123–24.

84. "It is not for you to know times or seasons [χρόνους ἢ καιρούς] that the Father has fixed by his own authority." Cf. Jervell, *Die Apostelgeschichte*, 450n259.

85. A process well described by Schnabel, *Acts*, 741.

86. Dupont, "Discours à l'Aréopage," 392.

87. Carson, *Gagging*, 500–501, rightly notes that v. 31 shows history to be teleological (i.e., redemptive-historical) by nature: it has a sovereignly decreed direction and termination point with an account to be given to a personal, transcendent and provident/immanent God. This is strictly antithetical to any Greek conception of time or history, even the Stoic idea of final reckoning.

88. "Paul montre par ces paroles qu'il faut prêter l'oreille à Dieu aussitôt qu'il parle, comme il est écrit : 'Si aujourd'hui vous entendez sa voix, n'endurcissez pas votre cœur' (Psaume 95 : 7–8)." Calvin,

The characterization of the instrument appointed for this worldwide lawsuit is intriguing, to say the least: God will judge the inhabited world ἐν ἀνδρί.⁸⁹ The context leaves no doubt that Jesus is in view (obvious to the reader and probably to the depicted audience also in view of v. 18 and the reference to the resurrection in v. 31), rendering the ellipsis quite striking.⁹⁰ At the very least this ensures that God remains in the foreground and the judgment is seen as his, while also climaxing with the person and role of Jesus.⁹¹ Jesus is the Isaianic Servant who serves in Yahweh's lawsuit.⁹² Though anarthrous ("a man"), the expression is made definite and very specific by the following clause.⁹³ Besides, the use of ἀνήρ rather than ἄνθρωπος or τίς characterizes Jesus as a real and individualized (even sexed!) human being rather than as an ideal or timeless model.⁹⁴ It is also probable that this affirmation contributes to Paul's defense against the charge of introducing strange deities. In any case, it seems that in view of Acts 7:55–56—which appears to suggest that the Son of Man is just about to judge the world—the expression should be understood in relation to the Son of Man of Daniel (7:13–14)⁹⁵ as well as the ἐξ ἑνός of v. 26 and what is said of Jesus in Acts 10:39–42. It has therefore unmistakable messianic and eschatological overtones, especially as it suggests that the judge is a "second Adam" who defines or establishes the final redemptive-historical age.⁹⁶ In view of 10:43, this means that his appointment as judge simultaneously establishes him as savior.⁹⁷

Actes, 477.

89. Though the perspective is cosmic (in both space and time), it is not abstract and disincarnate ideas such as the world (κόσμος) or idolatry (εἰδωλολατρία) or impiety (ἀσέβεια) or even "unknowing" (ἄγνοια) that will be judged and condemned, but human beings.

90. So also Rowe, *World Upside Down*, 172n201. As could be expected, D adds Ιησου to make explicit what was otherwise implicit.

91. See Gaventa, *Acts*, 253; Barrett, *Acts*, 2.853; Parsons, *Acts*, 248; Marguerat, *Actes*, 2.163; and Schnabel, *Acts*, 742. The phrase ἐν ἀνδρί is better understood in the instrumental sense for a personal agent (see BDF §219, [1]; contra Harris, *Prepositions and Theology*, 120 and the hesitating Turner, *Syntax*, 262). Charles' opinion ("Engaging," 59) that the speech presents history as beginning and ending with a man misses the theocentric focus of the speech as a whole and of these verses in particular (especially since v. 31 does not imply that Jesus is himself the last man).

92. But note Luke 20:30 (Matt 19:28) where Jesus promises his disciples that *they* will "sit on thrones judging the twelve tribes of Israel" in his kingdom. Rothschild's interpretation of ἀνήρ as "a hero, divine agent, even demi-god (i.e., δαίμων)" (Rothschild, *Paul in Athens*, 35n67) misses the point.

93. As noted by Hackett, "Discourse of Paul," 355.

94. See Kee, *Every Nation*, 330n38.

95. See Owen, "Stephen's Vision"); cf. Bruce, "Eschatology in Acts," 56; Bruce, *Acts Greek*, 386; and Bock, *Acts*, 570. The lexical and thematic overlap with 10:41–42 is quite remarkable—though most commentators limit their observations to the link between final judgment and call to repentance. Both passages speak of God "commanding" (παραγγέλλειν), of heralds proclaiming that God has "appointed" (ὁρίζειν) Jesus as judge (κριτής/κρίνειν) in connection with the fact that he raised him from the dead (ἀναστῆναι . . . ἐκ νεκρῶν). See also 2:23–24, 32–36.

96. So Evans, "Jesus and the Spirit," 37. Cf. Acts 13:33 and Luke 3:38.

97. "As second Adam, Christ stands in a solidaric relationship to all men, either as Redeemer or as judge." Tipton, "Resurrection Proof," 48–49.

The asyndetic juxtaposition and the grammatical parallelism of ἐν δικαιοσύνῃ and ἐν ἀνδρί indicate that the two are interrelated but do not specify in what way exactly.[98] Such an indeterminate conjunction is rhetorically suggestive and effective in closely associating the two ideas in the hearer/reader's mind. Even the use of a simple καί would imply a sharper distinction between the two coordinated terms. It is very unlikely that a specific logical or causal relationship between the two is intended by the speaker/writer, or he would have made it clear through the use of the corresponding conjunction. It seems better to understand the two to be concurring and mutually reinforcing characteristics of God's activity. Verse 31 is perfectly in line with the LXX use of ἐν δικαιοσύνῃ with the various cognates of κρίνειν, either to prescribe the divinely-ordained norm to Israelite kings and judges (in their time and place) or to express the perfection of Yahweh's judicial activity (typically in eschatological contexts).[99] The convergence of the two expressions thus achieves at least two effects. First, it highlights the rightness and lawfulness of God's appointment of Jesus, thereby emphasizing the unique legitimacy and authority of Jesus and of his verdict.[100] Second—and reciprocally—the appointment of Jesus is a constitutive aspect of the equity and justice of God's judgment, since his perfect personal righteousness necessitated his resurrection (Acts 2:24).[101] In this way Luke develops his christological exposition by shedding more light on what it means for Jesus to be made Lord and Christ (Acts 2:36).[102] Finally, v. 31 places Jesus at the heart of Paul's anti-idol polemic by heralding him as the Lord whose claims are established in opposition to every other ruler, power, or authority.[103]

The present divine summon to mankind is therefore determined by an event in the imminent future that is caused—and even *proved*—by a historical event

---

98. They are both constituted of the preposition ἐν and an anarthrous dative noun. Ἐν δικαιοσύνῃ is a dative of manner (see BDF §219, [4]; Harris, *Prepositions and Theology*, 119; and Zerwick, *Biblical Greek*, §117). The interconnection is reinforced by the intertextual link with Isa 42:6, where God says to the Servant: ἐκάλεσά σε ἐν δικαιοσύνῃ.

99. See Lev 19:15 for the Mosaic norm (Isa 1:21 for Israel's lack of conformity); for the Solomonic ideal, see 1 Kgs 3:9; 10:9; Ps 71:2; Sir 45:26; for the divine judgment, see Ps 9:9; 95:13; 97:9; as well as *Pss. Sol.* 8:23–25 and Rev 19:11 (the white horseman).

100. Not the lenient and sympathetic nature of the judge, as claimed by Kurz, *Acts*, 275. Cf. Pervo, *Acts*, 440 and Schnabel, *Acts*, 741.

101. See 2:22–36 and Luke 23:47; cf. Luke 20:17 and Acts 4:10–11 (Ps 117:22 LXX); 3:13–15; 13:28–30. In Luke, divine declarations of Jesus' innocence and perfection are many (from Scripture, heavenly voice, prophets, even his enemies and Gentiles). "The distinctive positive characteristic of Luke's account is its presentation of Jesus' righteousness. His innocence is a feature of the other gospels too, but in Luke it has become the unifying theme and, seemingly, an important purpose of the narrative." Seccombe, "Luke and Isaiah," 257. For fuller discussions, see Fitzmyer, "Today" and Larkin, "OT and Soteriology."

102. See Dennis E. Johnson, *Message of Acts*, 200 and Fitzmyer, *Acts*, 612.

103. This has also substantial implications concerning what makes worship legitimate and acceptable in God's eyes after the resurrection and ascension of Jesus. See the arguments in O'Toole, "Paul at Athens"; Dennis E. Johnson, "Jesus Against"; and Pao, *Acts and INE*, 193–212.

in the past that eschatologically fulfilled God's eternal plan.[104] The one event that brought redemptive history to its *telos* and birthed the eschaton is, in Lukan shorthand, the resurrection of Jesus.[105] Since Jesus' death "inaugurates" the eschatological lawsuit (proleptically, it represents the judgment of all of humanity), mankind is now arraigned before God's eschatological tribunal to answer for its idolatry.[106] In the words of Chrysostom: "If Christ rose not, we shall not be judged: but if he rose, we shall without doubt be judged."[107] The transition to the "now" of eschatology for Paul's audience was effected by Jesus' death and resurrection, not by Paul's proclamation of the gospel.[108] It is a matter of historical objectivity rather than epistemic or existential subjectivity. Thus, the proof is redemptive-historical in nature, not kerygmatic.[109] After that epoch-defining eschatological act of God, no one can be "BC" or "pre-messianic" as far as God's redemptive history—and therefore one's soteric status—is concerned.[110] Thus, the person of Jesus together with the fact and significance of his resurrection are the heart and climax of both story and speech, just as they were the substance of Paul's proclamation of the gospel (and of Luke's scriptural theology).[111] The intratextual links with v. 18 and the final negative reaction of the depicted audience make that crystal clear.[112]

104. The only use of πίστις in the NT (out of 243) where it carries its common Hellenistic forensic sense of "proof." It is unlikely that this would be another case of double-entendre, *pace* Klauck, *Magic and Paganism*, 92; Given, *Paul's True Rhetoric*, 74; and Marguerat, *Actes*, 2.163. Such amphibology would have no use for either Luke's or Paul's purposes. Besides, the forensic context and nature of the speech leave no doubt as to what is meant by the term. Rothschild, *Paul in Athens*, 35n68, considers the expression πίστις παρασχὼν itself to be forensic in nature.

105. That is the life-death-resurrection-ascension-glorification of Jesus. Cf. Stonehouse, "Areopagus Address," 39–40.

106. Jesus' work defines both the character (covenantal) and the certainty of the eschatological judgment. See Gaffin, *Perspectives*, 14–20 as well as Kline, *By Oath Consigned*, 50–62. Note how Paul equates faith in the resurrection of Jesus with the hope of general resurrection in his defense speeches and pointedly identifies both as the reason why he is being persecuted and prosecuted (see especially Acts 23:6, 8; 24:14–15, 20–21, 24–25; 26:6–8, 21–23; 28:20).

107. Chrysostom, Homily XXXVIII, 238.

108. "For in raising Christ from the dead God had revealed with sufficient clearness that the age to come had begun to be realized and that the One who had gained preeminence by the divine power which raised Him from the dead was One with whom men were compelled to reckon as a unique servant of God." Stonehouse, "Areopagus Address," 39. Cf. Jervell, *Die Apostelgeschichte*, 450n258.

109. See the demonstration in Tipton, "Resurrection Proof."

110. Cf. references in Larkin, *Acts*, 260 and Strange, *Possibility of Salvation*, 163–98.

111. See, e.g., Stenschke, *Luke's Portrait*, 219–20; Given, *Paul's True Rhetoric*, 75–76; and Marguerat, *Actes*, 2.163; contra Mark S. Smith, *God in Translation*, 309.

112. Remarkably, the audience reacts at the mention of the resurrection, not of the judgment, *pace* Keener, *Acts*, 3.2669; cf. Pervo, *Acts*, 440, who claims it is a literary device; Dupont, "Discours à l'Aréopage," 407; and Stenschke, *Luke's Portrait*, 222. For a nuanced and informed discussion of how the Christian doctrine of the resurrection would be perceived and understood in the Graeco-Roman world, see Martin, *Corinthian Body*, 108–20; cf. des Places, *Religion grecque*, 120–25, for traditional Greek paganism. The classic case for an overall lack of interest in immortality in the Roman empire is found in MacMullen, *Paganism*, 51–57. Cf. Marcus, "Paul at the Areopagus," 148, for a different reading of the epigraphic evidence.

EXEGETICAL EPILOGUE

Paul the Servant-Figure in Luke's New Exodus Judgment

WE SEE THAT PAUL'S apology for the gospel is built on a redemptive-historical—and therefore biblical-theological—interpretation of the history of the "nations" from creation to consummation. This construal presupposes and builds on revealed (i.e., scriptural) categories such as creation, covenant, providence, eschatology, etc. It starts, ends and centers, not on man, not on a pagan deity, not on an abstract concept of "god," but on Yahweh—the Creator-Lord-Judge of the universe who bound himself to his elect people (corporately known as Israel in the OT and the ἐκκλησία in the NT) by a covenant of grace—and on Jesus whom he raised from the dead and appointed Christ and Lord (and thus judge).

This scriptural redemptive-historical framework provides the *necessary* grid of interpretation for the historical facts of Jesus and the resurrection.[1] Luke's narrative framework stresses that the precipitating cause of Paul's speech—and therefore what it immediately addresses—is the Athenians' inability to make sense of the message of the gospel, summarized in their words as τὸν Ἰησοῦν καὶ τὴν ἀνάστασιν. As Carson puts it: "In short, the good news of Jesus Christ is virtually incoherent unless it is securely set into a biblical worldview."[2] Thus, vv. 32 and 34 depict the "informed" response of various groups of Athenians after they start grasping the meaning and implications of Paul's message concerning Jesus' resurrection.[3] We can concur with Witherington that, rhetorically speaking, Paul is pushing his audience to a decision regarding the risen Jesus—just like he does in his defense before Festus and Agrippa (Acts 26:27–28).[4] In Rowe's words: "To agree with the logic of the Areopagus speech

---

1. In fact it offers the contours of a complete worldview, and therefore provides the basic categories for interpreting *any* historical fact or event. Cf. Carson, *Gagging*, 501–3; Carson, "Athens Revisited," 391–94; Van Til, *Paul at Athens*, 11–14; Van Til, *Who Do You Say*, 8–11; and Tipton, "Resurrection Proof," 57–58.

2. Carson, *Gagging*, 502; cf. Carson, "Athens Revisited," 394.

3. Contra Haenchen, *Acts*, 526.

4. This confirms the *forensic* nature of the speech and argument, *pace* Witherington, *Acts*, 531. "In fact, Paul's appearance before the court of the Areopagus is a trial. Luke's Paul is enough of a rhetor to

in the end, therefore, is not to see the truth of the gospel in pagan philosophical terms (translation) but to abandon the old interpretive framework for the new. It is, plainly said, to become a Christian."[5]

At the same time the Areopagitica composes a remarkable and complete example of anti-idol polemic set in the Isaianic tradition. Pao's conclusion that Paul's address "is constructed with many of the prominent themes of the anti-idol program in Isaiah 40–55" is confirmed by the numerous parallels identified throughout our study (see index of Scripture citations), especially extensive and programmatic intertexts like Isaiah 42:1–9 (5!), 44:6–20, 45:15–25 and 55:5–11.[6] The profound similarity of thought and conception (themes, patterns, arguments, even language) between the two indicates that these individual passages should be seen as intertextual gateways into Isaiah's program and theology more broadly.[7] Moreover, the speech weaves into the Isaianic framework a number of themes and stories coming from various parts of the OT, especially the Pentateuch and the Psalms, and even some Hellenistic textual material—thereby impressing his own interpretation and meaning upon them—the whole being expressed in an idiom that is perfectly adapted to Paul's audience.[8]

The Athens episode is an integral part of Luke's New Exodus program, representing the highest peak of its narrative anti-idol mountain-range-like argument. *It must therefore be read in its historical, narrative, intertextual and theological context.* Seen within the narrative framework of Luke-Acts, this particular story depicts how the Word of God—the agent of the New Exodus—has traveled ἕως ἐσχάτου τῆς γῆς in relation to human culture and religion, in a redemptive-historical and eschatologically proleptic (therefore representative) way. In the same manner the last section of Acts tells how that same Word/gospel reached the symbolic geopolitical "end of the earth": Rome, where Paul is to appear before the Emperor himself (a "journey" that begins narratively in Jerusalem, in the temple precinct to be precise!). Together they show that the promise-mandate of Acts 1:8 was fulfilled through the apostolic witness in an "already and not yet" manner typical of the messianic age (cf. Acts 2:16–17 and 13:47).[9] Both show that God is indeed in the process of accomplishing his eternal plan

---

combine a skillful avoidance of the capital charge—bringing in strange deities, as did Socrates—with a comprehensive critique of pagan 'piety' as 'superstitious' idolatry." Rowe, *One True Life*, 136.

5. Rowe, *World Upside Down*, 41.

6. So Pao, *Acts and INE*, 194 (full argument on pp. 193–197).

7. The influence of the *book* of Isaiah on the Areopagitica is of one cloth with the impact it has on Luke-Acts as a whole or on Paul's epistles (see Hays, "Who Has Believed?"). Luke was clearly conversant with the Greek text, the themes and the theology of the book of Isaiah in an original and unmediated way. It seems that the parallels existing between Luke and Hellenistic Judaism are better explained by the fact that both drew from Isaiah rather than by some purported dependence. See the discussions in Pao, *Acts and INE*, 213–16 and Snodgrass, "Streams of Tradition."

8. Cf. Carson, "Athens Revisited," 392 and Gaventa, "You Will Be," 422.

9. "It needs to be stressed that Acts 1:8 is not addressed indiscriminately to all believers, regardless of time and place, but directly only to the *apostles* (cf. v. 2 where the 'you' of v. 8 is explicitly identified as the apostles), and concerns the foundational task of bringing the gospel from Jerusalem to Rome

of salvation for the κόσμος (which is revealed throughout the OT), for his agent, the Word/Way, is at work and truly unstoppable (cf. 17:33 and 28:28). "To [his readers], and to us, Luke writes a reminder that the power of God's word is greater than its enemies; it is also greater than the weakness of the vessels of witness."[10]

Paul is narratively and intertextually framed as the divinely-commissioned herald or word-bearer, God's instrument for the task. In typical Lukan narration, the scene of the Areopagitica "shows" (rather than "tells") Paul performing the properly divine prerogative of *commanding* all men to repent (v. 30).[11] Paul's words are God's words, and so are both his mission and authority. Luke paints Paul as the eschatological Isaianic Servant who acts in the name and on behalf of the Lord, viz. Jesus, in a way reminiscent of the Moses-Joshua and Elijah-Elisha transfer pattern. His preaching of the gospel effects the New Exodus by bringing judgment to the Lord's enemies and thereby extending the way of salvation to his eschatological people in exile among the nations. In both the Mosaic and the Isaianic Exodus God's people are understood to be in slavery to their masters' gods. Hence the motif of the Exodus is not an attempt at *keeping* God's people away from idols, but at *making* them "idol-free." It is a redemption and deliverance from the sway these false gods and their earthly representatives (pharaoh, the king of Babylon, the Roman emperor) have over them. Thus, the Exodus is inseparable from the divine covenantal commandment to put away idols and consecrate oneself to the Lord alone.[12]

In absolute contrast to the "gods, so-called," Yahweh is the sole legitimate and benevolent Lord of mankind, by virtue of being its maker. He alone can demand obedience, service, and worship from his creature. He alone has the right, the power, the authority, and the wisdom to judge (and therefore to condemn and execute the sentence) all people, nations, and religions.[13] He alone is the Σωτήρ, the warrior who liberates his people from spiritual exile and slavery by shining light to give sight, by pouring his Spirit to create contrite and believing hearts to them, and by pouring on them the many benefits of a covenant whose terms have been perfectly and finally fulfilled on their behalf by Jesus, *the* Servant and second Moses.[14]

---

completed by them (cf. Col 1:6, 23). . . . Rather [than 'Jerusalem'] we today are part of 'the ends of the earth' reached by the gospel in the period beyond its foundational spread." Gaffin, *Perspectives*, 23–24.

10. Gaventa, "You Will Be," 424.

11. To use a category from speech-act theory, Paul's speech appears to be *performative* in nature: as Paul utters the words of the address with his mouth God is concurrently commanding all men to repent. For the distinction between "showing" and "telling" modes of narration, see Ska, *Our Fathers*, 53–54.

12. Cf. Pao, *Acts and INE*, 212. Tellingly, the first two commandments of the Decalogue deal directly and explicitly with the issue of idolatry.

13. "Yahweh is the sovereign one who is in control, and only the people that belong to him will survive. Again, the attack on the idols is an attack on the nations. The survival of the Israelite community is ensured by the power of Yahweh. It is only within this context that the Isaianic anti-idol polemic can be understood." Pao, *Acts and INE*, 185.

14. Cf. Watts, "Consolation or Confrontation," 49–58.

Paul is the Servant (in a derivative manner) of that Lord, the agent or instrument through whom these New Exodus tasks are performed. It is with that Isaianic mantle on that Paul pronounces *eschatological judgment* upon God's and the church's enemies, i.e., on all who do not worship Yahweh in and through the risen Jesus.[15] This proclamation of condemnation is for that very same reason a proclamation of salvation, for God has acted in a final and eschatological manner in Jesus to save his people from the power of sin and evil through the condemnation and destruction of their idols and false gods.[16] This Word of God is the very agent that effects the salvation of God's elect (as in Romans 10). Paul's proclamation therefore brings *eschatological salvation* to those who are blind and in darkness in accordance with the Isaianic commission he received from Christ (see Acts 13:47; 26:18; cf. Luke 4:18-19, 21). This salvation is made theirs by means of their heeding God's summon to repent of their sin, and therefore to turn away from idols to the only true God and Lord who shares his praise with no one else (just as in 1 Thess 1:9-10).[17] Hence, Paul is the preacher of *eschatological repentance* par excellence, whose message is Jesus and the resurrection. There is no question that the perspective is one of absolute and eschatological antithesis between the Way/church/Christianity—which solely and exclusively belongs to God and is entrusted with his truth and salvation—and all other faiths.[18]

---

15. Inclusivists follow Legrand's theory that Romans 1 is very negative about other religions while Acts 17 is rather positive on the basis that the former offers an "eschatological" perspective on them and the latter a "historical" one (cf. Legrand, "Unknown God," 166-67). This dichotomy is simply groundless, failing to understand the *redemptive-historical*—we dare say "eschatological-historical"—nature of both texts. Pitting eschatology against history does not simply distort but destroys the nature of the biblical record.

16. Cf. Stonehouse, "Areopagus Address," 38-39.

17. As Rowe puts it: "To embrace the theological vision of Acts is in principle at once to abandon traditional cultic practice; *it is not to add yet another name to the high god atop the pyramid of powers but is to reject all other claims to ultimate divine power*. The early Christians thus differed substantially from pagan philosophy—the closest pagan analogue to early Christianity, as Nock saw long ago—and from pagan polytheism." "Acts and Cultural Explication," 265 (emphasis added).

18. As Pao argues, "in both Isaiah and Acts, the anti-idol polemic appears primarily in contexts that affirm the sovereignty of the Lord over against the challenges of the other peoples and their idols/deities. The Isaianic and Lukan communities are therefore portrayed as the sole bearer [sic] of the divine truth. The rhetorical annihilation of the idols serves to strip away the power of those who oppose the (renewed) people of God of the New Exodus. The delineation of the true people of God is therefore accomplished through such language." Pao, *Acts and INE*, 212; see also pp. 182 and 192. This people alone can worship Yahweh in a divinely-sanctioned manner. The Exodus (both original and new) is a journey from false and idolatrous worship to true worship in God's temple. This is one of the three elements of the pattern of the prophet like Moses identified by Moessner, "The Christ Must" (see especially his conclusion on p. 255). See also Beale, *Temple*, 201-44.

Conclusion

Much has been discussed, argued, and demonstrated in the various chapters of this book already. There is no need to repeat it here. We will limit our remarks to a few methodological "metacomments" and programmatic conclusions related to the three main concerns we identified in the introduction: hermeneutics/exegesis, inclusivism, and theology of religions.

First, it seems to us that the necessity of developing and adopting a holistic and integrative exegetical methodology has been demonstrated by our study. Its superior heuristic capability is evident in its ability to offer a unified, coherent, nuanced, multi-layered, and meaning-rich interpretation of a text that has vexed generations of highly qualified scholars. Instead of censuring the text for its purported fragmented, incoherent, incomplete, or alien nature, such an approach allows the reader to hear it speak with its own voice and artistry. One does not have to choose between the historical, theological, intertextual, narrative, or linguistic dimensions that make up the text but can enjoy the organic synergy that their interweaving produces under the pen of a skilled writer and storyteller such as Luke.

Thus the meaning and import of each individual element of Paul's speech is accessible through reading that particular bit of language within its various levels of context: sentence, paragraph, speech, episode, thematic or character development, book, etc. Moreover, we can appreciate the multi-perspectival riches that the medium of narration offers to someone who simultaneously seeks to recount historical events and expose their theological meaning. However, failing to take stock of this essential property of stories (and all historical studies are stories by nature) can only lead to reductionistic, partial, contradictory, and impoverished readings of the speech, of Paul's visit in Athens, and of Luke-Acts.

Second, this kind of result is precisely what we see in the interpretations of this text offered by both inclusivists and defenders of contextualization-controlled models for mission.[1] Their readings of the various parts of the text de-contextualize

---

1. See Appendix for more details. The term "contextualization" is notoriously slippery as it nearly has as many definitions as there are authors using it. Obviously, our issue is not with the idea of "contextualization" *per se*, but with particular ways of defining and construing both the concept and the practice. For further study of the topic, see Moreau, *Contextualization in World Missions* and Conn,

it by abstracting it from its Lukan setting, both at a micro- and a macro-level. Then, they re-contextualize it in an alien and abstract framework resulting from a form of "encyclopaedic mode of knowing" typical of modern comparative studies.[2] Doing so destroys the unity of Luke's writings and leads to conclusions that are in direct contradiction with his thought and message. It is therefore excluded by the very nature of the case.

Both schools of thought use a (historical, linguistic, cultural and textual) hermeneutical paradigm that depends on the notion of the translatability of the Christian gospel in Hellenistic terms without loss or transformation of meaning. That notion, however, turns the Areopagitica on its head and shows thereby its unfounded and mistaken nature. It is *de facto* denying the contextual nature of meaning as well as the embeddedness of both language and concept in life and community. Its outcome is the exact opposite of what it sought to facilitate, viz., the effective cross-cultural (and linguistic) communication of the gospel in settings where there is no biblical literacy. If one thing is clear from the story of Paul's "post-evangelistic" speech, it is that the gospel can *only* make sense in the context of biblical history and the biblical-theological framework it reveals!

Third, it seems that this very framework should constitute the backbone of any theology of religions that claims to be "biblical" in any sense of the term.[3] Of course, this simple outline does not exhaust what Scripture says about the human natural religiosity and the multiple forms in which we encounter it in history or in everyday life. But it does encapsulate its essential features and general pattern. Its fundamental attitude and outlook too.[4] To be properly scriptural, such a theology of religions would have to be especially sensitive to the epochal and eschatological—therefore progressive and teleological—nature of both the history of redemption it records and the history of revelation that produced it. A "smorgasbord" reading of the Scriptures that erases the resulting complexity and ignores the necessary nuances and distinctions to be made can only produce theological confusion and missiological aberration.[5] Finally, it should be driven by the same passion for the exclusive glory and worship of the one Creator-Lord-Judge-Savior of the universe, the Triune Father, Son, and Holy Spirit.

Eternal Word.

2. The concept of "encyclopaedic" mode of enquiry comes from MacIntyre, *Three Rival Versions*. For an illuminating application of MacIntyre's analysis to the comparison of ancient "traditions of life" (in this case, Stoicism and Christianity), see Rowe, *One True Life*, 176–99.

3. "The greatest missionary document in the New Testament" according to Deissmann, *Light*, 384.

4. "Thus on the total evidence adduced from our analysis so far of Luke-Acts we may conclude that Luke regarded the Areopagus speech as the final climactic part of his exposition of the whole plan of God." Schubert, "Place," 260.

5. "Smorgasbord comparison prohibits the examination of a philosophical tradition as a tradition and replaces the textual home of particular words with generalized scholarly reconstruction; the smorgasbord therefore hinders rather than aids understanding." Rowe, *One True Life*, 2.

APPENDIX

Some Further Reflections on the Subject of Theology of Religions[1]

Our study of the Areopagus story with its various levels of contexts confirms our intuition that this passage might be the best starting point for developing a sound and biblical Christian theology of religions. It also demonstrates that the Areopagitica is a powerful scriptural evidence *against* the theories of inclusivism (to which we can add missiological theories such as Insider Movements, CAMEL, "Qur'an as a bridge," etc.). We will now summarize our findings in those two regards.

The Areopagitica and Inclusivism

Inclusivists generally argue that two elements of the Athens story support a positive or "hopeful" estimation of non-Christian religions: the attitude displayed by Luke and Paul regarding pagans, and a message that accentuates the continuity between the Christian faith and other religions.[2] We believe that such an interpretation of Acts 17 is possible only when the passage is read in an atomistic way that fails to see its deep unity, its participation in the larger Lukan program, and its purpose.[3]

In the light of our exegesis, it is impossible to claim that Luke or Paul demonstrate an attitude of appreciation for the "truth" that is found in other religions, or

---

1. This appendix is a slightly revised version of the original conclusion of our dissertation—which focused especially on theology of religions and inclusivism, its claims, arguments and interpretations of Paul's Areopagitica. It is reproduced here for the sake of interested readers who might find the book's (new) conclusion a bit too terse on the subject.

2. Two of the most substantial representative studies of the Areopagus speech published by self-identified inclusivists are Sanders, *No Other Name*, 244–47 and Samuel, "Paul on the Areopagus." All depend to a significant extent on the seminal Schlette, "Religions."

3. This is certainly why the biblical scholars most often cited by inclusivists on this text are Dibelius, Conzelmann, and Haenchen. The same mindset expresses itself at the semantic level, for the meaning and theology of the passage is often sought in the *words* (such as δεισιδαιμονεστέρους) or phrases (such as ἀγνοοῦντες εὐσεβεῖτε) seen independently from the sentences and paragraphs (and books) they belong to and which provide the necessary hermeneutical context for their meaning.

call for discernment to sort out what is "good" from what is "bad" in them.[4] Every single religious belief or practice that is not according to God's covenantal ways—i.e., a repentant and obedient response to the claims of the risen Jesus—is defined as idolatry. And idolatry is considered *sin* as such. Here, it is not idolatry or paganism as an abstract and disincarnate concept that is in view, but it is the concrete expression and pursuit of men *qua* subjects in open revolt against their Maker, Benefactor, Lord and Judge. To put it bluntly: human beings, and not religious movements or institutions, are the ones who will suffer eternal punishment on account of idolatry.

Luke/Paul is not either acknowledging the presence of "salvific truth" in other religions. Just as there are no brute facts, there are no brute truths. Whatever kernel of truth paganism or Greek philosophy may hold, this truth is turned into darkness and "ignorance" by the pagan framework in which it finds its *actual* meaning. The speech makes it clear: the (apostolic) Christian church is the sole depository and possessor of divine truth. Only those who receive the gospel of the resurrection of Jesus are truly *seeking* Yahweh (in the biblical sense of the term) and *know* him, and can therefore genuinely and acceptably serve and worship God. Idolaters are serving and worshipping things that are truly "nothings" that cannot save, in stark and absolute opposition to the one God and Lord. They are in exile and in bondage far away from Yahweh.

Far from encouraging an "inclusive" or "dialogical" approach to other religions,[5] the speech is a radical and uncompromising critique and condemnation of everything else than the "way," i.e., the church or "Christianity." The Areopagitica is a powerful anti-idol polemic which demonstrates the foolish and culpable nature of man's religiosity outside of God's covenant statutes. It proclaims a final and eschatological judgment on all men who are in Adam but not in Christ, i.e., who belong to "this age" which is set for destruction rather than to the "age to come" that broke through in the person and work of Jesus. There is simply no hope whatsoever in the world of man, except for God's New Exodus being effected by Jesus the Messiah through his word and Spirit in the person of his disciples. Salvation is obtained not by supplementing, complementing, correcting, or improving one's false religion, but by condemning and abandoning it altogether to turn to the "way," thus joining the people of Jesus Christ *en route* for the eschatological Jerusalem-kingdom-temple of God.[6]

---

4. As typically claimed by inclusivists (e.g., Pinnock, "Toward an Evangelical," 364–65) on the basis of Legrand, "Unknown God." Cf. Jennings, "Deity of Christ for Missions" for a similar view argued in defense of missiological models like Insider Movements.

Though Paul displays an altogether respectful attitude vis-à-vis his audience, in spite of the fierce anger mentioned in v. 16, he does not insult the Athenians in response to their mocking, nor does he point out their ignorance to them in an arrogant attitude. He treats them with the dignity that their being made in the image of God requires, and he shows the humility of someone who knows that he also walked in deep darkness and was shown infinite mercy (cf. Johnson, "Jesus Against," 349–51).

5. As most contributors to the *International Journal of Frontier Missions* (like Higgins, "Key to Insider Movements") and Mbuvi, "Missionary Acts" claim, for example.

6. Hence, "the Christian sources are uniformly clear that the move into the Christian tradition is made possible by the God and Father of Jesus Christ and is not something that can be achieved by

In the end, we must conclude that inclusivism does not have the least ground to stand upon in Luke-Acts in general, and in Acts 17:16–34 in particular. Luke's theology and this climactic expression of his anti-idol polemic militate wholly against its claims.

The Areopagitica and Theology of Religions

At the same time, this passage points to the starting point and proper perspective to use when developing a biblical theology of religions. The first, and possibly most obvious, principle is that a biblical theology must be truly biblical. This means that it seeks to give expression to the Bible's intrinsic theology, not to extrapolate a theology for which Scripture is only one source read through an extra biblical grid.[7] This methodological commitment has at least three major corollaries. The first is that a biblical theology of religion must receive and read the Bible as a whole, and engage its message as a unified system (Luke makes use of all the main parts of the Old Testament). The second is that it must appreciate and benefit from its various authors both on their own terms and in their canonical context. The third is that such a theology must be consistent with and patterned after the very structure and nature of biblical revelation: it must therefore be theocentric, trinitarian, covenantal, and eschatological.[8]

Therefore, a biblical theology of religions can only be redemptive-historical in method, organization and perspective. This means that it ought to follow the basic creation-fall-redemption-consummation pattern of biblical revelation. The Areopagitica begins with creation and concludes with the parousia, having alluded to the stories of Noah and Babel as well as the Sinaitic covenant with Israel. It considers human religiosity from the perspective of Yahweh's original design, the post-Babel condition, God's covenant of grace—and its eschatological fulfillment—, and of the final judgment. It therefore offers a proper hermeneutic allowing a nuanced and balanced understanding of man's religious psychology who is both aware and ignorant of the Creator-God at the same time. Finally, it defines true and false religion on the basis of a simple contrast between idolatry—which is characterized by arrogance and a drive to "invent" and control the god(s) for one's benefit—and covenant-keeping.[9]

---

human effort of mind or will. It is, rather, a setting free, . . . For Luke, the name of the sort of knowledge Christian knowledge is for pagans is 'apocalypse,' a revealing of the truth from God's side of the Creator/creature distinction (see Luke 2:32)." Rowe, *One True Life*, 253.

7. See the methodological model offered by Gaffin, *Resurrection and Redemption*, 19–30.

8. We use "eschatological" in its Vosian sense. Creation—and therefore also history—is essentially teleological, tending towards its consummation from its very inception by divine design and decree. See Gaffin, "Introduction," ix–xxiii.

9. From his study of Paul's speeches in Lystra and Athens together with 1 Corinthians 8–10, Winter concludes: "The reason that the matter of religious pluralism was discussed in public preaching was simply that *it was an essential component of the gospel presentation*." Winter, "Public and Private," 142 (emphasis ours).

In fine, a biblical theology of religions must give its full weight to the eschatological fulfillment of God's salvation plan in the person of Jesus. The epoch-changing event of Jesus' life-death-resurrection-ascension is the single most important for one's understanding of the nature and standing of man's religion before God today. Man is now living in the last days, when God's grace and forgiveness is offered in an unprecedented way to the whole world and his final judgment is imminent. This is a time when the division between Yahweh's people and his enemies is climactic and the participation in God's eschatological New Exodus depends on one's Spirit-produced response to the divine word. This is no time for compromise or rapprochement, but rather for a loving, humble, and bold summon to all men everywhere to repent from their idolatry and to turn to the God who extends the way of salvation through the proclamation of the gospel of Jesus the crucified and risen Christ.

Bibliography

Achtemeier, Paul J. "Gods Made with Hands: The New Testament and the Problem of Idolatry." *Ex Auditu* 15 (1999) 43–61.

Adams, Sean A. *The Genre of Acts and Collected Biography*. SNTSMS 156. Cambridge: Cambridge University Press, 2013.

Adams, Sean A., and Michael Pahl, eds. *Issues in Luke-Acts: Selected Essays*. Gorgias Handbooks 26. Piscataway, NJ: Gorgias, 2012.

Aletti, Jean-Noël. *L'art de raconter Jésus Christ: L'écriture narrative de l'évangile de Luc*. Paris: Seuil, 1989.

———. *Quand Luc raconte: Le récit comme théologie*. Lire la Bible. Paris: Cerf, 1998.

Alexander, J. A. *Acts of the Apostles*. Geneva Series of Commentaries. 1857. Reprint, Carlisle, PA: Banner of Truth, 1963.

Alter, Robert. *The Art of Biblical Narrative*. 2nd ed. New York: Basic, 2011.

Anderson, Bernhard W. "Exodus and Covenant in Second Isaiah and Prophetic Tradition." In *Magnalia Dei, The Mighty Acts of God: Essays on the Bible and Archaeology in Memory of G. Ernest Wright*, edited by F. M. Cross et al., 339–60. Garden City, NY: Doubleday, 1976.

———. "Exodus Typology in Second Isaiah." In *Israel's Prophetic Heritage: Essays in Honor of James Muilenburg*, edited by Bernhard W. Anderson and Walter Harrelson, 177–95. New York: Harper, 1962.

Arnold, Bill T. "Luke's Characterizing Use of the Old Testament in the Book of Acts." In *History, Literature, and Society in the Book of Acts*, edited by Ben Witherington, III, 300–323. Cambridge: Cambridge University Press, 1996.

Athanassiadi, Polymnia, and Michael Frede, eds. "Pagan Monotheism in Late Antiquity." Oxford: Clarendon, 1999.

Attridge, Harold W. "The Philosophical Critique of Religion Under the Early Empire." In *ANRW* 2.16.1, 45–78.

Auffret, Pierre. "Essai sur la structure littéraire du discours d'Athènes (Ac xvii 23–31)." *Novum Testamentum* 20, no. 3 (1978) 185–202.

Augustine. *The Confessions*. Translated by Carolyn J.-B. Hammond. LCL 26. Cambridge, MA: Harvard University Press, 2014.

Aune, David E. *The New Testament in Its Literary Environment*. Library of Early Christianity 8. Philadelphia: Westminster, 1987.

Bahnsen, Greg L. *Always Ready: Directions for Defending the Faith*. Edited by Robert R. Booth. Texarkana, AR: Covenant Media Foundation, 1996.

Bailey, James L., and Lyle D. Vander Broek. *Literary Forms in the New Testament: A Handbook.* Louisville, KY: Westminster John Knox, 1992.

Baker, David L. "Typology and the Christian Use of the Old Testament." *Scottish Journal of Theology* 29 (1976) 137–57.

Balch, David L. "The Areopagus Speech: An Appeal to the Stoic Historian Posidonius Against Later Stoics and the Epicureans." In *Greeks, Romans, and Christians: Essays in Honor of Abraham J. Malherbe*, edited by David L. Balch et al., 52–79. Minneapolis: Fortress, 1990.

Bale, Alan J. *Genre and Narrative Coherence in the Acts of the Apostles.* LNTS 514. London: Bloomsbury T. & T. Clark, 2015.

Barnes, Timothy D. "An Apostle on Trial." *Journal of Theological Studies* 20 (1969) 407–19.

Barr, James. *The Semantics of Biblical Language.* Oxford: Oxford University Press, 1961.

Barrett, C. K. "Acts and the Pauline Corpus." *Expository Times* 88 (1976–77) 2–5.

———. *A Critical and Exegetical Commentary on the Acts of the Apostles.* 2 vols. ICC. Edinburgh: T. & T. Clark, 1994–98.

———. "Luke/Acts." In *It Is Written: Scripture Citing Scripture: Essays in Honour of Barnabas Lindars, SSF*, edited by D. A. Carson and H. G. M. Williamson, 231–44. Cambridge: Cambridge University Press, 1988.

———. "Paul at Athens and Paul to Rome." In *On Paul: Aspects of His Life, Work, and Influence in the Early Church*, 139–54. London: T. & T. Clark, 2003.

———. "Paul's Speech on the Areopagus." In *New Testament Christianity for Africa and the World: Essays in Honour of Harry Sawyer*, edited by M. E. Glasswell and E. W. Fasholé-Luke, 69–77. London: SPCK, 1974.

———. "The Third Gospel as a Preface to Acts? Some Reflections." In *The Four Gospels 1992: Festschrift for Frans Neirynck*, vol. 2, edited by F. Van Segbroeck et al., 1451–66. BETL 100. Leuven: Leuven University Press, 1992.

———. "What Minorities?" In *Mighty Minorities? Minorities in Early Christianity—Positions and Strategies: Essays in Honour of Jacob Jervell on His 70th Birthday 21 May 1995*, edited by David Hellholm et al., 1–10. Oslo: Scandinavian University Press, 1995.

Bartholomew, Craig G., et al., eds. *Reading Luke: Interpretation, Reflection, Formation.* Scripture and Hermeneutics Series 6. Grand Rapids: Zondervan, 2005.

Bauckham, Richard J., ed. *The Gospels for All Christians: Rethinking the Gospel Audiences.* Grand Rapids: Eerdmans, 1998.

———. *Bible and Mission: Christian Witness in a Postmodern World.* Easneye Lectures and Frumentius Lectures. Carlisle, UK: Paternoster, 2003.

———. *God Crucified: Monotheism and Christology in the New Testament.* Didsbury Lectures, 1996. Carlisle, UK: Paternoster, 1998.

———. "James and the Gentiles." In *History, Literature, and Society in the Book of Acts*, edited by Ben Witherington, III, 154–84. Cambridge: Cambridge University Press, 1996.

———. *Jesus and the Eyewitnesses: The Gospels as Eyewitness Testimony.* Grand Rapids: Eerdmans, 2006.

———. "Kerygmatic Summaries in the Speeches of Acts." In *History, Literature, and Society in the Book of Acts*, edited by Ben Witherington, III, 185–217. Cambridge: Cambridge University Press, 1996.

Baugh, Steven M. "'Savior of All People': 1 Tim 4:10 in Context." *Westminster Theological Journal* 54 (1992) 331–40.

Bavinck, Herman. "Common Grace." Translated by Raymond C. Van Leeuwen. *Calvin Theological Journal* 24 (1989) 35–65.

———. *God and Creation*. Vol. 2 of *Reformed Dogmatics*. Edited by John Bolt. Translated by John Vriend. Grand Rapids: Baker Academic, 2004.

———. *Prolegomena*. Vol. 1 of *Reformed Dogmatics*. Edited by John Bolt. Translated by John Vriend. Grand Rapids: Baker Academic, 2003.

Bavinck, J. H. *An Introduction to the Science of Missions*. Translated by David H. Freeman. Phillipsburg, NJ: Presbyterian and Reformed, 1960.

Bayer, Hans F. "Christ-Centered Eschatology in Acts 3.17–26." In *Jesus of Nazareth: Lord and Christ*, edited by Joel B. Green, 236–50. Grand Rapids: Eerdmans, 1994.

———. "The Preaching of Peter in Acts." In *Witness to the Gospel: The Theology of Acts*, edited by I. Howard Marshall and David Peterson, 257–74. Grand Rapids: Eerdmans, 1998.

Beale, G. K., ed. *The Right Doctrine from the Wrong Texts?* Grand Rapids: Baker, 1994.

———. "The Eschatological Conception of New Testament Theology." In *Eschatology in Bible and Theology: Evangelical Essays at the Dawn of a New Millennium*, edited by Kent E. Brower and Mark W. Elliott, 11–52. Downers Grove, IL: IVP, 1999.

———. "Isaiah 6:9–13: A Retributive Taunt against Idolatry." *Vetus Testamentum* 41, no. 3 (1991) 257–78.

———. "Other Religions in New Testament Theology." In *Biblical Faith and Other Religions: An Evangelical Assessment*, edited by David Baker, 79–105. Grand Rapids: Kregel, 2004.

———. "Review Article." Review of *Acts and the Isaianic New Exodus* by David W. Pao. *Trinity Journal* 25NS (2004) 93–101.

———. *The Temple and the Church's Mission: A Biblical Theology of the Dwelling Place of God*. NSBT 17. Downers Grove, IL: IVP, 2004.

———. *We Become What We Worship: A Biblical Theology of Idolatry*. Downers Grove, IL: IVP Academic, 2008.

Bentzen, Aage. "On the Ideas of 'the Old' and 'the New' in Deutero-Isaiah." *Studia Theologica* 1, no. 1–2 (1948) 183–87.

Berger, Peter L. *A Rumor of Angels: Modern Society and the Rediscovery of the Supernatural*. 2nd ed. New York: Doubleday, 1990.

———. *The Sacred Canopy: Elements of a Sociological Theory of Religion*. 2nd ed. New York: Anchor, 1990.

Berkouwer, G. C. *General Revelation*. Studies in Dogmatics. Grand Rapids: Eerdmans, 1955.

———. *Man: The Image of God*. Studies in Dogmatics. Grand Rapids: Eerdmans, 1962.

Betz, Hans Dieter, and Edgar W. Smith, Jr. "De Iside et Osiride (Moralia 351C–384C)." In *Plutarch's Theological Writings and Early Christian Literature*, edited by Hans Dieter Betz, 36–84. Leiden: Brill, 1975.

Block, Daniel I. *The Gods of the Nations: Studies in Ancient Near Eastern National Theology*. 2nd ed. ETS Studies. Grand Rapids: Baker Academic, 2000.

Boccaccini, Gabriele. *Middle Judaism: Jewish Thought 300 B.C.E. to 200 C.E.* Minneapolis: Fortress, 1991.

Bock, Darrell L. *Acts*. BECNT. Grand Rapids: Baker Academic, 2007.

———. *Proclamation from Prophecy and Pattern: Lucan Old Testament Christology*. JSNTSup 17. Sheffield, UK: Sheffield Academic Press, 1987.

———. "Scripture and the Realisation of God's Promises." In *Witness to the Gospel: The Theology of Acts*, edited by I. Howard Marshall and David Peterson, 41–62. Grand Rapids: Eerdmans, 1998.

———. *A Theology of Luke and Acts.* Biblical Theology of the New Testament. Grand Rapids: Zondervan, 2012.

Boismard, M.-E., and A. Lamouille. *Le texte occidental des actes des apôtres: reconstitution et réhabilitation.* 2 Vols. Synthèse 17. Paris: Editions Recherche sur les Civilisations, 1984.

Bonnard, Pierre-Emile. "Le Psaume 72: ses relectures, ses traces dans l'œuvre de Luc?" *Recherches de science religieuse* 69 (1981) 259–78.

Bossuyt, P., and J. Radermakers. "Rencontre de l'incroyant et inculturation: Paul à Athènes (Ac 17, 16–34)." *Nouvelle Revue Théologique* 117 (1995) 19–43.

Bovon, François. *L'Évangile Selon Luc.* 4 vols. CNT, Deuxième Série 3a-d. Genève: Labor et Fides, 1991–2009.

———. *Luc le théologien: Vingt-cinq ans de recherche (1950–1975).* Genève: Delachaux & Niestlé, 1978.

———. *Luke the Theologian: Fifty-Five Years of Research (1950–2005).* 2nd ed. Waco, TX: Baylor University Press, 2006.

Bowker, J. W. "Speeches in Acts: A Study in Proem and Yelamedenu Form." *New Testament Studies* 14 (1967–68) 96–111.

Boyarin, Daniel. *Border Lines: The Partition of Judaeo-Christianity.* Divinations: Rereading Late Ancient Religion. Philadelphia: University of Pennsylvania Press, 2004.

———. *The Jewish Gospels: The Story of the Jewish Christ.* New York: New Press, 2012.

Bréhier, Emile. *Antiquité et Moyen Age.* Vol. 1 of *Histoire de la Philosophie.* 5th ed. Paris: Presses Universitaires de France, Quadrige, 1989.

Brodie, Thomas L. *Luke the Literary Interpreter: Luke-Acts as a Systematic Rewriting and Updating of the Elijah-Elisha Narrative.* Rome: Pontifical University of Thomas Aquinas, 1987.

———. "Luke-Acts as an Imitation and Emulation of the Elijah-Elisha Narrative." In *New Views on Luke and Acts,* edited by Earl Richard, 78–85, 172–74. Collegeville, MN: Liturgical, 1990.

Brooks, James A., and Carlton L. Winbery. *Syntax of New Testament Greek.* Lanham, MD: University Press of America, 1979.

Brosend, William F., II. "The Means of Absent Ends." In *History, Literature, and Society in the Book of Acts,* edited by Ben Witherington, III, 348–62. Cambridge: Cambridge University Press, 1996.

Bruce, F. F. *The Acts of the Apostles: The Greek Text with Introduction and Commentary.* 3rd revised and enlarged ed. Reprint, Eugene, OR: Wipf and Stock, 1990.

———. *The Book of the Acts.* NICNT. Grand Rapids: Eerdmans, 1954.

———. *The Defence of the Gospel in the New Testament.* Grand Rapids: Eerdmans, 1959.

———. "Eschatology in Acts." In *Eschatology in the New Testament: Essays in Honor of George Beasley-Murray,* edited by W. H. Gloer, 51–63. Peabody, MA: Hendrickson, 1988.

———. "Is the Paul of Acts the Real Paul?" *Bulletin of the John Rylands Library* 58 (1975–76) 282–305.

———. "Paul and the Athenians." *Expository Times* 88 (1976–77) 8–12.

———. *Paul: Apostle of the Heart Set Free.* Exeter, UK: Paternoster, 2000.

———. "Paul's Use of the Old Testament in Acts." In *Tradition and Interpretation in the New Testament: Essays in Honor of E. Earle Ellis for His 60th Birthday,* edited by Gerald F. Hawthorne and Otto Betz, 71–79. Grand Rapids: Eerdmans, 1987.

Bryan, Steven M. *Jesus and Israel's Traditions of Judgment and Restoration.* SNTSMS 117. Cambridge: Cambridge University Press, 2002.

Bultmann, Rudolph. "Prédication: Actes 17/22–32." Translated by François Vouga. *Etudes Théologiques et Religieuses* 59, no. 4 (1984) 453–62.

Butticaz, Simon David. *L'identité de l'Eglise dans les Actes des apôtres: De la restauration d'Israël à la conquête universelle.* BZNW 174. Berlin: De Gruyter, 2011.

Cadbury, Henry J. *The Book of Acts in History.* London: Black, 1955.

———. "Commentary on the Preface of Acts." In *BegC* 2.489–510.

———. *The Making of Luke-Acts.* 2nd ed. 1958. Reprint, Peabody, MA: Hendrickson, 1999.

Calloud, Jean. "Paul devant l'Aréopage d'Athènes: Actes 17, 16–34." *Recherches de science religieuse* 69 (1981) 209–48.

Calvin, Jean. *Les Actes des Apôtres.* Edited by Roger Barilier. Commentaires Bibliques. Aix-en-Provence: Kerygma, 2005.

———. *L'institution de la religion chrétienne.* Aix-en-Provence: Kerygma, 1978.

Cameron, Euan. *Enchanted Europe: Superstition, Reason, and Religion, 1250–1750.* Oxford: Oxford University Press, 2010.

Carroll, John T. "The Uses of Scriptures in Acts." In *Society of Biblical Literature 1990 Seminar Papers.* SBLSP 29, 512–28. Atlanta: Scholars, 1990.

Carson, D. A. "Athens Revisited." In *Telling the Truth: Evangelizing Postmoderns*, 384–98. Grand Rapids: Zondervan, 2000.

———. *The Gagging of God: Christianity Confronts Pluralism.* Grand Rapids: Zondervan, 1996.

Casey, Maurice. "Where Wright Is Wrong: A Critical Review of N. T. Wright's *Jesus and the Victory of God*." *Journal for the Study of the New Testament* 69 (1998) 95–103.

Cerfaux, Lucien. *Saint Paul et le "Serviteur de Dieu" d'Isaïe.* SA 27–28, 351–65. Editrice Anselmiana, 1951.

Charles, J. Daryl. "Engaging the (Neo-)Pagan Mind: Paul's Encounter with Athenian Culture as a Model for Cultural Apologetics (Acts 17:16–34)." *Trinity Journal* 16NS (1995) 47–62.

Chavasse, Claude L. "The Suffering Servant and Moses." *Church Quarterly Review* 165, no. 255 (1964) 152–63.

Chrysostom, John. "Homily XXXI." In *NPNF¹* 11.195–201.

———. "Homily XXXVIII." In *NPNF¹* 11.232–39.

Clark, Gordon H. *Thales to Dewey.* 3rd ed. Trinity Paper 26. Hobbs, NM: Trinity Foundation, 1997.

Clarke, Andrew D., and Bruce W. Winter, eds. *One God, One Lord: Christianity in a World of Religious Pluralism.* 2nd ed. Tyndale House Studies. Grand Rapids: Baker, 1992.

Clarke, William K. L. "The Use of the Septuagint in Acts." In *BegC* 2.66–105.

Clifford, Richard J. "The Function of Idol Passages in Second Isaiah." *Catholic Biblical Quarterly* 42 (1980) 450–64.

Conn, Harvie. *Eternal Word and Changing Worlds: Theology, Anthropology, and Mission in Trialogue.* Grand Rapids: Zondervan, 1984.

Conzelmann, Hans. *Acts of the Apostles: A Commentary on the Acts of the Apostles.* Edited by Eldon Jay Epp and Christopher R. Matthews. Translated by James Limburg, et al. Hermeneia. Philadelphia: Fortress, 1987.

———. "The Address of Paul on the Areopagus." In *Studies in Luke-Acts*, edited by Leander E. Keck and J. Louis Martyn, 217–30. Nashville: Abingdon, 1966.

———. "Luke's Place in the Development of Early Christianity." In *Studies in Luke-Acts*, edited by Leander E. Keck and J. Louis Martyn, 298–316. Nashville: Abingdon, 1966.

———. *Die Mitte der Zeit*. BHT 17. Tübingen: Mohr, 1953.

———. *The Theology of St. Luke*. Translated by Geoffrey Buswell. New York: Harper and Row, 1961.

Copleston, Frederick Charles. *Greece and Rome*. Vol. 1 of *A History of Philosophy*. Rev. ed. Westminster, MD: Newman, 1959.

Croy, N. Clayton. "Hellenistic Philosophies and the Preaching of the Resurrection (Acts 17:18, 32)." *Novum Testamentum* 39, no. 1 (1997) 21–39.

Culy, Martin M., and Mikeal C. Parsons. *Acts: A Handbook on the Greek Text*. Baylor Handbook on the Greek New Testament. Waco, TX: Baylor University Press, 2003.

Currid, John D. *Ancient Egypt and the Old Testament*. Grand Rapids: Baker, 1997.

Dahl, Nils Alstrup. "The Purpose of Luke-Acts." In *Jesus in the Memory of the Early Church: Essays*, 87–98. Minneapolis: Augsburg, 1976.

———. "The Story of Abraham in Luke-Acts." In *Studies in Luke-Acts*, edited by Leander E. Keck and J. Louis Martyn, 139–58. Nashville: Abingdon, 1966.

Darr, J. A. *On Character Building: The Reader and the Rhetoric of Characterization in Luke-Acts*. Louisville, KY: Westminster John Knox, 1992.

Daube, David. *The Exodus Pattern in the Bible*. All Souls Studies 2. London: Faber and Faber, 1963.

Dawsey, James M. "The Literary Unity of Luke-Acts: Questions of Style—A Task for Literary Critics." *New Testament Studies* 35 (1989) 48–66.

Deissmann, Adolph. *Light from the Ancient East: The New Testament Illustrated by Recently Discovered Texts of the Graeco-Roman World*. 2nd ed. Translated by Lionel R. M. Strachan. 1927. Reprint, Grand Rapids: Baker, 1978.

Demarest, Bruce A. *General Revelation: Historical Views and Contemporary Issues*. Grand Rapids: Zondervan, 1979.

Dennison, William D. *Paul's Two-Age Construction and Apologetics*. Eugene, OR: Wipf and Stock, 2000.

Denniston, John D., and Kenneth J. Dover. *The Greek Particles*. 2nd ed. Oxford: Oxford University Press, 1978.

Denova, Rebecca I. *The Things Accomplished Among Us: Prophetic Tradition in the Structural Pattern of Luke-Acts*. JSNTSup 141. Sheffield, UK: Sheffield Academic Press, 1997.

Des Places, Édouard. "Actes 17,27." *Biblica* 48 (1967) 1–6.

———. "Actes 17,30–31." *Biblica* 52 (1971) 526–34.

———. "*Deisidaimôn* (Actes 17, 22)." In *La religion grecque: Dieux, culte, rites et sentiment religieux dans la Grèce antique*, 330–33. Paris: Picard, 1969.

———. "'Des temples faits de main d'homme' (Actes des Apôtres, 17,24)." *Biblica* 42 (1961) 217–23.

———. "'Quasi Superstitiosiores' (Act. 17:22)." In *Studiorum Paulinorum Congressus 1961*, vol. 2. AnBib 18, 183–91. Rome: Pontificio Istituto Biblico, 1963.

———. *La religion grecque: Dieux, culte, rites et sentiment religieux dans la Grèce antique*. Paris: Picard, 1969.

Dibelius, Martin. *Aufsätze zur Apostelgeschichte*. FRLANT 60. Göttingen, 1951.

———. "Paul in Athens." In *Studies in the Acts of the Apostles*, edited by Heinrich Greeven, translated by Mary Ling, 78–83. London: SCM, 1956.

———. "Paul on the Areopagus." In *Studies in the Acts of the Apostles*, edited by Heinrich Greeven, translated by Mary Ling, 26–77. London: SCM, 1956.

———. "The Speeches in Acts and Ancient Historiography." In *Studies in the Acts of the Apostles*, edited by Heinrich Greeven, translated by Mary Ling, 138–85. London: SCM, 1956.

———. *Studies in the Acts of the Apostles*. Edited by Heinrich Greeven. Translated by Mary Ling and Paul Schubert. London: SCM, 1956.

Dio Chrysostom. *De Dei Cognitione*. Translated by J. W. Cohoon. LCL 339. Cambridge, MA: Harvard University Press, 1977.

Doble, Peter. "The Psalms in Luke-Acts." In *The Psalms in the New Testament*, edited by Steve Moyise and Maarten J. J. Menken, 83–117. NTSI. London: T. & T. Clark, 2004.

———. "Something Greater Than Solomon: An Approach to Stephen's Speech." In *The Old Testament in the New Testament*, edited by Steve Moyise, 181–207. JSNTSup 189. Sheffield, UK: Sheffield Academic Press, 2000.

Dodd, C. H. *According to the Scriptures: The Sub-Structure of New Testament Theology*. London: Nisbet, 1952.

———. *The Apostolic Preaching and Its Developments*. 2nd ed. London: Hodder and Stoughton, 1964.

———. "The Old Testament in the New." In *The Right Doctrine from the Wrong Texts?* edited by G. K. Beale, 167–81. Grand Rapids: Baker, 1994.

Downing, F. Gerald. "Common Ground with Paganism in Luke and Josephus." *New Testament Studies* 28 (1982) 546–59.

———. "Ethical Pagan Theism and the Speeches in Acts." *New Testament Studies* 27 (1981) 544–63.

Dozeman, Thomas B. *God at War: Power in the Exodus Tradition*. New York: Oxford University Press, 1996.

Drury, John. *Tradition and Design in Luke's Gospel: A Study in Early Christian Historiography*. Atlanta: John Knox, 1976.

Dubarle, André-Marie. "Le discours à l'Aréopage (Act. 17,22–31) et son arrière-plan biblique." In *La manifestation naturelle de Dieu d'après l'Écriture*. LD 91, 155–200. Paris: Cerf, 1976.

Dumbrell, William J. *Covenant and Creation: A Theology of Old Testament Covenants*. Grand Rapids: Baker, 1993.

———. *The End of the Beginning: Revelation 21–22 and the Old Testament*. Moore Theological College Lectures. Grand Rapids: Baker, 1985.

Dunn, James D. G. *The Acts of the Apostles*. Narrative Commentaries. Valley Forge, PA: Trinity, 1996.

———. "ΚΥΡΙΟΣ in Acts." In *Christology*. Vol. 1 of *The Christ and the Spirit: Collected Essays of James D.G. Dunn*, 241–53. Grand Rapids: Eerdmans, 1998.

Dupont, Jacques. "La conversion dans les Actes des Apôtres." In *Etudes sur les Actes des Apôtres*. LD 45, 459–76. Paris: Cerf, 1967.

———. "Le discours à l'Aréopage (Ac 17, 22–31), lieu de rencontre entre christianisme et hellénisme." In *Nouvelles études sur les Actes des Apôtres*. LD 118, 380–423. Paris: Cerf, 1984.

———. "Etudes sur les Actes des Apôtres." LD 45. Paris: Cerf, 1967.

———. *Gnosis: La connaissance religieuse dans les épîtres de saint Paul*. Universitas Catholica Lovaniensis Dissertationes Ad Gradum Magistri in Facultate Theologica Consequendum Conscriptae, Series 2, no. 40. Paris: Gabalda, 1949.

———. "L'interprétation des Psaumes dans les Actes des Apôtres." In *Etudes sur les Actes des Apôtres*. LD 45, 283–305. Paris: Cerf, 1967.

———. "Je rebâtirai la cabane de David qui est tombée (Ac 15, 16 = Am 9:11)." In *Glaube und Eschatologie: Festschrift W.G. Kümmel zum 80. Geburtstag*, edited by E. Grässer and O. Merk, 19–32. Tübingen: Mohr, 1985.

———. "Repentir et conversion d'après les Actes des Apôtres." In *Etudes sur les Actes des Apôtres*. LD 45, 421–57. Paris: Cerf, 1967.

———. "Le salut des Gentils et la signification théologique du livre des Actes." *New Testament Studies* 6 (1959–60) 132–55.

———. "L'utilisation apologétique de l'Ancien Testament dans les discours des Actes." *Ephemerides Theologicae Lovanienses* 29 (1953) 289–327.

Edwards, Mark J. "Quoting Aratus: Acts 17,28." *Zeitschrift für die neutestamentliche Wissenschaft und die Kunde der älteren Kirche* 83 (1992) 266–69.

Ellis, E. Earle. *Eschatology in Luke*. Facet Books, Biblical Series 30. Philadelphia: Fortress, 1972.

———. *The Old Testament in Early Christianity: Canon and Interpretation in the Light of Modern Research*. WUNT 54. Tübingen: Mohr [Siebeck], 1991.

———. "Present and Future Eschatology in Luke." *New Testament Studies* 12 (1965–66) 27–41.

———. "'The End of the Earth' (Acts 1:8)." *Bulletin for Biblical Research* 1 (1991) 123–32.

Ellis, Nicholas J. "Aspect-Prominence, Morpho-Syntax, and a Cognitive-Linguistic Framework for the Greek Verb." In *The Greek Verb Revisited: A Fresh Approach for Biblical Exegesis*, edited by Steven E. Runge and Christopher J. Fresch, 122–60. Bellingham, WA: Lexham, 2016.

Ellis, Nicholas J., et al. "The Greek Verbal System and Aspectual Prominence: Revising Our Taxonomy and Nomenclature." *Journal of the Evangelical Theological Society* 59, no. 1 (2016) 33–62.

Eltester, Walther. "Gott und die Natur in der Areopagrede." In *Neutestamentliche Studien für Rudolf Bultmann zu seinem siebzigsten Geburtstag am 20. August*. BZNW 21, 202–27. Berlin: Töpelmann, 1954.

Enns, Peter. *Inspiration and Incarnation: Evangelicals and the Problem of the Old Testament*. Grand Rapids: Baker Academic, 2005.

Epp, Eldon Jay. "The 'Ignorance Motif' in Acts and Anti-Judaic Tendencies in Codex Bezae." *Harvard Theological Review* 55, no. 1 (1962) 51–62.

———. *The Theological Tendency of Codex Bezae Catabrigiensis in Acts*. SNTSMS 3. Cambridge: Cambridge University Press, 1966.

Evans, Craig A. "Jesus and the Continuing Exile of Israel." In *Jesus and the Restoration of Israel: A Critical Assessment of N. T. Wright's Jesus and the Victory of God*, edited by Carey C. Newman, 77–100. Downers Grove, IL: IVP Academic, 1999.

———. "Jesus and the Spirit: On the Origin and Ministry of the Second Son of God." In *Luke and Scripture*, edited by Craig A. Evans and James A. Sanders, 26–45. 1993. Reprint, Eugene, OR: Wipf and Stock, 2001.

———. "Prophecy and Polemic: Jews in Luke's Scriptural Apologetic." In *Luke and Scripture*, edited by Craig A. Evans and James A. Sanders, 171–211. 1993. Reprint, Eugene, OR: Wipf and Stock, 2001.

———. "The Prophetic Setting of the Pentecost Sermon." In *Luke and Scripture*, edited by Craig A. Evans and James A. Sanders, 212-24. 1993. Reprint, Eugene, OR: Wipf and Stock, 2001.

Evans, Craig A., and James A. Sanders. *Luke and Scripture: The Function of Sacred Tradition in Luke-Acts*. 1993. Reprint, Eugene, OR: Wipf and Stock, 2001.

Fanning, Buist M. *Verbal Aspect in New Testament Greek*. Oxford Theological Monographs. Oxford: Clarendon, 1990.

Fekkes, Jan, III. *Isaiah and Prophetic Traditions in the Book of Revelation: Visionary Antecedents and Their Development*. JSNTSup 93. Sheffield, UK: JSOT, 1994.

Fishbane, Michael A. "The 'Exodus' Motif: Paradigm of Historical Renewal." In *Biblical Text and Texture: A Literary Reading of Selected Texts*. Oxford: Oneworld, 1998.

Fitzmyer, Joseph A. *The Acts of the Apostles: A New Translation with Introduction and Commentary*. AB 31. New York: Doubleday, 1998.

———. "The Ascension of Christ and Pentecost." In *To Advance the Gospel*, 2nd ed., 265-94. The Biblical Resource Series. Grand Rapids: Eerdmans, 1998.

———. *The Gospel According to Luke*. 2 vols. AB 28A-B. Garden City, NY: Doubleday, 1981-85.

———. "Jesus in the Early Church through the Eyes of Luke-Acts." In *To Advance the Gospel*, 2nd ed., 249-64. The Biblical Resource Series. Grand Rapids: Eerdmans, 1998.

———. "Jewish Christianity in Acts in Light of the Qumran Scrolls." In *Studies in Luke-Acts*, edited by Leander E. Keck and J. Louis Martyn, 233-57. Nashville: Abingdon, 1966.

———. "The Lucan Picture of John the Baptist as Precursor of the Lord." In *Luke the Theologian*, 86-116. New York: Paulist, 1989.

———. *Luke the Theologian: Aspects of His Teaching*. New York: Paulist, 1989.

———. "Mary in Lucan Salvation History." In *Luke the Theologian*, 57-85. New York: Paulist, 1989.

———. *To Advance the Gospel: New Testament Studies*. 2nd ed. The Biblical Resource Series. Grand Rapids: Eerdmans, 1998.

———. "'Today You Shall Be with Me in Paradise' (Luke 23:43)." In *Luke the Theologian*, 203-33. New York: Paulist, 1989.

———. "The Use of Explicit Old Testament Quotations in Qumran Literature and in the New Testament." In *Essays on the Semitic Background of the New Testament*, 3-58. London: Chapman, 1970.

———. "The Use of the Old Testament in Luke-Acts." In *Society of Biblical Literature 1992 Seminar Papers*. SBLSP 31, 524-38. Atlanta: Scholars, 1992.

Flemming, Dean. *Contextualization in the New Testament: Patterns for Theology and Mission*. Downers Grove, IL: IVP, 2005.

———. "Contextualizing the Gospel in Athens: Paul's Areopagus Address as a Paradigm for Missionary Communication." *Missiology: An International Review* 30, no. 2 (2002) 199-214.

Flender, Helmut. *St. Luke: Theologian of Redemptive History*. Translated by Reginald H. and Ilse Fuller. Philadelphia: Fortress, 1967.

Foulkes, Francis. "The Acts of God: A Study of the Basis of Typology in the Old Testament." In *The Right Doctrine from the Wrong Texts?* edited by G. K. Beale, 342-71. Grand Rapids: Baker, 1994.

Frame, John M. *The Doctrine of God*. A Theology of Lordship. Phillipsburg, NJ: Presbyterian and Reformed, 2002.

———. *The Doctrine of the Knowledge of God*. A Theology of Lordship. Phillipsburg, NJ: Presbyterian and Reformed, 1987.

France, R. T. "The Formula-Quotations of Matthew 2 and the Problem of Communication." In *The Right Doctrine from the Wrong Texts?* edited by G. K. Beale, 114–34. Grand Rapids: Baker, 1994.

———. "Servant of Yahweh." In *DJG*, 744–47.

Franklin, Eric R. *Christ the Lord: A Study in the Purpose and Theology of Luke-Acts*. Philadelphia: Westminster, 1975.

Fudge, Edward. "Paul's Apostolic Self-Consciousness at Athens." *Journal of the Evangelical Theological Society* 14 (1971) 193–98.

Fuller, Michael E. *The Restoration of Israel: Israel's Re-Gathering and the Fate of the Nations in Early Jewish Literature and Luke-Acts*. BZNW 138. Berlin: De Gruyter, 2006.

Gaffin, Richard B., Jr. "Introduction." In *Redemptive History and Biblical Interpretation: The Shorter Writings of Geerhardus Vos*, 2nd ed., by Geerhardus Vos, edited by Richard B. Gaffin, Jr., ix–xxiii. Phillipsburg, NJ: Presbyterian and Reformed, 2001.

———. *Perspectives on Pentecost: New Testament Teaching on the Gifts of the Holy Spirit*. Phillipsburg, NJ: Presbyterian and Reformed, 1979.

———. "The Place and Importance of Introduction to the New Testament." In *Studying The New Testament Today*, edited by John H. Skilton, 143–51. The New Testament Student 1. Phillipsburg, NJ: Presbyterian and Reformed, 1974.

———. *Resurrection and Redemption: A Study in Paul's Soteriology*. 2nd ed. Phillipsburg, NJ: Presbyterian and Reformed, 1987.

Garland, R. *Introducing New Gods: The Politics of Athenian Religion*. Ithaca, NY: Cornell University Press, 1992.

Garner, David B. "The First and Last Son: Christology and Sonship in Pauline Soteriology." In *Resurrection and Eschatology: Theology in Service of the Church: Essays in Honor of Richard B. Gaffin Jr.*, edited by Lane G. Tipton and Jeffrey C. Waddington, 255–79. Phillipsburg, NJ: Presbyterian and Reformed, 2008.

Gasque, W. Ward. *A History of the Interpretation of the Acts of the Apostles*. 2nd ed. Peabody, MA: Hendrickson, 1989.

———. "The Speeches of Acts: Dibelius Reconsidered." In *New Dimensions in New Testament Study*, edited by R. N. Longenecker and M. C. Tenney, 232–50. Grand Rapids: Zondervan, 1974.

Gaventa, Beverly R. *The Acts of the Apostles*. ANTC. Nashville: Abingdon, 2003.

———. "The Eschatology of Luke-Acts Revisited." *Encounter* 43 (1982) 27–42.

———. "Toward a Theology of Acts: Reading and Rereading." *Interpretation* 42 (1988) 146–57.

———. "'You Will Be My Witnesses': Aspects of Mission in the Acts of the Apostles." *Missiology: An International Review* 10, no. 4 (1982) 413–25.

Gärtner, Bertil. *The Areopagus Speech and Natural Revelation*. Translated by Carolyn Hannay King. ASNU 21. Uppsala: Gleerup, 1955.

———. "Paulus und Barnabas in Lystra: Zu Apg. 14,8–15." *Svensk exegetisk årsbok* 27 (1962) 83–88.

Geagan, Daniel J. *The Athenian Constitution After Sulla*. Hesperia Supplement 12. Princeton, NJ: American School of Classical Studies at Athens, 1967.

———. "Ordo Areopagitarum Atheniensium." In *Φορος: Tribute to Benjamin Dean Meritt*, edited by D. W. Bradeen and M. F. McGregor, 51–56. Locust Valley, NY: Augustin, 1974.

———. "Roman Athens: Some Aspects of Life and Culture, 86 B.C.–A.D. 267." In *ANRW* 2.7.1, 371–437.

Gempf, Conrad H. "Before Paul Arrived in Corinth: The Mission Strategies in 1 Corinthians 2:2 and Acts 17." In *The New Testament in Its First Century Setting: Essays on Context and Background in Honour of B. W. Winter on His 65th Birthday*, edited by Peter J. Williams et al., 126–42. Grand Rapids: Eerdmans, 2004.

George, Timothy, et al. "The SBJT Forum: Responses to Inclusivism." *Southern Baptist Journal of Theology* 2, no. 2 (1998) 50–60.

Gill, David W. J. "Achaia." BAFCS, 2.433–53.

———. "Behind the Classical Façade: Local Religions of the Roman Empire." In *One God, One Lord*, edited by Andrew D. Clarke and Bruce W. Winter, 72–87. Cambridge: Tyndale House, 1991.

Given, Mark D. "Not Either/Or but Both/And in Paul's Areopagus Speech." *Biblical Interpretation* 3, no. 3 (1995) 356–72.

———. *Paul's True Rhetoric: Ambiguity, Cunning, and Deception in Greece and Rome*. Emory Studies in Early Christianity 7. Harrisburg, PA: Trinity, 2001.

Glöckner, Richard. *Die Verkündigung des Heils beim Evangelisten Lukas*. Walberberger Studien der Albertus-Magnus-Akademie: Theologische Reihe 9. Mainz: Matthias Grünewald Verlag, 1976.

Goette, Hans Rupprecht, et al. "Athens." In BNP 2.254–82.

Goppelt, Leonhard. *Typos: The Typological Interpretation of the Old Testament in the New*. Translated by Donald H. Madvig. Grand Rapids: Eerdmans, 1982.

Goulder, Michael D. *Type and History in Acts*. London: SPCK, 1964.

Gourgues, Michel. "La littérature profane dans le discours d'Athènes (Ac 17, 16–31): Un dossier fermé ?" *Revue Biblique* 109, no. 2 (2002) 241–69.

Gray, Patrick. "Athenian Curiosity (Acts 17:21)." *Novum Testamentum* 47, no. 2 (2005) 109–16.

———. *Godly Fear: The Epistle to the Hebrews and Greco-Roman Critiques of Superstition*. AcBib 16. Atlanta: Society of Biblical Literature, 2003.

———. "Implied Audiences in the Areopagus Narrative." *Tyndale Bulletin* 55, no. 2 (2004) 205–18.

Green, Joel B. *Conversion in Luke-Acts: Divine Action, Human Cognition, and the People of God*. Grand Rapids: Baker Academic, 2015.

———. "Internal Repetition in Luke-Acts: Contemporary Narratology and Lucan Historiography." In *History, Literature, and Society in the Book of Acts*, edited by Ben Witherington, III, 283–99. Cambridge: Cambridge University Press, 1996.

———. "Luke-Acts, or Luke and Acts? A Reaffirmation of Narrative Unity." In *Reading Acts Today: Essays in Honour of Loveday C. A. Alexander*, edited by Steve Walton et al., 101–19. LNST 427. London: T. & T. Clark, 2011.

———. "The Problem of a Beginning: Israel's Scripture in Luke 1–2." *Bulletin for Biblical Research* 4 (1994) 61–85.

———. "'Salvation to the End of the Earth' (Acts 13:47) God as the Saviour in the Acts of the Apostles." In *Witness to the Gospel*, edited by I. Howard Marshall and David Peterson, 83–106. Grand Rapids: Eerdmans, 1998.

———. *The Theology of the Gospel of Luke*. New Testament Theology. Cambridge: Cambridge University Press, 1995.

Green, Michael. *Evangelism in the Early Church*. 2nd ed. Grand Rapids: Eerdmans, 2004.

Gregory, Andrew F., and C. Kavin Rowe, eds. *Rethinking the Unity and Reception of Luke and Acts*. Columbia, SC: University of South Carolina Press, 2010.

Grundmann, Walter. "The Christ-Statements of the New Testament." In *TDNT* 9.527–73.

Hackett, H. B. "The Discourse of Paul at Athens: A Commentary on Acts 17:16–34." *Bibliotheca Sacra* 6, no. 22 (1849) 338–56.

Haenchen, Ernst. *The Acts of the Apostles: A Commentary*. Oxford: Blackwell, 1971.

Hansen, G. Walter. "The Preaching and Defence of Paul." In *Witness to the Gospel*, edited by I. Howard Marshall and David Peterson, 295–324. Grand Rapids: Eerdmans, 1998.

Hanson, R. P. C. *The Acts: In the Revised Standard Version with Introduction and Commentary*. New Clarendon Bible. Oxford: Clarendon, 1967.

Harris, Murray J. *Prepositions and Theology in the Greek New Testament: An Essential Reference Resource for Exegesis*. Grand Rapids: Zondervan, 2012.

Harris, Rendel, and Vacher Burch. *Testimonies*. 2 vols. Cambridge: Cambridge University Press, 1916–20.

Hatina, Thomas, ed. *The Gospel of Luke*. Vol. 3 of *Biblical Interpretation in Early Christian Gospels*. SSEJC 16. London: T. & T. Clark, 2010.

Hatina, Thomas R., and Michael Kozowski. "Introduction: Complexity of Contexts and the Study of Luke's Use of Scripture." In *The Gospel of Luke*. Vol. 3 of *Biblical Interpretation in Early Christian Gospels*, edited by Thomas Hatina. SSEJC 16, 1–17. London: T. & T. Clark, 2010.

Hays, J. Daniel. *From Every People and Nation: A Biblical Theology of Race*. NSBT 14. Downers Grove, IL: IVP, 2003.

Hays, Richard B. *Echoes of Scripture in the Letters of Paul*. New Haven, CT: Yale University Press, 1989.

———. "The Liberation of Israel in Luke-Acts: Intertextual Narration as Countercultural Practice." In *Reading the Bible Intertextually*, edited by Richard B. Hays et al., 101–17. Waco, TX: Baylor University Press, 2009.

———. *Reading Backwards: Figural Christology and the Fourfold Gospel Witness*. London: SPCK, 2015.

———. "'Who Has Believed Our Message?' Paul's Reading of Isaiah." In *Society of Biblical Literature 1998 Seminar Papers*. 2 vols. SBLSP 37, 205–25. Atlanta: Scholars, 1998.

Hays, Richard B., et al., eds. *Reading the Bible Intertextually*. Waco, TX: Baylor University Press, 2009.

Hemer, Colin J. *The Book of Acts in the Setting of Hellenistic History*. Edited by Conrad H. Gempf. Winona Lake, IN: Eisenbrauns, 1990.

———. "Paul at Athens: A Topographical Note." *New Testament Studies* 20 (1973–74) 341–50.

———. "Speeches of Acts: II. The Areopagus Address." *Tyndale Bulletin* 40, no. 2 (1989) 239–60.

Hengel, Martin. *Acts and the History of Earliest Christianity*. Eugene, OR: Wipf and Stock, 2003.

———. *Crucifixion in the Ancient World and the Folly of the Cross*. Translated by John Bowden. Philadelphia: Fortress, 1977.

———. "The Effective History of Isaiah 53 in the Pre-Christian Period." In *The Suffering Servant: Isaiah 53 in Jewish and Christian Sources*, edited by Bernd Janowski and Peter Stuhlmacher, translated by Daniel P. Bailey, 75–146. Grand Rapids: Eerdmans, 2004.

———. "Historische Methoden und theologische Auslegung des Neuen Testaments." *Kerygma und Dogma* 19, no. 2 (1973) 85–90.

———. *Judaism and Hellenism: Studies in Their Encounter in Palestine During the Early Hellenistic Period*. Translated from the German second revised and enlarged edition 1973. Translated by John Bowden. Minneapolis: Fortress, 1981.

———. "Der Jude Paulus und sein Volk: Zu einem neuen Acta-Kommentar." Review of *Die Apostelgeschichte: Übersetzt und Erklärt* by Jacob Jervell. *Theologische Rundschau* 66, no. 3 (2001) 338–68.

———. "Kerygma oder Geschichte." *Theologische Quartalschrift* 151 (1971) 323–36.

———. *Zur urchristlichen Geschichtsschreibung*. 2nd ed. Stuttgart: Calwer, 1984.

Higgins, Kevin. "The Key to Insider Movements: The 'Devoteds' of Acts." *International Journal of Frontier Missions* 21, no. 4 (2004) 155–65.

Hodge, A. A., and B. B. Warfield. "Inspiration." *The Presbyterian Review* 6 (April 1881) 225–60.

Holladay, Carl R. *Acts: A Commentary*. The New Testament Library. Louisville, KY: Westminster John Knox, 2016.

Holter, Knut. *Second Isaiah's Idol-Fabrication Passages*. BBET 28. Frankfurt am Main: Lang, 1995.

Hommel, Hildebrecht. "Platonisches bei Lukas: Zu Act 17,28a (Leben–Bewegung–Sein)." *Zeitschrift für die neutestamentliche Wissenschaft und die Kunde der älteren Kirche* 48 (1957) 193–200.

Hugenberger, G. P. "Introductory Notes on Typology." In *The Right Doctrine from the Wrong Texts?* edited by G. K. Beale, 331–41. Grand Rapids: Baker, 1994.

———. "The Servant of the Lord in the 'Servant Songs' of Isaiah: A Second Moses Figure." In *The Lord's Anointed: Interpretation of Old Testament Messianic Texts*, edited by Philip E. Satterthwaite et al., 105–40. Grand Rapids: Baker, 1995.

Jacquier, E. *Les Actes des Apôtres*. Paris: J. Gabalda, 1926.

Jaeger, Werner W. *The Theology of the Early Greek Philosophers*. The Gifford Lectures 1936. Translated by Edward S. Robinson. Oxford: Clarendon, 1947.

Jennings, J. Nelson. "The Deity of Christ for Missions, World Religions, and Pluralism." In *The Deity of Christ*, edited by Christopher W. Morgan and Robert A. Peterson, 253–81. Theology in Community. Wheaton, IL: Crossway, 2011.

Jeremias, Joachim. "Παῖς θεοῦ in Later Judaism in the Period after the LXX." In *TDNT* 5.677–700.

Jervell, Jacob. "The Acts of the Apostles and the History of Early Christianity." *Studia Theologica* 37 (1983) 17–32.

———. "Apostelgeschichte." In *Evangelisches Kirchenlexikon. Internationale theologische Enzyklopädie*. 5 vols, edited by Erwin Fahlbusch et al., 1.225–29. Göttingen: Vandenhoeck & Ruprecht, 1986.

———. *Die Apostelgeschichte*. KEK. Göttingen: Vandenhoeck & Ruprecht, 1998.

———. "The Center of Scripture in Luke." In *The Unknown Paul*, translated by Roy A. Harrisville, 122–37, 179–83. Minneapolis: Augsburg, 1984.

———. "The Church of Jews and Godfearers." In *Luke-Acts and the Jewish People*, edited by Joseph B. Tyson, 11–20. Minneapolis: Augsburg, 1988.

———. "The Divided People of God: The Restoration of Israel and Salvation for the Gentiles." In *Luke and the People of God*, 41–74. Minneapolis: Augsburg, 1972.

———. "The Future of the Past: Luke's Vision of Salvation History and Its Bearing on His Writing of History." In *History, Literature, and Society in the Book of Acts*, edited by Ben Witherington, III, 104–26. Cambridge: Cambridge University Press, 1996.

———. "God's Faithfulness to the Faithless People. Trends in Interpretation of Luke-Acts." *Word and World* 12, no. 1 (1992) 29–36.

———. "The History of Early Christianity and the Acts of the Apostles." In *The Unknown Paul*, 13–25, 158–62. Minneapolis: Augsburg, 1984.

———. "The Lucan Interpretation of Jesus as Biblical Theology." In *New Directions in Biblical Theology: Papers of the Aarhus Conference, 16–19 September 1992*, edited by Sigfred Pedersen, 77–92. NovTSup 76. Leiden: Brill, 1994.

———. *Luke and the People of God: A New Look at Luke-Acts*. Minneapolis: Augsburg, 1972.

———. "The Mighty Minority." In *The Unknown Paul*, 26–51, 162–64. Minneapolis: Augsburg, 1984.

———. "Paul in the Acts of the Apostles: Tradition, History, Theology." In *Les Actes des Apôtres*, edited by Jacob Kremer. BETL 48, 297–306. Leuven: Leuven University Press, 1979.

———. *The Theology of the Acts of the Apostles*. New Testament Theology. Cambridge: Cambridge University Press, 1996.

———. "The Unknown Paul." In *The Unknown Paul*, 52–67. Minneapolis: Augsburg, 1984.

———. *The Unknown Paul: Essays on Luke-Acts and Early Christian History*. Minneapolis: Augsburg, 1984.

Jewett, Paul K. "Concerning the Allegorical Interpretation of Scripture." *Westminster Theological Journal* 17, no. 1 (1954) 1–20.

Jipp, Joshua W. "Paul's Areopagus Speech of Acts 17:16–34 as *Both* Critique *and* Propaganda." *Journal of Biblical Literature* 131, no. 3 (2012) 567–88.

Jobes, Karen H. "Distinguishing the Meaning of Greek Verbs in the Semantic Domain for Worship." In *Biblical Words and Their Meaning: An Introduction to Lexical Semantics*, Moisés Silva, 201–11. Grand Rapids: Zondervan, 1990.

Jobes, Karen H., and Moisés Silva. *Invitation to the Septuagint*. Grand Rapids: Baker Academic, 2000.

Johnson, Dennis E. "Jesus Against the Idols: The Use of Isaianic Servant Songs in the Missiology of Acts." *Westminster Theological Journal* 52, no. 2 (1990) 343–53.

———. *The Message of Acts in the History of Redemption*. Phillipsburg, NJ: Presbyterian and Reformed, 1997.

Johnson, L. T. *The Acts of the Apostles*. SP 5. Collegeville, MN: Liturgical, 1992.

Kaiser, Walter C., Jr. *Mission in the Old Testament: Israel as a Light to the Nations*. Grand Rapids: Baker, 2000.

Kärkkäinen, Veli-Matti. *An Introduction to the Theology of Religions: Biblical, Historical and Contemporary Perspectives*. Downers Grove, IL: IVP, 2003.

Keck, Leander E., and J. Louis Martyn, eds. *Studies in Luke-Acts: Essays Presented in Honor of Paul Schubert Buckingham Professor of New Testament Criticism and Interpretation at Yale University*. Nashville: Abingdon, 1966.

Kee, Howard Clark. *Good News to the End of the Earth: The Theology of Acts*. Philadelphia: Trinity, 1990.

———. *To Every Nation Under Heaven: The Acts of the Apostles*. The New Testament in Context. Harrisburg, PA: Trinity, 1997.

Keener, Craig S. *Acts: An Exegetical Commentary*. 4 vols. Grand Rapids: Baker Academic, 2012–15.

Kennedy, George A. *New Testament Interpretation through Rhetorical Criticism*. SR. Chapel Hill, NC: University of North Carolina Press, 1984.

Keyes, Richard. "The Idol Factory." In *No God But God*, edited by Os Guinness and John Seel, 29–48. Chicago: Moody, 1992.

Kidd, Douglas, ed. and trans. *Aratus:* Phaenomena. Cambridge Classical Texts and Commentaries 34. Cambridge: Cambridge University Press, 1997.

Kilgallen, John J. "Acts 17,22b–31—What Kind of Speech Is This?" *Revue Biblique* 110, no. 3 (2003) 417–24.

———. *The Stephen Speech: A Literary and Redactional Study of Acts 7:2–53*. AnBib 67. Rome: Pontifical Biblical Institute Press, 1976.

Kilpatrick, George D. "Some Quotations in Acts." In *Les Actes des Apôtres*, edited by Jacob Kremer. BETL 48, 81–97. Leuven: Leuven University Press, 1979.

Kinzig, Wolfram. "Pagans and the Bible." In *From the Beginnings to 600*. Vol. 1 of *The New Cambridge History of the Bible*, edited by James Carleton Paget and Joachim Schaper, 752–74. Cambridge: Cambridge University Press, 2013.

Klauck, Hans-Josef. *Magic and Paganism in Early Christianity: The World of the Acts of the Apostles*. Translated by Brian McNeill. Edinburgh: T. & T. Clark, 2000.

———. *The Religious Context of Early Christianity: A Guide to Graeco-Roman Religions*. Translated by Brian McNeil. SNTW. London: T. & T. Clark, 2000.

Kline, Meredith G. *By Oath Consigned*. Reprint, Eugene, OR: Wipf and Stock, 1998.

———. *Kingdom Prologue*. South Hamilton, MA: M. G. Kline, 1993.

———. *The Structure of Biblical Authority*. 2nd ed. Reprint, Eugene, OR: Wipf and Stock, 1997.

———. *Treaty of the Great King: The Covenant Structure of Deuteronomy: Studies and Commentary*. Grand Rapids: Eerdmans, 1963.

Knox, Ronald A. *Essays in Satire*. 1928. Reprint, London: Sheed and Ward, 1954.

Koet, Bart J. "Isaiah in Luke-Acts." In *Dreams and Scripture in Luke-Acts: Collected Essays*. CBET 42, 51–79. Leuven: Peeters, 2006.

———. "Why Does Jesus Not Dream? Divine Communication in Luke-Acts." In *Dreams and Scripture in Luke-Acts: Collected Essays*, 11–24. CBET 42. Leuven: Peeters, 2006.

Koets, P. J. Δεισιδαιμονία: *A Contribution to the Knowledge of the Religious Terminology in Greek*. Purmerend: Muusses, 1929.

Kremer, Jacob, ed. *Les Actes des Apôtres: Traditions, rédaction, théologie*. BETL 48. Leuven: Leuven University Press, 1977.

Krodel, Gerhard A. *Acts*. Proclamation Commentaries: The New Testament Witnesses for Preaching. Philadelphia: Fortress, 1981.

Kugel, James L. *The Bible as It Was*. Cambridge, MA: Belknap Press of Harvard University Press, 1997.

———. *Traditions of the Bible: A Guide to the Bible as It Was at the Start of the Common Era*. Cambridge, MA: Harvard University Press, 1998.

Kuhn, Thomas S. *The Structure of Scientific Revolutions*. 4th ed. With an introductory essay by Ian Hacking. Chicago: Chicago University Press, 2012.

Kurz, William S. *Acts of the Apostles*. Catholic Commentary on Sacred Scripture. Grand Rapids: Baker Academic, 2013.

———. "Narrative Approaches to Luke-Acts." *Biblica* 68 (1987) 195–220.

———. *Reading Luke-Acts: Dynamics of Biblical Narrative*. Louisville, KY: Westminster John Knox, 1993.

Kümmel, Werner G. "Current Theological Accusations against Luke." *Andover Newton Quarterly* 16 (1975) 131–45.

Lane Fox, Robin. *Pagans and Christians*. New York: Knopf, 1986.

Larkin, William J., Jr. *Acts*. IVP New Testament Commentary 5. Downers Grove, IL: IVP, 1995.

———. "Luke's Use of the Old Testament as a Key to His Soteriology." *Journal of the Evangelical Theological Society* 20 (1977) 325–35.

Lee, Archie C. C. "Genesis 1 and the Plagues Tradition in Psalm 105." *Vetus Testamentum* 40, no. 3 (1990) 257–63.

Legrand, Lucien. "The Unknown God of Athens: Acts 17 and the Religion of the Gentiles." *Indian Journal of Theology* 30, no. 3–4 (1981) 158–67.

Levinsohn, Stephen H. *Discourse Features of New Testament Greek: A Coursebook on the Information Structure of New Testament Greek*. 2nd ed. Dallas: SIL International, 2000.

———. *Textual Connections in Acts*. SBLMS 31. Atlanta: Scholars, 1987.

Lightfoot, J. B. *The Acts of the Apostles: A Newly Discovered Commentary*. Edited by Ben Witherington, III and Todd D. Still. The Lightfoot Legacy Set 1. Downers Grove, IL: IVP Academic, 2014.

Lindars, Barnabas. *New Testament Apologetic: The Doctrinal Significance of the Old Testament Quotations*. Philadelphia: Westminster, 1961.

———. "The Place of the Old Testament in the Formation of New Testament Theology: Prolegomena." *New Testament Studies* 23 (1976–77) 59–66.

Lints, Richard. *Identity and Idolatry: The Image of God and Its Inversion*. NSBT 36. Downers Grove, IL: IVP, 2015.

Litwak, Kenneth D. "A Coat of Many Colors: The Role of the Scriptures of Israel in Luke 2." In *The Gospel of Luke*. Vol. 3 of *Biblical Interpretation in Early Christian Gospels*, edited by Thomas Hatina. SSEJC 16, 114–32. London: T. & T. Clark, 2010.

———. *Echoes of Scripture in Luke-Acts: Telling the History of God's People Intertextually*. JSNTSup 282. London: T. & T. Clark, 2005.

———. "Israel's Prophets Meet Athens' Philosophers: Scriptural Echoes in Acts 17:22–31." *Biblica* 85, no. 2 (2004) 199–216.

———. "Use of the Old Testament in Luke-Acts: Luke's Scriptural Story of the 'Things Accomplished among Us.'" In *Issues in Luke-Acts*, edited by Sean A. Adams and Michael Pahl, 147–69. Gorgias Handbooks 26. Piscataway, NJ: Gorgias, 2012.

Loisy, Alfred. *Les Actes des Apôtres*. Paris: Nourry, 1920.

Longenecker, Richard N. *The Acts of the Apostles*. Rev. ed. Expositor's Bible Commentary 10, 663–1102. Grand Rapids: Zondervan, 2007.

Losie, Lynn Allan. "Paul's Speech on the Areopagus: A Model of Cross-Cultural Evangelism, Acts 17:16–34." In *Mission in Acts: Ancient Narratives in Contemporary Context*, edited by Robert L. Gallagher and Paul Hertig, 220–38. Maryknoll, NY: Orbis, 2004.

McGiffert, A. C. *A History of Christianity in the Apostolic Age*. Rev. ed. International Theological Library. New York: Scribner, 1903.

MacIntyre, Alasdair. *Three Rival Versions of Moral Enquiry: Encyclopedia, Genealogy, and Tradition*. Notre Dame, IN: University of Notre Dame Press, 1990.

MacMullen, Ramsay. *Christianizing the Roman Empire (A.D. 100–400)*. New Haven, CT: Yale University Press, 1984.

———. *Paganism in the Roman Empire.* New Haven, CT: Yale University Press, 1981.

Malherbe, Abraham J. *Paul and the Popular Philosophers.* Minneapolis: Fortress, 1989.

Mallen, Peter. *The Reading and Transformation of Isaiah in Luke-Acts.* LNTS 367. London: T. & T. Clark, 2008.

Marcus, Joel. "Idolatry in the New Testament." In *The Word Leaps the Gap*, edited by J. Ross Wagner et al., 107–31. Grand Rapids: Eerdmans, 2008.

———. "Paul at the Areopagus: Window on the Hellenistic World." *Biblical Theology Bulletin* 18, no. 4 (1988) 143–48.

Marguerat, Daniel. *Les Actes des Apôtres.* 2 vols. CNT, Deuxième Série 5a-b. Geneva: Labor et Fides, 2007–15.

———. "Luc-Actes entre Jérusalem et Rome: un procédé lucanien de double signification." *New Testament Studies* 45, no. 1 (1999) 70–87.

———. *La première histoire du christianisme.* LD 180. Paris: Cerf, 1999.

Marshall, I. Howard. "Acts." In *Commentary on the New Testament Use of the Old Testament*, edited by G. K. Beale and D. A. Carson, 513–606. Grand Rapids: Baker Academic, 2007.

———. *Acts of the Apostles: An Introduction and Commentary.* TNTC. Grand Rapids: Eerdmans, 1980.

———. "The Christology of Luke's Gospel and Acts." In *Contours of Christology in the New Testament*, edited by Richard N. Longenecker, 122–47. Grand Rapids: Eerdmans, 2005.

———. *The Gospel of Luke: A Commentary on the Greek Text.* NIGTC. Exeter, UK: Paternoster, 1978.

———. *Luke: Historian and Theologian.* 3rd ed. New Testament Profiles. Downers Grove, IL: IVP, 1988.

Marshall, I. Howard, and David Peterson, eds. *Witness to the Gospel: The Theology of Acts.* Grand Rapids: Eerdmans, 1998.

Martin, Dale B. *The Corinthian Body.* New Haven, CT: Yale University Press, 1995.

———. "Hellenistic Superstition: The Problems of Defining a Vice." In *Conventional Values of the Hellenistic Greeks*, edited by Per Bilde, et al., 110–27. Studies in Hellenistic Civilization 8. Aarhus: Aarhus University Press, 1997.

———. *Inventing Superstition: From the Hippocratics to the Christians.* Cambridge, MA: Harvard University Press, 2004.

Martin, Hubert M., Jr. "Areopagus." In *ABD* 1.370–72.

Mather, P. Boyd. "Paul in Acts as 'Servant' and 'Witness.'" *Biblical Research* 30 (1985) 23–44.

Mattill, Andrew J., Jr. *Luke and the Last Things: A Perspective for the Understanding of Lukan Thought.* Dillsboro, NC: Western North Carolina Press, 1979.

Mánek, Jindřich. "The New Exodus in the Books of Luke." *Novum Testamentum* 2 (1957) 8–23.

Mbuvi, Andrew M. "Missionary Acts, Things Fall Apart: Modeling Mission in Acts 17:15–34 and a Concern for Dialogue in Chinua Achebe's *Things Fall Apart.*" *Ex Auditu* 23 (2007) 140–56.

Meijer, P. A. "Philosophers, Intellectuals and Religion in Hellas." In *Faith, Hope and Worship: Aspects of Religious Mentality in the Ancient World*, edited by H. S. Versnel, 216–63. Studies in Greek and Roman Religion 2. Leiden: Brill, 1981.

Melugin, Roy F. *The Formation of Isaiah 40–55.* BZAW 141. Berlin: De Gruyter, 1976.

Metzger, Bruce M. *A Textual Commentary on the Greek New Testament.* 2nd ed. Stuttgart: Deutsche Bibelgesellschaft, 1994.

Mitchell, Stephen, and Peter Van Nuffelen, eds. *One God: Pagan Monotheism in the Roman Empire*. Cambridge: Cambridge University Press, 2010.

Moellering, H. Armin. "Deisidaimonia, a Footnote to Acts 17:22." *Concordia Theological Quarterly* 34, no. 8 (1963) 466–71.

———. *Plutarch on Superstition: Plutarch's* De Superstitione, *Its Place in the Changing Meaning of* Deisidaimonia *and in the Context of His Theological Writings*. Rev. ed. Boston: Christopher, 1963.

Moessner, David P. "The Ironic Fulfillment of Israel's Glory." In *Luke-Acts and the Jewish People*, edited by Joseph B. Tyson, 35–50. Minneapolis: Augsburg, 1988.

———. "Jesus and the 'Wilderness Generation': The Death of the Prophet Like Moses According to Luke." In *Society of Biblical Literature 1982 Seminar Papers*, 319–40. SBLSP 21. Chico, CA: Scholars, 1982.

———. *Lord of the Banquet: The Literary and Theological Significance of the Lukan Travel Narrative*. Minneapolis: Fortress, 1989.

———. "Luke 9:1–50: Luke's Preview of the Journey of the Prophet Like Moses of Deuteronomy." *Journal of Biblical Literature* 102, no. 4 (1983) 575–605.

———. "Paul and the Pattern of the Prophet Like Moses in Acts." In *Society of Biblical Literature 1983 Seminar Papers*, 203–12. SBLSP 22. Chico, CA: Scholars, 1983.

———. "Paul in Acts: Preacher of Eschatological Repentance to Israel." *New Testament Studies* 34 (1988) 96–104.

———. "The 'Script' of the Scriptures in Acts: Suffering as God's 'Plan' (Βουλή) for the World for the 'Release of Sins.'" In *History, Literature, and Society in the Book of Acts*, edited by Ben Witherington, III, 218–50. Cambridge: Cambridge University Press, 1996.

———. "'The Christ Must Suffer': New Light on the Jesus-Peter, Stephen, Paul Parallels in Luke-Acts." *Novum Testamentum* 28, no. 3 (1986) 220–56.

Montanari, Franco. *The Brill Dictionary of Ancient Greek*. Edited by Madeleine Goh and Chad Schroeder. Leiden: Brill, 2015.

Moore, Thomas S. "To the End of the Earth: The Geographical and Ethnic Universalism of Acts 1:8 in Light of Isaianic Influence on Luke." *Journal of the Evangelical Theological Society* 40 (1997) 389–99.

Moreau, A. Scott. *Contextualization in World Missions: Mapping and Assessing Evangelical Models*. Grand Rapids: Kregel, 2012.

Morlan, David S. *Conversion in Luke and Paul: An Exegetical and Theological Exploration*. LNTS 464. London: T. & T. Clark, 2013.

Morris, Leon. "Luke and Early Catholicism." In *Studying The New Testament Today*, edited by John H. Skilton, 60–75. The New Testament Student 1. Phillipsburg, NJ: Presbyterian and Reformed, 1974.

Moscato, Mary. "A Critique of Jervell's Luke and the People of God." In *Society of Biblical Literature 1975 Seminar Papers*, 2 vols., 2.161–68. SBLSP 9. Missoula, MT: Scholars, 1975.

———. "Current Theories Regarding the Audience of Luke-Acts." *Currents in Theology and Mission* 3 (1976) 355–61.

Moule, C. F. D. "The Christology of Acts." In *Studies in Luke-Acts*, edited by Leander E. Keck and J. Louis Martyn, 159–85. Nashville: Abingdon, 1966.

———. *An Idiom Book of New Testament Greek*. 2nd ed. Cambridge: Cambridge University Press, 1959.

Moyise, Steve, ed. *The Old Testament in the New Testament: Essays in Honour of J. L. North.* JSNTSup 189. Sheffield, UK: Sheffield Academic Press, 2000.

———. "Intertextuality and Historical Approaches to the Use of Scripture in the New Testament." In *Reading the Bible Intertextually*, edited by Richard B. Hays et al., 23–32. Waco, TX: Baylor University Press, 2009.

———. "Intertextuality and the Study of the Old Testament in the New Testament." In *The Old Testament in the New Testament*, edited by Steve Moyise, 14–41. JSNTSup 189. Sheffield, UK: Sheffield Academic Press, 2000.

———. *The Old Testament in the New: An Introduction.* Continuum Biblical Studies Series. London: Continuum, 2001.

Muñoz-Larrondo, Rubén. *A Postcolonial Reading of the Acts of the Apostles.* Studies in Biblical Literature 147. New York: Lang, 2012.

Murray, John. *The Imputation of Adam's Sin.* Phillipsburg, NJ: Presbyterian and Reformed, 1959.

Nash, Ronald H. *Christianity and the Hellenistic World.* Grand Rapids: Zondervan, 1984.

Nave, G. D. *The Role and Function of Repentance in Luke-Acts.* AcBib 4. Atlanta: Society of Biblical Literature, 2002.

Neagoe, Alexandru. *The Trial of the Gospel: An Apologetic Reading of Luke's Trial Narratives.* SNTSMS 116. Cambridge: Cambridge University Press, 2002.

Newman, Carey C., ed. *Jesus and the Restoration of Israel: A Critical Assessment of N. T. Wright's Jesus and the Victory of God.* Downers Grove, IL: IVP Academic, 1999.

Newsom, Carol A. *Self as Symbolic Space: Constructing Identity and Community at Qumran.* STDJ 52. Leiden: Brill, 2004.

Neyrey, Jerome H. "Acts 17, Epicureans, and Theodicy: A Study in Stereotypes." In *Greeks, Romans, and Christians: Essays in Honor of Abraham J. Malherbe*, edited by D. L. Balch et al., 118–34. Minneapolis: Fortress, 1990.

Nock, Arthur D. *Essays on Religion and the Ancient World.* 2 vols. Edited by Zeph Stewart. Oxford: Clarendon, 1972.

Nolland, John L. *Luke.* 3 vols. WBC 35A-C. Waco, TX: Word, 1989–93.

Norden, Eduard. *Agnostos Theos: Untersuchungen zur Formengeschichte religiöser Rede.* Darmstadt: Wissenschaftliche Buchgesellschaft, 1956.

Nurmela, Risto. *The Mouth of the Lord Has Spoken: Inner-Biblical Allusions in Second and Third Isaiah.* Studies in Judaism. Lanham, MD: University Press of America, 2006.

O'Neill, J. C. *The Theology of Acts in Its Historical Setting.* London: SPCK, 1961.

O'Toole, Robert F. "Paul at Athens and Luke's Notion of Worship." *Revue Biblique* 89 (1982) 185–97.

Owen, H. P. "The Scope of Natural Revelation in Romans 1 and Acts 17." *New Testament Studies* 5 (1958–59) 133–43.

———. "Stephen's Vision in Acts 7:55–6." *New Testament Studies* 1 (1954) 224–26.

Padilla, Osvaldo. *The Speeches of Outsiders in Acts: Poetics, Theology and Historiography.* SNTSMS 144. Cambridge: Cambridge University Press, 2008.

Pao, David W. *Acts and the Isaianic New Exodus.* BSLib. Grand Rapids: Baker Academic, 2000.

———. Review of *A Critical and Exegetical Commentary on the Acts of the Apostles. Vol. II: Introduction and Commentary on Acts XV-XXVIII* by C. K. Barrett. *Journal of the Evangelical Theological Society* 44, no. 2 (2001) 346–49.

Parsons, Mikeal C. *Acts*. Paideia Commentaries on the New Testament. Grand Rapids: Baker Academic, 2008.

———. "Luke and the *Progymnasmata*: A Preliminary Investigation into the Preliminary Exercises." In *Contextualizing Acts: Lukan Narrative and Greco-Roman Discourse*, edited by Todd C. Penner and Caroline Vander Stichele, 43–63. SBLSymS 20. Atlanta: Society of Biblical Literature, 2003.

Parsons, Mikeal C., and Richard I. Pervo. *Rethinking the Unity of Luke and Acts*. Minneapolis: Fortress, 1993.

Penner, Todd. "Madness in the Method? The Acts of the Apostles in Recent Study." *Currents in Biblical Research* 2, no. 2 (2004) 223–93.

Pervo, Richard I. *Acts: A Commentary*. Hermeneia. Minneapolis: Fortress, 2009.

———. *Dating Acts: Between the Evangelists and the Apologists*. Santa Rosa, CA: Polebridge, 2006.

———. *Profit with Delight: The Literary Genre of the Acts of the Apostles*. Philadelphia: Fortress, 1987.

Pesch, Rudolph. *Die Apostelgeschichte*. 2 vols. EKKNT 5. Zürich; Neukirchen-Vluyn: Benziger; Neukirchener Verlag, 1986.

Peterson, David G. *The Acts of the Apostles*. PNTC. Nottingham, UK: Apollos, 2009.

———. "The Motif of Fulfilment and the Purpose of Luke-Acts." In BAFCS 1.83–104.

Pinnock, Clark H. "The Finality of Jesus Christ in a World of Religions." In *Christian Faith and Practice in the Modern World: Theology from an Evangelical Point of View*, edited by Mark A. Noll and David F. Wells, 152–68. Grand Rapids: Eerdmans, 1988.

———. "Toward an Evangelical Theology of Religions." *Journal of the Evangelical Theological Society* 33, no. 3 (1990) 359–68.

———. *A Wideness in God's Mercy: The Finality of Jesus Christ in a World of Religions*. Grand Rapids: Zondervan, 1992.

Piper, Otto A. "God's Good News: The Passion Story according to Mark." *Interpretation* 9 (1955) 165–82.

———. "The Origin of the Gospel Pattern." *Journal of Biblical Literature* 78 (1959) 115–24.

———. "Unchanging Promises: Exodus in the New Testament." *Interpretation* 11, no. 1 (1957) 3–22.

Plummer, Alfred. *A Critical and Exegetical Commentary on the Gospel according to Luke*. ICC 5. Edinburgh: T. & T. Clark, 1981.

Pohlenz, Max. "Paulus und die Stoa." *Zeitschrift für die neutestamentliche Wissenschaft und die Kunde der älteren Kirche* 42 (1949) 69–104.

Porter, Stanley E. *Idioms of the Greek of the New Testament*. Biblical Languages: Greek 2. Sheffield, UK: Sheffield Academic Press, 1994.

———. "Paul and His Bible: His Education and Access to the Scriptures of Israel." In *As It Is Written: Studying Paul's Use of Scripture*, edited by Stanley E. Porter and Christopher D. Stanley, 97–124. SBLSymS 50. Atlanta: Society of Biblical Literature, 2008.

———. *Paul in Acts*. Library of Pauline Studies. Peabody, MA: Hendrickson, 2001.

Porter, Stanley E., and Bryan R. Dyer. "Oral Texts? A Reassessment of the Oral and Rhetorical Nature of Paul's Letters in Light of Recent Studies." *Journal of the Evangelical Theological Society* 55, no. 2 (2012) 323–41.

Porter, Stanley E., and Andrew W. Pitts. "Paul's Bible, His Education and His Access to the Scriptures of Israel." *Journal of Greco-Roman Christianity and Judaism* 5 (2008) 9–41.

Poythress, Vern S. "Counterfeiting in the Book of Revelation as a Perspective on Non-Christian Culture." *Journal of the Evangelical Theological Society* 40, no. 3 (1997) 411–18.

———. "Dispensing with Merely Human Meaning: Gains and Losses from Focusing on the Human Author, Illustrated by Zephaniah 1:2–3." *Journal of the Evangelical Theological Society* 57, no. 3 (2014) 481–99.

———. "Divine Meaning of Scripture." In *The Right Doctrine from the Wrong Texts?* edited by G. K. Beale, 82–113. Grand Rapids: Baker, 1994.

Praeder, Susan Marie. "Jesus-Paul, Peter-Paul and Jesus-Peter Parallelisms in Luke-Acts: A History of Reader Response." In *Society of Biblical Literature 1984 Seminar Papers*, 23–39. SBLSP 23. Chico, CA: Scholars, 1984.

Rackham, Richard B. *The Acts of the Apostles: An Exposition*. 5th ed. WC. London: Methuen, 1910.

Rahlfs, Alfred. *Septuaginta*. Stuttgart: Deutsche Bibelgesellschaft Stuttgart, 1979.

Ramsay, William M. "The Firstfruits of Achaia." In *The Bearing of Recent Discovery on the Trustworthiness of the New Testament*. 2nd ed., 385–411. London: Hodder and Stoughton, 1915.

———. *St. Paul the Traveller and the Roman Citizen*. London: Hodder and Stoughton, 1897.

Renehan, Robert. "Classical Greek Quotations in the New Testament." In *The Heritage of the Early Church: Essays in Honor of the Very Reverend Georges Vasilievich Florovsky*, edited by David Neiman and Margaret Schatkin, 17–46. Rome: Pontificum Institutum Studiorum Orientalium, 1973.

Rese, Martin. *Alttestamentliche Motive in der Christologie des Lukas*. Bonn: Rheinische Friedrich-Wilhelms-Universität, 1965.

———. "Die Funktion des alttestamentlichen Zitate und Anspielungen in den Reden der Apostelgeschichte." In *Les Actes des Apôtres*, edited by Jacob Kremer, 61–79. BETL 48. Leuven: Leuven University Press, 1979.

Rhodes, Peter J. "Areopagus." In BNP 1.1046–47.

Ricœur, Paul. "The Narrative Function." *Semeia* 13 (1978) 177–202.

Ridderbos, Herman N. *The Coming of the Kingdom*. Philadelphia: Presbyterian and Reformed, 1962.

Rius-Camps, Josep, and Jenny Read-Heimerdinger. *Acts 13.1—18.23: The Ends of the Earth—First and Second Phases of the Mission to the Gentiles*. Vol. 3 of *The Message of Acts in Codex Bezae: A Comparison with the Alexandrian Tradition*. LNTS 365. London: T. & T. Clark, 2007.

———. *The Message of Acts in Codex Bezae: A Comparison with the Alexandrian Tradition*. 4 Vols. LNTS 257; 302; 365; 415. London: T. & T. Clark, 2004–9.

Robertson, A. T. *A Grammar of the Greek New Testament in the Light of Historical Research*. Nashville, TN: Broadman, 1934.

Robertson, O. Palmer. *The Flow of the Psalms: Discovering Their Structure and Theology*. Phillipsburg, NJ: Presbyterian and Reformed, 2015.

Robinson, W. C., Jr. *Der Weg des Herrn: Studien zur Geschichte und Eschatologie im Lukas-Evangelium: Ein Gespräch mit Hans Conzelmann*. TF 36. Hamburg-Bergstedt: Reich, 1964.

Roloff, Jürgen. *Die Apostelgeschichte*. NTD 5. Göttingen: Vandenhoeck und Ruprecht, 1988.

Rosner, Brian S. "The Progress of the Word." In *Witness to the Gospel*, edited by I. Howard Marshall and David Peterson, 215–33. Grand Rapids: Eerdmans, 1998.

Ross, James F. "The Prophet as Yahweh's Messenger." In *Israel's Prophetic Heritage: Essays in Honor of James Muilenburg*, edited by Bernhard W. Anderson and Walter Harrelson, 98–107. New York: Harper, 1962.

Roth, Wolfgang M. W. "For Life, He Appeals to Death (Wis 13:18): A Study of Old Testament Idol Parodies." *Catholic Biblical Quarterly* 37 (1975) 21–47.

Rothschild, Clare K. *Paul in Athens: The Popular Religious Context of Acts 17*. WUNT 341. Tübingen: Mohr Siebeck, 2014.

Rowe, C. Kavin. "The Book of Acts and the Cultural Explication of the Identity of God." In *The Word Leaps the Gap*, edited by J. Ross Wagner et al., 244–66. Grand Rapids: Eerdmans, 2008.

———. *Early Narrative Christology: The Lord in the Gospel of Luke*. 2006. Reprint, Grand Rapids: Baker Academic, 2009.

———. "The Grammar of Life: The Areopagus Speech and Pagan Tradition." *New Testament Studies* 57, no. 1 (2011) 31–50.

———. "Literary Unity and Reception History: Reading Luke-Acts as Luke and Acts." *Journal for the Study of the New Testament* 29, no. 4 (2007) 449–57.

———. *One True Life: The Stoics and Early Christians as Rival Traditions*. New Haven, CT: Yale University Press, 2016.

———. *World Upside Down: Reading Acts in the Graeco-Roman Age*. New York: Oxford University Press, 2009.

Runge, Steven E. *Discourse Grammar of the Greek New Testament: A Practical Introduction for Teaching and Exegesis*. Lexham Bible Reference Series. Peabody, MA: Hendrickson, 2010.

Runge, Steven E., and Christopher J. Fresch, eds. *The Greek Verb Revisited: A Fresh Approach for Biblical Exegesis*. Bellingham, WA: Lexham, 2016.

Samuel, S. Johnson. "Paul on the Areopagus: A Mission Perspective." *Bangalore Theological Forum* 18, no. 1 (1986) 17–32.

Sanders, Jack T. "The Prophetic Use of the Scriptures in Luke-Acts." In *Early Jewish and Christian Exegesis: Studies in Memory of William Hugh Brownlee*, edited by Craig A. Evans and W. F. Stinespring, 191–98. Homage 10. Atlanta: Scholars, 1987.

Sanders, James A. "From Isaiah 61 to Luke 4." In *Luke and Scripture*, edited by Craig A. Evans and James A. Sanders, 46–69. Minneapolis: Fortress, 1993.

———. "Isaiah in Luke." In *Luke and Scripture*, edited by Craig A. Evans and James A. Sanders, 14–25. Minneapolis: Fortress, 1993.

Sanders, John E. *No Other Name: An Investigation Into the Destiny of the Unevangelized*. Grand Rapids: Eerdmans, 1992.

Sandmel, Samuel. "Parallelomania." *Journal of Biblical Literature* 81, no. 1 (1962) 1–13.

Sandnes, K. O. "Paul and Socrates: The Aim of Paul's Areopagus Speech." *Journal for the Study of the New Testament* 50 (1993) 13–26.

Sawyer, John F. A. *The Fifth Gospel: Isaiah in the History of Christianity*. Cambridge: Cambridge University Press, 1996.

Schlette, Heinz R. "Religions." In *Encyclopédie de la foi*, edited by H. Fries, 59–68. Paris: Cerf, 1965–67.

Schnabel, Eckhard J. *Acts*. ZECNT. Grand Rapids: Zondervan, 2012.

———. *Paul and the Early Church*. Vol. 2 of *Early Christian Mission*. Downers Grove, IL: IVP, 2004.

Schneider, Gerhard. *Die Apostelgeschichte*. HThKNT 5. Freiburg: Herder, 1980–82.

Scholes, Robert, et al. *The Nature of Narrative*. 2nd ed. Oxford: Oxford University Press, 2006.

Schubert, Paul. "The Final Cycle of Speeches in the Book of Acts." *Journal of Biblical Literature* 87 (1968) 1–16.

———. "The Place of the Areopagus Speech in the Composition of Acts." In *Transitions in Biblical Scholarship*, edited by J. Coert Rylaarsdam, 235–61. Essays in Divinity 6. Chicago: University of Chicago Press, 1968.

———. "The Structure and Significance of Luke 24." In *Neutestamentliche Studien für Rudolf Bultmann zu seinem siebzigsten Geburtstag am 20. August 1954*, edited by W. Eltester. BZNW 21, 165–86. Berlin: Töpelmann, 1954.

Schwartz, Daniel R. "The End of the *Gē* (Acts 1:8) Beginning or End of the Christian Vision?" *Journal of Biblical Literature* 105, no. 4 (1986) 669–76.

Schwartz, Joshua, and Peter J. Tomson, eds. *Jews and Christians in the First and Second Centuries: The Interbellum 70–132 CE*. CRINT. Leiden: Brill, 2018.

Schweizer, Eduard. "The Concept of the Davidic 'Son of God' in Acts and Its Old Testament Background." In *Studies in Luke-Acts*, edited by Leander E. Keck and J. Louis Martyn, 186–93. Nashville: Abingdon, 1966.

———. "Concerning the Speeches in Acts." In *Studies in Luke-Acts*, edited by Leander E. Keck and J. Louis Martyn, 208–16. Nashville: Abingdon, 1966.

Scobie, Charles H. H. "A Canonical Approach to Interpreting Luke: The Journey Motif as a Hermeneutical Key." In *Reading Luke*, edited by Craig G. Bartholomew et al. Scripture and Hermeneutics Series 6, 327–47. Milton Keynes, UK: Paternoster, 2005.

Scott, James M. "Luke's Geographical Horizon." In BAFCS, 2.483–544.

Seccombe, David. "Luke and Isaiah." *New Testament Studies* 27 (1980–81) 252–59.

Seitz, Christopher R. *Figured Out: Typology and Providence in Christian Scripture*. Louisville, KY: Westminster John Knox, 2001.

Shields, Bruce E. "The Areopagus Sermon and Romans 1:18ff: A Study in Creation Theology." *Restoration Quarterly* 20 (1977) 23–40.

Silva, Moisés. *Biblical Words and Their Meaning: An Introduction to Lexical Semantics*. 2nd ed. Grand Rapids: Zondervan, 1994.

———. "Review of TDNT." *Westminster Theological Journal* 43 (1980–81) 395–99.

Ska, Jean-Louis. *"Our Fathers Have Told Us": Introduction to the Analysis of Hebrew Narratives*. SubB 13. Rome: Editrice Pontifico Istituto Biblico, 1990.

Smith, Daniel Lynwood. *The Rhetoric of Interruption: Speech-Making, Turn-Taking, and Rule-Breaking in Luke-Acts and Ancient Greek Narrative*. BZNW 193. Berlin: de Gruyter, 2012.

Smith, Mark S. *God in Translation: Deities in Cross-Cultural Discourse in the Biblical World*. FAT 57. Tübingen: Mohr Siebeck, 2008.

Smith, Morton. "*De Superstitione* (Moralia 164E–171F)." In *Plutarch's Theological Writings and Early Christian Literature*, edited by Hans D. Betz, 1–35. Leiden: Brill, 1975.

Smyth, Herbert Weir. *Greek Grammar*. Cambridge, MA: Harvard University Press, 1956.

Snodgrass, Klyne R. "Streams of Tradition Emerging from Isaiah 40:1–5 and Their Adaptation in the New Testament." *Journal for the Study of the New Testament* 8 (1980) 24–45.

———. "The Use of the Old Testament in the New." In *The Right Doctrine from the Wrong Texts?* edited by G. K. Beale, 29–51. Grand Rapids: Baker, 1994.

Soards, Marion L. *The Speeches in Acts: Their Content, Context, and Concerns*. 3rd ed. Louisville, KY: Westminster John Knox, 1994.

Sommer, Benjamin D. *A Prophet Reads Scripture: Allusion in Isaiah 40–66*. Contraversions: Jews and Other Differences. Stanford: Stanford University Press, 1998.

Span, John. "The Areopagus: A Study in Continuity and Discontinuity." *St Francis Magazine* 6, no. 3 (2010) 517–82.

Spencer, F. Scott. "Acts and Modern Literary Approaches." In BAFCS 1.381–414.

———. *Journeying through Acts: A Literary-Cultural Reading*, 278. Peabody, MA: Hendrickson, 2004.

Spencer, Patrick E. "The Unity of Luke-Acts: A Four-Bolted Hermeneutical Hinge." *Currents in Biblical Research* 5 (2007) 341–66.

Spicq, Ceslas. *Notes de lexicographie néo-testamentaire*. 3 vols. OBO 22. Göttingen: Vandenhoek & Ruprecht, 1978–82.

Squires, John T. *The Plan of God in Luke-Acts*. SNTSMS 76. Cambridge: Cambridge University Press, 1993.

Stanley, Christopher D. *Arguing with Scripture: The Rhetoric of Quotations in the Letters of Paul*. London: T. & T. Clark, 2004.

Stählin, Gustav. *Die Apostelgeschichte*. 11th ed. NTD 5. Göttingen: Vandenhoek and Ruprecht, 1966.

Stenschke, Christoph W. *Luke's Portrait of Gentiles Prior to Their Coming to Faith*. WUNT 2/108. Tübingen: Mohr Siebeck, 1999.

Sterling, Gregory E. *Historiography and Self-Definition: Josephos, Luke-Acts and Apologetic Historiography*. NovTSup 64. Leiden: Brill, 1992.

Sternberg, Meir. *The Poetics of Biblical Narrative: Ideological Literature and the Drama of Reading*. Indiana Literary Biblical Series. Bloomington, IN: Indiana University Press, 1985.

Stonehouse, Ned B. "The Areopagus Address." In *Paul Before the Areopagus: And Other New Testament Studies*, 1–40. Grand Rapids: Eerdmans, 1957.

———. *The Witness of Luke to Christ*. Grand Rapids: Eerdmans, 1951.

Stott, John R. W. *The Message of Acts: The Spirit, the Church, and the World*. BST. Downers Grove, IL: IVP, 1990.

Strahan, Joshua M. *The Limits of a Text: Luke 23:34a as a Case Study in Theological Interpretation*. Journal of Theological Interpretation Supplement 5. Winona Lake, IN: Eisenbrauns, 2012.

Strange, Daniel. *"For Their Rock Is not as Our Rock": An Evangelical Theology of Religions*. Nottingham, UK: Apollos, 2014.

———. *The Possibility of Salvation Among the Unevangelised: An Analysis of Inclusivism in Recent Evangelical Theology*. Paternoster Biblical and Theological Monographs. Carlisle, UK: Paternoster, 2002.

Strauss, Mark L. *The Davidic Messiah in Luke-Acts: The Promise and Its Fulfilment in Lukan Christology*. JSNTSS 110. Sheffield, UK: Sheffield Academic Press, 1995.

Stuart, Douglas. *Hoseah-Jonah*. WBC 31. Waco, TX: Word, 1987.

Sundberg, Albert C., Jr. "On Testimonies." *Novum Testamentum* 3 (1959) 268–81.

Swartley, Willard M. *Israel's Scripture Traditions and the Synoptic Gospels: Story Shaping Story*. Peabody, MA: Hendrickson, 1994.

Sweeney, James P. "Stephen's Speech (Acts 7:2–53) Is It as 'Anti-Temple' as Is Frequently Alleged?" *Trinity Journal* 23, no. 2 (2002) 185–210.

Talbert, Charles H. "Promise and Fulfillment in Lucan Theology." In *Luke-Acts: New Perspectives from the Society of Biblical Literature Seminar*, 91–103. New York: Crossroad, 1984.

———. *Reading Acts: A Literary and Theological Commentary on the Acts of the Apostles.* Rev. ed. Macon, GA: Smyth and Helwys, 2005.

———. "Shifting Sands: The Recent Study of the Gospel of Luke." *Interpretation* 30 (1976) 381–95.

Tannehill, Robert C. *The Acts of the Apostles.* Vol. 2 of *The Narrative Unity of Luke-Acts: A Literary Interpretation.* Minneapolis: Fortress, 1990.

Tannen, Deborah. "What Is a Frame? Surface Evidence for Underlying Expectations." In *Framing in Discourse,* edited by Deborah Tannen, 15–56. Oxford: Oxford University Press, 1993.

Taylor, Charles. *A Secular Age.* Cambridge, MA: Belknap Press of Harvard University Press, 2007.

Thom, Johan Carl. "Cleanthes' *Hymn to Zeus* and Early Christian Literature." In *Antiquity and Humanity: Essays on Ancient Religion and Philosophy Presented to Hans Dieter Betz on His 70th Birthday,* edited by Adela Yarbro Collins and Margaret M. Mitchell, 477–99. Tübingen: Mohr Siebeck, 2001.

———. *Cleanthes' Hymn to Zeus: Text, Translation, and Commentary.* STAC 33. Tübingen: Mohr Siebeck, 2005.

Thompson, Alan J. *The Acts of the Risen Lord Jesus: Luke's Account of God's Unfolding Plan.* NSBT 27. Downers Grove, IL: IVP, 2011.

———. *One Lord, One People: The Unity of the Church in Acts in Its Literary Setting.* LNTS 359. London: T. & T. Clark, 2008.

Thompson, Mark D. "The Uniqueness of Christ as the Revealer of God." In *Christ the One and Only: A Global Affirmation of the Uniqueness of Jesus-Christ,* edited by Sung Wook Chung, 90–110. Grand Rapids: Baker Academic, 2005.

Tiede, David L. "The Exaltation of Jesus and the Restoration of Israel in Acts 1." *Harvard Theological Review* 79, no. 1–3 (1986) 278–86.

Tipton, Lane G. "Resurrection, Proof, and Presuppositionalism: Acts 17:30–31." In *Revelation and Reason: New Essays in Reformed Apologetics,* edited by K. Scott Oliphint and Lane G. Tipton, 41–58. Phillipsburg, NJ: Presbyterian and Reformed, 2007.

Townsend, John T. "The Speeches in Acts." *Anglican Theological Review* 42, no. 2 (1960) 150–59.

Trites, Allison A. "The Importance of Legal Scenes and Language in the Book of Acts." *Novum Testamentum* 16, no. 4 (1974) 278–84.

Turner, Nigel. *Syntax.* Vol. 3 of *A Grammar of New Testament Greek.* James H. Moulton. Edinburgh: T. & T. Clark, 1963.

Tyson, Joseph B., ed. *Luke-Acts and the Jewish People: Eight Critical Perspectives.* Minneapolis: Augsburg, 1988.

———. "The Date of Acts: A Reconsideration." *Forum* 5, no. 1 (2002) 33–51.

Van de Sandt, Huub. "The Fate of the Gentiles in Joel and Acts 2: An Intertextual Study." *Ephemerides Theologicae Lovanienses* 66 (1990) 56–77.

———. "The Minor Prophets in Luke-Acts." In *The Minor Prophets in the New Testament,* edited by Maarten J. J. Menken and Steve Moyise, 57–77. LNTS 377. London: T. & T. Clark, 2006.

———. "The Quotations in Acts 13:32–52 as a Reflection of Luke's LXX Interpretation." *Biblica* 75 (1994) 26–58.

Van der Horst, Pieter W. "The Altar of the 'Unknown God' in Athens (Acts 17:23) and the Cults of 'Unknown Gods' in the Graeco-Roman World." In *Hellenism-Judaism-Christianity: Essays on Their Interaction*, 165–202. CBET 8. Kampen: Kok Pharos, 1994.

———. "A New Altar of a God-Fearer?" In *Hellenism-Judaism-Christianity: Essays on Their Interaction*, 65–72. CBET 8. Kampen: Kok Pharos, 1994.

———. "The Unknown God (Acts 17:23)." In *Knowledge of God in the Graeco-Roman World*, edited by R. Van den Broek et al., 19–42. EPRO 112. Leiden: Brill, 1988.

Van Nuffelen, Peter. *Rethinking the Gods: Philosophical Readings of Religion in the Post-Hellenistic Period*. Greek Culture in the Roman World. Cambridge: Cambridge University Press, 2011.

Van Til, Cornelius. *A Christian Theory of Knowledge*. Grand Rapids: Baker, 1969.

———. *Christianity and Idealism*. Philadelphia: Presbyterian and Reformed, 1955.

———. *Common Grace and the Gospel*. Phillipsburg, NJ: Presbyterian and Reformed, 1972.

———. *An Introduction to Systematic Theology: Prolegomena and the Doctrines of Revelation, Scripture, and God*. 2nd ed. Edited by William Edgar. In Defense of the Faith 5. Phillipsburg, NJ: Presbyterian and Reformed, 2007.

———. "Nature and Scripture." In *The Infallible Word: A Symposium by Members of the Faculty of Westminster Theological Seminary*, 263–301. Philadelphia: Presbyterian and Reformed, 1946.

———. *Paul at Athens*. Phillipsburg, NJ: Presbyterian and Reformed, c. 1956.

———. *A Survey of Christian Epistemology*. In Defense of the Faith 2. Phillipsburg, NJ: Presbyterian and Reformed, 1977.

———. *Who Do You Say That I Am?* Nutley: Presbyterian and Reformed, 1975.

Van Unnik, W. C. "Der Ausdruck ἕως ἐσχάτου τῆς γῆς (Apostelgeschichte 1:8) und sein alttestamentlischer Hintergrund." In *Evangelia, Paulina, Acta*. Vol. 1 of *Sparsa Collecta: The Collected Essays of W. C. Van Unnik*, 386–401. NovTSup 29. Leiden: Brill, 1973.

———. "The 'Book of Acts' the Confirmation of the Gospel." *Novum Testamentum* 4 (1960–61) 26–59.

———. "Luke-Acts, A Storm Center in Contemporary Scholarship." In *Studies in Luke-Acts*, edited by Leander E. Keck and J. Louis Martyn, 15–32. Nashville: Abingdon, 1966.

Van Winkle, D. W. "The Relationship of the Nations to Yahweh and to Israel in Isaiah 40–55." *Vetus Testamentum* 35, no. 4 (1985) 446–58.

Vanhoozer, Kevin J., et al., eds. *Theological Interpretation of the New Testament: A Book-by-Book Survey*. Grand Rapids: Baker Academic, 2008.

Verheyden, Joseph, ed. *The Unity of Luke-Acts*. BETL 142. Leuven: Peeters, 1999.

———. "The Unity of Luke-Acts: One Work, One Author, One Purpose?" In *Issues in Luke-Acts*, edited by Sean A. Adams and Michael Pahl, 27–50. Gorgias Handbooks 26. Piscataway, NJ: Gorgias, 2012.

Vielhauer, Philip. "The 'Paulinism' of Acts." In *Studies in Luke-Acts*, edited by Leander E. Keck and J. Louis Martyn, 33–50. Nashville: Abingdon, 1966.

Vos, Geerhardus. *The Pauline Eschatology*. The Student Library. 1930. Reprint, Phillipsburg, NJ: Presbyterian and Reformed, 1994.

———. "Some Doctrinal Features of the Early Prophecies of Isaiah." In *Redemptive History and Biblical Interpretation: The Shorter Writings of Geerhardus Vos*, 2nd ed., edited by Richard B. Gaffin, 271–87. Phillipsburg, NJ: Presbyterian and Reformed, 2001.

Vriezen, Theodorus C. "Essentials of the Theology of Isaiah." In *Israel's Prophetic Heritage: Essays in Honor of James Muilenburg*, edited by Bernhard W. Anderson and Walter Harrelson, 128–46. New York: Harper, 1962.

Wagner, J. Ross, et al., eds. *The Word Leaps the Gap: Essays on Scripture and Theology in Honor of Richard B. Hays*. Grand Rapids: Eerdmans, 2008.

Wallace, Daniel B. *Greek Grammar Beyond the Basics: An Exegetical Syntax of the New Testament*. Grand Rapids: Zondervan, 1996.

Walters, Patricia. *The Assumed Authorial Unity of Luke and Acts: A Reassessment of the Evidence*. SNTS 145. Cambridge: Cambridge University Press, 2009.

Waltke, Bruce K., and Charles Yu. *An Old Testament Theology: An Exegetical, Canonical, and Thematic Approach*. Grand Rapids: Zondervan, 2007.

Warfield, B. B. "The Divine and Human in the Bible." In *Evolution, Science, and Scripture: Selected Writings*, edited by Mark A. Noll and David N. Livingstone, 51–58. Grand Rapids: Baker, 2000.

———. "On the Emotional Life of Our Lord." In *The Person and Work of Christ*, edited by Samuel G. Craig, 93–145. Phillipsburg, NJ: Presbyterian and Reformed, 1950.

Watts, Rikki E. "Consolation or Confrontation? Isaiah 40–55 and the Delay of the New Exodus." *Tyndale Bulletin* 41, no. 1 (1990) 31–59.

———. *Isaiah's New Exodus in Mark*. BSLib. 1997. Reprint, Grand Rapids: Baker Academic, 2000.

Weißenberger, Michael. "D. Cocceianus of Prusa." In BNP 4.466–68.

Wendel, Susan J. *Scriptural Interpretation and Community Self-Definition in Luke-Acts and the Writings of Justin Martyr*. NovTSup 139. Leiden: Brill, 2011.

Wénin, André. "Le jeu de l'ironie dramatique dans les récits de ruses et de tromperies." In *L'intrigue dans le récit biblique: Quatrième colloque international du RRENAB, Université Laval, Québec, 29 mai–1er juin 2008*, edited by Anne Pasquier, et al., 159–70. BETL 237. Leuven: Université Catholique de Louvain; Peeters, 2010.

Whitmarsh, Tim. *Battling the Gods: Atheism in the Ancient World*. London: Faber and Faber, 2016.

Wilckens, Ulrich. "Interpreting Acts in a Period of Existentialist Theology." In *Studies in Luke-Acts*, edited by Leander E. Keck and J. Louis Martyn, 60–83. Nashville: Abingdon, 1966.

———. "Χάραγμα." In *TDNT* 9.416–17.

Wilkinson, T. L. "Acts 17: The Gospel Related to Paganism: Contemporary Relevance." *Vox Reformata* 35 (1980) 1–14.

Wilson, Stephen G. *The Gentiles and the Gentile Mission in Luke-Acts*. SNTSMS 23. Cambridge: Cambridge University Press, 1973.

———. "Lukan Eschatology." *New Testament Studies* 16 (1969–70) 330–47.

Winter, Bruce W. "In Public and in Private: Early Christians and Religious Pluralism." In *One God, One Lord*, 2nd ed., edited by Andrew D. Clarke and Bruce W. Winter, 125–48. Grand Rapids: Baker, 1992.

———. "On Introducing Gods to Athens: An Alternative Reading of Acts 17:18–20." *Tyndale Bulletin* 47, no. 1 (1996) 71–90.

———. "Theological and Ethical Responses to Religious Pluralism—1 Corinthians 8–10." *Tyndale Bulletin* 41, no. 2 (1990) 209–26.

Witherington, Ben, III, ed. *History, Literature, and Society in the Book of Acts*. Cambridge: Cambridge University Press, 1996.

———. *The Acts of the Apostles: A Socio-Rhetorical Commentary*. Grand Rapids: Eerdmans, 1998.

———. *Conflict and Community in Corinth: A Socio-Rhetorical Commentary on 1 and 2 Corinthians*. Grand Rapids: Eerdmans, 1994.

———. "Editing the Good News: Some Synoptic Lessons for the Study of Acts." In *History, Literature, and Society in the Book of Acts*, edited by Ben Witherington, III, 324–47. Cambridge: Cambridge University Press, 1996.

———. "Finding Its Niche: The Historical and Rhetorical Species of Acts." In *Society of Biblical Literature 1996 Seminar Papers*, 67–97. SBLSP 35. Atlanta: Scholars, 1996.

———. "Jesus as the Alpha and Omega of New Testament Thought." In *Contours of Christology in the New Testament*, edited by Richard N. Longenecker, 25–46. Grand Rapids: Eerdmans, 2005.

———. *The Many Faces of the Christ: The Christologies of the New Testament and Beyond*. Companions to the New Testament. New York: Crossroad, 1998.

———. *New Testament History: A Narrative Account*. Grand Rapids: Baker Academic, 2001.

———. *New Testament Rhetoric: An Introductory Guide to the Art of Persuasion in and of the New Testament*. Eugene, OR: Cascade, 2009.

———. *The New Testament Story*. Grand Rapids: Eerdmans, 2004.

———. "Salvation and Health in Christian Antiquity: The Soteriology of Luke-Acts in Its First-Century Setting." In *Witness to the Gospel*, edited by I. Howard Marshall and David Peterson, 145–66. Grand Rapids: Eerdmans, 1998.

———. "Transcending Imminence: The Gordian Knot of Pauline Eschatology." In *Eschatology in Bible and Theology: Evangelical Essays at the Dawn of a New Millennium*, edited by Kent E. Brower and Mark W. Elliott, 171–86. Downers Grove, IL: IVP, 1997.

Wolfe, Robert F. "Rhetorical Elements in the Speeches of Acts 7 and 17." *Journal of Translation and Textlinguistics* 6, no. 3 (1993) 274–83.

Wright, Christopher J. H. *The Mission of God: Unlocking the Bible's Grand Narrative*. Downers Grove, IL: IVP Academic, 2006.

Wright, N. T. *Acts for Everyone*. 2 vols. Louisville, KY: Westminster John Knox, 2008.

———. *The New Testament and the People of God*. Vol. 1 of Christian Origins and the Question of God. Minneapolis: Fortress, 1992.

Wycherley, R. E. "St Paul at Athens." *Journal of Theological Studies* 19 (1968) 619–21.

Young, Frances M. *Biblical Exegesis and the Formation of Christian Culture*. Cambridge: Cambridge University Press, 1997.

Zakovitch, Yair. *"And You Shall Tell Your Son . . .": The Concept of the Exodus in the Bible*. Jerusalem: Magnes, 1991.

Zerwick, Maximilian. *Biblical Greek Illustrated by Examples*. 4th ed. Translated by Joseph Smith. Scripta Pontificii Instituti Biblici. Rome: Editrice Pontificio Istituto Biblico, 1994.

Zuck, Roy B. Review of *The Possibility of Salvation among the Unevangelized: An Analysis of Inclusivism in Recent Evangelical Theology* by Daniel Strange. *Bibliotheca Sacra* 161 (2004) 497–98.

Zweck, Dean. "The *Exordium* of the Areopagus Speech, Acts 17.22, 23." *New Testament Studies* 35 (1989) 94–103.

Index of Modern Authors

Achtemeier, Paul J., 92n59
Adams, Sean A., 4n13, 5n14
Aletti, Jean-Noël, 4n7, 7, 8n13
Alexander, J. A., 134n31, 135n36, 142n71, 142n74, 143n80, 148n21, 154n67, 172n80, 193n59, 196n81, 203n20
Anderson, Bernhard W., 60n124, 60n126, 60n128, 61n132, 73-74, 74n214, 74n216, 77n238
Argyle, A. W., 3n2
Arnold, Bill T., 48n54, 52n74, 56n102, 83n10
Attridge, Harold W., 138n50, 142n72, 150n39, 150n41
Auerbach, Eric, 8n13
Auffret, Pierre, 103
Aune, David E., 45n31

Bahnsen, Greg L., 152n52, 153-54, 181n136, 183n144, 187n19, 188n29, 189n33, 199n98
Bailey, James L., 53n82, 61n133, 62
Baker, David L., 60n126
Balch, David L., 151n46, 195n69, 195n72, 213n83
Bale, Alan J., 5n14, 213n81
Barnes, Timothy D., 121n122, 122n132, 122,133
Barr, James, xxixn16, 8n13, 176n102
Barrett, C. K., xxviii, 3–5, 8n12, 40-46, 51n71, 65-66, 84-85, 102, 102n9, 103n18, 105, 109n50, 110n59, 110n62, 111n64, 112n70, 113n75, 115, 116, 117n102, 120, 121n122, 121n124, 122n132, 122n133, 123n136, 127n154, 131, 132n16, 135n32, 135n37, 136n40, 136n42, 138n52, 138n55, 139n56, 140n62, 142n71, 144n4, 145n6, 146n14, 148n23, 149, 153n61, 157n82, 157n85, 157n87, 157n89, 161n3, 161n4, 162, 162n6, 162n7, 162n8, 163n19, 164n24, 165n32, 166, 167n52, 167n53, 170n64, 172n78, 172n79, 173, 173n87, 173n88, 173n89, 175, 179, 181n135, 185, 187n12, 187n13, 187n18, 188n22, 188n25, 188n28, 188n29, 189, 189n32, 190n43, 192n53, 193n60, 196n77, 196n80, 197n84, 198n92, 199n99, 200n2, 202n17, 203n28, 207, 209n57, 209n63, 210n64, 210n67, 211n74, 212n77, 212n78, 214n91
Bauckham, Richard J., 4n9, 5n16, 24n108, 25n115, 27n124, 37n181, 40n5, 41n6, 44n29, 49n56, 54n87, 127n152, 147n18, 147n19, 179n123, 209n63
Baugh, Steven M., 158n91
Baur, F. C., xxviii, 10n21, 84n19
Bavinck, Herman, 152n50, 153n59, 154n65, 158n92, 192n50, 199n95
Bavinck, J. H., 199
Bayer, Hans F., 173n85, 203n27, 204n32, 205n39
Beale, G. K., 17n63, 67n168, 69n182, 71n197, 73, 76n233, 78n241, 91n55, 93n61, 93n63, 144n4, 153n61, 154n67, 154n70, 155n72, 167n48, 168n55, 192n52, 210n65, 220n18
Bentzen, Aage, 74n216
Berger, Peter L., 180n128, 180n129
Berkouwer, G. C., 153n59, 191n50
Betz, Hans Dieter, 182n143
Block, Daniel I., 168n54
Boccaccini, Gabriele, 10n21
Bock, Darrell L., 4n6, 4n13, 7n8, 11n25, 52-66, 72, 75n220, 106n34, 114n78, 116n94, 122n130, 127n154, 130n4, 134n26, 143n80, 149n27, 158n92, 173n88, 181n134, 181n135, 201n11, 204n30, 209n58, 214n95
Boismard, M.-E., 4n12
Bonnard, Pierre-Emile, 68n173
Bossuyt, P., xxixn18, 115n86, 122n133, 167n51, 170n65, 192n53
Bovon, François, xxviin12, 7, 58n115, 206n42
Bowker, J. W., 4n9

INDEX OF MODERN AUTHORS

Boyarin, Daniel, 10n21, 32n155, 38n187, 72n198
Brodie, Thomas L., 36n179, 52n74, 52n77
Brooks, James A., 165n31
Brosend, William F., 87n31
Bruce, F. F., 88n33, 104n21, 108n49, 109n51, 114n80, 121n122, 122n133, 123n136, 128n158, 130n4, 131n7, 132n16, 136n43, 142n71, 143n80, 148–152, 148n23, 151n48, 152n52, 153n63, 159n95, 163n16, 165n38, 167n53, 171, 172n76, 187n15, 187n19, 188, 189n32, 192n53, 195n70, 196n79, 203n27, 209n57, 213n81, 214n95
Bryan, Steven M., 70n187
Bultmann, Rudolph, 6, 156n77
Burch, Vacher, 49n56
Butticaz, Simon David, 131n5, 137n48, 144n4, 176n105, 183n149, 204n35

Cadbury, Henry J., xxviii, 4n13, 7, 31n146, 82n7, 102n8, 109n56, 112n71, 113n74, 117n100, 119, 120n121, 121n122, 121n123, 122n132, 122n133, 122n135, 123n136, 124, 133n20, 139n56, 157n86, 164n24, 165n32, 171n71, 172n82, 173, 187n16, 187n20, 188n21, 188n22, 191n45, 197n84, 198n92
Calloud, Jean, 167n49, 170n63, 202n18, 210n66, 213n81
Calvin, Jean, 99, 105n32, 106, 135n37, 175, 175n95, 180n128, 184n150, 194n66, 199n95, 209n59, 213n83, 213n88
Cameron, Euan, 131n10
Carroll, John T., 50
Carson, D. A., xxixn16, 155n75, 158n93, 180n127, 183n148, 208n56, 213n87, 217, 217n1, 218n8
Cerfaux, Lucien, 134n25
Charles, J. Daryl, xxixn18, 85n21, 179n123, 195n70, 214n91
Chavasse, Claude L., 75n223
Clark, A. C., 3n2
Clark, Gordon H., 151n44
Clarke, William K. L., 49
Clifford, Richard J., 88n36, 89, 90n46, 91n49, 91n52, 159n96
Conzelmann, Hans, xxviii, xxxn19, 4n6, 6, 6n1, 7, 13n40, 15–20, 31n146, 42n9, 44, 45, 58, 81n1, 88n33, 101n2, 102n9, 107n39, 111n64, 114n80, 115n85, 124n142, 130n4, 135n37, 138n51, 152n52, 154n66, 164n21, 164n27, 165n32, 167n51, 171, 171n73, 172n81, 172n83, 173n88, 173n89, 175n98, 185n2, 187n12, 187n19, 188n28, 189n32, 191n46, 197n84, 200n1, 204n33, 223n3
Creed, J. M., 31n146
Croy, N. Clayton, 116n92
Culy, Martin M., 110n59, 114n80, 116n94, 121n127, 139n56, 165n32, 181n132, 182n139, 196n80, 203n21, 208n54
Currid, John D., 90n44

Dahl, Nils Alstrup, 5n14, 52–59
Darr, J. A., 83n11
Daube, David, 62
Dawsey, James M., 4n13
Deissmann, Adolph, 222n3
Dennison, William D., 123n136, 151n44
Denniston, John D., 201n7
Denova, Rebecca I., 60, 60n125, 62n138
Des Places, Édouard, 103, 103n13, 130n3, 154n66, 162n8, 163n15, 183n146, 186n9, 187n12, 202, 203, 205n40, 210n64, 216n112
Dibelius, Martin, xxviii, xxixn17, xxxn19, 7, 47n46, 56n103, 79n249, 81–82, 84n19, 86, 86n28, 88n33, 101–2, 101n1, 101n2, 126n150, 127n152, 127n154, 137n50, 149, 158n93, 158n94, 161n2, 161–62, 163, 165n32, 165n39, 167n53, 171–72, 175–76, 179n123, 185n2, 185n5, 187, 188n21, 197n83, 200, 209n57, 211n68, 223n3
Doble, Peter, 25n116, 68, 96n77, 126n147
Dodd, C. H., 31n146, 40, 49n56, 50, 50n62, 50n63, 127n152
Dover, Kenneth J., 201n7
Downing, F. Gerald, 149n30
Dozeman, Thomas B., 91n54
Drury, John, 52n76
Dubarle, André-Marie, 140n66, 203n27, 206n45
Dumbrell, William J., 74n214
Dunn, James D. G., 96n77, 107n38, 109n53, 122n133, 123n136, 128n161, 130n4, 152–53, 184n154, 187n19, 195n68, 198n90, 209n63, 212n76
Dupont, Jacques, 48n51, 51n70, 54n85, 57n111, 63, 64n149, 65n156, 68n173, 96n77, 103n13, 105n26, 137n49, 139n59, 162n8, 163n17, 163n19, 165n35, 165n36, 167n49, 192n55, 193n60, 200n2, 203n26, 205–7, 210n64, 210n65, 210n67, 211n69, 211n70, 212n75, 212n76, 213n81, 213n86, 216n112
Dyer, Bryan R., 41

Edwards, Mark J., 191n45

Ellis, E. Earle, 16–17, 24n111, 52n76
Ellis, Nicholas J., 145n7
Eltester, Walther, 163n18, 171n73
Enns, Peter, 4n9
Epp, Eldon Jay, 206n42, 207n46
Evans, Craig A., 70n188, 75n224, 191n49, 203n27, 206n42, 214n96

Fanning, Buist M., xxixn16, 148n22
Fekkes, Jan, III, 66n166, 69n182
Fitzmyer, Joseph A., xxvii–xxix, 3–5, 6–39, 40–59, 93n61, 102, 105n25, 109, 119n114, 122n131, 124n143, 127n154, 128n158, 130n4, 146, 148n25, 149, 151n47, 164n26, 180n128, 188n21, 188n23, 188n28, 189n30, 189n33, 190n39, 191n45, 197n84, 203n20, 203n28, 209n57, 210n67, 215n101, 215n102
Flemming, Dean, xxixn18, 204n35
Flender, Helmut, xxviiin14, 16n59
Foakes-Jackson, F. J., 191n45, 187n19
Foulkes, Francis, 61, 61n131
Frame, John M., 152n50
France, R. T., 38n185, 68n177
Franklin, Eric R., xxviiin14, 16–17, 96n77
Frei, Hans, 8n13
Fresch, Christopher J., xxixn16
Fudge, Edward, 84
Fuller, Michael E., 70–71

Gaffin, Richard B., Jr., xxxn20, 3n1, 18n73, 63n144, 216n106, 218n9, 225n7, 225n8
Garland, R., 121n127
Garner, David B., 191n49
Gärtner, Bertil, 81, 85, 101–2, 112n70, 122n133, 151n46, 152n50, 154n67, 257n82, 161n2, 161n5, 161–62, 167n49, 170n63, 175n95, 175n98, 177n108, 179n123, 185–86, 187–90, 192n54, 206n45, 207n46, 209n59
Gasque, W. Ward, xxviin12, xxviiin14, 81n1, 101n2, 101n3
Gaventa, Beverly R., 6–7, 11n25, 16–20, 45n32, 85, 103n18, 106–9, 116n97, 117n98, 119–120, 122n130, 122n133, 130n4, 158n93, 162n10, 167n46, 190n38, 203n22, 204n34, 206n44, 214n91, 218n8, 219n10
Geagan, Daniel J., 121n129
Gempf, Conrad H., 88n33
Gill, David W. J., xxvin3, 105n29, 105n32, 120n121, 121n128, 121n129
Given, Mark D., xxxn20, 82–84, 131n5, 132n15, 141n69, 142n73, 208n52, 210n67, 216n104, 216n111
Glöckner, Richard, 30n142

Goppelt, Leonhard, 60n122
Goulder, Michael D., 17n66, 43n18, 50n68, 60n123, 61n131, 75n221
Gourgues, Michel, 85–86, 137n49, 145n5, 149, 151n48, 154n66, 155n73, 165n38, 166n40, 182n143, 200n3
Gray, Patrick, 82n6, 104n21, 107n40, 108n47, 112n71, 114n80, 114n81, 115, 115n87, 118n104, 131n5, 132n12, 137n50, 142n72, 207n51
Green, Joel B., 3n2, 4n6, 4n13, 25n116, 28n130, 31n148, 43n16, 52n74, 58–59, 60n127, 61n134, 62n136, 63n141, 65n159, 79n249, 158n91, 207n48, 207n49
Green, Michael, 67n167
Gregory, Andrew F., 4n13
Grundmann, Walter, 35n168

Hackett, H. B., 116n94, 138n51, 209n59, 214n93
Haenchen, Ernst, xxviii, xxxn19, 47n46, 81n1, 88n33, 101n2, 102n9, 104, 106n37, 110n58, 111n66, 112n71, 113, 114n78, 115n85, 118n107, 119n11, 120, 121, 122n133, 130n4, 136n40, 144n4, 146n12, 148n23, 148n24, 156n79, 157n83, 158n93, 158n94, 160n98, 161n2, 164n24, 165n36, 165n37, 165n39, 167n52, 167n53, 171n73, 171n75, 175–77, 187n12, 188n23, 190, 191, 195, 198n92, 201n6, 209n57, 217n3, 223n3
Hansen, G. Walter, 142n75, 151n46, 182n143, 195n69, 209n57
Hanson, R. P. C., 81n2, 85, 130n4, 153n61, 180n127, 187n15, 192n55, 192–93
Harris, Murray J., 214n91, 215n98
Harris, Rendel, 49n56
Hatina, Thomas R., xxixn16
Hays, J. Daniel, 168n56
Hays, Richard B., 5n17, 52n73, 53n80, 65n160, 218n7
Hemer, Colin J., xxixn17, 4n5, 103n13, 105n30, 176
Hengel, Martin, xxviin6, 4n5, 6n3, 9–10, 32n155, 38n187, 40n5, 107n41
Higgins, Kevin, 110n57, 142n76, 183n149, 199n96, 224n5
Hodge, A. A., 41n6
Holladay, Carl R., 110n61, 139n57, 208n56
Holter, Knut, 159n96
Hommel, Hildebrecht, 187n19, 188n28, 191n46
Hugenberger, G. P., 61n133, 75n223

Jacquier, E., 133n22, 134n28
Jennings, J. Nelson, 199n96, 224n4

INDEX OF MODERN AUTHORS

Jeremias, Joachim, 38n185
Jervell, Jacob, xxviii—xxix, 3–5, 6–39, 40–65, 76n229, 86n29, 87n32, 104, 110n62, 111n65, 115n82, 115n86, 126–29, 130n4, 146n16, 148n25, 152n54, 161n5, 164n27, 164n28, 165n34, 183n146, 183n149, 193n63, 195, 197n84, 201n11, 203n28, 204n30, 209n57, 211n73, 213n84, 216n108
Jewett, Paul K., 61n131
Jipp, Joshua W., 81n3, 121n127, 121n129, 122n133, 121n5, 152n53, 164n25, 181n132, 200n3, 211n68
Jobes, Karen H., 4n8, 138n55
Johnson, Dennis E., 69, 74–76, 78n240, 93n60, 142–43, 163n19, 196n81, 199n98, 199n99, 209n57, 209n58, 209n60, 209n63, 213n82, 215n102, 215n103, 224n4
Johnson, Luke Timothy, 53n80, 104n21, 108n49, 116, 130n4, 139n57, 163n19, 176n107, 180n130, 188n24, 190n38, 190n42, 209n57, 209n63

Kaiser, Walter C., Jr., 27n123, 37n181, 76n226
Kärkkäinen, Veli-Matti, xxvin4
Karris, Robert, 53n80
Käsemann, Ernst, 6, 31n146, 208n56
Keck, Leander E., xxviii
Kee, Howard Clark, 161n6, 213n83, 214n94
Keener, Craig S., xxviin11, xxixn17, 3n3, 4n10, 103n17, 107n38, 109n55, 110n62, 111n65, 112n71, 113n75, 114n78, 114n80, 115n82, 118n106, 118n107, 119n115, 120n121, 121, 122n133, 131n7, 132n15, 134n27, 139n59, 147n17, 151n44, 151n48, 156n81, 167n46, 167n53, 173n84, 180n126, 181n132, 182n138, 188n27, 190n37, 195n73, 197n87, 200n1, 200n4, 207n46, 213n83, 216n112
Keil, Carl Friedrich, 104
Kennedy, George A., 123n139, 196n77, 204n32
Keyes, Richard, 156n78, 180n129
Kidd, Douglas, 191n45
Kilgallen, John J., 54n90, 111n66, 126n151, 128n159, 128n161, 128n162
Kilpatrick, George D., 49n56
Kinzig, Wolfram, xxvn1
Klauck, Hans-Josef, xxvin3, xxixn17, 82n6, 82n7, 82n8, 105n31, 110n62, 113n75, 118n106, 122n133, 136n41, 136n44, 141n69, 150n40, 150n41, 188n21, 190n38,
198n94, 203n23, 206n44, 213n81, 216n104
Kline, Meredith G., 167n48, 177n111, 191n50, 216n106
Knowling, R. J., 110n61
Knox, Ronald A., 33
Koet, Bart J., 62n135, 67n170, 67n171, 69, 77n235, 78n244, 79
Koets, P. J., 130–33
Kozowski, Michael, xxixn16
Krodel, Gerhard A., 117n99, 118n103, 123n136, 158n91, 180n128
Kugel, James L., 4n9, 36n179, 59n121
Kuhn, Thomas S., xxviii
Kümmel, Werner G., xxviiin14, 58n115
Kurz, William S., xxviiin14, 53n80, 82n6, 113n76, 139n57, 140n64, 161n6, 166n44, 178n119, 203n19, 208n56, 215n100

Lake, Kirsopp, 102n8, 109n56, 112n71, 113n74, 117n100, 119n109, 119n112, 120n121, 121n122, 121n123, 122n132, 122n133, 122n135, 123n136, 124n140, 124n141, 133n20, 139n56, 157n86, 164n24, 165n32, 172n82, 173n84, 187n16, 187n19, 187n20, 188n22, 191n45, 197n84, 198n92
Lamouille, A., 4n12
Lane Fox, Robin, xxvin3, xxviin7
Larkin, William J., Jr., 10n22, 32, 38, 183n147, 196n77, 215n101, 216n110
Lee, Archie C. C., 74n214
Legrand, Lucien, xxxn19, 127n154, 129n164, 151n47, 161n6, 178–79, 211n70, 220n15, 224n4
Levinsohn, Stephen H., 108n45, 108n48, 138n53, 162n9, 201n8, 202n14
Lightfoot, J. B., 120n121
Lindars, Barnabas, 40, 50n62, 56n100, 60n122
Lints, Richard, 204n32, 211n71
Litwak, Kenneth D., 4n13, 5n14, 5n17, 23n104, 43n16, 51n71, 52n74, 52n77, 56n99, 65n159, 65n161, 79n249, 83n11, 139n59, 144n4, 176n105
Loisy, Alfred, 82n4, 113, 161n5
Longenecker, Richard N., 104, 104n21, 122n133, 187n19, 198n90
Losie, Lynn Allan, xxixn18
Luck, U., 58n115

MacIntyre, Alasdair, 222n2
MacMullen, Ramsay, xxvn2, xxviin3, 134n31, 150n41, 195n72, 195n73, 211n72, 216n112

Malherbe, Abraham J., 151n46
Mallen, Peter, 52n74, 52n77, 79n249
Mánek, Jindřich, 52n77, 66n164, 75
Marcus, Joel, 107n41, 211n72, 216n112
Marguerat, Daniel, 4n6, 25n116, 82n7, 84n16, 131n5, 136n44, 146n12, 154n70, 165n32, 181n132, 188, 191n50, 193n61, 194n66, 198n94, 200n4, 204n35, 208n55, 214n91, 216n104, 216n111
Marshall, I. Howard, xxviiin14, xxviiin15, 4n6, 4n10, 6n3, 31n148, 84n19, 88n33, 114n80, 136n40, 137n47, 144n4, 146n13, 149, 164n23, 168n55, 171n73, 171n75, 173n89, 176n105, 188n26, 195n70, 203n19
Martin, Dale B., 130n3, 131n10, 132n11, 132n14, 132n15, 132n16, 137n50, 142n70, 149n34, 149–51, 216n112
Martin, Hubert M., Jr., 121n129
Mather, P. Boyd, 75n223, 90n48, 91n53, 134n25
Mattill, Andrew J., Jr., 16
Mbuvi, Andrew M., xxixn18, 224n5
McGiffert, A. C., 209n57
Meijer, P. A., 132n11, 150n41, 151n44
Melugin, Roy F., 91n50
Metzger, Bruce M., 110n61, 206n42
Minear, Paul S., 53n80
Moellering, H. Armin, 132n13, 132n16, 133n20
Moessner, David P., 13n43, 20, 23n103, 31, 36n179, 39, 52n74, 52n77, 66n164, 75, 83n9, 134n25, 220n18
Montanari, Franco, 166n43, 208n52
Moore, Thomas S., 69n179
Morlan, David S., 115n82, 210n67
Morris, Leon, 6n3
Moscato, Mary, 5n15, 8n11
Moule, C. F. D., 34, 37n182, 106n37, 108n46
Moyise, Steve, xxviiin14, 46n40, 50n62, 65n161
Muñoz-Larrondo, Rubén, 107n38
Murray, John, 191n49

Nash, Ronald H., 171n68
Nave, G. D., 207n49
Neagoe, Alexandru, 87n30, 124n140, 124n142, 124n144, 127n156
Newsom, Carol A., 23n104
Neyrey, Jerome H., 102n5, 112n71, 113–14, 200n4
Nock, Arthur D., 115n85, 121n122, 220n17
Nolland, John L., 206n42
Norden, Eduard, 82n4, 117n100, 118n107, 138n51, 161n5, 185n2, 188n28
Nurmela, Risto, 67n168

O'Neill, J. C., 24n112
O'Toole, Robert F., 103, 113n75, 139n60, 178n118, 183n146, 215n103
Owen, H. P., 143n80, 144n1, 151n43, 151n44, 151n46, 152n54, 153n61, 175n98, 181n134, 183n144, 204n30, 214n95

Pahl, Michael, 4n13
Pao, David W., 8n12, 25, 40–80, 88–97, 126n148, 129n163, 140n66, 144n4, 159n96, 175n95, 179n123, 202n12, 203n27, 215n103, 218, 219n12, 219n13, 220n18
Parsons, Mikeal C., 4n13, 10n23, 103, 103n13, 110n59, 114n80, 116n94, 121n127, 133n21, 136n43, 139n56, 149n28, 165n32, 181n132, 182n139, 190n40, 192n53, 194n66, 196n80, 200n4, 203n21, 208n54, 209n57, 210n67, 213n81, 214n91
Penner, Todd, xxviiin12
Pervo, Richard I., xxixn17, 4n10, 4n13, 10n23, 83n14, 101–2, 105n27, 106n35, 108n46, 112n71, 114n78, 118n108, 120n118, 122n130, 122n131, 146n11, 149, 161n6, 167n49, 183n149, 195n68, 198n90, 204n35, 207n46, 212, 213n81, 215n100, 216n112
Pesch, Rudolph, 104n19, 121n123, 121n125, 165n32, 210n65
Peterson, David G., xxviiin15, 4n6, 55n97, 58n113, 106n34, 107n42, 170n63, 180n126, 196–97, 201n6
Pinnock, Clark H., xxxn19, 139n57, 161n6, 178n119, 208n56, 211n70, 224n4
Piper, Otto A., 40, 66n164
Pitts, Andrew W., 40n5
Plummer, Alfred, 82n7
Pohlenz, Max, 163n18, 179n123, 185n2, 188, 210n67
Porter, Stanley E., xxixn16, 3n3, 40n5, 103n13, 127n152, 173n86, 174, 181n132, 182n139, 182n143, 187n19, 213n83
Poythress, Vern S., xxixn16, xxxn20, 41n6, 89n38
Praeder, Susan Marie, 59n120

Rackham, Richard B., 104n24, 114n80, 116n90
Radermakers, J., xxixn18, 115n86, 122n133, 167n51, 170n65, 192n53
Ramsay, William M., xxixn17, 88n33, 123n136
Read-Heimerdinger, Jenny, 103n17, 108n48, 121n127
Renehan, Robert, 188n21, 188n22, 188n26
Rese, Martin, 49n59, 54–59

Ricœur, Paul, 8n13, 83n10, 83n11, 83n12, 119n116
Ridderbos, Herman N., xxxn20, 6n3, 16–17, 64n148
Rius-Camps, Josep, 103n17, 108n48, 121n127
Robertson, A. T., 198n93, 201n7
Robinson, W. C., Jr., xxviiin14
Roloff, Jürgen, 106n36, 112n71, 115n82, 128n161, 165n32, 194n66, 206n43
Rosner, Brian S., 44–45, 56
Ross, James F., 141n67
Roth, Wolfgang M. W., 88n36
Rothschild, Clare K., 110n59, 111n65, 111n67, 112n71, 114n79, 119n112, 120n118, 137n50, 154n64, 188n22, 188n27, 195n73, 196n80, 203n28, 210n67, 213n81, 214n92, 216n104
Rowe, C. Kavin, xxvn2, xxvii, xxxn20, 3–5, 7n8, 8, 8–11, 33–34, 38n188, 39n194, 65n161, 82n8, 85n25, 102n5, 102n7, 106n36, 115n85, 115n88, 118n104, 118n106, 118n107, 118n108, 120n119, 120n121, 121n122, 121n125, 121n127, 131, 133n17, 134n31, 139n58, 139n59, 140n64, 141–43, 149n35, 151n45, 152n51, 154n66, 154n69, 160n99, 180n127, 184n152, 189n35, 193n60, 194n66, 195n71, 195n72, 197n85, 197n88, 199n96, 203n20, 205n37, 207n50, 211n68, 213n81, 214n90, 217–18, 220n17, 222n2, 222n5, 224n6
Runge, Steven E., xxixn16, 107–8, 116, 116n92, 134n30, 135, 136n44, 138n53, 144n2, 193n62, 201n8, 202n14, 202n16, 203n21

Samuel, S. Johnson, 109n55, 142n76, 158n93, 161n6, 175n98, 185n3, 211n68, 211n70, 223n2
Sanders, Jack T., 53n78
Sanders, James A., 68n177, 69n179, 69n183, 72n199, 72n203, 74n219
Sanders, John E., xxxn19, 115n88, 139n57, 143n79, 157n88, 161n6, 175n98, 178n119, 185n3, 211n70, 223n2
Sandmel, Samuel, 59n120
Sandnes, K. O., 119n110
Sawyer, John F. A., 66n166
Schlette, Heinz R., xxxn19, 223n2
Schnabel, Eckhard J., 4n10, 88n33, 107n42, 108n46, 111, 112n71, 121n127, 122n130, 122n133, 128n158, 130n4, 137n48, 151n46, 172n77, 180n126, 195n69, 202n13, 204n31, 213n85, 214n91, 215n100

Schneider, Gerhard, 118n107, 137n45, 165n32
Scholes, Robert, 83n10, 83n12
Schubert, Paul, 52–59
Schwartz, Daniel R., 24
Schwartz, Joshua, 10n21
Schweizer, Eduard, 35, 127n152, 198n90
Scobie, Charles H. H., 25n116
Scott, James M., 168n54, 170n63, 171n69
Seccombe, David, 67, 68, 72n202, 74n219, 76n228, 215n101
Shields, Bruce E., 127n155, 151n47, 153n56, 153n59, 153n60, 208n56
Silva, Moisés, xxixn16, xxxn20, 1, 4n8, 99, 133n18, 176n102
Ska, Jean-Louis, 84n16, 219n11
Smith, Daniel Lynwood, 201n5
Smith, Edgar W., Jr., 182n143
Smith, Mark S., 144n3, 216n111
Smith, Morton, 131n10
Smyth, Herbert Weir, 111n66, 114n79, 180n130
Snodgrass, Klyne R., 40, 51n72, 54n87, 60n124, 66n166, 69n181, 71, 78n242, 79n245, 218n7
Soards, Marion L., 63n141, 86, 123n139, 137n49, 155n75, 163n20, 172n76, 172n80, 174n92, 179, 184n150, 203n24
Sommer, Benjamin D., 67n168
Span, John, xxixn18
Spencer, F. Scott, 4n7, 113n72
Spencer, Patrick E., 4n13
Spicq, Ceslas, 130n1, 135n39, 142n70, 171n71, 208n52
Squires, John T., 13n43
Stählin, Gustav, 139n59
Stanley, Christopher D., 40n5, 41n6
Stenschke, Christoph W., 10n23, 83n11, 101n1, 105n30, 110n62, 112n71, 115n83, 116n94, 118n104, 179n123, 180n127, 182n143, 193n60, 209n57, 216n111, 216n112
Sterling, Gregory E., 23n104, 72n202
Stonehouse, Ned B., xxxn20, 4n5, 88n33, 102n8, 136n40, 139n58, 139n60, 140n63, 142n70, 161n4, 166n41, 180, 184, 187n19, 189n33, 190n42, 199n95, 216n105, 216n108, 220n16
Stott, John R. W., 106n33
Strahan, Joshua M., 205n38, 206n41, 207n48
Strange, Daniel, xxxn19, 183n149, 199n97, 216n110
Strauss, Mark L., 44n29
Stuart, Douglas, 27n123
Sundberg, Albert C., Jr., 50n62
Swartley, Willard M., 52n74, 59, 66n164

Sweeney, James P., 93n63

Talbert, Charles H., 7, 31n146, 53–59, 60n125, 195n69
Tannehill, Robert C., xxxn20, 104n19, 145n5, 152n50, 179n121, 192n56, 195n69
Tannen, Deborah, 83n11
Taylor, Charles, xxvin5
Thom, Johan Carl, 188n22, 191n45, 210n67
Thompson, Alan J., 10n22, 11n26, 12n33, 19n78, 19n79, 26n119, 30n141, 31n151, 37n182
Thompson, Mark D., 180n129
Tiede, David L., 70n185, 76
Tipton, Lane G., 173n86, 183n149, 203n25, 203-4, 209n57, 214n97, 216n109, 217n1
Tomson, Peter J., 10n21
Townsend, John T., 42n10
Trites, Allison A., 124n144, 125n146
Turner, Nigel, 106n37, 167n50, 180n130, 201n10, 208n54, 214n91
Tyson, Joseph B., 4n10

Van de Sandt, Huub, 27n123, 49n57, 50n63, 67n171, 157n84, 203n27
Van der Horst, Pieter W., 107n41, 135n36, 138n51, 138n52, 154n70
Van Nuffelen, Peter, 130n3, 137n50, 149n34, 150, 196n74, 196n76
Van Til, Cornelius, 63n144, 84n15, 153n59, 154n65, 158n92, 197n86, 209n58, 217n1
Van Unnik, W. C., xxviin9, 5n16, 24n111,
Van Winkle, D. W., 77
Vander Broek, Lyle D., 53n82, 61n133, 62
Verheyden, Joseph, 4n13
Vielhauer, Philip, xxviii, 3n3, 6, 7, 204n35, 210n67, 212n76
Vos, Geerhardus, xxxn20, 17n65, 17n66, 72–73, 90n41, 225n8,
Voss, G., 31n146
Vriezen, Theodorus C., 45n36, 73n206, 73n207, 73n210, 78n239

Wallace, Daniel B., 148n22, 181n132, 201n7, 202n16, 208n54
Walters, Patricia, 3n2

Waltke, Bruce K., 159n57, 167n48, 191n50
Warfield, B. B., 33n157, 41n6
Watts, Rikki E., 66n164, 66n166, 69n182, 71–80, 91n51, 92, 159n97, 219n14
Weiss, Bernhard, 167n52
Weißenberger, Michael, 196n76
Wendel, Susan J., 5n17, 23n104, 72n202, 152n53
Wenham, J., 3n2
Wénin, André, 84n17
Wilckens, Ulrich, xxviiin14, 3n3, 6–7, 10, 194n65
Wilkinson, T. L., 108n49, 184n151, 191n47, 199n98, 206n44
Wilson, Stephen G., 16, 164n22, 167n49, 171n70 172n78, 181n133, 183n149, 197n88, 204n35
Winbery, Carlton L., 165n31
Winter, Bruce W., xxvin3, 89n38, 112n70, 113n72, 115n83, 117n102, 121–22, 123n136, 151n46, 195n72, 213n83, 225n9
Witherington, Ben, III, xxviii—xxix, 3–5, 6–39, 40–65, 76n229, 102n8, 102n9, 103n13, 103n18, 106n34, 106n37, 115n83, 115n85, 116n93, 121n125, 123n139, 130n4, 131n7, 132n16, 133n22, 139n58, 142n75, 152n49, 155n73, 158n91, 161, 163n20, 164n25, 165n32, 165n33, 165n37, 167n47, 167n53, 168n55, 170n61, 170n67, 171, 172n77, 178n118, 181n133, 181n135, 181n136, 182n138, 182n143, 187n15, 187n17, 190n40, 195n70, 197n88, 198n91, 200n2, 200n4, 207n46, 209n57, 210n67, 217
Wolfe, Robert F., 140n65, 174, 212n76
Wright, Christopher J. H., 37n181
Wright, N. T., 70–71, 112n71, 121n127
Wycherley, R. E., 105n29

Young, Frances M., 134n31
Yu, Charles, 159n57, 167n48, 191n50

Zakovitch, Yair, 89n37
Zerwick, Maximilian, 215n98
Zuck, Roy B., xxvin4
Zweck, Dean, 103n18, 130n4, 139n57

Index of Scripture Citations

Genesis

1–11	169
1–10	170n63
1–2	89n37, 145, 146n15, 165n33
1	146n10, 149
1:1	89n38, 144n4, 153n58
1:26	146n10, 164n23, 191
1:27	164n23, 191, 192n52
1:28	155n74, 164n25, 169n59, 170
2:1	144n4, 146n13, 147
2:7	144n4, 157n83
3:15	177
5:1	191
5:3	191
6:7	146n10
8:20–21	169n59
8:21–22	169n59
9:1	155n74, 169n59, 170
9:7	169n59, 170
9: 8–17	169n59
9:27	170n66
10	155n74, 168–69
10:19	171
11	168
11:2	170n66
11:4	169, 169n58
11:8	155n74, 169n58
11:9	155n74, 169n58
11:31	170n66
12	169, 177
12:2	168
12:6	170n66
14: 18	154n68
14:19	145n8, 148n25, 154n68
14:20	154n68
14:22	145n8, 154n68
15	177
17	177
19:11	181
22:1	35n173
25	169n57
27:12	181
27:21	181
27:22	181
43:3	201n9

Exodus

4:23	201n9
5:2	140, 141
6:7	178n112
9:2	201n9
10:21	181
12:12–13	91
12:12	90n44
15:11	194n64
18:11	194n64
18:14–26	36n178
18:15	177n109, 178n116
20:2–6	90n44
20:3	194n64
20:11	47n46, 144n4, 146n10
20:23	194n64
23:31	171
25:40	155n75
29:45	178n112
32:1–10	90n44
33:7–11	155n72
33:7	177n109, 178n116
33:9	178n116
34:13	194n65
35:3	170n66
40:38	155n72

Leviticus

5:17–19	205
16:2	155n72
17:7	189
19:15	215n99
26:1	194n65
26:12	178n112
26:37	208n53
26:40	208n53
26:43	208n53
26:44	208n53

Numbers

3:10	136n41
15:22–31	205
33:4	90n44

Deuteronomy

3:26	208n53
4:15–40	178n114
4:19	146n13
4:28–29	194n64
4:29–30	178n115
4:29	178n114
4:33	194n64
5:26	194n64
7:5	194n65
7:25	194n65
8:5	209n60
9:7–8	106n34
12:11	155n72, 178n112
13:7	206n45
14:23	155n72
16:2	155n72
16:6	155n72
16:11	155n72
17:3	146n13
18–19	106n34
18:15	36n178
21:23	32n155
23:16	155n72
28:15–68	178n114
28:29	181
29:21–27	178n114
31:20	106n34
32:5	168n55
32:8–9	170
32:8	168, 171, 154n68
32:9	168n55
32:16	106n34
32:19	106n34
32:31	194n64
32:39	194n64
32:41	106n34

Joshua

1:5	208n53
3:10	194n64
13:8	36n176
14:7	36n176
24	89n37
24:23	90n44

Judges

2:12	106n34
2:14	106n34
16:26	181

1 Samuel

5–6	155n73
13:14	50
17:36	194n64

1 Kings

3:9	215n99
6:13	178n112
8	155n75
8:10–11	155n72
8:12–13	155n75
8:16	155n75
8:17	144n4
8:20	155n75
8:23	155n75
8:27	144n4, 155n75, 178n112
8:29–30	155n75
8:33–34	155n75
10:9	215n99
18	26

2 Kings

17:6–23	194n65
17:11	194n65

19:4	194n64
19:16	194n64

1 Chronicles

1:1—2:2	170n63
16:10–11	178n117
28:9	178n113

2 Chronicles

6:34	36n176
7:12	155n72
7:13–14	178n115
7:14	178n113, 178n116
11:16	178n117
12:14	178n117
15:12–15	178n117
17:3–4	178n114, 178n117
24:9	36n176
28:2	194n65
32:1–22	90n44

Nehemiah

1:9	155n72

Esther

6:13	194n64

Job

5:14	181
6:14	208n53
12:25	181
34:13	146n10
38:8–11	171n73

Psalms

2	45, 49n58, 67, 68, 126n147, 129n163, 140
2:1–12	192n51
2:1–2	126n147, 206
2:7	35n173, 67, 79, 126n147
8:6–7	192n51
9:9	47n46, 215n99
9:10	178n113
9:22 (LXX)	208n53
9:25 (LXX)	106n34
9:34 (LXX)	106n34
10:4	178n115
13:2 (LXX)	184
14:2–3	180n126
16	68
16:10	67
19	184n150
22:26	178n117
24:7	205
27:4	178n113
27:7–8	178n113
27:9	178n114
34:10 (LXX)	194n64
40:16	178n117
41:3 (LXX)	194n64
45:5 (LXX)	154n68
46:3 (LXX)	154n68
49 (LXX)	158n94
49:12 (LXX)	158n94
49:13 (LXX)	158n94
49:14 (LXX)	158n94
50	158, 159
50:12–13	159
50:7–15	158
50:8–13	144n4
70:19 (LXX)	194n64
71:2 (LXX)	215n99
73:17 (LXX)	171
77:17 (LXX)	154n68
77:35 (LXX)	154n68
77:41 (LXX)	106n34
77:56 (LXX)	154n68
77:59 (LXX)	208n53
77:62 (LXX)	208n53
78:6 (LXX)	206n45
81:1–2	209n60
82:19 (LXX)	154n68
83:3 (LXX)	194n64
86:5 (LXX)	154n68
88:7 (LXX)	194n64
88:9 (LXX)	194n64
95:7–8	213n88
95:13 (LXX)	215n99
96:9 (LXX)	154n68
96:13	47n46
97:9 (LXX)	215n99
98:9	47n46
104:5–9	171n73
105	74n214
105:29 (LXX)	106n34

Psalms (continued)

106:36 (LXX)	170n66
109:1 (LXX)	96n77
110	68, 126n147
110:1–7	192n51
110:1	37n181, 126n147, 129n163
113:12 (LXX)	194n64
113:13–15 (LXX)	194n64
113:15 (LXX)	181
113:16 (LXX)	194n64
113:23–24 (LXX)	174n90
115:4–8	67
117:22 (LXX)	215n101
118	126n147
132:13–14	155n72, 178n112
134:17 (LXX)	181
135:15–18	67
139:7–12	190
141:8	178n116
145:6 (LXX)	144n4, 146n10

Proverbs

8:17	178n113
12:9	158n94
28:5	178n117
29:26	178n116

Isaiah

1:11–17	159
1:21	215n99
2	73n206
2:2–4	73n206
2:3–4	37n181, 44n29
2:3	45n36
2:20	189
5:24	45n36, 106n34
6	72
6:1–8	155n72
6:3	73n206
6:9–10	80
6:9–13	73
6:13	78n241
8:16	45n36
8:20	45n36
10:10	194n65
10:13	171
11:16	78n242
13:10	146n13
14:1–4	37n181
14:14	154n68
19:18–25	37n181
24:21	146n13
29:13	159
32:15	76n227
35:8	78n242
37:4	194n64
37:17	194n64
40–66	67n168
40–55	69, 70, 71, 72, 73, 74, 80, 88, 90n45, 91, 93n61, 147n18, 218
40	79
40:1–11	69, 79
40:1–5	71, 79
40:1	90n45
40:3–4	78n242
40:3	71, 72, 76n229, 78n242, 79, 79n245, 94n66
40:9	111n63
40:12–31	89
40:12–14	89
40:15–17	89
40:18–20	194n64
40:19–20	90n45, 185n5
40:21–24	89
40:25–26	89
41:1–4	199n99
41:21–24	199n99
41:28	194n64
42–53	69
42:1–9	147, 192n51, 210n65, 218
42:1–4	76n226
42:1	35n173, 67
42:2	152n52
42:5–9	147
42:5	47n46, 144–47, 156, 157, 157n84, 184n154, 218
42:6–9	175n96
42:6–7	184
42:6	27n123, 144n4, 147, 157n84, 174, 215n98
42:7	144n4
42:8	144n4, 174, 184n154, 194n65
42:16–17	76n232
42:17	194n65
42:18–19	199n99
43:8–12	199n99
43:18	74n216
43:19	78n242
43:24	144n4
44:1–8	76n227
44:6–20	218

44:6	194n64
44:8	194n64, 199n99
44:9–20	67, 185n5, 194n64
44:9	189, 199n99
44:17–20	199n99
45	142
45:5	194n64
45:6	194n64
45:12	144n4
45:14–25	140
45:14–15	140
45:15–25	173, 218
45:15–24	210n65
45:15	141, 143n81, 209n58
45:17	209n58
45:18	104n19, 144n4, 174, 175n96
45:19	178n113, 209n58
45:20–25	175n96
45:20–24	202
45:20–22	199n99
45:20	178n116, 180n126, 206n45
45:21	174, 179n123, 194n64
45:22	174, 178n116, 206n45
45:23–24	213
46:1–7	194n64
46:1	194n65
46:6	185n5
46:7	156
46:8	210n65
46:9	194n64
46:13	27n123, 92n56
48:5	194n65
49:6	27, 27n123, 71, 76n227, 80, 88, 147, 209n61, 210n65
49:11	78n242
49:20	174n90
51:1	176, 178n117
52:7	111n63
52:10	27n123
53	74
53:12	32, 38, 38n188
54:17	156n79
55	67n168
55:3	67, 67n168, 126n147
55:5–11	218
55:6–7	178n115, 178n116
55:6	175n96, 176, 213
55:8–9	178n116
56	26n119
57:14	78n242
57:15	154n68, 156
58:6	68n177
58:7	208n53
59:7	181
59:10	181
60:6	111n63
61	22n97, 28, 68n177, 69, 74, 75
61:1–2	22, 35n173, 43, 68n177, 72, 80, 93n63
61:1	111n63
61:11–12	44n29
62:10	78n242
65:3	106n34
66:1–2	144n4, 154, 154n69, 156
66:15ff.	76n229
66:15–19	18

Jeremiah

3:12–16	205n39
6:8	174n90
7:3–25	205n39
8:19	189
10:1–16	180n126
10:25	206n45
12:15	179n123
14:6–7	205n39
23:23–24	190
26:19 (LXX)	174n90
31:31–34	23

Ezekiel

7:20	146n13
18:30	205n39
37	26n119
38:12	174n90
48:1–14	171

Daniel

2:36–45	172n81
4:22	194n64
4:37	145n8, 146n10
5:23	194n64
6:21	194n64
6:27	194n64
7–9	172n81
7	34
7:13–14	214
7:13	36
12:7	172n82, 194n64

Hosea

2:1	194n64
5:5	178n115
5:6	178n114
5:15—6:6	206n45
5:15	178n115
7:10	178n115
13:4	145n8, 194n64

Joel

2:27	194n64
2:28–32 (LXX)	18, 22, 43, 48
2:28 (LXX)	27
2:29 (LXX)	182n140
2:32 (LXX)	211n69
3:5	211n69

Amos

5:5–6	178n114
5:25–27	154n69
9:11–12	179n123
9:11	27

Micah

6:6–8	159

Nahum

3:11	208n53

Zechariah

1:3	205n39
1:12	208n53
7:8–10	205n39

Malachi

3:1–5	79n245
3:1–2	203n27
3:1	44n29, 78n242, 178n116
3:7	205n39

Matthew

5:23	136n41
5:24	136n41
5:25	213
5:45	158n92
11:25	148n25
16:16	194n64
19:4	145n8
19:26	184n153
19:28	214n92
20:37	196n81
22:38–40	108
22:40	47n43
23:18	136n41
23:19	136n41
23:20	136n41
23:35	136n41
26:56	47n43

Mark

10:27	184n153
12:30	196n81
13:19	145n8
14:58	154n70

Luke

1–2	43 79n249
1	28n128
1:1	14, 44
1:3	43
1:7	211n74
1:9	154n69
1:10	13
1:11	136n41
1:17	65, 76n229, 78n242, 79, 203n27
1:19	111n63
1:21	154n69
1:22	154n69
1:27	33
1:32–33	36n174
1:32	33
1:34–35	33
1:47	21n91, 33
1:54–55	60n129
1:54	36n176
1:68–70	60n129
1:69	29, 36n176
1:76	79

INDEX OF SCRIPTURE CITATIONS

2	147	9:43	33
2:4	33	9:47	121n125
2:6–7	32	9:51–56	61n134
2:10	111n63	9:54–55	207n47
2:11	29, 34, 35	10:21–22	33
2:25–32	18	10:21	33, 148n25
2:30–32	27n123	10:27	108, 196n81
2:31–32	206	11:13	12, 155n71
2:32	224n6	11:29	205n37
2:49	33	11:50	146
3–4	79n249	11:51	136n41
3	79	12:30	146, 206
3:4–6	79	12:47	13n42
3:16	12	12:50	35n173
3:21–22	155n71	12:58	213
3:22	33, 35n173	14:4	121n125
3:28	111n63	15	28
3:31	33	15:1	28
3:38	33, 191, 214n96	16:16	8n9, 16, 111n63
4	22n97, 28, 35n173, 68, 72, 74, 75	16:19	121n125
		17:3	38
4:1–13	93	17:22–30	63n145
4:1	33	18:17	121n125
4:11–12	43	18:27	184n153
4:14	33	18:31–33	39
4:16–30	69, 80	18:34	207n47
4:16	33	19	28
4:18–21	22, 28	19:9	29, 211n74
4:18–19	68n177, 220	19:38	36n174
4:18	33, 111n63	20:1	111n63
4:21	220	20:9–18	205
4:43	111n63	20:17	215n101
5	28	20:30	214n92
5:18–26	33	20:41–43	192n51
5:36	118n105	20:42	49n58
5:38	118n105	21:12	116n96
6:3	64n151	21:24	13
6:20–21	68n177	21:24	172, 173
6:35	158n92	21:30	121n125
7	28	22:16	14n46
7:22	29	22:19–20	31
7:22	68n177, 111n63	22:20	118n105
7:27	78n242, 203n27	22:22	13
7:30	13n42	22:24–27	207n47
7:34	28	22:28–30	23
8:1	111n63	22:37	32, 38
8:39	33	22:42	13n42
9:6	111n63	22:49–51	207n47
9:25	146	22:69–70	36n177
9:31	14n46	23:2–5	36n174
9:32–35	207n47	23:13–25	205
9:35	33	23:25	13n42
9:41	14n46	23:26	121n125
9:43–45	207n47	23:27	207

269

Luke (continued)

23:34	32, 206
23:34a	205, 206n42
23:37–38	36n174
23:45	154n69
23:46	33
23:47	215n101
23:51	13n42
24	53, 57n109
24:5–9	53n81
24:6a	33
24:19	37n82
24:25–27	207n47
24:26–49	14n46
24:26–27	39
24:27	38
24:31	207, 207n47
24:32	64n152
24:39	181n134
24:44–49	69, 80, 207, 207n47
24:44–47	39, 42
24:44	64, 51n69, 53n81, 207
24:45–49	31
24:45	64n152
24:46–47	30, 31
24:46	38, 207
24:47	210n64
24:49	12, 23, 76
24:50–53	53n81
24:51	33
24:52–53	93n62
24:52	33

John

1:45	47n43
5:39	47n43
5:46	47n43
20:9	47n43

Acts

1–15	47
1–4	47n45
1–2	20
1	16
1:1	44n26
1:2	218n9
1:4–11	14n46
1:4	14n46
1:5	12, 35n173
1:6–11	20n85
1:6–8	36n174, 69, 76n227, 126n147, 207n47
1:6	18, 76
1:7–8	19
1:7	13, 173, 213
1:8	12, 18, 24, 25, 27, 44, 44n26, 69, 76, 80, 86, 87, 125, 147, 170n62, 207, 210, 210n64, 210n65, 218
1:8a	11n28
1:9–11	61n134
1:9	33
1:11	20n85, 133n23, 155n71
1:15–26	31n150
1:16	133n23
1:18	201n9
1:20	49n58
2–6	23
2	22, 22n97, 57n112, 87
2:1–11	170n62
2:1–6	12
2:1ff.	14n46
2:7–13	114n78
2:9–12	168n56
2:14–40	31n150
2:15–21	22
2:16–41	207
2:16–17	218
2:17–21	18, 43
2:17ff.	14n46, 26n122
2:17	27, 210
2:18	182n140
2:21	29
2:22–36	215n101
2:22	32, 37n182, 133n23, 172
2:23	13n42, 205
2:24–36	39
2:24–32	33
2:24	211n74, 215
2:26	12n32
2:29–36	22n99
2:29	133n23
2:30	36n178
2:32–36	192n51
2:32	18n73
2:33–38	31
2:33	14n46, 18n73
2:34–36	37n181
2:34–35	96n77, 126n147
2:36	205, 215
2:37	133n23
2:38	210
2:41	22n100

INDEX OF SCRIPTURE CITATIONS

2:45	211n74	7:2	133n23
2:47	22n100, 31	7:11	93n63
3	20, 42n10	7:13	93n63
3:11–26	205–7	7:26	133n23
3:12–26	31n150	7:41	154n67
3:12–16	11n28	7:42	14n47
3:12	133n23	7:43	154n69
3:13–15	215n101	7:44	154n69, 184n150
3:13	12, 67	7:47	154n69
3:17–18	42n10	7:48	93n63, 144n4, 148n22, 154, 158n94
3:17	173n85, 207n46		
3:18–21	39	7:49–50	154
3:18	47n43	7:51–53	205
3:19	173n85	7:51–52	42n10
3:20	173	7:55–56	155n71, 214
3:24	14n46, 47n43, 140n63	7:56	34, 36n177
3:25	57	7:58	25n117
3:26	67	7:60	206
3:29	134n29	8	26, 47n45, 68n176
4:2	128n161, 140n63	8:1	25n117
4:4	22n100	8:4–24	94
4:7	120	8:4	22n100, 111n63
4:10–12	39	8:9	94n64
4:10–11	215n101	8:10	94n64
4:10	11n28	8:11	94n64
4:12	28, 29	8:12	22n100, 111n63
4:23–31	31n150	8:25	111n63
4:24	146n10, 148n25	8:26–40	31n150
4:25–27	206	8:30–38	207
4:25–26	126n147	8:30–35	48n53
4:25	36n176	8:31	64n152
4:27	67, 68n177	8:35	64n152, 111n63
4:28	13n42	8:40	111n63
4:29	46n37	9:1–18	31n150
4:30	11n28, 36n176, 67	9:3–19	207
4:31	46n37	9:3	155n71
4:35	211n74	9:15	26, 109, 120n121, 125
5–6	28	9:20	36n176
5:27–42	31n150	9:22	38
5:14	22n100	9:27	121n125
5:31	21n91, 31, 34	9:31	22n100
5:35	133n23	9:35	22n100
5:38–39	46n37	9:42	22n100
5:38	13n42	10	26, 47, 209n61
5:39	94	10:6	118n105
5:40	46n37	10:9–16	206
5:42	46n37, 111n63	10:15–18	31
6–8	25	10:18	118n105
6:1	22n100	10:23	118n105
6:7	22n100	10:25–26	94n68
7	14n47, 42n10, 47, 47n42, 47n45, 89n37, 95, 124n141, 142, 154n69	10:32	118n105
		10:34–43	27n126
		10:34–35	179
7:2–53	4n9, 21n90, 93–94, 174	10:36	111n63

271

Acts (continued)

10:38	68n177	14:1	22n100
10:39–42	214	14:4	11
10:41–43	15n51	14:5–19	94–95
10:41–42	214n95	14:7	111n63
10:42	13, 33, 36	14:14	11
10:43	47n43, 214	14:15–17	xxviin8, 47n46, 66n163, 171n75
11	26, 209n61	14:15–16	14n47
11:18	209n61	14:15	47n46, 111n63, 117n101, 146n10, 152n51, 189, 194n64
11:20	111n63		
11:21	22n100		
11:24	22n100	14:16–17	207
11:26	22n100	14:16	206, 209n58, 209n60
12	25n117, 26	14:17	152, 158n92, 171, 172, 173, 179, 179n123, 184, 190n40, 193
12:1–25	94		
12:3	94		
12:24	22n100	14:21	22n100, 111n63
13	42n10, 44, 47, 47n42, 47n45, 55n95, 57n112, 67, 87, 127n155	15	25n117, 26, 47n45, 209n61
		15:1–21	31n150
		15:4	11n28
13:2	11n28	15:5	27n124
13:5	140n63	15:7	133n23
13:6–12	94	15:12	11n28
13:9	25n117	15:13–21	4n9, 27n124
13:13–52	31n150	15:13	133n23
13:15	133n23	15:14	157n84
13:16–25	174	15:16–20	179n123
13:16	133n23	15:16–17	27
13:17–25	14n47, 21n90	15:16b—17	179
13:22	13n42, 50	15:16	96n77
13:23–26	79	15:21	42
13:23	21n91, 24, 29, 34	15:29	206
13:26	133n23	15:35	111n63
13:27–28	42n10	15:36	104n21, 140n63
13:27	38, 205, 206	15:39	106
13:28–30	215n101	16	25n118
13:32–33	126n147	16:5	22n100
13:32	111n63	16:7	12n32
13:33–37	39	16:10	111n63
13:33	35n173, 36, 49n58, 214n96	16:16–40	124n140
13:34	126n147	16:16–24	95n75
13:36	13n42	16:17	140n63
13:37	13	16:19	121
13:38	133n23, 140n63	16:21	140n63
13:40–41	23	16:31	29
13:43	22n100	17–24	110
13:46–47	23, 69, 80	17	87, 93n61, 95, 96n77, 114n78, 124n141, 177n110, 220n15
13:46	13n44, 26		
13:47	25, 27, 69, 88, 125, 157n84, 210n65, 218, 220	17:2–3	39, 110, 127n155
		17:2	110
13:48–49	87n32	17:3	42, 47n43, 64n152, 139, 140n63
13:48	209n61		
13:50	171	17:4	22n100

272

INDEX OF SCRIPTURE CITATIONS

17:6	121	17:24	47n46, 51n72, 136, 137, 186, 192, 193, 200n3, 201
17:11–12	22n100, 42n11, 115n83	17:25–31	156n80
17:12	123n136	17:25	38, 135n39, 137, 178n116, 193
17:13–15	104		
17:13	139, 140n63	17:25a	166
17:15	111n69	17:25b	163, 188, 189, 190, 191n46
17:16–34	xxxi, 80, 97, 101–4, 223–25	17:26–28	176, 192
17:16–23	206	17:26–27	149, 152, 161–84, 186, 189, 190, 192, 213
17:16–22a	101–29		
17:16–21	126n151	17:26	13, 155, 158, 192, 200n3, 211n73, 214
17:16–20	111, 119–20		
17:16–18	104–9, 111	17:26a	157, 191, 193n59
17:16	93n61, 123n138, 125, 128, 130n4, 134n26, 135, 135n39, 136, 160, 194n65, 200n3, 212n80, 224n4	17:26b	137, 148n20
		17:27–28	196
		17:27	133n21, 137, 139, 185–99, 200n3, 210n65
17:17–21	112–18	17:27a	148n20
17:17–20	114	17:27b	148n20
17:17–18	110–12, 114, 127n155, 202	17:27c	148n20
17:18–22a	140	17:28–31	186
17:18–21	113, 117–18, 122–23	17:28–29	157n89, 168n54, 162, 182, 183, 185–99
17:18–20	109, 113, 116, 121, 125, 141		
		17:28	139, 151, 156n81, 162n8
17:18–19	124n142, 200n3	17:28a	137, 148n20, 156, 157n82, 163, 182
17:18	112, 113, 113n75, 114n78, 127, 128, 200n3, 212, 214		
		17:28b	137, 148n20
17:19–20	112	17:29	106n36, 137n45, 148n23, 151n46, 182, 184n154, 200n3, 201
17:19	111n69, 121, 124n142, 200n3		
17:19b	121	17:29a	137, 148n20
17:21	113, 114, 114n78	17:29b	148n20
17:22–31	47n46, 66n163, 86, 124n142	17:30–31	15n51, 81, 84n19, 153n57, 168, 174, 178, 183, 186, 189, 200–216
17:22–29	212		
17:22–23	130–43, 183, 198	17:30	14n47, 113, 137, 157, 173, 184, 186, 189, 219
17:22	107, 109, 113, 115, 120, 120n120, 133, 180n128		
		17:30a	148n20
17:22b	201	17:30b	148n20
17:23–29	81	17:31–34	16
17:23	105n27, 109, 122, 128n159, 140n63, 153n62, 199, 200n3, 201n11, 204, 205n36, 206, 207n48, 207n51	17:31	13, 14, 32, 33, 36, 37n182, 47n46, 51n72, 111n63, 113, 122, 125, 127, 128, 167, 172, 178n118
17:24–31	193n59	17:31a	148n20
17:24–29	104n19, 149, 161n4, 192, 206, 207n48	17:31b	137, 148n20
		17:31c	148n20
17:24–28	186, 194, 207	17:32–34	115–16, 122–23
17:24–27	186	17:32–33	119–20
17:24–27b	189	17:32	109, 112, 113, 113n75, 114, 114n78, 126, 127, 134, 186, 200n3, 201, 202, 206, 217
17:24–26	186n11, 189		
17:24–25	144–60, 162, 163, 166, 174, 183, 184n154, 186, 190, 192		
		17:32b	113
		17:33–34	101–29

273

Acts (continued)

17:33	120, 219
17:34	113, 114n78, 120n117, 121, 127, 212n80, 217
18:1	104
18:4	110
18:6	23, 26
18:8	22n100
18:10	22n100, 157n84
18:19	110
19	87, 95, 120n119
19:8	110
19:9	110
19:11–20	95
19:20	22n100
19:23–41	87, 95
19:24	154n69
19:26	95n73
19:27	95n73, 154n69
19:35	133n23
19:37	95n73, 137n46
19:38	201n9
20:7	110
20:9	110
20:21	207
20:24	125
20:27	13n42
20:28	31, 32, 33
21–28	87
21:14	13n42
21:16	118n105
21:19	11n28
21:20	22n100
21:25	206
21:28	133n23, 210n64
21:33	121n125
22:1	133n23
22:14–15	69
22:14	13, 13n42
22:15	125
22:18–21	69
22:21	26
22:37	38
23	47n45, 113, 114n78
23:1–5	134n25
23:1	133n23
23:5	47
23:6	128n161, 133n23, 216n106
23:8	216n106
23:11	25, 125
23:11c	44n26
23:19	121n125
24:7	38
24:12	110
24:14–15	216n106
24:14	57n109
24:20–21	216n106
24:24–25	216n106
24:25	110
24:26	38
24:44	38
25:11	201n9
25:19	132
26	213n81
26:1–23	31n150
26:4	201n9
26:6–8	216n106
26:9	201n9
26:16–18	69
26:16	13, 125
26:17–18	26
26:18	94, 206, 220
26:19–23	127n153
26:20	207
26:21–23	216n106
26:22–23	39
26:22	57n109
26:23	140n63, 207
26:27–29	127n153
26:27–28	217
27:42	13n42
28	47n45
28:7	118n105
28:14	44n26
28:17	133n23
28:20	216n106
28:25–28	23, 69, 80
28:26–27	47
28:28	26, 219
28:30	24
28:31	44, 45, 86

Romans

1	176, 220n15
1:2–3	47n43
1:8	140n63
1:16	25
1:18–32	193
1:18–23	143n78
1:19–23	184n150
1:20	209n57
1:25	145n8
1:28	209n60
3:11	184
3:15	181

3:21	47n43	**Colossians**	
3:25	209n58		
5	191n49	1:6	218n9
9:26	194n64	1:15–17	188n29
10	220	1:16	145n8
10:9	110n62	1:23	218n9
11:3	136n41	1:28	140n63
11:13	201n9	2:11	154n70
11:36	188n29	3:20	134n29
16:26	47n43	3:22	134n29
		4:14	3

1 Corinthians

1 Thessalonians

1:18–25	123n136		
1:23–24	37n183	1:9–10	89n38, 95n69, 128n158, 220
2:1–2	xxixn17		
2:1	140n63		
2:2	88n33		

1 Timothy

6:4	201n9		
6:7	201n9		
8–10	225n9	1:13	206
8:5–6	xxvin3, 158	5:4	138n55
9:13	136n41		
9:14	140n63		
9:25	201n9		

2 Timothy

10:18	136n41		
11:26	140n63	4:1	203n28
13:5	106	4:11	3
15	18n70, 191n49		
15:3–4	47n43		
16:15	123n136		

Titus

		1:12	188

2 Corinthians

Philemon

5:1	154n70		
6:16	194n64	24	4

Ephesians

Hebrews

2:11	154n70		
4:18	206	1:1	47n43
		2:17	134n29
		4:15	134n29

Philippians

		7:11	201n9
		7:13	136n41
1:17	140n63	8:1–5	155n75
1:18	140n63	8:4	201n9
2:9–11	xxvin3	9:1	201n9
2:23	201n9	9:11	154n70, 155n71, 155n75
		9:14	194n64

Hebrews (continued)

9:24	154n70, 155n71, 155n75
10:24	106
11	47n42
11:3	153n61
11:10	149n28
12:18	181n134
13:10	136n41

James

2:12	203n28
2:21	136n41

1 Peter

1:14	206
1:23	194n64
3:14–16	128n160
3:16	134n26

2 Peter

2:12–13	206

1 John

1:1	181n134
5:21	89n38

Jude

10–11	206

Revelation

4–5	155n71
4:11	145n8
6:9	136n41
7:2	194n64
8:3	136n41
8:5	136n41
9:13	136n41
10:6	145n8, 146n10
11:1	136n41
13:4	194n64
13:16	194n65
13:17	194n65
14:9	194n65
14:11	194n65
14:18	136n41
15:7	194n64
16:2	194n65
16:7	136n41
19:11	215n99
19:20	194n65
20:4	194n65
21	170
21:2	155n71
21:3	178n112
22:8–9	89n38

Index of Ancient Sources

Apocrypha and Septuagint

Additions to Daniel

Bel and the Dragon
1:27 — 136n40

Additions to Esther

4:17g (Sinaiticus) — 208n53
8:12a–x — 194n64

Judith

8:20 — 208n53

2 Maccabees

4:1 — 149n28
7:11 — 208n52
7:23 — 157n83, 208n52
8:36 — 140n63
9:17 — 140n63
10:2 — 149n28
14:35 — 158n94

3 Maccabees

2:9–10 — 158n94
2:29 — 194n65

4 Maccabees

1:7 — 201n9
1:9 — 208n52
1:10 — 201n9
1:22 — 201n9
7:8 — 149n28
9:6 — 208n52

Sirach/Ecclesiasticus

4:3 — 158n94
11:12 — 158n94
13:3 — 158n94
18:32 — 158n94
23:3 — 206n45
28:7 — 206n45
42:21 — 158n94
45:26 — 215n99
50:12 — 136n41
50:14 — 136n41
50:27 — 194n65

Tobit

7:17 — 148n25

Wisdom of Solomon

13:1–10 — 180n126
13:10—14:2 — 185n5
13:16 — 201n9
14:20 — 136n40
14:22–31 — 206n45
14:27 — 206n45
15:7–17 — 185n5
15:13 — 149n28
15:17 — 136n40
19:6 — 74n214
19:22 — 208n53

Pseudepigrapha

Joseph and Aseneth

13.9 — 206n45

Psalms of Solomon

8.15	24, 44n26
8.23–25	215n99
8.30	208n53
17	35n171

Dead Sea Scrolls

1QapGen

22.16	148n25
22.21	148n25

1QH

1.13–15	144n4

1QM

10.12ff.	173

4QIsaiah Pesher[a] (4Q161 [4QpIs[a]])

	71n192

4QIsaiah Pesher[b] (4Q162 [4QpIs[b]])

	71n192

4QIsaiah Pesher[c] (4Q163 [4QpIs[c]])

	71n192

4QIsaiah Pesher[d] (4Q164 [4QpIs[d]])

	71n192

4QIsaiah Pesher[e] (4Q165 [4QpIs[e]])

	71n192

Ancient Greek, Roman, and Jewish Writings

Aelius Aristides

Orationes

1	133n22

Aeschylus

Eumenides

647–48	213n83

Andronicus

On Passions

3 (*SVF* 3.99.13)	207n51

Apuleius

Metamorphoses

10.7	131n7

Aratus

Phaenomena

5	191n45

Aristobulus

	191n45

Cleanthes

Hymn to Zeus

4	191n45

Dio Chrysostom

De Dei Cognitione (*Orationes* 12)

44–48	196n77
44	196
47	196
48	196
60–61	196n77

Diodorus Siculus

32.12.1–2	142n72

Diogenes Laertius

Vitae Philosophorum

1.110	135n37

INDEX OF ANCIENT SOURCES

Homer
Odyssea
9.415–16	181

Horace
Epistulae
2.2.81	104n24

Josephus
Contra Apionem
2.130	134n28
2.266–68	119n113

Livy
The History of Rome
45.27	134n28

Lucian
Anacharsis (De Gymnastica)
19	131n7

Demonax
11	133n22, 134n24

Juppiter Tragoedus
7–13	142n72
34–52	149n28

Pausanias
Graeciae Descriptio
1	105n30
1.1.4	135n37
1.17.1	134n28
1.24.3	134n28
5.14.8	135n37

Petronius
Satyricon
1.17	135n39

Philostratus
Vita Apollonii
6.3	135n37

Plato
Phaedrus
249C	151

Timaeus
28A	149n28
29A	149n28
40D	150n41
41A	150n41

Plutarch
De Iside et Osiride
1 (351D–E)	196n74
9 (354C)	196n78
10 (354F–355A)	196n78
20 (358E–F)	196n74
28 (362A)	182n143
36 (365B–C)	196n78
45 (369B)	196n74
57 (374C)	196n74
66 (377D–F)	196n74
71 (379C–D)	196
71 (379C–D)	142n72
71 (379C–E)	196n78

De Superstitione
1 (164E)	142n72, 207n51
3–4 (165D–167A)	142n72
11 (170E)	142n72
2 (165B–C)	207n51
3 (165E)	196n74
3 (165F)	213n83
3 (166B)	196n74
4 (166F–167A)	213n83
8 (169B–C)	196n74

Porphyry
Contra Christianos (fragment)
	xxv

Sophocles

Oedipus Coloneus

260	134n28

Stobaeus

Eclogae

2.92 (SVF 3.98.42)	207n51

Strabo

Geographica

1.2.7–9	196n77
9.1.16	134n28

Theophrastus

Characters

16	142n72
16.1	207n51

On Piety

fr. 584A–588	132n13

Early Christian Writings

Augustine

The Confessions

1.1.1	142n77

Epistulae

102.8	xxvn1

John Chrysostom

Homilies on the Acts of the Apostles

Homily XXXI	95n69
Homily XXXVIII	184n150, 209n61, 216

1 Clement

25.4	136n41

2 Clement

8.2	209n62
9.7	209n62
16.1	209n62

Diognetus

1.1	132n16
4.1	132n16

Eusebius

Demonstratio Evangelica

4.9	171n71

Praeparatio Evangelica

13.12.6	191n45

www.ingramcontent.com/pod-product-compliance
Lightning Source LLC
Chambersburg PA
CBHW080729300426
44114CB00019B/2525